T0202832

Lecture Notes in Computer Science   13316

More information about this series at https://link.springer.com/bookseries/558

Gabriele Meiselwitz (Ed.)

Social Computing and Social Media

Applications in Education and Commerce

14th International Conference, SCSM 2022
Held as Part of the 24th HCI International Conference, HCII 2022
Virtual Event, June 26 – July 1, 2022
Proceedings, Part II

 Springer

Editor
Gabriele Meiselwitz
Towson University
Towson, MD, USA

ISSN 0302-9743 ISSN 1611-3349 (electronic)
Lecture Notes in Computer Science
ISBN 978-3-031-05063-3 ISBN 978-3-031-05064-0 (eBook)
https://doi.org/10.1007/978-3-031-05064-0

This Springer imprint is published by the registered company Springer Nature Switzerland AG
The registered company address is: Gewerbestrasse 11, 6330 Cham, Switzerland

Foreword

Human-computer interaction (HCI) is acquiring an ever-increasing scientific and industrial importance, as well as having more impact on people's everyday life, as an ever-growing number of human activities are progressively moving from the physical to the digital world. This process, which has been ongoing for some time now, has been dramatically accelerated by the COVID-19 pandemic. The HCI International (HCII) conference series, held yearly, aims to respond to the compelling need to advance the exchange of knowledge and research and development efforts on the human aspects of design and use of computing systems.

The 24th International Conference on Human-Computer Interaction, HCI International 2022 (HCII 2022), was planned to be held at the Gothia Towers Hotel and Swedish Exhibition & Congress Centre, Göteborg, Sweden, during June 26 to July 1, 2022. Due to the COVID-19 pandemic and with everyone's health and safety in mind, HCII 2022 was organized and run as a virtual conference. It incorporated the 21 thematic areas and affiliated conferences listed on the following page.

A total of 5583 individuals from academia, research institutes, industry, and governmental agencies from 88 countries submitted contributions, and 1276 papers and 275 posters were included in the proceedings to appear just before the start of the conference. The contributions thoroughly cover the entire field of human-computer interaction, addressing major advances in knowledge and effective use of computers in a variety of application areas. These papers provide academics, researchers, engineers, scientists, practitioners, and students with state-of-the-art information on the most recent advances in HCI. The volumes constituting the set of proceedings to appear before the start of the conference are listed in the following pages.

The HCI International (HCII) conference also offers the option of 'Late Breaking Work' which applies both for papers and posters, and the corresponding volume(s) of the proceedings will appear after the conference. Full papers will be included in the 'HCII 2022 - Late Breaking Papers' volumes of the proceedings to be published in the Springer LNCS series, while 'Poster Extended Abstracts' will be included as short research papers in the 'HCII 2022 - Late Breaking Posters' volumes to be published in the Springer CCIS series.

I would like to thank the Program Board Chairs and the members of the Program Boards of all thematic areas and affiliated conferences for their contribution and support towards the highest scientific quality and overall success of the HCI International 2022 conference; they have helped in so many ways, including session organization, paper reviewing (single-blind review process, with a minimum of two reviews per submission) and, more generally, acting as goodwill ambassadors for the HCII conference.

This conference would not have been possible without the continuous and unwavering support and advice of Gavriel Salvendy, founder, General Chair Emeritus, and Scientific Advisor. For his outstanding efforts, I would like to express my appreciation to Abbas Moallem, Communications Chair and Editor of HCI International News.

June 2022   Constantine Stephanidis

HCI International 2022 Thematic Areas and Affiliated Conferences

Thematic Areas

- HCI: Human-Computer Interaction
- HIMI: Human Interface and the Management of Information

Affiliated Conferences

- EPCE: 19th International Conference on Engineering Psychology and Cognitive Ergonomics
- AC: 16th International Conference on Augmented Cognition
- UAHCI: 16th International Conference on Universal Access in Human-Computer Interaction
- CCD: 14th International Conference on Cross-Cultural Design
- SCSM: 14th International Conference on Social Computing and Social Media
- VAMR: 14th International Conference on Virtual, Augmented and Mixed Reality
- DHM: 13th International Conference on Digital Human Modeling and Applications in Health, Safety, Ergonomics and Risk Management
- DUXU: 11th International Conference on Design, User Experience and Usability
- C&C: 10th International Conference on Culture and Computing
- DAPI: 10th International Conference on Distributed, Ambient and Pervasive Interactions
- HCIBGO: 9th International Conference on HCI in Business, Government and Organizations
- LCT: 9th International Conference on Learning and Collaboration Technologies
- ITAP: 8th International Conference on Human Aspects of IT for the Aged Population
- AIS: 4th International Conference on Adaptive Instructional Systems
- HCI-CPT: 4th International Conference on HCI for Cybersecurity, Privacy and Trust
- HCI-Games: 4th International Conference on HCI in Games
- MobiTAS: 4th International Conference on HCI in Mobility, Transport and Automotive Systems
- AI-HCI: 3rd International Conference on Artificial Intelligence in HCI
- MOBILE: 3rd International Conference on Design, Operation and Evaluation of Mobile Communications

List of Conference Proceedings Volumes Appearing Before the Conference

1. LNCS 13302, Human-Computer Interaction: Theoretical Approaches and Design Methods (Part I), edited by Masaaki Kurosu
2. LNCS 13303, Human-Computer Interaction: Technological Innovation (Part II), edited by Masaaki Kurosu
3. LNCS 13304, Human-Computer Interaction: User Experience and Behavior (Part III), edited by Masaaki Kurosu
4. LNCS 13305, Human Interface and the Management of Information: Visual and Information Design (Part I), edited by Sakae Yamamoto and Hirohiko Mori
5. LNCS 13306, Human Interface and the Management of Information: Applications in Complex Technological Environments (Part II), edited by Sakae Yamamoto and Hirohiko Mori
6. LNAI 13307, Engineering Psychology and Cognitive Ergonomics, edited by Don Harris and Wen-Chin Li
7. LNCS 13308, Universal Access in Human-Computer Interaction: Novel Design Approaches and Technologies (Part I), edited by Margherita Antona and Constantine Stephanidis
8. LNCS 13309, Universal Access in Human-Computer Interaction: User and Context Diversity (Part II), edited by Margherita Antona and Constantine Stephanidis
9. LNAI 13310, Augmented Cognition, edited by Dylan D. Schmorrow and Cali M. Fidopiastis
10. LNCS 13311, Cross-Cultural Design: Interaction Design Across Cultures (Part I), edited by Pei-Luen Patrick Rau
11. LNCS 13312, Cross-Cultural Design: Applications in Learning, Arts, Cultural Heritage, Creative Industries, and Virtual Reality (Part II), edited by Pei-Luen Patrick Rau
12. LNCS 13313, Cross-Cultural Design: Applications in Business, Communication, Health, Well-being, and Inclusiveness (Part III), edited by Pei-Luen Patrick Rau
13. LNCS 13314, Cross-Cultural Design: Product and Service Design, Mobility and Automotive Design, Cities, Urban Areas, and Intelligent Environments Design (Part IV), edited by Pei-Luen Patrick Rau
14. LNCS 13315, Social Computing and Social Media: Design, User Experience and Impact (Part I), edited by Gabriele Meiselwitz
15. LNCS 13316, Social Computing and Social Media: Applications in Education and Commerce (Part II), edited by Gabriele Meiselwitz
16. LNCS 13317, Virtual, Augmented and Mixed Reality: Design and Development (Part I), edited by Jessie Y. C. Chen and Gino Fragomeni
17. LNCS 13318, Virtual, Augmented and Mixed Reality: Applications in Education, Aviation and Industry (Part II), edited by Jessie Y. C. Chen and Gino Fragomeni

39. CCIS 1582, HCI International 2022 Posters - Part III, edited by Constantine Stephanidis, Margherita Antona and Stavroula Ntoa
40. CCIS 1583, HCI International 2022 Posters - Part IV, edited by Constantine Stephanidis, Margherita Antona and Stavroula Ntoa

http://2022.hci.international/proceedings

Preface

The 14th International Conference on Social Computing and Social Media (SCSM 2022) was an affiliated conference of the HCI International (HCII) conference. The conference provided an established international forum for the exchange and dissemination of scientific information related to social computing and social media, addressing a broad spectrum of issues expanding our understanding of current and future issues in these areas. The conference welcomed qualitative and quantitative research papers on a diverse range of topics related to the design, development, assessment, use, and impact of social media.

The importance of social computing and social media in today's society has dramatically increased during the COVID-19 pandemic, as people worldwide have been forced to communicate, work, study, shop, and spend their free time online. This has brought about a renewed interest in renovating the design and user experience of online environments, as well as the analysis of their impact on society in general and on critical application domains such as education and commerce more specifically.

Two volumes of the HCII 2022 proceedings are dedicated to this year's edition of the SCSM conference, entitled Social Computing and Social Media: Design, User Experience and Impact (Part I) and Social Computing and Social Media: Applications in Education and Commerce (Part II). The first focuses on topics related to novel approaches to design and user experience in social media and social live streaming, text analysis and AI in social media, and social media impact on society and business, while the second focuses on topics related to social media in education as well as customer experience and consumer behavior.

Papers of these volumes are included for publication after a minimum of two single-blind reviews from the members of the SCSM Program Board or, in some cases, from members of the Program Boards of other affiliated conferences. I would like to thank all of them for their invaluable contribution, support, and efforts.

June 2022   Gabriele Meiselwitz

14th International Conference on Social Computing and Social Media (SCSM 2022)

Program Board Chair: **Gabriele Meiselwitz,** Towson University, USA

- Rocio Abascal Mena, Universidad Autónoma Metropolitana-Cuajimalpa, Mexico
- Francisco Alvarez Rodríguez, Universidad Autónoma de Aguascalientes, Mexico
- Andria Andriuzzi, Université Jean Monnet, France
- Karine Berthelot-Guiet, Sorbonne University, France
- James Braman, Community College of Baltimore County, USA
- Adheesh Budree, University of Cape Town, South Africa
- Adela Coman, University of Bucharest, Romania
- Tina Gruber-Muecke, Anton Bruckner Private University, Austria
- Hung-Hsuan Huang, University of Fukuchiyama, Japan
- Ajrina Hysaj, University of Wollongong in Dubai, United Arab Emirates
- Aylin Imeri, Heinrich Heine University Düsseldorf, Germany
- Ayaka Ito, Reitaku University, Japan
- Carsten Kleiner, University of Applied Sciences and Arts Hannover, Germany
- Jeannie Lee, Singapore Institute of Technology, Singapore
- Ana Isabel Molina, University of Castilla-La Mancha, Spain
- Takashi Namatame, Chuo University, Japan
- Hoang D. Nguyen, University of Glasgow, Singapore
- Kohei Otake, Tokai University, Japan
- Oronzo Parlangeli, University of Siena, Italy
- Daniela Quiñones, Pontificia Universidad Católica de Valparaíso, Chile
- Cristian Rusu, Pontificia Universidad Católica de Valparaíso, Chile
- Virginica Rusu, Universidad de Playa Ancha, Chile
- Christian W. Scheiner, Universität zu Lübeck, Germany
- Tomislav Stipancic, University of Zagreb, Croatia
- Simona Vasilache, University of Tsukuba, Japan
- Yuanqiong Wang, Towson University, USA
- Brian Wentz, Shippensburg University, USA

The full list with the Program Board Chairs and the members of the Program Boards of all thematic areas and affiliated conferences is available online at

http://www.hci.international/board-members-2022.php

HCI International 2023

The 25th International Conference on Human-Computer Interaction, HCI International 2023, will be held jointly with the affiliated conferences at the AC Bella Sky Hotel and Bella Center, Copenhagen, Denmark, 23–28 July 2023. It will cover a broad spectrum of themes related to human-computer interaction, including theoretical issues, methods, tools, processes, and case studies in HCI design, as well as novel interaction techniques, interfaces, and applications. The proceedings will be published by Springer. More information will be available on the conference website: http://2023.hci.international/.

General Chair
Constantine Stephanidis
University of Crete and ICS-FORTH
Heraklion, Crete, Greece
Email: general_chair@hcii2023.org

http://2023.hci.international/

Contents – Part II

Customer Experience and Consumer Behavior

Contents – Part I

Text Analysis and AI in Social Media

Social Media Impact on Society and Business

Social Media in Education

Design and Evaluation of a Programming Tutor Based on an Instant Messaging Interface

Claudio Alvarez[1]([⊠])[ID], Luis A. Rojas[2][ID], and Juan de Dios Valenzuela[1]

[1] Universidad de los Andes, Facultad de Ingeniería y Ciencias Aplicadas,
Santiago, Chile
calvarez@uandes.cl, jdvalenzuela@miuandes.cl
[2] Facultad de Ciencias Empresariales, Departamento de Ciencias de la Computación
y Tecnologías de la Información, Universidad del Bío-Bío, Concepción, Chile

Abstract. Computer programming skills are essential for a variety of disciplines in the fields of Science, Technology, Engineering and Mathematics (STEM). To support learning of programming in personalized ways, Programming Tutors (PTs) have been utilized in higher education contexts for decades. However, implementation of PTs with mobile devices has remained unexplored from both design and adoption standpoints. In this research, we designed, implemented, and trialled a PT based on Telegram Messenger. The tutor was introduced to a cohort of engineering freshmen ($N = 227$) in a computer programming course; however, it was introduced as an optional learning tool with no extrinsic incentives for fostering its adoption. Under these conditions, students' activity with the tool was monitored for 11 days. A total of 99 students (44.7%) chose to use the tutor and did so at least once. In average, students who used the tutor solved 9.2 tasks out of a maximum of 18 ($SD = 5.49$). The use of notifications was found highly influential to motivate tutor use: within 3 days of a student receiving a reminder notification, 80.6% of responses to tasks were registered. The tutor scored a mean of 73.8 ($SD = 13.81$) in the Systems Usability Scale. Students suggestions for improvement emphasized the need for more elaborate feedback after submitting their responses to problems and leveling of task difficulty. Regarding the tutor's best features, mobility and ease of use of the interface were found the most prominent.

Keywords: Programming tutor · Instant messaging · User study

1 Introduction

Computer programming is an essential skill in Science, Technology, Engineering and Mathematics (STEM) disciplines [6]. Virtually every STEM major will comprise at least one computer programming subject. Despite that most students in higher education nowadays are digital natives, instruction of programming literacy in K-12 levels is still scarce around the world and freshmen often enroll in

G. Meiselwitz (Ed.): HCII 2022, LNCS 13316, pp. 3–20, 2022.
https://doi.org/10.1007/978-3-031-05064-0_1

STEM curricula without these competencies. Failure rates in introductory computer programming courses (i.e., 'CS1' courses) are close to 30% in average [4]. That is, roughly one in every three students in a CS1 course will fail.

Pedagogical philosophies advocating greater personalization of teaching and active learning in CS1, such as active learning [21] and mastery learning [11], are becoming influential towards improving teaching effectiveness. Moreover, technological tools have been developed aiming to further personalize and improve students' learning. Specifically, Intelligent Tutoring Systems (ITS) [15,20] are computer programs that model learners' psychological states to provide individualized instruction [18]. An ITS presents students with new information, asks questions or assigns learning tasks, provides feedback or hints, and offers prompts to induce cognitive, motivational and metacognitive change. Additionally, an ITS can respond to questions posed by students.

In past decades, several ITS have been developed for the computer programming domain, known as Intelligent Programming Tutors (IPTs) [9]. Traditionally, these have been designed to be used in formal learning settings, such as computer laboratories with traditional PCs that have fixed screen and keyboard arrangements. This contrasts with the fact that nowadays students spend most of their time using mobile devices rather than PCs, and that through mobile devices, it is possible for students to study in informal contexts, with the freedom to choose the place and time. Additionally, text messaging is one of the most widely used applications on mobile devices, and several mobile messaging platforms allow the use of 'chatbots', or conversational agents, which can provide a friendly interface. With easy access and low interaction costs, text messaging is an alternative to a web interface or a full-fledged mobile application on the mobile device.

In this study, we present the design, implementation and evaluation of an IPT based on Telegram Messenger [24], a major text messaging platform accessible from mobile devices and PCs, that allows the development of chatbots. Our aim has been to develop an programming tutor based on this type of interface, which can be used for fostering learning of conceptual programming knowledge, based on any text-based programming language. Our proposal includes the interface and interaction design, and the incorporation of a basic tutor model based on fixed teacher-defined task sequences with multiple-choice items.

In the next sections, we present a review of related work, the design and implementation of the proposed tutor, followed by a pilot study, analysis of results, conclusions and future work.

2   Related Work

2.1   Programming Tutors

Tutoring Systems (TS) are computer programs that model learners' psychological states to provide individualized instruction [18]. A TS presents the learner with new information, asks questions or assigns learning tasks, provides feedback or hints, and offers prompts to induce cognitive, motivational, and metacognitive change.

In the domain of education of computer programming, Programming Tutors (PT), a specialized form of TS, have been developed over the past decades. A majority of PTs have been created for individual university courses, designed for specific programming languages and programming paradigm (such as imperative procedural, object-oriented, and functional) [12], and focused on a specific set of skills. Several PT teach foundation concepts like conditionals and loops, while others are based on specific concepts that have been identified as difficult to learn and in need of more structured tuition, such as recursion.

With the advent of web technologies and distance education, web-based tutors have become common, which can be scaled to large student cohorts. However, limitations still remain regarding the specificity of the programming language, paradigm, and skills that are addressed. Research gaps exist in the development of programming tutors, regarding the possibility that tutor models, domain models, and the user interface of a tutor can support multiple programming languages, and adjust to run on devices based on mobile form factors. These gaps can be solved by using mobile technologies that higher education students are familiar with [8].

2.2   Educational Chatbots

Constant interactions with mobile devices and applications are part of digital natives' lifestyles and interests. Text messaging through dedicated platforms and social media continues to be a prominent application of mobile devices for current generations [16,23].

Instant messaging platforms, such as Facebook Messenger [22] and Telegram [24], allow third parties to develop conversational agents, or chatbots. Such conversational characters can provide instruction to students, with varying degrees of sophistication. A chatbot can keep track of the user's task and context and can be accessed from devices with different form factors, enabling multi-modal interactions. Chatbots based on text messaging platforms are a convenient means of delivering software to the end-user, facilitating its accessibility, and not requiring installation of additional software. A chatbot is usually represented by a static or animated avatar and can be used to deliver notifications, messages, and instructional dialogs.

For the reasons discussed above, chatbots can be a convenient means for implementing pedagogical agents. For example, programming tutors can pervasively integrate with students' lifestyles and patterns of use of mobile technology [8]. However, this poses a research challenge as the development of PT based on current text messaging platforms is scarce [22].

3 Design and Implementation

3.1 Educational Context

Development of the tutor proposed in this research was part of a research agenda with the goal to improve engineering freshmen experience and learning in their introductory computer programming course based on Python 3. The student cohort in this study comprised 227 engineering freshmen at Universidad de los Andes, Chile. A fundamental step in the research agenda was to reform the programming course based on a mastery learning approach [11]. That is, provide instruction to students according to their own demonstrated learning progress. To enable this, the course was modified to be composed of four successive modules, wherein each module builds on knowledge taught in the preceding ones [1]. The student thus must achieve a pass grade in a module in order to be promoted to the next. As a result, a student may fail and repeat modules without necessarily failing the entire course in the semester, as long as the four modules are passed. In this way, the modular course offers students a greater degree of personalization than possible in a traditional course, as the students may follow different trajectories according to their own pace of learning.

As a means for fostering students' self-regulated learning [26] and foster effective personal study beyond what is possible in formal activities such as lectures and laboratory assignments, the research agenda included development of a mobile tutor for programming practice that could be utilized by students in their free time.

3.2 Elicitation of Requirements and Features

Definition of requirements and features for the tutor was initiated by the present authors through brainstorming sessions. User-tutor interactions were modeled by means of state diagrams and user interface mockups. Later, basic ideas were refined and reoriented through focus groups conducted with engineering students belonging to the target population, and with graduate students in an educational technology program. The first focus group activity was conducted at Universidad de los Andes, Chile, involving a cohort of seven freshman students in engineering (henceforth referred to as 'Cohort A'), who had passed the programming course in the previous semester. The second focus group was conducted with students from the Master of Arts in Digital Media Design for Learning at New York University, USA ('Cohort B'). Features initially considered by the present authors were as follows:

- Instant Messaging Interface: Use of an instant messaging application/platform as the primary means of interaction with the tutor.
- Conversational Interaction: Give the tutor human traits and behavior by supporting textual, conversational interactions for accessing its features.
- Persuasive Notifications: Incorporate persuasive notifications with humorous cues to invite the student to engage in new learning tasks, or resume unfinished tasks.

- Support for open and close-ended tasks: Support live coding tasks, as well as closed-ended tasks such as multiple-choice questions.
- Multi-modal interface: Give the student the choice to work on their computer, or on their mobile device. The tutor would pose problems suited to the platform being used by the student. That is, problems requiring writing or editing lengthy pieces of code were considered appropriate when accessing the tutor from a computer, though not from a mobile device. On the other hand, closed-ended items, such as multiple-choice questions were considered better suited for mobile devices.
- Help-seeking support: Allow a means for the student to communicate with teaching assistants to seek for help when dealing with a task.

The set of features described above was discussed with Cohort A in their focus group. The following observations were raised in this event:

- Utilize a mobile messaging platform that appeals most students and that is easy to use. Possibilities of adopting WhatsApp, Instagram o Snapchat were discussed with the students. A later investigation on available alternatives led the present authors to conclude that Telegram Messenger offered the best set of development features; particularly, a complete chatbot API [25].
- Minimize conversational interaction with the tutor for accessing its functions. It was considered that no apparent benefits stemmed from asking students to engage in a casual conversation with the tutor to start training, access their profile, see progress statistics, etc. Interaction design and mockups were modified to include structured menu-based navigation for accessing common features. Nevertheless, support for free conversation was maintained in case the student wanted to access a function directly, without requiring to navigate through a sequence of nested menus.
- Focus on supporting study in informal settings and in students's free time. The students welcomed the possibility of utilizing a tutor supporting their study of programming anywhere and anytime, and regarded this as the most desirable feature. In this regard, they did not consider a multi-modal interface to support study on a PC as a feature of critical importance. For this reason, design of the first version of the tutor was later limited to only support tasks based on multiple-choice questions, with hints and feedback, on the mobile device.

Based on the abovelisted considerations, a refined version of the design was finally presented to students in Cohort B in a focus group session. The students proposed the following features in order to promote the adoption of the tool:

- Adopt a character for the tutor based on a conversational avatar that can be friendly to the students, with a realistic biography and cultural identity, along with communication cues that can be attractive and interesting to the students.
- Develop the character with humorous traits and behavior, such as use of memes, as typically used in social networks.

- Develop the tutor in such a way that it provides a scaffolding for students' training of their self-regulation skills in the study of computer programming. Have the tutor incorporate reminder notifications, help-seeking functions.
- Introduce gamification mechanics in the tutor's design to maximize students' engagement.

Considering the above characteristics, 'Professor Murasaki' was developed by the present authors as the tutor's character. Murasaki is a guest lecturer visiting from a Japanese institution, who encourages discipline, hard work, and cares for every student's success. These traits were inspired by the sensei character in Karate Kid movies, Mr. Miyagi [14]. Other gamification characteristics were inspired by martial arts video games, such as Ninja Gaiden [10]. The intent was to convey students the idea that the experience of learning programming is rewarding, and that it bears similarities to learning martial arts, as for self-improvement, merit and skill mastery. Professor Murasaki greets students in Japanese, addresses students by their name followed by the honorific suffix 'san', and rewards students' achievements with ancient ninja and samurai weapons, such as shurikens (i.e., ninja stars), katana swords, and uchiwa (i.e., hand fans).

3.3   Functional Requirements

Tutor features discussed in focus groups were mainly student-facing. The present authors had further conversations on how the tool must support the teacher's role. Thus based on their prior experience with Learning Management Systems (LMS) and instructional design platforms, functional requirements for the tutor emerged as follows:

- **Task and content authoring:** The tutor and its supporting infrastructure shall provide teachers and administrators authoring tools to create, manage and organize tasks and content.
- **Task formats:** The tutor shall support closed-ended (i.e., multiple-choice questions) tasks, and support any text-based programming language.
- **Support for different tutoring modes:** The tutor shall permit teachers to organize, enable, and track progress of training in their courses. The tutor must support different operation modes (e.g. task selection algorithms), however, initially only fixed task sequence mode will be implemented, to focus in validating the usability of the user interface and adoption of the tutor.
- **User and Role management:** The system shall allow administrators to manage user accounts and to associate users with courses. Furthermore, administrators shall be able to assign roles to users in courses. On the other hand, the system shall permit administrators and teachers to *tag* students in a course, in order to target specific learning activities and notifications to students matching specific tags.
- **Student support:** The role of teaching assistant shall be able to receive inquiries from students as they perform learning activities. The students shall be able to access responses to their inquiries from teaching assistants.

- **Student monitoring:** Teachers shall be able to access dashboards in their courses, wherein they can constantly monitor students' progress and achievements, and spot specific tasks in which students have greater difficulties. In this way, the tutor provides teachers information by which they can provide students formative feedback in class.
- **Notifications:** The tutor shall provide teachers the possibility to send push-style notifications to students' mobile devices, in order to inform them about new activities available, or to persuade them to continuously train.
- **Chatbot Characters:** The tutor shall support adopting and configuring different chatbot characters, according to the preferences and needs of the target educational context. Characters shall be identified by a name, a background story, an avatar and a behavior.
- **Gamification:** With the intent of fostering students' progress and engagement, the tutor shall provide mechanics as typically found in gamified learning environments, including a scoring system, badges and achievements.

3.4   Non-functional Requirements

- **Usability:** The tutor and its supporting infrastructure must be easy to use for higher education students and teachers. Both roles must be able to adopt the tool with minimum training and support. A minimum average score of 70/100 in the Systems Usability Scale (SUS) [3] is considered acceptable from students' standpoint.
- **Availability:** The tutor and its supporting infrastructure must be operational and accessible by students and teachers at all times, in order to support learning, as well as monitoring of activities, in both formal and informal settings.

3.5   User Interface Design

Professor Murasaki's interface is accessible through the Telegram Messenger application, from a web browser, as a standalone application on a desktop computer, or through a mobile application in a smartphone or tablet device. The student begins by adding the tutor as a contact to Telegram Messenger (see Fig. 1(a)). An authentication process is implemented so that the student identifies themselves with their institutional email address. For this, after the tutor is added by the student as a contact, the tutor greets the student asking them for their institutional email address. After the student enters their email address, they receive a One-Time Password by email, which can then be entered on the tutor. After authentication succeeds, the student can start accessing the tutor's features, through a menu-based interface, or by asking the tutor to open them via text conversation (see Fig. 1(b)).

The student can access training task sets available, see their progress reports, communicate with teaching assistants, and see their achievements by navigating through menus displayed on the Telegram Messenger interface (see Fig. 2).

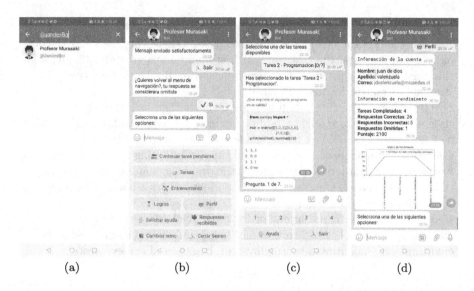

Fig. 1. (a) Professor Murasaki in a student's contact list. (b) Conversation and menu-based navigation (c) Student's response to a task. (d) Student profile and performance information.

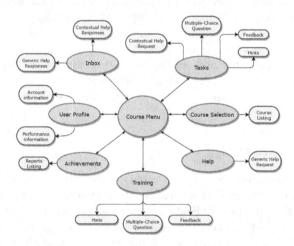

Fig. 2. Menu navigation in the Telegram-based tutor.

In the initial version of the tutor presented here, only tasks based on Multiple Choice Questions (MCQs) are supported (Fig. 1(c)). Reasons for this decision were threefold: (1) user interactions are simplified in the mobile device as the student does not need to type code, nor the tutor is required to analyze it. Nevertheless, items can include hints which can be displayed as required by the student, as well as feedback on correct and incorrect responses; (2) a standardized menu is embedded in the Telegram interface allowing the student to submit their response to each MCQ easily, either by taping the option number or by entering it manually; (3) any programming language can be used as item stems and options are based as rich text based on markdown format [13], and rendered as PNG images (see Fig. 1(c)).

The student may reach teaching assistants for help in two different contexts. Firstly, the student may freely ask any question related to the course, through an option available in the main navigation menu. Also, the student may see responses to their questions in an inbox, also accessible from the main menu. On the other hand, when the student is solving a given task, they can enter questions specific to the task, which then the teaching assistant can respond to asynchronously.

3.6   Architecture

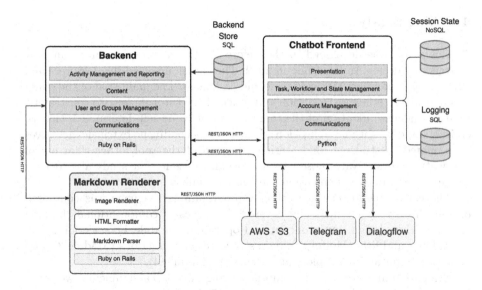

Fig. 3. Architecture of the proposed tutoring system.

An architecture comprising back-end and front-end subsystems was defined as shown in Fig. 3. The front-end subsystem provides tutor functionality in collaboration with the Telegram Messenger platform. On the other hand, the back-end is used to manage chatbot configuration, content, courses, notifications, etc.

The backend subsystem comprises four layers. The 'Activity Management and Reporting' layer is intended for managing learning activities, providing teachers with dashboards and reports for monitoring students' progress, and keeping track of gamification information. The 'Content' layer permits managing item banks, which includes item creation and modification. This layer communicates with a service that renders markdown text as bitmap images.

The 'Users and groups Management' layer permits managing users and roles, with operations such as associating users with a course, or assigning a user a role within a course. Lastly, the 'Communications' supports sending students email messages and push notifications through the text messaging service.

The front-end subsystem is also composed of four layers. The 'Presentation' layer refers to content (e.g. menus, images, instructions, etc.) when students interact with the tutor. The 'Task, Workflow and State Management' layer consists of the logic implemented by the tutor, such as task control, the student's status in the application, input mapping, among others. The 'Account Management' layer implements students' authentication and identity information. Lastly, the 'Communications' layer implements a messaging system to enable communication among students and the teaching staff, and notifications that can be sent from the backend system to Telegram Messenger executing in students' devices.

4   Pilot Study

A pilot study was developed in the before-mentioned programming course at Universidad de los Andes, Chile in 2019. The course involved five lecturers and 227 students, of which 189 were male and 38 female. The main goal of the study was to evaluate students' adoption and usage of the tutor under two constraints: Firstly, students' adoption of the tool was meant to be self-determined, that is, entirely optional with no obligation of any kind. Secondly, no extrinsic incentives were offered to students for fostering adoption of the tool, other than use of notifications to motivate those who had begun to use it. The study also focused on capturing students' perceptions on tutor usability.

The course based on the Python 3 programming language was composed of four three-week modules and covered the basics of computational thinking and algorithm design, input-output and operators (Module 1); selection statement, loops and lists (Module 2); data structures and functions (Module 3), and numeric computation, 2D plots and recursion (Module 4).

Evaluation in every module comprised two graded lab assignments (weighted 7.5% each), class and recitation attendance (7.5%), and a summative examination (70%).

The pilot study was conducted with students in modules two to four, in the fourth time block of the semester, that is, weeks 10 to 12.

4.1   Measurements

Tasks intended to foster students' mastery of programming skills were created targeting each module in the trial. Table 1 shows task sets created per each module, with their descriptions. Design of tasks was based on the taxonomy proposed by [19], which combines structural complexity based on categories of the SOLO taxonomy developed by [5], and cognitive categories from the revised Bloom's taxonomy [2] with an interpretation for the context of CS education. Tasks were based on the multistructural-understanding [19] level of the taxonomy; that is, problems requiring understanding the workings of a given code, by combining multiple programming skills and concepts.

Per each module, three task sets were elaborated. In Modules 2 and 3, six tasks were comprised in each set, with a total of 18 tasks administered. In Module 4, 15 tasks were comprised.

Students' grades in the course time block in which the intervention was undertaken were considered as a means to explore correlation among students' academic performance and tutor use. Grades considered include both lab assignments and the final exam. Evidently, as the design of this study does not comprise balanced control and experimental groups in the different course modules, analysis of impact of tutor use on students' learning is beyond the scope of the present work.

At the end of the intervention, the students responded an online version of the Systems Usability Scale questionnaire [3], to which two open-ended questions were added asking about aspects of the tutor that should be improved, and aspects considered the most positive.

Table 1. Description and number of questions in each module.

Module	Set	Tasks	Description
2	1	6	Code tracing problems involving flow control (i.e., selection statement and loops), requiring determining program behavior or output
	2	6	Similar to above, plus problems involving loops over collections (for statement)
	3	6	Similar to above
3	1	6	Code tracing problems involving lists, nested lists, slices and iterative control flow, requiring determining program behavior or output
	2	6	Similar to above
	3	6	Similar to above, plus list methods in Python (i.e., append, index, count, etc.)
4	1	6	Code tracing problems involving text file access and read/write operations, requiring determining program behavior or output
	2	6	Similar to above, plus algorithms for processing text input from files
	3	3	Similar to above

4.2 Method

The intervention began in a Friday morning (i.e., May 24th, 2019), four days before the second graded lab assignment in the fourth module of the course, which was to take place in the following Tuesday morning (i.e., May 28th, 2019). In the initial Friday, the tutor was introduced to the students by means of a live demonstration at the computer lab in their regular recitation session. In addition, an announcement was published in the course's LMS introducing the tutor, with indications on how to enable it on the mobile phone.

The intervention lasted for a total of eleven days. From the outset, all task sets were made available to the students in the different modules. However, these had to be solved sequentially; that is, after they finished a task set they could continue to the next one immediately.

Notifications were sent via Telegram to the students in the second, fourth and fifth days of the intervention, at noon, reminding them to complete the training tasks available in the tutor. In the fifth day of the intervention, the students had a graded laboratory assignment. The notification in the previous day hinted them about the tutor tasks being useful to prepare for it. The final notification in the fifth day was intended to encourage students to finish the remaining tasks in case they had not.

5   Results

5.1   Tutor Adoption

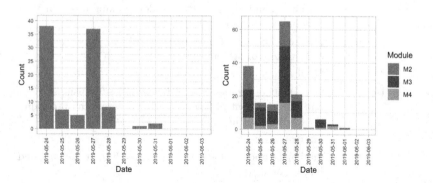

Fig. 4. Left: Users accessing the tutor for the first time each day. Right: Daily users from different course modules.

Table 2 shows the total number of students per module, and the share of students who chose to use the tutor, by accessing it at least once during the pilot study. In the first day of the intervention, only a few students (i.e., 38; 17.4%) began using the tutor, that is, considering the 218 total students in modules two to four who were introduced to the tutor either in the recitation session that took place in the morning of that day, or through the LMS announcement. In the two following days (weekend), only twelve additional students began using the tutor. A surge of tutor adoption and activity was observed in the fourth day of the intervention (Monday), after the students had been sent a notification about the tasks being useful to prepare for the lab assignment that was to take place in the following day.

In the day of the lab assignment, the increase of tutor activity and new users joining dropped substantially. After the assignment, tutor use decreased to a minimum.

Table 2. Students per module and share of tutor users.

Module	Total students	Tutor users	% Tutor users
1	3	–	–
2	55	25	45.5%
3	107	47	43.9%
4	56	27	48.2%
Total	221	99	44.7%

5.2 Tutor Usage

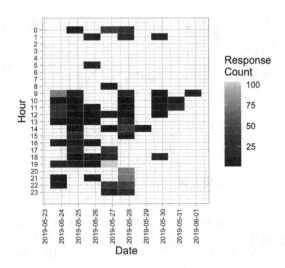

Fig. 5. Students' submission of task responses per hour in each day of the intervention.

Figure 5 shows students' usage of the tutor, in terms of submission of responses to tasks per each hour of the day, for the entirety of the intervention. In the first day there was peak activity during the recitation session in which the tutor was introduced to the students, then moderate to minor use of the tutor continued to be observed during that day. This information is complemented by Fig. 6. There it can be seen that activity in the first day, and in the ensuing weekend was mainly dedicated to the first task sets available for each module (i.e., M2T1, M3T1 and M4T1). On Saturday, the tutor was utilized constantly throughout the day, while on Sunday greater activity was observed at nighttime. On Monday, the greatest student engagement in the intervention was observed between 18:30 and 19:30, after classes, with some activity also being observed at lunchtime. The tutor continued to be used at night that day. In the fifth day of the intervention, in which a lab assignment took place, few students continued working on tutor tasks. According to Fig. 4, it can be seen that 12 new students began using the tutor. Consistently, these students began using the tutor that day possibly out of curiosity after the lab assignment took place, and solved the first tasks available to their module (Fig. 6). Other students in modules three and four continued progressing in the tasks available.

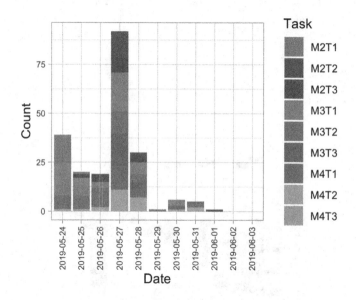

Fig. 6. Daily users per task set.

Figure 7 shows that tutor users' dedication to tasks in the different modules was clearly unequal. The mean number of tasks completed by students during the intervention was 9.2 ($SD = 5.49$, $min = 1$, $max = 18$), and 80.6% of task response submissions were observed in three days in which students were sent reminder notifications. In Module 2, no student completed all tasks. Few students (about five) reached the third task set but did not complete it. It is likely that task difficulty in the last set demotivated these students to strive further. In Module 3, it is observed that a substantial part of that group completed all task sets. However, it remains apparent that a comparable number of students only completed the first task set. In Module 4, a similar outcome was observed.

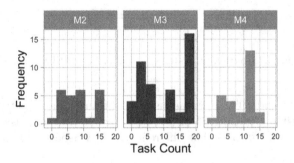

Fig. 7. Distributions of completed tasks per user, per module.

Lastly, Fig. 8 shows students' grade distributions in the course's time block in which the intervention with the tutor was conducted. It is observed that especially in Module 4 tutor users outperformed non-users. This result was not consistently observed in Module 3 (the most numerous), however, it was observed to a slight extent in Module 2. In terms of skills and difficulty, Module 3 requires that students understand and code algorithms that are substantially more complex that in Module 2, and even in Module 4. Tasks in Module 4 are more structured and predictable, as students are expected to learn to consume well-defined APIs and libraries to produce 2D plots and implement basic numeric computation. On the other hand, students in Module 4 were the most advanced and successful in the course at the time of the intervention. Thus their decision to use the tutor and practice likely correlates with greater self-regulation, motivation and engagement with the course.

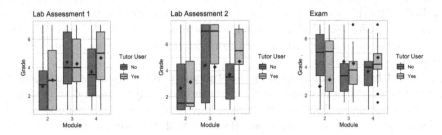

Fig. 8. Comparison of grade distributions among tutor users and non-users in (a) Lab Assignment 1, (b) Lab Assignment 2, and (c) Summative Exam.

5.3 Usability Evaluation

Figure 9 shows the distribution of scores in the SUS scale ($M = 73.8$, $SD = 13.81$, $median = 72.5$), considering a total of 23 responses collected. According to [17], the average SUS score of systems is 68.0, and only the top 10% have a score over 80.8. In the sample, 52.2% of the students gave the tutor a score under 68, and by having an average score of 73.8, the system falls into a percentile in

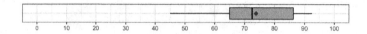

Fig. 9. Distribution of Systems Usability Scale (SUS) scores.

between the 65th and 69th. This means that the tutor has a better SUS score than 65% of systems considered in [17]'s sample. It can be considered a good score but the result indicates that different usability aspects can be improved.

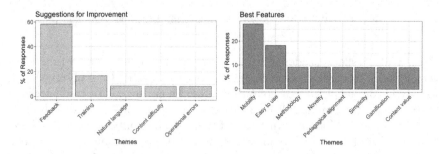

Fig. 10. Left: Suggestions for improvement. Right: Best tutor features.

Qualitative open-ended responses to survey items asking students to report on aspects in need of improvement were coded inductively. Figure 10 shows each response category and its relative frequency. The most common aspect in need of improvement was tutor's feedback. That is, the feedback given to the students on submitting wrong answers to the tutor was considered incomplete and/or insufficient. In the second place, some students considered that task difficulty should be adjustable, or that it should adjust automatically to their ability. Other aspects were in regard to the tutor's limited conversational capabilities and software bugs in that regard.

The best features emphasized by the students were mobility, i.e., understood as the possibility to practice course concepts and skills anywhere, and at anytime. Also, ease of use, and the training methodology were also valuable aspects in the students' opinion. Other positive aspects align with the present authors' intent to provide students a tool that could provide motivating and meaningful study possibilities in informal settings.

6   Conclusions and Future Work

This research set out to investigate the design, implementation and adoption of a programming tutor based on an instant messaging interface based on Telegram Messenger [24], which is intended to support students' learning of programming in informal settings. The initial version of the tutor was implemented supporting close-ended tasks, presenting the code involved to the student as images, thus supporting virtually any text-based programming language. The tool was used in a modular computer programming course for engineering freshmen, based on a mastery learning approach, and evaluated for a period of eleven days.

The tutor was presented to the students as an optional tool, without any obligation to use it. During the pilot, three notifications were to encourage use of the tutor by students who had began using it. In the study 99 students (44.7% of the cohort) used the tutor at least once. Usability evaluation based on the Systems Usability Scale (SUS) resulted in scores with $M = 73.8$ ($SD = 13.81$). Students suggestions for improvement emphasized the need for more elaborate feedback after submitting their responses to problems (58.3% of responses), and further training and assistance to use the tool (16.7%). Regarding the tutor's best features, the students considered mobility (27.2%) and ease of use of the interface (18.2%).

Results of the experience lead us to conclude that the use of the tutor varies among students when left as an optional tool, even if it delivers tasks that are related to the class content. The use of the tutor does not motivate students equally, and the further promotion of its adoption and frequent use requires greater facilitating conditions and incentives [7]. It is possible that a greater teacher involvement with the tool, by including it in the course in a systematic way, encourages greater student use. In the future, we will focus on improving the usability of the tutor based on the results obtained, and we will carry out a new study on the adoption of the tool, incorporating it as part of the pedagogical and evaluation strategy of the programming course. We also plan to introduce a continuous-adaptive training mode in the tutor, based on mastery learning, allowing the student to progress through different skills and task complexity at their own pace.

Acknowledgements. We thank Dr. Alyssa F. Wise for her cooperation with this research. This research was funded by ANID/FONDECYT Initiation into Research grant 11160211.

References

1. Alvarez, C., Wise, A., Altermatt, S., Aranguiz, I.: Predicting academic results in a modular computer programming course. In: 2nd Latin American Conference on Learning Analytics, LALA, vol. 2425, pp. 21–30 (2019)
2. Anderson, L.W., Krathwohl, D.R.: A Taxonomy for Learning, Teaching, and Assessing: A Revision of Bloom's Taxonomy of Educational Objectives. Longman, Harlow (2001)
3. Bangor, A., Kortum, P., Miller, J.: Determining what individual SUS scores mean: adding an adjective rating scale. J. Usability Stud. **4**(3), 114–123 (2009)
4. Bennedsen, J., Caspersen, M.E.: Failure rates in introductory programming: 12 years later. ACM Inroads **10**(2), 30–36 (2019)
5. Biggs, J.B.: Teaching for Quality Learning at University: What the Student Does. McGraw-Hill Education (UK), London (2011)

6. Bocconi, S., Chioccariello, A., Dettori, G., Ferrari, A., Engelhardt, K., et al.: Developing computational thinking in compulsory education-implications for policy and practice. Technical report, Joint Research Centre (Seville site) (2016)

7. Chao, C.M.: Factors determining the behavioral intention to use mobile learning: an application and extension of the UTAUT model. Front. Psychol. **10**, 1652 (2019)

8. Crompton, H., Burke, D.: The use of mobile learning in higher education: a systematic review. Comput. Educ. **123**, 53–64 (2018)

9. Crow, T., Luxton-Reilly, A., Wuensche, B.: Intelligent tutoring systems for programming education: a systematic review. In: Proceedings of the 20th Australasian Computing Education Conference, pp. 53–62 (2018)

10. Foxhack: Ninja Gaiden series. https://www.mobygames.com/game-group/ninja-gaiden-series. Accessed 28 Jan 2022

11. Garner, J., Denny, P., Luxton-Reilly, A.: Mastery learning in computer science education. In: Proceedings of the Twenty-First Australasian Computing Education Conference, pp. 37–46 (2019)

12. Gerdes, A., Heeren, B., Jeuring, J., van Binsbergen, L.T.: Ask-Elle: an adaptable programming tutor for Haskell giving automated feedback. Int. J. Artif. Intell. Educ. **27**(1), 65–100 (2017). https://doi.org/10.1007/s40593-015-0080-x

13. Gruber, J.: Markdown (2002). https://daringfireball.net/projects/markdown/. Accessed 19 May 2021

14. Kamen, R.M., Avildsen, J.G.: (nd). https://www.imdb.com/title/tt0087538/. Accessed 19 Jan 2022

15. Kulik, J.A., Fletcher, J.: Effectiveness of intelligent tutoring systems: a meta-analytic review. Rev. Educ. Res. **86**(1), 42–78 (2016)

16. Kumar, V., Nanda, P.: Social media in higher education: a framework for continuous engagement. Int. J. Inf. Commun. Technol. Educ. (IJICTE) **15**(1), 97–108 (2019)

17. Lewis, J.R., Sauro, J.: Item benchmarks for the system usability scale. J. Usability Stud. **13**(3), 158–167 (2018)

18. Ma, W., Adesope, O.O., Nesbit, J.C., Liu, Q.: Intelligent tutoring systems and learning outcomes: a meta-analysis. J. Educ. Psychol. **106**(4), 901 (2014)

19. Meerbaum-Salant, O., Armoni, M., Ben-Ari, M.: Learning computer science concepts with scratch. Comput. Sci. Educ. **23**(3), 239–264 (2013)

20. Mousavinasab, E., Zarifsanaiey, N., R. Niakan Kalhori, S., Rakhshan, M., Keikha, L., Ghazi Saeedi, M.: Intelligent tutoring systems: a systematic review of characteristics, applications, and evaluation methods. Interact. Learn. Environ. **29**, 1–22 (2018)

21. Pirker, J., Riffnaller-Schiefer, M., Gütl, C.: Motivational active learning: engaging university students in computer science education. In: Proceedings of the 2014 Conference on Innovation & Technology in Computer Science Education, pp. 297–302 (2014)

22. Smutny, P., Schreiberova, P.: Chatbots for learning: a review of educational chatbots for the Facebook messenger. Comput. Educ. **151**, 103862 (2020)

23. So, S.: Mobile instant messaging support for teaching and learning in higher education. Internet High. Educ. **31**, 32–42 (2016)

24. Telegram: Telegram messenger (2020). https://telegram.org/. Accessed 20 Dec 2020

25. Telegram: Telegram chatbot API (nd). https://core.telegram.org/bots/api. Accessed 19 Jan 2022

26. Zimmerman, B.J.: Investigating self-regulation and motivation: historical background, methodological developments, and future prospects. Am. Educ. Res. J. **45**(1), 166–183 (2008)

Embedding Social, Community Projects Within Contemporary Curricular

Pranit Anand[✉] [ID]

Queensland University of Technology, Brisbane, Australia
pranit.anand@qut.edu.au

Abstract. Social media continues to influence the online behaviours of humans in some of the most profound ways. Furthermore, COVID-19 pandemic has highlighted immense opportunities that social media provides to keep people connected and engaged through difficult circumstances. Unfortunately, it also attracts various dubious users, eager to take advantage to the anonymity of these platforms to conduct unethical and illegal practices.

Typical computing studies courses do not focus on developing the skills and attitudes to enable students to work in a globalised environment, and certainly do not focus on exposing many of the social challenges in our societies. Authentic learning experience are not common.

An activity was created between the UOW College Australia and UOW College Hong Kong where students from these respective institutions collaborated with each other to identify, explore and suggest a social media-based solution to challenges faced by a NGO located in a third country, that is, not located in Australia or Hong Kong. This gave students to experience working with each other, and through that navigate the various linguistic, cultural and other norms and differences. They also had to identify and communicate with a NGO from a third country, in many cases who had their own linguistic, cultural and other norms about work and communications.

This paper will discuss some of the knowledge, skills and attitudes that can be gained from engaging in cross border collaborative social projects. It will also outline some of the challenges and opportunities that exist in establishing these types of learning activities.

Keywords: Collaboration · Cross-institutional · Transdisciplinary

1 Introduction

The Internet and the World Wide Web has continued to have a profound impact on our lives ever since its creation. The World Wide Web in particular has allowed sharing and access to information to the masses, prior to which the Internet remained the domain of the information technology experts. The research and academic communities have benefited immensely through the WWW and continue to do so. Various large scale research collaborations now depend on reliable, accessible and global Internet connections, and the COVID-19 pandemic has demonstrated its significance in no uncertain terms.

© The Author(s), under exclusive license to Springer Nature Switzerland AG 2022
G. Meiselwitz (Ed.): HCII 2022, LNCS 13316, pp. 21–29, 2022.
https://doi.org/10.1007/978-3-031-05064-0_2

While the impact of the Internet on research and academic communities is unquestionable, the business and private sector have really driven many of the innovations around the use of the WWW. From innovations in business-to-business collaborations, to development of completely new business models, the business sector has embraced the WWW to add significant value for consumers and continue to re-define the way we do business. The WWW has allowed innovations in many types of business models that would not exist without the Internet and the WWW, Google, Facebook, Amazon are cases in point. Many of these businesses are leaders in innovations, not just on the business model side, but in leading edge technologies in connectivity, security, and the like, with some of the most innovative patents held by these Internet dependant businesses.

It is fair to say that the world of work, play and even they way we interact with each other is being redefined by many of these technologies, and driven by the businesses leading these innovations.

Regardless, there is no denying most young people are growing up within social media, and their thinking, perceptions of the world and behaviour is easily influenced by their engagement with social media. Studies have shown how social media can impact young people to live their lives in a manner that displays a 'glossier' way they live rather than the reality. Enveloped in this social media world many young people do not realise many of the inequalities and challenges that exist around us, but significantly how can social media be used in positive ways to address many of the global challenges.

Despite the hyper connectivity world that we live in, it can still be argued that we continue to live very isolated lives, with little understanding of other cultures, religions, ideologies, challenges, and perceptions. Most students enter higher education with little to no experience and appreciation of different cultures, communications norms, and ways of doing things. As the world of work becomes more and more global there is an expectation that every person will be able to navigate the hyperconnected world with ease. Students need to be provided with appropriate transformative experiences to develop these 21st century skills.

The traditional student study exchange program often provides opportunities for those involved to experience these firsthand, however these types of programs can be expensive and challenging to implement. Appropriate use of technology can help overcome many of these challenges, and yet give students the transformative experiences that is needed. While social media tools are not developed for education it can be used to learn about social causes. Through its scalable connectivity of ideas and ideologies, social media technologies have the capability of connecting people from diverse backgrounds. Connections often do not need to speak the same language, and many technologies exist to help manage these divides.

The students often used commonly used social media tools to collaborate, and that gave them an opportunity to experience a very different way of using these tools. Rather than looking at glossy pictures of other people, they were using it to do meaningful conversation about their university work, and how to help their chosen NGO. These activities were informed by and evaluated using existing theories and frameworks around situated learning and social constructivism.

2   Social Media and Social Good

Social media is arguably one of the most impactful platforms to come out of the innovations in WWW technologies (Tess 2013; Willems et al. 2016). While most readers are likely to be familiar with at least some form of social media, it is worth pointing out some of its features. Social media platforms operate on the easy to use and access WWW infrastructure but also provide accessibility via various mobile platforms such as iOS and Android. Most allow users to connect with other people and ideas from across the world. Users are able to easily search for and connect with other people, or ideas. Accessibility and connect ability is the primary feature of most social media platforms. Although there is a plethora of social media platforms for different demographics of users and interests, some of the common social media platforms include Facebook, Twitter, LinkedIn, Instagram, Snapchat, Tinder, TikTok, Pinterest, YouTube, QQ, and many more to name. Almost all of these social media platforms are free, with only some very selective platforms requiring pay for use service. They all service different purposes, for example Instagram allows the sharing of pictures and images, while LinkedIn is considered a professional social media platform for work and professional networking and resume sharing, TikTok on the had generally appeals to the younger users, allowing them to sharing quick short videos.

These social media companies are sophisticated enterprises, usually employing some of the best technologists, and innovators. Their main goal is to harvest as much user information as possible, which is used for targeted marketing and other business-related strategies. It's through these marketing, advertising and other business uses of the harvested data that provide lucrative incomes for these social media companies, allowing them to remain free for the users. The longer that the users remain on their platform, the more data about their interest, likes and dislikes, connections, even thinking patterns can be collected by the social media companies and therefore the user interaction of these platforms are extremely innovative and 'sticky', that is they are able get the users to be on their platforms for considerable long times. Social media that is accessed via mobile phones provide particularly rich data sources of the social media companies, as they are able to track the physical movement of their users, and their usage patterns in different geographical locations.

For many users, social media provides an opportunity to connect with others through family, friends, and other acquaintances or connecting with people with ideas and interests similar to ones own, or of interest to one. Many of the social media algorithms continuously curate the content and interactions for individual users, making these interactions innately personalised and therefore generates increasing interest of the users to remain on these sites.

Withstanding the profitability motivations of the social media companies, these platforms do provide users the ability to connect with each other and as has been demonstrated during the COVID-19 lockdowns, allows some semblance of social connections so important for many people regardless of the lockdown restrictions. These social media platforms are increasingly used by many NGOs and social enterprises to increase about what they are doing and seek support from a global user-base (Backholm and Hornmoen 2018).

There are numerous examples where social media has been utilised constructively to mobilise global support for victims of natural disasters, increase awareness about various social causes, organise support for various orphanages and other children's charities, and many more. Meaningful use of social media ensures people remain connected to each other and provide, albeit remote, support and comfort in times of need.

Social media is increasingly used by law enforcement agencies to identify and bring criminals to justice. It becomes so much more convenient to pursue people using algorithms and digital footprints than it is to pursue them physically (Brunty et al. 2015). Through these strategies many high-profile global criminal rings involved in money laundering, human and child trafficking, and pornographic and paedophilia rings have been dismantled. Business have benefitted from the use of social media as well. Many small businesses do not necessarily need to develop and host their own website to promote their services as this can be done conveniently and with little or no cost on exiting social media platforms. They also benefit by being able to access a vast network of potential customers from around the global and not limited to their traditional geographical locations.

So, despite its many negative consequences, social media used in a meaningful way does provide significant value to society, and adds immense value to our existing personal, professional, and business connections.

3 Computer Science Courses and Social Responsibility

It is sometime difficult to imagine that as a discipline, computer and information sciences have had such a huge impact of the lives of humans and continues to redefine the way we interact with each other. Advances in computers sciences and other related information technologies have led to profound changes to types of businesses, such as Google and Facebook, as well as changes to existing and traditional business practices, such as 'click and collect' at food and grocery stores. Most of these advances have been driven by advances in our understanding about new and emerging technologies and driven by professionals at the cutting edge of these technology revolution, in most cases competent information technologists and information scientists.

Computer science and other related information sciences and technology courses tend to be very specialised fields of study (Sinclair 2014). In many cases it needs to be to ensure students can grasp the intricacies of the discipline at the current and previous states, but significantly to ensure that they develop the necessary requisites to model future development and advances in that discipline. Students of computer science need to ensure they have the requisites to continue to experiment and explore new frontiers in technology through experimentation and exploration. These students do need to be immersed in these technologies to ensure they are exploring these new frontiers in a safe way, without affecting any existing setups.

Training and education programs used to prepare students to work within this space understand these inherent requirements and have developed curricula to reflect that. There is inherent reason for students getting into computers science to be deeply embedded within that discipline, however given the impact of that discipline on society it is also important that these students are provided with a well-balanced opportunity to appreci-ate the impact of their work and respect the types of work that continues in many other disciplines.

Most of the computer science curricula is not designed to include content from out-side disciplines. Some courses may give students opportunity to undertake electives from different areas, but the content of often not embedded within computer science disci-plines and therefore indirectly not encouraged. This inherently then creates a learning environment that is inward looking and leaves not much room to explore different ways of thinking and doing things. It certainly often insulates students from the various equity issues facing an increasing number of people around the world.

There is therefore important to embed social responsibility into contemporary com-puter science curricula so that as student engage and go through learning the important computer science content they are also developing a sense of community and social responsibility along the way. Through this, it is more likely the various solutions that many of them would be developing post-graduation are more likely than not to at least recognise the equity challenges for many, and hopefully improve the lives of many marginalised communities.

4   Educating to Improve the Future Through Social Community Project

Recognising the need to improve transdisciplinary skills among computer science (Fam et al. 2018; Khoo et al. 2019) and other discipline graduates, and particularly to increase their awareness about the impact of various technology tools and associated strategies in various equity groups around the world, a transformative learning activity was developed at the University of Wollongong College in Australian and the University of Wollon-gong College in Hong Kong (formerly known as the Community College of the City University of Hong Kong). The pathways study program at University of Wollongong College in Australia is designed for students, mainly from various disadvantaged and marginalised communities, who have not been able to get direct entry to a university course due to personal circumstances affecting their high school grades. As a conse-quence, these courses often get students diverse backgrounds, study preferences, life circumstances, and the like. As a common pathway to University qualification, the stu-dents in these program are made of student who aim to study a range of different courses at university, not necessarily computer science, although there are some students who do aim to get into computer science studies. Many of the students undertaking these courses struggle with motivations and other study skills necessary for university study. This background of students then provides an excellent opportunity to provide students with a transdisciplinary learning experience that can be meaningful and transformative.

The subject coordinator at the University of Wollongong College in Australia wrote to a number of similar institutions in Malaysia, Hong Kong and Fiji to seek interest in developing collaborations to develop a cross institutional, cross border social community project for student at both institutions. Initially the Sunway University responded and an initial activity was developed where students worked on an assigned project together (Anand and Latt 2015). This initial collaboration provided the impetus for a much more comprehensive initiative between University of Wollongong College in Australia and the Community College of the City University of Hong Kong (now known as the University of Wollongong College Hong Kong).

The main aim was to give students the opportunity to develop transdisciplinary skills and attitudes, and awareness about using technology to solve some challenges faced by various equity groups around the world. Students would be given opportunity to work with other students from different institutions located overseas, and also work with NGOs located in a third country to identify and solve some of their challenges.

After getting a positive, interested reply from the subject coordinator at the Community College of the City University of Hong Kong, the subject coordinator at University of Wollongong in Australia undertook to develop the learning activity plan and present this to the counterpart in Hong Kong. After some robust and very constructive discussions between both parties, various negotiations were agreed upon to ensure that both institutions perspectives and values were respectfully represented and embedded with the learning activities. This also ensured that any learning activity was not an attempt at 'neo-colonialism' by the Australian institution (Anand and Lui 2019). Common criteria and rubrics were developed, and timelines were adjusted to accommodate different start and end dates between the two institutions.

The activity itself involved 2 or 3 students from Australia put in a group with about 2 or 3 students from Hong Kong. The students were required to contact a NGO of their own choosing to discussion some of the challenges that they may be facing and then develop solution strategies and initiate and implementation plan for these strategies. For many students this was one of the most novel activities that had been required to work on and recognising that this would be challenging, the subject coordinators at both Australia and Hong Kong institutions collaboratively developed a detailed week by week activity plan to guide the students through this project. The activity plan looked something as follows:

1. Week 1, day 1 – read and understand what needs to be done. Spend sometime thinking about the types of NGOs you would like to support.
2. Week1, day 2 – contact the students in Hong Kong/Australia and introduce yourselves. Seek to find out about hobbies, interests, studies, etc.
3. By end of week 1 – zoom/phone meeting with all group members. Sort out individual responsibilities, identify type of NGO the group will be working for.
4. By start of week 2 – contact identified NGO. Start exploring the NGO operations and likely needs.
5. By end of week 3 – organise zoom/phone meeting with NGO. Discuss the project and seek their guidance in developing a solution for them.
6. By end of week 4 – provide a first draft of solution to NGO. Seek their feedback.
7. By end of week 5 – finalise and present their work to the NGO.
8. Week 6/7 – prepare portfolio and presentation for in class presentation. Hong Kong students record short section of presentation for their Australian group members and similarly the Australian students for their Hong Kong group members.

The groups of students submitted their portfolios to their respective institutions, that is, the Australian students submitted one portfolio to their Australian teachers and the

Hong Kong students submitted one portfolio to their Hong Kong teachers for marking and grading.

As can be seen from the activity plan above, this was a very intense activity, and there was not room for students to procrastinate. Students really had to depend on each other to ensure the work gets done on time and because they were accountable to their NGOs, they had to do it to a satisfactory standard too (Davies 2009; Jaques 2007). There is no room for group members to free load, or delay the activity, however appropriate and timely support was provided by the teaching team to ensure students were progressing as expected.

5 Discussion

Authentic, real-world projects are rare in higher education studies (Herrington and Oliver 2000; Herrington et al. 2014; Karakas-Özür and Duman 2019; Villarroel et al. 2019). Projects that also involve cross-institutional, overseas institutions and community groups are even more uncommon. For educators who have implemented authenticity in their teaching, learning and assessments, the benefits are obvious. Students tend to learn more effectively through authentic activities and the learning become a lot more transferable (Meyers and Nulty 2009; Rieger and Rolfe 2018).

Activities that involve students to work with social community project helps student develop a sense of responsibility and awareness about the plight of many disadvantaged communities around the world. These experiences tend to be transformative whereby students are transformed in they way they think, they way they approach problems, how they interact with each other, particularly with those from different cultural and linguistic backgrounds, and how they identify solutions to problems (Boyd 1989; Clifford and Montgomery 2015; 2017; Nelson et al. 2016; Shultz 2007).

The feedback from students and the NGOs that the students worked for have been extremely positive. Students report that they found the groupwork activities meaningful and worthwhile, even going as far as suggesting that the groupwork was in fact the best part about the subject. Most other groupwork experiences in the literature often differ these positive experiences (Davies 2009; Jaques 2007). Many students, both from Hong Kong and Australia comment that they have developed long term friendships among each other and were likely to visit each other when they get the opportunity to travel to the respective countries.

As the world of work becomes more and more global, the workforce of the future will be expected to possess characteristics such as intercultural competencies, accepting of diverse views and ways of doing things, adaptability with different ideas and opinions, negotiation and working with people from different background, etc. (OECD 2018). These are the same qualities that students working on this project report as having developed.

Some of the challenges of implementing such a program or learning activity often involves finding the right partner institution in the first place, but perseverance pays off. Activities of this nature also tend to be challenging for students, and in some ways it has to be (Davies 2009; Jaques 2007), but providing step by step, weekly schedule helps the student keep on track.

6 Conclusion

Project of this nature tend to be novel in higher education. Even when educators are willing to explore these opportunities, the various institutional policies and compliance requirements often prevents educators from exploring these types of learning experiences. The benefits however far outweigh the challenges associated with implementing these types of projects. In our experience the biggest challenge can be finding a willing partner institutions and then persuading them about the benefits of these projects, perhaps this paper, along with other similar ones, would help.

Providing students, the opportunity to engage in community based social projects, involving the use of social media is a transformative experience for many students, particularly those from various disadvantaged communities themselves. For educators it can also be a satisfying to see the positive impact their students end up making for others, and the impact on their own development.

References

Anand, P., Latt, S.: Authentic assessments for promoting inclusivity and computing mindset. In: International Conference on Advances in Social Sciences, Wuhan, China (2015)

Anand, P., Lui, B.: Developing 21st Century Intercultural and Collaborative Competencies Through Transformative Internationalisation Projects: A Post Neo-Colonialism Approach. IADIS Press (2019)

Backholm, K., Hornmoen, H.: Social Media Use in Crisis and Risk Communication Emergencies. Bingley, Concerns and Awareness. Emerald Group (2018)

Boyd, R.D.: Facilitating personal transformations in small-groups. Small. Group. Behav. 20(4), 459–474 (1989)

Brunty, J., Helenek, K., Miller, L.: Social Media Investigation for Law Enforcement. Routledge, London (2015)

Clifford, V., Montgomery, C.: Transformative learning through internationalization of the curriculum in higher education. J. Transform. Educ. 13(1), 46–64 (2015). https://doi.org/10.1177/1541344614560909

Clifford, V., Montgomery, C.: Designing an internationalised curriculum for higher education: embracing the local and the global citizen. High. Educ. Res. Dev. 36(6), 1138–1151 (2017). https://doi.org/10.1080/07294360.2017.1296413

Dave, E.M., Lawrence dela, P., Jade, K., Joy, D.: The design of a gamified responsible use of social media. Front. Educ. (Lausanne) 6, 84 (2021). https://doi.org/10.3389/feduc.2021.635278

Davies, W.: Groupwork as a form of assessment: common problems and recommended solutions. High. Educ. 58(4), 563–584 (2009). https://doi.org/10.1007/s10734-009-9216-y

Fam, D., Neuhauser, L., Gibbs, P.: Transdisciplinary Theory, Practice and Education The Art of Collaborative Research and Collective Learning, 1st edn. Springer, Cham (2018). https://doi.org/10.1007/978-3-319-93743-4

Herrington, J., Oliver, R.: An instructional design framework for authentic learning environments. Educ. Tech. Res. Dev. 48(3), 23–48 (2000). https://doi.org/10.1007/BF02319856

Herrington, J., Parker, J., BoaseJelinek, D.: Connected authentic learning: reflection and intentional learning. Australian J. Educ. 58(1), 23–35 (2014). https://doi.org/10.1177/0004944113517830

Jaques, D.: Learning in Groups : A Handbook for Face-to-Face and Online Online Environments, 4th edn. Routledge, Abingdon, Oxon (2007)

Jonassen, D.H., Rohrer-Murphy, L.: Activity theory as a framework for designing constructivist learning environments. Educ. Tech. Res. Dev. **47**(1), 61–79 (1999). https://doi.org/10.1007/bf0 2299477

Karakas-Özür, N., Duman, N.: The trends in authentic learning studies and the role of authentic learning in geography education. Int. Educ. Stud. **12**(12), 28 (2019)

Khoo, S.-M., Haapakoski, J., Hellstén, M., Malone, J.: Moving from interdisciplinary research to transdisciplinary educational ethics: bridging epistemological differences in researching higher education internationalization(s). Eur. Educ. Res. J. EERJ **18**(2), 181–199 (2019). https://doi.org/10.1177/1474904118781223

Leask, B.: Embracing the possibilities of disruption. High. Educ. Res. Dev. **39**(7), 1388–1391 (2020). https://doi.org/10.1080/07294360.2020.1824211

Meyers, N.M., Nulty, D.D.: How to use (five) curriculum design principles to align authentic learning environments, assessment, students' approaches to thinking and learning outcomes. Assess. Eval. High. Educ. **34**(5), 565–577 (2009). https://doi.org/10.1080/02602930802226502

Nelson, K.J., Clarke, J.A., Stoodley, I.D., Creagh, T.A.: Establishing a framework for transforming student engagement, success and retention in higher education institutions (2016)

OECD: The future of education and skills: Education 2030, Paris (2018). https://www.oecd.org/education/2030/E2030%20Position%20Paper%20(05.04.2018).pdf

Rieger, J., Rolfe, A.: So close and yet so far away: teaching design students to design for differences through reflective practice and authentic learning (2018)

Robinson, K.: The interrelationship of emotion and cognition when students undertake collaborative group work online: an interdisciplinary approach. Comput. Educ. **62**, 298–307 (2013). https://doi.org/10.1016/j.compedu.2012.11.003

Shultz, L.: Educating for global citizenship: conflicting agendas and understandings. Alberta J. Educ. Res. **53**(3), 248–258 (2007)

Sinclair, I.: Computer Science, 1st edn. Newnes, London (2014)

Tess, P.A.: The role of social media in higher education classes (real and virtual) – a literature review. Comput. Hum. Behav. **29**(5), A60–A68 (2013). https://doi.org/10.1016/j.chb.2012.12.032

Villarroel, V., Boud, D., Bloxham, S., Bruna, D., Bruna, C.: Using principles of authentic assessment to redesign written examinations and tests. Innov. Educ. Teach. Int. **54**, 1–12 (2019). https://doi.org/10.1080/14703297.2018.1564882

Willems, J., et al.: The promise and pitfalls of social media use in higher education. In: Australasian Society for Computers in Learning in Tertiary Education (2016)

Zammit, K., Martins, R.: Learning through community service: assisting others, learning themselves. Australasian J. Univ. Commun. Engage. **2**(2), 226–234 (2007)

Emergency Remote Teaching in the University Context: Responding to Social and Emotional Needs During a Sudden Transition Online

Magdalena Brzezinska[1]([⊠]) [iD] and Edward Cromarty[2] [iD]

[1] WSB University, Poznan, Poland
magdalena.brzezinska@wsb.poznan.pl
[2] Northeastern University, Boston, MA, USA
cromarty.e@northeastern.edu

Abstract. This empirical paper is a collaboration of two university educators from the USA and Poland who undertook to share their experiences of transitioning in-person classes to an online emergency environment. Some economic and humanitarian causes underlying the process have been discussed. The authors have presented a brief review of the topic and case studies related to Emergency Remote Teaching (ERT), as contrasted with online education specially designed for virtual delivery (Kagawa (2005) or Hodges, Moore, Lockee, Trust, and Bond (2020)).

Strategies and consequences of introducing ERT in a university course, such as content adjustment, repurposing, and personalization, have been discussed along with the difficulties, inclusive of the growing gap between the underprivileged and privileged members of society (McKenzie 2021). Advantages of synchronous and asynchronous modes in specific educational situations have also been identified. Additionally, it has been pointed out that in ERT student assessment needs to be rethought and made inclusive utilizing student feedback (Bates 2019).

Based on the evidence examined, the authors have recommended solutions to facilitate an ERT transition, with particular emphasis on creating an online community, providing university students with regular personalized feedback and non-grade-based assessment. The authors explained why it is essential that ERT should be trauma-sensitive and focused on developing strong student-student and student-instructor connections. It has been stressed that learning is **fundamentally a social activity**, which should be carefully considered in teaching practice during a sudden transition online. The authors believe such an approach may result in heightened student perseverance, increased engagement, active collaboration, and help students grow as human beings.

Keywords: Emergency remote teaching · Bichronous instruction · University education · Social computing · Social and emotional learning

1 Introduction

This article considers the transition of university educators from traditional teaching formats to emergency remote teaching (ERT) during a crisis. Recently, the coronavirus epidemic accelerated an unexpected shift from traditional in-person, hybrid, and online course designs toward emergency remote teaching, with which educators and students were unfamiliar. This article will focus on the underlying process and practical applications of emergency remote teaching in a crisis environment.

The purpose of this paper is to examine the reasons, strategies, and consequences of engaging ERT in a university course. This will include a review of teaching remotely in emergency situations and the possibilities offered by the transition to ERT, such as content adaptation and personalization. Learners ought to be provided with an amount of control over the learning process (Darby and Lang [5], Tucker [34]) to develop critical thinking skills and become more self-reliant. Course adaptation and personalization allow the instructor to engage the virtual learner and create inclusive learning environments.

Emergency remote teaching, while a subset of distance learning, differs in that ERT is an alternative and temporary method of teaching that emerges in a crisis environment (Wang et al. [36]). It usually emphasizes remote online teaching and learning methods with the intent of returning to normal classroom and hybrid environments after the crisis (Hodges et al. [13]). Due to the temporary nature of ERT, professors are usually given the responsibility of adapting courses to meet the situation (Shim and Lee [32]).

The underlying need for emergency remote teaching will usually be a humanitarian crisis such as an issue of social justice or the after-effects of a natural disaster. Important areas of emergency remote teaching inclusive of social computing, social-emotional learning, equity, and the development of high-level skills relevant to higher education are examined. Graham, Woodfield, and Harrison [11] implied that blended learning may fall anywhere in the spectrum of learning methods from face-to-face to online. Graham [10] suggested that blended learning depends not on percentages, but on the elements being blended, such as time, media, and method of instructional delivery. Therefore, the authors explore the flexibility of blended learning as a possible teaching modality allowing for the diversity and situational adaptability with which to improve the effectiveness of emergency remote teaching.

2 Emergency Remote Teaching Background

Emergency Remote Teaching (ERT) usually exists due to a humanitarian crisis which has a social, economic, medical, or environmental origin (Shim and Lee [32]). Its methods may vary by location and situation, depending on the needs of the region and the students. Students and teachers may have difficulty adjusting to ERT, which is planned differently than the usual class design, and because its temporary emergency nature will not be of the same quality as the traditional educational system [31]. The Covid-19 crisis has created an emergency environment which has lent itself to a flexible variety of online and hybrid methods that allow students to learn at a distance with the objective of preventing the spread of coronavirus.

The use of ERT may have specialized benefits in higher education with its ability to utilize professional skills and knowledge to alleviate humanitarian and crisis situations. On a professional level, ERT may provide for the transfer of agricultural, medical, educational, and technical training in emergency situations and regions which have become isolated. Instances in which ERT helps provide educational and training opportunities benefit society. However, consideration of the social effects of ERT on student learning over extended periods of time is more complex.

In a study conducted by Shim and Lee [32] of university students in South Korea during the Covid-19 crisis the largest number of students reported studying from home (87.21%) or a café (10.47%), with the most common source of dissatisfaction being overcrowding. In the USA 95% accessed the internet through home internet, 3% through school, and 1% in a public place, with 44% reporting connectivity issues serious enough to interfere with the study (Means and Neisler [24]). It should be noted that the Means and Niesler [24] research did not include the effect of income, regional, ethnic, or health differentials on accessing internet connectivity. In Poland, 24.68% to 30.77% of instructors and 31.05% of students reported technological problems, such as connectivity issues (19.96%), faulty devices (9.07%) or mobile application issues (2.02%), while 13% to 19% of students needed to share devices with family members (Romaniuk and Łukasiewicz-Wieleba [31]). Lack of access to internet and computer technology may hinder student ability to take part in ERT, therefore it is essential to assure that all students have equitable access to technological resources.

While ERT affords opportunity to students who have the privilege of access to internet and technical resources, it can limit the students who do not have that privilege. ERT may provide educational opportunities, breaking down traditional barriers and providing new discussion formats for students (Javeri [15]). However, inequity and connectivity issues exclude diverse students in poor rural and urban locations, ethnic minorities, and students having physical and emotional challenges. High costs can make ERT unaffordable and may create barriers of equity resulting in exclusion.

Emergency remote teaching contrasts with high-quality online/hybrid learning, because ERT is employed in emergency situations, and not focused on providing the full benefits of online/hybrid learning (Hodges et al. [13]). The ERT learning platform must be easy for students to navigate and motivate student interest. The creation of adaptable culturally responsive environments is vital in emergency remote teaching because learning may not be of primary concern to students preoccupied with family and social issues related to the crisis. The pandemic has served to illuminate the human and social diversity of students and the need to adapt teaching and learning in ERT to meet various educational needs (Vignare et al. [35]).

Institutions must realize that standardized one-size-fits-all environments increase social inequities and exclude poverty-affected and minority students, as well as those with disabilities (2020). In the USA and Poland, it is difficult to find higher education teacher training programs and programs that address diversity issues in higher education, even though in the USA 45% of incoming higher education students have minority backgrounds and 42% of independent students are poverty-affected (2020). In Poland, in 2019, foreign students constituted 6.8%, with Ukrainian students being the largest group at 47.5%, and in the academic year 2019–2020 the number of all foreign students increased. However, among higher education students there were only 1.8% students with disabilities, and here the trend was downward (Main Statistical Office [21]), which may be indicative of the fact that the students did not get sufficient support and assistance.

The temporary nature of ERT and the effects of anxiety on student well-being and behavior indicate the need for alternative methods of assessment in times of crisis (Bates, [2]; Darby [5]). Studies of students during ERT reveal not only increased feelings of stress and uncertainty but lowered self-efficacy and academic integrity (Mudenda et al.

[25]; Li et al. [20]). Długosz [6] discovered that the number of university students who experience health issues increased by 10–12%, those who have problems falling asleep by 20%, and those who experience bad mood by over 20% (p. 5). At the same time, 40% of the surveyed students felt they lost control of their lives. Odriozola-Gonzalez et al. [29] suggested that teachers should reduce unnecessary workload and increase interaction with students during ERT. Emphasis should be placed on the emotional well-being of students.

Due to the temporary and emergency nature of ERT, grading should be deemphasized. In high-level professional education, such as the training of teachers, doctors, and emergency workers, the learning of useful skills takes precedence over grading and may be applied through experiential learning. The University of Alberta replaced grades with Credit/No Credit (CR/NC) evaluation during ERT to reduce the risks to institutional integrity. To alleviate questions regarding the academic honesty of students working from home, traditional assignments may be replaced with oral presentations, research papers, take-home exams, and group activities (Gares, Kariuki, and Rempel [8]). Group learning within online and hybrid ERT may provide the emotional support networks of culturally sensitive environments, foster exchange of alternative ideas, and include the local knowledge of ethnically diverse and poverty-affected communities.

The health and well-being of students and teachers is a primary concern in ERT. The Yale Center for Intelligence and the Collaborative for Social Emotional Academic Learning (CASEL) in March of 2020, in a study of teachers, revealed the most common feelings during the pandemic as anxious, worried, overwhelmed, and sad (Brackett and Cipriano [3]). According to the study, teachers' primary concerns shifted from meeting students' needs and high-stakes testing in 2017 to fear of family contracting Covid-19 and adapting new educational technologies for teaching during the pandemic. Inflexible institutions, negative environments, increased job demands, handling students' needs and lack of training in SEL, defined as "the process through which all young people and adults acquire and apply the knowledge, skills, and attitudes to develop healthy identities, manage emotions and achieve personal and collective goals, feel and show empathy for others, establish and maintain supportive relationships, and make responsible and caring decisions" (CASEL [4]), were primary causes of teacher stress [3]. Brackett and Cipriano [3] found that the emotional well-being of educators is of critical concern to teaching and learning and the creation of positive environments as it affects attention, memory, and learning; decision-making; relationships; health and well-being; and performance. When teachers display positive emotions in the ERT classroom, it helps to motivate and engage students. Positive thinking and resilience in communicating with students has been shown to reduce the negative effects of crisis (Yang et al. [39]).

It has been shown that flexibility in lesson planning, the ability to adapt to the needs of students, and the need to pay special attention to students at risk of social isolation help provide a positive environment during ERT (Mukhtar et al. [26]; Hamza et al. [12]). A study by Jeffery and Bauer [16] found that excessive stress magnified individual differences and cognitive limitations. It also increased the need for peer and social interaction, discourse, visualization of problem solving, and hands-on activities (2020). A multi-institutional study by Astin [1] in Jeffery and Bauer [16] found that collaborative group study with peers and a student-centered faculty are the two most crucial drivers of learning and intellectual development in students inside and outside of the classroom. The creation of holistic culturally responsive environments in which the teacher may adapt and personalize content to the needs of the students in crisis is essential.

2.1   Practical Research in ERT for University Students

In Poland, the SpołTech project prepared a report on Polish higher education institutions during the pandemic, based on three focus group interviews and supplemented with individual interviews with e-learning experts. The author of the report, Marta Klimowicz [19], quoted Hodges et al. [13] focusing on Emergency Remote Teaching, clearly aware of the difference between ERT and online learning. Employing qualitative research, Klimowicz [19] explained how the sudden introduction of new technologies during the Covid pandemic of 2019–2020 had affected the practices of higher education faculty.

5 key overlapping phases were identified:

1. Suspension and chaos,
2. Support (or lack thereof),
3. The New Normal,
4. Overload and coming to terms with the situation, and
5. Drawing conclusions.

Suspension and Chaos. The first phase was an immediate consequence of the necessity to move university (and other) classes online during the first national lockdown. Initially, the interviewed faculty and their students assumed that the situation was temporary and might last for about 2–3 weeks. Therefore, some instructors discontinued teaching and waited for the situation to "normalize". Others stayed in touch with their students, emailing presentations or materials and announcing that the content would be discussed when the lockdown was over. Numerous institutions were not prepared to teach classes online: instructors may not have had sufficient skills, and some did not own appropriate devices, hence the use of new technologies was often limited to email communication.

Support (or Lack Thereof). As the lockdown prolonged, faculty and students gradually understood that the use of technologies practiced in ERT would become a new mode of instruction. Some institutions undertook to teach classes synchronously, using videoconferencing platforms while some decided to rely on asynchronous instruction, distributing materials, assigning tasks based on the materials shared, evaluating the tasks, and offering remote office hours. Institutional decisions were made selecting the instructional platform such as ZOOM or Teams, most of which, at that time, offered emergency free services for educators, or instructors were given freedom to choose from among the available options. Most faculty learned how to use new tools and remote education techniques "in combat", helped by their peers. The predominant faculty emotions were a sense of overload and perceived lack of support. Respondents emphasized that they were often forced to look for solutions to their problems on their own, and particularly those who were less digitally proficient were at an obvious disadvantage.

As universities suspended in-person classes till the end of the semester, some students returned home, which had both positive and negative effects. This might have been beneficial for student budgets as accommodation and additional expenses did not need to be paid. Yet, some students found themselves in circumstances which may have made it difficult or impossible to participate in asynchronous and even more so synchronous classes due to poor housing conditions, insufficient number of IT devices, numerous family members using technology at the same time, and similar social difficulties.

The New Normal. During this phase, it was realized that the ERT situation could last indefinitely, and it was impossible to transfer in-person classes online without adjustments. The educators who were new to online education were becoming aware of the differences between in-situ and remote education. The teaching method that was seen as the least effective was transmissive teaching, or learning by listening, mostly because students' attention span was shorter. Some instructors undertook recording video lectures, tutorials or supplementary materials, and some professors understood that to engage students, content needed to be broken down into smaller pieces to avoid cognitive overload. Simultaneously, it was discovered that certain techniques that instructors preferred in the classroom, e.g., synchronous pair work or group work, were in fact possible online if appropriate functionalities, such as breakdown rooms, with which the faculty had previously been unfamiliar, were utilized. This raised awareness of the urgent need for professional development in the area of information and communication technology.

A surprising discovery was that during this phase students seemed engaged, present, and disciplined. Another - perhaps counterintuitive - finding was that some learners who previously did not actively participate in classes became more courageous and outspoken. Initial conclusions were drawn that the unprecedented situation may have been favorable for introverts, who felt less overwhelmed, or judged. At the same time, a reverse phenomenon of the so-called "dead souls" was also discovered, where students would log in but not unmute microphones, be passive and practically invisible all the time, and even forget to log out when the meeting was over. In addition to interactive tasks, to increase student engagement, SEL techniques were adopted.

Despite the efforts undertaken, many instructors experienced "talking to the screen", as if they were the only participant. Sometimes the lack of social interactions and inability to gain feedback through non-verbal communication resulted in frustration or a sense of disconnection with reality. Frustration was also growing in students due to depression related to the uncertainty and gravity of the circumstances, technological inequality and exclusion, insufficient IT skills, and housing conditions inappropriate for remote studying. Many students were reluctant to share their private space with instructors and peers, which was their justification for refusing to turn on their cameras. In fact, 50% of students surveyed by Długosz [6] claimed that it was stressful for them to show themselves and their surroundings on camera. The group that seemed to be suffering the most were international students, who, in addition to all the problems listed, had to cope with deficient language skills and unfamiliarity with local systems, including healthcare.

Overload. Because of the ERT shift and the required unplanned professional development, instructors in both Poland and the USA began to experience severe exhaustion. The process of preparation of interesting interactive ERT classes was seen as much more time-consuming than in-person classes. Another factor contributing to overload was a different form of providing feedback to students, perceived as extremely tedious, and the feeling that constant availability was required. Some faculty felt that they were in front of the computer 24/7. Instructors felt increased control from authorities, experienced lack of trust on the part of administrators, and felt that disproportionate stress was put on employee accountability, especially for reporting teaching time. With instructors employed by non-public institutions, the exhaustion was deepened by the uncertainty of further employment and/or a decrease in salary due to market unpredictability.

Coming to Terms with the Situation and Drawing Conclusions. In this phase, most instructors and higher education institutions believed that the new academic year, when classes would probably need to be conducted online, would require significant adjustments or even radical changes in curricula, which might ultimately lead to reform in education. Individual strategies adopted or developed by faculty were perceived as insufficient. It was felt that systemic solutions were needed. In Poland, it was discovered that one of the weaknesses of higher education was its focus on scientific development without a simultaneous emphasis on an increase of didactic competencies of the faculty, which the pandemic proved to be key. It was also understood that a substantial investment should be made in technology, both on the individual level, such as better-quality microphones, and in institutional infrastructure. As for the social aspect, it was feared that a sense of community was disappearing due to a lack of encounters in the physical space. While e-learning experts argued that creating online communities was possible, the process required additional effort and it was not clear who should be responsible.

2.2 Bichronous Education as an ERT Alternative

According to Martin, Polly, and Ritzhaupt [22], bichronous learning is defined as the blending of both asynchronous and synchronous online learning in which students may participate any time and in any place during the asynchronous parts of the course and take part in real-time activities at synchronous sessions. Thus, designed appropriately, it may become a hybrid variation of online learning.

Bichronous learning is one mode of learning that may be implemented during ERT. Research suggests such an approach to be highly beneficial for the learner, with 57.43% of over 9000 European students preferring the synchronous mode (Mazur [23]). The Pedagogical University of Cracow research showed a significant preference of 48% over the next preferred mode, instructors sharing self-prepared materials, evaluated at 20% (Długosz [6]). When both synchronous and asynchronous elements are blended, the positive aspects are maximized and leveraged towards student success. Self-paced learning and no scheduling conflict (asynchronous education) and immediate feedback, enhanced interaction, and audio-visual communication (synchronous education) increase student accountability, motivation, and opportunity to structure time (Yamagata-Lynch [38]; Martin, Polly, and Ritzhaupt [22]). This, in turn, results in relatively low student dropout and a comparatively high level of student motivation and satisfaction (Means and Neisler [24]).

3 Emergency Remote Teaching During COVID-19: Practical Application

At the time of the first emergency shift, this author was an experienced foreign and business language teacher in higher education, instructional methodologist, teacher trainer, and researcher employed as an instructor and lecturer at the WSB University, a private university in Poznan, Poland, belonging to a group of state-recognized non-public universities. Before the transition, the author's classes were taught solely in person, using a laptop, an overhead projector, and the BYOD (Bring Your Own Device). Course materials and resources were uploaded to Moodle for students to access at their convenience, but most frequently photocopies and professor-created printouts were used in class.

There were two ERT transitions of in-person classes in the course of two subsequent academic years. The first one took place in March 2020, and the other – in November 2021. Both instances were related to the COVID-19 pandemic, and both happened instantaneously. When the first transition occurred, bichronous learning was utilized where the asynchronous mode involved an extensive use of a Learning Management System (LMS) while the synchronous one relied on regular meetings on a virtual conference platform. During the second emergency transition, the strategies and practices effective during the first transition were employed. Additionally, new solutions learned through professional development in online education were applied. The experiences in this section were shared in common with the teacher from the USA.

3.1 ERT Experience in Poznan, Poland

The fact that WSB was a private university and students could afford tuition and additional expenses (thanks to personal resources or scholarships and assistance programs) provided greater opportunities in comparison with many Polish public higher education institutions. However, many ERT aspects and challenges were common for the public and private sector.

Equitable access was a priority, so the instructor and the students took proactive steps to create inclusivity in an unfavorable emergency learning environment. Additionally, the instructor undertook to use anonymous polls and surveys to collect student feedback in order to improve the teaching process. Following Tucker's [34] recommendations, a partnership model was embraced, which was particularly justified in a higher education course. Mutual respect and trust became foundations for structuring classes, for example, tardiness, connectivity problems and the need to temporarily log out were not penalized. Honesty and open communication became key, and various reliable and clearly specified channels of such communication (such as university email, the LMS chat and the videoconferencing chat, both synchronous and asynchronous) were established.

The students were given voice and choice (France [7]), for example, final projects could be submitted in any equitable format. Flexible deadlines and a variety of mediums (a short video, a presentation, or an essay) ensuring student-led workflow for written assignments, were provided, with synchronous and asynchronous, regular, actionable instructor and peer feedback (Darby [5]). When deemed required, short explanatory videos or feedback videos were recorded by the professor in addition to providing students with written information, so that various learning styles were addressed. Moreover, the instructor employed SEL-recommended measures, such as incorporating culturally and linguistically responsive elements, and, when needed, using students' native languages (Polish and Russian) in addition to English, with the view of creating a safe and inclusive learning community that valued diversity.

Student-instructor and student-student interactions were modeled in accord with Vygotsky's theory, which states that:

"...learning awakes a variety of internal developmental processes that are able to operate only when [the student] is interacting with people in his environment and in cooperation with his peers."

(1935/1978, in Darby [5], p. 78).

and, following the recommendations of Garrison, Anderson and Archer [9] that an educational experience can only be effective when three presences: the Teaching Presence, the Cognitive Presence and the Social Presence intersect.

The author was aware that in ERT it was instrumental to revisit the initial assumptions made about the course being taught, particularly regarding its social aspect. One of the detrimental aspects of ERT was that students were not required to turn on their cameras during synchronous classes on video-conferencing platforms, which made the experience alienating, particularly for the instructor, who taught classes from an empty university room. Since very few students uploaded personal photos to the platform, and most of the time the microphones were turned off to avoid echo, the instructor, aware of the growing sense of distance and isolation, undertook to implement certain strategies to re-introduce elements of social interaction.

First (still in person, but, with COVID cases on the rise, aware that instruction might move to the ERT mode again), following Darby's [5] recommendations, the instructor made an introduction to the students and revealed her personality through a presentation with some unexpected and interesting information. Then students were asked to talk to three peers they had not had a chance to interact with and share three pieces of intriguing personal information, which helped to engage students with one another. Also, sometimes students were asked to self-assign peers to complete a task, using first names (which was appropriate in the context) to become more deeply involved with the content and with each other. When classes were moved online in the ERT mode, the practice was continued.

Community-building and additional support for international learners were also expressed by increasing everyone's awareness of each other's cultural contexts, for example, a short video featuring a well-known British actor and directed by a Belarussian director was used during a review-writing class, and Christmas and New Year customs were discussed prior to the season. In addition, constant empathy and support was conveyed by asking students how they were doing, inquiring (both in person and in writing) if they needed assistance, expressing support for their ongoing efforts, and informing them of sources of institutional help and assistance, such as national and self-governmental programs to fight student depression (such as The Zone of Comfort of The Parliament of the Students of the Republic of Poland, Parlament Studentów Rzeczypospolitej Polskiej [30] or Studencki Osrodek Wsparcia i Adaptacji [33] including a crisis intervention hotline and assistance in English). "Demonstrating this kind of understanding of students' lives and pressures shows that you know they are real people too, that you care about them, and that you're invested in relating with them in a way that allows them to persist." (Darby [5], p. 98).

At the beginning of a synchronous session, each student was asked to select an emoji that would reflect individual feelings and attitudes. The instructor commented on the emojis in real time, in a sensitive, empathetic, non-judgmental way. When a "sick" or "unwell" emoji appeared, the students would be encouraged to support the ill-disposed peer. The support could be expressed by reacting to the emoji with a heart, sending the peer a private message, or by individually selecting an alternative manner of assistance. That was one of the elements of the culture of mindfulness and care being recreated online.

Other aspects of social presence which served a similar purpose were:

- synchronous verbal interactions in the common room and breakout rooms,
- synchronous interactions in the chat box,
- informal "office minutes" before or after the class,
- asynchronous Moodle chat and email exchanges between the students and the instructor.

In addition to the instructor-introduced measures, during the first transition, students developed methods of transferring instructional materials (such as handouts and links to online tasks and websites) and providing help to peers through the use of mobile phones and Whatsapp, Discord, or social platforms (including Messenger) in instances in which access to Moodle or the videoconferencing platform was limited by technical issues. Similar measures were reintroduced during the second transition.

Additionally, students created Google Drive folders to upload hard-to-get sources and materials. In personal communication, the professor learned about individualized methods of socializing and strategies of bottom-up community building, invented by students, such as organizing spontaneous ZOOM meetings with peers to silently study together, with cameras turned on, to feel the presence of other young people. After lectures and in between classes, students engaged in playing Among Us, the League of Legends and other multiplayer games. In free time, they organized "Netflix Parties", when an appropriate plug-in was used, and one student would send a link for everyone to watch the same movie at the same time. When one person paused the movie, it paused for everyone, and students could use the chat box to comment on the motion picture in real time. Discord was also used in this way, with a movie or other content shared, watched together, and commented on in real time. Sometimes Listening Parties on Spotify were also organized via the Start a Group Session option, or students created playlists and mixed them up, so that two friends' lists were combined, and songs were played in turn. Games such as Words with Friends, Ludo, or 8-Ball Pool were also played on Messenger.

Such community-building through IT tools and platforms seemed beneficial to student wellbeing but also to the cognitive aspect, as research conducted by Community College Research Centre in 2013 and cited by Mazur [23] shows that a student's grade point average gets increased by 0.8 in environments with a high level of interpersonal relations.

3.2 ERT Experience in New York, USA

During Covid-19 teachers have experienced difficulties coping with high stress levels and inflexible institutions. At the time of the pandemic this author was participating in higher education at multiple levels. The author was an experienced teacher of design, language, and education in higher education, a mentor of graduate students, an academic researcher, and a student in professional development who had already completed a doctoral degree.

The educational experience in the USA with ERT is unique in the human, economic, and geographic diversity of a large nation. Due to the harsh nature of the pandemic in the USA, schools were closed for a substantial length of time, which varied in different states and regions. In the New York region the colleges began to initiate restrictions and closures in approximately March of 2020. The initial ERT response to the pandemic differed in that various forms of online learning had already taken root because of the expansive geographic distances and high costs involved in the American higher education system. One result being that online program capabilities differed between larger institutions which were operationally prepared and smaller colleges which were forced to initiate new programs. To meet the need for online learning, some smaller colleges offered self-branded online courses, licensed using the infrastructure of major universities, which had the technology and resources available.

One area of difficulty confronted by US higher educational institutions in ERT situations was technological and financial inequity. This refers to inequality of access to the internet and the technology resources that make it possible for students to participate in online learning. Students who cannot afford internet services, and who may live in remote rural or poor urban areas may not have access to the technological facilities necessary to attend online courses (Vignare et al. [35]). Working students temporarily unemployed found the high costs of internet access and computer technology increasingly prohibitive. The inability of students to afford required internet and technological resources resulted in a lack of skills, in students facing economic difficulties, and a lack of experience in using computers. Digital equity includes more than just access to technology, it includes course materials and opportunity for learning (Holland [14]). It is therefore necessary in ERT that equity to learning be assured by the educational institution.

In practice, equal access to technology has been accomplished through the establishment of computer rooms and campus library technology facilities that are accessible to all students for use in studying, researching, and partaking in class activities. Public libraries offer another venue which may provide online access to students. Because of limitations in the time allowed to use public library computers, it may be advisable for the university to assure students have adequate time and access to public library facilities. In some states it may be possible for schools to integrate technological equity through the public library system (New York State Education Department [28]). It has been the practice in some colleges to provide students with free laptop computers upon admittance and enrollment in the program. Another popular method of obtaining internet facilities is through local coffee houses, hotels, and similar public locations which offer free online Wi-Fi services. For example, during a serious blizzard which took electricity offline for over a week, students studied in a local Starbucks, which offered free Wi-Fi and heat during the long subzero evenings.

The complexities of creating equity of access to technology may be compounded when students live in different states and countries which have needs that must be handled individually. This is particularly applicable to overseas students who may have returned home to study. Accommodating the needs of international students is a critical issue in American schools, which include a high percentage of students from nations around the world. The author has taught and mentored students from many different nations who were impacted by closures and travel restrictions during the pandemic. Moreover, during emergency situations working students and families may suffer increased financial hardship and emotional stress (Vignare et al. [35]; Jurisevic et al. [17]). While emergency responses may differ between cultures and situations, it is essential in ERT that equity of access be addressed so all students are offered the resources required to participate.

An area of considerable concern during emergency remote teaching are the effects of the increased workload on student and teacher well-being. This included the effects of radical change on emotional health (Brackett and Cipriano [3]). Faculty showed dissatisfaction with the demands of insensitive institutions requiring increased workloads without providing the necessary resources and training. Required to work at home, teachers were forced to use personal laptops and home technology for long hours during the day without fair compensation. Voicemails and emails became clogged with questions and teachers were unable to reach students to give assistance. Teachers required to teleconference 6 h per day suffered from zoom fatigue (Javeri [15]). They were unable to spend time with families due to intolerant institutional employers refusing to allow flexible work hours (personal communication, 2021). Teacher frustration and dissatisfaction with working conditions increased the risks of student trauma (Brackett and Cipriano [3]). In ERT, which occurs during a crisis, the quality of courses may be diminished, and the emotional health of students and teachers should take priority (Hodges et al. [13]). It is critical that institutions provide the resources, training, flexibility, and positive work environments to help teachers create a good experience that enhances the well-being of students and teachers alike.

When considering the coping methods used during Covid-19 it must be remembered that ERT is intended to be transitional in nature. At present the USA and Poland are undergoing another surge in Covid cases related to the Omicron variation that far surpasses the initial Covid rates (Worldometer [37]). The situation in some areas is tenuous with mention of continuing restrictions and loss of teaching positions.

ERT is not utilized in traditional situations, and therefore institutional flexibility is vital to assist the teacher in meeting increased workloads and adapt class design and learning to meet student needs. A one-size-fits-all approach to learning does not work in ERT (Vignare et al. [35]). Personalization of lessons helps to adapt for the diverse needs of students in crisis during which ethnically diverse, special education, international, and low-income students may be disproportionately adversely affected. Culturally responsive teaching reduces cultural and technological barriers. Building the trust of students and using the cultural knowledge of diverse students makes learning relevant (2020).

The emotional health of the teacher influences the educational environment and the attitude of students (Brackett and Cipriano [3]). It is essential that teachers care for their own emotional, physical, and social well-being. Yoga and meditation are two effective methods of releasing tension. Occasionally attending a yoga studio may have the social benefits of group practice. Hiking and bicycling provide the physical and emotional health benefits of exercise and the touring aspect. Javeri [15] suggests embodying learning, letting students express how the lesson makes them feel different physically. Another method of stress reduction used by teachers is professional development in the form of certifications, courses, and research, which is a worthwhile career builder in an increasingly competitive crisis job environment. Whether one's interest is health and well-being or career development, it is recommended to develop group and personal activities that assist with the SEL needs of a high stress educational environment.

Involving students in group activities helps to prevent loneliness, keeping students socially active while creating a positive ERT learning environment. Research by Astin [1] in Jeffery and Bauer [16] showed that student learning is most effective using activity-based and collaborative learning, and when students interact with peers. Allowing for a variety of styles of communication creates an interactive atmosphere and allows students to share experiences (Yamagata-Lynch [38]). Diversity of communication includes more than methods of communication, digital or face-to-face, it allows freedom for the diverse methods of human expression of each individual student.

4 Recommendations

In making suggestions, personal experience is combined with the available research to provide practice-based flexible techniques which may be adapted for the situationality of future crises. It is impossible to tell a teacher "how to teach", as every student and circumstance is different. This is especially true in ERT. A few key educational principles upon which ERT practice may be effectively based are offered.

First, it is necessary to move away from a profit-based motivation of education toward implementation of diversity and inclusive teaching practices (Javeri [15]). Second, one-size-fits-all factory education does not work: ERT must be personalized and adjusted to the needs of each student and to the crisis-situation (Ng [27]). Third, it is necessary to utilize culturally responsive teaching practices that adapt lessons for student diversity, reduce inequality, offer equal access to technology, and include local knowledge (Vignare et al. [35]). Applying these key principles may provide a flexible guide for educators.

One viable ERT alternative which is a variant of the hybrid mode is bichronous education, where synchronous and asynchronous methods allow for the creation of the three CoI presences: the teaching presence, the cognitive presence, and the social presence (Garrison, Anderson, and Archer [9]). The teacher's role is deciding what is relevant to include and integrating asynchronous self-motivated learning with synchronous lessons utilizing teacher-student and student-student interaction in the form of group discussions, activities, and problem-based learning to improve student engagement, reduce stress, and create positive learning environments.

As for the teaching and cognitive presence, it needs to be borne in mind that synchronous education allows for clarification of content, tasks, and procedures, and it offers greater flexibility (Darby [5]). Therefore, when considering the two modes of bichronous instruction, it is worthwhile to either secure the time for synchronous assignment analysis or to carefully divide each module into asynchronous manageable tasks. In both cases, it is crucial to utilize student feedback to cultivate effective progress towards the specified goal.

Experts agree that in ERT the social presence requires particular attention. It should be proactively fostered through synchronous and asynchronous activities. Taking into account student feedback gathered through personal communication, in addition to digital course tools, opportunities for social interaction may be provided by VoIP, instant messaging, and distribution platforms. When flexible and adaptable, these platforms can be used for communication and for uploading and sharing media.

Another issue which must be considered is the institutional flexibility to accommodate the complex personal needs of teachers working in difficult scenarios. Tucker perceptively noticed that "lack of time and exhaustion are barriers to innovation" (Tucker [34], p. 30). It can be justifiably assumed that in ERT lack of time and exhaustion can impede the whole teaching process, especially in view of faculty stress related to the emergency situation and its consequences.

Providing teacher training programs that meet the needs of diverse student populations through culturally responsive teaching practices coupled with social-emotional learning may help to alleviate the frustration and stress of ERT (Brackett and Cipriano [3]). Improving the teachers' ability to provide positive environments in crisis situations will assist SEL enhancing the development of student attention, decision-making skills, relationships, well-being, performance, and holistic growth. One technique that may assist in accomplishing this is holding a private interview and together creating a flexible learning agreement that promotes the development of each student within the crisis ERT environment to establish adjustable goals that engage and motivate.

Institutional assistance in creating online learning communities appropriate to the emergency may provide social and collaborative opportunities for student-student instructional support (Hodges et al. [13]). Low-income and minority students may be more severely impacted by inequalities of internet connectivity and technology in ERT. With inclusive and equitable ERT in view, it is essential to provide access to devices and a reliable internet connection, for example, by temporarily adapting university computer laboratories for ERT. It can also be done through creating provisionary safe spaces on campuses with several devices and university-provided Wi-Fi. Another suggestion would be for universities to collaborate with libraries and community centers that are already equipped with laptops, computers, and LAN/WLAN.

The flexibility of hybridization enhances the creativity that helps teachers to adapt and design emergency learning. It fosters development of inclusive courses that meet the individual needs of students through personalization and Universal Design for Learning (UDL), which utilizes student-centered educational principles to provide accessible and equitable learning environments and activities (Hodges et al. [13]). The flexibility to assist students in adjusting to ERT will impact all aspects of learning from the design of web portals and learning platforms to the cultural relevance of course lessons. The hybridization of ERT can include the integration of online learning methods such as computer-based, videoconferencing, and radio education with collaborative and personalized teaching practices which promote alternative ideas and improve communication among students.

Flexibility is a concept that permeates all aspects of ERT. The teacher's ability to adapt coursework for the emotional and physical diversity of students is essential in crisis settings as the emphasis is not on content learning, but on the well-being and development of the learners (Hodges et al. [13]; Jurisevic et al. [17]). The institution and teacher may have to work with social issues that arise in emergencies. The use of local cultural knowledge and diversity may be of great assistance in adapting learning for traditional and unanticipated social responsibilities. Whether in ERT or classroom learning, the holistic human development of the student is the primary objective (France [7]).

5 Conclusion

In conclusion, properly applied emergency remote teaching may be of great assistance in fostering well-being and learning in times of crisis. The sensitivity and flexibility of the institution and the teacher to adapt to the situationality of emergency is vital to cultivate a rewarding ERT experience. The creation of positive work environments that enhance well-being helps teachers to provide a positive atmosphere for students. The flexibility to humanize ERT through hybridization and adaptation to the unique needs of diverse students assists in providing caring class spaces in which social activities and local community knowledge may be used to help engage and motivate learning. Offering equal access to technology and learning opportunities is a crucial ingredient in nurturing a sensitive environment in which all students are welcome to become active participants.

It must be remembered that ERT is a temporary solution in which well-being and human development take priority over course content. It may be necessary to reduce workloads, alleviate student isolation, and find alternative methods of grading that are suitable for the crisis climate. Through ERT the hardships which are inherent in emergency settings may become learning opportunities which teach lessons of kindness, hone critical decision-making skills, and help students grow as human beings.

References

1. Astin, A.W.: What Matters in College? Four Critical Years Revisited. Jossey-Bass, San Francisco, CA (1995)
2. Bates, A.W.: Teaching in a Digital Age. Second Edition. Tony Bates Associates Ltd., Vancouver, B.C. (2019). https://pressbooks.bccampus.ca/teachinginadigitalagev2/. Accessed 3 Feb 2022
3. Brackett, M., Cipriano, C.: Teachers are anxious and overwhelmed. They need SEL now more than ever. EdSurge Soc. Emotion. Learn. (2020)
4. CASEL: Fundamentals of SEL, 26 October 2021. https://casel.org/fundamentals-of-sel/. Accessed 10 Feb 2022
5. Darby, F., Lang, J.M.: Small Teaching Online. Applying Learning Science in Online Classes. Jossey-Bass, San Francisco, CA (2019)
6. Długosz, P.: Raport z II etapu badań studentów UP. Opinia na temat zdalnego nauczania i samopoczucia psychicznego [Report from the 2nd stage of research of the students of the Pedagogical University of Cracow. Opinion on remote teaching and mental wellbeing] (2020). https://rep.up.krakow.pl/xmlui/handle/11716/7488. Accessed 3 Feb 2022

7. France, P.E.: 4 Steps for Humanizing Personalized Learning. EdSurge (2021). https://www.eds urge.com/news/2021-05-17-4-steps-for-humanizing-personalized-learning. Accessed 3 Feb 2022
8. Gares, L., Kariuki, J.K., Rempel, B.P.: Community matters: student-instructor relationships foster student motivation and engagement in an emergency remote teaching environment. J. Chem. Educ. **2020**(97), 3332–3335 (2020). https://doi.org/10.1021/acs.jchemed.0c00635
9. Garrison, D.R., Anderson, T., Archer, W.: Critical inquiry in a text-based environment: computer conferencing in higher education. Internet Higher Educ. **2**, 87–105 (1999)
10. Graham, C.R.: Blended learning systems: definition, current needs, and future directions. In: Bonk, C.J., Graham, C.R. (eds.) The Handbook of Blended Learning: Global Perspectives, Local Designs, pp. 3–21. Pfeiffer, San Francisco (2006)
11. Graham, C.R., Woodfield, W., Harrison, J.B.: A framework for institutional adoption and implementation of blended learning in higher education. Internet Higher Educ. **18**, 4–14 (2013). https://doi.org/10.1016/j.iheduc.2012.09.003
12. Hamza, C., Moore, S., Lockee, B., Trust, T., Bond, A.: When social isolation is nothing new: a longitudinal study psychological distress during COVID-19 among university students with and without pre-existing mental health concerns. Can. Psychol. **62**(1), 20–30 (2020). https://doi.org/10.1037/cap0000255
13. Hodges, C., Moore, S., Lockee, B., Trust, T., Bond, A.: The difference between emergency remote teaching and online learning. Educause Review, 27 March 2020. https://er.educause.edu/articles/2020/3/the-difference-between-emergency-remote-tea ching-and-online-learning. Accessed 3 Feb 2022
14. Holland, B.: Strategies for tackling digital equity. GettingSmart.com, Equity & Access, 18 April 2019
15. Javeri, J.: How remote learning subverts power and privilege in higher education. EdSurge, Teach. Learn. (2021)
16. Jeffery, K.A., Bauer, C.F.: Students' responses to emergency remote online teaching reveal critical factors for all teaching. J. Chem. Educ. **2020**(97), 2472–2485 (2020). https://doi.org/10.1021/acs.jchemed.0c00736
17. Jurisevic, M., Lavrih, L., Lisic, A., Podlogar, N., Zerak, U.: Higher education students' experience of emergency remote teaching during the Covid-19 pandemic in relation to self-regulation and positivity. CEPS J. **11**, 241–262 (2021). https://doi.org/10.26529/cepsj.1147
18. Kagawa, F.: Emergency education: a critical review of the field. Comp. Educ. **41**(4), 487–503 (2022). http://www.jstor.org/stable/30044557
19. Klimowicz, M.: Polskie uczelnie w czasie pandemii. Raport projektu Społ-Tech. [Polish universities during the pandemic. A Społ-Tech Project report]. Fundacja Centrum Cyfrowe Projekt SpołTech, Warsaw (2020). https://centrumcyfrowe.pl/spoltech/polskie-uczelnie-w-czasie-pandemii/. Accessed 3 Feb 2022
20. Li, H.Y., Cao, H., Leung, D.Y.P., Mak, Y.W.: The psychological impacts of a COVID-19 outbreak on college students in China: a longitudinal study. Int. J. Environ. Res. Public Health **17**(11), 1–11 (2020). https://doi.org/10.3390/ijerph17113933
21. Main Statistical Office: Szkolnictwo wyższe i jego finanse w 2019 roku. Raport. [Higher education and its finances in 2019. A report] (2020). https://stat.gov.pl/obszary-tematyczne/edu kacja/edukacja/szkolnictwo-wyzsze-i-jego-finanse-w-2019-roku,2,16.html. Accessed 3 Feb 2022
22. Martin, F., Polly, D., Ritzhaupt, A.: Bichronous online learning: blending asynchronous and synchronous online learning. Educase Review (2020). https://er.educause.edu/articles/2020/9/bichronous-online-learning-blending-asynchronous-and-synchronous-online-learning. Accessed 3 Feb 2022

23. Mazur, J.: Remote learning. Taming the (un)known. Impact of COVID-19 on higher education. University of Warsaw, DELab UW (2021). https://www.delab.uw.edu.pl/wp-content/upl
oads/2021/01/ENG-Report_Remote-Learning-Taming-the-Unknown-Impact-of-COVID-
19-on-higher-education.pdf
24. Means, B., Neisler, J., with Langer Research Associates: Suddenly Online: A National Survey
of Undergraduates During the COVID-19 Pandemic. Digital Promise, San Mateo, CA (2020)
25. Mudenda, S., et al.: Impact of coronavirus disease 2019 (COVID-19) on college and university
students: a global health and education problem. Aquademia **4**(2), 1–2 (2020). https://doi.
org/10.29333/aquademia/8494
26. Mukhtar, K., Javed, K., Arroj, M., Sethi, A.: Advantages, limitations and recommendations
for online learning during COVID-19 pandemic era. Pakistan J. Med. Sci. **36**(COVID19-S4),
27–31 (2020). https://doi.org/10.12669/pjms.36.COVID19-S4.2785
27. Ng, B-Y.: Engaging students in emergency remote teaching: strategies for the instructor. IGI
Global (2021). https://orcid.org/0000-0002-6670-4102, https://doi.org/10.4018/978-1-7998-
4658-1.ch004
28. New York State Education Department, New York State Library: Division of Library
Development. https://www.nysl.nysed.gov/libdev/ Accessed 26 Jan 2022
29. Odriozola-Gonzalez, P., Planchuelo-Gomez, A., Jesus-Irurtia, M., de Luis-Garcia, R.: Psychological effects of the COVID-19 outbreak and lockdown among students and workers of
a Spanish university. Psych. Res. **290**, 1–8 (2020). https://doi.org/10.1016/j.psychres.2020.
113108
30. Parlament Studentów Rzeczypospolitej Polskiej [The Parliament of the Students of the Republic of Poland] and The Ministry of Science and Higher Education of the Republic of Poland.
(n.d.). Strefa komfortu PSRP [The Zone of comfort of The Parliament of the Students of the
Republic of Poland]. https://wsparciepsychologiczne.psrp.org.pl/. Accessed 3 Feb 2022
31. Romaniuk, M.W., Łukasiewicz-Wieleba, J.: Zdalna edukacja kryzysowa w APS w okresie
pandemii COVID-19 z perspektywy rocznych doświadczeń. Raport z badań. [Emergency
Remote Teaching at The Maria Grzegorzewska University during the COVID-19 pandemic
from the perspective of one year of experience. A research report]. Akademia Pedagogiki
Specjalnej im. Marii Grzegorzewskiej, Warsaw (2021)
32. Shim, E.S., Lee, Y.L.: College students' experience of emergency remote teaching due to
COVID-19. Child Youth Serv. Rev. **119**(2020), 105578 (2020). https://doi.org/10.1016/j.chi
ldyouth.2020.105578
33. Studencki Osrodek Wsparcia i Adaptacji - Uniwersytet Jagiellonski: Studencki Ośrodek
Wsparcia i Adaptacji [Student Center of Support and Adaptation]. https://sowa.uj.edu.pl/
english. Accessed 3 Feb 2022
34. Tucker, C.R.: Balance with Blended Learning: Partner With Your Students to Reimagine
Learning and Reclaim Your Life, 1st edn. (Corwin Teaching Essentials) Corwin, Thousand
Oaks (2020)
35. Vignare, K., Lorenzo, G., Tesene, M., Reed, N.: Improving critical courses using digital
learning & evidence-based pedagogy. Joint Publication of Association of Public and Land-
grant Universities and Every Learner Everywhere (2020)
36. Wang, G., Zhang, Y., Zhao, J., Zhanh, J., Jianh, F.: Mitigate the effects of home confinement
on children during the Covid-19 outbreak. The Lancet **395**(10228), 21–27 (2020). https://doi.
org/10.1016/S0140-6736(20)305-47-XReferences
37. Worldometer: Coronavirus statistics live, 26 January 2022. https://www.worldometers.info/
coronavirus/. Accessed 26 Jan 2022

38. Yamagata-Lynch, L.C.: Blending online asynchronous and synchronous learning. Int. Rev. Res. Open Distance Learn. **15**(2), 189–212 (2014)
39. Yang, D., Tu, C.-C., Dai, X.: The effect of the 2019 novel coronavirus pandemic on college students in Wuhan. Psychol. Trauma Theory Res. Pract. Policy **12**(S1), 6–14 (2020). https://doi.org/10.1037/tra0000930

Development of an Explicit Agent-Based Simulation Toolkit for Opening of Schools: An Implementation of COMOKIT for Universities in the Philippines

Maria Regina Justina Estuar$^{(\boxtimes)}$ ⓘ, Roland Abao ⓘ, Jelly Aureus ⓘ,
Zachary Pangan ⓘ, Lenard Paulo Tamayo ⓘ, Elvira de Lara-Tuprio ⓘ,
Timothy Robin Teng ⓘ, and Rey Rodrigueza ⓘ

Ateneo de Manila University, Quezon City, Philippines
restuar@ateneo.edu
https://www.ateneo.edu

Abstract. Since the start of the pandemic in early 2020, there have been numerous studies related to the design and use of disease models to aid in understanding the transmission dynamics of COVID-19. Output of these models provide pertinent input to policies regarding restricting or relaxing movements of a population. Perhaps the most widely used class of models for COVID-19 disease transmission is the compartmental model. It is a population model that assumes homogeneous mixing, which means that each individual has the same likelihood of contact with the rest of the population. Inspite of this limitation, the approach has been effective in forecasting the number of cases based on simulated scenarios. With the shift from nationwide lockdowns to granular lockdown as well as gradual opening of limited face to face classes, there is a need to consider other models that assume heterogeneity as reflected in individual behaviors and spatial containment strategies in smaller spaces such as buildings. In this study, we use the COVID-19 Modeling Kit (COMOKIT, 2020) as a basis for the inclusion of individual and spatial components in the analysis. Specifically, we derive a version of COMOKIT specific to university setting. The model is an agent-based, spatially explicit model with the inclusion of individual epidemiological and behavior parameters to show evidence of which behavioral and non-pharmaceutical interventions lead to reduced transmission over a given period of time. The simulation environment is set up to accommodate the a) minimum number of persons required in a closed environment including classrooms, offices, study spaces, laboratories, cafeteria, prayer room and bookstore, b) parameters on viral load per building or office, and c) percentage of undetected positive cases going on campus. The model incorporates the following interventions: a) compliance to health protocol, in particular compliance to wearing masks, b) vaccine coverage, that is, the percentage distribution of single dose, two doses and booster, c) distribution of individuals

Ateneo Research Institute for Science and Engineering, Ateneo de Manila University.

G. Meiselwitz (Ed.): HCII 2022, LNCS 13316, pp. 48–66, 2022.
https://doi.org/10.1007/978-3-031-05064-0_4

into batches for alternating schedules. For mask compliance, as expected, results showed that 100% compliance resulted to lowest number of cases after 120 days, followed by 75% compliance and highest number of cases for 50% compliance. For vaccine coverage, results showed that booster shots play a significant role in lowering the number of cases. Specifically, those who are fully vaccinated (2 doses) and 100% boosted produce the lowest number of cases, followed by the 50% of the population fully vaccinated and have had their booster shots. Intervals of no onsite work or class in between weeks that have onsite classes produce the lowest number of cases. The best scenario is combining the three interventions with 100% compliance to mask wearing, 100% fully vaccinated with booster, and having two batches or groups with interval of no onsite classes.

Keywords: Agent-based user behavior modeling · COVID-19 modeling · Social behavior

1   Context of Pandemic in the Philippines

On March 12, 2020, the Philippine government announced that Metro Manila would be placed on lockdown from March 14, 2020 to April 15, 2020 due to detected local transmission of COVID-19 [9]. Within this time period, government agencies were advised to go on skeletal workforce and private agencies were to have flexible working arrangements. Consequently, schools were closed and needed to prepare for alternative classes. As early as May 2020, the President of the Philippines has publicly stated that schools shall remain closed and can resume only when vaccination program for the country has been rolled out [1]. As such, the government rolled out alternative learning methods and prepared for blended learning [10]. In January 26, 2021, the Philippine government approved limited face to face classes for allied health programs [26]. The partial opening of medical universities paved the way for development of implementation guidelines in opening of schools including: development of modular courses to limit the amount of time for face to face classes, comprehensive health screening and contract tracing protocols to avoid local transmission, and adjustments in physical spaces to ensure that minimum public health standards are implemented. The Philippines began the roll out of its vaccination program last March 1, 2021 [34]. Last November 15, 2021, the Department of Education began a pilot implementation of limited face to face classes for the public schools [12]. In recent months, more and more schools are preparing for resumption of classes with the issuance of the nationwide implementation of the alert level systems where alert levels 1, 2 and 3 provide options for limited face to face classes [21].

There is a need to extend modeling to include individual behaviors as the country transitions to the new normal where mobility is expected to increase. Modeling the transmission dynamics of COVID-19 can be extended to studying possible outcomes for select scenarios in limited face to face classes. However, individual behaviors need to be incorporated into the model to represent heterogeneous mix. Unlike standard compartmental disease models where population is considered a homogeneous mix, increased mobility results to increased individual behaviors which may not be captured by standard compartmental models.

In this study, we developed an explicit agent-based model for face to face classes in a Philippine university setting using COMOKIT[1] (COVID-19 Modeling Kit for analyzing COVID-19 interventions at a city scale). Specifically, we developed a submodel we call EASE which stands for Explicit Agent-based Simulation for Education, extending the standard disease compartmental model to an agent-based approach that incorporates individual characteristics of agents in scenarios and simulations. This paper describes outcomes of simulations resulting from scenarios that measure effectiveness of vaccine based on vaccine coverage, compliance to wearing of masks and batch scheduling within a university setting. Outcomes of the simulations using agent-based modeling in this paper can be used as inputs in planning for the gradual opening of onsite classes in the Philippines.

2   Literature Review

Two of the most commonly used types of models for studying COVID-19 transmission are the compartmental models and the agent-based simulation models. The former, which is more popular and widely used, has been at the forefront in guiding decisions about various interventions to limit the spread of the virus in the population especially in the early stages of the pandemic [28]. The latter, although more complex and computationally expensive [24], is more reliable in situations where predicting the impact of localized interventions in a smaller heterogeneous group of population is one of the key aspects to consider [17].

2.1   Compartmental Mathematical Models

Deterministic Models. Multiple studies adapted the use of deterministic compartmental models to forecast the spread of COVID-19 in the community. One of the early attempts to forecast the trajectory of COVID-19 cases was in Russia using the classic "susceptible-infected-removed" (SIR) and the "susceptible-exposed-infected-removed" (SEIR) deterministic models [35]. In the absence of good initial data about the virus, SIR and SEIR models made it possible to obtain acceptable quantitative forecast in the early stages of the pandemic due to their simplicity and small number of parameters requirement. A similar SEIR model analyzed the transmission in Brazil and India, but one that includes birth and death rates [29]. From the model, they were able to compare the disease spread and mortality rates between the two countries.

The aforementioned compartmental models assume that the infected population is able to freely interact with the susceptible population. But actual practice involves isolating infected individuals through active case detection to mitigate the spread of the disease. This necessitated the development of COVID-19 models that incorporate the effect of quarantine, where quarantined infectious

---

[1] https://comokit.org/.

individuals are assumed to be not capable of transmitting the virus to other members of the population. An example would be the modification of the SIR to include this intervention by dividing the infected population into two sub-groups - quarantined and unquarantined - correlated by the factor of testing [2]. Another variation of the SEIR model is where the undetected and infectious individuals are either asymptomatic (I_a) or symptomatic (I_s) [15]. From among them, individuals will be detected to have the COVID-19 disease, and hence will transition to the confirmed compartment C. These individuals are assumed to undergo isolation over the entire span of their infectious period, and are receiving treatment. The SIDARTHE model considered eight stages of the infection: susceptible (S), infected (I), diagnosed (D), ailing (A), recognized (R), threatened (T), healed (H) and extinct (E) [19]. Aside from distinguishing between detected and undetected infections, the SIDARTHE model also considers different degrees of disease severity. With this more delineated model, the risk of underestimating case fatality ratios is minimized.

Furthermore, in the Philippines, the severity of COVID-19 disease can vary greatly across different age groups. Therefore, an age-structured SEEIIR model was developed, with the following compartments: susceptible, non-infectious exposed, infectious exposed, early actively infectious, late actively infectious, and recovered/removed [7]. The model included the effects of various interventions in the transmission dynamic of the disease including time-varying mobility, testing, and personal protective behaviors. A few more studies adapted the use of age-structured transmission models to observe the epidemic progression in France [14] and to evaluate the effects of control measures in Netherlands [31].

Stochastic Models. While the classic deterministic model assumes that infectiousness is averaged out across the population over a certain time interval [28], stochastic models consider variations in individual's infectiousness, thereby introducing stochasticity in the behavior of the population across time. Several stochastic individual-based models had been developed over the course of this pandemic, such as the one presented in [16] where transmission is driven by interactions of individuals within the household, work and school settings, and the general community. Another study formulated a stochastic SEIR model where the transmission dynamic follows a geometric random walk process, and is fitted to the available data on COVID-19 cases within Wuhan and those originating from Wuhan [25]. A sequential Monte Carlo simulation was then used to estimate the transmission rate over time and projected number of cases. A similar study was also done for Australia and United Kingdom where the progression of COVID-19 cases in a SIR structure via Monte Carlo simulation was used to estimate the daily number of new and cumulative cases [38].

2.2 Agent-Based Models (ABM)

One of the early adoptions of agent-based modelling in the pandemic was to evaluate the transmission risks of COVID-19 in a simulated environment.

Specifically, a simplistic model was designed to simulate the spatio-temporal transmission of the virus in a 300 × 300 matrix facility between two types of agent-representing individuals: the susceptible group and the infected group [11]. A sample application of this kind of agent-based model has was done in a simulated supermarket environment to estimate the number of infections with respect to varying exposure times [39]. The study also modeled several possible interventions inside the store, which includes restricting the maximum number of customers, re-arranging the layout of the store, and implementing face mask policy among the individuals.

Agent-Based Modeling in COMOKIT. Agent-based Modeling is useful when: interaction between individuals are complex, nonlinear, discontinuous, or discrete; space is crucial and the agents' positions are not fixed; population is heterogeneous; topology of the interactions is heterogeneous and complex and; each agent exhibit complex behavior such as learning and adaptation [4]. While population-based model are more suited for when the number of agents considered becomes large or more 'global', ABM is more applicable in a 'local perspective' or individual-based [5, 6].

COMOKIT or COVID-19 Modeling Toolkit is an integrated model running on GAMA platform for evaluating and comparing intervention options in the face of Covid-19 pandemic [17]. The simulation model was designed to be run at the scale of a closed commune city-like setting, where individual buildings are the smallest spatial units that can be evaluated.

In COMOKIT, individual agents (or species) are the central component where they represent individual residents with unique characteristics (age, sex, work status), as well as individual epidemiological status and related variables. They go about their daily lives according to their own schedule. Depending on the age and family status of the Individual agent, this agenda is a created collection of Activities that can be shared by numerous individuals (e.g., going to a restaurant with some friends). The qualities of individual agents include their family (i.e., the household), friends, coworkers (or classmates), and their home, workplace, and school building. Individual agents can infect other Individual agents directly or indirectly through building contamination as represented by the variable viral load.

Agent-Based Modeling in Schools. Agent-based Modeling is applicable in school setting because the model can consider individual characteristics that represent behavior of individual in a community. For example, agent-based Modeling has been used to study evacuation of humans during disasters because of its capacity to include heterogeneity, randomness, and interactions among the individuals or agents being represented [30]. An agent-based evacuation model was developed to simulate human evacuation process which was validated with real data from an evacuation drill of a K-12 school (Kindergarten to 12th grade children and staff) in the city of Iquique, Chile. The model assumed that the agent will choose the shortest path in exiting the building. Actual drill showed similar results, especially for those who have knowledge or are informed of the surroundings and of evacuation routes, as in the case of those who attend school daily.

In one study, ABM was used to simulate prevention of the spread of measles in schools developed an agent-based model for schools to prevent the spread of measles[18]. Using NOVA modeling platform, a stochastic, spatially-structured, individual-based SEIR model of outbreaks was built with assumed $R_0 = 7$. In this study, results showed that the policy of sending home students without proof of vaccination had significantly lowered the number of cases in communities with both relatively high (95%) and relatively low (85%) vaccination rates. The mean duration of outbreak was also significantly lower when 'send unvaccinated students home' policy was implemented as compared to 'no action'. In another study a hybrid model that combines an agent-based model with an equation-based model was built to simulate the effect of school closure during measles outbreak [20]. In the study, the degree centrality of towns in a network is considered and is determined based on the number of agents commuting in and out of a town. The results showed that closing schools in a town with high in degree centrality is more beneficial than closing schools in a town where the outbreak started or with the closest distance from it because an agent tends to commute to a town with high centrality bringing the disease into the town.

Use of ABM has also been used to study disease spread and school closures [33]. Specifically, the model examined the impact of partial or full reopening of schools. Results showed that there is a significant increase in cases if the school will be re-opened completely (100%). Relaxing school safety protocols such as use of mask and social distancing will also result in small increase in cases. But partial re-opening (up to 75%) has no significant impact on the number of cases. Hence, the recommendation was to keep the level of student return below a threshold with a modest campus safety protocol in order to reduce incremental infections from school reopening. A similar study simulated school re-opening and vaccination scenarios in an urban city in the Philippines [8] where an Age-Stratified, Quarantine-Modified SEIR with Non-Linear Incidence Rates (ASQ-SEIR-NLIR) model was embedded into an ABM coupled it contact matrices. Results showed that schools may re-open at only 25% capacity as a precautionw with students vaccinated with a minimum of 55% vaccination coverage, and strict health safety protocols must be observed such as wearing of masks and social distancing.

This paper further explores the use of agent-based modeling in a university setting as the country prepares for the gradual opening of face to face classes. Specifically, we develop and simulate scenarios on EASE: an explicit agent-based simulation for opening of schools considering three conditions: compliance to wearing of masks, vaccine effectiveness based on vaccine coverage and scheduling of campus entry by groups.

3   Methodology

3.1   Data Source and Data Sets

The test university is a private university located in a highly urbanized city in the National Capital Region (NCR), Philippines. Like all universities, the campus has been closed for face to face classes since the onset of the pandemic last March 2020. The campus covers 83 hectares of land with interspersed with greenery and vegetation amidst office buildings, classrooms and laboratories.

In November 2021, the university began working on the requirements for limited face to face classes as a response to IATF Resolution 148G and Joint Memorandum Circular 2021-001 [22] indicating that schools are allowed to conduct limited face to face classes under Alert Levels 1, 2 and 3 under certain conditions that apply to ensuring compliance to minimum public health standards, approval of the local government units and participation of fully vaccinated students, teaching and non-teaching personnel.

Geographic Data and Shapefile. The geographic data was acquired by searching for the location in OpenStreetMap (OSM)[2] and exporting the result into an OSM file, which contains the full street map information of the selected site. Using an online Geodata Converter Tool[3], the exported OSM file was then converted into a Shapefile format comprising of multiple layers of structured geographic data.

COMOKIT requires two Shapefiles to be present in the dataset folder during the simulation: the boundary and buildings Shapefiles. The boundary Shapefile contains the bounding polygon information of the whole university in the map while the buildings Shapefile contains the polygon information of each building inside the university. Both necessary Shapefiles were generated by modifying the amenity-polygon and buildings-polygon layers of the converted OSM file respectively using the open-source Quantum GIS (QGIS)[4] software.

A total of 24 buildings with reduced maximum seating capacity per room were included in the study. Seats in classrooms, laboratories and offices were arranged 1.5 m apart to fulfill requirements on social distancing. Rooms were retro-fitted to incorporate prescribed ventilation requirements. Hallways, corridors and walkways were marked with arrows that serves as a guide to proper pedestrian flow.

A building with multiple floors was modeled by duplicating the building's row entry accordingly in the Shapefile's attribute table, effectively simulating different floors occupying the same land area in the map. In a limited face-to-face class opening, not all buildings in the campus are to be opened and the maximum capacity of the amenities are reduced. To accommodate these reduced capacity policy, three new columns were added into the Shapefiles's attribute table: one

---

[2] https://www.openstreetmap.org/.
[3] https://mygeodata.cloud/converter/osm-to-shp.
[4] https://www.qgis.org/en/site/.

of which was used to indicate whether a particular building is to be opened or not; another one was used to indicate the number of opened rooms within the building; and the last one was used to indicate the new maximum capacity of the building. Actual data of new building capacities to be implemented was used to adjust the values in the Shapefile's attribute table for the simulation.

Epidemiological Parameters. Table 1 shows the summarized assumed epidemiological parameters used in EASE. Both the human and building contact rates were calculated by dividing the basic reproduction number of the virus with the period length of it being infectious. As of the time of writing, Omicron is the dominant variant in the Philippines. Omicron's basic reproduction number is estimated to be 7.0 or greater [3] with an effective infectious period of 10 days [32]. The proportion of asymptomatic infections valued at 19.51% was estimated based on the vaccine effectiveness reported in UK Health Security Agency (UKHSA) technical briefing on SARS-CoV-2 [36] and the vaccination data from the National Capital Region. The basic viral release and decrease parameters were adopted from COMOKIT's default values. Omicron's median incubation period has been described to be approximately 3 days [23]. The average time duration between first infection and reinfection is 63.6±48.9 days [13] while the protection against reinfection is set around 87.02% [27].

3.2 Base Model

The original COMOKIT code was modified to accommodate the following university related considerations and assumptions:

1. The number of synthetic population (also called as reduced population) generated in each simulation run is based on the sum of the new normal seating capacity per room per building to be opened.
2. An individual agent is assigned to a particular building and room, dictating who will be their colleagues for social interaction when inside the university.
3. Once infected, symptomatic individuals are not allowed to enter the university until they recover. However, asymptomatic individuals can still enter the university undetected, causing internal viral transmission.
4. The university opens and closes at a pre-defined opening and closing hours. Outside of these working hours, all individuals are placed outside the university premises.
5. There is a probability for an individual to be infected when outside the university. This probability value is calculated based on the current effective reproduction number where the test university is located and the incubation period of the virus.
6. After recovering from the disease, an individual receives natural immunity from the virus by a certain percentage, defined by the factor of natural immunity parameter. After a period of time (as dictated by the reinfection interval parameter), the recovered individual may become reinfected again but with higher protection from infection.

Table 1. Epidemiological parameters assumed in EASE.

Parameter	Definition	Value
Human contact rate	Probability of any infectious agent to infect a susceptible one during a contact	7.0/10
Building contact rate	Successful contact rate for environment to human transmission	7.0/10
Proportion asymptomatic	Proportion of asymptomatic infections as compared to the total number of infections	0.1951
Basic viral release	Value to increment to the viral load of the building from an infectious individual	0.03
Basic viral decrease	Value to decrement in the viral load from the building to the environment	0.01375
Incubation period	Time in days from the earliest possible exposure until symptom onset	3
Infectious period	Time in days from being infectious to being recovered	10
Reinfection interval	The average time duration in days between first infection and reinfection	63.6±48.9
Factor natural immunity	Protection against reinfection	0.8702

3.3 Interventions and Scenarios

The simulation environment is set up to evaluate different intervention strategies including: mask compliance (3 scenarios), vaccination (4 scenarios), batch scheduling (4 scenarios), and combined interventions (3 scenarios).

Mask Compliance. One of the scenarios considered in compliance with government memorandum is the wearing of face masks in closed environments. There are three cases considered as scenarios, namely: a) 50%, b) 75%, and c) 100% of the total synthetic population properly wearing a mask. The effectiveness of masks against contracting the COVID-19 virus was set to 85% instead of the standard value of 95% [37] to accommodate for the different types of masks incorporating a number of individuals possibly wearing low quality masks.

Vaccine Intervention. Vaccine intervention is defined as the percentage of individuals who are vaccinated and boosted. In this study, four scenarios are considered:

1. 100% of the population have completed two doses of vaccine but without a booster shot;
2. 50% of the population have completed two doses only while the remaining 50% received two doses plus booster shot;

3. 100% of the population have completed the two doses of vaccine plus booster shot;
4. 77% of the population have completed two doses only and an additional 17% receiving two doses plus booster shot, leaving 6% unvaccinated. This scenario replicates the real vaccine proportion in NCR as of the time of writing, where the test university is located

Batch Scheduling. The reduced population is further distributed into two groups that will be assigned alternate schedules in the onsite classes. Specifically, each group or batch are scheduled to be on campus on alternating weeks. An interval is defined as the week where there are no onsite classes for both groups. Four scenarios were considered, namely:

1. one batch without interval (the entire population is back on campus);
2. one batch with intervals (the entire population is back on campus but with every other week interval of no onsite classes);
3. two batches without interval (batch A and batch B have alternate weekly onsite classes; and
4. two batches with intervals (batch A and batch B have alternate weekly onsite classes with an interval of one week with no onsite classes for both groups).

Combined Interventions. Mask compliance, vaccine doses and batch scheduling when considered as separate interventions are not sufficient to comply with the minimum public health standards. A more realistic scenario considers combination of these three interventions. We consider three combined intervention scenarios for the simulation.

1. **Minimum acceptable case**, where
   (a) Mask compliance is at 70%
   (b) 80% of the population have completed two doses of vaccine and 0% have received their booster shots
   (c) one batch with interval
2. **Close to reality scenario**, where
   (a) Mask compliance is at 85%
   (b) 77% of the population have completed two doses of vaccine only and an additional 17% have received their booster shots
   (c) two batches with intervals
3. **Ideal case scenario**, where
   (a) Mask compliance is at 100%
   (b) 100% of the population have completed two doses of vaccine plus booster shots
   (c) two batches with intervals

3.4 Simulation and Analysis

A total of 500 simulations over a period of 120 days or 18 weeks was performed for each of the 14 scenarios to produce the median frequency count of daily infected cases and cumulative cases. One way analysis of variance was performed to test for significant differences in the median of cumulative cases among scenarios per intervention in four different time periods, namely 30th day, 60th day, 90th day and 120th day.

4 Results and Discussion

A total of 1,995 synthetic population was generated for each simulation run. All scenarios per intervention were simulated 500 times with a 120 day time period approximating one semester. This section first presents the results of single intervention with accompanying scenarios for each intervention to serve as a baseline in understanding on the effects of single interventions. The succeeding section present results of select scenarios combining the three interventions to depict close to reality scenarios.

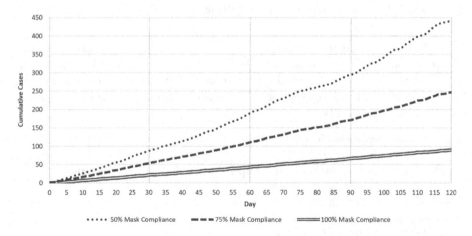

Fig. 1. Cumulative graph of cases on levels of mask compliance (median of 500 runs).

4.1 Mask Compliance

Figure 1 shows the resulting median cumulative graph in three mask compliance levels from 500 simulation runs. Scenario 1.1 (dotted-line on Fig. 1) shows the cumulative graph of cases when the population is 50% compliant in properly wearing their face masks. Scenario 1.2 (dashed-line on Fig. 1) shows the cumulative graph of cases for 75% mask compliance. Scenario 1.3 (double-line on Fig. 1) shows the cumulative graph cases for 100% mask compliance.

As expected, results show that 50% mask compliance has the highest cumulative case count of 441 cases at the end of 120 days, followed by 75% mask compliance at 247 cases at the end of 120 days and lowest count of 90 cases at the end of 120 days for 100% mask compliance. Results also showed that there is a significant difference in median case counts for the 500 simulation runs per level of compliance at 30, 60, 90 and 120 days. This means that higher level of compliance to wearing masks results to lower case counts (see Table 2).

Table 2. Cumulative case count on levels of mask compliance at the end of 120 day simulation period.

Scenario	Level	Cumulative case	% reduction
1.1	50% mask compliance	441	Baseline
1.2	75% mask compliance	247	43.99%
1.3	100% mask compliance	90	79.59%

Note: Day 30 $F[(2, 1497)= 6319.54, p < 0.00]$; Day 60 $F[(2, 1497)=$ $8752.13, p < 0.00]$ & Day 90 F $[(2, 1497)= 9374.09, p < 0.00]$ & Day 120 F $[(2, 1497) = 8056.39, p < 0.00]$

4.2 Vaccine Coverage

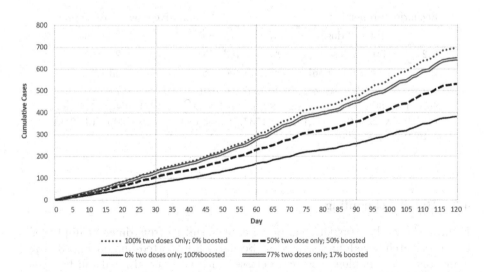

Fig. 2. Cumulative graph of cases based on vaccine coverage (median of 500 runs).

Figure 2 shows the median cumulative graph of cases for 500 simulation resulting from varying vaccine coverage levels. Scenario 2.1 (dotted-line on Fig. 2) shows the cumulative graph of cases when the entire simulated population received two doses only; Scenario 2.2 (dashed-line on Fig. 2) is for the case when half of the population received a booster shot aside from the basic two doses; Scenario 2.3 (full-line on Fig. 2) is for the case when the entire simulated population received a booster shot already; and Scenario 2.4 (double-line on Fig. 2) shows the cumulative graph of cases simulating the actual vaccine proportion where the university is located, that is 77% for the two doses and 17% for the booster shot, leaving 6% unvaccinated.

Results showed that the scenario where the lowest case count of 381 individuals at the end of the 120 day simulation period, will occur when the entire population is fully vaccinated (with 2 doses) and also received booster shots. The second lowest case count of 531 cases will occur if 50% of the population is fully vaccinated and have received booster shots. Higher case counts of 646 individuals and 695 individuals will occur if only 77% of the population is fully vaccinated with 17% of them receiving booster shots (which is based on the current actual scenario in NCR) and if the population is fully vaccinated with no booster shots, respectively.

Analysis of variance on the median of the total number of cases at the 30th, 60th, 90th and 120th day of the simulation all showed significant differences (see Table 3).

Table 3. Cumulative cases based on vaccine coverage at the end of 120 day simulation period.

Scenario	Proportion	Cumulative case	% reduction
2.1	100% 2 doses only; 0% boosted	695	Baseline
2.2	50% 2 doses only; 50% boosted	531	23.60%
2.3	0% 2 doses only; 100% boosted	381	45.18%
2.4	77% 2 doses only; 17% boosted	646	7.05%

Note: Day 30 $F[(3,1996)= 1386.89, p < 0.00]$; Day 60 $F[(3,1996)= 1493.36, p < 0.00]$ & Day 90 $F[(3,1996)= 1737.71, p < 0.00]$ & Day 120 $F[(3,1996) = 1689.18, p < 0.00]$

4.3 Batch Scheduling

Figure 3 shows the cumulative graph of cases resulting from different implementation of batch scheduling strategies. Scenario 3.1 (dotted-line on Fig. 3) simulates one batch implementation of classes with no interval breaks in between. Scenario 3.2 (dashed-line on Fig. 3) simulates again one batch but now with a recurring week-long break interval in between. Scenario 3.3 (double-line on Fig. 3) simulates two batches without interval while Scenario 3.4 (full-line on Fig. 3) simulates two batches with recurring break intervals in between.

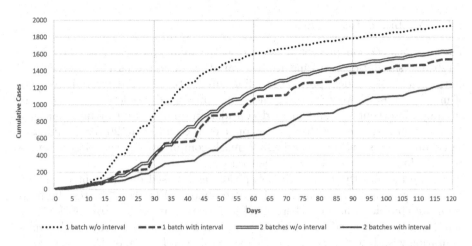

Fig. 3. Cumulative graph of cases based on batch scheduling (median of 500 runs).

Table 4. Case Counts at variation of batch schedule strategy at the end of 120 day simulation period.

Scenario	Set-up	Cumulative case	% reduction
3.1	No batching without interval	1,939	Baseline
3.2	No batching with interval	1,538	20.68%
3.3	2 batches without interval	1,637	15.58%
3.4	2 batches with interval	1,242	35.95%

Note: Day 30 $F[(3, 1996)= 3697.95, p < 0.00]$; Day 60 $F[(3, 1996)= 7260.52, p < 0.00]$; Day 90 $F[(3, 1996)= 7624.42, p < 0.00]$; Day 120 $F[(3, 1996) = 6897.99, p < 0.00]$

Results show that the scenario with lowest case count of 1,242 cases at the end of a 120 day simulation is when the population is divided into two batches that go on campus in alternate weeks with an interval of one week of no onsite classes in between alternating weeks. This is followed by a case count of 1,538 which occurs when the entire population goes onsite all at once every other week alternating with interval of no onsite classes. Dividing the population into two batches and having them onsite in alternating weeks results to a higher case count of 1,637 cases. Baseline set up where the entire population goes onsite without interval results into almost everyone in the population getting infected with a total of 1939 case counts at the end of a 120 day simulation.

Analysis of variance on the median of the total number of cases at the 30th, 60th, 90th and 120th day of the simulation all showed significant differences (see Table 4).

4.4   Combined Intervention

The previous section presented results on the number of cases at the end of
a 120 day simulation resulting from a variation of scenarios per intervention.
Output of these models provide baseline information in understanding effects
of interventions. However, management of a prolonged pandemic does not rely
on single interventions and instead considers a combination of interventions.
This section discusses resulting case count at the end of a 120 day simulation
based on select scenarios that include mask compliance, vaccination coverage
and scheduling of onsite visits to the campus.

Figure 4 shows the cumulative graph of cases based on different combined
intervention strategies. Scenario 4.1 (dotted-line on Fig. 4) simulates the minimum acceptable situation where mask compliance is set to 70%, 80% of the
population is vaccinated with two doses only, and classes are on one batch implementation with interval. Scenario 4.2 (dashed-line on Fig. 4), on the other hand,
simulates the close to reality situation where assumptions and parameters are
taken from NCR where the test university is located. In this close to reality scenario, mask compliance is set to 85%, 77% of the population received two doses
of vaccines only with an additional 17% receiving a booster shot, and classes
are on two batches implementation with interval breaks in between. Scenario 4.3
(double-line on Fig. 4) simulates the ideal case situation where 100% mask compliance is assumed, the entire population is assumed to have received a booster
shot, and class are on a two batch implementation with one week interval in
between.

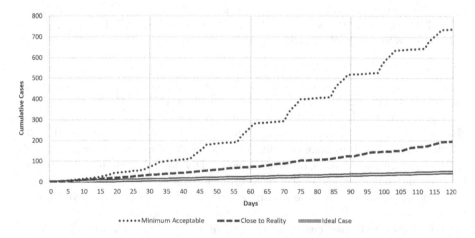

Fig. 4. Cumulative graph of cases based on different combined intervention strategies
(median of 500 runs).

Results show that case counts will remain low, at 48 cases based on a 120
day simulation if the the entire population will comply 100% to wearing masks,

are fully vaccinated and boosted 100% and go onsite in alternating weeks for 2 batches. However, this scenario seems ideal as reality and experience tells us that not everyone will comply to mask wearing at all times on campus. At the same time, the roll out of the vaccination program already includes booster shots.

When the simulation was set to mimic January 2022 National Region Data on compliance and vaccination coverage, results further show that if mask compliance is at 85%, population fully vaccinated at 77% with 17% and apply two batches with one week interval of no onsite classes, case numbers would reach 196 cases at the end of the 120 day simulation.

Finally, running the simulation to mimic acceptable compliance rate of 70%, with 80% of the population fully vaccinated but none of which have had a booster shot, and having just intervals in between onsite classes for the entire population resulted to more cases, reaching a high of 736 cases at the end of the 120 day cycle.

Analysis of variance on the median of the total number of cases at the 30th, 60th, 90th and 120th day of the simulation all showed significant differences. (see Table 5).

Table 5. Cumulative case count on levels of combined intervention at the end of 120 day simulation period.

Scenario	Level	Cumulative case	% reduction
4.1	70% mask compliance, 80% 2 doses only, 0% boosted, one batch with interval	736	Baseline
4.2	85% mask compliance, 77% 2 doses only, 17% boosted, two batches with interval	196	73.37%
4.3	100% mask compliance, 0% 2 doses only, 100% boosted, two batches with interval	48	93.48%

Note: Day 30 $F_{(2, 1497)}= 2865.13$, $p < 0.00$]; Day 60 $F_{(2, 1497)}= 4074.91$, $p < 0.00$]; Day 90 F $[(2, 1497)= 7947.31$, $p < 0.00$]; Day 120 F $[(2, 1497) = 12585.58$, $p < 0.00$]

5   Conclusion

In this study, we use the COVID-19 Modeling Kit (COMOKIT, 2020) as a basis for the inclusion of individual and spatial components in the analysis of possible behaviors of individuals as the country returns to onsite classes in 2022. Specifically, we derive a version of COMOKIT specific to university setting. The model is an agent-based, spatially explicit model with the inclusion of individual epidemiological and behavior parameters to show evidence of which behavioral and non-pharmaceutical interventions lead to reduced transmission over a given period of time. Three intervention strategies were applied to the model, namely: compliance to wearing masks, vaccination status and coverage, and dividing population into two groups for pre-scheduled onsite classes.

When interventions are applied and viewed separately, wearing of face mask, despite varying degrees of compliance, produced the lowest case numbers at the end of a simulation run, which covers close to one semester of onsite classes. Vaccine intervention scenarios show that having significant portion of the population with booster shots produces less number of cases compared to the scenario when none or minimal portion only have booster shots. Dividing the population into two groups with predetermined schedules of onsite classes produces lower cases if the two groups go onsite on alternating weeks with a one week interval of no onsite classes. However, this type of intervention alone is not an effective measure as shown by the large number of cases at the end of the simulation, for all four scenarios. Combined interventions are consistent with intended effects where higher mask compliance, larger vaccination coverage and batched scheduling produce the lowest case numbers.

Explicit spatial agent-based modeling is applicable to simulate effects of behavioral and pharmaceutical interventions for limited face to face classes in a university setting. Further studies need to consider increase in vaccination coverage, change in reproduction rate, and possibly additional interventions within the span of a one semester simulation.

References

1. Al Jazeera Media Network: No school until coronavirus vaccine is available: Duterte, May 2020. https://www.aljazeera.com/news/2020/5/26/no-school-until-coronavirus-vaccine-is-available-duterte
2. Anand, N., Sabarinath, A., Geetha, S., Somanath, S.: Predicting the spread of COVID-19 using SIR model augmented to incorporate quarantine and testing. Trans. Indian Natl. Acad. Eng. **5**(2), 141–148 (2020). https://doi.org/10.1007/s41403-020-00151-5
3. Boarman, A.: Omicron is the Dominant COVID Variant for Two Reasons. Sutter Health, December 2021. https://vitals.sutterhealth.org/omicron-is-the-us-dominant-covid-variant-for-two-reasons/
4. Bonabeau, E.: Agent-based modeling: methods and techniques for simulating human systems. Proc. Natl. Acad. Sci. USA **99**(3 Suppl.), 7280–7287 (2002)
5. Bosse, T., Gerritsen, C., Hoogendoorn, M., Jaffry, S.W., Treur, J.: Agent-based vs. population-based simulation of displacement of crime: a comparative study. Web Intell. Agent Syst. **9**(2), 147–160 (2011)
6. Bosse, T., Mogles, N.: Spread of situation awareness in a group: population-based vs. agent-based modelling. In: 2014 IEEE/WIC/ACM International Joint Conferences on Web Intelligence (WI) and Intelligent Agent Technologies (IAT), IEEE, August 2014
7. Caldwell, J.M., et al.: Understanding COVID-19 dynamics and the effects of interventions in the Philippines: a mathematical modelling study. Lancet Reg. Health Western Pacific **14**, 100211 (2021). https://doi.org/10.1016/j.lanwpc.2021.100211

8. Celeste, J.J., Bongolan, V.P.: School re-opening simulations with COVID-19 agent-based model for Quezon City, Philippines. ISPRS Int. Arch. Photogramm. Remote Sens. Spat. Inf. Sci. **XLVI-4/W6-2021**, 85–90 (2021)

9. CNN Philippines: Metro Manila to be placed on "lockdown" due to COVID-19, March 2020. https://cnnphilippines.com/news/2020/3/12/COVID-19-Metro-Manila-restrictions-Philippines.html

10. dela Cruz, R.C.: No face-to-face classes until COVID-19 vaccine is available. Philippine News Agency, June 2020. https://www.pna.gov.ph/articles/1105226

11. Cuevas, E.: An agent-based model to evaluate the COVID-19 transmission risks in facilities. Comput. Biol. Medi. **121**(January), 103827 (2020). https://doi.org/10.1016/j.compbiomed.2020.103827, https://linkinghub.elsevier.com/retrieve/pii/S001048252030192X

12. Department of Education: Youth group: Vaccines for students first before resuming face-to-face classes. GOVPH, November 2021. https://www.deped.gov.ph/2021/11/14/on-the-opening-of-the-pilot-implementation-of-limited-face-to-face-classes/

13. Dhillon, R.A., et al.: The mystery of COVID-19 reinfections: a global systematic review and meta-analysis. Ann. Med. Surg. **72**(December), 103130 (2021)

14. Di Domenico, L., Pullano, G., Sabbatini, C.E., Boëlle, P.Y., Colizza, V.: Modelling safe protocols for reopening schools during the COVID-19 pandemic in France. Nat. Commun. **12**(1), 1–10 (2021). https://doi.org/10.1038/s41467-021-21249-6

15. Estadilla, C., Uyheng, J., de Lara-Tuprio, E., Teng, T., Macalalag, J., Estuar, M.R.J.: Impact of vaccine supplies and delays on optimal control of the COVID-19 pandemic: mapping interventions for the Philippines. Infect. Dis. Poverty **10**(107), 1–14 (2021). https://doi.org/10.1186/s40249-021-00886-5

16. Ferguson, N.M., et al.: Impact of non-pharmaceutical interventions (NPIS) to reduce COVID-19 mortality and healthcare demand (2020)

17. Gaudou, B., et al.: COMOKIT: a modeling kit to understand, analyze, and compare the impacts of mitigation policies against the COVID-19 epidemic at the scale of a city. Front. Public Health **8**(September), 1–18 (2020). https://doi.org/10.3389/fpubh.2020.563247

18. Getz, W.M., Carlson, C., Dougherty, E., Porco, T.C., Salter, R.: An agent-based model of school closing in under-vaccinated communities during measles outbreaks. Simulation **95**(5), 385–393 (2019)

19. Giordano, G., et al.: Modelling the COVID-19 epidemic and implementation of population-wide interventions in Italy, vol. 26. Springer, US (2020). https://doi.org/10.1038/s41591-020-0883-7

20. Hunter, E., Kelleher, J.D.: Using a hybrid agent-based and equation based model to test school closure policies during a measles outbreak. BMC Public Health **21**(1), 499 (2021)

21. Inter-Agency Task Force: Guidelines on the Nationwide Implementation of Alert Level System For COVID-19 Response. GOVPH, November 2021. https://www.officialgazette.gov.ph/downloads/2021/11nov/20211118-IATF-GUIDELINES-RRD.pdf

22. Inter-Agency Task Force: Planned Implementation Of Limited Face To Face Classes. GOVPH, November 2021. https://mirror.officialgazette.gov.ph/downloads/2021/11nov/20211116-RESO-148G-RRD.pdf

23. Jansen, L., et al.: Investigation of a SARS-CoV-2 B.1.1.529 (Omicron) variant cluster - Nebraska, November–December 2021 MMWR. Morbidity Mortal. Weekly Report **70**(5152), 1782–1784 (2021). https://doi.org/10.15585/mmwr.mm705152e3

24. Kerr, C.C., et al.: Covasim: an agent-based model of COVID-19 dynamics and interventions. PLOS Comput. Biol. **17**, e1009149 (2021). https://doi.org/10.1371/journal.pcbi.1009149
25. Kucharski, A.J.: Early dynamics of transmission and control of COVID-19: a mathematical modelling study. Lancet Infect. Dis. **20**(5), 553–558 (2020). https://doi.org/10.1016/S1473-3099(20)30144-4
26. Lalu, G.P.: Youth group: Vaccines for students first before resuming face-to-face classes. INQUIRER.net, February 2021. https://www.pna.gov.ph/articles/1105226
27. Mao, Y.J., Wang, W.W., Ma, J., Wu, S.S., Sun, F.: Reinfection rates among patients previously infected by SARS-CoV-2. Chinese Med. J. Publish Ah. **135** 1–8 (2021). https://doi.org/10.1097/CM9.0000000000001892, https://journals.lww.com/10.1097/CM9.0000000000001892
28. Panovska-Griffiths, J.: Can mathematical modelling solve the current Covid-19 crisis? BMC Public Health **20**(1), 1–3 (2020). https://doi.org/10.1186/s12889-020-08671-z
29. Paul, S., Mahata, A., Ghosh, U., Roy, B.: Study of SEIR epidemic model and scenario analysis of COVID-19 pandemic. Ecol. Genetics Genomics **19**(May), 100087 (2021)
30. Poulos, A., Tocornal, F., de la Llera, J.C., Mitrani-Reiser, J.: Validation of an agent-based building evacuation model with a school drill. Transp. Res. Part C Emerg. Technol. **97**, 82–95 (2018)
31. Rozhnova, G., et al.: Model-based evaluation of school- and non-school-related measures to control the COVID-19 pandemic. Nat. Commun. **12**(1), 1–11 (2021). https://doi.org/10.1038/s41467-021-21899-6
32. Schuster-Bruce, C.: Here's how long people with COVID-19 might remain contagious, according to the best available data. Business Insider, January 2022. https://www.businessinsider.com/covid-how-long-contagious-infectious-period-omicron-delta-rapid-test-2022-1
33. Tatapudi, H., Das, T.K.: Impact of school reopening on pandemic spread: a case study using an agent-based model for COVID-19. Infect. Dis. Model. **6**, 839–847 (2021)
34. Tomacruz, S.: Philippines begins legally rolling out first COVID-19 vaccines. Rappler, March 2021. https://www.rappler.com/nation/philippines-begins-legally-rolling-out-covid-19-vaccine-march-1-2021/
35. Tomchin, D.A., Fradkov, A.L.: Prediction of the COVID-19 spread in Russia based on SIR and SEIR models of epidemics. IFAC-PapersOnLine **53**(5), 833–838 (2020). https://doi.org/10.1016/j.ifacol.2021.04.209
36. UK Health Security Agency: SARS-CoV-2 variants of concern and variants under investigation in England: Technical briefing 34 (2022). https://www.gov.uk/government/publications/investigation-of-sars-cov-2-variants-technical-briefings. Accessed January 2022
37. Wang, Y., Deng, Z., Shi, D.: How effective is a mask in preventing COVID-19 infection? Med. Dev. Sens. **4**(1), e10163 (2021)
38. Xie, G.: A novel Monte Carlo simulation procedure for modelling COVID-19 spread over time. Sci. Rep. **10**(1), 1–9 (2020). https://doi.org/10.1038/s41598-020-70091-1
39. Ying, F., O'Clery, N.: Modelling COVID-19 transmission in supermarkets using an agent-based model. PLoS ONE **16**(4 April), 1–13 (2021). https://doi.org/10.1371/journal.pone.0249821

Exploring Faculty Members Perception of Utilizing Technology to Enhance Student Engagement in the United Arab Emirates: Technology and the ICAP Modes of Engagement

Georgina Farouqa[1] and Ajrina Hysaj[2]([envelope])

[1] Georgina Farouqa, Walden University, Minneapolis, MN, USA
[2] Ajrina Hysaj, UOW College, University of Wollongong, Dubai, UAE
ajrinahysaj@uowdubai.ac.ae

Abstract. Many university students across the United Arab Emirates (UAE) as well as other countries around the world are struggling to improve their academic achievement. In the context of online teaching and learning, this can be related to low levels of student engagement, which can be related to faculty's choice of modern technologies to enhance students' engagement. The purpose of this qualitative study was to understand how faculty utilize technology to enhance student engagement. The conceptual framework for the study consisted of Chi and Wylie's interactive, constructive, active, and passive learning framework, which emphasizes the relationship between students' academic achievement and their engagement in the learning activity. The research question addressed faculty members' choice of modern technologies to enhance students' engagement at 4-year universities in the UAE. Qualitative research was chosen for the study, and data were collected through an open-ended online questionnaire from 106 faculty members teaching at universities in the UAE. The findings potentially contribute to a better understanding of ways that technology is utilized in higher education and suggest ways for promoting students' engagement through modern technologies. Educators and policymakers can use our findings to enhance student engagement and suggest strategies that promote the use of technology in higher education.

Keywords: ICAP framework · Modern technologies · Student engagement

1 Introduction

The problem of low academic achievement of university students in the United Arab Emirates (UAE) as well as other countries in the world can be caused by low level of student engagement in their learning. The purpose of this study was to understand how university faculty utilize technology to support student engagement. The UAE government believes that the development of the nation depends highly on education and technology. Therefore, in the UAE the learning process encourages active and experiential learning [13, 21]. According to Al Kaabi [2] education in the UAE depends

© The Author(s), under exclusive license to Springer Nature Switzerland AG 2022
G. Meiselwitz (Ed.): HCII 2022, LNCS 13316, pp. 67–76, 2022.
https://doi.org/10.1007/978-3-031-05064-0_5

on traditional ways of teaching, like face-to-face and teacher-centered learning. The motivation of students who were taught in a traditional way and others who were more engaged in their learning activities were highlighted in a study presented by Al Kaabi which showed that students were less motivated when taught in a traditional while those who were actively engaged in their learning were more motivated to learn. Understandably, faculty who use proper technologies in their classroom can help students enhance important skills like collaboration, creativity, communication, and critical thinking [1, 3, 11].

It is worth mentioning that although many studies have been conducted to measure the effectiveness of the use of technology like social media and smartphones, yet the ways that faculty use these technologies in their teaching needs to be further explored [1, 17, 18]. There is a gap in the literature pertaining to ways that faculty utilize technology to promote active learning in the context of higher education in the UAE. A possible cause of this problem lies in the low engagement of students and lack of technology use in the teaching and learning process [3, 4, 11, 14, 17]. This can be related to lecturing which remains the main mode of teaching in UAE higher education institutions. Students learn in a passive way, and they are expected to use their passive learning during exams. A pre-course survey showed results showed that 95.2% of students viewed working on projects to help them learn more while 92% of students did not enjoy lectures [21].

The purpose of this study was to understand how university faculty support student engagement level and subsequently improved students' achievement through the use of technology. This study is needed to develop a deeper professional understanding of student engagement in higher education. By highlighting the issue of student engagement using technology, our study revealed ways that technology is utilized in higher education that promotes students' engagement and prepares students of the UAE to face the challenges of the 21st century. Therefore, to fill the existing gap and provide information to educators and decision-makers in higher education. We used the ICAP four modes of engagement to analyze ways that technology can be used to enhance student engagement in the current study. The purpose of this study was to understand how university faculty support student engagement. According to Mohammed [21] It is important that students are encouraged to be actively engaged in their classrooms and have the opportunity to achieve experiential learning. However, a number of faculty members seem to choose strategies that do not promote student engagement which leads to low academic achievement [21].

2   Literature Review

2.1   Technology in the Middle East

The Middle East has witnessed significant growth in internet usage since early 2000. Studies by Rashidi, Arani and Kakia [24] and Stephens [26] indicate that teachers in the Middle East have noticed that students consider using mobile phones and technology to access information about other cultures. Furthermore, digital technologies can support students in enhancing their perceptions of cultures and the rapid advancement of technology. For instance, according to Halaweh [10] the number of smartphone users in the United Arab Emirates are increasing. Smartphones are used on daily basis by students for many reasons including learning and instruction. Halaweh [10] investigated using smartphones in classrooms as well as restrictions placed by universities when students are using their phones in an unplanned manner as the university implemented a clear policy not allowing the use of smartphones and restricting the use of technology to laptops and projectors to present material in class.

However, Halaweh [10] proposed ways that smartphones can be used in class to enhance student engagement by asking students to look for new information online, using their calculators, presentation, and sharing information to enhance discussion. In order to control the use of smart phones, Halaweh suggested that instructors ask students to keep phones silent until they are requested to use them. Ethics and awareness related to the use of smartphones in class are clarified by the instructor. Technical issues related to the use of smartphones were also presented by Halaweh like ensuring the compatibility of files and providing chargeable devices. Halaweh recommended the integration of smartphones as a teaching tool used by faculty with clear regulations to the use of this technology.

Abdelouarit, Sbihi, and Aknin [1] studied the use of online research by students and explored new methods for a solution of open massive data to develop research in the UAE. Users are exposed to a large amount of heterogeneous data that might not improve learning in the academic community. This kind of data might not meet the requirements of students and can add to their confusion in relation to the reliability of sources. Abdelouarit, Sbihi, and Aknin [1] explored new ways to encourage students to use online research. The authors proposed a tool that can structure and integrate data to enhance research and self-learning of students in the UAE. This tool can make the consumption of data easier through a detailed analysis, specified future solutions through processing big data information into single layers that classify metadata based on the search of providing ergonomic presentation that will make it easier for learners to find results for their search which will support learners' online research in the UAE.

Educators are expected to be up to date and create a digital learning environment that matches the expectations in the 21st century [15] According to Barber and King [6], educators need different kinds of competencies other than the traditional way of teaching. Barber and King presented a study that showed students were more engaged in an online environment. Barber and King explored ways that problem-based learning (PBL) can help students to take responsibility for their learning, create communities, and achieve collaboration through feedback from their peers and educators which creates a shift in teacher-student roles. When students are engaged in PBL they can play a role in their learning and assessment which will help them gain skills like teamwork and personal management skills needed to join the workforce and improve their competencies for the economy of the 21st century. However, students who were used to traditional ways of learning felt frustrated when exposed to PBL as they did not develop self-directed skills and they needed constant instruction on how to succeed in this method of learning [7].

3   The ICAP Framework

The use of the ICAP framework in science, technology, engineering, and mathematics (STEM) classrooms showed that the learning performance of students improved significantly in interactive classrooms. Hyun et al. [16] highlighted the importance of this improvement as well as ways that faculty can develop activities to enhance student engagement. The study focused on ways to redesign STEM courses to achieve active learning. The STEM classes examined in this study were a good example to evaluate the learning outcome using the ICAP framework, especially because these courses are mainly taught using traditional methods. According to Hyun et al. [16], interactive activities require students to exchange ideas to come up with a new understanding that can help students achieve better learning than constructive activities require students to generate their own ideas while active activities require motor movements. The learning performance of students who were involved in interactive activities improved their learning performance which can indicate that the interactive mode of activity is effective for STEM classrooms [12, 16]. However, educators have noted that interactive activities require more planning and management of classrooms [13–16]. More research is required to further explore moving from active to constructive or constructive to interactive by actively exploring the benefits of implementing the ICAP modes of engagement to help students improve their learning outcomes [27]. In the United States, some schools adopted the ICAP to support students and help them meet their graduation requirements [20]. Therefore, students were trained on how to use the ICAP model and ICAP activities were facilitated by counselors at schools. Faculty supporting students were familiar with the model, yet they needed the support of the technology department. Utilizing technologies to promote active learning. This study hopes to contribute in filling a gap in the literature in relation to the use of technology in higher education in the United Arab Emirates.

4   The Conceptual Framework of the Study

The conceptual framework for this study was based on Chi and Wylie's [8] ICAP framework. This framework emphasizes the relationship between students' engagement in the learning activity and their learning performance. The ICAP framework categorizes students' engagement into four styles: interactive, constructive, active, and passive. Subsequent research and ICAP applications might offer guidance on how to improve student achievement. Subsequent researchers have explored the effects of implementing active learning strategies in classrooms on students' satisfaction with their learning experiences [16]. The researchers provided information related to faculty members' practice that can be useful to stakeholders like university deans and academic administrators who supervise faculty. In this qualitative study, faculty members were invited to complete a survey that provided information on how university faculty choose their teaching strategies to enhance university students' engagement and improve their achievement. Data were analyzed through qualitative data analysis software and the results included concepts that are central in the essays and converge with Chi and Wylie's [8] framework.

4.1   Research Design and Methodology

This study was a part of a larger scale Ed.D. study done to investigate the perception of faculty members of student engagement in the UAE. The qualitative approach was regarded appropriate for the study, as we sought to explore how faculty members utilize technology to enhance student engagement at 4-year universities in the UAE. A basic qualitative methodology was employed to help understand the perception of faculty members which required the collection of data through an online questionnaire.

The selection of participants was through purposeful random sampling to ensure they have experience and knowledge so they can provide sufficient information needed to answer the research questions.106 faculty members participated in the study. This number helped in better understanding of the perception of faculty members from various universities. Faculty members teaching at different universities in UAE were contacted through Social Networking Service SNS and invited to participate in the study. As positions held by faculty members affect their practice and ways of knowing [5], which contributed to the examination of the research question. The instrument used to collect data was a researcher-developed online open-ended questionnaire, open-ended questions enabled participants to provide long answers providing data that helped in extracting codes and categories to answer the research questions.

4.2 Thematic Data Analysis

Thematic analysis was used to address the research questions. We used QDA Miner Lite 2.0.7, software for data analysis [23]. QDA Miner Lite provided the statistics related to the codes as displayed in the following section.

4.3 Research Questions:

Which modern teaching strategies do you use in your classrooms to help students get engaged in their learning?

Do you consider using technology-based tools in your teaching?

4.4 Testing and Results

See Fig. 1.

Passive: Approximately one-third of the interviewed faculty (34 of responses, or 35.4%) stated that students use technology in a Passive way like "watching videos" "YouTube", "slides" "media sources", and "online teaching". One participant stated, "I still follow the classical way but based on examples, study cases or video contents sometimes".

Constructive: A Quarter of the responses (25 Participants 26%) encouraged students to use technology in a Constructive way through "gamification" "augmented learning" "class presentations using PowerPoint applications" "simulations" "news broadcast" "specific software that can be used to solve practical cases" as well as "games relevant to the theme of teaching using digital tools and games successfully support student engagement".

Active: Similar number of responses (21 participants 21.9%) enhanced student engagement using technology in an active way like "online activities including applications such as "Kahoot", "fun tech tools" "google forms and "Socrative to give quizzes for

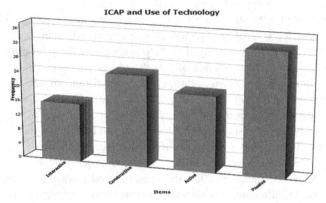

Fig. 1. ICAP and use of technology

the students." "using software" "online platforms" "online exercises" "Blended Learning System" "e-resources" in addition to" Khan Academy".

Interactive: Some 16 responses or 16.7% consisted of statements that faculty members got students engaged using technology through interactive tools like "social media as a learning tool" "Student sharing work on wiki's created by them is also effective". "Webinar," "technology and communicative approach" "WhatsApp" "interactive online videos" "social media channel" "Blackboard discussion boards" "Zoom and Blackboard" video conferencing" (Fig. 2).

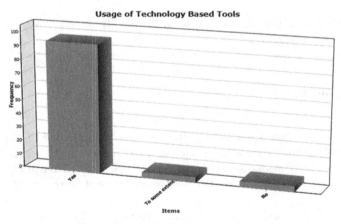

Fig. 2. Usage of technology-based tools

Most of (95) participants 92.2% stated that they would consider technology-based tools stressing that "I used many technology during my tenure in the current college and the previous universities" "sure as it's one aspect of the 21st-century skills" considering it a "strategy that keeps students on task" "describing technology as "a great tool if used appropriately" "as long as they are safe and efficient because they encourage the students and help them feel the importance and practicality of their learning"

"Sure, I used many technologies such as Blackboard, Moodle, smart boards, YouTube, Socrative, personal presenters,… etc." "I use technology-based tools already, such as YouTube, movie screening, practical applications, and digital communication with students" "Today, even in STEM fields, Ed Tech simulations are fast replacing physical lab sessions. "I also use eLearning as part of a blended learning approach" " just the computer and drawing tablet" "definitely. It is indispensable in modern education" "I always use interactive videos and ask students to answer online surveys and prepare their own technology-based materials". As "this generation is very internet savvy" " it is an integral part of my job. "Audio-visual aids, discussion boards, online assessments" "I am using blackboard collaborate ultra for blended learning".

Few (4) participants 3.9. % responded that they use technology "to some extend" "I try" "not always" "not much". Similarly, another 4 participants 3.9. % responded that "in my current environment, it still can be a barrier for student learning" "I am using old fashion type lectures where I use a marker to write everything on the board." One participant rejected the use of technology stating that "it's the worst, students can only keep concentrate for 3 min, so it's sincerely better not to use smartphones, tablets" (Fig. 3).

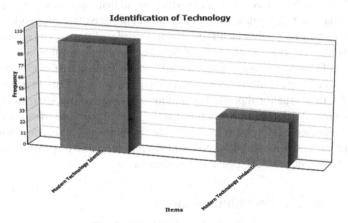

Fig. 3. Identification of technology

Technology Identified: Most of the participants 71% responses identified the technology they are using in their classrooms to enhance student engagement.

Technology unidentified: 29% did not identify technologies used instead responses included examples like "discussion, role plays" "integrate technology into my teaching plans" "case studies and discussions" "strategies, debates, discussion, sometimes asking students to state their positions on a given topic and then argue against themselves" "brainstorming activities." "comparison study" "open discussions and being friendly to students to build a good relationship" "Think Plan act and develop" project-based learning, research-based learning, and student-assisted learning" "focus on creating a collaborative approach where everyone is considered as a team member and must provide some effort to help the team do the task in hand. On the other hand, some participants stated that they "remain pretty much very classical. It's all about personal interactions in face-to-face classes" "I still follow the classical way but based on examples, study cases or video contents".

5 Discussion

The constructive use of technology by students that was highlighted by faculty members as they encourage students to conduct research aligns with the findings of Abdelouarit, Sbihi, and Aknin [1] that focus on the importance of online research and exploration of new ways to utilize and benefit from open data. Findings related to active engagement through online quizzes are in line with the literature by Salas-Morera, Arauzo-Azofra and García-Hernández [25] that online quizzes are considered important as they pay attention to these activities, students found online quizzes helpful with a positive impact on their grades.

Furthermore, the study echoed the findings of Halaweh [10] and Rashidi et al. [24] that consider the use of social media as beneficial to students' learning because it enhances their engagement levels and improves their understanding of cultures and nations. Nevertheless, student interaction through social media was contended by Nadelson et al. [22] that emphasized the findings which found that students who were engaged in social media like Facebook and Instagram and considered the information they get as facts. This study found that faculty members considered the use of communication technologies like Skype as beneficial to students' active engagement which is a finding similar to that of Duranczyk and Pishcherskaia [9] which highlighted that communication technologies like Skype conferences and video chat, can give students an opportunity to get engaged with international peers. The findings also showed that some faculty members did not identify specific technologies that they use in their classrooms to enhance students' engagement, and few preferred the old fashion ways of teaching which is in line with Barber and King [6] article that highlights the need to enhance educators' competencies to match the 21st century expectations.

6 Conclusion and Recommendations

The key findings of the study suggested ways that faculty members can use to encourage students to use technology efficiently in their learning. The findings suggest that although faculty members are for the use of technology in teaching and learning they may unknowingly promote (a) passive use of technology by students rather than active or interactive use of technology. Other faculty members promote (b) constructive use of technology as well as (c) active mode of engagement using technology. While some get students engaged through interactive use of technology, most faculty members stressed the importance of using technology in their classrooms. Some faculty members did not identify specific kinds of technologies that they consider using while most were specific in identifying the technology they use to get students engaged in their learning. The findings derived from the analyzed data related to how faculty use technology to enhance student engagement. The findings suggest that one-third of faculty members encourage students to use technology in a passive way. This is in line with Chi and Wylie [8] definition of passive mode of engagement as learners remain isolated able to remember information but in a certain context. Resulting from thematic analysis, the findings suggested that most faculty members use technology that requires students to be passive in their learning. While a similar number of participants use technologies that enhance active and constructive engagement of students. As for the interactive use of technology, it was used by some of the participants. The limitation of the study is that faculty members did not elaborate on the exact ways that they use technology to enhance student engagement. Therefore, further exploration of specific ways technology is used would be recommended for future research.

References

1. Abdelouarit, K.A., Sbihi, B., Aknin, N.: Big data at the service of teaching and scientific research within the UAE. J. Educ. Voc. Res. **6**(4), 72–75 (2015). https://doi.org/10.22610/jevr.v6i4
2. Al Kaabi, S.A.: Determinants that impact first year male students' motivation to learn at UAE public colleges (Doctoral dissertation, University of Southern Queensland) (2016). https://eprints.usq.edu.au/28742/1/Al%20Kaabi_2016_whole.pdf
3. Al-Qirim, N., Tarhini, A., Rouibah, K., Mohamd, S., Yammahi, A.R., Yammahi, M.A.: Learning orientations of IT higher education students in UAE University. Educ. Inf. Technol. **23**(1), 129–142 (2017). https://doi.org/10.1007/s10639-017-9589-y
4. Andrew, M., Taylorson, J., Langille, D.J., Grange, A., Williams, N.: Student attitudes towards technology and their preferences for learning tools/devices at two universities in the UAE. J. Inf. Technol. Educ. Res. (2018)
5. Avci, O.: Positionalities, personal epistemologies, and instruction: an analysis. J. Educ. Train. Stud. **4**(6), 145–154 (2016). https://doi.org/10.11114/jets.v4i6.1462
6. Barber, W., King, S.: Teacher-student perspectives of invisible pedagogy: new directions in online problem-based learning environments. Electron. J. e-Learn. **14**(4), 235–243 (2016). https://issuu.com/academic-conferences.org/docs/ejel-volume14-issue4-article509/2
7. Cheon, S.H., Reeve, J., Song, Y.G.: Recommending goals and supporting needs: an intervention to help physical education teachers communicate their expectations while supporting students' psychological needs. Psychol. Sport Exerc. **41**, 107–118 (2019)
8. Chi, M., Wylie, H.: The ICAP framework: linking cognitive engagement to active learning outcomes. Educ. Psychol. **49**(4), 219–243 (2014). https://doi.org/10.1080/00461520.2014.965823
9. Duranczyk, I., Pishcherskaia, E.: Bridging countries and cultures through accessible global collaborations. Educ. Sci. **8**(4), 199 (2018). https://doi.org/10.3390/educsci8040199
10. Halaweh, M.: Using mobile technology in the classroom: a reflection based on teaching experience in UAE. TechTrends **61**(3), 218–222 (2017). https://doi.org/10.1007/s11528-017-0184-2
11. Hamam, D., Hysaj, A.: Technological pedagogical and content knowledge (TPACK): higher education teachers' perspectives on the use of TPACK in online academic writing classes. In: Stephanidis, C., Antona, M., Ntoa, S. (eds.) HCII 2021. CCIS, vol. 1421, pp. 51–58. Springer, Cham (2021). https://doi.org/10.1007/978-3-030-78645-8_7
12. Hysaj, A.: COVID-19 pandemic and Online Teaching from the Lenses of K-12 STEM Teachers in Albania. In: 2021 IEEE International Conference on Teaching, Assessment, and Learning for Engineering (TALE), pp. 755–760 (2021)
13. Hysaj, A., Hamam, D.: The Journal of Asia TEFL (2021)

14. Hysaj, A., Hamam, D.: Does delivery method matter for multicultural undergraduate students? A case study of an Australian University in the United Arab Emirates. In: Meiselwitz, G. (ed.) HCII 2020. LNCS, vol. 12195, pp. 538–548. Springer, Cham (2020). https://doi.org/10.1007/978-3-030-49576-3_39

15. Hysaj, A., Suleymanova, S.: Safeguarding academic integrity in crisis induced environment: a case study of Emirati engineering and it students in a private university in the UAE. In: Meiselwitz, G. (ed.) HCII 2021. LNCS, vol. 12775, pp. 236–245. Springer, Cham (2021). https://doi.org/10.1007/978-3-030-77685-5_19

16. Hyun, J., Ediger, R., Lee, D.: Students' satisfaction on their learning process in active learning and traditional classrooms. Int. J. Teach. Learn. Higher Educ. 29(1), 108–118 (2017). http://www.isetl.org/ijtlhe/pdf/IJTLHE2452.pdf

17. Khan, Z., Sivasubramaniam, S., Anand, P., Hysaj, A.: The role e-tools play in supporting teaching and assessments with integrity during the COVID-19 pandemic. In: European Conference on Academic Integrity and Plagiarism 2021: Book of abstracts, pp. 52–54 (2021)

18. Khan, Z.R., Sivasubramaniam, S., Anand, P., Hysaj, A.: 'e'-thinking teaching and assessment to uphold academic integrity: lessons learned from emergency distance learning. Int. J. Educ. Integr. 17(1), 1–27 (2021). https://doi.org/10.1007/s40979-021-00079-5

19. Kivunja, C.: The efficacy of social media technologies in academia: a pedagogical bliss or digital fad? Int. J. Higher Educ. 4(4), 33–44 (2015). https://doi.org/10.5430/ijhe.v4n4p33

20. Moeder-Chandler, M.: School counselor lead initial individual career and academic plan implementation design. J. Educ. Pract. 8(19), 198–207 (2017). https://www.iiste.org/Journals/index.php/JEP/article/view/37896/38978

21. Mohammed, N.A.: Project-based learning in higher education in the UAE: a case study of Arab students in Emirati studies. Learn. Teach. Higher Educ. Gulf Perspect. 14(2), 1–14 (2017). http://lthe.zu.ac.ae/index.php/lthehome/article/view/294/181

22. Nadelson, L., Sias, C., Matyi, J., Morris, S., Cain, R., Cromwell, M.: A world of information at their fingertips: college students' motivations and practices in their self-determined information seeking. Int. J. Higher Educ. 5(1), 220 (2016). https://doi.org/10.5430/ijhe.v5n1p220

23. Onwuegbuzie, A.J., Frels, R.K., Hwang, E.: Mapping Saldana's coding methods onto the literature review process. J. Educ. Issues 2(1), 130–150 (2016). https://doi.org/10.5296/jei.v2i1.8931

24. Rashidi, H., Arani, A.M., Kakia, L.: E-learning, state and educational system in Middle East countries. Bulgarian Comparative Education Society (2012). https://www.learntechlib.org/p/194933/

25. Salas-Morera, L., Arauzo-Azofra, A., García-Hernández, L.: Analysis of online quizzes as a teaching and assessment tool. J. Technol. Sci. Educ. (JOTSE). 2(1), 39–45 (2012). https://doi.org/10.3926/jotse.30

26. Stephens, G.: Digital liminality and cross-cultural re-integration in the Middle East. ICEA Forum. 45(1), 20–50 (2016). https://journals.tdl.org/ceaforum/index.php/ceaforum/article/view/7085

27. Wiggins, B.L., Eddy, S.L., Grunspan, D.Z., Crowe, A.J.: The ICAP active learning framework predicts the learning gains observed in intensely active classroom experiences. AERA Open 3(2), 2332858417708567 (2017)

Active Learning in the Lenses of Faculty: A Qualitative Study in Universities in the United Arab Emirates

Georgina Farouqa[1] and Ajrina Hysaj[2]

[1] Georgina Farouqa, Walden University, Minneapolis, MN, USA
[2] Ajrina Hysaj, UOW College, University of Wollongong, Dubai, UAE
ajrinahysaj@uowdubai.ac.ae

Abstract. Many university students across the United Arab Emirates (UAE) and the world face the problem of low achievement when compared to students graduating from other countries. This may be due to lower student engagement, which in turn may be a result of faculty's perception of student engagement. The purpose of the study was to investigate the perception of faculty members on the ways that students are actively engaged in their learning process. The conceptual framework for the study consisted of Chi and Wylie's interactive, constructive, active, and passive learning framework, which emphasizes the relationship between students' academic achievement and their engagement in the learning activity. The research questions addressed faculty members' definition and description of students being engaged in the teaching and learning process at 4-year universities in the UAE, and the ways faculty members perceive active learning that can successfully support student engagement. Qualitative research was chosen for the study, and data were collected through an open-ended online questionnaire from 106 faculty members teaching at universities in the UAE. Resulting from thematic analysis, the findings suggested that faculty members defined active students as those who participate in class are motivated, pay attention, ask questions, interact with others, take responsibility, and submit assignments on time. The study results further showed that participants described students being engaged as interactive, inquisitive, autonomous, diligent, attentive, collaborative, and punctual students as engaged in their learning. The findings potentially contribute to a better understanding of the teaching and learning process in higher education and suggest ways for deans and academic leaders to enhance student engagement, thus improving higher education institutions and leading to positive social change.

Keywords: Active learning · Faculty perceptions · Interactive dialogue

1 Introduction

The problem of low achievement of university students can be related to the low level of engagement of students in their learning. The purpose of the study was to investigate the perception of faculty members on the ways that students are actively engaged in their learning process. Ways that faculty members can facilitate learning are too many

G. Meiselwitz (Ed.): HCII 2022, LNCS 13316, pp. 77–90, 2022.
https://doi.org/10.1007/978-3-031-05064-0_6

to count [32]. Nevertheless, lack of skills to encourage student' engagement can result in dissatisfaction on the side of students and frustration on the side of educators [5]. For instance, faculty members might lack skills like the ability of providing appropriate instructions, which can enhance student engagement levels and improve students' satisfaction [11]. On the other side, faculty may be equipped with skills that can enhance student motivation through adequate preparation and utilizing technology [47].

Low achievement level of university students has been a major concern of students and their families [16]. It is important that educators use andragogical strategies to enhance students' engagement and encourage students to share their knowledge and experience to become independent active learners. To improve student engagement, it is important that educators understand the needs of students and ways to help them use their knowledge in their professional life in addition to improving their academic skills [14]. Although pedagogical and andragogical ways of teaching and learning have similarities, they are different in many too [36]. For instance, a comparison between the two methods showed that the andragogical method of teaching increases students' creativity and improves their achievement while the pedagogical method leads to higher dependency on the teacher which leads to reduced creativity [46]. Understandably, in a university setting it is important to put students as the center of the learning to increase independence and creativity [39]. In the context of higher education in the UAE, education depends on teacher-centered and traditional methods of teaching that affect students' performance. However, educators in universities are trying to change the traditional ways of teaching to get students more engaged in their learning [2]. According to Al Kaabi students that were taught in a traditional way were less motivated in their studies compared to others who were taught through creative forms such as projects, reports, and handson activities. The comparison showed that students who were traditionally taught were less motivated than the others and subsequently were lacking behind in their learning. Therefore, the study highlights the matter of student engagement and the effective strategies that can enhance student achievement. Furthermore, the study emphasizes the fact that students who engage in their learning develop many skills like creativity, collaboration, communication, and critical thinking [29].

Students of all ages seek progress in their studies and choose the best program that fits their needs. Bugge and Wikan [6] presented a study investigating types of programs that meet the needs of students and the difference between flexible and full-time students. The study included 511 students of which 110 were flexible and 168 were full-time students. The findings show that although students have different learning styles, they were engaged in flexible studies, as flexible studies meet the needs of the diversity present in them. Students who found flexible studies suitable for their needs were older in age than on-campus students they were more female students as well as students with different family needs or employed which can prevent them from attending face to face classes. Therefore, flexible learning can be adopted by a larger number of students than face to face learning as it allows them to continue learning throughout their life regardless of the obstacles or limitations. Therefore, higher education institutions need to provide learners with the opportunity to be engaged in flexible learning and meet the needs of students through study programs designed without prejudice to the advantages of traditional studies.

2 Problem Statement

This study addresses the views of faculty members with regard to undergraduate students' active engagement in the learning process. The possible reasons for the low engagement of students can be related to a widespread form of teaching practice that depends heavily on lecturing to teach [40]. When students learn through lecturing, their learning can be classified as passive and would lack the qualities of creativity, knowledge sharing, interaction, and may result in low academic progression [7]. According to a study by Mohamed [35], undergraduate students do not feel motivated when attending lectures and feel more bonded with the matter being taught when working in groups to complete assessments tasks such as projects or reports. The main reason why they consider the latter more interesting is due to the increased levels of independence and creativity required to complete the tasks [13, 19, 23]. High school students in the Gulf region depend substantially on the knowledge and guidance provided by their teachers [21, 24, 28] with the majority of students considering their teachers as possessors of the ultimate knowledge required to score high and progress academically [17].

In a university setting, where the number of students enrolled in any given subject and attending any given lecture may go well above 100, it is practically impossible for most educators to focus on the specific needs of each student and to facilitate their learning while paying attention to the curriculum alignment and the method of delivery. Moreover, as emphasized in the study by Al Kaabi [2] students from the Gulf region have adaptation difficulties when starting their studies in college because they are not accustomed to high levels of independence and less reliance on teachers. Many students who start college years seem to be unprepared for active learning and show passive learning behavior [33]. Understandably, if students are used to passive learning they tend to memorize the information rather than apply the concepts they learned which can lead to a lack of essential skills like problem-solving and critical and analytical thinking [20, 33]. Alternatively, when students are engaged their levels of motivation, self-reliance, and engagement are enhanced and their interest in further learning is improved [39, 43]. Furthermore, students with higher engagement levels as highlighted in the study by Ahmed and Ahmed [1], are more involved in the learning process and are able to score higher cumulative grades and achieve higher academic progress. One of the factors that have the potential of resulting in increased engagement levels of students is the involvement of faculty staff in creating inclusive and interesting lessons that encourage inquisitiveness and allow students to express their thoughts freely [22, 26, 33]. Faculty members need to use teaching strategies to get students more engaged in their studies in order to improve their academic achievement [43].

3 Literature Review

3.1 Understanding Concepts of Andragogy and Adult Learning Aiming to Facilitate Students' Active Learning

Active learning is important to prepare students to achieve positive social change in their communities. It is important to consider a serious change in the curriculum and instructional design to improve college teaching and to offer differentiating levels of teaching and preparation as well as to reach a proficient level of teaching. Furthermore, it is important to adopt the andragogical rather than the pedagogical approach. The andragogical approach allows university students to focus on content delivery and concept exploration rather than on rote learning and fact memorization [15, 30]. As the boundaries between concepts of pedagogy and andragogy are not always clearly defined, faculty members may differ in the ways they perceive teaching and learning should take place in a university setting [4]. Moreover, they may have difficulty in shifting to project-based learning techniques that require students' active involvement in the learning process [27, 45]. The study by Nikolaros [38] that presented the Socratic method of applying questioning to encourage deep learning and improved reasoning, as well as the study by Malik [34] and Mohammed [35] that focus on the importance of feedback, emphasizes the need to place students in the center of teaching and learning process. Understandably, the approach of placing undergraduate students in the center of their learning process can play a major role in their academic growth [45]. Furthermore, the provision of feedback can facilitate improvement of undergraduate students' efficiency levels and give them value for their work. By providing feedback college instructors give undergraduates the chance to mature intellectually and emotionally and move away from teacher-centered learning to a new and independent method of learning that helps them eliminate self-doubt and support them to achieve their academic goals [19, 22].

According to Al-Hadithy [3] students who are not actively engaged in their learning are considered passive learners. It is worth mentioning that adequate ways of teaching should provide learners with a long-lasting learning experience to improve their ability to be independent and to work effectively with teams [35]. Furthermore, assessments should be conducted in a format which helps undergraduates succeed in their future careers. This approach was supported by the study of Ahmed and Ahmed [1] which presented a comparison of active versus passive learning and emphasized the correlation between preferences of learning methods of undergraduate students and their academic results. As expected the results showed that the majority of students especially high achievers prefer deep learning rather than memorization that does not allow them to improve their essential skills like creativity, critical thinking, and problem-solving [1]. Furthermore, this study stressed the important role of educators in using deep learning methods to support undergraduate students and help them improve their academic achievement. One way that the authors of this study suggested to achieve this was by facilitating training sessions for educators to enhance understanding of methods through which active learning, as well as the development of students' cognitive abilities are achieved.

Muneja [37] reviewed multiple journals articles focusing on the theory of andragogy and the theory of pedagogy, as well as on the elements of adult learning that include cooperative, self-directed, experiential activities, and active learning. The author highlighted the notion of Knowles [31] that adults are more motivated by internal than external factors, and that this approach can affect their learning styles and learning effectiveness. It is a well-known fact that Piaget's constructivism theory of learning as cited in the study by Wadsworth [47] by which adult learners learn through hands-on activities and collaboration more than they learn through fact and matter remembrance. Therefore, it is valuable that educators are equipped with adequate knowledge of adult education and learning theories that are more applicable to them [45]. Furthermore, it is important that adult learning theories and elements of andragogy are implemented in universities worldwide while considering the uniqueness of cultures and languages present in different nations [21, 22].

3.2 Concepts of Active Learning and Their Effects on Undergraduate Students

Ways by which educators can support active learning of students are of academic, psychological, and personal nature [8]. For instance, students as learners are expected to benefit from the matter being taught in lectures and tutorials, while transferring this knowledge to their future academic environments [44]. Furthermore, students can be supported through content, method of delivery, feedback provided, and curriculum alignment [12]. According to a study by Hwang et. al [18], one of the ways that students can be supported academically is by engaging them with real-world problems in an environment that encourages the development of their inquisitive skillsets and facilitates the development of their creativity and cognitive skills. Correlating theoretical concepts with those of practical nature can increase students' desire to explore more and to correlate the reality with the matter taught in a university setting [12]. Although the academic approaches of educators may vary, just like their personalities and prior experiences vary, all educators can provide students with a memorable learning experience if they consider their students' learning needs as more important than the matter being taught in lectures or tutorials [22]. The academic needs of undergraduate students are interconnected with their learning experience in the university and subsequently with the academic progression and the rewarded grades [8, 44].

The academic progression of undergraduate students requires active involvement in the learning process which can be achieved through a variety of methods. For instance, it is a well-known fact that undergraduate students enjoy working in teams or groups and consider the process of learning done through exploration as more productive and memorable [9]. Furthermore, undergraduate students construct knowledge through social-constructivism and as such learn from their experiences of working in teams and feel highly engaged with their learning process [12]. Moreover, concepts of work ethics, integrity, and self- confidence can be supported by working in teams and receiving feedback from peers on projects, reports, or presentations [9, 19, 22, 42]. Students as individuals learn many concepts and apply a large number of theories during their university years [12]. These concepts and theories may be of academic, psychological, or personal nature and may support students' growth in a variety of forms. On the other hand, students first internalize these concepts and theories and then they connect them with their prior and present experiences to built their notions of future actions. Therefore, learning that takes place in a university setting has an effect on student's psychological and personal nature and it can support or otherwise their present and future life goals and the ways they view the reality and the environment around them [42, 44].

4   The Conceptual Framework of the Study

The conceptual framework for this study was based on the ICAP framework Chi and Wylie's [10]. The ICAP focuses on the level of student engagement and the relationship between engagement and learning performance. According to the ICAP framework students' engagement levels are categorized into four modes: interactive, constructive, active, and passive. Researchers have explored the effects of implementing active learning strategies in classrooms and the relationship between the same and students' academic satisfaction [25]. This study aimed to provide information related to faculty members' practice that can be useful to stakeholders like university deans and academic administrators who supervise faculty. In this qualitative study, faculty members were invited to complete a survey that provided information on how university faculty define and describe students being actively engaged in their studies that can improve their academic achievement. Data were analyzed through qualitative data analysis software and the results included concepts that are central in the essays and converge with Chi and Wylie's [10] framework.

5   Materials and Methods

5.1   Research Design and Methodology

The purpose of the study was to investigate the perception of faculty members on the ways that students are actively engaged in their learning process. The study was conducted in the United Arab Emirates and the participants were faculty members of federal and private universities in the country. The approach chosen for this study was qualitative as it was found the most suitable one because we sought to explore how faculty members perceive and describe active learners. Social Networking Services (SNS) were used to contact faculty members and invite them to take part in the study. The data was collected through an online questionnaire and its analysis was done qualitatively. Purposeful random sampling was used to select respondents to ensure that they were qualified to provide us with significant information to answer the research questions. The responses of over 100 faculty members who worked in different universities in the United Arab Emirates, were analyzed by the authors of this study to get a broader perspective over the way they described active learners. An online questionnaire that included open-ended questions was used as an instrument to collect data. Open-ended questions gave the participants the opportunity to elaborate their knowledge perception related to active learners and provided enough data that enabled us to extract quotes and categories to answer the research question.

5.2   Thematic Data Analysis

To address the research question, we used Thematic analysis. QDA Miner Lite 2.0.7, a data analysis software analysis tool was used to analyze data [41]. After the coding categorizing was completed, QDA Miner Lite provided the statistics needed to present the findings.

5.3 Research Questions:

How would you define student engagement?
Describe typical students being engaged in their learning.

5.4 Testing and Results

See Fig. 1.

Faculty Definition of Student Engagement

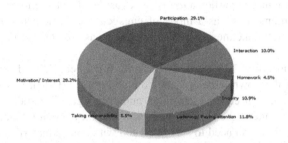

Fig. 1. Faculty **Definition of Student Engagement**

Participation: Approximately one-third of the interviewed faculty (32 participants, or 29.1%) stated that they defined students who participate in the classroom activities as engaged. Participants considered student participation as "central in the teaching process...physically and psychologically". They also stressed the importance of "the engagement of students throughout the entire duration in a variety of activities - written tasks, verbal presentation, group work, etc." and for students "to be fully engaged in the learning process by focusing on learning and participation in all classroom academic activities" as well as students ability "to contribute in the class and be effective members" as well as "physical and mental participation in the study" stressing on "involvement of students in their learning activities that are meaningful and progressing their knowledge, skills, and abilities" participants indicated that: "active participation in and outside class regarding matters of their studies" as "student engagement is any form of student's active participation to aid learning process".

Motivation: Around one-quarter of 31 participants (28.2%) considered motivation as a definition of student engagement and defined engaged students as those who show "curiosity, interest, and passion". Participants defined motivation as student engagement stating that students who are "motivated during the class and willing to put effort in learning" "have the ability to focus and be interested in the curriculum" as they are "enthusiastic to learn" as "students take an interest in their studies and actively seek out learning opportunities while enjoying what they are learning and they seek more knowledge about the content". They have the "initiative and a desire to keep improving with commitment to learning, and they are interested and motivated". The role of the educator was highlighted in participants responses that "most students engagements are proportional to how instructor motivates them" through "sharing thoughts and ideas during discussions" as well as being interactive inside the classroom, work effectively outside classroom" as students "should be active in group work in class" achieving "collaboration" through "exchange of useful and meaningful information between the student and teacher".

Listening/Paying attention: 13 participants or 11.8% thought that students "paying attention" through "active listening" and the "degree of attention in the learning process" and those who "listen" are defined as engaged students. A similar number (12 participants 10.9%) contented that inquiry is a mode of student engagement "through raising questions" and "asking relevant questions" "that are out of curiosity and taking part in Q and A sessions".

Interaction: Another 11 participants or 10% considered "interaction in class" through "interactive communication" as a mode of engagement. Participants highlighted the role of educators to "Make the sessions as interactive as possible" through "interactive sessions".

Taking responsibility: Few participants, only 6 of them defined "students taking responsibility for their own learning" and "the ability of a student to sustain progress without rewards and consequences from an authority figure." Participants added that "first students must attend the classes" and show that they "want to learn and enhance their knowledge" they also need to stay "updated with course material" "which would keep them engaged in their learning".

Homework/Completing assignments: A similar number (5 participants 4.5%) considered "giving more assignment and practice" and students' ability to "respond to assignments and tasks on time" and "submitting assignments on time" as well as "doing their homework and other duties assigned to them" were defined as engaged students by faculty (Fig. 2).

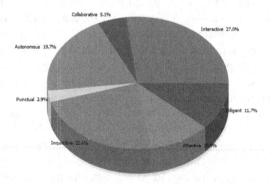

Faculty Description of Student Engagement

Fig. 2. Faculty **Description of Student Engagement**

Interactiveness: The study showed that 37 participants or 27% described student engagement as interactive. As students who "participate in the class discussion" "communicate actively together" and are "involved in peer learning in the classroom", "respond with examples and suggestions", and get engaged in "class presentations" "contribute actively to classwork, group work, and pair work" are more engaged in their learning. Participants stressed that the role of educators is to get students engaged through "making the sessions more interactive" encouraging students to "participate in activities" through "dialogue, debate and brainstorming" they also need to "comment, provide feedback, and answer questions". Participants also highlighted the importance of communication with students during office hours as stated "they come regularly to my office for discussion". Participants also commented on the importance of students feeling comfortable and able to "discuss their ideas" "speak their minds freely", and "express their feelings openly", "I expect students to speak and "discuss issues related to the subject being taught".

Inquisitiveness: 31 respondents or 22.6% described inquisitive students as engaged in their learning. Students "being inquisitive in most of the learning sessions" they "should actively seek for help, either from their classmates, their tutor, their mentor or their teachers" they ask valid questions" to "clarify doubts by raising questions directly" a "typical student would ask at least two questions" that "reflect over the topic covered" and being able "to contact faculty members during office hours for further questions or comments".

Autonomy: Another 27 participants 19.7% described students who have high autonomy as engaged in their learning. Students who "prepare in advance", "read and develop thoughts before coming in class" and are "regularly prepared and have knowledge what the lesson or the lecture is about" these "show intrinsic motivation to study content" and are able to conduct research on their own", "prepare for the lecture" and complete activities on their initiative, not because of a rule" they are"initiating their own actions" and "honest in their own study progress" "students should develop self-monitoring skills" "reading at home, activities and class preparation" students have the ability to "find out more about the content and to share it with others". They show "curiosity, interest, optimism, and passion" participants described students as " proactive", "motivated" and" excited".

Diligence: Some 16 participants or 11.7% described engaged students as being diligent in submitting their assignments. Students are "expected to do their assignments and projects independently without any external help whether from friends or paid". They need to "complete homework, submit assignments on time" and "be on task the whole lesson" they need to"deliver assignments within the time limit", and "get deeper knowledge on the subject and achieve excellence by working on inter-disciplinary projects" "follow up on tasks independently" through "reading, studying, and submitting assignments until they pass the module", "complete exercises/activities on specified allocated time" "production of work in each session".

Attentiveness: Similarly, (15 participants 10%) described engaged students as being attentive in class. Students are expected to "pay attention", "be attentive", and "listen carefully to their teachers and mentors in the classes" their concentration during the lecture" was perceived as important, and their ability to "focus during the lecture so it will be easier for them to study later" and listen for new content or ideas".

Collaboration: Few (7 participants 5.1%) described students being engaged as those who are Collaborative. Students who "collaborate with classmates and teachers" and those who are involved in "writing, speaking" are more engaged than others who do more "listening or reading" activities. Students who "share, and challenge others" "mainly in a seminar or group settings" through "active participation in the in-class activities" work in groups/teams" are considered more engaged in their learning.

Punctuality: Another (4 participants 2.9%) described punctual students as engaged in their learning as students "should not miss the classes intentionally" and "turn up to lecture on time" and "attend classes regularly" (Fig. 3).

Level of Student Engagement

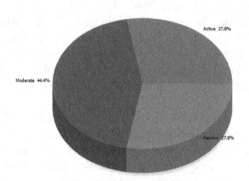

Fig. 3. Level **of Student Engagement**

Active: While 27.8% described them as "excellent" "very active" "great" "very good". Moderate: Some faculty members expanded on their answers and further described the level of student engagement in their classrooms. 18 participants described the different levels of engagement of their students with the majority 44.4% described them as "moderate", "some are engaged and some are not" it is" relatively acceptable" "average, like everywhere in the world". Passive: The same number of faculty 27.8% described them as "passive", "less engaged, distracted", "discouraged" "not active" "zero level of activity" as "students do not care at all about their studies".

6   Discussion

The current study was conducted to better understand the faculty perception of student engagement. This qualitative study was based on Chi and Wylie's [10] conceptual framework, ICAP. Data were collected through an online questionnaire, and participants were faculty members teaching at 4-year universities in the UAE. The preliminary findings showed that faculty members defined student engagement as (a) student participation in-class activities, (b) motivation, (c) listening, (d) asking questions, (e) Interactive, (f) taking responsibility, (g) those who submit their assignments on time are defined as active learners. The study results further showed that participants described students being engaged as (a) interactive, (b) inquisitive, (c) autonomous, (d) diligent, (e) attentive, (f) collaborative, (g) punctual students as engaged in their learning. The study findings showed that faculty further described the level of student engagement in their classrooms. Most faculty members described student engagement as (a) moderate while others described it as (b) active and (c) passive.

The findings derived from the analyzed data related to faculty definition and description of engaged students. Student participation in-class activities are in line with literature by Giannoukos, et.al [14] and Ntombela [39] that stressed the importance of students sharing their experience and knowledge. Student motivation, and taking responsibility for their learning are in line with Al Kaabi [2] findings that students who are more engaged in their studies are more motivated than those taught in the old fashion way. Describing students who are engaged in their learning as autonomous comes in line with Knowles assumption that learners are self-directed and motivated by internal factors in Muneja [37] reviewed articles. Faculty members defined students who listen and are attentive as engaged. However, as highlighted by Rismiyanto et al.,[46] students who rely on teachers will not be able to develop their creativity unlike those who are taught using the andragogical approach that increases creativity. As for defining students as interactive, this comes in line with Al-Hadithy [3] that stresses on the importance of building students' ability to work within teams. Passive learners are evident in the study by Al-Hadithy [3] that due to traditional ways of teaching learners remain passive in their studies and faculty members need to provide learners with a learning experience that will help them improve their ability and work independently.

7   Conclusion and Recommendations

This paper has several important implications for researchers, educators, and institutional administrators. The findings can provide evidence on possible ways that faculty members define and describe student engagement which can guide deans of faculties on steps that can be taken to improve the practice of faculty members which can result in increasing student engagement. Enhancing student engagement can help students improve their academic achievement, develop learning skills, and improve their ability to utilize their learning in their professional future. Moreover, the study highlighted the need for enhancement of the learning process through effective teaching forms and most importantly through understanding of students' needs to develop life-long skills like collaboration, proactive connection with the learning process, and subsequently improved academic performance. Nevertheless, this study needs to be followed by further research that analyses the impact of steps taken to empower faculty with the understanding of ways to provide active and interactive learning experiences for undergraduate students.

References

1. Ahmed, A., Ahmad, N.: Comparative analysis of rote learning on high and low achievers in graduate and undergraduate programs. J. Educ. Educ. Dev. 4, 111 (2017). https://doi.org/10.22555/joeed.v4i1.982

2. Al Kaabi, S.A.: Determinants that impact first year male students' motivation to learn at UAE public colleges (Doctoral dissertation, University of Southern Queensland) (2016). https://eprints.usq.edu.au/28742/1/Al%20Kaabi_2016_whole.pdf

3. AlHadithy, T.M.: The traditional vs. the modern translation classroom: a need for new directions in the UAE undergraduate translation programs. Proc. Soc. Behav. Sci. **192**, 180–187 (2015). https://doi.org/10.1016/j.sbspro.2015.06.026

4. Badr, H.M.: Exploring UAE teachers' attitude towards the successful implementation of the general rules in the "school for all" initiative. J. Lang. Teach. Res. **10**(1), 92 (2019)

5. Ballen, C.J., Wieman, C., Salehi, S., Searle, J.B., Zamudio, K.R.: Enhancing diversity in undergraduate science: Self-efficacy drives performance gains with active learning. CBE Life Sci. Educ. **16**(4), 56 (2017)

6. Bugge, L.S., Wikan, G.: Flexible studies as strategy for lifelong learning. Turkish Online J. Educ. Technol. **15**(4), 46–52 (2016). http://www.tojet.net/articles/v15i4/1545.pdf

7. Cazden, C.B.: Communicative Competence, Classroom Interaction, and Educational Equity: The Selected Works of Courtney B. Routledge, Cazden (2017)

8. Cheon, S.H., Reeve, J., Song, Y.G.: Recommending goals and supporting needs: an intervention to help physical education teachers communicate their expectations while supporting students' psychological needs. Psychol. Sport Exerc. **41**, 107–118 (2019)

9. Cherney, I.D.: The effects of active learning on students' memories for course content. Active Learn. Higher Educ. **9**(2), 152–171 (2008)

10. Chi, M., Wylie, H.: The ICAP framework: linking cognitive engagement to active learning outcomes. Educ. Psychol. **49**(4), 219–243 (2014). https://doi.org/10.1080/00461520.2014.965823

11. Chiu, P.H.P., Cheng, S.H.: Effects of active learning classrooms on student learning: a two-year empirical investigation on student perceptions and academic performance. High. Educ. Res. Dev. **36**(2), 269–279 (2017)

12. De Freitas, S.A.A., Silva, W.C., Marsicano, G.: Using an active learning environment to increase students' engagement. In: 2016 IEEE 29th International Conference on Software Engineering Education and Training (CSEET), pp. 232–236 (2016)

13. Evnitskaya, N., Berger, E.: Learners' multimodal displays of willingness to participate in classroom interaction in the L2 and CLIL contexts. Classroom Disc. **8**(1), 71–94 (2017)

14. Giannoukos, G., Hioctour, V., Stergiou, I., Kallianta, S.: Andragogy: prerequisites for adult educators. World J. Educ. **6**(4), 53–57 (2016). https://doi.org/10.5430/wje.v6n4p53

15. Hartree, A.: Malcolm Knowles' theory of andragogy: a critique. Int. J. Lifelong Educ. **3**(3), 20321 (1984)

16. Hatherley-Greene, P.: The border crossing index: implications for higher education teachers in the UAE. Learn. Teach. Higher Educ. Gulf Perspect. **11**(2), 1-21 (2014). http://lthe.zu.ac.ae

17. Hojeij, Z., Atallah, F., Baroudi, S., Tamim, R.: Challenges for practice teaching in UAE schools: Supervisors' and pre-service teachers' perceptions. Issues Educ. Res. **31**(2), 513–536 (2021)

18. Hwang, G.-J., Chang, S.-C., Chen, P.-Y., Chen, X.-Y.: Effects of integrating an active learning-promoting mechanism into location-based real-world learning environments on students' learning performances and behaviors. Educ. Tech. Res. Dev. **66**(2), 451–474 (2017). https://doi.org/10.1007/s11423-017-9567-5

19. Hysaj, A., Hamam, D.: Understanding the development of critical thinking through classroom debates and online discussion forums: a case of higher education in the UAE. J. Asia TEFL **18**(1), 373 (2021)

20. Hysaj, A., Suleymanova, S.: The analysis of developing the application of critical thinking in oral and written discussions: the case of Emirati students in the United Arab Emirates. In: 2020 IEEE International Conference on Teaching, Assessment, and Learning for Engineering (TALE), pp. 819–824 (2020)
21. Hysaj, A., Suleymanova, S.: Safeguarding academic integrity in crisis induced environment: a case study of Emirati engineering and IT students in a private university in the UAE. In: Meiselwitz, G. (ed.) HCII 2021. LNCS, vol. 12775, pp. 236–245. Springer, Cham (2021). https://doi.org/10.1007/978-3-030-77685-5_19
22. Hysaj, A., Elkhouly, A., Qureshi, A.W., Abdulaziz, N.: Analysis of engineering students' academic satisfaction in a culturally diverse university. In: 2018 IEEE International Conference on Teaching, Assessment, and Learning for Engineering (TALE), pp. 755–760 (2018)
23. Hysaj, A., Elkhouly, A., Qureshi, A.W., Abdulaziz, N.: Study of the impact of tutor's support and undergraduate student's academic satisfaction. Am. J. Hum. Soc. Sci. Res. 3(12), 70–77 (2019)
24. Hysaj, A., Hamam, D., Baroudi, S.: Efficacy of group work in the online platform: an exploration of multicultural undergraduates' attitudes in online academic writing classes. In: Meiselwitz, G. (ed.) HCII 2021. LNCS, vol. 12775, pp. 246–256. Springer, Cham (2021). https://doi.org/10.1007/978-3-030-77685-5_20
25. Hyun, J., Ediger, R., Lee, D.: Students' satisfaction on their learning process in active learning and traditional classrooms. Int. J. Teach. Learn. Higher Educ. 29(1), 108–118 (2017). http://www.isetl.org/ijtlhe/pdf/IJTLHE2452.pdf
26. Ismail, T.: Towards Learner Centredness in Higher Education: Exploring English Language Classrooms in the UAE (2019)
27. Khan, Z.R., Hysaj, A., John, S.R., Khan, S.: Gateway to preparing k-12 students for higher education–reflections on organizing an academic integrity camp. In: European Conference on Academic Integrity and Plagiarism, p. 66 (2021)
28. Khemakhem, S.: Investigating the predictive validity of IELTS for a teacher education program in UAE (Doctoral dissertation, University of the West of England) (2016)
29. Kivunja, C.: The efficacy of social media technologies in academia: a pedagogical bliss or digital fad? Int. J. Higher Educ. 4(4), 33–44 (2015). https://doi.org/10.5430/ijhe.v4n4p33
30. Knowles, M.S.: Andragogy. NETCHE (1972)
31. Knowles, M.S.: Andragogy: Adult learning theory in perspective. Commun. Coll. Rev. 5(3), 9–20 (1978)
32. Lugosi, E., Uribe, G.: Active learning strategies with positive effects on students' achievements in undergraduate mathematics education. Int. J. Math. Educ. Sci. Technol. 53, 1–22 (2020)
33. Mahrous, A.A., Ahmed, A.: A cross-cultural investigation of students' perceptions of the effectiveness of pedagogical tools: The Middle East, the United Kingdom, and the United States. J. Stud. Int. Educ. 14(3), 289–306 (2009). https://doi.org/10.1177/1028315309334738
34. Malik, M.: Assessment of a professional development program on adult learning theory. Librar. Acad. Portal 16(1), 47–70 (2016)
35. Mohammed, N. A.: Project-based learning in higher education in the UAE: a case study of Arab students in Emirati studies. Learn. Teach. Higher Educ. Gulf Perspect. 14(2), 1–14 (2017). http://lthe.zu.ac.ae/index.php/lthehome/article/view/294/181
36. Muduli, A., Kaura, V., Quazi, A.: Pedagogy or andragogy? Views of Indian postgraduate business students. IIMB Manag. Rev. 30(2), 168–178 (2018)
37. Muneja, M.S.: A theoretical basis for adult learning facilitation: review of selected articles. J. Educ. Pract. 6(31), 54–61 (2015). https://iiste.org/Journals/index.php/JEP/article/view/27299/27982
38. Nikolaros, J.: College philosophy and teaching. World J. Educ. 5(1), 144–148 (2015). https://doi.org/10.5430/wje.v5n1p144

39. Ntombela, B.: Project based learning: in pursuit of andragogic effectiveness. Engl. Lang. Teach. **8**(4), 31–38 (2015). https://doi.org/10.5539/elt.v8n4p31

40. Onwuegbuzie, A.J., Frels, R.K., Hwang, E.: Mapping Saldana's coding methods onto the literature review process. J. Educ. Issues **2**(1), 130–150 (2016). https://doi.org/10.5296/jei.v2i1.8931

41. Park, E.L., Choi, B.K.: Transformation of classroom spaces: traditional versus active learning classroom in colleges. Higher Educ. **68**(5), 749–771 (2014)

42. Plush, S.E., Kehrwald, B.: A supporting new academics' use of student-centered strategies in traditional university teaching. J. Univ. Teach. Learn. Pract. **11**(1), 5 (2014). https://ro.uow.edu.au/cgi/viewcontent.cgi?referer=&httpsredir=1&article=1340&context=jutlp

43. Poedjiastutie, D., Oliver, R.: Exploring students' learning needs: expectation and challenges. Engl. Lang. Teach. **10**(10), 124–133 (2017)

44. Poonpon, K.: Enhancing English skills through project-based learning. Engl. Teach. **2017**, 10 (2017)

45. Rismiyanto, S., Mursid, M., Januarius, W.: The effectiveness of andragogically oriented teaching method to improve the male students achievement of teaching practice. Engl. Lang. Teach. **11**(2), 113–121 (2018). https://doi.org/10.5539/elt.v11n2p113

46. Sogunro, O.A.: Quality instruction as a motivating factor in higher education. Int. J. Higher Educ. **6**(4), 173–184 (2017). https://doi.org/10.5539/hes.v8n2p47

47. Wadsworth, B.J.: Piaget's Theory of Cognitive and Affective Development: Foundations of Constructivism. Longman Publishing, White Plains (1996)

Food Sector Entrepreneurship: Designing an Inclusive Module Adaptable to Both Online and Blended Learning Environments in Higher Education

Marco Garcia-Vaquero[✉]

School of Agriculture and Food Science, University College Dublin, Belfield Campus, Dublin 4, Ireland
marco.garciavaquero@ucd.ie

Abstract. This work focuses on the re-structure work of a module previously delivered face-to-face to more interactive approaches, capable to adapt to both online and/or blended learning environments and accommodating the changing needs of the learners due to the variable health and safety guidelines in relation to teaching in Higher Education during 2021–2022 due to the COV-19 pandemic. Several complex threshold concepts were identified, and the learning objectives of the module were modified and aligned with new learning activities and assessment strategies to create meaningful and clear associations for the learners. The principles of universal design for learning (UDL) were applied when re-designing new online/blended materials. The module included asynchronous delivery of theoretical contents related to business that served as the main scaffolds supporting active learning group work. The group work was organized as a research-based scenario in which the learners develop a business idea and specify all the different elements needed for a realistic business to work by the completion of a "business canvas". The alignment of the new learning objectives, activities and assessments was evaluated by a peer-observation of a session and the student's feedback. Overall, the design of a flexible module that could be delivered in both fully online and blended learning environments facilitated the delivery of the content and promoted active learning in a way that was suitable and capable to adapt and engage with the learners during the challenging and ever-changing learning environment created by the COV-19 pandemic.

Keywords: Food business · Universal design for learning · Threshold concepts · Constructive alignment

1 Introduction

The module "Food Sector Entrepreneurship" is an optional module offered to learners at stage 4 of the Food Science Programme at University College Dublin (UCD, Ireland). The overall aim of this module is to integrate new knowledge related to business and business management to previous learners' knowledge of food science.

© The Author(s), under exclusive license to Springer Nature Switzerland AG 2022
G. Meiselwitz (Ed.): HCII 2022, LNCS 13316, pp. 91–102, 2022.
https://doi.org/10.1007/978-3-031-05064-0_7

The original module was delivered face-to-face mainly via lectures, introducing key concepts of business to the learners as well as practical exercises related to business in the context of the food sector. Complementary to this work, the learners had meetings and interviews with several food industries, aiming to gain insights into their businesses and real issues. Once these issues were identified, the groups of learners acted as consultants proposing solutions and reverting to the companies to check if those solutions could potentially be implemented. Although these active learning activities with industry allowed the learners to gain valuable insights from several food businesses, the problems identified rarely related to the theoretical contents of the module and thus, these activities did not allow the students to gain a deep learning of business concepts as originally intended. This situation resulted in two differentiated pieces of work that were not related to each other and also in a poor engagement of the learners with the activities proposed. In 2020, due to COV-19, the module was adapted to an online environment, resulting in a reactive adaptation of its contents that exacerbated the previously identified lack of integration of the different activities of the module as well as the lack of options in activities and assessment for learners with special learning requirements. Similar issues of fragmented learning due to poor integration of the contents of the module were also appreciated in modules related to Food Science delivered both face-to-face and online [1, 2]; being these challenges addressed by re-designing the learning activities and aligning them with the learning objectives of the modules [1, 2]. Moreover, UDL offers a framework for proactively anticipate diverse learners' needs [3] and the UDL principles have been applied successfully when designing curricula in multiple disciplines in Higher Education [4].

As the health and safety guidelines in relation to teaching in Higher Education during the 2021–2022 academic term continue to evolve due to the COV-19, the module needs to be able to provide the desired learning outcomes whether its activities take place in blended or fully online environments. Thus, this work focuses on the re-structure work of the module "Food Sector Entrepreneurship", addressing the previously identified challenges of integration and inclusivity of its contents. Moreover, the newly re-designed module will focus on implementing "learning by doing" approaches that could be suitable for both online and/or blended learning environments due to the changing learner's needs and variable health and safety guidelines in relation to teaching in Higher Education during the 2021–2022 academic term as a reflection of the COV-19 pandemic.

2 Material and Methods

2.1 Threshold Concepts and Constructive Alignment

A threshold concept is a "akin to a portal, opening up a new and previously inaccessible way of thinking about something. It represents a transformed way of understanding, or interpreting, or viewing something without which the learner cannot progress" as mentioned by Meyer and Land [5]. Threshold concepts differs from the previously referred 'core concepts' or 'building blocks' in University in the sense that these need to be understood to progress, however their understanding does not necessarily lead to new understandings on the subject matter [5]. From the previous module materials as well as current state of the discipline and the needs of the curriculum, several threshold concepts were identified and were key for the modification of the learning outcomes of the module.

The variety of the thresholds identified and the need to integrate the contents of the module, while maintaining the curriculum coherence and aligning these with new activities and assessment will be key for the success of the re-designed module. The principles of constructive alignment were applied when re-designing this module by making modifications first in the learning outcomes, followed by modifications in learning activities and assessments aligned with the learning needs previously identified. Constructive alignment has been defined as an outcome-based approach in which the learning outcomes are defined before the teaching takes place and the teaching activities and assessments are designed to guide the students to achieve them [6]. This theory is based on the principles of alignment between course objectives and assessment targets defined by instructional designers [7] and previous teaching philosophies of "constructivism". Constructivism focuses on developing teaching activities that create meaning or "learning by doing", focusing on the idea that the learning takes place by the active behavior of the learners rather than from the activities/work performed by the lecturer [8].

2.2 UDL in Module Design

UDL is a principle-based approach to designing curricula that meets the needs of all students in the increasingly diverse Higher Education environment [4]. The guidelines developed by the Center for Applied Special Technology (CAST) were used for the implementation of the principles of UDL in "Food Sector Entrepeneurship" [9]. Several strategies were analyzed in the context of the re-designed module for online/blended learning to introduce:

- Means of engagement. Engagement refers to the differences in which the learners get motivated to learn. As the engagement of the learners can be affected for multiple factors inherent to individuals (i.e. culture, background knowledge) providing multiple options for engagement can benefit the engagement of a wide variety of learners [9].
- Means of representation. Presenting the information represented in multiple ways to ensure it is perceived and accessible to learners with multiple needs (i.e. sensory or learning disabilities) [9].
- Means of action and expression. Learners may differ in the ways to express what they know. Flexible and multiple ways of working and assessment methods accounting for these multiple ways of expression will contribute to foster an inclusive environment [9].

2.3 Evaluation of Re-designed Module

Peer Observation. The modifications of the module were qualitatively evaluated by a peer observation process. The main objectives of the observation were to evaluate the overall quality of the delivery of a session, as well as to check the alignment of the designed contents of the module covered in a session towards achieving the newly proposed learning objectives. These objectives and information of learning outcomes of the module and proposed activities for the session were discussed in advance. Moreover, the criteria for the evaluation of the session were also discussed and agreed in advance and a rubric for the evaluation of different aspects the session was established.

Students' Feedback. The pedagogical practices introduced in the module design "Food Sector Entrepreneurship" during the autumn 2021–2022 semester were further evaluated by the learners as an anonymous "module feedback questionnaire" managed independently of the module coordinators by UCD. The learners evaluated the module anonymously by replying to 5 questions on a scale of 1 to 5, being 5 "Strongly Agree". The questions posed to the students by UCD as part of this process were:

- Q1. I have a better understanding of the subject after completing this module.
- Q2. The assessment was relevant to the work of the module.
- Q3. I achieved the learning outcomes for this module.
- Q4. The teaching on this module supported my learning.
- Q5. Overall I am satisfied with this module.

Ethical exemption as a low-risk study was sought and granted by the Human Research Ethics Committee – Sciences at UCD. The data available to module coordinators is anonymized data showing the mean response of the students to each question posed.

3   Results and Discussion

3.1   Threshold Concepts

Several complex threshold concepts were identified in "Food Sector Entrepeneurship". These threshold concepts will bring together different aspects of the subject that previously did not appear to be related [10] covering the new concepts of: (1) Food sector and market, (2) Food business theory and practice, (3) Food business planning and projections and (4) Food business and team work. Thus, the comprehension of these threshold concepts may transform the internal view of the subject by the student and influence their future professional practice. The main threshold concepts identified can be grouped into:

- Food sector and market. Understanding the needs of multiple markets that will guide food production and innovation as well as how local and global trends and increased appreciation for food may limit or contribute to expand businesses. The learners will understand where to place their food business and what values they are targeting within a local and global context i.e. currently there is a global trend favoring the change towards more sustainable diets including diets high in plant-based products and low in meat [11]. However, there is huge variability on the pathways towards this transition between countries in terms of food as well as agricultural practices [12]. Thus, understanding the production of food and the business in the context of local and global markets will enable the students to understand the economic efforts and predict future hurdles of new food businesses which is a threshold in this module.

- Food business theory and practice. Simple modifications in a food business can influence the finances and future viability of a company. i.e. small modifications of the food packaging systems have huge implications to consider within a company, including legal and financial requirements, current workflow and management of several sectors of the company, implications on the price of the product and even in their shelf-life [13]. Understanding the main concepts of business management and how to put them in practice in the context of the food sector will be key for their future professional activities in the sector.
- Food business planning and projections. The need to rapidly adapt to the changing needs of the clients is currently favoring the development of start-ups aiming to provide innovative products, processes and services [14]. Based on previous business research, the entrepreneurial conditions of the company including its goal-orientation and business competence are factors that significatively influence the success of start-ups [14]. Thus, understanding and working towards the creation of a successful food business will benefit their understanding of the sector and increase their research into already existing entrepreneurial food ventures.
- Food business and teamwork. An essential part of any food business is based on relationships, with suppliers, clients and also within the organization, being relationship management one of the most practical aspects that will take place inside any business. Active cooperation and interaction with customers in innovation networks has been proven to be beneficial supporting food innovation [15]. Soft skills related to communication, group work and leadership skills will benefit the learners in multiple aspects of the food sector, particularly food business and innovation.

Based on the complex threshold concepts identified, the learning outcomes of the module "Food Sector Entrepreneurship" were re-designed as follows:

1. Develop an appreciation of the Irish and global food markets.
2. Ability to understand and explain the challenges and opportunities presented in dealing with the retail multiples.
3. Analysis of the existing and potential segmentation of the food market.
4. Identify possible new product opportunities in segmented markets.
5. Achieve a competence in creating and developing new food product or service opportunities.
6. Understand the basic principles of management, including operations, marketing and finance management of food businesses.
7. Apply the basic principles of management, business development and entrepreneurship by developing a realistic business plan.
8. Develop and implement team and leadership skills by significantly contributing to a team project.

3.2 Curriculum Implementation Plan

Constructive alignment, an outcome-based approach in which the learning outcomes or general objectives of the modules are designed first; and the teaching activities and subsequent assessment strategies are designed to be aligned with those learning outcomes [6, 7]. Previous studies have identified that constructive alignment is necessary for effective learning [16]. The alignment of the curriculum with learning outcomes of the modules as well as with the teaching and learning approaches, assessment and evaluation have been described in multiple disciplines and scarcely explored in food science [1, 2, 16]. The re-designed elements of the module include new (1) learning activities and (2) assessment methods towards achieving the previously mentioned learning outcomes.

Learning Activities. The main learning activities of the module are suitable for both blended and online learning scenarios created by COV-19 in Higher Education. These activities included:

Asynchronous Learning Activities. These activities aimed to introduce the learners to new concepts related to business and the food sector from an industry perspective. The learning activities were organized as pre-recorded lectures, hand-outs/notes, media (blogs and webpages from official business organizations) and additional readings via the online platform Brightspace.

Synchronous Learning Activities. These activities consisted in group work (3–4 learners, 6 groups) guided weekly online (Zoom using breakout rooms functionality) or face-to-face. The students were posed with the problem-based scenario of creating and presenting as part of their group an innovative food business idea and plan. A "business canvas" containing 9 key points to sustain a successful business as described by Osterwalder and Pigneur [17] served as the main scaffoldings supporting problem solving. The main research areas of the business canvas to develop an innovative food business included: (1) customer segments, (2) value proposition, (3) channels, (4) customer relationships, (5) revenue streams, (6) key resources, (7) key activities, (8) key partnerships and (9) cost structure. Moreover, all the asynchronous materials provided were also related to each of the research areas of the business canvas, providing the learner with efficient tools to engage in high quality research. An overview of the main re-designed elements of "Food Sector Entrepreneurship" including learning activities and assessment strategies is provided in Fig. 1.

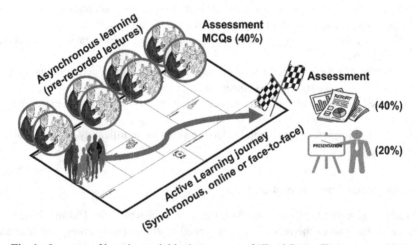

Fig. 1. Structure of learning activities/assessment of "Food Sector Entrepreneurship".

This instructional design follows the principles of the constructivism theories as it is based on recognizing that each individual builds their own learning by connecting it to their prior experiences and knowledge and thus, the learning involves an active re-structuring of how one thinks [18]. Moreover, these learning activities are designed to increase "active learning" or "learning-by-doing", focusing on the idea that learning takes place as an active behavior of the learners [8]. Previous studies analyzing the efficiency of these scenario-based learning demonstrated that problem-based learning approaches achieved higher student competency compared to lecture-based environments and active learning aspects related to these scenarios were perceived as motivating by the learners [19]. The practical application of the new business knowledge and critical thinking are hugely emphasized in "Food Sector Entrepreneurship" as these are considered high order cognitive skills requiring a deeper conceptual understanding compared to those of simple memorization [20] and most learners have difficulties performing at this level [21]. As remarked by Napoleon, Freedman, Seetharaman and Sharma [22] the development of these high order cognitive skills in food science will require the development of a creative curriculum linked to real-life scenarios linked to the real needs of the industry.

The development of pedagogical approaches in teaching and learning that include problem-based scenarios, active learning and presentation-discussion of the work aim to engage the learners with the theoretical frameworks of food science by putting them into practice on real based scenarios and to develop critical thinking of their work and the one of their peers. The use of "real-life" scenarios and problems has been previously described as motivating and helpful to retain knowledge by learners [23]. As described by Gagnon and Collay [24] there are 6 elements involved in a constructivist learning design (CLD) "Situation element is designed to answer three key questions so that you can determine your purpose, topic, and assessment. The topic is understanding the six elements of CLD and the relationship between them. The assessment of learning is your definition of each of the six elements". However, research specific to food science education and the use of problem-based learning approaches is scarce [25–27]. Choo [27] emphasized that when designing these scenarios and activities in food science needed careful consideration to align the intended learning outcomes and activities independently on the learning strategy followed to facilitate the learning.

Assessment Strategy. The new content related to business of the asynchronous activities were assessed by 3 multiple choice question test that overall accounted for 40% grade. These assessment activities were adapted to be performed remotely online or face-to-face via the Brightspace platform. Sambell, McDowell and Brown [28] evaluated the opinion of students to different assessment methods, and reported a negative opinion towards conventional assessment methods, while the alternative assessment methods were seeing as enablers of quality learning beyond simple memorization of learning materials. Thus, the re-designed module included additional assessment strategies. The assessment of the synchronous activities related to innovative food business included the completion of a full report or business canvas portfolio containing the main elements of the proposed business (40% grade). Moreover, the presentation and pitch of their business ideas to investors accounted for 20% of the grade.

3.3 Inclusion and Application of UDL

As promoting inclusion of all learners in the module was one of the main objectives of this re-designed content, an inclusivity statement was shared with all students aiming to encourage them to specifically mention some of their needs that may not be fully considered within the module.

The inclusivity statement shared with all the learner was as follows: "The School of Agriculture and Food Science and the section of Food and Nutrition strive to create a community that nurtures the talents of everyone regardless of socioeconomic status, disability, race, religion, culture, gender or sexual orientation. Our modules and learning environment are designed inclusively, so that they can be accessed, understood and used to the greatest extent possible, removing all barriers to learning. Students are provided with equal opportunities to access, participate and succeed, regardless of background, personal circumstances, age or disability. Students are encouraged to approach staff to discuss their learning needs and any information disclosed will be treated with confidentiality and respect."

Moreover, several modifications were introduced in the module aiming to meet the needs of the diverse student population by applying the principles of UDL during the process of curriculum design as previously explored in multiple disciplines in Higher Education [4]. The practical modifications in activities/assessments aiming to take into account the principles of UDL were:

Means of engagement

- Provide multiple media (pre-recorded lectures, slides) and materials (links to videos (TED talks, Blinkists) and also books and articles) were made available online, via Brightspace without any additional cost to the student and in advance of the sessions.
- Use of intelligent agents were set up in Brightspace to identify students that have not accessed materials or log in into the class for certain periods of time, allowing the module coordinator to identify and contact them to inquiry for possible issues when accessing the content or engaging in the class.

Means of representation

- The accessibility of all the materials was checked using the "accessibility checker" from Microsoft [29].
- The individual learning will be evaluated in multiple choice question test that will include several questions using images and asking relevant questions about that representation rather than all of them being text.

Means of action and expression

- The learning outcomes, assignment, grading and proposed activities of the module will be explained in the class using a mind map developed for the module that mirror the information of the one provided within the syllabus.

- During the group work the learners are allowed to present using the media that better suits their needs (i.e. video format, PowerPoint, poster, podcast, blog).
- To promote transparency on grading, rubrics for all the graded activities were shared and explained in class in week 1.

3.4 Evaluation of the Module

Peer-Observation Feedback. The peer-observation session was a synchronous online group work (1 hour) in which the learners were building up on previous work to develop further their business knowledge by analyzing the activities and key resources needed by their proposed innovative businesses.

The online session was designed as an introduction to the tasks of the day (10–15 min) interacting with the learners by posing questions and practical examples of the activities that they had to undertake as part of their groups. After this, the learners split into their groups to perform the proposed tasks for 20–25 min. After its completion all the groups received feedback on their performance and listened to the feedback received also by other groups (15 min). The session finished with 10 min allocated for questions that different groups of learners may have in relation to previous tasks towards the completion of their report as well as other aspects of the module related to both group and individual learning.

Overall the feedback of the peer-observation was positive, highlighting few points for improvement mainly related to the delivery of the sessions as seen in Table 1.

Table 1. Observation form completed by the peer-observer.

Prompts	Strengths	Weaknesses
Clarity of objectives	The objectives were clear during the session as there was a framework of work that was being referenced, enabling to get a sense of what the students should achieve in the tutorial and what will they be producing	The lecturer could have given an overview of the general objectives of the module and how the session related to those could be relevant at the beginning of the session
Planning and organization	The tutorial was well organized, mentioning a week-by-week module organizer giving a clear sense of the activities that the tutorial will be focusing on at first sight. The session was in their timetable from the beginning of the module and the contents were also provided in advance	The accessibility of few slides could be improved. A summary slide at the end could also be beneficial to understand all the content covered in the tutorial at a glance

(continued)

Table 1. (*continued*)

Prompts	Strengths	Weaknesses
Methods/Approach	The delivery of the content was quite interactive with practical examples that they can apply to their final report of work. The students were also allowed to develop exercises related to the work they will have to do in their breakout rooms	The methods were designed for online delivery and worked out nicely. These will need to be re-assessed if the sessions are meant to be in person
Delivery and pace	The delivery was online and the lecturer took time waiting for the students to reply to the questions posed. He read the comments from the chat out loud to enrich discussions	The lecturer's speech is good, but can be quite fast at times. Although everything was really clear, it would be good to introduce certain breaks to allow the lecturer to slowdown the pace of delivery
Content (use of relevant examples, level of the content appropriate...)	The examples used were relevant to the work the students have to perform with practical examples analyzing food businesses that will allow them to develop their own work. The contents of this online lecture were also related to the theoretical contents of the module, which contributes to guide the students as the theoretical contents covered were not new to them	A brief reminder of key concepts could be beneficial at the beginning. Like a short intro of 3 min with key terms, although they have covered that topic for weeks. Further a short summary (1 slide) at the end of the session would wrap up the session nicely
Student participation	The students participated mainly via chat and continued discussions later in breakout rooms were the engaged better with the coordinator	More breakout rooms would be beneficial through the tutorial to boost participation as this seems to be their preferred method for participation
Use of learning resources	The main learning resources use were PowerPoint, zoom polls, annotation tools in zoom and whiteboard	Maybe videos and animations could also be a good alternative for this session

Overall quality of the session and further comments:
The overall objectives of the session were achieved. The lecturer was patient allowing students' participation even when that created certain delays in the progress of the tutorial. Most of the participation of the students was done via chat, and all the queries/participation of the students were mentioned in the main session and discussed. The structure of the session was overall really interactive and engaged the students
Putting the students into breakout rooms and moving from one room to the other worked very well. It gave the students the possibility to clarify questions specific to their group work
With respect to the main objective of the observation, the contents of this tutorial are clearly aligned with the theoretical contents previously delivered. The work structure-flow is cohesive and the learning is build up over time to help the students deliver on the practical elements of the course

Student Feedback. Only 4.35% of the learners engaged in the feedback questionnaire during the Autumn semester 2021–2022. Despite the fact that the overall evaluation of the module by the learners was really positive (5 points for each question), these results cannot be used without an increased participation of the learners. Further feedback will be necessary from new cohorts of learners to gain an insight into their perceptions of the changes implemented in this module.

4 Conclusions and Future Work

Overall, the re-designed learning objectives of the module were clearly aligned with the new active learning approaches and assessment strategy and were capable to adapt to both an online and/or blended learning environments, allowing the learners to construct and build a deeper understanding of key business concepts when compared to the module delivered face-to-face, based almost exclusively on the delivery of theoretical business concepts. Moreover, sharing an inclusivity statement and the flexibility and multiple choices provided when designing the learning activities and assessments following the principles of UDL provided an inclusive environment, with equal opportunities for learning to all by considering the individual needs of the learners during both individual and group work. This new module design was flexible allowing the delivery of the content in both fully online and blended learning environments while promoting active learning in a way that was suitable and capable to adapt and successfully engage with the learners during the challenging and ever-changing learning environment created by the COV-19 pandemic. Future work will be necessary to engage the learners in the evaluation process of the module to gain a deeper understanding on their perceptions of this new and flexible module design.

Acknowledgement. Marco Garcia-Vaquero acknowledges the funding received from the Ad Astra Start Up Award from UCD to attend this conference. Marco Garcia-Vaquero would like to thank his family, specially Blanca Vaquero Martín and América Martín Mezquita for their constant support, wisdom and passion for education that was passed on to everyone around them. América Martín Mezquita "Study, learn and get educated! Money can come and go; Knowledge will always stay with you and it will help you forever".

References

1. Alae-Carew, C., Green, R., Stewart, C., Cook, B., Dangour, A.D., Scheelbeek, P.F.D.: The role of plant-based alternative foods in sustainable and healthy food systems: consumption trends in the UK. Sci. Total Environ. **807**, 151041 (2022)
2. Bailin, S.: Critical thinking and science education. Sci. Educ. **11**(4), 361–375 (2002)
3. Basham, J.D., Blackorby, J., Marino, M.T.: Opportunity in crisis: the role of universal design for learning in educational redesign. Learn. Disabil. Contemp. J. **18**(1), 71–91 (2020)
4. Biggs, J.: Enhancing teaching through constructive alignment. High. Educ. **32**(3), 347–364 (1996)
5. Biggs, J.: Teaching for Quality Learning at University (2003)

6. Biggs, J.: Constructive alignment in university teaching. HERDSA Rev. Higher Educ. **1**, 5–22 (2014)
7. CAST: Universal Design for Learning Guidelines version 2.2 (2018). http://udlguidelines.cast.org. Accessed 10 Feb 2022
8. Choo, W.S.: Student perspectives of various learning approaches used in an undergraduate food science and technology subject. J. Food Sci. Educ. **20**(4), 146–154 (2021)
9. Colurcio, M., Wolf, P., Kocher, P.Y., Spena, T.R.: Asymmetric relationships in networked food innovation processes. Br. Food J. **114**(5), 702–727 (2012)
10. Crowe, A., Dirks, C., Wenderoth, M.P.: Biology in bloom: implementing bloom's taxonomy to enhance student learning in biology. CBE. Life. Sci. Educ. **7**(4), 368–381 (2008)
11. Duffrin, M.W.: Integrating problem-based learning in an introductory college food science course. J. Food Sci. Educ. **2**(1), 2–6 (2003)
12. Gagnon, G.W., Jr., Collay, M.: Constructivist Learning Design: Key Questions for Teaching to Standards. SAGE Publications, Thousand Oaks (2005)
13. Garcia-Vaquero, M.: Design thinking online: approaching constructive learning in food science. In: 18th International Conference on Cognition and Exploratory Learning in Digital Age (2021)
14. HLPE: Nutrition and food systems. HLPE, Rome (2017)
15. https://support.microsoft.com/en-us/office/improve-accessibility-with-the-accessibility-checker-a16f6de0-2f39-4a2b-8bd8-5ad801426c7f. Accessed 10 Feb 2022
16. Jideani, V.A., Jideani, I.A.: Alignment of assessment objectives with instructional objectives using revised bloom's taxonomy—the case for food science and technology education. J. Food Sci. Educ. **11**(3), 34–42 (2012)
17. Kim, B., Kim, H., Jeon, Y.: Critical success factors of a design startup business. Sustainability **10**(9), 2981 (2018)
18. Meyer, J., Land, R.: Threshold concepts and troublesome knowledge: linkages to ways of thinking and practising within the disciplines. Citeseer (2003)
19. Morris, S.A.: Basic Elements of Food Processing and Packaging Food and Package Engineering, pp. 3–16 (2011)
20. Napoleon, L., Freedman, D., Seetharaman, K., Sharma, P.: An educational needs assessment of pennsylvania workforce: opportunities to redefine secondary career and technical education to meet food industry needs. J. Food Sci. Educ. **5**(2), 19–23 (2006)
21. Oliveira, L., Cardoso, E.L.: A project-based learning approach to promote innovation and academic entrepreneurship in a master's degree in food engineering. J. Food Sci. Educ. **20**(4), 120–129 (2021)
22. Osterwalder, A., Pigneur, Y.: Business Model Generation: A Handbook for Visionaries, Game Changers, and Challengers, vol. 1. John Wiley & Sons, Hoboken (2010)
23. Padden, L., O,Connor, J., Barrett, T.: Universal Design for Curriculum Design: UCD Access and Lifelong Learning (2017)
24. Pelech, J.: The comprehensive handbook of constructivist teaching: from theory to practice. IAP (2010)
25. Sambell, K., McDowell, L., Brown, S.: "But is it fair?": an exploratory study of student perceptions of the consequential validity of assessment. Stud. Educ. Eval. **23**(4), 349–371 (1997)
26. Sjöö, M., Östman, E., Rayner, M.: Concept circuit training: a new pedagogic approach for better teaching and learning. In: LTHs 6:e Pedagogiska Inspirationskonferens (2010)
27. Tyler, R.W.: Basic Principles of Curriculum and Instruction. University of Chicago Press, Chicago (2013)
28. Vardi, I., Ciccarelli, M.: Overcoming problems in problem-based learning: a trial of strategies in an undergraduate unit. Innov. Educ. Teach. Int. **45**(4), 345–354 (2008)
29. Wijnia, L., Loyens, S.M.M., Derous, E.: Investigating effects of problem-based versus lecture-based learning environments on student motivation. Contemp. Educ. Psychol. **36**(2), 101–113 (2011)

Dimensions of Formative Feedback During the COVID-19 Pandemic: Evaluating the Perceptions of Undergraduates in Multicultural EAP Classrooms

Ajrina Hysaj[1]([⊠]) [iD] and Doaa Hamam[2] [iD]

[1] UOWD College, University of Wollongong in Dubai, Dubai, UAE
Ajrinahysaj@uowdubai.ac.ae
[2] Higher Colleges of Technology, Dubai, UAE
dhamam@hct.ac.ae

Abstract. This study aimed to understand the attitudes and challenges faced by multicultural undergraduate students enrolled in academic writing classes. The focus of the study was on the use of formative feedback to scaffold the development of academic writing skills, including ways of conducting research and writing essays and reports using the online platform. The approach involved collecting and extracting relevant data from a survey that included questions related to the provision of formative feedback in academic writing classes for aspects of research related to analysing journal articles and summarising them while considering appropriate grammar use, vocabulary development, and research structure. Responses were obtained from 67 multicultural undergraduate students enrolled in different majors in a private university in the United Arab Emirates. The study results revealed a fair awareness of students' existing difficulties with research and academic writing skills and their awareness of the importance of receiving constructive formative feedback in different ways to improve their written work.

Keywords: Academic writing · Online platform · Formative feedback · Research skills · Multicultural students

1 Introduction

Providing or not providing formative feedback in academic writing classes is no longer a debatable matter due to the large number of studies proving the positive aspects that it has for multicultural students and tutors alike [3, 4, 9, 17, 19, 20, 58]. All students, especially multicultural students require formative feedback to construct their cognitive abilities and fill in their knowledge gaps. At the same time, tutors recognise the necessity to give feedback, take notice of the outcomes and alter further actions to make comprehensive decisions in their instructional practices to facilitate learning. Undoubtedly, students whose first language is not English develop their language abilities when receiving written formative feedback from their tutors or peers. Such feedback could be

G. Meiselwitz (Ed.): HCII 2022, LNCS 13316, pp. 103–114, 2022.
https://doi.org/10.1007/978-3-031-05064-0_8

direct or indirect but, in both cases, students need to be actively involved in receiving feedback and making amendments to their work, sometimes in its form, format or content. Undoubtedly, academic writing is a crucial skill in academia, the workplace, and social life. Effective academic writing skills require incorporating acquired knowledge and sources to show the depth of understanding of a particular topic [43]. Academic writing is crucially related to the successful completion of studies in the university level as most subjects in undergraduate or postgraduate levels require students to think critically and analytically and display the same when writing academically. Several scholars debate that educators need to focus on the skills' development of multicultural students across a variety of academic contexts and not only on the assessed tasks [35, 42, 55]. In other words, when giving feedback for writing as a productive task, cognitive factors need to be considered as they are equally important to the finished work itself. Several scholars agree that students should know their weaknesses and strengths through feedback so that they can build on that acquired knowledge and produce better work later [10, 32, 53]. Weaver [53] further points out that some academics believe that feedback is generally not beneficial to the students because they are only concerned about the grade they receive for their assignments and not about the overall development of their writing skills. On the other hand, Chokwe [13] suggests that effective feedback is an important teaching tool in the online platform, facilitating the students' learning process by addressing the issues with which they struggle.

Nevertheless, tutors need to consider the learners before giving feedback. Numerous researchers suggest effective feedback strategies in academic writing pedagogy to suit the learners' needs [12, 26, 46, 51]. Such effectiveness may relate to the first language of the learners, their previous schooling system or their individual preferences. In other words, feedback should address the needs of the learners while guiding them towards a better and more comprehensive language construction and thinking development process. Writing as a productive task takes a whole lifetime to be mastered, and while students struggle to understand concepts and get marks for their work, they also learn a long-life skill that can be utilised later as per their needs [18, 29]. As feedback is directed from tutors to students, the first ones are in the position of understanding its value and power, and they figure out effective ways of passing the information to the learners to facilitate a life-long learning process. On the other hand, learners are in authority to receive their tutors' feedback and make changes to their writing pieces to better develop their academic literacies [4, 44]. Although feedback is given on specific written work presented by students to tutors as part of a graded or non-graded academic writing task, the careful consideration of it by the tutors is the only way to improve the learners' abilities in writing/thinking critically, analytically and presenting work in an academically acceptable format [32, 44].

2   Literature Review

2.1   Importance of Feedback in Academic Writing Classes

The first year of university studies is academically, personally and socially demanding for many undergraduates, and it can also be challenging for some [5, 28, 32, 40]. The demands and challenges associated with the first year of the tertiary level can be academic, personal, and social. Despite the variances between the angles of these challenges, they address issues related to undergraduate students, and their variety of needs and perspectives, which are highly interconnected. Being new in an unknown environment can be daunting for students. Moreover, as the undergraduate students come from a variety of schooling systems and are not necessarily familiar with the types of assessments required to be in a private university setting or with the required level of academic language, some difficulties they have can be of linguistic and cognitive nature [2, 17, 27]. Therefore, because these students lack some linguistic and cognitive skills, they require support from educators and peers. Academic writing assessment types in undergraduate subjects vary from essays to case studies, individual, pair or group reports, and final individual or group projects. Although these assessment tasks differ in length and format, they always lead to each other because they include research, critical and analytical writing, and elements of referencing.

Multicultural students, whose English is not their mother tongue, are known to face problems not only with the conventional rules of academic writing in the English language but also with the vocabulary and grammatical forms used in it [32, 39, 50]. The process of writing appropriate academic texts depends on the understanding and the application of many factors connected with academic writing that can be divided into form, structure and content. Most undergraduate students whose first language is not English are enrolled in academic writing classes, the pathway to university classes or general education classes that are usually designed as a bridging program between high school and university. Although the level of difficulties of undergraduate students could relate to any of the four language skills, e.g. reading, speaking, listening or writing, according to several authors [1, 5, 32], a large number of students struggle more with academic writing along with the other language skills.

The most significant difficulties that multicultural students face with academic writing are noticeable in academic writing classes; hence, it becomes valuable to explore and analyse them [36, 56]. The diversity of difficulties present in each student may be related to their individual skillset, learning preferences and the various schooling systems they were enrolled in before joining university [2, 16, 23]. While it is not expected and is not reasonably possible that academic writing instructors cater to the needs of all students and that they miraculously fix all the issues that students have, it is valuable to analyse possible ways and approaches to facilitate the students' learning process. Academic language tutors may give direct or indirect feedback to students aiming to correct content, structure, grammar, vocabulary, research or referencing skills [16, 29]. They may also decide to focus on one aspect at a time and micro-manage their students' academic writing process. Once the academic writing process seems to fulfil the requirements of structure and content and contains elements of research and referencing skills, the tutors can focus on providing indirect feedback to students and guide them towards correcting their errors through proofreading and editing their work. Peer feedback can come in handy in this process as peers have a different perspective and approach from tutors, and they sound less authoritative and can manage several aspects of the academic writing process of their peers.

2.2 Methods and Approaches of Providing Feedback in Academic Writing Classes

Feedback methods are to be analysed based on the target students and the required outcomes needed. These two factors must be considered to achieve effectiveness and prove that the targets are well-achieved. Moreover, Ferris [19] maintains that clear and selective feedback could assist student writers. For example, when students are given an academic writing task well ahead of the deadline submission and receive formative feedback, their level is likely to improve. In such a case, the learners take the initiative, and therefore, tutors are required to be highly considerate of the learners' academic and individual needs.

Bandura, Freeman and Lightsey [6] claim that although certain behaviours will attain the desired outcomes, individuals will not exert control unless they believe they can produce these behaviours. In the case of summative feedback, students are not required to apply any changes to a complete academic writing task, when instead all they are worried about maybe the given grade. For that reason, comments from tutors have to address the strengths and weaknesses displayed in students' work and contribute substantially as a proof of the given mark. However, some tutors may opt to provide more detailed feedback and focus specifically on the structure of the students' argument. In this case, feedback becomes summative as well as formative. Shute [49] has an innovative approach towards addressing the purposes of formative feedback by analysing the development of cognitive mechanisms, the length and complexity of the feedback, and the importance of feedback as a scaffolding tool and source of motivation. All such goals can be achieved by providing direct, metalinguistic, and indirect feedback [48]. As the name indicates, direct feedback gives explicit directions to learners by providing them with clear examples of where the errors have occurred and how they can be corrected. Metalinguistic feedback focuses on providing codes to show the nature of the errors without correcting them, and indirect feedback provides learners only with an indication of where the errors have occurred by underlining the errors or using cursors to indicate omissions in the students' texts. Bitchener and Knoch [9] argue that indirect and metalinguistic feedback are considered to employ guided learning and problem-solving techniques hence, can have a long-lasting effect on learners. Ferris and Roberts [20] recommended that direct feedback is more beneficial to ESL learners with low levels of competency that do not necessarily understand the English language complexity and cannot produce critically and analytically well-thought speech.

Therefore, the spread of online teaching necessitates exploring and analysing the effectiveness of providing formative feedback to multicultural undergraduate students in the online platform [37]. Although the switch from face-to-face to the online platform at the start of 2020 due to the COVID-19 pandemic did not allow enough time for tutors to consider ways of providing feedback, it exposed them to the need to explore the same. Amid material and assessment adaptations to achieve the appropriate curriculum alignment, tutors utilised online tools such as individual emails and audio or video recordings to provide formative feedback [34, 41]. Furthermore, tutors used the online forums for general feedback, and the software embedded in learning management systems (LMS), created PowerPoints with common errors and uploaded them to LMS for all students to view and reflect. Although tutors individually considered the ways they used to provide formative feedback, it is also worth checking the students' evaluations and points of view about those ways. In general, students expectations of formative feedback during the outbreak of COVID-19 were higher than usual, mainly because of the disconnection created by the online platform [37, 45]. Moreover, the conditions by which the shift happened from the face-to-face classes to the online platform and the social isolation created because of the spread of the worldwide pandemic impacted how students learnt and tutors taught [45].

2.3   Multicultural Students' Perspectives on Formative Feedback on Academic Writing Assignments

According to studies by Bader et al. [4], Rabab'ah and Belgrimet [47], and Knight et al. [42], formative feedback practices and their impact on students' academic performance are under-researched. Furthermore, despite the impact that formative feedback can have on students' desire to learn and progress in any given subject, they are yet to be understood and analysed [57]. Aspects of formative feedback that require understanding are personal and academic and inclusive of students from a multicultural, and multilingual background and different majors as well as the variety of educational institutions [24]. Multilingual and multicultural students may vary in the ways they expect to receive formative feedback, and this could be based on their prior experiences during their schooling years [25, 38, 52, 54]. Another aspect of formative feedback, which could vary from one student to the other refers to the person who provides formative feedback, the form of feedback, the degree of scaffolding that is offered and the tendency of the learner to work with the received feedback [11, 25]. The forms by which formative feedback can be provided could vary and include direct or indirect feedback provided by the teacher (teacher feedback), student to student feedback (peer feedback), group feedback, reflective feedback and artificial intelligence (AI) feedback (feedback provided by a programme) [4, 42]. Irrespective of the method being used to provide formative feedback, it is crucial for students to accept feedback as a constructive form of self-evaluation and fix their writing according to it.

Nevertheless, as expected, this is not always the case. For instance, Bader et al. [4] revealed that the analysed reflective notes of 128 students showed that students did not perceive peer feedback as beneficial and were reluctant to make changes based on it. At the same time, they wholeheartedly worked on the formative feedback received by their instructors and considered it as substantial to their academic writing progression.

On the one hand, providing formative feedback in academic writing requires focusing on content, structure, language and vocabulary development [54]. Moreover, formative feedback in such courses should align with the requirements described in the marking criteria of assessments that count for the marks and accumulated grades. One format of providing formative feedback to undergraduate students is that of positive reinforcement from the side of teachers [4], which can encourage students to work on the received formative feedback, consider it as a necessary part of their learning process and use it in bridging the gap between the existing knowledge and the newly constructed knowledge. Furthermore, the newly-constructed knowledge could be a blend of the provided formative feedback, individual reflections on the feedback provided, adequate practice on drafting and redrafting pieces of academic writing, and finally implementing the feedback in all aspects of academic writing [49, 53, 55]. Multiple revisions of academic writing drafts offer support to the students' learning through reflections and can enhance the process of life-long learning [21].

During the Covid-19 pandemic, delving into forms of providing and receiving formative feedback becomes more complex than ever. These forms can contain but are not restricted to the inclusion of asynchronous forms of provision of formative feedback from teachers through emails, general groups' notice boards, peer feedback, discussion boards and many other frameworks that require exploration and utilisation [47]. Although providing formative feedback is not easy, the frameworks utilised for it can be transferred from teachers to students, so the process of providing formative feedback can be possible on a larger scale. For instance, Bartholomew Strimel and Yoshikawa [7] and Rabab'ah and Belgrimet [47] highlighted the positive aspects of coaching students to provide peer feedback and reflect on their individual goals academic pieces of writing. Therefore, it is important to consider the process of the provision of formative feedback as an internal and external process, which requires the implementation of sets of rules based on certain frameworks [21].

With the widespread internet use, it seems worthwhile to consider how automated assessment tools can be utilised to provide formative feedback to students and to study the impact this type of feedback has on students [7, 57]. One way that formative feedback can support learning is by pointing out the undergradutes' errors to improve their skillsets by learning from their mistakes. Another form, however, can be that formative feedback is provided through automated assessment tools, and this can help scaffold learning by providing clues to instructors about the common errors noticed in students' work [15, 22]. These clues can help instructors understand the gap present in undergraduate students' knowledge and address the gap simultaneously while addressing students' learning needs [57]. In this context, it is important to consider the alignment of students' learning needs with the requirements of the assessment tasks, so the solutions used to fix the errors present in their work address their individual needs and the requirements present in the assessment marking criteria [7, 24, 33, 57].

3   Methodology

The present study contributes to the ongoing research on measuring undergraduate students' attitudes, experiences and challenges faced when producing pieces of academic writing and the expectations of receiving formative feedback. The study utilised quantitative methods to obtain conclusive data from the participants [14]. A survey comprised of 12 Likert-scale items was designed to collect the data. The survey was based on the Likert scale to critically analyse how students respond to their existing needs when it comes to formative feedback in research and academic writing. For clarity of responses, the survey was piloted first on a random group of students to test its validity and reliability, and as a result, some items were amended to make it easier for the students to understand. The target population for the study were undergraduate students in a private English medium university in the United Arab Emirates. These students were enrolled in academic writing classes, and as part of their coursework, they were required to write research essays and reports. The majority of the students were first-year students. However, some of the students postponed taking the course to a later date as they were in their final semester. Students completed the survey anonymously, and the survey completion required around 10 min. The survey was conducted online. Students responded to Likert-scale items related to their difficulties and preferences in research and academic writing and the role of formative feedback. The survey was distributed to approximately 130 students; however, only 67 students responded (n = 67), so the response rate was 51.5%. The researchers also explained the purpose of the research study and explained the meaning of the term "formative feedback" to the participants before sending the survey. Students completed the survey anonymously, and the incomplete responses were disqualified. Data were then extracted from the survey, organised and tabulated within the contingency tables using descriptive methods where necessary.

4 Results

The table shows the 12 Likert scale items and the percentage of each response. The options for the Likert-scale items were: 1-To a great extent, 2 = Somewhat, 3 = Neutral, 4 = Very little, and 5 = Not at all. The survey's overall results show that most students were interested in receiving formative feedback for their written work. 67% of students believed that their academic writing skills required significant improvement, and over 57% of students indicated that they were open to receiving help to produce good pieces of academic writing. An overwhelming majority of over 70% were enthusiastic about receiving formative feedback on their academic writing from their teachers, while 46% of the respondents agreed on receiving formative feedback from online software. Interestingly, only 25% of students believed that receiving formative feedback from peers was beneficial to them, while over 60% of them responded that their peers' formative feedback was not helpful or important. Two of the most challenging issues for the respondents were the comprehension of journal articles and the summarising process required to conduct research and write essays and reports. Respectively, over 60% of students were interested in receiving scaffolding from teachers to comprehend journal articles, and over 38% of students believed they needed support to summarise the information gathered from journal articles. Although a considerable number of students -over 50%- thought that their academic writing structure required major development, precisely 45% of them believed it was difficult to amend their written work by making changes and editing the draft of their work before the final submission. However, despite the increased difficulty in amending the written work, which may be connected with the students' inadequately developed academic writing skills, over 62% of respondents expressed their interest in correcting their written work based on the teachers' suggestions which were given through formative feedback. Furthermore, the provision of formative feedback from teachers seems to encourage students to ask for further clarifications; hence over 40% of students were comfortable asking their teachers questions about their formative feedback, especially the grammatical and structural aspects of their written work. To conclude, the survey respondents needed formative feedback in their academic writing classes and considered editing their work integral to their learning process. Nevertheless, the ways and forms of this process that could prove to be more fruitful and beneficial to students, and teachers alike require further exploration and understanding (Table 1).

Table 1. Formative feedback survey results

Survey item	1	2	3	4	5
Do you think that your academic writing requires improvement?	32%	35%	23%	10%	10%
Do you prefer to receive formative feedback from your tutor on your written work?	47%	28%	12%	8%	5%
Do you prefer to receive formative feedback from your peers?	12%	13%	14%	31%	30%
Do you prefer to receive formative feedback through online software?	22%	24%	15%	28%	12%
Do you need support with the comprehension of journal articles?	35%	30%	10%	15%	10%
Do you find it easy to summarise journal articles and write your literature review?	15%	12%	33%	15%	25%
Do you need help with your academic vocabulary and grammar?	37%	25%	23%	15%	15%
Do you need help with the structure of academic writing?	38%	20%	10%	25%	17%
Is it easy for you to make changes to your draft after receiving formative feedback?	22%	23%	25%	20%	10%
Do you enjoy correcting your work upon receiving formative feedback?	35%	25%	10%	20%	10%
Do you ask for clarification if you do not understand the feedback given by the tutor?	25%	25%	18%	12%	20%
Do you find it convenient to make changes to your draft before the final submission?	33%	25%	17%	15%	10%

5 Discussion

This current study revealed that students who were enrolled in academic writing classes appreciate receiving formative feedback on their written and research assignments. Moreover, they consider this as a way to reflect on their learning process and its continuous improvement. They recognised the need to improve their academic writing and research skills and felt that formative feedback and the subsequent changes they made to their work provided them with the possibility of learning from their errors and helped them in mastering their academic writing skills. This finding concurs with the findings of Huisman, et al. [35], who concluded that feedback benefited students and improved the drafts of their essays. Furthermore, despite finding the editing process somehow difficult, the students enjoyed making changes and improving their work because they felt connected with the matter and indicated that their linguistic, cognitive and research skills improved. Consequently, the students' self-confidence level in academic writing skills and their interaction with the teachers and their engagement with the subject and written assessments were enhanced. The study also concluded that several strategies are needed to overcome the difficulties encountered by students in academic writing classes and this agrees with the findings of Ismiati and Pebriantika [36] who stated that it is important to add new strategies, including formative feedback, to the process of teaching and learning to improve the students' academic writing. Therefore, in alignment with our work [31], we strongly believe that formative feedback enriches the students' academic writing skills as well as their online engagement and paves the way to a successful online learning experience. Finally, we believe that the use of feedback software, AI, and automatic analytical tools can be beneficial to help students in academic writing classes. The study results show students' reasonable level of acceptance of using online software to receive feedback about their academic writing. This finding is in line with the recommendations of Knight, et al. [42], who stated that there must be a system to evaluate and analyse students' writing using different tools.

6 Conclusion and Recommendations

To conclude, this study stressed the importance of providing formative feedback in academic writing classes. Also, students revealed that they benefited from feedback and stated that it helped them improve their writing. They also reported a decrease in the level of assessment difficulty due to the formative feedback they received. The study also concluded that students prefer to receive feedback from their tutors more than their peers, and they showed a certain level of acceptance to receiving feedback via software or automated tools. Students also revealed that they need help with analysing journal articles and summarising them. All in all, it is evident that formative feedback plays a vital role in improving the students' writing. This feedback can inform tutors of the steps to provide more appropriate and comprehensive feedback for a successful online learning experience. Furthermore, this study opens the way to understand the benefits of thought negotiations skills acquired in receiving and dealing with formative feedback. Also, this study highlighted that feedback led to the enrichment of students' academic and linguistic skills through the stimulation of deeper learning. So, it is essential to conduct continuous research to explore the perceptions of multicultural undergraduate students about the best ways and forms to give and utilise formative feedback, especially in the online platform.

References

1. Altınmakas, D., Bayyurt, Y.: An exploratory study on factors influencing undergraduate students' academic writing practices in Turkey. J. Engl. Acad. Purp. **37**, 88–103 (2019)
2. Akhtar, R., Hassan, H., Saidalvi, A.: The effects of ESL student's attitude on academic writing apprehensions and academic writing challenges. Int. J. Psychosoc. Rehabil. **24**(05), 5404–5412 (2020)
3. Ashwell, T.: Patterns of teacher response to student writing in a multi-draft composition classroom: is content feedback followed by form feedback the best method? J. Second. Lang. Writ. **9**(3), 227–257 (2000)
4. Bader, M., Burner, T., Iversen, S.H., Varga, Z.: Student perspectives on formative feedback as part of writing portfolios. Assess. Eval. High. Educ. **44**(7), 1017–1028 (2019)

5. Baik, C., Naylor, R., Arkoudis, S., Dabrowski, A.: Examining the experiences of first-year students with low tertiary admission scores in Australian universities. Stud. High. Educ. **44**(3), 526–538 (2019)
6. Bandura, A., Freeman, W.H., Lightsey, R.: Self-efficacy: The exercise of control (1999)
7. Bartholomew, S.R., Strimel, G.J., Yoshikawa, E.: Using adaptive comparative judgment for student formative feedback and learning during a middle school design project. Int. J. Technol. Des. Educ. **29**(2), 363–385 (2018). https://doi.org/10.1007/s10798-018-9442-7
8. Bitchener, J.: Evidence in support of written corrective feedback. J. Second Lang. Writ. **17**(2), 102–118 (2008)
9. Bitchener, J., Knoch, U.: The value of written corrective feedback for migrant and international students. Lang. Teach. Res. **12**(3), 409–431 (2008)
10. Bitchener, J., Ferris, D.R.: Written Corrective Feedback in Second Language Acquisition and Writing. Routledge, Milton Park (2012)
11. Black, P.: Formative assessment: views through different lenses. Curric. J. **16**(2), 133–135 (2005)
12. Breeze, R.: Rethinking Academic Writing Pedagogy for the European University. Brill, Leiden (2012)
13. Chokwe, J.M.: Students' and tutors' perceptions of feedback on academic essays in an open and distance learning context. Open Praxis **7**(1), 39–56 (2015)
14. Creswell, J.W.: Research Design: Qualitative, Quantitative, and Mixed Methods Approaches. Sage Publications, Thousand Oaks (2014)
15. Daradoumis, T., Puig, J.M.M., Arguedas, M., Liñan, L.C.: Analysing students' perceptions to improve the design of an automated assessment tool in online distributed programming. Comput. Educ. **128**, 159–170 (2019)
16. Eberle, J., Hobrecht, J.: The lonely struggle with autonomy: a case study of first-year university students' experiences during emergency online teaching. Comput. Hum. Behav. **121**, 106804 (2021)
17. Ellis, R., Sheen, Y., Murakami, M., Takashima, H.: The effects of focused and unfocused written corrective feedback in an English as a foreign language context. System **36**(3), 353–371 (2008)
18. Estaji, M., Karimabadi, M.: Iranian ESP students' and professors' perceptions of plagiaristic behaviors in academic writing: the case of veterinarian course. Iran. J. Engl. Acad. Purp. **10**(2), 11–22 (2021)
19. Ferris, D.: The case for grammar correction in L2 writing classes: a response to Truscott (1996). J. Second Lang. Writ. **8**(1), 1–11 (1999)
20. Ferris, D., Roberts, B.: Error feedback in L2 writing classes: how explicit does it need to be? J. Second Lang. Writ. **10**(3), 161–184 (2001)
21. Fluckiger, J., Vigil, Y.T.Y., Pasco, R., Danielson, K.: Formative feedback: involving students as partners in assessment to enhance learning. Coll. Teach. **58**(4), 136–140 (2010)
22. Gao, Y., Passonneau, R.J.: Automated assessment of quality and coverage of ideas in students' source-based writing. In: Roll, I., McNamara, D., Sosnovsky, S., Luckin, R., Dimitrova, V. (eds.) AIED 2021. LNCS (LNAI), vol. 12749, pp. 465–470. Springer, Cham (2021). https://doi.org/10.1007/978-3-030-78270-2_82
23. Gezmiş, N.: Difficulties of students in process writing approach. J. Lang. Linguist. Stud. **16**(2), 565–579 (2020)
24. Hao, Q., Tsikerdekis, M.: How automated feedback is delivered matters: formative feedback and knowledge transfer. In: 2019 IEEE Frontiers in Education Conference (FIE), pp. 1–6. IEEE (2019)

25. Harrison, C.J., Könings, K.D., Dannefer, E.F., Schuwirth, L.W.T., Wass, V., van der Vleuten, C.P.M.: Factors influencing students' receptivity to formative feedback emerging from different assessment cultures. Perspect. Med. Educ. **5**(5), 276–284 (2016). https://doi.org/10.1007/s40037-016-0297-x
26. Hill, G.: Making the assessment criteria explicit through writing feedback: a pedagogical approach to developing academic writing. Int. J. Pedagogies Learn. **3**(1), 59–66 (2007)
27. Hysaj, A., Elkhouly, A., Qureshi, A.W., Abdulaziz, N.: Analysis of engineering students' academic satisfaction in a culturally diverse university. In: 2018 IEEE International Conference on Teaching, Assessment, and Learning for Engineering (TALE), pp. 755–760. IEEE (2018)
28. Hysaj, A., Elkhouly, A.: Why do students plagiarise? The case of multicultural students in an Australian university in the United Arab Emirates. In: Integrity in Education for Future Happiness, pp. 64–77 (2020)
29. Hysaj, A., Hamam, D.: Academic writing skills in the online platform-a success, a failure or something in between? A study on perceptions of higher education students and teachers in the UAE. In: 2020 IEEE International Conference on Teaching, Assessment, and Learning for Engineering (TALE), pp. 668–673. IEEE (2020)
30. Hysaj, A., Hamam, D.: Exploring the affordance of distance learning platform (DLP) in COVID19 remote learning environment. In: Stephanidis, Constantine, et al. (eds.) HCII 2020. LNCS, vol. 12425, pp. 421–431. Springer, Cham (2020). https://doi.org/10.1007/978-3-030-60128-7_32
31. Hysaj, A., Suleymanova, S.: The analysis of developing the application of critical thinking in oral and written discussions: the case of Emirati students in the United Arab Emirates. In: 2020 IEEE International Conference on Teaching, Assessment, and Learning for Engineering (TALE), pp. 819–824. IEEE (2020)
32. Hysaj, A., Hamam, D.: Understanding the development of critical thinking through classroom debates and online discussion forums: a case of higher education in the UAE. J. Asia TEFL **18**(1), 373 (2021)
33. Hockly, N.: Automated writing evaluation. ELT J. **73**(1), 82–88 (2019)
34. Howe, E.R., Watson, G.C.: Finding our way through a pandemic: teaching in alternate modes of delivery. Front. Educ. **6**, 187 (2021)
35. Huisman, B., van den Saab, N., Broek, P., van Driel, J.: The impact of formative peer feedback on higher education students' academic writing: a meta-analysis. Assess. Eval. High. Educ. **44**(6), 863–880 (2019)
36. Ismiati, I., Pebriantika, E.: Designing strategies for university students' writing skill. J. Lang. Lang. Teach. **8**(1), 8–19 (2020)
37. Jiang, L., Yu, S.: Understanding changes in EFL teachers' feedback practice during COVID-19: implications for teacher feedback literacy at a time of crisis. Asia Pac. Educ. Res. **30**(6), 509–518 (2021). https://doi.org/10.1007/s40299-021-00583-9
38. Juwah, C., Macfarlane-Dick, D., Matthew, B., Nicol, D., Ross, D., Smith, B.: Enhancing student learning through effective formative feedback. High. Educ. Acad. **140**, 1–40 (2004)
39. Khan, Z.R., et al.: Initiating count down-gamification of academic integrity. Int. J. Educ. Integr. **17**(1), 1–15 (2021)
40. Khan, Z.R., Hysaj, A., John, S.R., Khan, S., Gateway to preparing k-12 students for higher education–reflections on organising an academic integrity camp. In: European Conference on Academic Integrity and Plagiarism, p. 66 (2021)
41. Kim, D., et al.: Formative education online: teaching the whole person during the global COVID-19 pandemic. AERA Open **7**, 23328584211015228 (2021)
42. Knight, S., et al.: AcaWriter: a learning analytics tool for formative feedback on academic writing. J. Writ. Res. **12**(1), 141–186 (2020)
43. Lea, M.R., Street, B.V.: Student writing in higher education: an academic literacies approach. Stud. High. Educ. **23**(2), 157–172 (1998)

44. Máñez, I., Vidal-Abarca, E., Kendeou, P., Martínez, T.: How do students process complex formative feedback in question-answering tasks? A think-aloud study. Metacognition Learn. **14**(1), 65–87 (2019)
45. Peimani, N., Kamalipour, H.: Online education and the covid-19 outbreak: a case study of online teaching during lockdown. Educ. Sci. **11**(2), 72 (2021)
46. Saito, H.: Teachers' practices and students' preferences for feedback on second language writing: a case study of adult ESL learners. TESL Can. J. **11**(2), 46–70 (1994)
47. Rabab'ah, G., Belgrimet, S.: Postgraduate instructors' formative feedback on EFL students' assignments in email communication: a gender-based study. JALT CALL J. **16**(2), 85–105 (2020)
48. Sheen, Y., Ellis, R.: Corrective feedback in language teaching. Handb. Res. Second Lang. Teach. Learn. **2**, 593–610 (2011)
49. Shute, V.J.: Focus on formative feedback. ETS Res. Rep. Ser. **1**, 1–47 (2007)
50. Singh, M.K.M.: International graduate students' academic writing practices in Malaysia: challenges and solutions. J. Int. Stud. **5**(1), 12–22 (2019)
51. Strobl, C., et al.: Digital support for academic writing: a review of technologies and pedagogies. Comput. Educ. **131**, 33–48 (2019)
52. Watling, C.: The uneasy alliance of assessment and feedback. Perspect. Med. Educ. **5**(5), 262–264 (2016). https://doi.org/10.1007/s40037-016-0300-6
53. Weaver, M.R.: Do students value feedback? Student perceptions of tutors' written responses. Assess. Eval. High. Educ. **31**(3), 379–394 (2006)
54. Wiliam, D.: Keeping learning on track: formative assessment and the regulation of learning. Rev. Process **20**, 20–35 (2005)
55. Xiao, Y., Yang, M.: Formative assessment and self-regulated learning: how formative assessment supports students' self-regulation in English language learning. System **81**, 39–49 (2019)
56. Yu, S.: Giving genre-based peer feedback in academic writing: sources of knowledge and skills, difficulties and challenges. Assess. Eval. High. Educ. **46**(1), 36–53 (2021)
57. Zamprogno, L., Holmes, R., Baniassad, E.: Nudging student learning strategies using formative feedback in automatically graded assessments. In: Proceedings of the 2020 ACM SIGPLAN Symposium on Splash-E, pp. 1–11 (2020)
58. Zhang, H., et al.: eRevise: using natural language processing to provide formative feedback on text evidence usage in student writing. In: Proceedings of the AAAI Conference on Artificial Intelligence, vol. 33, no. 01, pp. 9619–9625 (2019)

Online Formative Assessment and Feedback: A Focus Group Discussion Among Language Teachers

Ajrina Hysaj[1](✉) [iD] and Harshita Aini Haroon[2] [iD]

[1] University of Wollongong Dubai, Dubai, UAE
`ajrinahysaj@uowdubai.ac.ae`
[2] Universiti Malaysia Perlis, Arau, Malaysia

Abstract. Formative assessment and the provision of formative feedback are key factors in effective teaching and learning. Generally, while teachers understand the role of feedback, studies show there is a tendency for them to provide it when a task comes to a complete. When teaching took to the online mode due to forced conditions imposed by COVID-19, questions arise about the provision of formative feedback particularly since teachers have been found to struggle teaching online. In this paper, we report on a preliminary study involving five university faculty who teach language courses. We present the respondents' (1) views and practices on using the computer for teaching online (2) practices of providing formative assessment and feedback online and (3) their intentions to proceed with online formative assessment and feedback. By and large, the faculty were comfortable teaching online. While they did agree on the importance of formative feedback and attempted to provide these in their classes, they reported issues on using the appropriate tools or assigning the appropriate tasks for the purpose. They also talked of the stress in doing so, relating it with pedagogical, technical and institutional management factors. With effective learning in mind, the group was divided on whether or not they would proceed with online formative assessment and feedback, if the choice was available to them. This paper concludes with recommendation for further research and consideration for teaching online.

Keywords: Formative assessment · Formative feedback · Online learning · Language teachers

1 Introduction

Formative assessment refers to a variety of methods that teachers use to conduct evaluation of students' academic progress while learning is in process with the aim of ascertaining the latter's grasp of learning points. Whether students are found to have successfully understood the learning objectives, or if they are facing difficulties comprehending them will determine the teacher's teaching direction. They may progress with their teaching plan, or they will need to adjust the lessons, in other words to improve instruction and student learning while it is happening. Findings from the assessment

© The Author(s), under exclusive license to Springer Nature Switzerland AG 2022
G. Meiselwitz (Ed.): HCII 2022, LNCS 13316, pp. 115–126, 2022.
https://doi.org/10.1007/978-3-031-05064-0_9

allows the teacher to provide formative feedback to students, which is considered as a key factor in influencing teaching and learning processes [1] and is an important component of students' development and improvement [2]. In order to be able to provide formative feedback, teachers need to be able to utilize appropriate formative assessment tools. The importance of such tools is recognized by the Organization for Economic Cooperation and Development (OECD), which has delineated six key elements of formative assessment [3]. These relate to a culture that promotes interaction and use of assessment tools, use of varied approaches to assess students' understanding, feedback and adaptation of instruction, students' active involvement, having learning goals and tracking them, and the use of a variety of instruction methods in serving a variety of students' needs.

Research has shown that feedback is not a one-way process but requires student engagement for learning to be effective [4]. Interaction between students and teachers is important in creating the level of trust needed to open up and ask for help, and also for the success of feedback in the teaching-learning process. van der Kleij [5, p. 176–177] in a study on feedback perceptions among teachers and students, used a conceptual model where "feedback is an interpretative process which may or may not result in learning", which is then "perceived by students in a certain way. Although it is a well-known fact that teachers understand the role of feedback [6] and are always available to offer feedback [7, 8] when it comes to formative feedback, there is a tendency for them to provide feedback when a task comes to a complete end [6].

The mass adoption of online learning globally in 2020 due to the forced conditions imposed by the spread of Covid-19 meant that formative assessment and hence formative feedback both were required to also be conducted online. Studies reveal that virtual learning can offer optimal possibilities of growth and academic satisfaction to students and teachers alike [9, 10] is considered a very interactive and innovative method of teaching and learning [11, 12] and that the alignment of course outlines, online activities and assessment tasks is substantial for students' active engagement in the online platform and improved academic satisfaction [9]. In addition, the online platform offers a broad range of ways to provide formative feedback to students and the utilization of these technologies efficiently can prove to support the mechanisms of giving and receiving formative feedback [13, 14]. Despite these positive support and evidence, studies have also revealed that educators have generally been found to struggle teaching online [15–20] with challenges including lack of student participation, student engagement, inadequate supporting infrastructures, insufficient resources, student differentiation, students lack of access to technology, and having to learn new technology. The online mode that teachers have had to adopt adds a further layer of challenge with regard to conducting formative assessment and providing formative feedback. Questions therefore arise about teachers' implementation of both formative assessment and formative feedback online.

1.1 Formative Assessment and Formative Feedback

Transference of knowledge via feedback is substantial to teaching and learning. Understanding how it can be achieved purposefully and efficiently either via conventional face-to-face teaching or online is equally important [14], where it should be supported by theoretical and conceptual knowledge [9]. According to the Organization for Economic Cooperation and Development feedback is recognized as a key skill that teachers should have [21], particularly since it is one of the factors that have the strongest influence on learning [22, 23]. Generally, despite teachers' employment of many good teaching strategies in the classroom, formative assessment remains to be an area of weakness [24]. Specifically, these include classroom discussion, questioning techniques, the use of assessment in instruction, and the provision of student feedback. Teachers' insufficient knowledge of formative assessment has been well documented and is recognized as contributing to inadequate formative feedback given to learners [6, 25]. This notion is supported by Schildkamp et al. [26] whose study concluded that knowledge and skills are in fact among the prerequisites for teachers' effective use of formative assessment. However, studies suggest that lack of appropriate implementation of formative assessment in the classroom may not necessarily be due to lack of knowledge of such mechanisms, and may be contributed by situational factors, such as being faced with students' ideas [24, 27].

Online provision of teacher formative feedback has recently drawn the attention of researchers and educators mainly due to the widespread of online learning. The complexity of the methods by which formative feedback can be applied in the online platform and the readiness of students to accept and act upon, it is still unraveled by scholars [28] and academic approach towards it is still unfocused and less explored [29]. Generally, the benefits of online formative assessment are well documented in studies such as Wilson et al. [30], Marriott and Lau [31], and Baleni [32]. However, this is not to say that online formative assessment is seen as an easy task, as challenges in implementation have also been much discussed [33–36]. Research has also found that if a system is perceived as being easy to use, it will influence the attitudes towards using it [37]. Numerous studies have found that users' perception of usefulness of online tools bears positive relationship with their intention to use them, such as in regard to Google Classroom, Buabeng-Andoh [38] on mobile learning, and Nurkhin and Saputro [39] in reference to intention to use e-learning in schools.

1.2 Computer Self-efficacy and Computer Use for Teaching-Learning

Studies on computer self-efficacy have found positive relationship between the variable and attitudes towards digital technology [40], the ability to integrate technology in the classroom [41, 42], level of educational technology use [37, 43, 44] and with blended learning practices [45]. In the context of computer use, Compeau and Higgins [46] found that self-efficacy plays a key role in shaping individuals' feelings and behaviors, where the individuals engaged more in computer use, and enjoyed the experience with having lesser anxiety. Compeau and Higgins' [46] outcome expectation variable is considered by Lopez and Manson [47] to be similar to perceived usefulness as they referred to "performance-related outcomes and personal outcome expectations" and found a positive relationship between the two variables.

Numerous studies have also found a positive relationship between computer self-efficacy and perceived ease of use and perceived usefulness [48, 49]. Studies have shown positive relationship between intention to use a system and its perceived ease of use [50, 51] and perceived usefulness [39, 51]. Davis [52], in proposing his Technology

Acceptance Model, posits the idea that a user's perception of how useful (perceived usefulness) and how easy it is to use (perceived ease of use) a technology is influenced by external variables. These perceptions, in turn, have bearings on the user's attitude towards using the technology. The model was enhanced by Abdullah and Ward [53], who specified the external factors. The study found that within the context of online learning, predictors of students' perceived ease of use are self-efficacy, enjoyment, experience, computer anxiety and subjective norm, whereas predictors of students' perceived usefulness of technology for online learning were identified as enjoyment, subjective norm, self-efficacy and experience.

1.3 Objectives of the Study

The general objective of the study is to explore and understand teachers' perspectives and experiences in the use of online formative assessment and the provision of formative feedback. Specifically, the study aimed to explore language teachers' perspective on usage of computer for online teaching, their knowledge of formative assessment, their preferred practices of providing formative feedback and their intentions to proceed with online formative assessment (OFA) and providing online formative feedback (OFF) in the future.

2 Methodology

Rooted within the qualitative approach, the study used focus group discussion to obtain the data. The qualitative research design was chosen to enable the researchers to deep dive into the complexities that teachers' might face in their online teaching with specific reference to OFA and OFF. Five language teachers were involved in the online discussion with the two researchers. The teachers were informed about the purpose of the focus group and willingly decided to participate. Their consent was also obtained for the recording of the discussion for the purpose of researchers' reference post-interview. Three of the teachers were from Malaysia and taught English in a university in Malaysia. The other two teachers were from Jordan and Egypt and taught English and Arabic in a university in United Arab Emirates. All the teachers had taught in a variety of institutions and had between 6 to 10 years teaching experience in higher education on full or part-time basis. At the time of the study three of the teachers were still teaching online and the other two in hybrid mode.

The questions asked during the focus group addressed issues related to teachers' perspectives on utilization of computer for online teaching, knowledge of formative assessment and feedback, techniques of providing formative feedback as well as their intentions to proceed with online formative assessment and feedback even after the restrictions imposed by COVID-19. These questions served as a general guide, but as with the nature of focus group discussions, issues not initially anticipated and planned by the researchers also surfaced during the discussion, and these too were considered as data. The analysis of data involved an interpretive process, in which the researchers systematically identified patterns within the data in order to answer the research questions. The discussion lasted for about two hours and teachers were able to express their thoughts openly.

3 Results

Based on data analysis, four key themes emerged from the data: computer self-efficacy, knowledge and implementation of OFA and OFF, stress and struggles, and usefulness of technological tools and intention to use them.

3.1 Computer Self-efficacy

The teachers generally expressed being comfortable in using the computer to teach online. This feeling is generally contributed by familiarity and experience in using the computer before, either as a learner (*"I studied my Masters and my PhD online so teaching online comes naturally to me."*) or in teaching. For the period of online learning, two teachers expressed reliance on the computer in helping them engage with their students, citing the utilization of online tools such as the 'comment box'.

The need to use the computer effectively was acknowledged as one of the teachers, who had been using an old computer, purchased a new laptop for the purpose: *"I was using an old computer and if it wasn't for the online teaching, I might still be using it. Nevertheless, it become necessary for me to change it as it wasn't helping me with my online classes"*. The fact that the teacher did not 'settle' and made do with an existing tool, albeit a poorly functioning one, suggests that she had been concerned about teaching in an impactful way. The use of the computer seems to spur the teachers to be more creative in their bid to teach better and develop more skills that can be used for teaching-learning purposes. The teachers showed keenness and enjoyment in exploring suitable applications, for example, a teacher commented that *"I enjoy teaching online and using different applications like PowerPoint, Jamboard, Kahoot, Flipgrid and others."*

The teachers expressed confidence in the benefits online learning bring to them and their students; *"Actually, I believe that if utilized appropriately, the online platform is very rewarding to students and teachers."*, with a teacher explicitly identifying the benefits as helping her to be more creative and to be able to better explain concepts in her lessons. In all, the teachers exhibited enjoyment, engagement and willingness to use the computer in their teaching-learning process.

3.2 Knowledge and Implementation of OFA and OFF

The teachers exhibited awareness of the necessity to have online formative assessments (OFA) and to provide online formative feedback (OFF). One respondent stressed on the importance of both to highlight weak points in their teaching and students learning which will enable them to reflect and make improvements. Another respondent was of the belief that OFA and OFF are equally important to both teachers and students:

> *"When I teach online, I focus on the material preparation and the delivery method as much as I can. Nevertheless, because I do not see my students, I cannot judge if my teaching has been at an adequate standard and if my students have understood the content and the concepts that I have taught. Therefore, OFA and OFF serve me to understand how much my students have comprehended and give me an idea of the concepts that were more difficult and on which I should focus my attention on. This helps me prepare quizzes that can support my students learning."*

Despite this general understanding of OFA and OFF and the affirmation that both are needed in education for all the concepts of academic study skills like, reading, writing, listening, speaking and research, a respondent expressed the view that the amount of work involved in conducting assessment and providing online feedback is an added challenge to language teachers. She cited students' demands which contributed to never-ending work as particular challenges, leading her to question the effectiveness of the process:

"Preparing OFA and providing OFF to students requires efforts and in the online platform the amount of work seems to not end. Students are more demanding when studying online and they expect off straight after each OFA. This does not allow me to focus on providing a fruitful OFF and the process does not serve its purpose".

It appears that student factors have a role to play in the implementation of OFA and OFF. The way in which the teachers generally provided OFA and OFF seems to be driven by their students' level of progress and their preferences. One of teachers felt the need to conduct mini OFA after every session in her effort to help weaker students become aware of their limitations immediately after the learning blocks, so that they can further improve effectively:

"Students of low-skills level lack confidence and require to be tested through simple and continuous tasks after every lesson. This allows them to revise the material immediately after is been taught and recall it later. Their cognitive abilities develop when they receive OFF after each OFA and their vocabulary and grammar improve organically".

While the focus of the shorter bursts of OFA and OFF was in aid of the weaker students, one respondent was of the belief that students of all levels will benefit from these, particularly in comparison to online summative assessment, as it is during the formative assessment and the feedback that follows do they get personal consideration from the teachers:

"Students appreciate receiving OFF from teachers and they look forward to receiving individual attention during their studies. I feel they connect more productively with the content and their studies when they receive OFF. This helps them build on their existing knowledge and progress academically".

This comment suggests that OFF serves not just the purpose of content and academic feedback but also touches on the affective domain to enhance students' motivation and self-esteem. This idea that OFF serves an affective purpose is further strengthened with one of the respondents citing the importance of students' enjoyment for them to be attentive in online lessons. One respondent was of the opinion that OFA and OFF are more purposeful when done through gaming applications like Kahoot, Quizlet and others: *"My students enjoy playing games and they do not feel that they are doing an exam when playing games. They get excited about participating in games and are more attentive in lessons".*

Other factors include the large number of assessments and students enrolled in most classes. The large number of teaching time and prolonged working hours imposed due to the online environment also posed a logistical, practical and emotional challenge to the teachers. While these are not deterrents to the teachers' desire to engage students in OFA and provide effectively, timely and well-written OFF, there is a sense of the need for a balance between meeting the pedagogical requirements and ensuring that teaching-learning conditions are considerably manageable for the process to be effective, particular as it is these that contribute to the quality of OFA and OFF. In this regard, institutional leadership is seen as having a role to play, for example, in setting the number of students in a class, in optimizing the time allocated for lessons, and in establishing relevant institutional policies at the institution. A respondent summarized this concern succinctly when she commented on the equilibrium that needs to be satisfied, between requiring the teachers to complete tasks (i.e., teaching, marking etc.) on time versus doing things right so that students are afforded 'deep learning experience, which will result in actual student progress and development.

3.3 Stress and Struggles of Online OFA and OFF

Teacher stress and struggles in relation to OFA and OFF can be broken down into several sources. The first relates to teachers having to become proficient in online learning. While there is a general sense of familiarity with computer use, the matter of online learning is another issue altogether. Two teachers expressed having been somewhat burdened to learn and teach themselves new skills and tools for online teaching, resulting in stress at the beginning of the online learning period. However, despite the exhaustion they felt, they took comfort that in the long run, the hard work will pay off and will leave them satisfied, particular when students show positive achievement and progress in their learning.

The second source of stress relates to the difficulties the teachers faced in providing constructive and meaningful feedback online. In particular they talked about effective ways to comment on the tasks they gave students, comparing this to the perceived efficiency that is afforded by the conventional face-to-face classroom. There is, however, a sense of acceptance of this setback considering that OFA and OFF needed to be pursued nonetheless. Added to this hurdle is the teachers' view that with the tools that they were employing now, the question of the trustworthiness of the assessment surfaced. In addition, the idea that online formative assessment and feedback require relatively more time made marking stressful and thus affected the whole process of checking the quality of teaching and student learning.

Thirdly, are stress and struggles in the form of challenges providing OFF for students with lower language proficiency. The teachers cited having to repeat feedback and shower them with praises in order to motivate the students who will otherwise become easily distracted during online sessions. This notion is supported by another respondent who believed that part of the role of feedback is not just on content but also to establish personal rapport with the students, *"to make them feel included, safe and someone to help them get to their goal"*. While the teachers agreed that motivating students is part of the teaching process, having to carry it out online repeatedly has been a source of the teachers' angst.

Another stressor is related to information and data management. One of the teachers expressed being intimidated by the amount of information he has had to process in a very short amount of time: "*I had to multitask constantly and learn computer programs at the same time while aligning the curriculum and focusing on my students' needs", including in providing feedback on students' progress"*. He also talked about being more comfortable in conventional teaching and attributed this preference to the idea that it is easier for him to monitor students and their learning in a physical classroom.

Despite these sources of anxiety, in all, the teachers seemed to have embraced the challenges faced while teaching online and felt their efforts were required and valued by their students.

3.4 Usefulness of Technological Tools and Intention to Use Them

Regardless of the challenges and stressors described, the teachers did agree on the usefulness of technological tools facilitating OFA and OFF. The teachers concurred that there is an option of doing so in an easy manner with the relevant tools, but which may not necessarily be effective; or to consistently and constantly provide OFF throughout the learning process. The former, for example, can be accomplished using a response template such as Google Form, while the latter may probably create less anxiety for the students but will be harder and trickier for the teacher to grade especially considering that the teacher is required to be as fair as possible. The use of tools such as chat boxes and Google Form were reported to also assist in student feedback analysis, so that these can be discussed with students and teachers can use them for teaching reflection purposes.

Teachers also acknowledged that as useful as the tools have been, they are worried that students may cheat in assessment. One teacher strategized by redistributing marks to projects, for which the students can discuss with the teachers. However, this move required a longer time for project completion.

Ultimately, the teachers were divided on their intention to use the tools for OFA and OFF. Some teachers seemed to prefer conventional teaching with in-person formative assessment and formative feedback. A factor cited is that teachers will be able to see students' facial expression and body language generally, and level of interactivity is believed to be higher when all the students and teacher are together in a physical classroom. On the other hand, other teachers felt that OFA and OFF are pedagogical repertoire that teachers teaching online will have to grapple with, especially with the current pandemic situation and uncertain future. Teachers cited practical logistical reasons, such as their ability to save time (as compared to having to travel to classes), and that there is no difference if feedback was provided online or in-person since it is given in writing, as reasons for them to continue implementing OFA and OFF.

4 Discussion

By and large, the faculty expressed being comfortable teaching online and exhibited understanding on the utilitarian role of the technological tools when teaching was migrated online. Their familiarity with the computer, and their willingness to explore ways in which they can deliver their lessons online are commendable and signal positively on teaching and learning online generally. The findings of this study suggest that teachers' implementation of OFA and OFF may be connected with their abilities in using technological tools, echoing findings by Molloy et al. [54] and Mackintosh-Franklin [55].

However, this positive finding is also coupled with several concerns. Despite them acknowledging the benefits of OFA and OFF academically and affectively for the students, and revealing that their actions in providing these were driven by the students' wants and preferences, the teachers expressed concerns on the extra burden that was present with OFA and OFF. Secondly are issues on choosing the appropriate tools or assigning the appropriate tasks for the purpose of formative assessment and feedback. Thirdly, there seems to be a sense that institutional leadership lacked sensitivity on the practical needs of the online classes which affected the way in which the teachers provided OFA and OFF, causing them to worry about the quality of their online teaching.

The need to train teachers on appropriate methods of OFA and OFF, therefore cannot be understated. While the sampling of this study is small, the findings on teachers' considerations and struggles in implementing OFA and OFF are in sync with the work of Abel et al. [2] which highlights the importance of teachers being given appropriate training to use technological tools appropriately. The teachers in this study self-taught themselves to teach online and seemed to develop the skills with experience. Furthermore, this study has shown that the teachers recognized the role OFA and OFF play in increase students' motivation and active engagement as well their increased academic performance, further supporting existing studies [11, 13, 56].

This study has also highlighted the need to consider students technological knowledge and their level of English language when choosing the appropriate method of providing formative feedback. This study suggests these to be stressors for teachers, which may contribute to ineffective online teaching-learning process. The findings resonate with previous studies [7, 12, 23].

5   Conclusion and Recommendation

It is encouraging to note that the teachers in this study understood and were willing to engage in OFA and OFF. However, the study points to the need for teacher professional development to enhance their online teaching skills, including in the execution of OFA and OFF. The teachers' input on pedagogical and technical concerns point to training opportunities and requirement, and underscores the need for institutions to not assume that just because a teacher is familiar and comfortable with using a computer, s/he will be able to teach online without glitches. In addition to the provision of training, institutional management needs to review teaching conditions such as class size, class duration, workload as well as key deadlines in order to ensure that teachers are able to carry out their online teaching responsibilities effectively. The study suggests that teaching online has not affected the teachers' sensitivity to students' learning and progress, as well as their engagement and motivational needs despite the former's report of being burdened in carrying out OFA and OFF. To ensure that these remain at an encouraging and even commendable level, it is imperative that institutional management provide the support that teachers require, especially since current global conditions seem to suggest that online teaching may be the norm in the foreseeable future.

References

1. Hoeg Karlsen, K.: The value of oral feedback in the context of capstone projects in design education. Des. Technol. Educ. **22**(3), 9–31 (2017)
2. Abel, S., Kitto, K., Knight, S., Shum, S.B.: ASCILITE 2018. In: 35th International Conference of Innovation, Practice and Research in the use of Educational Technologies in Tertiary Education: Open Oceans: Learning without Borders, pp. 15–24 (2018)
3. Organisation for Economic Cooperation and Development: 21st Century Learning: Research, Innovation and Policy. Directions from recent OECD analyses (2008). https://www.oecd.org/site/educeri21st/40554299.pdf
4. Winstone, N.E., Nash, R.A., Parker, M., Rowntree, J.: Supporting learners' agentic engagement with feedback: a systematic review and a taxonomy of recipience processes. Educ. Psychol. **52**(1), 17–37 (2017). https://doi.org/10.1080/00461520.2016.1207538
5. van der Kleij, F.M.: Comparison of teacher and student perceptions of formative assessment feedback practices and association with individual student characteristics. Teach. Teach. Educ. **85**, 175–189 (2019)
6. Park, M., Liu, X., Smith, E., Waight, N.: The effect of computer models as formative assessment on student understanding of the nature of models. Chem. Educ. Res. Pract. **18**(4), 572–581 (2017). https://doi.org/10.1039/C7RP00018A
7. Yaseeni, P.: Effects of written feedback on college students' academic writing performance. Lang. India **21**(1), 13–24 (2021)
8. Hysaj, A., Hamam, D.: Understanding the development of critical thinking through classroom debates and online discussion forums: a case of higher education in the UAE. J. Asia TEFL **18**(1), 373 (2021)
9. Novakovich, J.: Fostering critical thinking and reflection through blog-mediated peer feedback. J. Comput. Assist. Learn. **32**(1), 16–30 (2016)
10. Khan, Z., Sivasubramaniam, S., Anand, P., Hysaj, A.: The role e-tools play in supporting teaching and assessments with integrity during the COVID-19 pandemic. In European Conference on Academic Integrity and Plagiarism 2021: Book of Abstracts. European Network for Academic Integrity (ENAI), pp. 52–54 (2021)
11. Akbari, J., Tabrizi, H.H., Chalak, A.: Effectiveness of virtual vs. non-virtual teaching in improving reading comprehension of Iranian undergraduate EFL students. Turk. Online J. Dist. Educ. **22**(2), 272–283 (2021)
12. Thijssen, D.H.J., Hopman, M.T.E., van Wijngaarden, M.T., Hoenderop, J.G.J., Bindels, R.J.M., Eijsvogels, T.M.H.: The impact of feedback during formative testing on study behaviour and performance of (bio) medical students: a randomised controlled study. BMC Med. Educ. **19**(1), 1–8 (2019)
13. Goldin, I., Narciss, S., Foltz, P., Bauer, M.: New directions in formative feedback in interactive learning environments. Int. J. Artif. Intell. Educ. **27**(3), 385–392 (2017). https://doi.org/10.1007/s40593-016-0135-7
14. Mensa, E., Radicioni, D.P., Lieto, A.: COVER: a linguistic resource combining common sense and lexicographic information. Lang. Resour. Eval. **52**(4), 921–948 (2018)
15. An, Y., Kaplan-Rakowski, R., Yang, J., Conan, J., Kinard, W., Daughrity, L.: Examining K-12 teachers' feelings, experiences, and perspectives regarding online teaching during the early stage of the COVID-19 pandemic. Educ. Technol. Res. Dev. **69**(5), 1–25 (2021)
16. Joshi, A., Vinay, M., Bhaskar, P.: Impact of coronavirus pandemic on the Indian education sector: perspectives of teachers on online teaching and assessments. Interact. Technol. Smart Educ. **18**(2), 205–226 (2020). https://doi.org/10.1108/ITSE-06-2020-0087
17. Beck, D., Beasley, J.: Identifying the differentiation practices of virtual school teachers. Educ. Inf. Technol. **26**(2), 2191–2205 (2020). https://doi.org/10.1007/s10639-020-10332-y

18. Subekti, A.S.: Covid-19-triggered online learning implementation: pre-service English teachers' beliefs. Metathesis J. Engl. Lang. Lit. Teach **4**(3), 232–248 (2021)
19. Tamah, S.M., Triwidayati, K.R., Utami, T.S.D.: Secondary school language teachers' online learning engagement during the COVID-19 pandemic in Indonesia. J. Inf. Technol. Educ. Res. **19**, 803–832 (2020)
20. Nambiar, D.: The impact of online learning during COVID-19: students' and teachers' perspective. Int. J. Indian Psychol. **8**(2), 783–793 (2020)
21. Organisation for Economic Cooperation and Development: Education Policy Outlook 2015: Making Reforms Happen (2015). https://www.oecd-ilibrary.org/education/education-policy-outlook-2015_9789264225442-en
22. Hattie, J.A.: Visible Learning. A Synthesis of over 800 Meta-Analyses Related to Achievement. Routledge, New York (2009)
23. Hattie, J., Timperley, H.: The power of feedback. Rev. Educ. Res. **77**, 81–112 (2007)
24. Cotton, D.: Teachers' use of formative assessment. Delta Kappa Gamma Bull. **83**(3), 39 (2017)
25. Hussain, S., Shaheen, N., Ahmad, N., Islam, S.: Teachers' classroom assessment practices: challenges and opportunities to classroom teachers in Pakistan. Dialogue (1819–6462) **13**(4), 87–97 (2018)
26. Schildkamp, K., van der Kleij, F.M., Heitink, M.C., Kippers, W.B. Veldkamp, B.P.: Formative assessment: a systematic review of critical teacher prerequisites for classroom practice. Int. J. Educ. Res. **103**, 101602 (2020). https://doi.org/10.1016/j.ijer.2020.101602. ISSN 0883-0355
27. Cisterna, D., Gotwals, A.W.: Enactment of ongoing formative assessment: challenges and opportunities for professional development and practice. J. Sci. Teach. Educ. **29**(3), 200–222 (2018). https://doi.org/10.1080/1046560X.2018.1432227
28. Hoffmann, M.H.: Stimulating reflection and self-correcting reasoning through argument mapping: three approaches. Topoi **37**(1), 185–199 (2018)
29. Hagaman, J.L., Casey, K.J.: Paraphrasing strategy instruction in content area text. Interv. Sch. Clin. **52**(4), 210–217 (2017)
30. Wilson, K., Boyd, C., Chen, L., Jamal, S.: Improving student performance in a first-year geography course: examining the importance of computer-assisted formative assessment. Comput. Educ. **57**(2), 1493–1500 (2011)
31. Marriott, P., Lau, A.: The use of on-line summative assessment in an undergraduate financial accounting course. J. Acc. Educ. **26**(2), 73–90 (2008). https://doi.org/10.1016/j.jaccedu.2008.02.001
32. Baleni, Z.: Online formative assessment in higher education: its pros and cons. Electron. J. e-Learn. **13**(4), 228–236 (2015). www.eje.org
33. Omorogiuwa, K.O.: Benefits and challenges of feedback in formative assessment of distance learners (2012). https://uir.unisa.ac.za/handle/10500/8558
34. Xiong, Y., Suen, H.K.: Assessment approaches in massive open online courses: possibilities, challenges and future directions. Int. Rev. Educ. **64**(2), 241–263 (2018). https://doi.org/10.1007/s11159-018-9710-5
35. Webb, M.E., et al.: Challenges for IT-enabled formative assessment of complex 21st century skills. Technol. Knowl. Learn. **23**(3), 441–456 (2018). https://doi.org/10.1007/s10758-018-9379-7
36. Remmi, F., Hashim, H.: Primary school teachers' usage and perception of online formative assessment tools in language assessment. Int. J. Acad. Res. Progressive Educ. Dev. **10**(1), 290–303 (2021)
37. Buchanan, T., Sainter, P., Saunders, G.: Factors affecting faculty use of learning technologies: implications for models of technology adoption. J. Comput. High. Educ. **25**(1), 1–11 (2013). https://doi.org/10.1007/s12528-013-9066-6

38. Buabeng-Andoh, C.: Predicting students' intention to adopt mobile learning: a combination of theory of reasoned action and technology acceptance model. J. Res. Innov. Teach. Learn. **11**(2), 178–191 (2018). https://doi.org/10.1108/JRIT-03-2017-0004

39. Nurkhin, A., Saputro, I.H.: Teacher's intention to use online learning; an extended technology acceptance model (TAM) investigation. J. Phys. Conf. Ser. **1783**(1), 012123 (2021)

40. Gudek, B.: Computer self-efficacy perceptions of music teacher candidates and their attitudes towards digital technology. Eur. J. Educ. Res. **8**(3), 683–696 (2019). https://doi.org/10.12973/eu-jer.8.3.683

41. Litterell, A.B., Zagumny, M.J., Zagumny, L.L.: Contextual and psychological predictors of instructional technology use in rural classrooms. Educ. Res. Q. **29**(2), 37–47 (2005)

42. Zhao, Y., Pugh, K., Sheldon, S., Byers, J.L.: Conditions for classroom technology innovations. Teach. Coll. Rec. **104**(3), 482–515 (2002)

43. Turel, V., McKenna, P.: Design of language learning software. In: Zou, B., et al. (eds.) Computer-Assisted Foreign Language Teaching and Learning: Technological Advances, pp. 188–209. IGI-Global, Hershey (2013). http://www.igiglobal.com/chapter/design-language-learning-software/73265

44. Turel, V.: Teachers' computer self-efficacy and their use of educational technology. Turk. Online J. Dist. Educ. **15**(4), 130–149 (2014)

45. Noh, N.M., Abdullah, N., Teck, W.K., Hamzah, M.: Cultivating blended learning in teaching and learning: teachers' intrinsic and extrinsic readiness in Malaysia. Int. J. Acad. Res. Bus. Soc. Sci. **8**(2), 257–265 (2019)

46. Compeau, D.R., Higgins, C.A.: Computer self-efficacy: development of a measure and initial test. MIS Q. **19**(2), 189–211 (1995). https://doi.org/10.2307/249688

47. Lopez, D.A., Manson, D.P.: A Study of Individual Computer Self-efficacy and Perceived Usefulness of the Empowered Desktop Information System (1997). http://citeseerx.ist.psu.edu/viewdoc/summary?doi=10.1.1.217.5670

48. Usman, M.B.O., Septianti, A., Susita, D., Marsofiyati, M.: The effect of computer self-efficacy and subjective norm on the perceived usefulness, perceived ease of use and behavioural intention to use technology. J. Southeast Asian Res. (2020). https://doi.org/10.5171/2020.753259. Article ID 753259

49. Hasan, B.: Examining the effects of computer self-efficacy and system complexity on technology acceptance. Inf. Resour. Manage. J. **20**, 76–88 (2007)

50. Weng, F., Yang, R.-J., Ho, H.-J., Su, H.-M.: A TAM-based study of the attitude towards use intention of multimedia among school teachers. Appl. Syst. Innov. **1**(3), 36 (2018). https://doi.org/10.3390/asi1030036

51. Hong, X., Zhang, M., Liu, Q.: Preschool teachers' technology acceptance during the COVID-19: an adapted technology acceptance model. Front. Psychol. **12**, 691492 (2021). https://doi.org/10.3389/fpsyg.2021.691492. PMID: 34163416, PMCID: PMC8215170

52. Davis, F.D.: Perceived usefulness, perceived ease of use, and user acceptance of information technology. MIS Q. 319–340 (1989)

53. Abdullah, F., Ward, R.: Developing a general extended technology acceptance model for e-learning (GETAMEL) by analysing commonly used external factors. Comput. Hum. Behav. **56**, 238–256 (2016)

54. Molloy, E., Ajjawi, R., Bearman, M., Noble, C., Rudland, J., Ryan, A.: Challenging feedback myths: values, learner involvement and promoting effects beyond the immediate task. Med. Educ. **54**(1), 33–39 (2020)

55. Mackintosh-Franklin, D.C.: An evaluation of formative feedback and its impact on undergraduate student nurse academic achievement. Nurse Educ. Pract. **50**, 102930 (2021). https://doi.org/10.1016/j.nepr.2020.102930

56. Al-Fudail, M., Mellar, H.: Investigating teacher stress when using technology. Comput. Educ. **51**(3), 1103–1110 (2008). https://doi.org/10.1016/j.compedu.2007.11.004

Analyzing the Impact of Culture on Students: Towards a Student eXperience Holistic Model

Nicolás Matus[1]([✉]) [iD], Ayaka Ito[2] [iD], and Cristian Rusu[1] [iD]

[1] Pontificia Universidad Católica de Valparaíso, Av. Brasil 2241, 2340000 Valparaíso, Chile
nicolas.matus.p@mail.pucv.cl, cristian.rusu@pucv.cl
[2] Reitaku University, 2-1-1, Hikarigaoka, Kashiwa, Chiba 2778686, Japan
ayitou@reitaku-u.ac.jp

Abstract. Ensuring customer's satisfaction is an imperative for companies and institutions; as a result of a satisfactory experience, the customer will enhance their overall well-being, in addition to meeting their needs. The brand, similarly, benefits commercially from each positive customer experience. The User eXperience (UX) concept is closely related to user-product or user-service interactions. This is framed within the Human-Computer Interaction (HCI) area. The focus on UX, while useful, is unrealistic in everyday situations. This is because users generally interact with more than one service or product offered by a brand. Therefore, Customer eXperience (CX) is a relevant concept in many areas. It analyzes the perceptions and interactions of users with brands that offer products and services. Nowadays, Student eXperience (SX) has become a widely used term, with a great variety of approaches. One of them is from the CX point of view. In this way SX may be considered as a particular case of CX, where the customer is a student of a Higher Education Institution (HEI). Unfortunately, several aspects of the SX are usually omitted by scholars, mainly due to the high level of specialization of the solutions developed in the academic field. However, by not analyzing SX in a holistic way, studies may fall short. Culture is an aspect that is frequently underestimated when analyzing solutions regarding students' experiences. This is a problem considering the increasing number of exchange students at universities, and the culture shock entails for students, classmates, and academic staff. In this work we analyze the way in which cultural aspects are related to SX and its dimensions. For this, we analyze the concepts of culture and SX, the culture-communication and culture-perception relationship, and the culture role in education. In this way we expect to develop an SX model that explicitly incorporates cultural aspects. We expect this will help analyze SX in detail.

Keywords: Student eXperience · Customer eXperience · Culture · Cultural aspects · Higher education

1 Introduction

The Student eXperience (SX) concept is relatively new. It has been widely addressed in the literature, with dissimilar meanings, adapting to each case study. SX can be understood as a particular case of Customer eXperience (CX), where students are customers of

G. Meiselwitz (Ed.): HCII 2022, LNCS 13316, pp. 127–135, 2022.
https://doi.org/10.1007/978-3-031-05064-0_10

Higher Education Institutions (HEIs). Thus, when analyzed from a CX perspective, the SX refers to all the physical and emotional perceptions that a student or future student experiences in response to interaction with products, systems or services provided by a HEI. The SX includes student background elements, which are relevant to your relationship with the services and products offered by HEIs, and your relationship with peers and educational staff. Some of these elements are culture, gender, sexuality, physical disabilities, and students' perception of digital services, among others.

Among the most important student background elements are the cultural aspects. The cultural factors in the SX, from the CX approach, are little explored yet, despite the importance of the culture, especially for first year and exchange students. For this reason, we analyze the relationship between culture and SX. We believe that clarifying the SX-culture relationship, could offer a better theoretical basis that will allow the development of more complete SX models than those currently available. It should be noted that an SX model could be used to develop a wide variety of solutions aimed at evaluating and designing student experiences.

2 Background

2.1 Customer eXperience (CX)

To understand the SX concept it is necessary to talk about the CX. This, because in our view, the SX is a particular case of CX. Klaus & Maklan define CX as "the customer's cognitive and affective assessment of all direct and indirect encounters with the firm relating to their purchasing behavior" [1]. Lemon & Verhoef, have defined CX as "a multidimensional construct focusing on a customer's cognitive, emotional, behavioral, sensory, and social responses to a firm's offerings during the customer's entire purchase journey" [2]. A correct CX administration can lead to differential advantage for service organizations [3], for this reason nowadays the organizations invest more and more resources in analyzing the CX.

There are many specific tools that allow analyzing CX. One of these is the Customer Journey Map (CJM). This is "a visualization of the process that a person goes through in order to accomplish a goal". It includes points of contact and indicates the perceptions, thoughts, channels and emotions of users to create a narrative [5]. The concept touchpoints, meanwhile, refers to the combination of channel, device, and user task and emotions [4]. The student journey is relevant, as it has distinctive elements and student interactions are not merely referred to the classroom. It is important to understand the nature that underlies student interactions, as these may be related to the HCI area. This is because student interactions may be subject to the use of computerized products, systems or services.

It is important to correctly understand CX dimensions. Due to the complex nature of CX, there is no single, generally agreed CX model. Gentile et al. (2007) consider that CX has six dimensions: emotional, sensory, cognitive, pragmatic, lifestyle and relational [6]. The emotional component is related to the affective system, through the generation of affective states such as emotions, moods, and feelings. The sensory component is related to customer stimulation, which affects his senses. The cognitive component is related to customers' thinking and conscious mental processes. The pragmatic component is related to the practical act of doing something. The lifestyle component involves the values and beliefs of a customer, and the adoption of certain lifestyles and behaviors. The relational component involves the customer, social context, and interpersonal relationship.

Although for specific purposes it is possible to analyze the experience of customers at specific moments of their journey or focus on certain elements of it, it must be considered that CX implies a complete experience. Verhoef et al. (2009) consider that CX is "holistic in nature and involves the customer's cognitive, affective, emotional, social and physical responses to the retailer" [7]. Additionally, CX is an area unquestionably linked to consumers. As technology advances and changes the way consumers interact, it is expected that new CX models will be developed. A clear example of this is the development of the Mobile Application Customer eXperience (MACE) model, which focuses on analyzing customer interaction with mobile technology to ensure a quality experience [8]. In this way, to address new consumption scenarios, it is possible to develop new CX models.

An important point to mention is the complexity that suppose evaluate the CX. Considering that CX traditionally includes cognitive and emotional elements [9], a strong subjective component is evident. Different evaluation scales have traditionally been applied for specific purposes to analyze CX. An example is this is the Positive and Negative Affect Schedule or PANAS, used to assess emotional aspects of the customer [10]. There's also the SERVQUAL scale, which evaluates the service quality based on the customers perception and expectations with a product or service [11]. Similarly to CX, SX is very complex to assess given the subjectivity of perceptions and the ubiquity of student interactions. As with the CX, SX rely on different scales that are traditionally used to evaluate specific aspects.

2.2 Student eXperience (SX)

SX is a widely covered subject in literature. However, most studies do not agree a general SX definition. The SX is traditionally defined from pedagogical or academic approaches. Douglas et al. (2008) defined SX within the academic context as the "experience of higher education teaching, learning and assessment and their experience of other university ancillary service aspects" [12]. Obviously the SX does not refer to the merely academic field. Some definitions use terms such as "total student experience" to refer to experiences more diverse than those that occur strictly in the classroom [13, 14]. For the purposes of this article, we will use the concept proposed from the CX approach. According to Matus et al. (2021) "SX concept refers to all the physical and emotional perceptions that a student or future student experiences in response to interaction with products, systems or services provided by a HEI, and interactions with people related to the academic field, both inside and outside of academic spaces". The previous definition makes it clear that the student can be analyzed as a particular case of customer, in which HEIs provide products and services [15].

It has been observed that the SX is composed of 3 dimensions: i) Social Dimension, related to community relationship and institutional engagement; ii) Educational Dimension, related to Learning Engagement, Higher Education Quality, Learning Resources/Learning Environment, and Educational/Support Services; and iii) Personal

Dimension, related to Student Development and Outcomes, Student Feelings and Emotions, Environment Relationship, Student Thoughts, and students' Identity and Background. Within the personal dimension, there is the cultural factor. SX solutions generally do not analyze the cultural factor.

SX evaluation methods have been found to have specific applications. This implies that there are no SX assessment methods that contemplate the holistic experience of the student. In addition to not considering aspects of the student, such as culture, SX assessments are usually carried out at the end of the semesters or academic years. This is a problem, since by not analyzing intermediate points of the students' experiences, details of key experiences for the students are lost.

2.3 Culture

According to Hofstede (1991), culture refers to "the collective programming of the mind that distinguishes the members of one group or category of people from another" [16]. In this way, the implications that culture has for students are evident; culture can define the degree to which a student can adapt and integrate into an environment. This is important for freshmen, refugee, or exchange students. It is important to mention that the adaptation process can be observed early in the work of Lysgaard (1955) where he identifies a "U-shaped" curve to describe the process of cross-cultural transition. In this model, the curve begins in a good state of mind (honeymoon) and progresses in time towards a cultural crisis, before beginning an adjustment process [17]. Later, Gullahorn and Gullahorn (1963) extended the cross-cultural transition model to a "W-shaped" curve. This model contemplates the period of return of individuals to their places of origin. In this way, after a cultural adjustment in a foreign culture, individuals once again experience a cultural crisis and a process of adjustment when they return to their cultures [18]. We consider important the student cultural integration and re-integration process. This is because the student journey has a considerable temporal extension and throughout the student cycle there are interactions with their respective perceptions. To develop a hollistic SX model, it is necessary to consider, in addition to cultural factors, the processes of cultural adjustment (integration and re-integration).

A closely related concept to that of culture is the cultural identity. This refers to the subject's identification with a certain culture. In this way, culture is an unconscious attribute and cultural identity is a conscious one [16, 19]. Cultural identity could play an important role in SX, as it is related to the sense of belonging of the students. For this reason, although culture can define the degree to which a student can adapt to an environment, it is through cultural identity that the student can externalize their perceptions, feelings and emotions.

Hofstede's work is recognized as one of the most relevant regarding the influence and impact of culture on people [16, 20, 21]. Furthermore, his work has been used extensively to develop cross-cultural solutions. Hofstede has long developed a model in which he identifies six dimensions of national cultures: (i) Power distance, (ii) Uncertainty avoidance, (iii) Individualism/collectivism, (iv) Masculinity/Femininity, (v) Long/short term orientation and (vi) Indulgence/restraint. We believe that these dimensions, which have already been used to develop culturally focused solutions, can also be used to develop an SX model.

3 The Role of Culture in SX

The importance of cultural aspects for students is undeniable. This is not only for the academic field. Even so, the impact that cultural factors have on the lives of exchange or immigrant students may have an impact on their learning outcome and affective states. Todd (1994) pointed out some factors that can influence the integration or segregation of culturally dissimilar populations. In this way, elements such as the structures of family nuclei in the host country have a high impact on cultural assimilation [22]. This is an important aspect when proposing solutions with a cultural approach. Evidently it is almost impossible to propose a SX model that manages to correct all the problems of students caused by cultural asymmetries.

Another limitation of our research, related to the aforementioned point, lies in the social dimension of SX. It is not feasible to delve into the ways in which students' satisfaction with a social, spontaneous and personal process could be improved. Even so, this is not an impediment to point out the importance that technologies have today to facilitate and enable the social interaction of students.

It is possible to contribute to the development of an SX model based on cultural related works. These works provide valuable information on the culture-communication relationship [23], culture-perception, and culture-education, among others.

3.1 Culture and Communication

When we refer to culture and communication, it is common to speak of intercultural and cross-cultural communication. Although some scholars mention that intercultural communication is one form of cross-cultural communication, others defend that those are two completely different concepts. Gudykunst defines cross-cultural communication as the comparison of communication across cultures. Also, defines intercultural communication as the communication between people from different cultures [24]. In this way, in order to correctly analyze intercultural communication, it is necessary to understand cross-cultural communication. For his part, Ma (2004) in his work extends Wittgenstein's language-game of the builders. As a result of this work, she concludes that intercultural and cross-cultural communication are not far from each other concepts [25].

The relationship between communication and culture can be seen in technological solutions. Rau et al. (2009) investigated the effects of culture and the communication styles in relation to people's acceptance of the recommendations given by robots. Their results indicated a clear difference between groups of people, attributed to cultural differences regarding their language. This certainly shows the importance of culture in HCI solutions; in the digital age the way in which information is presented has a great impact on users [26]. We consider language a crucial element when developing an SX model taking into consideration that communication between subjects is carried out across all SX dimensions.

A remarkable element in terms of the cultural differences between subjects are the communicational contexts [27]. According to Dozier et al. (1998) communication context refers to "(...) the environment and circumstances surrounding the message itself, including history, knowledge, use of pauses and silences, assumptions about the other person's values, and so forth" [28]. In this way, cultures can be differentiated in terms of high or low context depending on the economy and dynamics of their language [29]. The SX personal dimension includes the students' relationship with their environment. With this information, the development of an efficient SX model must take inherent aspects of the communicational context into consideration. This is evident considering that students relate to their HEIs not only through their courses, but using support services, library, financial services, among others.

3.2 Culture and Perception

In view of a series of research based on the Hofstede works it is evident that cultural aspects have an impact on users' perception about technology, innovation adoption and use. Additionally, for the purposes of these articles, particular models have been used to relate technology systems/products attributes with the perception of the users. Hassan and Wood (2020) have investigated the influence of country culture in relation to the adoption of mobile banking systems. For this they focused on users from Egyptian and US cultures [30]. In their study is of special interest the use of the Technology Acceptance Model (TAM) [31] to analyze the technology innovation adoption and use of the users under analysis. Their results show that the country culture may influence user perceptions toward usage of innovative technological products or services. Similarly, Mohammed and Tejay (2017) analyzed the impact of users' perceptions and concerns in relation to e-commerce services, this with respect to culture [32]. In this work, the impact of cultural factors regarding the adoption of e-commerce technology is evidenced.

It is important to mention that based on what was stated by Parasuraman et al. (1985) [33] the perceived quality of a service or a product can be explained with the relationship between users' expectations and perceptions. In view of the clear relationship that exists between the culture of a certain user and their perception of a technological product or service, it is clear that cultural aspects could determine the perceived quality.

3.3 Culture and Education

The impact of cultural aspects related to technology in education can be evidenced in a wide range of studies. This can be observed in the literature, especially in articles referring to e-learning, distance learning, and mobile learning [34], and the role of cultural aspects in the adoption of technology. In this way, technology as a tool can help in educational processes, and cultural aspects determine the degree to which students are able to take advantage of such technology and adopt/accept it [30].

Although most of the research on technology and culture uses the cultural dimensions proposed by Hofstede, some researchers have added additional factors. Hamidi and Chavoshi (2018), for example, have proposed the factor "culture of using applications" or "culture of using" in their study [35]. This concept refers to the cultural elements that facilitate or hinder the mobile learning of students. This shows how theoretical models regarding culture and technology scale as technology advances.

It is evident in view of the existence of the educational dimension of SX [15] that the analysis of the culture-technology-education relationship is imperative to develop a holistic SX model.

4   Discussion

The SX dimensions are made up of the social, educational, and personal dimensions. The development of solutions regarding the social dimension should be explored further. This considers the ubiquity, variety and particularity of social interactions, which vary from student to student. Having clarified this, we will analyze the opportunities to improve the SX by analyzing the case of each dimension.

We believe that's great potential in analyzing the educational dimension. This takes the variety of technological solutions that facilitate and/or allow education into consideration. The efficient use and adoption of technology, we know, depends partially on cultural aspects. The use of technology can enable the education of students with highly limited physical disabilities or students in remote areas. Additionally, the design and language used in educational applications and platforms certainly influence student satisfaction.

The personal dimension is where the student's culture is explicitly manifested. This dimension lies in the student-environment relationship, student emotions and student identity. The development of solutions in this dimension may include the use of affective computing and non-invasive environment interventions. One way to improve the student experience, considering their cultural background, is the use of cross-cultural design in terms of developing solutions for students.

Communication is a widely explored element in terms of user culture [26–28]. This is an important element to develop solutions for students, since it is evident that communication is present transversely in the 3 dimensions of the SX. We find it necessary when developing an effective SX model to consider the importance of the form and medium through which students communicate. It is important to mention that the average student communicates throughout their student period with teachers, classmates, technical personnel, educational and support services, and digital applications, among others.

We found it feasible to use widely used and validated cultural dimensions, such as the Hofstede's model, as a basis for including cultural aspects to our SX model. The extension of the model will be done considering the special characteristics of the student as a consumer, such as special needs, spaces for interaction, and common communication channels.

5   Conclusion

Cultural aspects influence the way in which users perceive and interact with a product, system or service. We have observed that cultural factors determine the willingness to accept a certain technology. Also, we have seen how a model of cultural dimensions has been extended to analyze a specific case of mobile technology use by specific users. This highlights the feasibility of expanding existing models to meet the needs and requirements of specific users.

Additionally, we observe how communication processes are carried out, transversely, in all dimensions of the SX. Also, we observe that there are subtle differences in communication processes between subjects based on their culture. This certainly provides us with enough evidence to analyze in depth the communicative aspect in the design of a holistic SX model.

Based on the dimensions and factors identified in previous studies, and considering the works present nowadays in the literature, we will develop a SX model that incorporates cultural elements. To achieve this, we consider the use of widely acknowledged and validated cultural models feasible to extend our SX model. Also, its development must be supported by a broader review of the literature on culture and communication.

With a holistic SX model it will be possible to develop a wider range of solutions, such as usability heuristics, design guides, questionnaires, and evaluation scales. This model will allow to adequately analyze the perceptions and interactions of the students considering essential elements of their context and environment, such as culture, technology, services, emotions. To develop that model its necessary in first place to consider the dimensions and factors that make up the SX. Second, its necessary to consider the elements analyzed in previous sections, that is, the culture-communication & culture-perception relationship, and the culture role in education. Third, use a widely validated cultural model as reference, which can be extended and particularized to the student case of study. Finally, in view of technological progress and the way in which users interact with modern products and systems, we consider it necessary to analyze the technological solutions offered to students. This is especially important in cases where technological products or systems are directly or indirectly related to customers cultural aspects, as could be seen in the examples presented in this article.

References

1. Klaus, P., Maklan, S.: Towards a better measure of customer experience. Int. J. Market Res. **55**(2), 227–246 (2013)
2. Lemon, K.N., Verhoef, P.C.: Understanding customer experience throughout the customer journey. J. Mark. **80**, 69–96 (2016)
3. Sujata, J.: Customer experience management: an exploratory study on the parameters affecting customer experience for cellular mobile services of a telecom company. Procedia Soc. Behav. Sci. **133**, 392–399 (2014)
4. Nielsen Norman Group: Channels Devices Touchpoints. https://www.nngroup.com/articles/channels-devices-touchpoints/. Accessed 02 Dec 2021
5. Nielsen Norman Group: Journey Mapping 101. https://www.nngroup.com/articles/journey-mapping-101/. Accessed 21 Jan 2022
6. Gentile, C., Spiller, N., Noci, G.: How to sustain the customer experience: an overview of experience components that co-create value with the customer. Eur. Manage. J. **25**, 395–410 (2007)
7. Verhoef, P.C., Lemon, K.N., Parasuraman, A., Roggeveen, A., Tsiros, M., Schlesinger, L.A.: Customer experience creation: determinants, dynamics and management strategies. J. Retail. **85**(1), 31–41 (2009)
8. McLean, G., Al-Nabhani, K., Wilson, A.: Developing a mobile applications customer experience model (MACE)-implications for retailers. J. Bus. Res. **85**, 325–336 (2018)
9. Edvardsson, B.: Service quality: beyond cognitive assessment. Manage. Serv. Qual. Int. J. **15**(2), 127–131 (2005)
10. Watson, D., Clark, L.A., Tellegen, A.: Development and validation of brief measures of positive and negative affect: the PANAS scales. J. Pers. Soc. Psychol. **54**(6), 1063–1070 (1988)
11. Parasuraman, A., Zeithaml, V.A., Berry, L.L.: Servqual: a multiple-item scale for measuring consumer perceptions of service quality. J. Retail. **64**, 12–40 (1988)

12. Douglas, J., McClelland, R., Davies, J.: The development of a conceptual model of student satisfaction with their experience in higher education. Qual. Assur. Educ. **16**, 19–35 (2008)
13. Harvey, L., Knight, P.T.: Transforming Higher Education. Society for Research into Higher Education. Open University Press, London (1996)
14. Arambewela, R., Maringe, F.: Mind the gap: staff and postgraduate perceptions of student experience in higher education. High. Educ. Rev. **44**, 63–83 (2012)
15. Matus, N., Rusu, C., Cano, S.: Student eXperience: a systematic literature review. Appl. Sci. **11**(20), 9543 (2021)
16. Hofstede, G.: Cultures and Organization: Software of the Mind. McGraw-Hill, New York (1991)
17. Lysgaard, S.: Adjustment in a foreign society: Norwegian fulbright grantees visiting the United States. Int. Soc. Sci. Bull. **7**, 45–51 (1955)
18. Gullahorn, J.T., Gullahorn, J.E.: An extension of the U-curve hypothesis. J. Soc. Sci. **19**(3), 33–47 (1963)
19. Collier, M.J., Thomas, M.: Cultural identity: an interpretive perspective. Int. Intercult. Commun. Annu. **12**, 99–120 (1988)
20. Hofstede, G.: Culture's Consequences: Comparing Values, Behaviours, Institutions, and Organizations Across Nations, 2nd edn. Sage, London (1980)
21. Hofstede, G.: Dimensions of Culture, pp. 159–181 (1980)
22. Todd, E.: Le Destin des immigrés: Assimilation et ségrégation dans les démocraties occidentales. Seuil, France (1994)
23. Ito, A.: A Study of Location-Based Audio Guide System Promoting Cultural Understanding in Japan. Doctoral dissertation, Keio University, Tokyo, Japan (2018)
24. Gudykunst, W.B.: Cross-Cultural and Intercultural Communication. Sage, California (2003)
25. Ma, L.: Is There an Essential Difference between Intercultural and Intracultural Communication? J. Intercult. Commun. **6**, 1404–1634 (2004)
26. Rau, P., Li, Y., Li, D.: Effects of communication style and culture on ability to accept recommendations from robots. Comput. Hum. Behav. **25**(2), 587–595 (2009)
27. Hall, E.T.: Understanding Cultural Differences. Intercultural Press, Boston (1990)
28. Dozier, J.B., Husted, B.W., Mcmahon, J.T.: Need for approval in low-context and high-context cultures: a communications approach to cross-cultural ethics. Teach. Bus. Ethics **2**(2), 111–125 (1998). https://doi.org/10.1023/A:1009733101664
29. Hall, E.T.: Beyond Culture, 1st edn. Anchor, New York (1976)
30. Hassan, H.E., Wood, V.R.: Does country culture influence consumers' perceptions toward mobile banking? A comparison between Egypt and the United States. Telematics Inf. **46**(2), 101312 (2020)
31. Davis, F.D.: Perceived usefulness, perceived ease of use, and user acceptance of information technology. MIS Q. **13**(3), 319–340 (1989)
32. Mohammed, Z.A., Tejay, G.P.: Examining privacy concerns and ecommerce adoption in developing countries: the impact of culture in shaping individuals' perceptions toward technology. Comput. Secur. **67**, 254–265 (2017)
33. Parasuraman, A., Zeithaml, V.A., Berry, L.L.: A conceptual model of service quality and its implications for future research. J. Mark. **49**(4), 41–50 (1985)
34. Ariffin, S.A.: Mobile learning in the institution of higher learning for Malaysia students: culture Perspectives. Int. J. Adv. Sci. Eng. Inf. Technol. **1**(3), 283–288 (2011)
35. Hamidi, H., Chavoshi, A.: Analysis of the essential factors for the adoption of mobile learning in higher education: a case study of students of the university of technology. Telematics Inf. **35**(4), 1053–1070 (2018)

Enhancing Concept Anchoring Through Social Aspects and Gaming Activities

Marie J. Myers[✉]

Queen's University, Kingston, ON K7L 3Y7, Canada
myersmj@queensu.ca

Abstract. As equity is one of the fundamental criteria in the commitment to students at my university, when courses had to be taught on-line, new aspects had to be taken under scrutiny as regards the human-machine interface.

Promoting socialization is important for online activities. Not only was it crucial to ensure that all students could have access to all the materials, but more importantly, that they found contents to engage with in groups, that sparked their interests in order to be motivated [1], but that they also had a choice in navigating across different resources corresponding to personal styles to ensure a deep anchoring of concepts and gaming aspects were included where relevant.

Therefore, the course was devised around group work, plus individual support was provided by the instructor along the process.

The method used was qualitative [2] and based on the analysis of instructor's teaching and classroom observation notes. The courses consisted of professional pre-service courses for teachers of French. All students were used to the technology.

Results show that as the results on all assignments were superior the way activities were designed had been beneficial. The added listings of on-line resources including many varied types, and the additional internet surfing possibilities, enhanced overall satisfaction and learning. Moreover, the addition of a gaming approach to content learning improved engagement.

There was typically less directionality, although direction was given with choices always included. More intentionality was expected on students' part. Some areas of concern were connected to social aspects.

Keywords: Enhanced learning · Gains through socialization in breakout rooms · Impact of gaming aspects

1 Background

In the context of teacher education, students are new to professional learning having experienced academic learning situations thus far. To bridge the gap, in a flipped pedagogy approach, the directions initially given to students were to prepare contents for class discussions, as a means to explore contents along their own ways of being and doing, and then follow-up with reinforcement both, through group discussions, and whole class discussions on the questions remaining.

© The Author(s), under exclusive license to Springer Nature Switzerland AG 2022
G. Meiselwitz (Ed.): HCII 2022, LNCS 13316, pp. 136–146, 2022.
https://doi.org/10.1007/978-3-031-05064-0_11

The problem centers around bringing students in teacher training directly into capacity building as these young people often come somewhat unprepared or unaware of what it entails to get organized in order to carry through a project, like a detailed lesson plan or a larger unit plan. Without in-person contact, this has been increasingly challenging as many aspire at being fast-tracked through their professional program after having already spent several years at university.

1.1 Classroom Communication

Research on on-line teaching suggests added communication problems, shallowness in interactions, lack of engagement, in addition to technological difficulties [3–5]. In addition to that, the hidden sides of communication are the most challenging as complex activity takes place. Nevertheless, we are able to manage. In other research theories [6] it is suggested that perceptual, cognitive and motor activities come together when we concentrate on something while we make inferences around what we think are relevant invisible facets. Other researchers suggest that we develop a predictive ability [7, 8].

Having to express what one thinks is necessary to verify one's thoughts. Moreover, our thoughts are solidified in the context of our interactions with others.

Complex factors come into play during interaction. The question is about how we can tell which element influences which and how [9]. During on-line interactions more complexity comes into play and we may miss the whole picture with our attention to detail. It is of utmost importance that course instructors ensure that important contents are remembered.

A lack of cultural knowledge can cause distortions in interpreting [10]. The author tried to identify the problem by drawing up a list of metaphors of the self. These include a biological component, and others including, contextual, conventional and poetic components. By being aware of these one should be well positioned in relation to a judgment to be made.

The biological component relates to our physical aspects and mental traits as these dictate our behavior to some extent. The contextual component refers to environmental influences on us. These can impact our habits, our working conditions, and our responses to certain stimuli. The conventional component includes everything about culture, whatever formed us. In the multicultural context in which we are in Canada, it is necessary to question the various cultural influences surrounding conventions as these would be multifarious. For the poetic component the author refers to our creativity. The perspectives from which we approach issues can also be explained by the greater or lesser degree of creativity we have.

There should also be an openness to the multiplicity of possible cultural clues we are encountering. In addition, higher psychological processes have to be taken into account [11] when considering university courses at a professional development level. However, when teaching on-line, instructors are at a disadvantage due to the lack of proximity to students and the inability to glance across the whole group to identify clues. According to research [12], there is a range of aspects that influence us in each situation. The questions examined relate to eye movement, the importance attached to time, positioning, colors, noise and silence, and gestures.

Therefore, in line with equitable practice and in fairness for all, one or several models of expected outcomes for assignments were given in order to let students judge the distance between their working draft and the expected model and allow them to fill in the learning gap with the instructor's help.

In taking notes on student activity a displacement of interest is clearly happening based on the instructor envisioning the student's potential activity. As well, whatever gaps were anticipated by the instructor, as needing to be filled, which was indicative of remedial work to be prepared, which in turn allowed to expand upon didactic possibilities [13]. There are often very heavy ritualized elements in some conversations, yet there needed to be fluidity in the students' exchanges [14].

It was crucial that their understanding was articulate or else they could not grasp the contents. Thus students had to unpack their thoughts that could no longer remain 'as islands in the sea of [their] unformulated practical grasp on the world' [15:308].

What also had to be kept in mind was the fact that we frame our representations in an attempt at reducing complexity [16].

This researcher [17] also suggests taking into account socio-pragmatic and pragma-linguistic aspects in intercultural trans-linguistic language use. The idea to improve communication through a socio-semiotic approach [18] also has a lot of merit. However, the challenge had been to make working groups meeting on-line only, into well-functioning interactional communities, given the many limiting factors mentioned above.

1.2 The Problem

With suddenly mandated on-line teaching, instructors are especially looking for ways to improve on-line communication. In multicultural contexts like in Canada the inability to actually be in physical contact poses additional difficulties when one is concerned with inclusion. Problematic issues pointed to the need for further awareness-raising in interactions intended to enhance learning.

In multicultural contexts, many different features have to be taken into our conceptualization as noted above, providing added richness. As far as the instructor was concerned, with the way the course was designed the stage seemed to have been set for rich discussions to take place and deep learning to occur with improved students' intake and better possibilities for deeper conceptualization.

2 Method

2.1 Site

The observation notes were taken during class meetings at a Faculty of Education in central Ontario. Teachers in Canada, typically have to earn a university degree before entering the professional program for their teaching specialization. The students have to have two specialties, with a first subject in the area of their major and a second one, as a minor with at least three university courses in the subject. They are then required to take a full year course in curriculum in addition to other courses. In this case, the course under scrutiny was the French as a second language curriculum course.

2.2 Participants

The number of participants in the classes on which notes were taken was around 50, with some not always present when there were connection issues. The breakout rooms had on average five students per group, with fewer students at times due to absenteeism.

All students were familiar with the technology also presenting work through the share screen feature, using the whiteboard and moving in and out of breakout rooms.

In such courses students are usually between 24 and 27 years old with a few more mature students and are in their fifth or sixth year at university and therefore acculturated to academic settings. Among this population, for some of them French was the first subject and the second subject for the others. However, both groups will obtain the same teaching certificate from the Ministry of Education although their levels of proficiency in French vary.

Many of these students are new to education although we also have a consecutive program that allows them to take a few education courses while they pursue their bachelor's studies. They display different types of attitudes toward the program due to a number of factors, although they are overall very good students. Some are unprepared or unwilling to explore further thinking that they already are knowledgeable in the area.

2.3 The Instructor

In this case the instructor was very qualified in the subject area with over 20 years of experience teaching this type of course, always trying to adapt and improve based on leading edge information and practical considerations. On-line teaching was new and required a lot of additional work, reconversions and effort. Instructors are overall pretty well left to their own devices and had to learn how to use the technology on their own besides taking into consideration instructions provided by zoom. The on-line teaching situation was challenging for the instructor, yet it brought about renewed interest, creative ways to design the course, although the flipped classroom model had been adopted earlier, before on-line teaching was mandated.

2.4 Note Taking

As is common practice for instructors, notes are taken during class with the intention to support student learning make accommodations for further learning, keep track of developments and so forth. Teaching notes were also available for the instructional period and annotated as the course developed, either during or after class.

The observational notes analyzed in this study were taken during breakout room observations. Based on the flipped classroom model, students were assigned a great number of resources to unpack before class, while class meetings were devoted to the consolidation of items studied namely through group activities and whole class discussion. We only looked at breakout room discussions here.

The activities devised for this purpose were characterized by very active interactions.

As stated earlier the instructor made an effort to include a socializing aspect in group work. Questions surrounding Krashen's affective filter theory, led to students' brainstorming and exchanging thoughts and feelings on their own learning experiences.

Discussions on Socio-Economic-Status allowed to question ways of including all students on a field trip and whether or not the field trip should only be a virtual visit. 'Four Corners' activities prompted students to delve deeper into their understanding and beliefs about various theoretical tenets, inviting them to discuss them and position themselves as to whether they agreed, somewhat agreed, disagreed or totally disagreed and then in turn justify their positioning under the chosen heading. As well, for instance students were required to connect concepts under scrutiny to their own personal and or classroom experiences. In addition, students were given ample time so that each group member had time to contribute.

Wherever feasible, a gaming aspect was directing the whole activity or was tagged on the breakout room tasks. For instance, a tic-tac-toe competition was held while students answered a series of questions based on content that was to be studied, with each good answer giving the team a turn. For this game students have to line up three consecutive crossed or circles to be winning, these have to be within the confines of nine spaces in any direction. Filling a grid under the given headings requiring ten entries within a time limit for points, finding a concept with less than twenty questions, using charades to review a definition, coming up with the most innovative design of an emblem representing their teaching beliefs by collaborating using the whiteboard feature, are all examples of the types of gaming enhancements.

2.5 Methodological Approach

As we were interested in obtaining as much detail as possible and as we only could analyze the notes found in the instructor's journal, it was clear that a qualitative approach was most suitable [2]. Moreover, we wanted to uncover the type of learning that took place, therefore a phenomenological approach to looking at the notes was deemed appropriate. Phenomenology is said to be an approach to research that seeks to describe the essence of a phenomenon by exploring it from the perspective of those who have experienced it [19]. This was recorded in the instructor's notes. We were trying to understand what was experienced and how it was experienced as we tried to understand the meaning of those experiences. We adopted the hermeneutic approach to phenomenology which is interpretive. Researchers say that by examining an experience as it is subjectively lived, new meanings and appreciations can be developed to inform, or even re-orient, how we understand that experience. This required the researcher to suspend personal attitudes, beliefs, and suppositions in order to focus on the participants' experience of the phenomenon and identify the essences of the phenomenon. The idea was to identify what was going on as perceived by the researcher's consciousness, looking at what was given directly to the researcher's intuition based on the notes.

Data were analyzed after two readings, with the first one to uncover emerging themes and then with the second reading to regroup around major themes.

We looked for characteristics of successful exchanges, including a variety of factors based on the respect and awareness of persons' developmental needs, including linguistic, academic, cognitive, emotional, social and physical requiring consideration in the negotiation of persons' socio-cultural identities [20].

In group work students needed to develop a certain combination of skills, expertise and commitment in order to be successful. They needed to be able to recognize the patterns in their field of practice [21]. In addition to discussions, students also needed to complete practical assignments. According to research [22:136] to grasp a lot of complexity a system makes a selection and the process requires a reduction of complexity. Keeping these notions in mind, it was important to see if the design of learning units got and held students' interest and encouraged them to take advantage of the richness of their backgrounds to help them bridge new knowledge for the duration of the course [1]. In the process of sorting through all the complexity however, students had to make appropriate selections.

The limitations to the methodological approach are due to the on-line teaching delivery, which required more preparation, plus, was a new mode of delivery for these types of classes that often require a more hands-on approach.

This added complexity. Hence, with these on-line interactions one could only get sporadic views of what information could be gleaned because of interrupted breakout room contacts, of the instructor with the groups, which could lead to more possibilities for misunderstandings. In addition, the instructor is not bias free, as everyone's attitude to the world is encrypted in the way we carry ourselves, and therefore the notes were based on knowledge that could only be partial or truncated due to the circumstances and may have caused disruptions in what we know about what is right and fitting under normal circumstances.

3 Findings

What emerged from the results was that the assessment of handed-in students' work yielded superior results, which supports the fact that the approaches used with a concentration on socializing aspects and parameters around gaming factors, attached to a significant number of activities, were effective at deepening the learning of concepts to be mastered in the courses.

Themes uncovered are reported below around a better anchoring of knowledge and divided between social aspects and gaming strategies.

Results indicate that even with a model given, some students had trouble in figuring out tasks. The underlying reasons include among others the switch from an academic program to professional training. Some of these students experiencing major difficulties managed to complete the program successfully with on-going support from the instructor.

Breakout room discussions were very rich and followed by excellent whole class interactions. When it was noticed initially, that some students remained a little distant more aspects to encourage socializing were included, as for instance having groups connect outside of class through their preferred social media platform for class preparation, and devising ways to get them to open up more by including questions about their professional and life experiences in their breakout room assignments. As well to support more engagement, gaming aspects were included where feasible to allow the students to delve more readily into the complex issues.

There were many nuances of activity behind a number of success stories. As mentioned before, among the results we identified the positive influences of social aspects and also the increase in interest through the gaming aspect that impacted on student work. Therefore, we separated the two categories of findings although some aspects of gaming were also connected to the affective domain.

3.1 Enhanced Anchoring of Concepts Through Social Aspects

We identified how through group interactions, transactions took place, allowing transitioning across various questions and assignments as students came to understanding involving their different social systems despite only through on-line access to one another. These students did not start on 'common ground' [23], however it appears that through articulating diverse factors, they were in a sense finding common ground across the materials prepared for class, from sometimes a closed mind-set to a productive discussion [24]. In this context of inclusive teaching, multifarious skills and ways of being came into play and this constituted a great richness. Some unusual new ideas were brought forth, adding crucial information for education. These sometimes emerged from more relaxed conversations.

Collaboration. The Ministry of Education promotes collaboration among teachers as a useful strategy for support in both outcome-related aspects of their work but also to provide a system for social connectivity. As such, this measure could prevent teacher burn-out. Hence a number of assignments for the course were designed to require collaboration. Collaboration was explained and compared to cooperation. Breakout room observations indicate that few of the student groups truly collaborated although some students in the groups did. They basically did not stay within the parameters of collaboration with the idea of all coming together for the final product. Instead there was a back and forth between collaboration and cooperation. Some produced a part of the assignment to be fitted in to the final product instead of them all working together to complete the product. Only one group really collaborated but then a leader had them collaborate and oversaw the overall result although this leader did not influence the product through input, only by channeling the others' contributions. All their effort however showed a good understanding of the underlying concepts involved for the completion of assignments.

Cooperation. These students were obviously used to cooperate and they were quite efficient at demonstrating it. The carried out class presentation showed their level of cooperation and their understanding of course contents related to the activities.

Sharing Results of Autonomous Enquiry. As these students were new to the pre-service program when directed to find their own resources, in addition to instructor provided materials, in order to enrich their learning and make contents more accessible to their own learning styles and preferences, a few discrepancies were noticed. Autonomous search for their own resources also implied self-regulation. They were to identify the gaps between instructor recommended materials and finding their own 'digestible' resources around the class topic for discussion. One student was especially instrumental at doing this, was able to identify what was needed for their own learning style. In this case, the instructor placed the links to the resources into the chat room for all students to access for improved learning. Most students had accessed the English versions of the French materials they were required to read ahead of class. This demonstrated their effort to understand the materials and clearly the positive impact of multi-languaging. They shared these accesses to information in their own group platform.

Leadership Aspect Uncovered. At the beginning of breakout room meetings, to ease into group coordination, there was in each group a spontaneous recapping of the outlines of the task-at-hand. This way the groups came together, with one student taking the lead, as was evidenced in two groups, and co-directionality in four groups when two students filled the gaps for the others or they worked as an effective team, which was the case for the remaining four groups. In the latter case, they worked as a team to dissect the task and made it attainable by all in order to complete it.

Inquisitiveness. This feature centered round social aspects not only as the students explored many other resources through a research orientation but also in sharing these findings with others in their groups and with the whole class during full class discussions. This aspect greatly eased their way to mastering contents through their social ease with one another. This happened mostly at the beginning of the instructor joining breakout rooms, with more formality happening shortly after. If the resources added were mostly reflecting good choices, however three times, they were beside the point. The students left the second language learning context, as for instance when looking for competences, not just 'communicative competence', when extending backward design to more than unit planning and when scaffolding was only applied to assessment by a few groups instead of all aspects of teaching.

Risk Taking. In one case, learning was demonstrated by a student recording a video of her class presentation ahead of time, in order to keep a smooth social climate, and play a responsible part for her group because she was unsure she could be present the day of the presentation. Through the video, frozen in time, no amendments could be made at the last minute, although when other students' groups presented they were able to make slight adjustments after having observed what previous groups did. All students were supportive.

Connectivity. The ease they felt connecting to their breakout room groups, also impacted their learning as they were more relaxed. A definite advantage was that all students were familiar with the technology, as well since they were all in their 5th or 6th year at university they were also familiar with academic culture. Many of them had had contacts in previous years but many were new to the university. As well, they had different possibilities for internet connections. Some of them lived in the countryside, away from easy connection to internet and had to take their cars closer to a city to get connections. So on video, these students were in their car and in one case with also a baby in an adjacent seat. One student had difficulties with their computer and faded in and out and often had to connect through their phone. In several instances students' videos showed them on their bed while connected to their breakout room group, although they turned off their video during whole class discussions. They were all supporting one another.

Choice. The groups were given choices of topics for their group assignments and this led to very fruitful discussions as they had to come to a consensus and this helped the students get closer. Some of them however were unfamiliar with having to take on more responsibilities, having a choice for assignments, and also with the categories for grading being comprehensibility, quality, quantity, originality and creativity. These categories were intended for more inclusivity, which worked quite well given the very varied backgrounds of the students. They consulted each other especially to include creative aspects. In addition, having the possibility to get feedback on assignments before been graded certainly helped make groups more cohesive and they worked together for success. Nevertheless, a few competitive students were unhappy that they could not be the only ones to shine.

3.2 Gains Through the Gaming Aspect

Disruptions. With an added gaming feature to activities, students had to reconsider how to go about completing the assigned work. According to researchers in cognition, displacing the center of attention requires more concentration and a disruption that stimulates activity [7, 25–29]. This is particularly useful to attract the attention of new generations used to rapid eye movement, in order to get them to focus on something.

Competitiveness. Emulation was brought about through the competitive aspects attached to gaming and since these playful aspects were all centered around better mastery of course content and since no assessment was involved, this was utmost beneficial to the students' progress.

Innovation. In a certain sense, using innovative gaming ideas corresponded to a sort of transgression when compared to the regular academic functioning of courses. According to research [30] transgressions from the basic functioning students were used to, also increased their interest and motivation, which in turn helped enhance learning outcomes or at least helped them all to remain engaged until completion of the activity.

Contrasts. In line with equity and diversity, including contrasts and different ways of adjusting contents through gaming as well as allowing for students' success through creativity, appeared to have enabled students to internalize chunks of the content, either new or reviewed, through a different way of consolidating information. This was also a more inclusive way in terms of cultural differences [31].

4 Conclusion and Limitations

Gaming enhanced interest across the diverse students' socio-cultural backgrounds. Group work, with special attention given to social aspects, made discussions more lively and as assignments had to be completed, this in turn created deeper learning. Nevertheless, there were also different paths that had to be aligned. According to researchers, knowledge and cultural aspects allow for reflexive co-orientation [32, 33]. Sufficient similarity in their background knowledge allowed discussions based on assumed similar parameters.

Communication was freer during gaming versus regular class problem solving activities and gaming activities facilitated social connections.

There are several limitations to account for in this study. First of all, the instructor's observation notes did not include every aspect that could have come under scrutiny had there been a video available. However, even videos of breakout room observations would not have allowed to get the full picture due to limited access to the different breakout rooms during class time. Perhaps if one student in each breakout room was asked to record their session with a phone, all contents could have been examined, except that at the same time perhaps students would not have felt as free to communicate with one another due to being recorded. Despite these aspects, it is crucial to realize that instructor's notes were on the most salient aspects and therefore all the important data would have been contained in those notes.

Because of our analysis of observation notes, we were unable to connect specific factors to specific students' backgrounds, which could have influenced certain actions and reactions. Nevertheless since we were mainly interested in overall outcomes and based on the fact that thanks to group work students supported one another, in the end they all benefitted as is evidenced by superior outcomes on their graded assignments. In addition, we were not looking at individual strengths or weaknesses.

References

1. Renninger, K.A., Hidi, S.E.: The Power of Interest for Motivation and Engagement. Routledge, New York (2015). https://doi.org/10.4324/9781315771045
2. Creswell, J.W., Poth, C.N.: Qualitative Inquiry and Research Design. SAGE Publishing, Thousand Oaks (2017)
3. Caine, G., Caine, R.N.: The learning community as a foundation for developing teacher leaders (2000). https://doi.org/10.1177/019263650008461603l. Accessed 07 Feb 2022
4. Rogalsky, M.: Maintain radio silence: listening to the gaps between the words 2000–2003. Digit. Creativity 14(2), 115–118 (2003)
5. Kebritchi, M., Lipschuetz, A., Santiague, L.: Issues and challenges for teaching successful online courses in higher education: a literature review. J. Educ. Technol. Syst. 46(1), 4–29 (2017)
6. Cahan, D.: Hermann Ludwig von Helmholtz and the Foundations of Nineteen Century Science. University of California Press, Los Angeles (1993)
7. Biederman, I.: Visual object recognition. In: Kosslyn, S.M., Osherson, D.N. (eds.) Visual Cognition: An Invitation to Cognitive Science, pp. 121–165. The MIT Press, Cambridge (1995)
8. Lowe, D.G.: Probability theory as an alternative to complexity. Behav. Brain Sci. 13, 423–469 (1990)
9. Voinov, A.: Understanding and communicating sustainability: global versus regional perspectives. Environ. Dev. Sustain. 10(4), 487–501 (2007)
10. DeGramont, P.: Language and the Distortion of Meaning. New York University Press, New York (1990)
11. Vygotsky, L.S.: Mind in Society: The Development of Higher Psychological Processes. Harvard University Press, Cambridge (1978)
12. Borden, G.A.: Cultural Orientation: An Approach to Understanding Intercultural Communication. Prentice Hall, Hoboken (1991)
13. Dessus, P.: Quels sont les soubassements cognitifs de l'activite d'enseignement. Revue Internationale des Sciences de l'Education 14, 111–124 (2005)
14. Bourdieu, P.: Le sens pratique. Minuit, Paris (1980)

15. Taylor, C.: The dialogic self. In: Hiley, D., Bohman, J., Shusterman, R. (eds.) The Interpretive Turn. Cornell University Press, Ithaca and London (1994)
16. Luhmann, N.: Gesellzschaftstruktur und Semantik: Studien zur Wissensociologie der modernen Gesellschaft. Suhrkamp, Frankfurt (1980)
17. Myers, M.J.: Modalites d'apprentissage d'une langue seconde, DeBoeck Duculot, Bruxelles Paris (2004)
18. Halliday, M.A.K.: An Introduction to Functional Grammar, 1st edn. Edward Arnold, London (1985)
19. Gubrium, J.F., Holstein, J.A.: Analyzing interpretive practice. In: Denzin, N.K., Lincoln, Y.S. (eds.) Handbook of Qualitative Research, 2nd edn., pp. 487–508. Sage, Thousand Oaks (2000)
20. Duff, P.A., Uchida, Y.: The negotiation of teachers' sociocultural identities and practices in postsecondary EFL classrooms. TESOL Q. 31(3), 451–486 (1997)
21. Barton, D., Tusting, K.: Beyond Communities of Practice. Language, Power and Social Context. Cambridge University Press, Cambridge (2009)
22. Luhmann, N.: Social Systems, translated by John Bednarz. Stanford University Press, Stanford (1995)
23. Olson, D.R.: Psychological Theory and Educational Reform: How Schools Remake Mind and Society. Cambridge University Press, Cambridge (2003)
24. Nostrand, H.L., Noctrand, F.L., Imberton-Hunt, C.: Savoir vivre en francais. John Wiley & Sons, New York (1988)
25. Kosslyn, S.M.: Mental imagery. In: Kosslyn, S.M., Osherson, D.N. (eds.) Visual Cognition: An Invitation to Cognitive Science, pp. 267–296. The MIT Press, Cambridge (1995)
26. Pashler, H.: Attention and visual perception: analyzing divided attention. In: Kosslyn, S.M., Osherson, D.N. (eds.) Visual Cognition: An Invitation to Cognitive Science, pp. 267–296. The MIT Press, Cambridge (1995)
27. Farah, M.J., Wilson, D.K., Drain, M., Tanaka, J.N.: What is "special" about face perception? Psychol. Rev. 105(3), 482–498 (1998)
28. Milner, A.D., Goodale, M.A.: The Visual Brain in Action. Oxford Psychology Series 27. Oxford University Press, Oxford (1995)
29. Kowler, E.: Eye movement. In: Kosslyn, S.M., Osherson, D.N. (eds.) Visual Cognition: An Invitation to Cognitive Science, pp. 215–265. The MIT Press, Cambridge (1995)
30. Samara, T.: Design elements. A graphic style manual: Understanding the rules and knowing when to break them. Rockport, Beverley (2014)
31. Bringhurst, R.: The Elements of Typographic Style, 3rd edn. Hartley & Marks, Vancouver (2004)
32. Siegrist, J.: Das Consensus-Modell. Enke Verlag, Stuttgart (1970)
33. Siegrist, J., Bertram, H.: Schichtspezifische Variationen des Krankheitsverhaltens, Soziale Welt, pp. 206–218 (1970)

Work Organization and Effects of Isolation on the Perception of Misconduct in Italian Universities During Covid-19 Pandemic

Oronzo Parlangeli⬤, Margherita Bracci⬤, Stefano Guidi⬤, Enrica Marchigiani⬤, and Paola Palmitesta(✉) ⬤

Department of Social, Political and Cognitive Sciences, University of Siena, Via Roma, 56, 53100 Siena, Italy
`paola.palmitesta@unisi.it`

Abstract. Universities and institutions of higher education have been forced to move study and work activities remotely to contrast the spread of the pandemic due to Covid-19. Given the differences in roles, opportunities and operational functions of students, faculty members and university employees, it was deemed important to investigate whether any difficulties encountered in this condition of isolation may have led the three different groups to behave in an ethically inappropriate manner. To this end a questionnaire was developed and administered to a sample of 706 respondents, i.e. faculty members, students and technical and administrative staff. The study participants filled in a questionnaire aimed at investigating the operating conditions of working and studying at a distance, relating them to the perception of possible misbehavior by their own group and the other two subgroups. Results put in evidence that the three groups considered faced different difficulties that had different effects on perceptions in relation to the misconduct they experienced or perpetrated. Faculty appear to be essentially suffering from problems experienced even before the pandemic, such as an excess of competition that leads them to see their own colleagues as unfair. Students have less satisfactory housing conditions and demonstrate an awe of faculty that leads them to express less dissent when they witness misconduct. Technical and administrative staff appear disadvantaged in terms of technical tools and less equipped to process the negative feedback they receive about their work. However, they more than the other two groups are convinced that misbehaviors have decreased during home quarantine. On the contrary, faculty and students reported that misconduct have increased during the period of isolation.

Keywords: Faculty members · Administrative and technical staff · Students · Operational roles · Housing conditions · Technological tools · Unethical conduct

1 Introduction

Universities and institutions of higher education have had to respond to the outbreak of the Covid-19 pandemic promptly. Home isolation and a shift to remote working and training settings were among the most frequently undertaken countermeasures [1].

© The Author(s), under exclusive license to Springer Nature Switzerland AG 2022
G. Meiselwitz (Ed.): HCII 2022, LNCS 13316, pp. 147–160, 2022.
https://doi.org/10.1007/978-3-031-05064-0_12

A survey carried out by the International Association of Universities [2] about the impact of Covid-19 on 424 universities and other Higher Education Institutions in 109 countries from the 4 regions of the world (Africa, the Americas, Asia and Pacific, Europe) highlighted how almost all the countries experienced an important degree of stress and constraint in all the educational activities. Moreover, low-income countries are having a greater negative impact and inequality of learning opportunities are on the rise. Universities were differently prepared to face up this challenge. According to Multirank's data, just 17.6% of universities in the EU had a complete plan to undertake the transition to a digital model of education with specific aims and measures [3]. In some cases, remote teaching was just an "emergency teaching" [4].

Italy was the first country in Europe experiencing the Covid-19 outbreak and the first to close schools outside Asia.

The rapidity with which these pandemic response measures were taken has resulted in an obvious difficulty in interpersonal relationships in contexts where, in many cases, there is a very clear differentiation between roles and functions [5]. Faculty, in fact, have very different functions and roles from those of students, and these two sub-populations of the university community, in turn, have different functions and roles from those of administrative technical staff (henceforth AT staff) [6].

Universities as complex socio-technical organizations [7] have indeed an internal complexity resulting from the multiple sub-entities. Departments, research groups, laboratories, which have semi-autonomous status and a set of formal and informal rules that determine the functions and the different role of sub-populations such as professors, researchers, students, AT staff [8, 9].

The ability to continue the primary missions of education, research and service despite disruptive events, is what defines the University as a "resilient organization", and it depends on the possibility that resources such financial reserves, redundancy and positive relationship have to develop resilient capabilities [10]. Social relationships and forms of collaboration in the organization are, in the context of remote work, a particularly relevant issue [11]. Trust is a fundamental part of proper professional relationships between co-workers, between managers and employees, or between employees and managers [12, 13]. Inside organizational settings trust concerns the positive expectations individuals have about the intent and behaviors of other members based on working roles, relationships, experiences, and interdependencies [14]. The trust that individuals have about the intent and integrity in the behaviors of colleagues and of the other members of organizations derives not only from recognizing their competence (a trust dimension) but is also built by informal interaction, through verbal and nonverbal communication and through the leisure time spent together. Research [15] is finding that during the Covid-19 pandemic, people trust colleagues less than before.

A recent study by Microsoft [16] shows how remote working has reduced synchronous meeting and audio video call, and globally synchronous communication, while has increased asynchronous communication of emails and messages. Moreover, remote working seems to increase the interaction with the proximal working networks and decrease the interaction with the distant networks. The exchange of communication was more frequent with people who normally communicated more regularly while weaker relationships were gradually neglected [15, 16].

Given the differences between faculty, students, and AT staff in functions, available IT tools, and roles, it seems relevant to ask whether their further differentiation due to isolation - working and contact in spaces and through tools that cannot be assimilated - led to an increase in these differences.

This relationship difficulties may in turn exacerbate mutual negative considerations regarding the implementation of correct and ethically acceptable conduct [17–19].

In the last decades Universities have been operating in a competitive context with a funding system based on performance [20]. Ranking can have a positive (or negative) influence on the public perception regarding the educational quality of teaching institutions and on the occupational opportunities they can offer [21]. While competition can be useful to improve efficiency, effectiveness and sustainability, hyper competition can alter academic behavior, increasing the occurrence of different forms of unethical conduct [22–25]. Students and administrative-technical staff also experience performance pressure [26]. Numerous studies reported how academic cheating is a very common problem among students and a serious issue for academic integrity, and how this problem is getting worse during Covid-19 outbreak [27–29]. On the other hand, as far as we know, there are no specific studies that show if and how growing performance pressure is equally experienced or perceived within different roles in academic communities.

Starting from these considerations, the study presented here was conducted in order to verify whether, as a result of the periods of isolation due to Covid-19, unequal operating conditions occurred. These inequalities, in fact, could lead to different perceptions by teachers, students, and AT staff with respect to the frequency of occurrence of misconduct, perpetrated and suffered, within their own reference group and in relation to the other two groups.

2   The Study

The purpose of the study was to investigate how the lockdown period due to the COVID-19 pandemic was experienced by the entire academic community and how, in that period, changed the perception of misbehavior.

High educational institutions are a complex socio-technical system mainly based on a close interrelation between three different groups: faculty members, students and administrative and technical staff. Thus, it is crucial to investigate the effects of isolation on their relationships and working activities [30–34] and the nature of the perception of misbehaviors [18, 35, 36], in order to allow a good cooperative relationship fostered by mutual trust and collaboration among all the parties involved [37], in case of new periods of isolation and in any case, for study and work activities undertaken at a distance.

The research, therefore, intended to analyze life conditions and working and studying issues in relation to the perception of misconduct [17] by the main three subpopulations inside universities, i.e. faculty members, students, and AT staff [30, 32, 33, 38, 39].

Specifically, the research questions that guided this study are as follows:

- In which living and working conditions did students, faculties and AT staff experience, respectively, learning at distance, teaching on-line and working remote during the isolation?
- What issues did they encounter with respect to the environment in which they lived, the availability and use of technology and the Internet connection?
- In the context of isolation, what was their perception of incorrect behavior relative to their own group and to the other two?
- How did the perception of misconduct change, if at all, before and after the pandemic relative to their own group and to the other two?
- How did the demonstration of dissent, if at all, vary as a result of perceived misbehavior in one's own group and in the others?

3 Method

3.1 Participants and Procedure

The study involved 706 participants (380 faculty members, 179 students, and 147 AT staff) from three Tuscany Italian universities: Florence, Pisa and Siena.

Participants were contacted via their institutional e-mail. In the email text they were explained the aims of the study, and they were invited to connect to a link where they could voluntarily, and without any remuneration, fill in an anonymous self-reported questionnaire structured for this study on Google forms. They were also informed that filling in the questionnaire took about fifteen minutes.

The questionnaire was divided into three sections. Three versions of the questionnaire were developed for the study, adapted to the three different sub-groups in the sections relating to study or work activities.

The first section was aimed at gathering socio-demographic information, such as gender, age, residence, the role covered as a worker and the kind of course attended as a student. Furthermore, the duration of the working experience was requested to faculty members and administrative technical staff and the year of enrollment to students.

The second section included questions about the operating conditions during the isolation period due to the Covid-19 pandemic [18].

The questions were related to two aspects:

1. The living environment: the questions were related to where they lived and with whom, if alone, with family or with other roommates and how many in all. They were also asked to give a judgment, on a Likert scale from 1 to 5, on some specific characteristics, such as the width of the living environment (not very wide/very wide); the amount of people (few/many); the location with respect to the nearest city (badly/well positioned); the level of comfort (comfortable: not at all/a lot); its pleasantness (strongly disagree/strongly agree).
2. The technological equipment: they were asked if they could have access to a PC, if they had an exclusive access to a PC, the kind of adequacy of the technical characteristics and network connection (yes/no answers).

The third section was aimed at investigating three issues related to misconduct during the pandemic: their frequency, their increase/decrease, the respondent willingness to manifest their dissent when witness of a misconduct. For each of these issues five questions were asked. For instance, for the perception of frequency of misconduct one question was about the frequency of one's own group - e.g. faculty members misconduct in relation to other faculty members: "How often has it happened that your colleagues adopted unfair behaviors towards other colleagues? (i.e.: exchanging favors, promoting career advancement, not exchanging relevant information, speaking in unflattering terms about others, including/not including in publications, excluding from their "group", etc.)".

Four other questions were related to the other two groups within the university - e.g. faculty's perception of frequencies of misconduct perpetrated and suffered by both students and AT staff. (For more details see [17–19, 40, 41]).

The research protocol was subjected to evaluation and then approved by the Ethics Committee for Human and Social Sciences of the University of Siena - CAREUS - (act n. 6/2020).

4 Results and Discussion

4.1 The Sample

The sample included a higher percentage of females than males for students (73.7%) and AT staff (63.9%), while it was more balanced for teachers (females 45.5%, males 53.2%, does not declare = 1.3%).

Overall, the age of participants ranged between 18 and 70 years, but the distribution was different among the three groups. Faculties age ranged between 29 to 70 years (M: 49.35, SD: 10.81), students between 18 and 56 years (M: 21.89, SD: 4.49) and AT staff age between 28 and 66 years (M: 50.77, SD: 8.98).

Faculty were mostly researchers (of various types, 43.9%), associate professors (37.1%), and full professors (18.2%), with a quite homogeneous distribution among the scientific areas, except for a predominance of the literary area (28.7%). Most of the students (69.9%) were enrolled in a bachelor's degree program. The distribution of AT staff was very homogeneous both regarding position and seniority.

Household Environment Features. The ratings for the different household features were compared across groups using univariate ANOVAs. Significant differences were found between the group means for the ratings of crowdedness ($F(2, 699) = 8.642, p = .000$), goodness of location ($F(2, 698) = 15.255, p = .000$) and pleasantness ($F(2, 702) = 5.084, p = .006$). The mean scores for all the measures and groups are reported in Table 1. Students rated their household as significantly more crowded than faculty members, while AT staff ratings for this variable were not significantly different from those of the other groups. The ratings for pleasantness and goodness of location of the household were lowest for students, intermediate for AT staff and highest for faculty members.

Table 1. Average ratings for the dimensions of the household included in the survey across groups.

	Faculty members		Students		AT staff	
	M	*(SD)*	*M*	*(SD)*	*M*	*(SD)*
Wide (vs narrow)	3.70	(1.11)	3.59	(1.06)	3.72	(0.95)
Crowded (vs not)	2.24[a]	(1.07)	2.62[b]	(0.96)	2.50[ab]	(1.14)
Good location (vs bad)	4.35[a]	(0.88)	3.85[b]	(1.15)	4.21[c]	(0.98)
Well equipped (vs not)	2.05	(1.33)	2.06	(1.21)	2.03	(1.19)
Pleasant	4.17[a]	(0.95)	3.88[b]	(1.07)	4.05[c]	(0.95)

Note: Means in each row which do not share a letter in the superscript are significantly different from each other ($p < .05$). When no letters are reported, differences were not significant in the univariate ANOVA.

Technological Tools. Basically, all participants (99%) had access to a personal computer during the lockdown period. Chi-square tests comparing the distributions of responses concerning the availability of technological tools (see Table 2) showed significant differences across the groups in the responses to the items about having (vs not having) exclusive access to a personal computer ($Chi^2(4) = 26.294, p = .000$) and about the adequacy (vs inadequacy) of the features of the equipment available during the isolation period ($Chi^2(4) = 56.461, p = .000$). An ANOVA comparing the ratings for the adequacy of the internet connection available (1 = absolutely adequate, 7 = absolutely not adequate) showed significant differences in the mean ratings across the groups ($F(2, 699) = 8.642, p = .000$), with student rating their connection significantly less adequate for their need than AT staff, which in turn considered their connections less adequate than faculty members (see Table 3). Moreover, 61.9% of AT staff reported to not have a personal computer provided by their university.

Table 2. Distribution of the responses about the technological tools during the isolation period across the different groups.

	Faculty members (n = 380)		Students (n = 179)		AT staff (n = 147)	
	n	*%*	*n*	*%*	*n*	*%*
Access to a Personal Computer (PC)	377	99.2	179	100.0	143	97.3
Exclusive access to a PC	356	93.7[§]	155	86.6	118	80.3[§]
Adequacy of technical specifications to needs	357	93.9[§]	154	86.0[§]	107	72.8
Access to the Internet	378	99.5	176	98.3	146	99.3

Note: [§] Significative adjusted standardized residuals for Chi square test

Table 3. Average ratings for the (in)adequacy of the internet connection available during lockdown cross groups. Higher ratings indicate less adequate connection.

	Faculty members		Students		AT staff	
	M	(SD)	M	(SD)	M	(SD)
Inadequacy of the Internet connection	2.16[a]	(1.20)	2.68[b]	(1.29)	2.25[c]	(1.24)

Note: Means in each row which do not share a letter in the superscript are significantly different from each other ($p < .05$). When no letters are reported, differences were not significant in the univariate ANOVA.

Perception of Misconduct. In the following figures (Fig. 1, 2 and 3) are presented the average ratings about the perceived frequency of misconducts within and between the groups (Fig. 1), their perceived change in frequency of occurrence during the lock-down period (Fig. 2), and the frequency of manifestations of dissent by participants in front of misconducts (Fig. 3). Arrows connecting different groups represent perceptions of misconducts that each group either committed toward (outward direction) or received from (inward direction) other groups, and self-directed arrows represent perceptions of misconduct committed toward colleagues (same group). The colors represent the groups that provided the ratings. Statistically different (p = .000) averages for the same misconduct across pairs of groups (i.e. differences in point of view between two groups about the same misconduct) are marked with ***.

Concerning the perceived frequency of occurrence of misconducts (Fig. 1), all the average ratings were significantly lower (all $ps < .0001$) than the midpoint of the scale (midpoint = 3). Both faculty members and students reported that the frequency of misconducts toward them enacted by AT staff was higher than the frequency AT staff reported they had committed (toward each of the other groups). Moreover, the ratings about the perceived frequency of misconducts by colleagues (within each group) varied significantly across groups ($F(2, 686) = 99.562$, p = .000). Pairwise comparisons (adjusted with Tukey's method) showed that faculty members reported a higher frequency of misconducts among colleagues (other faculty members) than the other two groups did (all $ps < .0001$). AT staff also reported higher frequency of misconducts among colleagues than students did ($p = .007$) (Table 4).

Concerning the perceived change in the frequency of misconduct occurrence (Fig. 2), first of all it is interesting to notice that in most cases the average ratings are above the midpoint of the scale (midpoint = 3), showing that participants reported an increase of misconducts during lockdown, both perpetrated and received. Only the average ratings provided by AT staff (for all misconduct types), and the average ratings by faculty members about the change in the frequency of misconduct toward them by AT staff were not significantly different from 3. For all the other ratings the average values were significantly higher than 3 (all $ps = .007-.000$). Students reported increases in misconducts toward and from AT staff significantly more than AT staff themselves. Students also reported increases in misconduct toward faculty members (perpetrated by students) more than faculty members did. A significant ANOVA ($F(2, 684) = 4.075$, p = .017) showed that the ratings about the changes in the frequency of misconduct among colleagues varied across groups, and pairwise comparisons (Table 4) showed that the ratings expressed by faculty members were significantly higher than those expressed by students ($p = .05$).

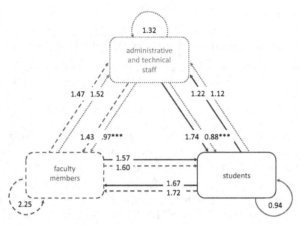

Fig. 1. Frequency of misconducts within the group, towards the other groups, and suffered by the other two groups. See the text for details.

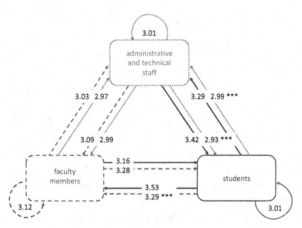

Fig. 2. Perception of the decrease/increase of misconducts within the group, towards the other groups, and suffered by the other two groups.

Concerning the manifestation of dissent in front of misconduct (Fig. 3), first of all the average ratings were significantly lower (all $ps < .0001$) than the midpoint of the scale. A significant ANOVA then showed that the ratings about the frequency of manifestations of dissent in front of misconducts by colleagues varied significantly across groups ($F(2, 654) = 3.484$, $p = 0.031$), and pairwise comparisons showed that faculty were significantly higher ($p < .05$) than the corresponding ratings expressed by students (Table 4). Faculty members' and AT staff's ratings of their manifestation of dissent in front of their misconducts toward students or of the misconducts they received from students were significantly higher than the corresponding ratings expressed by students (all *ps* < .000). Faculty members also expressed dissent in front of their misconduct toward AT staff more than AT staff did.

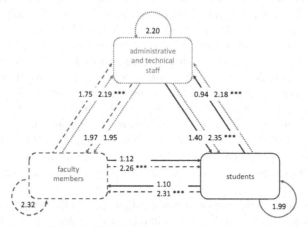

Fig. 3. Demonstration of dissent following the perception of misconducts in his own group, enacted toward other groups and suffered by the other two groups.

Table 4. Average ratings about misconduct among colleagues in each group.

	Faculty members		Students		AT staff	
	M	(SD)	M	(SD)	M	(SD)
Frequency of misconducts	2.25[a]	(1.08)	0.94[b]	(1.03)	1.32[c]	(1.16)
Perception of the decrease/increase of misconducts	3.12[a]	(0.49)	3.01[b]	(0.61)	3.01[bc]	(.56)
Demonstration of dissent	2.32[a]	(1.18)	1.99[b]	(1.43)	2.20[ab]	(1.36)

Note: Means in each row which do not share a letter in the superscript are significantly different from each other (p < .05). When no letters are reported, differences were not significant in the univariate ANOVA.

Discussion and Conclusions. The results obtained from the comparisons of perceptions, within and between the different groups, show several conditions of relational disharmony that require specific interventions [30].

First and foremost, with regard to faculty members, a high perception of misconduct within their own group (i.e. among colleagues) is evident compared to the other groups [40]. Moreover, faculty members reported more than other groups that misconduct among colleagues had increased during the isolation period. Given that this was the group that reported the better living conditions and technological equipment during this period, these factors cannot explain their perception about misconduct. Hence, it seems more likely that the perceived higher occurrence of misconduct within one's group by faculty is traceable to the occurrence of a more competitive context within the group [20, 42]. Within competitive context trust is essential and derives from recognizing competence and from working collaboration and communication, but also from informal interaction and communication out of work context [15]. During the pandemic, changes in the network and patterns of relationship among people [16] may have reduced trust and produced a lack of mutual respect and an increase of misconduct.

Not surprisingly, faculty members express dissent when witnessing misbehavior perpetrated towards or received by students, more than students do in front of the same behaviors. These data do not seem to be due to a sort of evaluative illusion in which the global perception, the one related to the whole context, influences the particular one [43], since the perceptions of misconduct in relation to the AT staff do not show any disharmony. In short, faculty members, in their relationships with students, sense a relational equity that is not perceived by students. This finding is likely to have to do with the definition of reciprocal roles [5], and it does not seem influenced by differences in the living and working conditions experienced during the isolation resulting from the pandemic.

AT staff appear to be the most disadvantaged group from the perspective of technological tools. Aside from what they report in reference to internet connection, they are the group that reports being least equipped. However, this does not lead them to believe that the misconducts among their colleagues or toward/from other groups became more frequent during the lockdown, as the other groups seem to believe. If anything, they express dissent in front of misbehaviors perpetrated against or received by students, and in front of misconduct received from faculty members more frequently than students and faculty members do in front of these behaviors. They also judge themselves particularly fair, toward both faculty members and students, significantly fairer than they are perceived to be by these same groups. Perhaps the issues related to technological tools make it difficult to have a dialogue on their own working activity, and to receive the feedback that could improve the mutual understanding. Consequently, it seems appropriate to try to provide this group with the necessary equipment for adequate home working. This problem, however, is likely to be not the only one, and it might sum up to the already highlighted difficulty of reconciling private life with working life in home contexts [44].

Students appear to be the most disadvantaged group from a housing conditions standpoint. Their technological tools, however, while not at the same level as faculty members, still appear more adequate than those of AT staff. It might be that students, despite being probably in a lower socio-economic condition than the other groups [45], simply prefer having an operational adequacy, and possessing efficient communication tools over the satisfaction of needs related to residential comfort. And this, in a complementary way to what the faculty reported, also manifests itself in a kind of awe (a sort of unbalanced self-perception with regard to teachers) that does not lead them to express their dissent about misconduct on the side of faculty members [41]. However, students reported more than the other two groups the perception that misconduct increased, both the ones they enact towards AT staff and faculty, as well as those they receive from AT staff.

Overall, then, the results of this study suggest that the sudden shift from usual operating conditions to periods of home isolation exacerbated the working, socio-economic, and relational inequalities found within the different groups that make up the university community [7]. These inequalities, in several cases, led to uneven perceptions between what was suffered, what was perpetrated, and judgments regarding these behaviors by other groups. Most importantly, however, it was apparent that AT staff during the pandemic perceived a decrease in misconduct, and this was especially so in relation to students. This finding is evident in how AT staff perceive both students' behaviors toward them as well as their own behavior toward students. This is probably also due, as mentioned earlier, to fewer relational opportunities due to inadequate operational and communication tools.

Future studies should be aimed at clarifying this relevant issue.

References

1. Crawford, J., Butler-Henderson, K., Rudolph, J., Malkawi, B., Glowatz, M., Burton, R., et al.: COVID-19: 20 countries' higher education intra-period digital pedagogy responses. J. Appl. Learn. Teach. 3, 1–20 (2020). https://doi.org/10.37074/jalt.2020.3.1.7
2. Marinoni, G., van't Land, H., Jensen, T.: The impact of Covid-19 on Higher Education around the world. Global Survey Report, International Association of Universities IAU (2020). https://www.iau-aiu.net/IMG/pdf/iau_covid19_and_he_survey_report_final_may_2020.pdf
3. UMultirank Homepage. https://www.umultirank.org/blog/universities-and-the-digitalis ation-of-teaching/. Accessed 15 Feb 2022
4. Hodges, C., Moore, S., Lockee, B., Trust, T., Bond, A.: The Difference between Emergency Remote Teaching and Online Learning. EDUCASE Review (2020). https://er.educause.edu/articles/2020/3/the-difference-between-emergency-remote-teaching-and-online-learning. Accessed 15 Feb 2022
5. Elias, N.: Scientific establishments. In: Elias, N., Martin, H., Whitley, R. (eds.) Scientific Establishments and Hierarchies. Sociology of the Sciences Yearbook VI, pp. 3–69. Dordrecht, Reidel (1982)
6. Seeber, M., Lepori, B., Montauti, M., Enders, J., de Boer, H., Weyer, E., et al.: European universities as complete organizations? understanding identity, hierarchy and rationality in public organizations. Public Manag. Rev. 17, 1444–1474 (2015). https://doi.org/10.1080/147 19037.2014.943268
7. Pinheiro, R., Young, M.: The university as an adaptive resilient organization. a complex systems perspective. In: Huisman, J., Tight, M. (eds.) Theory and Method in Higher Education Research, vol. 3, pp. 119–136. Emerald, Bingley (2017). https://doi.org/10.1108/S2056-375 220170000003007
8. Rapanta, C., Botturi, L., Goodyear, P., Guàrdia, L., Koole, M.: Online university teaching during and after the Covid-19 crisis: refocusing teacher presence and learning activity. Postdig. Sci. Educ. 2(3), 923–945 (2020). https://doi.org/10.1007/s42438-020-00155-y
9. Biswakarma, J., Rushworth, D., Srivastava, G., Singh, G., Kang, K., Das, S., et al.: Organizational level responses to the COVID-19 outbreak: challenges, strategies and framework for academic institutions. Front. Commun. 6, 573585 (2021). https://doi.org/10.3389/fcomm. 2021.573585
10. Duchek, S., Raetze, S., Scheuch, I.: The role of diversity in organizational resilience: a theoretical framework. Bus. Res. 13(2), 387–423 (2019). https://doi.org/10.1007/s40685-019-0084-8
11. van Zoonen, W., Sivunen, A., Blomqvist, K., et al.: Factors influencing adjustment to remote work: employees' initial responses to the COVID-19 pandemic. Int. J. Environ. Res. Public Health. 18, 6966 (2021). https://doi.org/10.3390/ijerph18136966

12. Kähkönen, T., Blomqvist, K., Gillespie, N., Vanhala, M.: Employee trust repair: a systematic review of 20 years of empirical research and future research directions. J. Bus. Res. **130**, 98–109 (2021). https://doi.org/10.1016/j.jbusres.2021.03.019
13. Krot, K., Lewicka, D.: The importance of trust in manager-employee relationships. Int. J. Electron. Bus. Manag. **10**, 224–233 (2012)
14. Shockley-Zalabak, P., Ellis, K., Winograd, G.: Organizational trust: what it means, why it matters. Organ. Dev. J. **18**, 35–48 (2000)
15. Baym, N., Larson, J., Martin, R.: What a year of WFH has done to our relationships at work. Harvard Business Review (2021). https://hbr.org/2021/03/what-a-year-of-wfh-has-done-to-our-relationships-at-work. Accessed 15 Feb 2022
16. Yang, L., Holtz, D., Jaffe, S., Suri, S., Sinha, S., Weston, J., et al.: The effects of remote work on collaboration among information workers. Nat. Hum. Behav. **6**, 43–54 (2022). https://doi.org/10.1038/s41562-021-01196-4
17. Parlangeli, O., Guidi, S., Marchigiani, E., Bracci, M., Liston, P.M.: Perceptions of work-related stress and ethical misconduct amongst non-tenured researchers in Italy. Sci. Eng. Ethics **26**(1), 159–181 (2019). https://doi.org/10.1007/s11948-019-00091-6
18. Parlangeli, O., Palmitesta, P., Guidi, S., Di Pomponio, I., Bracci, M., Marchigiani, E.: Social distancing, stress and unethical behavior: a study on Italian university students in the first period of isolation due to COVID-19. In: Goonetilleke, R.S., Xiong, S., Kalkis, H., Roja, Z., Karwowski, W., Murata, A. (eds.) AHFE 2021. LNNS, vol. 273, pp. 11–18. Springer, Cham (2021). https://doi.org/10.1007/978-3-030-80713-9_2
19. Parlangeli, O., Palmitesta, P., Bracci, M., Marchigiani, E., Di Pomponio, I., Guidi, S.: University teachers during the first lockdown due to SARS-CoV-2 in Italy: stress, issues and perceptions of misconduct. Sci. Eng. Ethics **28**(9) (2022). https://doi.org/10.1007/s11948-022-00362-9
20. Fumasoli, T., Huisman, J.: Strategic agency and system diversity: conceptualizing institutional positioning in higher education. Minerva **51**, 155–169 (2013). https://doi.org/10.1007/s11024-013-9225-y
21. Downing, K., Loock, P., Gravett, S.: The Impact of Higher Education Ranking Systems on Universities, 1st edn. Routledge, London (2021). https://doi.org/10.4324/9781003002543
22. Hall, J., Martin, B.: Towards a taxonomy of research misconduct: the case of business school research. Res. Policy. **48**, 414–427 (2019). https://doi.org/10.1016/j.respol.2018.03.006
23. Biagioli, M., Kenney, M., Martin, B.R., Walsh, J.P.: Academic misconduct, misrepresentation and gaming: a reassessment. Res. Policy. **48**, 401–413 (2019). https://doi.org/10.1016/j.respol.2018.10.025
24. Anderson, M.S., Ronning, E.A., De Vries, R., Martinson, B.C.: The perverse effects of competition on scientists' work and relationships. Sci. Eng. Ethics **13**, 437–461 (2007). https://doi.org/10.1007/s11948-007-9042-5
25. Edwards, M.A., Roy, S.: Academic research in the 21st century: maintaining scientific integrity in a climate of perverse incentives and hypercompetition. Environ. Eng. Sci. **34**, 51–61 (2017). https://doi.org/10.1089/ees.2016.0223
26. Giusti, L., Mammarella, S., Salza, A., Del Vecchio, S., Ussorio, D., Casacchia, M., et al.: Predictors of academic performance during the covid-19 outbreak impact of distance education on mental health, social cognition and memory abilities in an Italian university student sample. BMC Psychol. **9**, 142 (2021). https://doi.org/10.1186/s40359-021-00649-9
27. Janke, S., Rudert, S.C., Petersen, Ä., Fritz, T.M., Daumiller, M.: Cheating in the wake of COVID-19: how dangerous is ad-hoc online testing for academic integrity? Comput. Educ. **2**, 100055 (2021). https://doi.org/10.1016/j.caeo.2021.100055

28. Comas-Forgas, R., Lancaster, T., Calvo-Sastre, A., Sureda-Negre, J.: Exam cheating and academic integrity breaches during the COVID-19 pandemic: an analysis of internet search activity in Spain. Heliyon **7**, e08233 (2021). https://www.sciencedirect.com/science/article/pii/S2405844021023367

29. Blankenberger, B., Williams, A.M.: COVID and the impact on higher education: the essential role of integrity and accountability. Adm. Theory Prax. **42**, 404–423 (2020). https://doi.org/10.1080/10841806.2020.1771907

30. Odriozola-González, P., Planchuelo-Gómez, A., Irurtia, M.J., de Luis-García, R.: Psychological effects of the COVID-19 outbreak and lockdown among students and workers of a Spanish university. Psychiatry Res. **290**, 113108 (2020). https://doi.org/10.1016/j.psychres.2020.113108

31. Sahu, P.: Closure of universities due to coronavirus disease 2019 (COVID-19): impact on education and mental health of students and academic staff. Cureus **12**, e7541 (2020). https://doi.org/10.7759/cureus.7541

32. Biwer, F., Wiradhany, W., Egbrink Oude, M.G.A., Hospers, H., Wasenitz, S., Jansen, W., et al.: Changes and adaptations: how university students self-regulate their online learning during the COVID-19 pandemic. Front. Psychol. **12**, 642593 (2021). https://doi.org/10.3389/fpsyg.2021.642593

33. Knight, H., Carlisle, S., O'Connor, M., Briggs, L., Fothergill, L., Al-Oraibi, A., et al.: Impacts of the COVID-19 pandemic and self-isolation on students and staff in higher education: a qualitative study. Int. J. Environ. Res. Public Health **18**, 10675 (2021). https://doi.org/10.3390/ijerph182010675

34. Leal Filho, W., Wall, T., Rayman-Bacchus, L., Mifsud, M., Pritchard, D.J., Lovren, V.O., et al.: Impacts of COVID-19 and social isolation on academic staff and students at universities: a cross-sectional study. BMC Public Health **21**, 1–19 (2021). https://doi.org/10.1186/s12889-021-11040-z

35. King, C.G., Guyette, R.W., Piotrowski, C.: Online exams and cheating: An empirical analysis of business students' views. J. Educ. Online **6** (2009). https://doi.org/10.9743/JEO.2009.1.5

36. Watson, G.R., Sottile, J.: Cheating in the digital age: do students cheat more in online courses? OJDLA **13**, EJ877536 (2010). http://www.westga.edu/~distance/ojdla/spring131/watson131.html. Accessed 15 Feb 2022

37. Zorkic, T.J., Micic, K., Cerovic, T.K.: Lost trust? The experiences of teachers and students during schooling disrupted by the Covid-19 pandemic. Cent. Educ. Policy Stud. J. **11**(Special Issue, S), 195–218 (2021). https://doi.org/10.25656/01:23657

38. Corbera, E., Anguelovski, I., Honey-Rosés, J., Ruiz-Mallén, I.: Academia in the time of COVID 19: towards an ethics of care. Plan. Theory Pract. **21**, 191–199 (2020). https://doi.org/10.1080/14649357.2020.1757891

39. Cesco, S., et al.: Higher education in the first year of COVID-19: thoughts and perspectives for the future. Int. J. High Educ. **10**, 285–294 (2021). https://doi.org/10.5430/ijhe.v10n3p285

40. Parlangeli, O., Palmitesta, P., Bracci, M., Caratozzolo, M.C., Liston P.M., Marchigiani E.: Stress and perceptions of unethical behavior in academia. In: ICERI, 10th International Conference of Education Research and Innovation, Seville, Spain 16–19 Nov 2017. https://doi.org/10.21125/iceri.2017.0586

41. Parlangeli, O., Palmitesta, P., Bracci, M., Marchigiani, E., Liston, P.M.: Stress misconduct and reduced ability to express dissent: a study on a sample of students at the University of Siena. In: Arezes, P.M., et al. (eds.) Occupational safety and hygiene, vol. 6, pp. 443–446. CRC Press, Taylor & Francis Group, London (2018). https://doi.org/10.1201/9781351008884-78

42. Ali, I., Sultan, P., Aboelmaged, M.: A bibliometric analysis of academic misconduct research in higher education: current status and future research opportunities. Account. Res. **28**(6), 372–393 (2021). https://doi.org/10.1080/08989621.2020.1836620

43. Parlangeli, O., Roncato, S.: Draughtsmen at work. Perception **39**(2), 255–259 (2010). https://doi.org/10.1068/p6500
44. Ghislieri, C., Molino., M., Dolce., V, Sanseverino., D, Presutti., M.: Work-family conflict during the Covid-19 pandemic: teleworking of administrative and technical staff in healthcare. An Italian study. Med. Lav. **112**(3), 229–240 (2021). https://doi.org/10.23749/mdl.v112i3.11227
45. Devlin, M.: Bridging socio-cultural incongruity: conceptualising the success of students from low socio-economic status backgrounds in Australian higher education. Stud. High. Educ. **38**(6), 939–949 (2013). https://doi.org/10.1080/03075079.2011.613991

Re-imagining the Distributed Nature of Learner Engagement in Computer-Supported Collaborative Learning Contexts in the Post-pandemic Era

Andriani Piki[(⊠)] [iD]

University of Central Lancashire, Cyprus (UCLan Cyprus), 12-14 University Avenue, Pyla,
7080 Larnaca, Cyprus
apiki@uclan.ac.uk

Abstract. Learner engagement has become more fragmented and distributed than ever before due to the challenging and unpredictable circumstances amidst the pandemic. Social isolation, mobility restrictions, and the emergency transition to online education have influenced students' emotions, thoughts, and actions. The purpose of this study is to explore the factors that impacted learner engagement over time during the pandemic; to investigate students' perceptions on the role of social technology during remote education; and to capture students' reflections distilled through their recent and ongoing experiences with online learning. The findings from three exploratory case studies conducted during the pandemic with undergraduate students are collectively analysed and discussed. Four main themes emerged following a holistic, comparative data analysis: the distributed nature of learner engagement; the impact of the pandemic on the affective, behavioural, and cognitive dimensions of engagement within computer-supported collaborative learning contexts; the multifaceted and contradictory roles of social media and social technology while learning under lockdown; and finally, the lessons learnt and visions of students for learning in the post-pandemic era. The findings can inform the pedagogical design of inclusive, seamless, and accessible learning environments embracing social technology towards reactivating learner engagement.

Keywords: Learner engagement · Computer-supported collaborative learning · Undergraduate students · Social technology · Social media · Pedagogical design

1 Introduction and Motivation to the Research

The consequences of Covid-19 outbreak have undoubtedly challenged many aspects of modern life. Educational systems have witnessed unprecedented disruptions (Marinoni and van't Land 2020; Vijayan 2021) leading educational institutions to suspend their operations or rapidly shift from conventional, classroom-based teaching and learning to online education (Dhawan 2020; Hodges et al. 2020; Kara 2021; Veluvali and Surisetti 2022; Vijayan 2021; Vlachopoulos 2020). Within higher education, the persistence and

G. Meiselwitz (Ed.): HCII 2022, LNCS 13316, pp. 161–179, 2022.
https://doi.org/10.1007/978-3-031-05064-0_13

extent of the pandemic's consequences have compelled both students and educators to re-establish their discontinuous social interactions, fill the gaps caused by fragmented learning experiences, and reflect on social, family, and ethical values.

Although Covid-19 pandemic may have not been the solitary driver for recent technological developments, the measures for social distancing and restricted mobility – which were enforced for restricting the impact of the pandemic – have certainly speeded up the exploitation of social technologies in personal, educational, and professional contexts alike. The role of social media, collaborative platforms, learning management systems (LMS), and mobile apps has been instrumental in ensuring educational institutions continue functioning and supporting teachers and students during the rapid, imposed, and unplanned shift to online education (Dhawan 2020; Engelbrecht et al. 2020; Hodges et al. 2020; Marinoni and van't Land 2020; Muñoz-Carril et al. 2021; Piki 2020; Veluvali and Surisetti 2022; Vlachopoulos 2020). This exploitation has been particularly evident within higher education (Abu Elnasr et al. 2020; García-Peñalvo et al. 2021; Marinoni and van't Land 2020; Muñoz-Carril et al. 2021; Piki 2020). Without the utilisation of these technologies, it would not have been possible for universities to respond quickly and constructively to the unfolding disruptions. Still, despite the acceleration in the uptake of social technologies, their role and the impact on learner engagement and students' academic performance has been explored to a limited extend (Piki 2020; Abu Elnasr et al. 2020). Similarly, while the scale at which online teaching has been deployed at all levels of education has been unprecedented, the theoretical and empirical exploration of online teaching pedagogies has been limited (Vijayan 2021). These empirical gaps have attracted researchers' attention in recent months.

Personal experiences further fuelled the motivation for performing research on learner engagement during the shift to online education. Observing the variation in student engagement, and the sharp decline in student participation, following the emergency transition to online teaching, compared to the engagement and participation of the same groups of students a few days before the initial lockdown (in the first quarter of 2020), instigated a set of exploratory research questions towards investigating the reasons behind these variations, and how students experienced this transition from their point of view. Given the novelty of the situation at the time, there was limited empirical research into students' perspectives, feelings, and experiences, and on the role that social, mobile, and collaborative technology played during the emergency shift to remote education. Therefore, a case study was designed to address these nascent research questions. While a vast number of research studies has been published on teaching and learning since the outburst of Covid-19 pandemic, the fact that its consequences are ongoing invites further empirical research for understanding students' perspectives both during the emergency transition to online education in higher education and throughout successive isolation periods. Hence, guided by the initial findings, two additional case studies were deployed to explore and compare the impact of the pandemic on learning and engagement over time, across subjects, and between different modes of study (full-time and part-time students).

In addition to the empirical gaps, there exists a methodological discrepancy in the wider research into pedagogical design and the educational applications of digital and social technology. Research quality metrics often favour objectivist over interpretivist approaches (Twinning et al. 2017). As a result, many studies focus on evaluating specific technological interventions in a particular learning milieu or aim to capture quantitative data on student engagement and satisfaction (Muñoz-Carril et al. 2021; Wang et al. 2022). Conducting exploratory case studies in higher education can contribute to existing literature and instructional practice and help fill the identified empirical and methodological gaps.

The overarching purpose of this research is to conscientiously portray students' voices, viewpoints, and reflections on their learning experiences during Covid-19 pandemic, understand the factors that enabled or weakened their engagement over time and in different subjects, and finally explore the role of social and collaborative technology during remote education. Listening to 'student voice' creates a channel through which to understand how students experience a situation and why certain aspects are important to them, which has implications for educational quality and student performance (Grebennikova and Shah 2013; Kahu et al. 2020; Wang et al. 2022). Hence, students' perceptions and insights should not be neglected in the post-pandemic efforts towards reframing the educational system and re-establishing inclusive, accessible, and engaging teaching and learning environments.

The paper is organised as follows: Sect. 2 synthesises related literature and provides the background to the research. Section 3 presents the methodology and research design. Section 4 describes the key findings and overarching themes extracted from the case studies conducted. Finally, Sect. 5 synthesises the research insights towards re-imagining the distributed nature of learner engagement in computer-supported collaborative learning (CSCL) contexts in the post-pandemic era.

2 Background Research and Related Work

Prior to delving into the exploration of student perspectives, it is vital to study relevant literature, including previous empirical work and educational theory (Twining et al. 2017). This section synthesises research and empirical work that has informed the study of learner engagement with CSCL contexts before and during the pandemic.

2.1 Learner Engagement in Computer-Mediated Learning Contexts

Learner engagement is a complex and multifaceted concept (Ainley 2004), characterised by qualities such as vigour (high levels of intellectual effort, energy, and mental resilience during learning), dedication (strong involvement, active participation, inspiration and challenge), and absorption (being fully concentrated and deeply engrossed in learning) (Schaufeli et al. 2002). High degrees of engagement and motivation subsequently impact retention, understanding, and academic achievement (Hughes 2012). The 'Distributed Engagement Theory' (Piki 2012) portrays learner engagement in CSCL environments as a multi-dimensional concept, embracing emotional, behavioural, and intellectual constructs which are dynamically affected by a distributed collection of personal, social, group-level, and other situational factors. When this theory was originally proposed about a decade ago (Piki 2012) the aim was to understand the nature of learner engagement and capture the multifaceted enablers and barriers that dynamically interact and shape learner engagement to inform pedagogical design. Many aspects have changed since then (innovative collaboration tools and emerging social technologies have become readily available; virtual, mixed, and augmented learning environments are flourishing; the educational milieu has been greatly disrupted due to the pandemic), yet the primary aim remains the same in new research ventures.

Learner engagement has been increasingly attracting the interest of educators, instructors, and scholars in the pursuit of innovative pedagogies that respond to changes in the society (Ferguson et al. 2019). These efforts aim towards establishing rewarding learning activities, motivational assessment strategies, and student-centric and inclusive knowledge delivery methods (Piki 2017) catering to the needs of diverse learners (Veluvali and Surisetti 2022). Nevertheless, in recent months, the negative impact of the pandemic has been evident, and counter-engaging expressions such as boredom, anxiety, stress, and mental health issues are commonly featured in recent literature (Kara 2021; Vijayan 2021; Wang et al. 2022). The rapid and imposed changes which forced students to switch from the familiar learning environment to an unfamiliar, isolated situation, not only elevated student anxiety, uncertainty and distress but also negatively impacted their learning experiences, level of concentration, and degree of participation during online lectures (Piki 2020; Piki et al. 2022). The prolonged negative impact of the pandemic has reignited interest into the range of personal, pedagogical, technological, and social factors influencing students' engagement and satisfaction. Recent studies explore the aspects that impact learner engagement in online learning (Kara 2021; Wang et al. 2022) and CSCL contexts (Ma et al. 2020; Muñoz-Carril et al. 2021), as well as the role that social media played in engaging learners during remote education (Abu Elnasr et al. 2020; Piki 2020; Piki et al. 2022).

A keyword search using Scopus interdisciplinary abstract and citation database (Scopus Elsevier 2022) performed on January 31st, 2022, revealed that the number of papers discussing 'learner engagement' increased by more than four times between the years 2011 and 2021 (Fig. 1). Searching within the results demonstrated a similar trend for 'learner engagement and online learning' and 'learner engagement and online learning and social media'. Examining the number of new publications per year for the latter combination of key terms also revealed that the yearly count of papers was 2,5 times greater in 2020 compared to 2019, and almost doubled in 2021 compared to 2020 (Fig. 2). The novelty of the situation caused by the pandemic unsurprisingly launched new hypotheses and research questions driving scientific and exploratory research in the broader educational literature. Moreover, several academic journals and conferences dedicated special issues and thematic sessions, respectively, encouraging scholars to study the impact of Covid-19 pandemic on education. Naturally, a vast number of researchers started exploring the social, emotional, pedagogical, and technological disruptions caused by Covid-19 pandemic and their impact on teaching and learning (Muñoz-Carril et al. 2021; Vijayan 2021; Wang et al. 2022). With the crisis still unfolding, researchers have been eagerly sharing research findings on the strengths, weaknesses, opportunities, and challenges presented to students, educators, school leaders, and institutions through online teaching and learning (Aucejo et al. 2020; Dhawan 2020; Muñoz-Carril et al. 2021; Toquero 2020); the solutions and technological interventions being employed to engage learners (Piki et al. 2022); and the knowledge gleaned and lessons learned during this unprecedented period (Vijayan 2021). Research studies have been contacted at all educational levels, including higher education (Abu Elnasr et al. 2020; Cassibba et al. 2021; García-Peñalvo et al. 2021; Kara 2021; Marinoni and van't Land 2020; Muñoz-Carril et al. 2021; Piki 2020; Piki et al. 2022; Toquero 2020; Tractenberg 2021).

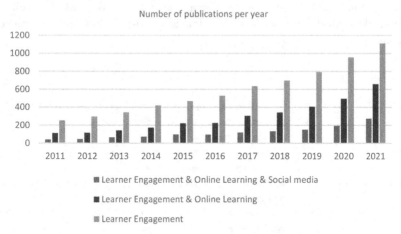

Fig. 1. Number of publications per year on 'Learner Engagement' and related search terms between 2011 and 2021. The search was performed on Scopus (Scopus Elsevier 2022).

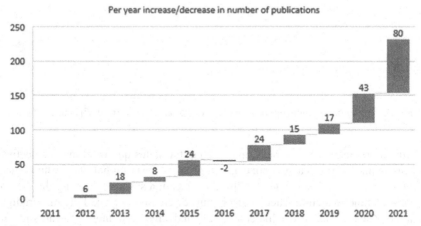

Fig. 2. Increase/decrease in number of new publications per year for the search terms 'Learner Engagement & Online Learning & Social media'. The search was performed on Scopus (Scopus Elsevier 2022).

While the continuous increase in the number of papers exploring learner engagement and related concepts is evidently illustrated in the column graph (Fig. 1) and the waterfall chart (Fig. 2) above, a recent topic modelling study (Vijayan 2021) revealed that student engagement, social media, and computer-based learning are amongst the least utilised keywords in the broader research area on teaching during Covid-19.

Figure 3 shows a subset of the keywords captured by the study. This observation suggests that there is a need for more empirical research focusing specifically on these concepts. Additionally, although higher education appears to be amongst the top three keywords featured in the articles analysed (Vijayan 2021), undergraduate education has received fewer mentions. Hence, conducting more studies at this level of education can enrich existing literature and help develop teaching and learning practices which specifically apply to undergraduate students, both full-time and part-time, studying in a range of subject areas.

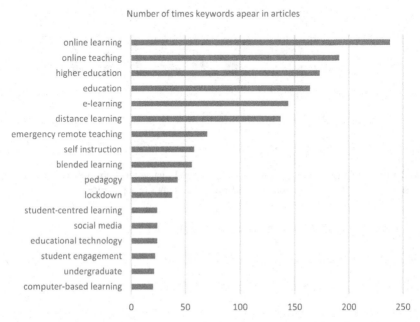

Fig. 3. Subset of common author-provided keywords (adapted from Vijayan 2021).

Furthermore, many papers focus on depicting the status quo from the perspectives of educators and school leaders, concentrating on the institutional and technological efforts undertaken to reframe and stabilise the education system following the disruptions caused by the pandemic. There is an ongoing discussion on an underlying paradigm shift in the education sector (Mehla et al. 2021) and a research interest towards identifying effective ways for delivering education online during a crisis (Dhawan 2020). At the same time, exploring students' experiences, perceptions, and expectations, understanding what affects their engagement and how they respond to various technologies and social interactions can also make valuable contributions and inform pedagogical design, theory, and practice (Aucejo et al. 2020; Muñoz-Carril et al. 2021; Piki 2020). The following section discusses key trends in the technologies used for learning.

2.2 Trends in Social, Mobile, and Collaborative Technologies for Learning

The role of social, mobile, and collaborative technology has been instrumental in ensuring learners and educators remain connected, both during the emergency transition to online learning (Hodges et al. 2020; Kara 2021; Piki 2020), and during subsequent periods of isolation which occurred in response to the national lockdowns and stringent governmental measures enforced around the world. Still, the core mobile, collaborative, educational, games-based, and social technologies which were embraced during this period have been around for a long time, and certainly pre-existed the pandemic. The ubiquity of mobile devices and the seamless integration of mobile technology into everyday tasks (Schindler et al. 2017) has long been shaping the way we communicate and collaborate, and the means through which information (and often misinformation) is diffused. The advent of social networking sites and social media mobile apps has evidently transformed the way we virtually socialise, interact, and keep in touch with family, friends, and the world around us.

Within education, various attempts have been made in recent years to incorporate social technology towards promoting motivation and learner engagement – ranging from web-based applications like blogs (Mansouri and Piki 2016), to educational games (Adams 2019; Behl et al. 2022; Krouska et al. 2021), massive open online courses (MOOC) and LMS (Veluvali and Surisetti 2022), social media and social networking sites (Abu Elnasr et al. 2020; Camus et al. 2016; Clements 2015; Hamid et al. 2015; Piki 2020), and multi-user virtual environments (Nisiotis and Kleanthous 2019). Still, until recently, the educational sector has been lacking behind thriving technological innovations (Gandhi et al. 2016). Within higher education this presents an oxymoron: on one hand, the majority of students and academics already own personal mobile devices and adeptly use collaboration platforms and social media apps to communicate, collaborate, and interact, while on the other hand, the role of these social technologies as channels for learning and educational purposes is not yet fully realised. There are many reasons this phenomenon can be attributed to, ranging from rigid institutional procedures at universities (Schindler et al. 2017), to educators being reluctant to incorporate these channels in their instructional approach due to lack of practical expertise (often leading to insecurity and apprehension not to be chastened in front of their students), concerns about the time and effort required to set up and seamlessly blend CSCL tasks within the established curriculum, as well as uncertainties on whether technology can indeed improve students' academic performance and learning outcomes (Gikas and Grant 2013; Schindler et al. 2017).

Beyond the barriers that keep CSCL practices from being realised to their full extent, there is a substantial amount of research demonstrating that utilising mobile, collaborative, and social technology, presents genuine opportunities for: (i) engaging learners into new knowledge construction through collaborative learning activities in physical, mobile, and virtual worlds alike (Ally and Tsinakos 2014; Gikas and Grant 2013; Muñoz-Carril et al. 2021; Nisiotis and Kleanthous 2020; Piki 2014; Piki 2017; Schindler et al. 2017; Tsinakos and Ally 2013); (ii) offering authentic and context-aware learning opportunities through mobile learning (Ally and Tsinakos 2014; Mottiwalla 2007; Sharples et al. 2007; Tsinakos and Ally 2013); (iii) promoting learner engagement through educational gamification (Adams 2019; Behl et al. 2022), mobile games-based learning (mGBL) approaches (Krouska et al. 2021), and immersive learning experiences both in the classroom and online (Nisiotis and Kleanthous 2020; Nisiotis et al. 2017); (iv) blending formal and informal learning contexts (Gikas and Grant 2013; Schindler et al. 2017; Sharples et al. 2007); and (v) inspiring learners to take ownership of their learning by blending self-directed learning with learning which is continuous, seamless, inclusive, and accessible from virtually everywhere (Ally and Tsinakos 2014; Tsinakos and Ally 2013; Mottiwalla 2007; Nisiotis et al. 2017; Veluvali and Surisetti 2022). Capitalising on these opportunities and leveraging the unique characteristics and educational capabilities of mobile, collaborative, and social technologies can contribute towards reimagining learner engagement. Nevertheless, what has led to the increased uptake of these tools extends beyond their technological affordances and engaging capabilities. In fact, during lockdowns and self-isolation periods, social technologies and collaborative platforms were not embraced solely as supplementary tools for engaging users and improving the learning outcomes. Technology was no longer a complementary tool for learning – it was the only means through which students could reach each other, their teachers, and the learning content. Under these unprecedented circumstances, online education is no more an alternative option, it becomes a necessity (Dhawan 2020).

During Covid-19 pandemic, institutions embraced communication and collaboration platforms (such as Microsoft Teams, Zoom, GoToMeeting, Skype, Google Meet, etc.) which offer a range of capabilities including shared workspaces, instant messaging and videoconferencing capabilities, file storage, screen sharing, video-recording, and attendance monitoring amongst other integrated functionality. The pandemic also accelerated the use of mobile applications in education, including mobile games (Krouska et al. 2021) and social media mobile apps (Piki 2020; Abu Elnasr et al. 2020). Social media broadly refer to Internet-enabled applications that allow the creation and exchange of user generated content while also creating a sense of community (Gikas and Grant 2013). Social media and social technologies extent the capabilities of mobile devices and have the capacity to enable interactions and collaborative activities both between students, and among educators and students, fading out the line between formal and informal learning activities (Camus et al. 2016; Mansouri and Piki 2016; Schindler et al. 2017). Nonetheless, it is also commonly argued in the literature that the application of any technology or tool needs to be appropriately structured, personalised, meaningful, and have a clear purpose in order to engage learners, be conducive to learning, and contribute towards achieving the desirable learning outcomes. This has been argued for social media (Abu Elnasr et al. 2020; Gikas and Grant 2013), educational gamification (Adams 2019; Behl et al. 2022; Piki 2020), and CSCL approaches in general (Ma et al. 2020; Muñoz-Carril et al. 2021; Piki 2012; Piki 2017; Schindler et al. 2017).

For universities which already had collaboration platforms in place, the transition to a fully online mode was logistically straightforward. Nevertheless, it was still deemed necessary to educate both students and academics on the technological capabilities of these platforms, and the conventional practices, social rules, and nuances pertaining to online educational communications. The ways technology was utilised after Covid-19 related measures were enforced, goes beyond the typical uses educators and students were accustomed to. Some educators were better prepared than others and quickly incorporated the newest features of mobile, social, and collaborative technologies into their teaching, formative feedback, and assessment approaches. Similarly, some students started utilising the state-of-the-art in mobile computing for learning, studying, and interacting with peers and lecturers. The rapid, emergency transition to online learning, however, meant that in many cases there was insufficient time for adjustment leading to a variability in the approaches used by different educators in the same institution (Piki 2020; Piki et al. 2022). Furthermore, institutions had to make impromptu decisions about practical aspects such as whether the lecturers' and students' web camera should be on or off during the lectures, whether to proceed with synchronous or asynchronous delivery of the lectures, whether or not to record the lectures and make the recordings available to students, the protocol regarding office hours and other routine issues suddenly had to be re-negotiated taking into account General Data Protection Regulations (GDPR), technological readiness, and health-related measures. This created an unstable situation which inevitably affected students' engagement and motivation (Piki 2020). It has long been established that students learn and engage differently during remote education compared to learning in a conventional classroom. These differences are evident in the ways students interact socially with their lecturers and their peers, and in the way they engage with the learning content and approach their learning in general (Bolliger and Martin 2018; Gikas and Grant 2013; Ma et al. 2020; Martin and Bolliger 2018; Molinillo et al. 2018; Schindler et al. 2017; Wang et al. 2022; Xie et al. 2019). With the consequences of the pandemic still unfolding, the role of social, mobile, and collaborative technologies is not yet fully realised. This widens the avenues for exploring how students perceive the opportunistic and interventional uses of technology for teaching and learning during the pandemic.

3 Research Methodology

3.1 Study Context and Research Participants

Empirical data was gathered through three exploratory studies conducted at a Higher Education Institution (HEI). The study participants were undergraduate students, studying in a range of subjects (including computing, finance and accounting, business administration, mathematics, economics, and marketing). Both female and male students participated in all studies. Teaching at the selected HEI is traditionally carried out face-to-face. Hence, neither communication platforms nor procedures for distance learning were in place before the first Covid-19 lockdown. This created a genuine opportunity for exploring the stories and voices of students and appreciating how they experienced the emergency transition to remote education. The first case study was conducted between April-May 2020 adopting an inductive, exploratory approach. This leading study illuminated both the positive experiences and frustrations undergraduate students faced while studying remotely, and how this affected their engagement and academic performance specifically with mathematics and other practical, applied modules. The study also shed light on the role of social media during the lockdown (Piki 2020). The second study was conducted in July 2020 and the goal was to capture the impact of the emergency transition to online education on students' experiences and the implications pertinent to mathematics education. The focus for this study was inspired by initial findings indicating that learner engagement was more severely affected in practical modules such as mathematics. Finally, a third study was performed approximately one year later, in June 2021, with the purpose to corroborate initial findings and observe prominent changes and persistent themes in students' perspectives over time and during a planned rather than an emergency transition to online learning, notwithstanding the successive lockdowns and other impacts the pandemic had on student life (Piki et al. 2022). Further to the formerly published findings (Piki 2020; Piki et al. 2022), the present study collectively analyses the gathered insights and discusses the aggregated findings aiming to highlight persistent themes that re-emerged over time, across subjects, and affected both part-time and full-time undergraduate students. Furthermore, this study critically examines the empirical findings in light of recently published research outcomes.

3.2 Data Collection Methods and Comparative Meta-analysis

In the initial study the in-depth perspectives of forty-three undergraduate students (22 female and 21 male students) were gathered through thorough, semi-structured interviews (Piki 2020). The sample included both full-time and part-time students (37 and 6, respectively). Each interview lasted approximately one hour and all interviews were audio- or video-recorded which facilitated both the discussion flow during the interview and the subsequent transcription process. Although an interview agenda was utilised to ensure the consistency across interviews, discussions encouraged openness and additional questions and probes were utilised to encourage deepening on issues raised by the students. This ensured that students felt comfortable to share and discuss their experiences, feelings, and thoughts. Creating a trusting space is essential for researchers to build a richer understanding of students' perceptions (Kahu et al. 2020). Data gathering and analysis were interleaved, and additional interviews were arranged until newly gathered data was no longer revealing new patterns or themes and saturation was achieved (Twining et al. 2017). Preliminary analysis involved reading transcripts and playing-back interview recordings, leading into the identification of emerging themes and recurring patterns. Colour-coding facilitated the identification of relationships between themes and through thematic analysis relevant ideas were grouped into thematic categories (Clarke and Braun 2017).

In the second and third studies, focus groups were organised (eight and five focus groups respectively). The sample was focused and purposeful, capitalising on the insights gained in the leading study. Consequently, the invited participants were undergraduate students who were registered on mathematics modules at the time the research was conducted. A total of twenty-eight students participated (19 female and 9 male students) in a total of thirteen focus groups. A semi-structured approach was utilised – aligned with the initial case study – allowing students to lead the discussion to issues that mattered to them. The rationale behind performing focus groups was to generate further insights on collective views promoted through facilitated, casual encounters amongst the participants (Gill et al. 2008; Krueger 2014; Patton 1990). The group dynamics and peer relations facilitated the flow of the discussion and engaged students into higher-order reflections which helped to yield deeper student insights, challenges, feelings, expectations, and overall experiences following the disruptions in their studies (and their lives, in general) due to Covid-19. Furthermore, a collaborative analytical approach was followed utilising techniques like keeping reflective diaries, maintaining joint research logs of emerging themes and codes, systematic researcher debriefing sessions for refining the emergent thematic categories and removing redundancies, and ultimately, an overarching analytical stage for eliminating researcher bias and achieving triangulation of the findings (Piki et al. 2022).

Following the analysis of each study and considering relevant literature published in the broader field of education in recent months, it was deemed necessary to proceed with a more critical, overarching interpretation and juxtaposition of the prominent findings. This holistic meta-analysis revealed four main themes which are discussed next.

4   Discussion of Key Research Findings

The main themes which emerged following the holistic data analysis are: the distributed nature of learner engagement; the impact of the pandemic on the emotional, cognitive and behavioural dimensions of engagement in CSCL contexts; the multifaceted and contradictory roles of social media and social technology while learning under lockdown; and finally, the lessons learnt and visions of students for learning in the post-pandemic era.

4.1   The Distributed Nature of Learner Engagement

The way students articulated their experiences during the pandemic indicates that their engagement with learning activities (both synchronous and asynchronous) was influenced by a dynamic combination of factors. The stories, feelings, and perceptions students voiced provided rich insights indicating that learner engagement is distributed across personal, pedagogical, social, group-level, and technological facets. This reinforces the notion that "learner engagement does not appear to be a stable, trait-like characteristic of the individual; rather it may shift and change according to a number of factors" (Piki 2012). Furthermore, students described how their learner engagement and degree of participation changed over time (before vs. during the pandemic; emergency transition to online education vs. subsequent lockdown periods); between places (classroom-based vs. online learning); and across process dimensions (monotonous, one-way instructional approach vs. interactive, responsive, empathetic educational strategy). In addition to time, space, and process, students also explained they engaged differently across different modules. During the holistic analysis this variation in learner engagement was attributed to the complex interplay between five factors.

First, personal characteristics and individual preferences, earlier experiences with computer-mediated learning, the inclination towards particular subjects, and other individual facets inevitably impacted the way students engaged and their overall level of satisfaction (Muñoz-Carril et al. 2021). Personality, selected approaches to studying and learning, familiarity and prior experiences with the tools and technologies employed, also affected the degree of student participation. Many students felt the need to express the adverse feelings of uneasiness, boredom, and anxiety they experienced during this unprecedented period. Students also explained how these feelings impacted their concentration, the degree of participation in the online lectures, and ultimately their overall academic performance. Recent studies also discuss the mediating role that personal learner characteristics and academic emotions play in learning engagement, particularly in online learning settings (Kara 2021; Molinillo et al. 2018; Wang et al. 2022). Nevertheless, there were a few students who explained that, after recovering from the initial anxiety they encountered due to the emergency transition to remote learning, they recognised some positive learning outcomes which, on-reflection, made them feel stronger and more well-prepared for the future. This 'upskilling' included strategies to self-regulate their learning, multi-tasking skills, as well as learning how to act and behave during synchronous online communications.

Second, pedagogical aspects, such as the nature of the curriculum (theoretical or practical) and the interactions with the learning content also affect learner engagement (Wang et al. 2022). In the studied context students explained that they found it particularly challenging to stay concentrated during the online lectures and follow the lecturer' line of thought in practical subjects such as mathematics (Piki et al. 2022). Similar findings regarding the subject of mathematics are also discussed in the literature (Aucejo et al. 2020; Barlovits et al. 2021; Cassibba et al. 2021). Other pedagogical factors such as the teaching style, the lecturer's approach during and in-between online lectures (formal, rigid vs. informal, caring), and the overall attitude of the lecturer had a great impact on how undergraduate students engaged in particular modules. As the literature confirms (Ferguson et al. 2019; Muñoz-Carril et al. 2021; Hernández-Sellés et al. 2019), educators play a significant role, not merely for content delivery and knowledge dissemination, but most importantly for supporting and guiding students, acting as facilitators in the learning process. Furthermore, the inconsistency in instructional approaches used among different lecturers, as well as institutional decisions regarding video-recording the online lectures were also linked with decline in learner engagement and overall academic performance (Piki 2020). Regarding the latter, students explained that as non-native English speakers, they did not feel confident to interrupt the lecturer to ask questions or contribute to interactive discussions while the lecture was recorded. This eventually made students feel emotionally and cognitively disconnected since this changed the natural flow of interaction they were accustomed to during traditional, face-to-face instruction (Piki 2020). At the same time, the HEI did not have a definite policy regarding joining lecturers with the web-camera on, thus with a few exceptions all students joined with their web-cameras off. As a result, lecturers did not have a visual while teaching and there was no direct way to know if students were following through or whether they were struggling with a certain concept or exercise. This contradicted students' habitual learning process where the lecturer can easily notice if there are questions or requests from students. This further fragmented the interactions between students and lecturers and among students as well (Piki 2020). On the positive side, on many occasions, students highlighted the empathy, compassionate attitude, responsiveness, and emotional support from some of their lecturers. An appealing finding was the fact that many students would join the online lectures merely as a respectful response to their lecturers' supportive attitude, even though they would not always contribute or participate actively during the lecture (Piki et al. 2022).

Third, social aspects affected learner engagement more than any other facet during Covid-19 pandemic. The imposed measures for social isolation and the negative consequences of the pandemic brought disruptions across all societal axes. Families, friends, peers, co-workers, students, and teachers had to find new ways to interact, communicate, collaborate, and keep in touch. The ongoing changes greatly impacted the phycology and wellbeing of young adults. The impact was more intense in the words of full-time students and students who were not working in parallel to their studies and hence were more isolated, whereas students who were working full-time or part-time viewed their experiences more holistically. Beyond the technical and practical barriers students had to overcome, the real challenge was that they were experiencing the transition to remote learning while in isolation and under restricted mobility measures (Piki 2020). It was this twinned experience that really inhibited their level of concentration, raised feelings of anxiety, fatigue, and tiredness, which altogether weakened their engagement with learning. The vast majority of students explained that over time they were experiencing these feelings more intensely. Recent literature has been refocusing on these negative feelings which emerged heavily during the pandemic (Kara 2021; Vijayan 2021; Wang et al. 2022). A key finding that emerged during the comparative analysis phase was that over time and on contemplation, many students truly appreciated the role of family bonds, and social values like caring for each other, and lifting each other's motivation up during periods of increased distress. Some students even admitted they would quit without the psychological support from their parents and family members (Piki et al. 2022). This finding raises important social implications as we emerge out the pandemic, such as the need to leverage emotional intelligence, re-establish broken social and family bonds, and redefine ethical and social values.

Four, group-level dynamics and peer relations also impacted student engagement. Some students recounted that during the lockdowns they developed stronger bonds with their peers compared to the pre-Covid period. Social media played a key role in establishing and supporting students' study groups by helping students keep track of their learning activities and fill the gap generated due to the lack of face-to-face contact time. Students who formed or joined a study group appeared to be more engaged during the lectures and generally more positive and energetic during distance learning, compared to students who were more isolated or did not try to connect with their peers. Constructive interactions among learners are commonly associated with positive academic emotions, learning self-efficacy, and higher levels of learner engagement, within online and CSCL learning contexts (Ma et al. 2020; Molinillo et al. 2018; Wang et al. 2022). Beyond the informal, social interactions among learners this finding re-emphasises the pedagogical implications of collaborative learning in general.

Finally, the technologies and tools utilised by different lecturers also had considerable impact on how students engaged. This included the means for delivering the lectures (i.e., the official educational platform selected by the HEI), technological interventions created by the lecturers to facilitate the feedback process and instruction (Piki 2020), as well as the social technologies employed by lecturers to provide more informal and immediate responses and ongoing feedback to their students (Piki 2020). In fact, the role of social media and social technologies during online teaching and learning was instrumental and was captured as one of the key themes, discussed below. When taken collectively, the set of personal, pedagogical, social, group, and technological factors that emerged in the studied context capture the distributed character of learner engagement.

4.2   Affective, Behavioural, and Cognitive Dimensions of Learner Engagement

The findings from the holistic meta-analysis appear to reconfirm the multidimensional nature of the learner engagement (Piki 2012; Piki 2014) encompassing affective, behavioural, and cognitive dimensions, which can be collectively referred to as the 'ABC structure of learner engagement'. In all three studies, students were inquired about how they experienced learning during the pandemic, what changed in the way they studied, compared to the usual way they were approaching their learning at higher or secondary level, and what were the main challenges and opportunities presented to them during this unparalleled situation, amongst other questions. Students explained how social isolation and restricted mobility negatively affected their aptitude to intellectually connect with their learning during the emergency transition to online learning and after successive lockdowns, the inability to concentrate and sustain their focus for a long period of time while looking at a screen, and the impact on their understanding and retention. Similarly, students' responses during the interviews and focus groups were rich in expressions of feelings ranging from frustration, annoyance, and boredom, to anxiety, uncertainty for the future, and stress. The array of (mostly negative and undesirable) emotions students experienced while learning under lockdown (joining online lectures, self-studying, or studying with peers in groups), was leading them towards passive, disengaged approaches which eventually impacted their academic performance, thus further sustaining the loop of negative emotions. Additionally, students expressed their experiences through sharing stories and incidents illustrating their actions, reactions, and behaviour during the online lectures (e.g., admitting they were cooking, eating, or sleeping during their lectures) and how they generally behaved as a response to the novel and challenging situations presented to them. The affective, behavioural, and cognitive dimensions of learner engagement appeared to be inextricably interwoven in the ways students expressed their perceptions, perspectives, and experiences. The multidimensional nature of engagement and the mediating role it plays in CSCL contexts is also discussed in recent literature (Kara 2021; Ma et al. 2020; Molinillo et al. 2018; Muñoz-Carril et al. 2021; Piki 2012; Piki 2017; Wang et al. 2022).

4.3   The Role of Social Technology While Learning Under Lockdown

The role of social media and social technology while learning under lockdown was multifaceted and contradictory. On one hand social media mobile apps (such as Messenger, Viber, and Facebook) had a significant contribution in supporting student learning and nurturing learner engagement during the lockdowns and helped students virtually circumvent the social restrictions enforced due to the pandemic. These tools provided an informal means through which students reached out to their peers and lecturers alike. Informality was discussed as one of the key 'qualities' of social media in terms of their learning capacity. Students explained they considered it less intimidating, quicker, and more natural and direct to contact their lecturers on Messenger simply sending a photo of their written answer, rather than having to type a formal email and attach their solutions. This encouraged students and helped them feel more comfortable to ask questions and seek formative feedback, which in turn facilitated their learning process (Abu Elnasr et al. 2020; Piki 2020). Communication through social media was highly appreciated by part-time students, as well as students with family and work obligations. Students in these groups explained that without their mobile devices and social media it would be impossible to stay connected with their learning tasks, peers and lecturers while maintaining their work-life balance amidst the crisis.

While overall social media contributed to student engagement, on the other hand they were considered by many students as a major distraction, both for the duration of the live online lectures and during self-study. Chatting on social media often distracted students for a long period of time hence impacting their concentration, level of participation, and overall academic performance. Furthermore, the flexibility and ubiquity of mobile and social technology, along with the lack of strict procedures for students to have the web-cameras on during the online lectures, meant it was impossible for lecturers to monitor student participation closely, and students could easily get away with simply joining the session through their mobile phones but without really engaging. Overall, however, the positive attributes of social technologies and social media surpassed the limitations, and largely helped students while learning remotely. Relevant literature also suggests that social media can enrich interactions with fellow students and lecturers and create a sense of belonging within a community (Bahati 2015; Bowman and Akcaoglu 2014; Camus et al. 2016; Clements 2015; Naghdipour and Eldridge 2016). These interactions constitute a viable channel for increasing and sustaining learner engagement in periods of social isolation.

4.4 Lessons Learnt and Visions for Learning in the Post-pandemic Era

Students appeared very direct and explicit about how they envision their future learning endeavours. Across all three studies, most students declared their preference for traditional, face-to-face, classroom-based instruction rather than distance education. This is aligned with recent studies (Gierdowski 2019). One of the key reasons for this was the fact that face-to-face instruction provides an effortless and natural learning process, which students consider as ideal particularly for practical subjects such as mathematics (Piki et al. 2022). Although this was by far the preferred way, students acknowledged that an online, virtual environment could also support remote learning as long as it could offer a seamless simulation of the whiteboard so they could watch their lecturer's writings clearly and synchronously while the lecturer is solving exercises step-by-step on the whiteboard live, but at the same time being able to watch their lecturer's facial expressions and body gestures. Essentially, students emphasised the need for a seamless, multimodal, and natural learning environment, which would make them feel involved and comfortable to ask for clarifications during the lecture or as the solution proceeds, be encouraged to contribute to the development of the solution and be able to do so actively and effortlessly. Although a few students also discussed the need for higher education to leverage augmented reality and virtual learning environments, the majority focused on lectures that 'simply work', with no connectivity hassles, technical quality or compatibility issues. Another emergent suggestion raised was that breaks are important, and that there should be ways to recreate 'social breaks' in online and virtual environments. Regarding the lessons learnt, the most remarkable was the students' appreciation of the value of family bonds, and the important role that their parents' encouragement played in remaining focused on their target goals. Similarly, students valued the psychological support, empathy, and mutual understanding from lecturers and peers alike. These lessons constitute some of the restricted positive outcomes reported during this challenging period.

5 Conclusion

The purpose of this study was to explore the factors that impacted learner engagement over time amidst the pandemic; to investigate students' perceptions on the role of social technology during remote education; and to capture students' reflections distilled through their recent and ongoing experiences with online learning. The findings from a holistic, meta-analysis of three exploratory case studies conducted during the pandemic with undergraduate students are discussed and synthesised. The gathered insights do not only accentuate the need to study and instigate learner engagement in current CSCL endeavours, but also re-emphasise the 'distributed nature' of learner engagement indicating that learner engagement is not a trait-like characteristic confined to an individual learner; rather, it is amalgamated through the complex interplay of personal, pedagogical, social, group-level, and technological factors. Beyond realising the role of social, mobile, and collaborative technologies, the unprecedented scale at which online teaching and learning has been studied since Covid-19 outbreak had significant beneficial outcomes. Firstly, understanding the impact of the pandemic on teaching and learning through the eyes and voices of students raised the level of awareness on the significance of making social and mobile technology more inclusive, seamless, and accessible. Secondly, research outputs have contributed to the upskilling of both students and teachers, in all levels of education. Thirdly, the unfolding Covid-19 crisis has enabled us to contemplate on the value of family and social bonds, and brought to the foreground social values, empathy, and emotional intelligence, which are often neglected in educational practices. Finally, while the full extent of the students' envisioned adaptations and the realisation of the long-term impact of this ever-changing situation on our mental health, wellbeing, and engagement is yet to be fully realised, the pandemic has certainly motivated the adoption of mobile, social, and collaborative technologies which are anticipated to continue playing a major role in higher education as we enter a new normal.

References

Abu Elnasr, E.S., Hasanein, A.M., Abu Elnasr, A.E.: Responses to COVID-19 in higher education: social media usage for sustaining formal academic communication in developing countries. Sustainability **12**(16), 6520 (2020). https://doi.org/10.3390/su12166520

Adams, S.: The role of gamification in the facilitation of student engagement: an exploratory industrial psychology application. Ph.D. thesis, Faculty of Economic and Management Sciences at Stellenbosch University (2019)

Ainley, M.: What do we know about student motivation and engagement? Paper presented at the annual meeting of the Australian Association for Research in Education, Melbourne (2004)

Ally, M., Tsinakos, A. (eds.): Increasing access through mobile learning. Commonwealth of Learning (COL): Perspectives on Open and Distance Learning (2014)

Aucejo, E.M., French, J., Araya, M.P.U., Zafar, B.: The impact of COVID-19 on student experiences and expectations: evidence from a survey. J. Public Econ. **191**, 104271 (2020)

Bahati, B.: Extending student discussions beyond lecture room walls via Facebook. J. Educ. Pract. **6**(15), 160–171 (2015)

Barlovits, S., Jablonski, S., Lázaro, C., Ludwig, M., Recio, T.: Teaching from a distance-math lessons during COVID-19 in Germany and Spain. Educ. Sci. **11**, 406 (2021)

Behl, A., Jayawardena, N., Pereira, V., Islam, N., Del Giudice, M., Choudrie, J.: Gamification and e-learning for young learners: a systematic literature review, bibliometric analysis, and future research agenda. Technol. Forecast. Soc. Chang. **176**, 121445 (2022)

Bolliger, D.U., Martin, F.: Instructor and student perceptions of online student engagement strategies. Distance Educ. **39**(4), 568–583 (2018). https://doi.org/10.1080/01587919.2018.152 0041

Bowman, N.D., Akcaoglu, M.: "I see smart people!": using Facebook to supplement cognitive and affective learning in the university mass lecture. Internet High. Educ. **23**, 1–8 (2014). https://doi.org/10.1016/j.iheduc.2014.05.003

Camus, M., Hurt, N.E., Larson, L.R., Prevost, L.: Facebook as an online teaching tool: effects on student participation, learning, and overall course performance. Coll. Teach. **64**(2), 84–94 (2016)

Cassibba, R., Ferrarello, D., Mammana, M.F., Musso, P., Pennisi, M., Taranto, E.: Teaching mathematics at distance: a challenge for universities. Educ. Sci. **11**, 1 (2021)

Clarke, V., Braun, V.: Thematic analysis. J. Posit. Psychol. **12**(3), 297–298 (2017). https://doi.org/10.1080/17439760.2016.1262613

Clements, J.C.: Using Facebook to enhance independent student engagement: a case study of first-year undergraduates. High. Educ. Stud. **5**(4), 131–146 (2015). https://doi.org/10.5539/hes.v5n4p131

Dhawan, S.: Online learning: a panacea in time of COVID-19 crisis. J. Educ. Technol. Syst. **49**(1), 5–22 (2020). https://doi.org/10.1177/0047239520934018

Engelbrecht, J., Borba, M.C., Llinares, S., Kaiser, G.: Will 2020 be remembered as the year in which education was changed? ZDM Math. Educ. **52**(5), 821–824 (2020)

Ferguson, R., et al.: Innovating Pedagogy 2019: Open University Innovation Report 7 (2019)

Gandhi, P., Khanna, S., Ramaswamy, S.: Which industries are the most digital (and why?) (2016). https://hbr.org/2016/04/a-chart-that-shows-which-industries-are-the-most-digital-and-why

García-Peñalvo, F.J., Corell, A., Rivero-Ortega, R., Rodríguez-Conde, M.J., Rodríguez-García, N.: Impact of the COVID-19 on higher education: an experience-based approach. In: García-Penalvo, F.J. (ed.) Information Technology Trends for a Global and Interdisciplinary Research Community, pp. 1–18. IGI Global (2021). https://doi.org/10.4018/978-1-7998-4156-2.ch001

Gierdowski, D.C.: ECAR Study of Undergraduate Students and Information Technology (Research report). Louisville, CO: EDUCAUSE Center for Applied Research, October 2019 (2019). http://www.educause.edu/ecar

Gikas, J., Grant, M.M.: Mobile computing devices in higher education: student perspectives on learning with cellphones, smartphones & social media. Internet High. Educ. **19**, 18–26 (2013)

Gill, P., Stewart, K., Treasure, E., Chadwick, B.: Methods of data collection in qualitative research: interviews and focus groups. Br. Dent. J. **204**, 291–295 (2008)

Grebennikova, L., Shah, M.: Student voice: using qualitative feedback from students to enhance their university experience. Teach. High. Educ. **18**(6), 606–618 (2013). https://doi.org/10.1080/13562517.2013.774353

Hamid, S., Waycott, J., Kurnia, S., Chang, S.: Understanding students' perceptions of the benefits of online social networking use for teaching and learning. Internet High. Educ. **26**, 1–9 (2015). https://doi.org/10.1016/j.iheduc.2015.02.004

Hernández-Sellés, N., Muñoz-Carril, P.C., González-Sanmamed, M.: Computer-supported collaborative learning: An analysis of the relationship between interaction, emotional support and online collaborative tools. Comput. Educ. **138**, 1–12 (2019). https://doi.org/10.1016/j.compedu.2019.04.012

Hodges, C., Moore, S., Lockee, B., Trust, T., Bond, A.: The difference between emergency remote teaching and online learning. EDUCAUSE Rev. **2020**, 3 (2020)

Hughes, K.: Impact of student engagement on achievement and well-being. A Literature Review Prepared for the Ottawa-Carleton District School Board, pp. 1–26 (2012)

Kahu, E.R., Picton, C., Nelson, K.: Pathways to engagement: a longitudinal study of the first-year student experience in the educational interface. High. Educ. **79**(4), 657–673 (2020). https://doi.org/10.1007/s10734-019-00429-w

Kara, M.: Revisiting online learner engagement: exploring the role of learner characteristics in an emergency period. J. Res. Technol. Educ. **54**, 1–17 (2021)

Krouska, A., Troussas, C., Sgouropoulou, C.: Mobile game-based learning as a solution in COVID-19 era: modeling the pedagogical affordance and student interactions. Educ. Inf. Technol. 1–13 (2021). https://doi.org/10.1007/s10639-021-10672-3

Krueger, R.A.: Focus Groups: A Practical Guide for Applied Research. SAGE, Thousand Oaks (2014)

Ma, X., Liu, J., Liang, J., Fan, C.: An empirical study on the effect of group awareness in CSCL environments. Interact. Learn. Environ. 1–16 (2020). https://doi.org/10.1080/10494820.2020.1758730

Mansouri, S.A., Piki, A.: An exploration into the impact of blogs on students' learning: case studies in postgraduate business education. Innov. Educ. Teach. Int. **53**(3), 260–273 (2016)

Marinoni, G., van't Land, H.: The impact of COVID-19 on global higher education. Int. High. Educ. **102**, 7–9 (2020)

Martin, F., Bolliger, D.U.: Engagement matters: student perceptions on the importance of engagement strategies in the online learning environment. Online Learn. **22**(1), 205–222 (2018). https://doi.org/10.24059/olj.v22i1.1092

Mehla, L., Sheorey, P.A., Tiwari, A.K., Behl, A.: Paradigm shift in the education sector amidst COVID-19 to improve online engagement: opportunities and challenges. J. Glob. Inf. Manag. **30**(5), 1–21 (2021)

Molinillo, S., Aguilar-Illescas, R., Anaya-Sánchez, R., Vallespín-Arán, M.: Exploring the impacts of interactions, social presence and emotional engagement on active collaborative learning in a social web-based environment. Comput. Educ. **123**, 41–52 (2018). https://doi.org/10.1016/j.compedu.2018.04.012

Mottiwalla, L.F.: Mobile learning: a framework and evaluation. Comput. Educ. **49**(3), 581–596 (2007)

Muñoz-Carril, P.C., Hernández-Sellés, N., Fuentes-Abeledo, E.J., González-Sanmamed, M.: Factors influencing students' perceived impact of learning and satisfaction in Computer Supported Collaborative Learning. Comput. Educ. **174**, 104310 (2021)

Naghdipour, B., Eldridge, N.H.: Incorporating social networking sites into traditional pedagogy: a case of Facebook. TechTrends **60**(6), 591–597 (2016). https://doi.org/10.1007/s11528-016-0118-4

Nisiotis, L., Kleanthous, S.: The relationship between students' engagement and the development of transactive memory systems in MUVE: an experience report. In: 24th Annual Conference on Innovation and Technology in Computer Science Education (ITiCSE), Aberdeen, Scotland. ACM (2019). https://doi.org/10.1145/3304221.3319743

Nisiotis, L., Kleanthous, S.: Lessons learned using a virtual world to support collaborative learning in the classroom. J. Univ. Comput. Sci. **26**(8), 858–879 (2020)

Nisiotis, L., Kleanthous Loizou, S., Beer, M., Uruchurtu, E.: The use of a cyber campus to support teaching and collaboration: an observation approach. In: Beck, D. (ed.) The Immersive Learning Research Network (iLRN) Conference, Portugal, 26–29 June 2017, pp. 193–194 (2017)

Patton, M.Q.: Qualitative Evaluation and Research Methods. SAGE Publications, Thousand Oaks (1990)

Piki, A.: Learner engagement in computer-supported collaborative learning environments: a mixed-methods study in postgraduate education. Ph.D. thesis. Royal Holloway University of London, UK (2012)

Piki, A.: Learner engagement in computer-supported collaborative learning activities: natural or nurtured? In: Zaphiris, P., Ioannou, A. (eds.) LCT 2014. LNCS, vol. 8523, pp. 107–118. Springer, Cham (2014). https://doi.org/10.1007/978-3-319-07482-5_11

Piki, A.: Learner engagement in mobile computer-supported collaborative learning contexts: an integrative framework. In: Proceedings of the 16th World Conference on Mobile and Contextual Learning (mLearn 2017), 30 October–1 November 2017, Larnaca, Cyprus. ACM (2017)

Piki, A.: An exploration of student experiences with social media and mobile technologies during emergency transition to remote education. In: The Proceedings of the 19th World Conference on Mobile, Blended and Seamless Learning (mLearn 2020), 2–4 November 2020, Cairo, Egypt (2020)

Piki, A., Andreou, L., Markou, M.: Students' perspectives on the emergency transition to online education – a case study in mathematics education. In: 16th Annual International Technology, Education and Development Conference (INTED 2022), 2–7 March 2022 (2022)

Schaufeli, W.B., Salanova, M., González-Romá, V., Bakker, A.: The measurement of burnout and engagement: a confirmatory analytic approach. J. Happiness Stud. **3**(1), 71–92 (2002)

Schindler, L.A., Burkholder, G.J., Morad, O.A., Marsh, C.: Computer-based technology and student engagement: a critical review of the literature. Int. J. Educ. Technol. High. Educ. **14**(1), 1–28 (2017). https://doi.org/10.1186/s41239-017-0063-0

Scopus Elsevier: Scopus – Expertly curated abstract & citation database (2022). https://www.elsevier.com/solutions/scopus

Sharples, M., Taylor, J., Vavoula, G.: A theory of learning for the mobile age. In: Andrews, R., Haythornthwaite, C. (eds.) The Sage handbook of Elearning research, pp. 221–247. Sage, London (2007)

Toquero, C.M.: Challenges and opportunities for higher education amid the COVID-19 pandemic: the Philippine context. Pedagog. Res. **5**(4), em0063 (2020). https://doi.org/10.29333/pr/7947

Tractenberg, R.E.: The assessment evaluation rubric: promoting learning and learner-centered teaching through assessment in face-to-face or distanced higher education. Educ. Sci. **11**, 441 (2021)

Tsinakos, A., Ally, M. (eds.): Global mobile learning implementation and trends (2013)

Twining, P., Heller, R.S., Nassbaum, M., Tsai, C.-C.: Some guidance on conducting and reporting qualitative studies. Comput. Educ. **106**, A1–A9 (2017)

Veluvali, P., Surisetti, J.: Learning management system for greater learner engagement in higher education—a review. High. Educ. Future **9**(1), 107–121 (2022)

Vijayan, R.: Teaching and learning during the COVID-19 pandemic: a topic modeling study. Educ. Sci. **11**, 347 (2021)

Vlachopoulos, D.: COVID-19: Threat or opportunity for online education? High. Learn. Res. Commun. **10**(1), 16–19 (2020). https://doi.org/10.18870/hlrc.v10i1.1179

Wang, Y., Cao, Y., Gong, S., Wang, Z., Li, N., Ai, L.: Interaction and learning engagement in online learning: the mediating roles of online learning self-efficacy and academic emotions. Learn. Individ. Differ. **94**, 102128 (2022)

Xie, K., Heddy, B.C., Vongkulluksn, V.W.: Examining engagement in context using experience-sampling method with mobile technology. Contemp. Educ. Psychol. **59**, 101788 (2019). https://doi.org/10.1016/j.cedpsych.2019.101788

Experiential Learning Through Virtual Tours in Times of COVID-19

Roxana Sandu[✉] [iD]

Toyo University, 5 Chome-28-20 Hakusan, Bunkyo City, Tokyo 112-8606, Japan
sandu@toyo.jp

Abstract. Many argue that experience plays a significant role in learning. However, previous research has shown that experience alone does not necessarily produce learning. This study describes the application of Kolb's experiential learning cycle (experiencing, reflecting, thinking and acting) as a framework to design assignments for an English for Tourism Industry course at a private university in Japan. The scope of the study was to ensure students a firsthand tourism experience through active participation in virtual tours and events during emergency remote teaching due to COVID-19 pandemic, as well as to explore the implications such an approach may have on students' learning, in acquiring new knowledge and reflecting on its further use. Through the use of free virtual tours available online, students completed three assignments over a 15-week semester. Each assignment included a different type of virtual activity: (1) a tour of a UNESCO World Heritage Site using Google Earth, (2) an online event, museum exhibition or concert, and (3) a walking tour of a major world city using 360° interactive video. Analysis of the collected data, in form of students' assignments, revealed how the implementation of such an approach not only allowed for various realizations about the perceived usefulness and benefits of virtual tours, but also motivated students themselves to think more about the use of virtual tours in the tourism industry beyond COVID-19 pandemic.

Keywords: Virtual tours · Experiential learning cycle · Reflection · English for Tourism

1 Introduction

The threat of the COVID-19 pandemic has presented unique challenges for higher education worldwide. As we all know, due to the urgency of the situation and in order to protect the health of their personnel (staff, faculty and students alike), many universities opted to switch their face-to-face classes to online classes. Different from carefully planned online programs, this emergency remote teaching (ERT) as a temporary measure led to myriad difficulties. In spite of the image Japan holds as being a technology leader, Aoki [1] and Funamori [2] pointed out that the use of technology for educational purposes in Japan is low compared to other developed countries. Therefore, when ERT was adopted for courses designed to be delivered face-to-face, it revealed not only a large digital gap among faculty members, but also a lack of adequate preparedness for such a radical

© The Author(s), under exclusive license to Springer Nature Switzerland AG 2022
G. Meiselwitz (Ed.): HCII 2022, LNCS 13316, pp. 180–198, 2022.
https://doi.org/10.1007/978-3-031-05064-0_14

change on the part of the institutions [3]. Apple and Mills [3, p. 2] describe the situation where university administrators were "scrambling to set guidelines for the new online classes yet had little or no knowledge of online teacher training, online course design and management, and online teaching pedagogy" as contributing to states of general confusion.

In the midst of this situation, students had to start or continue their studies where in many university programs, such as those related to tourism for example, field trips and/or in-person internships had to be cancelled, activities considered essential to fully understand the job requirements in such industries. With tourism being one of the industries hardest-hit due to the pandemic, tourism students were particularly affected, as activities that allowed them hands-on experiences were mostly cancelled. However, as physical tourism hit bottom, other means of tourism, such as virtual tours (VTs), allowed for entertaining potential tourists worldwide. Museums, nature parks, and heritage sites worldwide opened their virtual doors, and in no time people were able to virtually travel to places, attend events and partake of a variety of tours, many free of charge. For example, according to El-Said and Aziz [4], the Frank Lloyd Wright Foundation, the New York Botanical Garden, the Eiffel Tower, and the Vatican Museums began conducting VTs. The list could continue. Under these unprecedented circumstances, teaching Tourism Industry English courses with textbooks that focused only on the language used in interactions with tourists at hotels, airports and restaurants felt out of context.

Responding to this reality, the present research designed three different assignments in order to promote (1) a way for students to experience firsthand an emerging way of traveling (through VTs) and attending events (through virtual events), albeit in an English for Specific Purposes (ESP) course environment, while (2) encouraging reflection on their experiences. The aim of this approach was not only to provide students with the opportunity to live firsthand the online tourist experience, but also to examine how they perceive the "new normal" way of traveling through VTs, as well as the implications VTs have for their own future careers.

2 Background to the Study

2.1 Virtual Tours

VTs are defined as "a simulation of an existing location that is composed of a sequence of video images" [5, p. 173]. Such simulations can be accompanied by text descriptions, audio guides, or sound effects, and are most commonly experienced through the worldwide web using a computer. It is important to differentiate VTs from virtual reality (VR), which is defined as "the sum of the hardware and software systems that seek to perfect an all-inclusive, sensory illusion of being present in another environment" [6, p. 63]. VR is technology that "generates a simulated environment through head-mounted displays (HMDs) and creates an immersive and interactive experience for users" [7, p. 1].

More recently, due to the ongoing COVID-19 pandemic, VTs have attracted increased interest, especially in the tourism industry. The various opportunities that VTs can provide in tourism are mentioned in El-Said and Aziz [4, p. 530], as "enabling tourists to experience and learn about different sites and destinations during times of travel restrictions and bans while staying safe at home (UNESCO 2020), enabling museums and different touristic sites to remain engaged with their public (UNESCO 2020; Sallent 2020), and providing job opportunities for employees such as tour guides through the provision of VT-based tour guiding (Ramachandran, Subramani, and Ambrose 2020)". However, to my knowledge, little research has reported on integration of VTs in second language education, and ESP in particular. Prominent theories commonly associated with virtual technologies are constructivism [8], and experiential learning theory. One study reports on the theory of experiential learning being commonly associated with digital technologies in general, but also with VR in particular [7].

2.2 Experiential Learning

Experiential learning theory was developed by Kolb [9] based on several models of experiential learning, including those of Lewin, Dewey, and Piaget, which basically refer to learning from experience or learning by doing. Learning is defined as "the process whereby knowledge is created through the transformation of experience" [9, p. 38]. In other words, "to learn, one must go through a series of steps after an initial experience: There must be a reflection on the experience followed by an understanding of what the new learning means to the individual and a conceptualization of how it can be used in the future" [10, p. 53]. In experiential learning theory, the concern for the whole learner is central, as Kolb and Kolb state [11, p. 48]: "the learner 'touches all the bases' – experiencing, reflecting, thinking and acting", making it a holistic dynamic theory.

Experiential learning theory has at its core six distinctive characteristics [9, pp. 26–36]: (1) "learning is best perceived as a process not in terms of outcomes", (2) "learning is a continuous process grounded in experience", (3) "learning requires the resolution of conflicts between opposing modes of adaptation to the world", (4) "learning is a holistic process of adaptation to the world", (5) "learning involves transactions between the person and the environment", and (6) "learning is the process of creating knowledge". Thus, learning is, first, not an outcome and shall be accompanied by feedback. Second, learners' beliefs are challenged and new ideas and insights may take shape thanks to this. Third, the learning process is driven by differences and it is through the resolution of these differences that individuals learn. Fourth, adapting to an environment by feeling, thinking, perceiving, and behaving is learning. Fifth, learning results from connecting new experiences to existing concepts and vice versa. Finally, the learners themselves create new knowledge.

Based on these six characteristics, in order to become an effective learner and acquire new knowledge, learners need to approach all four modes of experiential learning; these four modes of learning are what came to be known as the experiential learning cycle as shown in Fig. 1 [12, p. 11] below. The learning modes include two opposing modes of grasping experiences and two opposing modes of transforming experiences. Grasping experience includes Concrete Experience and Abstract Conceptualization, whereas transforming experiences refers to Reflective Observation and Active Experimentation. In order for learning to occur, all four modes—experiencing, reflecting, thinking and acting—must be present. These learning modes occur in a four-stage cycle: (1) first, learners have concrete experiences by exposing themselves to a new situation, (2) second, learners reflect on and analyze their experiences, (3) third, the learners engage in abstract conceptualization, which enables them to discover the learning that took place during the experience and through reflection, and (4) fourth, learners make use of their new learning and put it into action. Kolb and Kolb [12, p. 15] explain the importance of the experiential learning cycle as it "describes the learning process as a recursive circle or spiral as opposed to the linear, traditional information transmission model of learning used in most education, where information is transferred from the teacher to the learner to be stored in declarative memory for later recall."

As the experiential learning cycle implies, experience alone does not produce learning; it must be followed by reflection, as a way to deepen the understanding of the new acquired knowledge. This way, both experience and reflection are at the centre of experiential learning. Kohonen [13, p. 32] explains this relation as "the process of extracting personal meanings from experience through reflection."

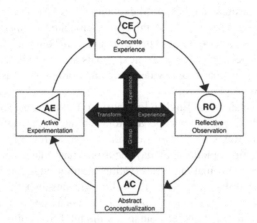

Fig. 1. Kolb's experiential learning cycle

The literature on the use of experiential learning of theoretical concepts as a base for curriculum design, courses and even activities design across different disciplines is vast. And so is the literature discussing the importance of integrating reflective activities into one's teaching. Young et al. [14, p. 38] suggest "that experiential learning activities that incorporated all four stages of the learning cycle led to a deeper approach to learning and a reporting of a higher level of perceived learning and more favorable attitudes by students." They further explain that for eliciting "deeper meaningful learning, faculty should design comprehensive learning activities that allow for concrete experiences, reflective observation, abstract conceptualization, and active experimentation." While critical reflection is a desirable skill for students of all disciplines, referring to students of tourism, Hughes et al. [15, p. 95] argue that "self-reflection is one of those 'hidden' skills embedded and implicit in effective performance of many other 'soft' skills required by employers," a description that fits well for the tourism industry. The current study adopts the use of the experiential learning cycle as a framework to design assignments for an English for Tourism Industry course. Based on previous studies, experiential learning approaches have been documented to be well suited for students of tourism [16].

3 Methodology

This section will first offer an account of the teaching context, and then discuss the design of each assignment within the framework of the experiential learning cycle, as well as the data collection and interpretation.

3.1 Teaching Context

Most English courses at Japanese universities are compulsory for all freshman students, independent of their chosen specialties. Many of these courses focus on the development of various skills, such as reading, writing, speaking, intercultural communication, presentation and so on. However, a small number of courses that are included in a Japanese university curricula are what would fit under the name of English for Specific Purposes (ESP). As Basturkmen [17, p. 8] explains, "[i]n ESP, the learner is seen as a language learner engaged either in academic, professional or occupational pursuits and who uses English as a means to carry out those pursuits." In contrast, she further explains that in an English for general purposes context "goals are generally linguistic (such as, development of oral competence or a wide vocabulary, or ability to use a wide range of grammatical structures)" [17, p. 8].

Based on these explanations, English for Tourism (EfT) is considered to be a branch of ESP. In a typical EfT course, concepts and topics related to the tourism industry are introduced through readings and various exercises such as role plays. Other learning activities include listening practice that may focus on situational conversations: English for hotels (checking in/out, making a reservation, dealing with common complaints), restaurants (describing dishes, taking orders, dealing with unsatisfied customers), airlines (bookings and check-in). This type of course, encompassing a variety of topics, is what Basturkmen [17] calls a "wide-angled course". Although ESP is often organized on the basis of student analysis, such wide-angled courses "are not based on an analysis of needs of a particular group of learners but on description of language use in a field or discipline" [17, p. 56]. To borrow Basturkmen's term, the course selected for this study was a wide-angled course, which focused on introducing students to some of the language used in various situations in the tourism industry, as well as on introducing students to several types of tourism, such as sustainable tourism, nature tourism, ecotourism, etc.

The study was carried out at a Japanese private university over one semester in the fall of 2021. All 18 class members (2 male and 16 female) were Japanese second-year undergraduates in the Faculty of International Management Tourism. The course, *English for the Tourism Industry*, was compulsory and taught over two semesters (thirty 90 min sessions in total). The spring semester was entirely taught online while the fall semester was a mixture of face to face (every other week between October and December, six classes in total) and online classes (every other week on Zoom, nine classes in total). Participants' English proficiency ranged between intermediate to pre-advanced (TOEIC scores ranged between 660 and 725, with an average 692), therefore English was the medium of instruction. For classroom instruction, a textbook especially designed for students of tourism and professionals working in the tourism industry was used. For the online sessions, Zoom, along with Edmodo, a learning management platform, were used for allowing students to work in small groups and share their ideas smoothly during class discussions.

3.2 Assignment Design and the Experiential Learning Cycle

Under normal circumstances, students would have been encouraged to visit tourist sites, travel agencies and hotels/restaurants for firsthand experiences, but due to the COVID 19 pandemic, that was not possible. For that reason, and as a means of providing opportunities to explore the realities of virtual tourism as an emerging sector of the tourism industry, three virtual activities were designed while taking into account Kolb's [9] experiential learning cycle. Each assignment complemented textbook units on similar topics. Students had about four weeks to complete and submit each assignment; they were encouraged to use a variety of media to prepare their assignments, such as photos, drawings, videos, graphs, infographics, etc.

In order to complete each assignment, students had to follow four steps: (Step 1) Choose a virtual tour or event to participate in, (Step 2) Write about the experience from the tourist's perspective (150–200 words), (Step 3) Write about the experience from the worker's perspective (virtual tour guide, virtual tour coordinator, etc.) (100 words), (Step 4) Reflect on the experience and write about what was learned (150 words). Other than the first step, that simply asked students to select a tour or event they would like to participate in, each of the other steps included all learning modes of the experiential learning cycle. During Steps (2) and (3), although students were not asked specifically to reflect on their experience, it was obvious that without actually reflecting and thinking about the experience, the writing would not be possible. The rationale behind this was to gradually introduce students to the reflection exercise and have them think about their experiences from various perspectives instead of just asking them to reflect on the experience in a general or universal way. The last step clearly brought students to reflect on what they had learned, evident in an emphasis on their learning in the form of newly acquired knowledge or realizations and the application of this learning to their future careers. The reflective type of writing expected in these assignments was meant to bring students to slowly immerse themselves in a reflection exercise that would hopefully show them a new way of learning.

Thus, for the first step of each assignment, students were clearly instructed how to select their virtual tours and examples were provided as necessary. The first assignment was titled World Heritage Sites. Students were told to choose a heritage site they would like to visit and go on a virtual tour. The objectives of this assignment were clearly stated as follows: (1) to experience firsthand a new way of traveling, through virtual tours, (2) to think about the future of the tourism industry and the new skills needed for it, and (3) to reflect on their learning process. About 30 UNESCO World Heritage Sites can be visited with Google Earth using the street view, and brief captions including information and descriptions of the heritage sites are available. This way, Google Earth was one platform provided as an example to help students find suitable tours for their assignments. Students were also told to choose a tour that allowed them to walk around so that the experience is as immersive as possible, and use a computer instead of their phones for a better experience.

Shellito [18, p. 1] defines Google Earth as: "... a virtual globe software program that allows you to utilize geospatial technology for a variety of very cool applications. You can zoom from Earth's orbit to see a satellite image or aerial photograph of your house, fly to any location on the globe, see cities and landscapes in 3D, and look at all sort of geographic content from around the world." Google Earth has been used in education, especially in disciplines such as geography. However, Wise [19, p. 192] explains how such a visual learning technique as Google Earth, "can be used to reinforce understandings of particular tourism-related practices by virtually taking learners to actual locations to reinforce understandings [...]." An easy entry to use of technology in tourism, Google Earth seemed the perfect choice as many students might have used it in their daily lives before, therefore some sort of familiarity to its functions was expected.

For the second assignment, titled Events, students were instructed to choose an online event (free of charge): a festival, a film festival, a concert, a talk, an art exhibition, a show, etc. The objectives were again clearly stated as follows: (1) to experience first hand a new way of entertainment, through online events, (2) to think about the future of the tourism industry and the new skills needed for it, and (3) to reflect on their learning process. Students were told to choose any type of event they participated in during the COVID-19 pandemic. Some links were again provided as examples and they were also directed towards Google Arts and Culture tours, which has a collection of virtual tours of renowned museums worldwide. The last assignment, Walking Tours, had the following objectives: (1) to experience first hand a new way of exploring cities, through virtual walking tours, (2) to think about the future of the tourism industry and the new skills needed for it, and (3) to reflect on their own learning process. This time, students were asked to choose a virtual walking tour, using a 360° interactive video, of a major city anywhere in the world. A YouTube channel was provided as an example, as it offered a large variety of short and long walking tours around major cities in the world.

Violante et al. [20, p. 730] wrote about 360° videos being completely immersive: "The viewer can see everything within the range of the camera, whereas traditional video is limited to wherever the camera is pointing." This allows the viewer to experience the environment from multiple perspectives, not only the director's view. They further explain that "360° videos are typically viewed via personal computers, mobile devices such as smartphones, or dedicated head-mounted displays for a completely immersive experience" [20, p. 731]. Therefore, a walking tour shot with this type of camera allows for a more immersive experience, and more opportunities for viewers to explore the sites.

As already stated, in order to provide students with several opportunities to look back at their experiences and reflect on them, reflection was encouraged in this study as follows: (1) as an initial reflection - description of the experience as an online tourist, (2) as a further reflection - assessment of the possible needed skills as future professionals making use of their experience, and (3) as an ultimate reflection - evaluation of their learning through the experience and its implications for their future careers.

Therefore, in the second step of the assignments students were instructed to write in detail about their experience as online tourists, as an initial reflection exercise. In the first two assignments, students were asked to pay particular attention to details, such as the people around them and their own feelings, during the virtual tours. Questions such as,

"What were you thinking or feeling during the experience?" were given to help students write not only about the descriptions of the sites, but also their emotions in that moment. In the last assignment, they were encouraged to pay attention not only to the people around them, but also to the stores, the buildings, etc., and also to answer questions such as, *"Was there anything that surprised you? Was there anything that was different from where you live?"* or *"Was there anything that was similar to where you live?"*. Such questions were provided to help students think deeper about their experiences, by comparing the new explored environments with the ones they are familiar with.

While the initial stage of reflection was meant to elicit descriptive narratives of their experiences, the further stages of reflective observation were meant to provide an opportunity for them to also start thinking of concrete examples based on the learning discoveries. As a result, the third step in the assignments was more of a visualizing exercise. For the first assignment, students were asked to imagine their job as an online tour guide and write their opinions by answering questions such as: *"Are the skills needed to be an online tour guide any different from a typical tour guide? What do you think?"*. For the second assignment, students were asked to imagine their job as an online event coordinator and think whether the same skills are needed in order to be an online event coordinator as opposed to an event coordinator in a typical environment. For the final assignment, students had to imagine they work in marketing, promoting travel destinations using interactive virtual walking tours. Questions were again provided to help them understand better what to write about: *"What skills do you think you need for this type of job? Do you think these virtual tours will replace the physical ones in the future?"*. This type of exercise, as in shifting perspectives from an online tourist to a worker in the tourism industry, was meant to prompt students to think critically about their future careers and the professional skills needed in such new environments.

Finally, as the fourth step of the assignments, students had to reflect on their experiences as a whole and write about what they learned. At the same time, they were also encouraged to think of how this experience helped them understand more about the future of tourism. The following questions were provided to guide students through this final step: (1) What did I learn? (I learned that ...), (2) How, specifically, did I learn it? (I learned this when ...), (3) Why does this learning matter, or why is it significant? (This learning matters because ...), (4) In what ways will I use this learning? (In light of this learning ...). These questions were adopted from Ash and Clayton's [21] study and are called "articulated learning". They explain that the above questions are similar to the "What? So What? Now What?" model developed by the Campus Opportunity Outreach League and based on Kolb's Experiential Learning Cycle of action and reflection (1984), embodying Dewey's theory that reflection leads to better understanding *and* more informed action" [21, p. 143]. The rationale behind using the articulated learning for this study was that it offers students an easy how-to guide as opposed to just a "write a reflection" or "reflect on your experience" type of writing prompt. As argued in Ash and Clayton [21, p. 142], "the *articulating learning* phase brings each reflection activity to a close and establishes a foundation for learners to carry the results of the reflection process forward beyond the immediate experience, improving the quality of future learning and of future experience (related to service or to other aspects of their lives)."

Moreover, for each of these assignments, the following evaluation rubric was provided for the students to understand what is expected of them. In Cheng and Chan [22, p. 181], the rubric was used to examine the impact of using such a rubric during reflective writing activities on students' reflection levels. Their study showed that "rubrics can effectively enhance students' learning in reflective writing with proper guidelines and training." In other words, its use and detailed explanations can help students in their reflective writing as they can evaluate themselves and better their writing according to the guidelines in the rubric. In the current study, the rubric (Fig. 2) was provided from the beginning as a mere guideline and the way students used these rubrics was not something that was closely examined as it was beyond the scope of this study.

LEVEL	POOR ★	FAIR ★★	AVERAGE ★★★	GOOD ★★★★	EXCELLENT ★★★★★
CRITERIA	Only includes mere descriptions of what you did in the activities; no reflection is demonstrated beyond the descriptions	Includes description of events and activities, and a little further consideration behind these events using a relatively descriptive style of language; no evidence of using multiple perspectives in analyzing the issues encountered	Showing satisfactory ability to relate acquired knowledge and experience to previous knowledge and experiences; demonstrating attempt to analyze the issues encountered from a number of different perspectives	Ability to proficiently demonstrate reflection and deep thinking of acquired knowledge and concepts, and integrate them into different issues from wide range of perspectives (e.g. different contexts, cultures, disciplines etc.); creative solutions and critical thinking skills demonstrated in the writing	Able to demonstrate excellent insights in their self-reflection. Able to apply past and present experiences to future situations and integrate into different issues from wide range of perspectives (e.g. different contexts, cultures, disciplines etc.); creative solutions and critical thinking skills demonstrated in the writing, including deep emotions.

Fig. 2. Cheng and Chan's evaluation rubric for reflective writing

In addition, following these three assignments, three structured activities were created for students to be able to share their reflections and realizations with their peers. During the final review, students were asked to share their opinions about the virtual experiences they had through the VTs and virtual events. This activity was first done through discussions in small groups, then followed by a class discussion. Next, during the final class, the teacher offered overall feedback with an emphasis on the importance of reflection in learning, and how to make use of it in future courses, as well as pointing out common mistakes encountered throughout students' assignments. Finally, students were asked to work in small groups and think of the definition of virtual tourism, its advantages and disadvantages, based on their own experiences. After the group discussions, a class discussion was held to share each group's findings. Furthermore, in order to allow students to put their findings into words, each student had to share on Edmodo, their virtual classroom, their own definitions of virtual tourism, its advantages and disadvantages. This activity completed the learning cycle in the hope that students will make use of the acquired knowledge in the future. The analysis of these final thoughts was not included in this study, as it meant to be a summary of their overall realizations; in other words, rewriting in a more succinct form what they had already written in their assignments.

3.3 Data Collection and Interpretation

The data of this study is comprised of students' narratives, collected from the three assignments described in the previous section. As shown above, each assignment included a three-step reflective writing exercise, in other words, three different paragraphs were written for each of the second, third and fourth steps of the assignments. In order to address the aim of this study, which is to explore the implications such an approach may have on students' learning, as in acquiring new knowledge (and/or realizations) and reflecting on its further use, only the narratives written for the fourth step of the assignments were collected and carefully analyzed. A qualitative approach was employed to interpret the data; by using content analysis to analyze students' narratives, several repeating patterns were found which allowed the author to create specific categories for the identified patterns, as the discussion below will show. Each participant was randomly allocated a number (i.e. S1, S2, etc.) for anonymity.

4 Results and Discussion

The results of the analysis of student narratives will be presented and discussed to highlight the repeating patterns found in the data. The main findings of these narratives were divided into two sub-sections; the first sub-section will offer an overall description of students' narratives, while the second will focus on what students perceived as learning following their virtual experiences.

4.1 Overall Descriptions of Students' Narratives

For their virtual tours, students selected a wide variety of places from around the world to visit. Some of the heritage sites students visited were the Taj Mahal Palace in India, Shirakawago in Japan, Vatican City, the Great Wall of China, and some of the major cities they selected for their walking tours included Dubai, Singapore, Venice, Seoul, London, Los Angeles. For the second assignment, most students chose to write about attending online concerts of their favorite artists, while some chose to visit online art exhibitions and write about them. Only one student chose to write about an online study abroad program that was held in collaboration with a university in Laos. For the third assignment, many students chose a video with voice over, which means they could actually listen to a guide as they were walking through the streets of their chosen destinations.

Although instructions were provided in written form, as well as orally during class, the narrative analysis collectively revealed students' misunderstanding of the type of platforms they were supposed to use. As a result, for the first assignment, few students chose to watch either a video or a 360° panorama photo instead of visiting the site using a virtual tour, as instructed. This could be due to the fact that students were not familiar with the concept of virtual tours. This confusion showed the author the necessity of providing clear definitions along with instructions; and rather than allowing students to freely choose a virtual tour from the Internet, compiling a list with links to a variety of virtual tours for students to choose from may have been a better way to avoid such confusion.

Despite the fact that VTs are not necessarily the newest tool available, students' narratives revealed the fact that many may have never used VTs before this assignment. After the first assignment, S2 wrote: "*It was first time for me to attend an online tour. I expected that online tours are not interesting, they will made me bored. It was a fun experience than expected.* I could know atmosphere. And I could see views and designs in detail [emphasis added]". Although the purpose of this study was not to measure students' enjoyment of the VT experience, it is interesting to find out how such an assignment changed students' minds about a tool that is probably going to be increasingly implemented in many sectors of the tourism industry, therefore becoming an essential part of what may constitute their jobs in the near future. As we can see from S2's example above, the actual experience exceeded the initial expectations. Similarly to S2, S14 writes in the second assignment how the experience prompted her to change her views about virtual events: "*This experience mattered for me because I could change my thought of online event and for my future job, it was good trigger to think about how to entertain people online.* To deepen my learning of online event, I will try to join many kinds of it [emphasis added]."

Other students' narratives also showed that many of them were neither familiar with VTs nor had knowledge about VTs' recent increasing use as a form of traveling during COVID-19 pandemic. For example, S12 wrote:

> *I learned that we could visit heritage sites and travel all over the worldat our own house.* I learned this when I went on virtual tours, especially, I saw inside the building. Before this experience, I knew that we could use Street View to see the streets and the outside of buildings, but through this experience I learned that we could also look around the inside of buildings. *This learning matters because we must adapt to the changing times. As the environment changes, so does the demand.* I think the virtual tour to be an example of this. [...] *This learning was a good opportunity to experience the service adapting to that change* [emphasis added].

Learning and thinking about the convenience of using VTs versus the hassle of physical traveling has given students a different perspective of the ongoing changes in the tourism industry and the implications these changes may have for their future careers. This simple realization, that by using VTs we can visit the world from the comfort of our homes, offered students an opportunity to start thinking about various ways of using VTs in their future careers, and prompted them to identify VTs advantages (and disadvantages), as well as who benefits from further development of such technology.

Furthermore, this type of assignment also sparked curiosity in some students and prompted them to further research the phenomenon in the Japanese context, as we can see in this S13's narrative: "Moreover, *according to a survey by Kankokeizai Shimbun, about 65 percent of respondents' purpose of online tour is information gathering*, too. I want to utilize online tour actively in the future because it must entertain my real travel more [emphasis added]." S5 also mentioned how this assignment motivated her to find out more information about the current use of VTs, and reports on the findings from an article she read, as shown in the example below:

In addition, through doing this activity, I was able to learn and reaffirm the future demand for virtual tours. *I actually learned this when I was researching virtual tours on the Internet. I saw an article that said that the number of participants who joined the tour had doubled.* I believe the pandemic is probably the biggest influence, but I felt that the demand is definitely increasing [emphasis added].

At the same time, some students referred to the importance of VTs as an educational tool. For example, S1 talks about her realization of how important it is to not only know about this technology but to also learn how to use it effectively. Through these assignments, she realized the importance of developing basic IT skills to keep up with the ever-changing trends in the industry.

This learning matters because *it may be new main education for young people.* Learning how to operate computers has already been one of the educations students should learn. I think it will be more important because online and offline services will be combined in the future in my opinion. In light of this learning, *I want to learn about computer. Editing is difficult for me, so I want to learn some kinds of enjoyable videos and think about what contents satisfy tourists* [emphasis added].

S8 writes about the future use of this new approach to traveling, while emphasizing the importance of being up to date with the latest technologies in the field in order to further improve customer service: "*Keeping up to date with the latest information and using state-of-the-art technology may add value to online tours more than traditional physical ones.* Demand varies, so I think that thoroughly investigating and responding to customer needs will lead to the development of new travel styles [emphasis added]."

Throughout their reflective narratives, students showed again and again what they learned, and most importantly, how they will make use of the new acquired knowledge and/or realizations in their future careers. While most students offered detailed explanations, some just pointed to the integration of VTs in tourism and their further development in very general terms. The next sub-section will discuss in more details these two aspects.

4.2 Students' Perceived Learning Discoveries Through Virtual Experiences

This sub-section will look at some of the things students perceived as learning through these three assignments. Specific information regarding the sites and places visited will not be noted here, as the ultimate step of reflection should go beyond just enumerating facts; students should have explained their learning discoveries in general terms so that they can apply it more broadly to other areas in their lives. One example of specific learning information is shown below in S8's narrative:

S8: I could find that Singapore is a city where even a short stay can be enjoyed enough because there are many tourist spots with many attractions in a small land area. In particular, I felt that Marina Bay Sands and Gardens by the Bay, which I mentioned before, are more like coming to the future than being in a foreign country.

This does not mean that such learning is insignificant, but its analysis goes beyond the scope of this study. Moreover, such descriptive explanations of the visited places or attended events, were expected to be found in the second step of their assignments, which encouraged a detailed description of their experiences.

Therefore, one common pattern found in the narratives was students' attempt at evaluating VTs' usefulness beyond COVID-19, while emphasizing VTs' advantages and disadvantages. In the reflections following their first assignment, many students tried to examine the potentiality of VTs from the perspective gained through their own virtual experiences. While some of them focused on the negative aspects of VTs, many students attempted to give examples of how to further develop and improve potential customers' virtual experiences. The lack of detailed guidance and information about a site in most of these virtual tours was given as an example of a disadvantage, as well as the lack of sensory and olfactory stimuli. Among the advantages mentioned, some students wrote about the luxury of exploring and examining sites without being bothered or interrupted by other tourists, while others wrote about temporary satisfaction, significant cost savings and short traveling time. S6 even explains how the use of VTs could probably help solve a problem frequently discussed in the industry, such as over tourism. Although an ambitious thought, her response shows her attempt to construct on the existing knowledge and past experience in order to integrate the newly acquired knowledge:

> In typical tour, sometimes we can't take enough time to watch scenery because there are many tourists. But in virtual tour, we can enjoy tour at our own pace. *This learning is important because I think some problems can be solved by implementing online tourism. For example, we can solve "over tourism" which is one of the problems in tourism industry.* By making the best use of virtual tour, the number of people who visit the tourism spots actually would be decreased and the problem would be solved [emphasis added].

S3 also writes about the advantages of VTs, showing her surprise at the fact that VTs not only allow the tourist to explore places otherwise difficult to reach, but also allow for further exploration of a site through the zoom in function. And S5s' narrative below shows the same enthusiasm in regard of such functions that allow for a clearer view of sites' out of reach places.

> S3: *When I participated in the virtual tour, I was very surprised that I could see things in the virtual tour that normally cannot see up close when I actually go there. I realized that this kind of things is the strength of virtual tours.* This learning matters because virtual tours are expected to grow in demand and develop further in the future [emphasis added].

> S5: Through experiencing this virtual walking tour, I could learn a lot of things. I had thought that visiting a place in person would be better, *but I found that the quality of the images made me see more clearly than with the naked eye, and the ability to zoom in and out was an advantage of the virtual tour.* By using the zoom-in and zoom-out functions, I was able to feel that the scenery around the Washington Monument was similar to the Shinjuku Gyoen in Japan. I also realized

that I can feel the atmosphere of a country or region through the expressions and actions of its people without actually going there [emphasis added].

Another merit that students mentioned is the use of VTs as a way of gathering information before actually visiting a place. S3 writes: "Virtual tours are not just about enjoying the scenery, but also about discovering new things. *It will help you learn about the city, and it will also help you gather information before you actually travel*" [emphasis added]. Other students also referred to the future use of VTs as a way of preparing for a trip. S1 refers to this use of VTs as a preview: "I want to actually visit because I could know what kind of place there is. In this way, *online tour will be a role of preview* [emphasis added].", while S11 talks about it from a promotional perspective, with potential tourists being attracted to actually visiting a site after participating in a VT: "[…] *using online is an effective promotion in the tourism industry. People can go around the world through the internet. After they participate in online tours, they want to visit real sites.* I think online events have significant potential [emphasis added]."

At the same time, students wrote about their learning discoveries from the perspective of a tourist and from the perspective of someone who will be working in the industry. Some of them even offered recommendations for future virtual tour guides, as in what should be done to enhance future customers' virtual experiences. For example, S1 wrote about the importance of our five senses when we are traveling somewhere. Through her experience, she found out that the lack of smell, for example, could have a negative impact on the whole experience, and the levels of enjoyment of potential customers may be affected by it. Therefore, she proposes that virtual tour guides should pay close attention to these details and include as many explanations as possible in order to offer a realistic and vivid image to the online tourists. On the other hand, S5 is imagining a future where technology will advance to the point that a simple VT will be able to offer such enhanced experiences to its customers, allowing them to enjoy a VT using all five senses.

In the future, technology will be even more advanced than now, and new features will be added too. Therefore, we might be able to enjoy virtual tours that allow us to travel with our five senses, such as smelling the local food and so on. Wouldn't it be exciting? Yes, it definitely is exciting. In light of this learning, I felt that I would like to learn more about the combination of tourism and technology. This assignment was very interesting! [emphasis added].

Next, analysis of students' narratives following the second assignment revealed a change in students' attitudes towards virtual experiences. Some admitted they had not expected much entertainment from virtual events, but the actual participation made them change their minds and prompted them to think more of the usefulness of this type of event in the future. Students also wrote specific suggestions for future online event coordinators based on their own observations during the events. S17 explained:

I learned that in order to give participants a sense of realism in an online event, it is important to pay more attention to audio and to shoot from different angles than in a typical event. […] Through this experience, I was able to learn what I should pay attention to when conducting events online, which I thought would be useful in the future. This learning matters because it has taught me the importance of organizing quality online live shows so that people who cannot go to live shows due to illness or old age can still have the same experience as normal people. In light of this learning, I thought it would be good if I could connect it to the planning of content that could entertain people at home [emphasis added].

Although there are no specific suggestions in S4's narrative below and it may seem superficial, the simple realization that such a job exists in the tourism industry is an important first step to getting more accustomed to what the future job market might be offering: "*I had never imagined or focused on online event coordinator, but I found the job interesting.* [...] I think that it is very important to experience such an event in order to think about the future of tourism [emphasis added]."

Finally, the analysis of the narratives collected from the third assignment showed a recurrent topic: a comparison between the use of virtual travel and in-person travel. While the majority acknowledged VTs' benefits under special circumstances, such as a global pandemic, few doubted a growth in use beyond COVID-19. Most students agreed that virtual tours will never replace physical tours; some mentioned the inability to feel the atmosphere of a place through a virtual tour, as in not being able to feel the wind or scorching sun, smell the flowers or the different aromas of the street food. S13 explains:

I don't think that these virtual walking tours can replace the physical ones in the future. It is because we cannot enough enjoy the travel through virtual walking tour. Even though the real pleasures of the walking tour are to look around traditional buildings, try traditional foods at each restaurant, and purchase some souvenirs, it is difficult to carry out latter ones through virtual tours. In fact, *we cannot experience the taste and the smell of traditional foods through this type of tour* [emphasis added].

And S11 emphasizes the same issues: "*I think there will be more virtual walking tours, but it won't replace the physical ones because to visit the spot where people have wanted to visit actually is exciting and it is difficult to smell, listen and feel genuinely on virtual tours* [emphasis added]."

However, other students, instead of totally denying probable growth in demand for VTs in the future, offered alternative ideas to their use beyond COVID-19. S1 writes: "I think it will be more important because *online and offline services will be combined in the future* in my opinion [emphasis added]." And S2 explains as follows:

S2: In my opinion, the situation won't change because *I thought that the virtual ones are not interesting compared with the physical ones. But we can take advantage of the virtual ones for some people such as elderly people. Some of them can't visit easily because of some physical problems. In conclusion, we should use them together and we should change method depend on the situation.* By doing so, virtual tours will develop more. And the future of tourism will change [emphasis added].

As in S2's response above, undeniably the most frequent example encountered in many of the narratives, is that VTs represent an opportunity to travel the world for people with disabilities, or people unable to travel because of illness, age or other causes, such as expense, etc. S12's narrative below shows the desire to make use of the knowledge gained through these assignments, and find a way to make traveling more inclusive, by helping people who cannot travel in-person experience the world through a different kind of traveling.

Although this virtual tour cannot replace the physical one, I think that it will allow people who have difficulty traveling due to mobility issues or physical disabilities to experience the feeling of traveling. By learning about these virtual tours, I was able to learn that there are many different forms of travel, and I have more ways to learn about other countries. In light of this learning, *I want to figure out a way for people who have difficulty traveling to enjoy traveling.* I also thought it would be a good way to prepare for a trip in advance [emphasis added].

Many other students make reference to the importance of delivering more inclusive services in the future, and such ideas can also be noticed in S18's narrative below.

S18: *I learned we have to make the world convenient not only for particular people but also everybody included people with disability.* For example, this virtual tour doesn't have a guide describing a site around like a voice over, as I wrote in STEP2, and it's not kind for people with visual disabilities. However, of course, everyone included those people can be the online tourists and we should never refuse their participation. [emphasis added].

S10 also suggests a similar approach to the use of VTs in the future, as the following example shows: "*I think that the number of customers who are aging and new viruses will appear, so, it will be difficult for many people to travel* [emphasis added]."

From analysis of these narratives, it becomes clear that the actual experience of participating in VTs and the reflection exercise served as a starting point for not only reevaluating their knowledge regarding virtual tourism and recent trends in the industry, but also for exploring new avenues for their future careers. Although not all students gave specific examples of how they plan on applying the acquired knowledge in their future careers, most of them referred of the use of VTs in very broad terms.

From S10's narrative below, we can see how this type of assignment acted as a starting point for rethinking traveling options as someone who is pursuing a career as a travel agent. She shows interest in finding ways to convey the charm of VTs to potential customers: "I want to be a travel planner in the future. I think that the number of customers who are aging and new viruses will appear, so, it will be difficult for many people to travel. *I would like to make use of it to convey the appeal of virtual tours to customers* [emphasis added]." Similarly, S17's reflection below, following the second and third assignments, also reveals a starting point for thinking of ways to incorporate the acquired knowledge in the tours she will be planning as a future tour agent.

This learning matters because it has taught me the importance of organizing quality online live shows so that people who cannot go to live shows due to illness or old age can still have the same experience as normal people. In light of this learning, *I thought it would be good if I could connect it to the planning of content that could entertain people at home* [emphasis added].

This learning matters because, as a tourist, I will be able to notice attractive points of travel destinations that I didn't know before, and *as a tour planner, I will learn what I need to pay attention to. In light of this learning, I will use this to plan better tours in the future* [emphasis added].

Although some of the students' reflections may seem superficial, in the sense that they do not provide detailed explanations of how the perceived learning discoveries can actually be used in their future careers, based on the analysis above it is not an exaggeration to suggest that this type of assignment was both (1) a starting point for students to reevaluate their knowledge about a certain phenomenon, as well as (2) a starting point for students to think about newly acquired knowledge and its possible use in their lives. Kolb [19] defines experiential learning as knowledge that is created through the transformation of experience; students' perceived learning discoveries point out how the exercise of gradual reflection on the experience forced them into thinking deeper, as many attempted to explain their understanding of what the new learning means to them, as future tourists, and to the future customers.

5 Conclusions and Practical Implications

The impact of COVID-19 and the consequential adoption of emergency remote teaching in Japan account for the undertaking of the current study. In order to make the best out of the restricted resources at hand, the author designed three assignments for an English for Tourism Industry course based on Kolb's [9] experiential learning cycle (experiencing, reflecting, thinking and acting), in the hope that providing for students a firsthand experience, through participation in virtual tours and events will instill the motivation to further look into the use of technology in the tourism industry and its possible applications. From the analysis of students' narratives, it can be suggested that such an approach may be a starting point for allowing students' reevaluation of existing knowledge. It can be concluded that the use of virtual tours had a positive impact on students' learning, in the sense that most students enjoyed the new experience and also used it as a way to rethink their future careers or the future of tourism. The research cannot conclude regarding whether such learning and its application is helpful in the long run, but one thing is sure: students' perceived learning discoveries allowed for deeper understanding of the implications such technologies will have for the future of tourism.

The details and conclusions of such practice-oriented research should be useful not only to language teachers, but also to teachers of other disciplines interested in engaging their students in ways they have never dared before. First, the use of Kolb's [9] experiential learning cycle as a framework for designing assignments has proved effective, as it provided a means for students to immerse themselves in a reflection exercise that allowed for a deeper understanding of the target phenomenon. The design of each assignment in such a way to generate gradual reflection should also be taken into consideration, as the process of reflection takes time and effort; a specific design element is therefore necessary. Second, the use of virtual tours can be an attractive way to teach students about something, whether it is a historical site, a cultural event, or even space. The possibilities of such approaches to teaching and learning are infinite and so are our resources, if only we force ourselves to step out of our educational comfort zones.

References

1. Aoki, K.: The use of ICT and e-learning in higher education in Japan. World Acad. Sci. Eng. Technol. **42**, 854–858 (2010)
2. Funamori, M.: The issues Japanese higher education face in the digital age—are Japanese universities to blame for the slow progress towards an information-based society? Int. J. Inst. Res. Manage. **1**(1), 37–51 (2017)
3. Apple, M.T., Mills, D.J.: Online teaching satisfaction and technostress at Japanese universities during emergency remote teaching. In: Giannikas, C.N. (ed.) Transferring Language Learning and Teaching From Face-to-Face to Online Settings, pp. 1–25. IGI Global (2022)
4. El-Said, O., Aziz, H.: Virtual tours a means to an end: an analysis of virtual tours' role in tourism recovery post COVID-19. J. Travel Res. **61**(3), 528–548 (2022)
5. Osman, A., Wahab, N.A., Ismail, M.H.: Development and evaluation of an interactive 360 virtual tour for tourist destinations. J. Inf. Technol. Impact **9**(3), 173–182 (2009)
6. Biocca, F., Delaney, B.: Immersive virtual reality technology. In: Biocca, F., Levy, M.R. (eds.) Communication in the Age of Virtual Reality, pp. 57–124. Lawrence Erlbaum Associates (1995)
7. Fromm, J., Radianti, J., Wehking, C., Stieglitz, S., Majchrzak, T.A., vom Brocke, J.: More than experience? - on the unique opportunities of virtual reality to afford a holistic experiential learning cycle. Internet High. Educ. **50**, 1–14 (2021)
8. Alizadeh, M.: Virtual reality in the language classroom: theory and practice. CALL-EJ **20**(3), 21–30 (2019)
9. Kolb, D.A.: Experience as the Source of Learning and Development. Prentice Hall, Upper Sadle River (1984)
10. Knutson, S.: Experiential learning in second-language classrooms. TESL Canada J. **20** (2) (2003)
11. Kolb, A.Y., Kolb, D.A.: Learning styles and learning spaces: A review of the multidisciplinary application of experiential learning theory in higher education. In: Sims, R.R. and Sims, S.J. (eds.) Learning Styles and Learning, pp. 45–91. Nova Science Publishers, New York (2006)
12. Kolb, A. Y. , Kolb, D. A.: Experiential learning theory as a guide for experiential educators in higher education. Exper. Learn. Teach. High. Educ. **1**(1) (2017)
13. Kohonen, V.: Towards experiential foreign language education. In: Kohonen, V., Jaatinen, R., Kaikkonen, P. Lhtovaara, J. (eds.) Experiential Learning in Foreign Language Education, Pearson Education. Routledge, London (2001)
14. Young, M.R., Caudill, E.M., Murphy, J.W.: Evaluating experiential learning activities. J. Adv. Mark. Educ. **13** (2008)
15. Hughes, K., Mylonas, A., Ballantyne, R.: Enhancing tourism graduates' soft skills: the importance of teaching reflective practice. In: Benckendorff, P., Zehrer, A. (eds.) Handbook of Teaching and Learning in Tourism. Edward Elgar Publishing (2017)
16. King, B., Zhang, H.Q.: Experiential tourism and hospitality learning: principles and practice. In: Benckendorff, P., Zehrer, A. (eds.) Handbook of Teaching and Learning in Tourism. Edward Elgar Publishing (2017)
17. Basturkmen, H.: Developing Courses in English for Specific Purposes. Palgrave MacMillan, New York, NY (2010)

18. Shellito, B.: Google Earth Exercises for World Regional Geography. W.H. Freeman, New York (2012)
19. Wise, N.: Integrating Google Earth into the lecture: visual approaches in tourism pedagogy. In: Benckendorff, P., Zehrer, A. (eds.) Handbook of Teaching and Learning in Tourism. Edward Elgar Publishing (2017)
20. Violante, M.G., Vezzetti, E., Piazzolla, P.: Interactive virtual technologies in engineering education: why not 360° videos? Int. J. Interact. Des. Manufac. **13**(2), 729–742 (2019). https://doi.org/10.1007/s12008-019-00553-y
21. Ash, S.L., Clayton, P.H.: The articulated learning: an approach to guided reflection and assessment. Innov. High. Educ. **29**(2), 137–154 (2004)
22. Cheng, M.W.T., Chan, C.K.Y.: An experimental test: Using rubrics for reflective writing to develop reflection. Stud. Educ. Eval. **61**, 176–182 (2019)
23. Ramachandran, S., Subramani, V., Ambrose, I.: COVID-19 and Opportunities for VR Based Tourism Economy. https://www.accessibletourism.org/?i=enat.en.news.2176. Accessed 10 Feb 2022
24. Sallent, M.: Tourism in Africa: Virtual Safaris Kick in as Countries Prepare to Reopen to Tourists. https://www.un.org/africarenewal/web-features/coronavirus/tourism-africa-virtual-safaris-kick-countries-prepare-reopen-tourists. Accessed 10 Feb 2022

Undergraduate Emirati Students' Challenges of Language Barrier in Meeting Expectations of English Medium University in the UAE

Sara Suleymanova[1] and Ajrina Hysaj[2]

[1] University of Dubai, Dubai, UAE
ssuleymanova@ud.ac.ae
[2] UOWD College, University of Wollongong in Dubai, Dubai, UAE
Ajrinahysaj@uowdubai.ac.ae

Abstract. This paper analyses the challenges faced by Emirati students who are admitted to universities in the UAE where the medium of instruction is in English. The study focuses mainly on the expectations of their performance during a full semester course where students are supposed to move from an intermediate level B1 user of English to upper intermediate B2 in a short span of one semester which is less than four months. The sample was collected from students' past assessments in correlation to their language admission requirement, who are enrolled in the first year in two compulsory general English courses in an undergraduate degree program. The paper examines the validity of whether the IELTS and EmSAT exam scores that are the standard tests accepted for the entrance of both courses is achievable within a little period of time and the effects of whether linguistic acquisition can be obtained. Two sections of entrance English courses samples are compared to the other data collected from two sections of follow on level English course, along with the test scores achieved by the same students to enter the university. The paper reveals the findings of discrepancies between students who start with entrance English course (English 1) and progress to the follow-on English course (English 2) as opposed to the students who are admitted directly to the higher-level English 2 course. The main purpose behind this study is to understand the challenges faced by nonnative speakers of English i.e. Emiratis in particular and bridging the gap of linguistic barriers that they face in their tertiary studies in the target language.

Keywords: Emirati students · Language barrier · Language acquisition · Linguistic comprehension · Subject content · EFL teaching

1 Introduction

English language is the core of education in the UAE higher education. Therefore, students are required to prove their English competency to enter a university in all around the Emirates. This study is designed to capture the effectiveness of one semester English courses aiming to progress students from a B1 level to B2. This is achieved by looking at entrance level English requirements and analyzing their results in passing English courses that are mandatory general subjects in the first year of their undergraduate degrees. The level of English knowledge abilities is a prominent and unceasing concern for English as foreign language students (EFL) [31, 50] and EFL instructors worldwide [17, 45]. English language abilities required to study in an English medium university are a combination of academic vocabulary [26], complex grammar skills [41] and adequate academic writing structure [34]. Furthermore, the English language abilities include composition skills [36, 37] as well as summarizing [16, 26, 38, 41] Therefore, each of the aspects of English language abilities is of an important worth and it requires appropriate consideration.

Standardized testing for entering universities is used commonly throughout the world [3, 34, 42, 43]. Despite the fact that English language abilities are considered crucial for a successful tertiary experience in an English medium university and require an adequate grasp of the English language, a considerable number of universities worldwide have traditionally had a low entrance level requirement [34, 42, 43, 50]. Furthermore, the benchmark set by universities worldwide may vary, nevertheless, for the last decade or so is seen a trend of lowering the entrance levels, mainly aiming to make universities more inclusive and open to a larger number of students [3, 5]. Furthermore, a fairly imbalanced importance is paid to comprehension and writing skills despite being crucial for a successful academic progression of undergraduate students [40, 41].

English level requirement for entering an English medium university in the UAE is generally lower compared to counterpart universities in English speaking countries [3, 5]. The rationale behind such set benchmark is related to the considerably lower levels of exposure to English language of UAE based students, especially Emirati students prior to attending university. The knowledge accumulated through high school and surrounding environment constitutes the amount of English knowledge that Emirati students possess prior to entering university. This knowledge is a combination of general knowledge accumulated through the different surroundings and the academic knowledge accumulated mainly in schools and especially during the English language classes. Many universities worldwide consider general English knowledge skills more substantial than academic writing skills [31]. The rationale behind this opinion is related to the undeniable truth that general English knowledge skills take time and effort to develop and are the basis of academic writing skills [26]. Furthermore, in the case of Emirati students this tends to be even more complicated because the majority of Emirati students attend Arabic medium schools and have limited exposure to the general and academic English [6]. General writing skills require progression to academic writing skills [40, 41] for the benefit of students while studying in university and for their successful work experience. For example, a degree holder is required to own the language of his field of study and use it efficiently while working as a professional person [36, 39]. In the case of Emirati students, progression in English language abilities during the university years and especially during the first year becomes more complex considering the low entrance levels of starting university studies [6]. Although it is true that general English skills are the basis of academic English skills [46, 30] yet the latter requires a whole range of reading and writing skills which are unique to academia [17, 18] and in the case of Emirati students because of low entrance levels they take longer to develop and master [6].

2 Literature Review

2.1 Language Assessment Criteria for University Entrance

According to the Ministry's website, students who are wishing to register in higher education institutions in the UAE are required to pass English language tests [28]. These tests are internationally recognized such as International English Language Testing System (IELTS), Test of English as a Foreign Language (TOEFL), or the national examination Emirates Standardized Test (EmSAT). Depending whether the student is international or the citizen of the Emirates, the examination board changes accordingly. Consequently, non-nationals can prove their linguistic competency for admission to the universities within the UAE with an IELTS, TOEFL or any internationally recognized English tests. However, for UAE nationals, recently the ministry has made the EmSAT exam as the only assessment tool to be measured for tertiary education. International language standards that commonly uses the Common European Framework for Reference for Languages (CEFR) uses a 6-point scale to measure one's linguistic ability in any given language [9]. The scale ranges from A1 being the basic user of the target language to C2 proficient or near native user. CEFR is mainly used to compare and to make equivalent to the different examination boards' language scores to identify their level. Generally, in the UAE the level of proficiency in English for higher education entrance purposes ranges between B1 (intermediate user of a language) to B2 (upper intermediate) which is classified by Cambridge English as 'Independent user' [9]. EmSAT score 1100 to 1550 which is equivalent to the IELTS band 5 to 6 (please refer to the Table 1 below for more details) falls under independent user category. Specific to this particular study, which was done in one of the private universities in the UAE, the entrance level requirements for the competency skills in the target language is either IELTS 5 or EmSAT 1100 to be able to register for the general requirement course English 1 that is taken as a first semester course in an undergraduate program. Nonetheless, those who score higher than the admission requirements for English, can ultimately skip the entrance level English 1 subject and enter directly to the English 2 course, which is a follow-on course from English 1, with a minimum of IELTS 6 or EmSAT 1400.

2.2 Language Acquisition

Language acquisition requires exposure to the target language and progressive practice of the same [10, 24]. Based on the methods and variety of encounters that children have with the native languages, they gain recognition of the vocabulary and grammar related to those languages [19, 27]. Usually first languages are taught at a young age and the early exposure to them constitutes the progression achieved through the years. Nevertheless, second languages are not always taught at an early age and progression achieved in learning and practicing them is known to be connected with learners' abilities of being fluent on their first languages. In the case of Emirati students in the United Arab Emirates,

English as second language is usually taught in the primary or secondary school and the focus is mainly on the speaking abilities of the students rather than on the writing and research abilities [6, 14, 21]. This trait tends to shape the way Emirati students perceive the value of English language skills and in many instances, it is continued during the tertiary education [21, 48, 51].

Components of English language abilities require individual focus, as they make sense when interconnected yet the ways that they develop are unique and equally challenging [35, 50]. The encounter of each of the components of English language acquisition shows the level of its development and it is an integral part of each specific assignment. In other words, the syntax and morphology are equally valuable in a piece of writing or speaking, in the same way that transition signals and grammatical forms of words are in any assignment [12, 52]. Language in a spoken or written depends on all the components of language formation in being in harmony and presenting a complete meaning [12, 26, 25]. Emirati students are exposed to English language learning during their second language classes in primary and secondary school, and through the spoken language of the people around them. As Emirati culture is a collective culture highly rooted in Islamic teachings, the spoken language comes as more natural to Emirati students compared to the written language [4, 38]. The issue of second language acquisition becomes more pressing when Emirati students enroll in English medium universities in the UAE or abroad. When enrolled in English medium universities, they are required to progress extensively in their chosen major which can only occur after they have progressed substantially in their English language acquisition [1, 10, 13, 48, 51]. Therefore, Emirati students are required to make a major shift from general English language skills that they have been more often exposed prior to attending university, to the academic language required for successful university studies [10, 13, 48, 51].

2.3 Importance of Language Comprehension in Tertiary Studies

Linguistic resources required for writing appropriate academic papers, necessitate adequate consideration of all aspects of academic writing and a considerable amount of continuous practice of them all [8, 22, 23]. According to Cheung and Low [11] educators are required to consider the notion of students' individual voice as substantial in producing a good essay. The notion of students' voice construction may appear to be too abstract but it is nevertheless the foundation of a linguistic resource that combines common sense of thought development and utilisation of lexicographic information [11, 33]. Thought development may be employed as a complete and diverse resource when a variety of tasks like conceptual categorization, keywords extraction, and conceptual similarity are considered as important and as integrated aspects of academic thought development. Studies by Saito [42], Sawaki [43] and Schalley [44] analyse conceptual categorization from the perspectives of instructors and learners. Conceptual categorization is relatively complex and not easily achievable or even understood and explained through words that mainly tend to be abstract.

In other words, learners may be able to understand the concepts when explained by the educators but not necessarily have the understanding or relevant skills to transfer the message across to their teachers or to their classmates. They may not undoubtably possess the abilities to interpret their conceptual categorization and this may hinder their academic writing process and ultimately their progress in the university or in their professional career [2, 7, 22, 23]. According to Zhang et al. [52] another substantial factor that may hinder students' success in academia are the incapacity to extract keywords and to mentally create a conceptual similarity based on previous work or prior understood concepts. Concept imagining requires an analysis of lexical semantics that is achieved through decomposition of the lexical semantics and analysis of the imagining of the words being used [29, 47] to specify noun phrases. Therefore, the continuous occurrence of collocated adjectives and the subsequent evaluative strength, the coordinated nouns with nominal genitives prior to the target word as well as prepositions connected with the target words are analyzed to understand the level of contribution in the adequate explanation of nouns phrases [13–15].

3   Methodology

The aim of this study was to examine the efficiency and the accuracy of the language skills assessed for the university entrance. Additionally, how the expectations of improving one's English competency in language skills is linguistically feasible in a period of one semester, where the gap between English competency skills of being accepted to English 1 course and English 2 course is too high. The sample was collected from students who are taking Electrical Engineering or Information Technology as their major. Two sections with a total of 58 participants who were registered in English 1 course compared to another two sections of 55 English 2 course students. All the students in this study were native Emirati speakers. Table 1 shows the measurement scale for the equivalency of EmSAT exams scores to the IELTS and is linked to the Cambridge international language standards. Independent user i.e. B1/B2 (Cambridge English, 2021) which is the minimum requirement for entrance to an undergraduate program in this particular university, is the benchmark that this study will be using. Both the exams IELTS and EmSAT assess students' capabilities in all the four language skills, i.e. receptive skills Listening and Reading as well as productive skills Writing and Speaking. The English course that they are required to take as part of the General Educational Requirements, which is mandatory for Ministry approved universities in the country, is also designed to improve all the four skills mentioned above.

Table 2 illustrates the results obtained at the end of the first semester in the English 1 course and the analysis show the correlation between the students who got the minimum required score (EmSAT 1100–1225 or IELTS 5) in relation to the medium (EmSAT 1250–1375 or IELTS 5.5) and higher scores (EmSAT 1400–1525 or IELTS 6) but not sufficient enough to be admitted to the English 2 course. The grading system used in this study is the general assessment tool used by the university to grade students' achievement levels in a particular course and is uniform across the board. Students obtaining *Excellent* A/A- which is the highest grade in the table equals to 87–100%, B+ to B— that is 77–86%, 67–76% are the ones who achieve *Satisfactory* C+ to C—, *Good* D+ to D is 60–66% and is considered *Poor* and everything below the 60% is given an F grade and the students need to retake the course in the following semester. Table 3 on the other hand, compares the students who attained higher results (EMSAT 1550 or IELTS 6.5) in their admission requirement to the university and skipped the first English course and were admitted straight to the advanced English 2 course. Moreover, their final grade at the end of the term along with those students who took the English course after passing the English 1 course the proceeding semester is demonstrated in the same table. In order to analyse the data gathered from the two courses, a quantitative approach has been applied.

4 Results

It is apparent from the results that naturally the students who were accepted to the entrance English course in Table 2 with the lowest language requirements (IELTS 5/EmSAT 1100–1225) obtained no grade A/A− and furthermore, had two students who did not pass the subject. Majority under this category 13 out of the total 58 were graded in the range of C+ to C− which is the average to below average grade. 5 students gained results B+ to B− with and equally the remaining 5 only managed to pass the course with *Poor* results of D+ or D grade. Nonetheless, those who were admitted with medium range (IELTS 5.5/EmSAT 1250–1325) English scores, performed considerably better with no F grades and at least one *Excellent* result of A to A−. There were also improvements in the number of students grading *Good* with 7 students an increase of 40% as opposed to the lowest acceptance range. In addition, the students who attained *Satisfactory* and *Poor* results also dropped by 23% and 75% respectively. All the students who had the highest admission requirement results in English, fared the best in their end of the course results for English 1 with 50% increase from the medium range in the *Excellent* grade category as well as 100% from the lowest. Comparatively, a drastic reduction in the Satisfactory grade of 3 students that is 77% reduction from the lowest admission rate and a rise in Good grade with 80%. No students obtained *Poor* or *Fail* grades with the highest language admission rate for English 1 course. Consequently, there is an organic tendency for students to perform better with higher admission results. Moreover, students with the lowest language assessment results seem to struggle to achieve better grades in English 1.

The results deduced from Table 3 seem to follow the similar pattern to the Table 2 results. In general, students progressing from the English 1 course achieved much lower grades, wherein the students who were exempt from taking English 1 course and were directly registered in the English 2 course seemed to have fared much desired results. None of the student who progressed from English 1 course to English 2 gained A/A− results, however, only one student did not pass the course out of the 55 student who took the subject. A huge portion, 16 of the students that is 61.5% out of the 26 in this category, attained *Satisfactory* grades. The second highest grade achieved for English 1 graduates was *Poor* with 5 students and the remaining 4 student achieved B+/B− results.

5 Discussion

Most tertiary level educators view the English language acquisition of undergraduate students as challenging for all parties involved, to say the least. Furthermore, they consider the process of developing of shifting from general knowledge of English language to the development of adequate academic writing skills required in university, as complex and life-long. The complexity of academic writing development is influenced by

Table 1. Criteria for English language assessments: test score comparison

EmSAT	CEFR	IELTS
675	A1/A2	4
950–1075	A2/B1	4.5
*1100–1225	B1/B2	5
1250–1375	B2	5.5
1400–1525		6
1550–1600		6.5
1625–1975	C1	7
		7.5
		8
2000	C2	8.5
		9

* University accepted entrance level for undergraduate programs

Table 2. Results for lower, medium and higher university entrance scores in comparison to the English 1 final subject grades

English 1 course passing grade and description	Student numbers from each category	A/A− excellent	B+/B− good	C+/C− satisfactory	D+/D poor	F fail
IELTS (5)/EmSAT (1100–1225)	25	0	5	13	5	2
IELTS (5.5)/EmSAT (1250–1375)	19	1	7	10	1	0
IELTS (6)/EmSAT (1400–1525) overall*	14	2	9	3	0	0
Total	58	3	21	26	6	2

* IELTS band 6 or EmSAT 1400–1525 needs to be achieved in all skills to be exempt from English 1

a variety of factors, starting from the material utilized in classes for scaffolding such process to the engagement levels of undergraduate students with the process of learning. The interconnection of teaching and learning processes necessitates the recognition of the value of adequate levels of English level skills prior to entering university. The level of English knowledge that undergraduate Emirati students accumulate through their schooling system is the basis of their knowledge upon entrance to their chosen university, where the medium of communication is in English language. This study opposed

Table 3. Results for Students Exempt from English 1 in Comparison to the Students Progressing from English 1 Course and their English 2 Final Subject Grades

English 2 course passing grade and description	Student numbers from each category	A/A− Excellent	B+ /B− Good	C+ /C− Satisfactory	D+ /D Poor	F Fail
Students entering from English 1	26	0	4	16	5	1
IELTS (6)/EmSAT (1400–1525) in each skill	16	1	6	8	1	0
IELTS (6.5)/EmSAT (1550) overall*	13	2	9	2	0	0
Total	55	3	19	26	6	1

* Exempt from taking English 1 but not from English 2 (IELTS (6.5)/EmSAT (1550) needs to be achieved in all skills to skip English 2 course)

the findings of Singh et al. [46, 49] which found that Emirati students enrolled in English medium universities found it easy to adapt and did not encounter any major obstacles in their adaptation process.

The andragogical approach of teaching and learning places undergraduate students in the centre of their learning process, and encourages the development of inquisitiveness and research base interest in undergraduate students. Nevertheless, none of the above can be achieved without an adequate level of understanding the English language from a general and degree related perspective. Therefore, it is crucial for Emirati undergraduate students to enter university with an overall score higher than the existing one. This study has proven that Emirati undergraduate students that entered with a higher score than the others, had a better chance in developing their writing skills compared to the ones who entered with a lower score. The findings of this research reaffirm the findings of Smarandache [47] Andrés et al. [32] and Geiger [20] that highlight the need to aim the development of skills in schools and universities alike. Furthermore, this study has reaffirmed the knowledge accumulated through an extensive schooling system accounts as more valuable than the knowledge accumulated through one semester in a university setting. Nevertheless, this study should be followed by further research that analyses the needs of Emirati students who have studied in English medium schools and with a majority of non-Arabic speakers upon entering an English medium university, to take into consideration the level of exposure to English language in a different schooling system and in a multicultural teacher and student body environment.

6 Conclusion and Recommendations

English is the basic requirement when it comes to tertiary education in the UAE. Emiratis wishing to study abroad or in the country have to be well equipped in the target language to not only pass the required English courses but also all the major courses that are offered in English. Thus, entrance requirements with lower levels such as B1 can prevent the students from progressing further in English and consequently effect their achievements in other courses that are offered in English. This may mainly be due to comprehension levels and writing skills along with other linguistic features. It is crucial that primary and secondary schools incorporate the English academic language skills well before the students join the university. One semester course for students to improve form B1 level to B2 is still unrealistic in linguistic terms. Once this is implemented in all the major schools then universities can raise the language competency level to B2 for their admission intake. Additionally, this could be followed with another study to see how B2 students perform in other subject as opposed to B1, which could give insight to more academic achievements being linked to their linguistic ability in English.

References

1. Adnan, M.: Professional development in the transition to online teaching: the voice of entrant online instructors. ReCALL **30**(1), 88–111 (2018)
2. Aitchison, C., Lee, A.: Research writing: problems and pedagogies. Teach. High. Educ. **11**(3), 265–278 (2006)
3. Al Awadi, F.: An investigation into the correlation between IETLS test preparation courses and writing scores. Perspectives on Language Assessment Literacy: Challenges for Improved Student Learning, p. 85 (2020)
4. Al Othman, F.H., Shuqair, K.M.: The impact of motivation on English language learning in the Gulf states. Int. J. High. Educ. **2**(4), 123–130 (2013)
5. Al Habbash, M., Alsheikh, N., Liu, X., Al Mohammedi, N., Al Othali, S., Ismail, S.A.: A UAE Standardized Test and IELTS Vis-À-Vis International English Standards. Int. J. Inst. **14**(4) (2021)
6. Al Murshidi, G.: Emirati and Saudi students' writing challenges at US universities. Engl. Lang. Teach. **7**(6), 87–95 (2014)
7. Alzu'bi, M.A.: The influence of suggested cornell note-taking method on improving writing composition skills of jordanian EFL learners. J. Lang. Teach. Res. **10**(4), 863–871 (2019)
8. Andueza, A.: Assessing academic writing: the construction and validation of an integrated task-based instrument to evaluate specific writing skills. Lang. Assess. Quar. Int. J. **25**(2), 1–20 (2019)
9. Cambridge English. https://www.cambridgeenglish.org/exams-and-tests/cefr/. Accessed 15 Nov 2021
10. Clark, E.V., Casillas, M.: First Language Acquisition, pp. 327–344. Routledge (2015)
11. Cheung, Y.L., Low, T.H.: Pre-university students' voice construction in argumentative essays. RELC J. **50**(2), 269–284 (2019)
12. Cronley, C., et al.: A multivariate analysis of writing skills in BSW case study papers. J. Baccalaur. Soc. Work **22**(1), 181–205 (2017)
13. Deveci, T.: Students' self-perceptions of creativity: the case of Emirati students in a first-year English program. Learn. Teach. High. Educ. Gulf Perspect. **17**(1) (2021)
14. Diallo, I.: Emirati students encounter Western teachers tensions and identity resistance. Learn. Teach. High. Educ. Gulf Persp. **11**(2) (2014)
15. Durkin, D.: What classroom observations reveal about reading comprehension instruction. Read. Res. Q. **14**(4), 481–533 (1979)
16. Abdul Azeez, E.P.: Academic writing and publishing in India: is quality a touchstone? J. Commun. Positive Pract. **17**(1), 13–24 (2017)

17. Fowler, J.: Academic essays part 1: the importance of academic writing. Br. J. Nurs. **29**(12), 718 (2020)
18. Fowler, J.: From staff nurse to nurse consultant: academic essays part 10: developing themes. Br. J. Nurs. **30**(8), 502 (2021)
19. Genesee, F., Nicoladis, E.: Bilingual First Language Acquisition. Blackwell Handbook of Language Development, pp. 324–342. McGill University, Canada (2007)
20. Geiger, R.L.: To Advance Knowledge: The Growth of American Research Universities, pp. 1900–1940. Routledge (2017)
21. Gitsaki, C., Robby, M.A., Bourini, A.: Preparing Emirati students to meet the English language requirements for higher education: a pilot study. Education, Business and Society: Contemporary Middle Eastern Issues (2014)
22. Hysaj, A., Suleymanova, S.: The analysis of developing the application of critical thinking in oral and written discussions: the case of emirati students in the United Arab Emirates. In: 2020 IEEE International Conference on Teaching, Assessment, and Learning for Engineering (TALE), pp. 819–824. IEEE (2020)
23. Hysaj, A., Suleymanova, S.: Safeguarding academic integrity in crisis induced environment: a case study of Emirati Engineering and IT students in a private university in the UAE. In: Meiselwitz, G. (ed.) HCII 2021. LNCS, vol. 12775, pp. 236–245. Springer, Cham (2021). https://doi.org/10.1007/978-3-030-77685-5_19
24. Ingram, D., David, I.: First Language Acquisition: Method, Description and Explanation. Cambridge University Press (1989)
25. Johnson, J.E., Rulo, K.: Problem in the profession: how and why writing skills in nursing must be improved. J. Prof. Nurs. **35**(1), 57–64 (2019)
26. Le Pham Hoai, H.: A survey study on academic vocabulary learning strategies by EFL university students. J. Lang. Teach. Res. **9**(5), 1009–1016 (2018)
27. Mayberry, R.I.: First-language acquisition after childhood differs from second-language acquisition: the case of American Sign Language. J. Speech Lang. Hear. Res. **36**(6), 1258–1270 (1993)
28. Ministry of Education. https://emsat.moe.gov.ae/emsat/Default.aspx. Accessed 15 Nov 2021
29. Makhoul, B., Sabah, K.: Academic vocabulary knowledge and reading comprehension skills among seventh-graders in Arabic as L1. J. Psycholinguist. Res. **48**(4), 769–784 (2019). https://doi.org/10.1007/s10936-019-09630-5
30. Makiko, K.: Good and poor summary writers' strategies: the case of Japanese high school EFL learners. J. Lang. Teach. Res. **9**(6), 1199–1208 (2018)
31. Marriot, H.: A programmatic exploration of issues in the academic interaction of Japanese students overseas. J. Asian Pac. Commun. **14**(1), 33–54 (2004)
32. Mateo Andrés, J., Escofet Roig, A., Martínez Olmo, F., Ventura Blanco, J.J., Vlachopoulos, D.: Evaluation tools within the European Higher Education Area (EHEA): an assessment guide for evaluating the competences of the Final Year Project in the social sciences. Eur. J. Educ. **47**(3), 435–447 (2012)
33. Mensa, E., et al.: COVER: a linguistic resource combining common sense and lexicographic information. Lang. Resour. Eval. **52**(4), 921–948 (2018)
34. Morrow, C.: Assessing entry-level academic literacy with IELTS in the UAE. In: Al-Mahrooqi, R., Coombe, C., Al-Maamari, F., Thakur, V. (eds.) Revisiting EFL Assessment. SLLT, pp. 151–169. Springer, Cham (2017). https://doi.org/10.1007/978-3-319-32601-6_10
35. Mousavi, T., Abdollahi, M.: A review of the current concerns about misconduct in medical sciences publications and the consequences. DARU J. Pharmaceut. Sci. **28**(1), 359–369 (2020). https://doi.org/10.1007/s40199-020-00332-1
36. Nagy, W., et al.: Words as tools: learning academic vocabulary as language acquisition. Read. Res. Q. **47**(1), 91–108 (2012)

37. Olson, C.B., et al.: The pathway to academic success: scaling up a text-based analytical writing intervention for Latinos and English learners in secondary school. J. Educ. Psychol. **112**(4), 701–717 (2020)
38. O'Sullivan, A.: Reading and Arab college students: issues in the United Arab Emirates higher colleges of technology. In: Proceedings of the First International Online Conference on Second and Foreign Language Teaching and Research: Beyond Borders (2004)
39. Pandey, A.K.: English for specific purpose vs. English for general purpose. Lang. India **18**(12), 377–382 (2018)
40. Patidar, J.: Evaluation of study skills in nursing students. Int. J. Nurs. Educ. **11**(3), 26–31 (2019)
41. Rai, L.: Academic writing and referencing for your social work degree, Jane Bottomley, Patricia Cartney and Steven Pryjmachuk. Br. J. Soc. Work. **49**(6), 1696–1698 (2019)
42. Saito, Y.: Impacts of introducing four-skill English tests into university entrance examinations. Lang. Teach. **43**(2), 9–14 (2019)
43. Sawaki, Y.: University faculty members' perspectives on English language demands in content courses and a reform of university entrance examinations in Japan: a needs analysis. Lang. Test. Asia **7**(1), 1–16 (2017). https://doi.org/10.1186/s40468-017-0043-2
44. Schalley, A.C.: The lexical semantics of imaginings–a corpus-based analysis. Nordic . English Stud. **19**(4), 218–228 (2020)
45. Scott, J.A., Hoffmeister, R.J.: Superordinate precision: an examination of academic writing among bilingual deaf and hard of hearing students. J. Deaf Stud. Deaf Educ. **23**(2), 173–218 (2018)
46. Singh, H., Bailey, F., Eppard, J., McKeown, K.: Partners in learning: an exploration of multi-cultural faculty and Emirati students' perspectives of university learning experiences. Learn. Cult. Soc. Interact. **31**, 100564 (2021)
47. Smarandache, F.: Collected Papers, vol. II. Infinite Study (1997)
48. Troudi, S., Jendli, A.: Emirati students' experiences of English as a Medium of Instruction. Peter Lang Publishers (2011)
49. Varga, M., Gradečak-Erdeljić, T.: English and Croatian citation practices in research articles in applied linguistics: a corpus-based study. Linguistics: Germanic & Romance Studies/Kalbotyra: Romanu ir Germanu Studijos, pp. 153–183 (2017)
50. Vekarić, G., Jelić, G.: Raising students' awareness of the importance of English language writing skills. Activ. Phys. Educ. Sport **3**(1), 29–31 (2013)
51. Wyatt, M., Midraj, J., Ayish, N., Bradley, C., Balfaqeeh, M.: Content teachers' perspectives of student challenges in processing science and mathematics texts in English at an Emirati university. Read. Psychol. **42**(2), 1–24 (2021)
52. Zhang, Y., Wang, M., Saberi, M., Chang, E.: Knowledge fusion through academic articles: a survey of definitions, techniques, applications and challenges. Scientometrics **125**(3), 2637–2666 (2020). https://doi.org/10.1007/s11192-020-03683-3

Building an Educational Social Media Application for Higher Education

Felix Weber[1,2]([envelope]) [iD], Niklas Dettmer[1,2] [iD], Katharina Schurz[2] [iD], and Tobias Thelen[1,2] [iD]

[1] Institute of Cognitive Science, Osnabrück University, Wachsbleiche 27, Osnabrück, Germany
[2] Center for Digital Teaching, Campus Management and Higher Education Didactics (virtUOS), Osnabrück University, Heger-Tor-Wall 12, Osnabrück, Germany
fweber@uos.de

Abstract. In this paper, we present an overview of an ongoing field study by the Siddata (Studienindividualisierung durch Digitale Datengestuetzte Assistenten [Joint project for Individualization of Studies through Digital, Data-Driven Assistants]) joint research project at the Universities of Bremen, Hannover, and Osnabrück in Northern Germany, with a digital data-driven study assistant (DSA), integrated into the local learning management system (LMS). Some of the included functions, especially those combining data from LMS, OER repositories, and user data with recommendation algorithms, are similar to functions of social media applications. Based on these similarities, we introduce the idea of educational social media applications (edSMA), which implement social media functions for educational purposes. Since 2018, four prototypes (P0, P1, P2, P3) have been developed, deployed, and tested in annual software development cycles. We overview the general user interaction schema, prototype, lifetimes, usage statistics, and features. A remarkable finding is a high demand for digital assistance in the early stages of the student life cycle. For any student differing from the default student, implicitly assumed by education systems, recommender systems can make less frequent educational opportunities accessible and consequently individualize educational pathways and increase equality. We conclude with an outlook on planned developments in the future, such as making the Siddata study assistant available for a broader range of students.

Keywords: Educational Social Media Applications (edSMA) · Digital Study Assistants (DSA) · Artificial intelligence · Higher education · Innovative education technologies · Learning Management Systems (LMS)

The authors acknowledge the financial support by the Federal Ministry of Education and Research of Germany for Siddata (project number 16DHB2124).

G. Meiselwitz (Ed.): HCII 2022, LNCS 13316, pp. 210–220, 2022.
https://doi.org/10.1007/978-3-031-05064-0_16

1   Introduction

While Social media applications (SMA) have increased the quantity and efficiency of digital networking and personalized media consumption, they are often criticized for toxic effects on individuals and societies, e.g., abuse of user data or fake profiles. Learning management systems (LMS) share essential properties with SMAs, such as media sharing, communication channels, and personal profiles but serve primarily to serve education by sharing true information among registered, trusted learners to foster personal knowledge, competencies, and intellectual growth. A subset of LMS functionalities can be understood as educational, social media applications (edSMA).

1.1   Social Media and Social Media Applications

Social Media[1] Aichner et al. [1] wrote a review about terminology and definitions, Social Networks, Virtual Communities, Social Networking Services, Networking Websites are only a subset of terms, describing web-based applications that

- allows users to present themselves and their identity in user profiles,
- exchange chat messages with other users or groups of users,
- to share various types of visual and auditory digital media,
- manage contact networks for personal, professional, political or commercial purposes
- to get contact to other users by algorithms or active search through profiles,
- and to publicly or semi-publicly react to messages and media posted by others.

Social media applications (SMA) have increased the quantity and efficiency of digital networking and personalized media consumption. They have often been criticized for toxic effects on individuals and societies. One reason for adverse effects is rooted in the commercial nature of platforms, which can cause systematic prioritization of profit over personal and societal well-being. A second reason is the business models where users pay with their data, which has historically been abused for commercial or, even worse, political interests. The third problems are fake profiles and bots used with intransparent and probably destructive intentions.

There is empirical evidence for harmful effects on individuals, such as amplifying effects of SMA on eating disorders [4], and societies, such as, for instance, significant effects of fake news on the 2016 presidential election in the US [2]. The separation of the role of content editors and curators in social media contexts has been identified as one reason for lower media quality and weakening of trusted editors [6].

---

[1] In this paper, we will consistently use the term social media in the sense that some but not necessarily all of the mentioned aspects are met for an application to be called social media.

1.2   Learning Management Systems (LMS)

Learning Management Systems (LMS), formerly known as Integrated Learning Systems (ILS), can be understood as frameworks handling all aspects of learning processes [9], ranging from organizational, communicative, administrative to educational aspects. In higher education, usually, University officials maintain LMS, and access is limited to enrolled students. LMS shares some structural properties with Social Media Platforms, such as user profiles, communication channels, and media sharing, to name a subset. In this paper, we explore the potentials of LMS to learn from Social Media Platforms under the minimization of their harmful effects.

1.3   Building an Educational Social Media Application (edSMA)

The primary motivation or purpose of LMS is education and personal growth, while most large SMA is run by global enterprises, following commercial goals. In LMS, users' identities are certified by University Officials, which anchors trust and accountability. In most SMA, an email address is sufficient to create user accounts, easily implemented on a large scale. Likes, comments, and other interactions significantly affect the visibility of opinions. Hence, in LMS, fake profiles and bots are very unlikely, while commercial platforms have not successfully prevented them. In LMS, the platform owners have an intrinsic interest in media quality, while commercial platform owners have an intrinsic interest in user interactions under ignorance concerning the triggering content.

Social Media Applications originated from commercial platforms, and significant efforts have been undertaken to meliorate user interaction patterns and algorithms. Educational Social Media Applications (edSMA) and related functionalities can build upon this groundwork. Combining design patterns from SMA into LMS is auspicious because many technical foundations, such as databases and platforms with active users, are already given. Due to the users' membership of the same educational institution or educational system, individual motivation for cooperative learning, and the accountability of users, it can be expected that toxic behaviors, such as trolling, harassment, off-topic content, and cyberbullying are less likely to occur than they do in commercial SMA. High standards for ethical data regulations and transparency concerning algorithms can be assured without conflicts with commercial goals. Consequently, the authors assume that there are vast potentials of edSMA to rebuild positive aspects of SMA while avoiding their downsides.

A DSA can be understood as an educational social media application (edSMA). While core aspects of SMA, such as recommendation and filtering algorithms, media sharing, personal profiles, and measurement of user characteristics, are part of the DSA, there are fundamental differences to commercial social media in terms of ethical data standards, transparency of algorithms, empowerment, and accountability of users, and the organizational context. The core component of the graphical user interface is a news feed of so-called activities, which are simple boxes with an image, text, and response modalities, such as choices and text input. This interaction schema is often used for streaming platforms and social network platforms and works very well on mobile devices and tiny touch screens.

1.4   The Siddata Study Assistant

The core idea o the Siddata DSA, as the acronym[2] states, is the individualization of studies by the DSA. Therefore, a software architecture was established that provides new functionalities within the known learning environment of the local LMS.

The software architecture supports separate recommender modules, allowing researchers to independently develop and evaluate innovative functionalities. Four prototypes have been released since the project started (including the technical baseline prototype P0). The feature set of the current prototype (P3) (see Fig. 1) includes the following social media-related recommender modules: The *academic interests module* implements an intelligent recommendation algorithm, based on BERT, a state-of-the-art neural network for language representation, to find personally relevant university courses, open educational resources (OER), and massive open online courses (MOOCs) from external repositories. The *academic contacts module* offers personal profiles and uses a matching algorithm to match and connect learners based on shared interests and individually selected criteria. The *personality module* offers psychometric tests for purposes of self-realization and self-reflection, and the resulting psychological profile is a digital mirror and personal property of the user. The *data ethics module* offers an online multimedia course on data ethics and data sovereignty from a philosophical perspective.

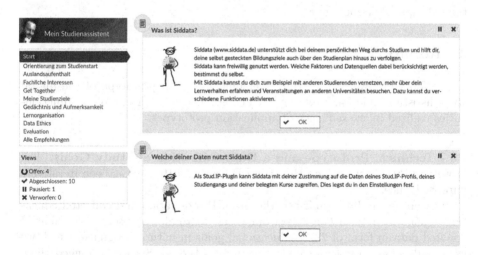

Fig. 1. Screenshot of the current study assistant. In the navigation bar at the left, the activated recommender modules of the user are listed. At the right the recommendation newsfeed, which is the main interaction element, is located.

---

[2] Studienindividualisierung durch Digitale Datengestuetzte Assistenten [Joint project for Individualization of Studies through Digital, Data-Driven Assistants].

Data sovereignty and transparency of data usage have been guiding principles for the user interface design, which we constantly monitor and improve. We implemented fine-grained data sharing and data donation settings for users and highlighted the trade-offs between data-sparseness and investing personal data in functionality whenever possible.

In this work-in-progress report, we try to answer the following questions:

– How did the Siddata study assistant evolve, and how did the set of features change?
– How many students interacted with Siddata, and which functionalities were used by students?
– Which implications about DSAs and edSMA can be derived from the experiences in this project?

2   Methods

Digital study assistants and educational, social media applications are novel digital approaches aiming to individualize educational paths in higher education. Therefore, the approach chosen in the Siddata project is to develop an assistant with yearly agile software development cycles. We evaluated the resulting prototypes concerning the functionality and user experience. Additionally, usage data allows us to conclude about the users and their usage of Siddata.

The evaluation of the prototypes was done with a mixed-methods approach. Quantitative data analyses were based on data donated by users, while qualitative evaluations were based on design-thinking workshops and evaluation questionnaires, as described in [8].

3   Results

In the following, we present the development of each prototype of the digital study assistant Siddata. Table 2 gives a comprehensive overview of the functionalities realized in the sequence of application prototypes.

P0 - Technical Prototype and a Data Collection of Study Goals. The prototype P0 was started on the 8th of February 2019 and has been iteratively improved since.

The prototype P0 established the Stud.IP integration and collected educational goals in natural language from users. In total, 732 users (see Table 1) donated data in form of 2.262 educational goals in natural language, which we used to develop a tagset for educational goals [12,14]. Six raters tagged these goals, and we could show, which goal characteristics can be unambiguously recognized from an external perspective, and which characteristics hold subjective qualities. This line of research continues, and the findings can be used to build conversational user interfaces.

Table 1. Release dates, end dates and users per prototype of Siddata.

Name	Start	End	Users
P0	2019-02-08	2019-05-16	732
P1	2020-06-01	2020-11-30	<1776 (subset of P2)
P2	2020-01-12	2021-10-30	1776
P3	2021-11-01	Currently active	890 (on January 25th 2022)

P1 - Start of the Field Study in Local LMS. The P1 prototype initiated the newsfeed interaction schema, which has proven itself. The function differentiation of the assistant leads to the foundation for separate recommender modules, which are technically still intertwined in P1. A feedback function for recommendations is implemented but rarely used, also in the following P2 version. Therefore, in P3, it was converted into an implicit feedback function, holding back essential information until users explicitly show their interest.

P2 - Expansion of the Set of Features. In the P2 version, recommender modules were strictly separated, allowing us to build and test a large set of features. The data from version P2, which 1776 students used in total, is explored from which 737 (41%) donated their data for scientific purposes. The results point at a high demand for assistive functions during the early stages of the student life cycle, which their need for orientation and information can explain (see Fig. 2). The data collected by P2 has been published as a free and open dataset [7]. Experimental empirical evidence from a field study shows demand for data and AI-driven tools in LMS. Social media-related functionalities, such as the academic interests recommender (60%), the academic contacts recommender (60%), and the personality recommender (80%), are popular among the offered functionalities. The report about the intensive mixed-methods-based evaluation was published by Schurz et al. [8].

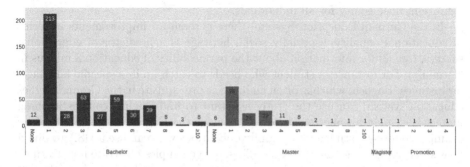

Fig. 2. The semester statistics of the study assistant version P2 shows a strong usage among students in their first semesters and a decrease with increasing semester.

P3 - Refinement and Consolidation. Based on user interactions, core functionalities were identified, recommenders were reduced, and essential functionalities were refined. Implicit feedback by progressive disclosure of relevant information was implemented to gather data for future applications using collaborative filtering and content-based filtering recommendation algorithms. Students in the early phase of the student life cycle are targeted by a specific recommender delivering relevant information. A nudging function was integrated, sending push notifications in case of new content, new personal matches, and reminders for critical tasks. Results from another line of research focused on educational goals [5,10,11] were integrated as an educational goal setting recommender. The study assistant has reached a technical and functional stage now, which allowed us to introduce it at a Workshop [13]. It has been active since the 1st of November 2021 and has more than 1100 (on the 11th of February 2022) active users already.

4   Discussion and Outlook

In this section, we elaborate on the potentials of edSMA to increase educational equality, summarize methodological limitations of the field study data and sketch SMA downsides, which may occur in edSMA, and considerations about data protection and data security. The outlook section highlights cooperation perspectives and the future development of the Siddata study assistant.

4.1   How edSMA Can Raise the Level of Equity in Higher Education

The stereotypical academic career starts after school and results in the first full-time employment. This idealized educational path is an underlying assumption behind higher education's curricular and organizational environments and can result in a one-size-fits-all approach. Any student with their traits can use a digital study assistant to individualize their educational paths, follow personal interests and distinguish themselves from the average. By helping students follow their interests and build up individually relevant competencies, DSAs, by definition, raise equity for all individuals.

In the German Education System, there is room for improvements in terms of educational equality, especially social heritage is a predictor of educational success. (see [3] for information about the permeability of educational milieus in Germany). For instance, a student who needs to catch up in a specific language, for instance, English, which is often an implicit prerequisite in the German higher education system, can use the study assistant to find English courses learning materials or plan a semester abroad, to master the English language. Another example could be a student with family obligations who can use a DSA to find a consistent weekly schedule of classes. These two examples illustrate how learners with individual educational goals and constraints can use DSAs to benefit most from higher education.

Table 2. Featureset of the study assistant prototypes. The column SM stands for social media relatedness, P stands for prototype.

Name	Functionality	SM	P0	P1	P2	P3
Academic Contacts (german: Get-together)	Social matching				✓	✓
Academic Interests (german: Fachliche Interessen)	Learning resources recommendation engine	✓		✓	✓	✓
Data Ethics (german: Souverän mit meinen Daten)	Education about data ethics to increase data sovereignty	✓			✓	✓
Evaluation (german: Evaluation)	User feedback for evaluation purposes				✓	✓
Funding (german: Studienfinanzierung)	Information about funding			✓	✓	
Learning Organization (german: Lernorganisation)	Education about learning organization techniques			✓	✓	✓
Open Educational Resources (german: Freie Bildungsmaterialien)	OER recommendation engine	✓			✓	(✓)
Personality Module (german: Gedächtnis & Aufmerksamkeit)	Personality, long-term memory, short-term memory and task-switching ability tests and personal feedback			✓	✓	✓
Scientific Career (german: Wissenschaftliche Karriere)	Information collection related to scientific careers				✓	
Study Abroad (german: Auslandssemester)	Information, reminders and nudging towards a semester abroad			✓	✓	✓
My Study Goals (german: Meine Studienziele)	Clarification of personal educational goals	✓	✓			✓

Furthermore, the modular architecture of DSA presented in this paper allows Universities to build recommender modules to support students with specific attributes. For instance, a recommender for students with kids or students from familiar non-academic backgrounds could be built and selectively used. The academic career recommender, which we built and tested in P2, provides insights about implicitly relevant knowledge that may be less familiar to students from non-academic backgrounds. This example shows that Universities can use DSAs to address specific target groups in their area of responsibility they think need specific support.

4.2   Limitations

The work presented in this paper is still in progress, and the empirical foundations in terms of data from the ongoing field study are limited. The reasons, among others, are the confoundation of the available data related to variables, such as willingness to donate data or openness, in general as a character trait, or openness to new technologies in particular. Furthermore, the data analyses were carried out exploratively, without prior hypotheses, which results in methodological constraints. Nevertheless, the data shows a row of characteristics, such as high usage by students in their early study phases, which seem to be robust. Building upon our preliminary findings, further empirical studies can be conducted to harden the insights empirically.

4.3   Which Downsides of Social Media Can Occur in LMS?

Although the authors assume that a row of downsides of SMA can be avoided in edSMA, some others, such as, for instance, social comparison issues caused by exaggerated self-presentation, leading to unhealthy behaviors, cannot be ruled out. The effects of social comparison in digital educational settings in general, and edSMA in particular, should be addressed in future studies.

4.4   Data Protection and Data Security Risks

In the database of the Siddata backend server, the amount of person-relatable data increases continuously. Although it is pseudonymized and protected by state-of-the-art IT security measures, it is principally not guaranteed that data can be lost or stolen. The risk of data loss has limited consequences for users because the previous state can be reestablished quickly by entering the same initial data again. In the worst case of data theft, if attackers succeeded in de-anonymizing the database, they could gain insights into individual educational interests or scores of psychometric tests from the personality module. Such an attack would require significant technical skills and effort, which raises the question, which attacker could be interested in such an endeavor? Buying the data legally from data brokers may be much cheaper. Nevertheless, data security and high ethical data standards are a core priority in the software development processes of Siddata.

4.5   Outlook

Although the generalizability from the field study data is limited because the sample is not representative, being influenced by variables, such as the willingness to donate data and being a student at a University in Northern Germany, it can be concluded that there is an unprecedented demand for data- and AI-driven assistive functions in LMS. The open-source web-based software architecture of our DSA allows other universities to join in by connecting their LMS to existing servers or by setting up a customized Siddata study assistant ecosystem.

User-generated data is a prerequisite for high-quality recommendations as recommender systems utilize historical ratings to predict personally relevant content. The body of implicit ratings of learning resources and other users' profiles is piling up during the ongoing field study. These ratings can be used for collaborative filtering algorithms to recommend personalized learning resources and potentially interesting personal contacts in the future.

References

1. Aichner, T., Grünfelder, M., Maurer, O., Jegeni, D.: Twenty-five years of social media: a review of social media applications and definitions from 1994 to 2019 (2021). https://doi.org/10.1089/cyber.2020.0134
2. Allcott, H., Gentzkow, M.: Social media and fake news in the 2016 election. J. Econ. Perspect. **31**(2), 211–236 (2017). https://doi.org/10.1257/jep.31.2.211
3. El-Mafaalani, A.: BildungsaufsteigerInnen aus benachteiligten Milieus. VS Verlag für Sozialwissenschaften, Wiesbaden (2012). https://doi.org/10.1007/978-3-531-19320-5
4. Holland, G., Tiggemann, M.: A systematic review of the impact of the use of social networking sites on body image and disordered eating outcomes. Body Image **17**, 100–110 (2016). https://doi.org/10.1016/j.bodyim.2016.02.008
5. Iwama, G.Y., Weber, F., Prentice, M., Lieder, F.: Development and Validation of a Goal Characteristics Questionnaire (2021). https://doi.org/10.31219/osf.io/dzhwv
6. Martens, B., Aguiar, L., Gomez-Herrera, E., Mueller-Langer, F.: The digital transformation of news media and the rise of disinformation and fake news - an economic perspective. Technical report 2, Joint Research Centre, European Commission, Seville, Spain (2018). https://doi.org/10.1017/S037346330002052X
7. Schrumpf, J., Weber, F., Schurz, K., Dettmer, N., Thelen, T.: A free and open dataset from a prototypical data-driven study assistant in higher education. In: Proceedings of the 14th International Conference on Computer Supported Education. SCITEPRESS (2022)
8. Schurz, K., Schrumpf, J., Weber, F., Seyfeli, F., Wannemacher, K.: Towards a user focused development of a digital study assistant through a mixed methods design. In: Sampson, D.G., Ifenthaler, D., Isaías, P. (eds.) 18th International Conference on Cognition and Exploratory Learning in the Digital Age, CELDA 2021, pp. 45–52, No. Celda. IADIS Press (2021)
9. Watson, W.R., Watson, S.L.: An argument for clarity: what are learning management systems, what are they not, and what should they become? TechTrends **51**(2), 28–34 (2007). https://doi.org/10.1007/s11528-007-0023-y
10. Weber, F.: Goal trees as structuring element in a digital data-driven study assistant. In: Sampson, D.G., Ifenthaler, D., Pedro, I., Mascia, M.L. (eds.) 16th International Conference on Cognition and Exploratory Learning in Digital Age (CELDA 2019), pp. 413–416, Cagliari, Italy, No. Celda. IADIS Press (2019). http://dx.doi.org/10.33965/celda2019_201911c053
11. Weber, F., Kernos, J., Grenz, M., Lee, J.: Towards a web-based hierarchical goal setting intervention for higher education. In: Sampson, D.G., Ifenthaler, D., Isaías, P. (eds.) 18th International Conference on Cognition and Exploratory Learning in the Digital Age, CELDA 2021, Lisbon. IADIS Press (2021)
12. Weber, F., Le Foll, E.: A tagset for university students' educational goals. In: 17th International Conference on Cognition and Exploratory Learning in the Digital Age, CELDA 2020 (2020). https://doi.org/10.33965/celda2020_2020141004

13. Weber, F., Schurz, K., Schrumpf, J., Seyfeli, F., Wannemacher, K., Thelen, T.: Digitale Studienassistenzsysteme Von der Idee zur Umsetzung im Projekt SID-DATA. In: Wollersheim, H.W., Karapanos, M., Pengel, N. (eds.) Medien in der Wissenschaft, Band 78, Bildung in der digitalen Transformation, pp. 239–244. Waxmann Verlag, Münster (2021)
14. Weber, F., Thelen, T.: Characterizing personal educational goals: inter-rater agreement on a tagset reveals domain-specific limitations of the external perspective. In: Ifenthaler, D., Sampson, D., Isaías, P. (eds.) Orchestration of Learning Environments in the Digital World. Cognition and Exploratory Learning in the Digital Age, 2nd edn., pp. 57–80. Springer, Cham (2021). https://doi.org/10.1007/978-3-030-90944-4_4

Customer Experience and Consumer Behavior

Augmented Reality Filters and the Faces as Brands: Personal Identities and Marketing Strategies in the Age of Algorithmic Images

Ruggero Eugeni[✉]

Università Cattolica del Sacro Cuore, Milan, Italy
ruggero.eugeni@unicatt.it

Abstract. This paper analyzes the so-called "augmented reality filters" (ARF), a technology that makes it possible to produce and spread widely on social media a particular type of video selfies that are manipulated live while filming – for example, by modifying the somatic characters of the producer's face. The first part of the paper analyzes ARFs in the light of a socio-semiotics of dispositives. This approach makes it possible to identify three interconnected aspects of ARFs: their technological consistency, which is closer to mixed reality than to augmented reality; their socio-psychological uses, and in particular personal identity construction through body image manipulation; and finally, their economic-political implications, linked to face recognition and social surveillance. The second part of the paper focuses on the marketing uses of ARFs and, in particular, on branded ARFs transforming users' faces. In these cases, the radical involvement of brands in defining the identity of users requires a profound rethinking of the mechanisms of trust that bind them to consumers.

Keywords: Media semiotics · Socio-semiotics · Digital advertising · Augmented reality · Mixed reality · Enunciation · Identity · Algorithmic capitalism · Media experience · Dispositive

1 Changing Images, Changing Branding

This paper deals with a particular image production technology, generally referred to as "Augmented Reality Filters" (hereinafter ARF). The ARFs allow you to manipulate video footage while filming – for example, by modifying the somatic characters of the portrayed subjects, or by introducing elements that are not physically present in the environments. I will particularly focus on ARFs manipulating users' faces, that have rapidly spread on social media platforms over the past five years. Among the reasons of interest in ARFs is their adoption by a growing number of brands as a new marketing tool – for example, to allow you to try some makeup or clothing products in virtual form, or to disseminate funny and personalized images of brands and of some of its products.

In this paper, after having presented a brief history of ARFs (Sect. 2), I will propose an analysis of them from the point of view of a socio-semiotics of dispositives; in this

G. Meiselwitz (Ed.): HCII 2022, LNCS 13316, pp. 223–234, 2022.
https://doi.org/10.1007/978-3-031-05064-0_17

way, I will bring to light three aspects of them: the technological, the social and micro-social, and finally the economic-political ones (Sect. 3). The second part of the paper is devoted to the analysis of the uses of ARFs in marketing and advertising, with a focus on branded ARFs manipulating users' faces (Sect. 4): I intend to analyze (still from the perspective of a socio-semiotics of dispositives) how these new types of images determine on the one hand the processes of identity constitution pursued by subjects, and on the other hand the relationships between subjects and brands.

2   Augmented Reality Filters: A Very Short History

In September 2015 Snapchat - a social platform facing some competition problems with Instagram - launches a new feature called "Lenses": users can add some dynamic effects to their video selfies. The innovation comes from having acquired a small Ukrainian startup, Looksery, which has invented this type of effect and introduced them to the app market the previous year. Although the first Lenses are only seven, they immediately prove to be a great success: the one that depicts the subjects vomiting a rainbow is partic-ularly trendy. In November, the platform opens a paid "lens store". Given this success, in May 2017 Instagram introduces a similar feature that it calls "augmented reality filters"; also in this case, the software comes from a Belarusian startup, Masquerade, acquired in 2016. At this point, the number of effects has significantly grown and includes fake glasses, animal muzzles, strange hats and so on. And the competition rate between the two platforms has raised correspondingly.

Snapchat takes the next move: in December 2017, it introduces their "Lens Studio AR developer tool", a free software that allows users to create original filters and upload them to Snapchat. In addition to end-users of social media, the software is aimed at creative agencies and intends to promote the design of branded ARFs, thus establishing a new market. Instagram understands the opportunity and launches the analogue "Spark AR Studio" between October 2018 and August 2019.

The combined effect of desktop software for creating filters on the one hand, and mobile platforms for their use on the other one, is disruptive. In the United States alone, ARF users were 43.7 million in 2020 [1]. The sector is rapidly growing: experts estimate that ARF users in the world are passing from 0.44 billion in 2019 to 1.73 billion in 2024 [2]; but some estimates increase to 3.5 billion in 2024 and 4.3 billion in 2025. And if 4.6 billion photos or videos applying ARF were uploaded in 2021, they are expected to reach 17.6 billion in 2025 [3].

3   The Many Faces of Augmented Reality Filters

3.1   ARF as Dispositives

In this paper, I will analyze ARFs in the light of a socio-semiotics of dispositives, the main lines of which I have drawn elsewhere [4]. In a nutshell, I consider a dispositive as a governmental instrument for managing a series of resources (that can be material, financial, informational, cognitive, emotional, etc.). Therefore, a dispositive allows you to produce or extract; to circulate and exchange; to valorize or devalue; to transform or destroy the resources it encompasses. Note the ambiguity of the term "governmental instrument": on the one hand, dispositives allow subjects involved within them to manage resources; on the other one, they regulate the subjects' agencies in a standardized and automated way, so to govern the subjects themselves and their behaviours.

Dispositives work and manifest themselves at three embedded levels of increasing generality. The first level is the *technological* one, about which we will talk of *devices*. The second level is the *social and micro-social* one: they regulate various experiential situations as *assemblages*. Finally, the third level is that of the more general mechanisms of *political economy*: here, dispositives appear as *apparatuses*. Let us examine how ARFs can be considered dispositives; and what types of resources they (allow to) manage at the different and interconnected levels of the device, assemblage and apparatus.

3.2   ARF as Devices

From a technological point of view, ARFs work in three steps. In the first one, that derives directly from face recognition procedures, some sensors (for example, my smartphone's camera) capture a pattern of photons (my face) and translate it into a set of data that express a model of the object portrayed (a 3D print of my face). Second, the data set that corresponds to this lens-based three-dimensional model is blended with computer-generated elements (for example, the various makeup elements that I apply to my face), according to the indications I provide through the interface: in this way, a data cube is obtained. Finally, this data cube is displayed on the smartphone screen: I see my face move, shift and change expression according to my behaviour, with the makeup elements I applied perfectly integrated into my image. Furthermore, this implies that my act of observation is in turn constantly captured by the sensors, and that the data cube is extremely dynamic, since it is reorganized moment by moment in real-time. At this point, I can observe the moving images like in a distorting mirror; broadcast live the video selfie that is being produced; or record it and make it subsequently available in my Stories.

Starting from this description, we can first observe that ARFs belong to a broader family of face-editing algorithms, which use various Artificial Intelligence tools to modify the expressions of faces within videos (face reenactment, or expression swap); replace a face with that of another subject (deep fakes, or identity swap), build non-existent faces (face synthesis); or – and this is the most typical case for ARFs – modify some features of the face (attribute manipulation) to create digital masks [5]. Consequently, the term "augmented reality" is not well applied. In fact, these algorithms are not limited to assuming a lens-based digital image and superimposing an additional digital layer on it; instead, they construct a three-dimensional digital model of the face and blend computer-based elements within it to produce a homogeneous and dynamic data cube to visualize it. Therefore, it would be necessary to speak more appropriately of "mixed reality". Virtual, augmented and mixed reality are all components of the broader meta-category of Extended Reality [6, 7] and constitute together the field of "reality media" [8]; however, it is essential to understand that, despite their naming, ARFs do not "augment" reality caught in photo-cinematographic terms: rather, they "mix" photo-cinematographic elements and computer-generated elements within the same dynamic algorithmic model before visualizing it.

To sum up, ARFs as devices (that is, as technological dispositives) regulate the connections and exchanges between three main types of resources: light, which can be measured in photons; images, quantifiable in pixels; and data, calculable in bytes. In the processes of switching between the three orders of resources, data has a central and strategic role: even if ARFs appear to be producers of images, more deeply they reveal to be dispositives to produce data, that eventually come to be partially displayed.

3.3   ARF as Assemblages

In October 2019, a few months after having introduced their Spark AR Studio, Instagram surprisingly suspended the use of ARF. Although temporary (ARFs were triumphantly reintroduced in August 2020), the decision is symptomatic of a certain unease surrounding ARFs. Effectively, social media using ARF have been accused by an increasing number of studies to promote "Snapchat dysmorphia" [9], a particular occurrence of body dysmorphic disorders (BDD), consisting in a misalignment between the desired image of one's body and the one actually perceived, due to continuous and intensive use of beautification ARF [10, 11]. In turn, Snapchat dysmorphia would lead to lower levels of self-esteem [12] and higher levels of depression [13–15]; to several disorders of nutritional behaviour [16] and more frequent use of plastic surgery [17–19]; to self-objectification [20, 21] and adaptation to stereotypical socio-cultural aesthetic standards [22] (including racial and skin-colours ones [23]); to "aesthetic labour" [24] and mutual surveillance through female "policing gazes" [25]. However, other studies have shown that beautification is neither the only reason for the use of ARFs nor the prevailing one; in fact, aesthetic motivations are flanked by entertainment, coolness, curiosity, social interaction, silliness, having fun, creativity, brand "fandomship" and so on [26–29]. Furthermore, many studies have issued the constitution of self-identity through the construction and diffusion of ARF moving images, asserting that it is a processual and inferential process involving not only body images but also body schemata (i.e., sets of sensorimotor abilities) [30]; and that it implies a constant oscillation between self-recognition and otherness in watching selfie images produced by ARFs [31]. Finally, some more theoretical interventions have proposed to consider ARFs and similar procedures in the light of a semiotic construction of identity [32], also within that particular type of identifying interaction between subjects and technological objects that has been defined as "radical mediation" [33, 34].

We can approach this literature in terms of a socio-semiotics of dispositives, by saying that ARFs as assemblages (that is, socio-psychological dispositives) are responsible for managing connections and exchanges between input resources such as energy (the labour of the user, the electrical power required for the operation of smartphones), time, attention; and output ones, such as identity, reputation and self-reputation. It is important to provide a more detailed description of how this happens, both for the importance of the issue itself and the consequences regarding the use of branded ARFs (see below, Sect. 4.2).

We can describe ARFs as identity and reputational dispositives starting from the fact that they allow and encourage the production of a discursive object (a video clip) and, therefore, of an audiovisual utterance (*enoncé*). The identity and reputational procedures of the ARF are consequently based on processes of technologically implemented enunciation (*énonciation*) [35–38].

As the event of the enunciation unfolds in its intertwined cognitive and material aspects, two main questions arise: to whom to attribute the utterance and its contents (who is the subject and who is the object of the discourse that is enunciated?); and what value to assign to them. In particular, users must determine how much and what of the audiovisual utterance and its contents belongs to themselves, and how much pertains to other subjects or objects. Semiotics has shown how this recognition occurs through the two operations of disengagement (*débrayage*) and engagement (*embrayage*). In a first phase, enunciation implies disengagement, so that the utterance is attributed to and inhabited by non-persons (I look at the product of an ARF but without feeling that it was I who produced the video, nor giving a precise identity to the figure whose face is shown). In a second phase, the engagement takes over: within a distribution of the actantial roles among different subjects, users recognize the audiovisual utterance as their own product, therefore qualifying as Enunciators (*Énonciateurs*); at the same time, users recognize themselves in the faces modified by the ARFs, so qualifying as Narrators (*Narrateurs*: actually, I am producing the video, and that face is mine). The criterion for attributing these qualities to the selves (and therefore also for determining the belonging, proximity, distance or otherness of other subjects and objects) is the sensorimotor activity that the subjects are deploying and proprio-perceiving by materially producing the utterance. In practice, I consider "mine" everything that depends on the movements I feel I am acting while producing the ARF video clip.

Therefore, the constitution of one's own conscious self takes place through repeated acts of enunciation, hence through the constant and repeated oscillation between disengagement and engagement, in a constantly dynamic and adaptive spiral process. Furthermore, the same dynamic involves not only the actantial dimension, but also the axiological one: after a first phase implying a suspension of values, a second one takes place in which subjects make a value judgment on both the utterance and its contents (I can consider my face beautiful or ugly, and my video successful or trash). Thus, the formal dispositive of enunciation makes it possible to transform the input resources mentioned above (visual, luministic, informational, operational, energetic, temporal, attentional) into other types of output resources and, in particular, into identity and reputation. It should be noted that this model allows us to comprehend and consider at the same time both cases of beautification and relative dysmorphic drifts, and the less dramatic cases of fun, entertainment and creativity.

3.4   ARF as Apparatuses

Within a few months, two little-publicized but significant events took place in the world of social media. In June 2021 Tik Tok, which belongs to the Chinese group Bytedance, modified its privacy policies valid in the US by introducing a clause according to which it "may collect biometric identifiers and biometric information as defined under US laws, such as faceprints and voiceprints, from your User Content" [39]. In the opposite direction, in November 2021 Facebook-Meta (which owns Instagram) announced that it had started the suspension of all face recognition activities - which allowed, for example, to automatically tag the faces of people in the photos posted on social. The two episodes are revelatory: the relief of the ARF is not simply technological, semiotic and social; they also involve an important *economic* dimension, linked both to the increase in traffic on social networks, and to the marketing exploitation – including micro-profiling of users for hyper-targeted advertisements; in turn, this economic dimension is linked to a *political* dimension relating to privacy problems and the face recognition procedures that the ARFs involve (see Sect. 3.2).

The link between ARFs and surveillance capitalism [40] through the application of soft biometrics [41, 42] is not always evident, but it is nonetheless present. The use of databases of facial images derived from social networks is increasingly used in the forensic field, to identify people responsible for crimes [43]; in these cases, if the original faceprint underlying the ARF is not available, biometric recognition adopts reverse engineering algorithms that cancel the face distortions introduced by ARFs [44, 45]. In other cases, the intent of political control is more evident. For example, the Face++ platform, implemented by the algorithms of the Chinese company Megvii, provides online ARF services for beautification. In May 2019, NGO Human Rights Watch reported that fragments of Megvii's code were being used (without the company's awareness) in the Integrated Joint Operations Platform, (IJOP), a surveillance app used by security forces of the Chinese government in the control of the Muslim community of Uyghurs in Xinjiang province [46].

Ultimately, there is a strong continuity between the strictly medial, semiotic and visual aspects of ARFs and their broader and more ramified economic and political implications. Therefore, the ARFs as apparatuses (that is, as dispositives of political economy) prove to be components of a mechanism that manages and exchanges informational, economic, financial and agentive resources.

4   From Ordinary to Branded ARF

In this paragraph, I apply the socio-semiotic analysis of dispositives to a specific type of ARF: those branded by different companies and used as a new marketing tool. As I mentioned, the introduction of ARF design software by social media platforms was also aimed at opening a new advertising market: that of branded ARFs (which I will avoid calling, with the usual use of acronyms, BARF), capable of integrating social media marketing [47] and AR marketing [48] tools. Although branded ARFs are of various types (some involve environments or entire bodies in motion), I will focus on those that manipulate users' faces.

4.1   A Typology of Branded ARF

I start by defining the possible categories of face-focused branded ARFs. The first category is that of *atmospheres*: in these cases, the user's face does not undergo substantial variations, but it is placed in an environment that refers to some values of the brand or some characteristics of the product: this is the case, for example, of the ARF that launches the new Aria collection by Gucci (2021) on Instagram: it immerse the users in a glamorous and glittering environment and superimpose the image of a heart on their bust; I can also cite many ARFs created by Netflix for Snapchat, which plunge the users, for example, in the sinister atmospheres of *Stranger Things* (2017) or other shows available on the OTP platform.

The second category of branded ARF is that of *try-on*: in these cases, filters allow users to virtually try on cosmetic products (single makeup elements or a combination of them) or clothing accessories (glasses, hats, jewels. etc.). The try-on category has two variations. The first is the mode that I will call *gaming*: animated elements such as strange machines (*Face-o-matic* and *Eyes-o-matic* ARF created by Max Siedentopf for Gucci Beauty in Instagram, 2020) or flying pencils and brushes (Disney Cruella by Mac Cosmetics in Snapchat, 2021) intervene to apply makeup on the user's face. The second mode is that of *shopping*: once users have completed the virtual makeup or the test of a pair of glasses, they can immediately check the price and possibly order the products (as in the "Checkout" function introduced by Instagram in 2019, or in the "AR Shopping Lenses", presented by Snapchat in 2022).

The third category of branded ARF is what I call *disguise*. Here too, we find some subcategories. In some cases, the filter superimposes graphic effects on the users' faces, for example, signboards placed above the foreheads and moving with the subjects ("What should I watch on Netflix?"). In other cases, the users' faces are masked by more complex objects: for example, Netflix on Snapchat allows you to wear the Dalì mask from *Money Heist* (2018). In some cases, the masking takes place "on sight": for example, the song *The eternal struggles of the howling man* by Rob Zombie was launched in 2021 on Instagram with an ARF that, as soon as users open their mouths threateningly, quickly transforms them into terrifying werewolves. Finally, among the category of disguise, it is appropriate to reserve a specific subcategory for ARFs that turn users' faces into living logos of well-known brands. Take for instance the case of Starbucks. The company has not invested heavily in branded ARFs, but various users have created ARFs based on the Starbucks logo. For example, a filter created by the yuho account (yu_xo0) in Instagram allows you to "wear" the hair and crown of the mermaid that appears in the Starbucks logo. Even more radically, the filter created by Shin Naka (Oknaka) still in Instagram allows you to fully inhabit the face of the mermaid: in this case, the users' expressions and grimaces are immediately expressed by the character that represents the brand.

4.2 Branded ARF as Dispositives

If at this point we consider the branded ARFs as dispositives, we immediately realize that all three levels of devices, assemblages and apparatuses are present and connected in their use. For example, from a political-economic perspective, it has been observed that branded ARFs constitute a model of delocalization and fragmentation of the work of brand promotion, which assigns advertising micro-tasks to individual users on the model of Amazon's Mechanical Turk [49]. Furthermore, the technological and political issue of face recognition is by no means unrelated to branded ARFs: some studies have shown that awareness and concern about surveillance issues by users discourage their adoption and suspend the "privacy paradox" (the behaviour for which, although defending in principle the right to privacy, we do not hesitate to make our data available in online requests) [50, 51].

In any case, the main reasons of interest in the branded ARFs are concentrated on their nature of *assemblages*, that is, of social, micro-social and experiential dispositives. Research on branded ARFs (still, at the moment, fragmentary) has highlighted various aspects of their user experience: they are perceived as more original, creative, fun, interactive and informative than non-branded ARFs [27]; furthermore, they imply (particularly in the case of try-ons of cosmetic products or clothing accessories) an increase in product purchase intentions and a positive attitude towards brands [52]. Yet, more relevant research in this sector leads back to the problem of users' definition (and appreciation) of selves, in relation this time with the identities and values of brands and products. In this direction, scholars observed that the use of try-on ARFs (and more generally of "virtual mirrors") enhances the self-brand connection (that is, the process in which consumers incorporate brands into their self-concepts) [53]; that they stimulate both the sense of belonging to the products virtually tested [54] and that of the artificial image of one's own body [55]; that they produce in this way "augmented selves" [56], able to renegotiate the gap between the current selves and the ideal and desired ones, with the help of the brands and products they use in the virtual try-on [57].

This literature focuses on try-on ARFs; however, the users' identity issue that it places at the centre of attention can also be extended to other types of branded ARFs. In this regard, we can return to the model of the enunciational constitution of identity introduced in Sect. 3.3, to apply it to branded ARFs. As I explained, this model envisages the two phases of disengagement (constitution of the utterance-discourse in a non-personal form) and subsequent engagement (attribution of actantial roles and value weights to the different entities identified as objects or subjects of the discourse). In the case of branded ARFs, the brand, possibly represented by its own products, is among the entities to which an actantial role and a value qualification are to be attributed. In this regard, three main possibilities can be defined, which broadly correspond to the three types of branded ARFs I have outlined in Sect. 4.1. Furthermore, each of the three roles implies the involvement of specific value universes [58].

In the case of *atmospheres*, the brand qualifies as the Helper (*Adjuvant*) of the Enunciators: the brand provides them with the apt tools to "make a good impression", creating elegant and compelling video clips. The values of the brand are mainly those of playful and aesthetic valorization. In the case of ARFs of the *try-on* type, the brand more easily assumes the role of Addresser (*Destinateur*), that is, the agent who transmits to the subjects the value criteria of their well-appearing and well-being (for example, the type of makeup best suited to their faces); the tools to realize this ideal (the different cosmetic tricks and makeups); and finally the material products themselves (the shopping offers of the apps). In this case, the directly involved values are those of practical and possibly critical valorization: the quality of the products counts and, in particular, their effectiveness in ensuring the required effects. Finally, in the case of branded ARFs belonging to the category of *disguise*, and especially in cases where the brand logo becomes the mask that the subjects wear and which move with the expressions of their faces, the brand assumes the role of *Narrator*, that is, it replaces more or less completely the Enunciators as a figurative presence within the audiovisual utterance. The values involved are those of utopian valorization, since they concern some basic existential choices that directly affect the subjects' way of feeling and being.

4.3   From Branded Selves to Selfed Brands

In conclusion, we can evaluate some consequences of what I have just described, both on the side of users' and on that of the brands' identities. On the first front, as I said, the type of self that derives from these processes has been defined as an "augmented self" [56]. However, the technological nature of ARFs as devices is not the "additional" one of augmented reality, but rather the connective, blending and fusional one of mixed reality (see Sect. 3.2). Hence, the images of themselves that the subjects enunciate through the branded ARFs imply a real fusion and a radical and intimate connection between themselves and the brands. I will therefore speak of a "mixed self".

On the front of the brands, this new intimacy with the subjects implied by the enunciational construction of the self through branded ARFs, has at least two consequences. First, the brands' identity, although linked to mythologies and world-building operations [59], must also deal with the capillary dimension of personal situations, of intimate stories, of personal expressions and emotions crossing the face of each user. Second, the construction of the value universes of brands [60] is increasingly filtered by networks of individual, intimate, embodied trust relationships embedded in the life, in the bodies, and in the experiences of social subjects. Ultimately, the "branded selves" of the past [61] are now taking over new semiotic entities, that we could at least temporarily define as *selfed brands*.

References

1. Social network augmented reality users U.S. 2018–2022. Statista, 28 Jan 2021. https://www.statista.com/statistics/1035436/united-states-social-network-ar-users/. Accessed 18 Feb 2022
2. Number of mobile augmented reality (AR) active users worldwide from 2019 to 2024. Statista, 29 Nov 2021. https://www.statista.com/statistics/1098630/global-mobile-augmented-reality-ar-users/. Accessed 18 Feb 2022
3. Deloitte Digital: Snap Consumer AR Global Report 2021. https://www2.deloitte.com/content/dam/Deloitte/nl/Documents/deloitte-digital/deloitte-digital-nl-snap-netherlands-report.pdf. Accessed 18 Feb 2022
4. Eugeni, R.: Capitale Algoritimico. Morcelliana-Scholè, Brescia (2021)
5. Tolosana, R., et al.: Deepfakes and beyond: a survey of face manipulation and fake detection". Inf. Fus. **64**, 131–148 (2020). https://doi.org/10.1016/j.inffus.2020.06.014
6. Liberatore, M.J., Wagner, W.P.: Virtual, mixed, and augmented reality: a systematic review for immersive systems research. Virtual Reality **25**(3), 773–799 (2021). https://doi.org/10.1007/s10055-020-00492-0
7. Shumaker, R. (ed.): ICVR 2007. LNCS, vol. 4563. Springer, Heidelberg (2007). https://doi.org/10.1007/978-3-540-73335-5
8. Bolter, J.D., Engberg, M., MacIntyre, B.: Reality Media. The MIT Press, Cambridge (2021)
9. Ramphul, K., Mejias, S.G.: Is "Snapchat dysmorphia" a real issue? Cureus **10**(3), e2263 (2018). https://doi.org/10.7759/cureus.2263
10. Ryan-Mosley, T.: Beauty filters are changing the way young girls see themselves. MIT Technology Review (2020). https://www.technologyreview.com/2021/04/02/1021635/beauty-filters-young-girls-augmented-reality-social-media/. Accessed 18 Feb 2022
11. Surace, B.: Culture del volto e sociosemiotica della selfie dysmorphia. Filosofi(e)Semiotiche **7**(2), 56–66 (2020)

12. Veldhuis, J., et al.: The relations between selfie behaviors, body image, self-objectification, and self-esteem in young women. Am. Psychol. Assoc. **9**(1), 3–13 (2020). https://doi.org/10.1037/ppm0000206

13. Abbas, L., Dodeen, A.: Body dysmorphic features among Snapchat users of "Beauty-Retouching of Selfies" and its relationship with quality of life. Media Asia (2021). https://doi.org/10.1080/01296612.2021.2013065

14. Fastoso, F., González-Jiménez, H., Cometto, T.: Mirror, mirror on my phone": drivers and consequences of selfie editing. J. Bus. Res. **133**, 365–375 (2021). https://doi.org/10.1016/j.jbusres.2021.05.002

15. Tiggemann, M., Anderberg, I., Brown, Z.: Uploading your best self: selfie editing and body dissatisfaction. Body Image **33**, 175–182 (2020). https://doi.org/10.1016/j.bodyim.2020.03.002

16. Rounsefell, K., et al.: Social media, body image and food choices in healthy young adults: a mixed methods systematic review. Nutr. Diet. **77**, 19–40 (2020)

17. Chen, J., et al.: Association between the use of social media and photograph editing applications, self-esteem, and cosmetic surgery acceptance. JAMA Facial Plast. Surg. **21**(5), 361–367 (2019). https://doi.org/10.1001/jamafacial.2019.0328

18. Rajanala, S., Maymone, M.B.C., Vashi, N.A.: Selfies—living in the era of filtered photographs. JAMA Facial Plast. Surg. **20**(6), 443–444 (2018). https://doi.org/10.1001/jamafacial.2018.0486

19. Rodner, V., Goode, A., Burns, Z.: "Is it all just lip service?": on Instagram and the normalization of the cosmetic servicescape. J. Serv. Mark. (2021). https://doi.org/10.1108/JSM-12-2020-0506

20. Caso, D., et al.: "Change my selfie": relationships between self-objectification and selfie-behavior in young Italian women. J. Appl. Soc. Psychol. **50**, 538–549 (2020). https://doi.org/10.1111/jasp.12693

21. Vendemia, M.A., DeAndrea, D.C.: The effects of engaging in digital photo modifications and receiving favorable comments on women's selfies shared on social media. Body Image **37**, 74–83 (2021). https://doi.org/10.1016/j.bodyim.2021.01.011

22. Senín-Calderón, C., Perona-Garcelán, S., Rodríguez-Testal, J.F.: The dark side of Instagram: predictor model of dysmorphic concerns. Int. J. Clin. Health Psychol. **20**(3), 253–261 (2020). https://doi.org/10.1016/j.ijchp.2020.06.005

23. Ryan-Mosley, T.: How digital beauty filters perpetuate colorism. MIT Technology Review (2021). https://www.technologyreview.com/2021/08/15/1031804/digital-beauty-filters-photoshop-photo-editing-colorism-racism/. Accessed 18 Feb 2022

24. Elias, A.S., Gill, R., Scharff C. (eds.). Aesthetic Labour. Rethinking Beauty Politics in Neoliberalism. Palgrave MacMillan, Cham (2017)

25. Winch, A.: Brand intimacy, female friendship and digital surveillance networks. New Form. **84**, 228–245 (2015). https://doi.org/10.3898/NewF:84/85.11.2015

26. Dodoo, N.A., Youn, S.: Snapping and chatting away: consumer motivations for and outcomes of interacting with Snapchat AR ad lens. Telematics Inform. **57**, 101514 (2021). https://doi.org/10.1016/j.tele.2020.101514

27. Flavián, C., Ibáñez-Sánchez, S., Orús, C.: User responses towards augmented reality face filters: implications for social media and brands. In: Tom Dieck, M.C., et al. (eds.) Augmented Reality and Virtual Reality. New Trends in Immersive Technology, pp. 29–42. Springer, Cham (2021). https://doi.org/10.1007/978-3-030-68086-23

28. Javornik, A., et al.: "What lies behind the filter?" uncovering the motivations for using augmented reality (AR) face filters on social media and their effect on well-being. Comput. Hum. Behav. **128**, 107126 (2022). https://doi.org/10.1016/j.chb.2021.107126

29. Rios, J.S., Ketterer, D.J., Wohn, D.Y.: How users choose a face lens on Snapchat. In: Evers, V., Naaman, M. (eds.) CSCW 2018. Proceedings of the Companion of the 2018 ACM Conference on Computer Supported Cooperative Work and Social Computing. Association for Computing Machinery, New York (2018). https://doi.org/10.1145/3272973.3274087
30. Tremblay, S.C., Essafi Tremblay, S., Poirier, P.: From filters to fillers: an active inference approach to body image distortion in the selfie era. AI Soc. **36**(1), 33–48 (2020). https://doi.org/10.1007/s00146-020-01015-w
31. Fribourg, R., Peillard, E., McDonnell, R.: Mirror, mirror on my phone: investigating dimensions of self-face perception induced by augmented reality filters. Paper presented at 2021 IEEE International Symposium on Mixed and Augmented Reality (ISMAR), 4–8 Oct 2021. Added to IEEE Xplore: 13 Nov 2021. https://doi.org/10.1109/ISMAR52148.2021.00064
32. Leone, M. (ed.): Artificial Faces, pp. 37–38. Lexia. Rivista di Semiotica (2021). https://doi.org/10.4399/97888255385331
33. Villa, F.: Filtred self. Few notes around recent self–technologies. In: Malavasi, L., Tongiani, S. (eds.) Technophobia and Technophilia in the Media, Art and Visual Culture, pp. 29–39. Aracne, Roma (2020). https://doi.org/10.4399/97888255398513
34. Grusin, R.: Radical mediation. Crit. Inq. **42**(1), 124–148 (2015)
35. Paolucci, C.: For a cognitive semiotics of subjectivity. In: Paolucci, C. (ed.) Cognitive Semiotics. Integrating Signs, Minds, Meaning and Cognition, pp. 27–61. Springer, Cham (2021). https://doi.org/10.1007/978-3-030-42986-7_2
36. Benveniste, É.: Problems in General Linguistic. Miami University Press, Coral Gables (Fl.) (1971)
37. Greimas, A.J., Courtes, J.: Semiotics and Language: An Analytical Dictionary. Indiana University Press, Bloomington (1982)
38. Fontanille, J.: The Semiotics of Discourse. Peter Lang, New York (2006)
39. TikTok Privacy Policy, Updated June 2 (2021). https://www.tiktok.com/legal/privacy-policy-us?lang=en. Accessed 18 Feb 2022
40. Zuboff, S.: The Age of Surveillance Capitalism. PublicAffairs, New York (2019)
41. Berle, I.: Face Recognition Technology. Compulsory Visibility and Its Impact on Privacy and the Confidentiality of Personal Identifiable Images. Springer, Cham (2021). https://doi.org/10.1007/978-3-030-36887-6_2
42. Fairhurst, M.: Biometrics. A Very Short Introduction. Oxford University Press, Oxford - New York (2018)
43. Ferguson, R., Littlefield, M.M., Purdon, J. (eds.): The Art of Identification. Forensics, Surveillance, Identity. The Pennsylvania State University Press, University Park (2021)
44. Hedman, P., et al.: On the Effect of Selfie Beautification Filters on Face Detection and Recognition. Pattern Recognition Letters (2021). arXiv:2110.08934v2
45. Powell, A., Haynes, C.: Social media data in digital forensics investigations. In: Zhang, X., Choo, K.-K. (eds.) Digital Forensic Education. SBD, vol. 61, pp. 281–303. Springer, Cham (2020). https://doi.org/10.1007/978-3-030-23547-5_14
46. Human Rights Watch: China's Algorithms of Repression. Reverse Engineering a Xinjiang Police Mass Surveillance App (2019). https://www.hrw.org/report/2019/05/01/chinas-algorithms-repression/reverse-engineering-xinjiang-police-mass
47. Dwivedi, Y.K., et al.: Setting the future of digital and social media marketing research: perspectives and research propositions. Int. J. Inf. Manage. **59**, 102–168 (2021). https://doi.org/10.1016/j.ijinfomgt.2020.102168
48. Rauschnabel, P.: Augmented reality is eating the real-world! The substitution of physical products by holograms. Int. J. Inf. Manage. **57**, 102–279 (2021). https://doi.org/10.1016/j.ijinfomgt.2020.102279

49. Hawker, K., Carah, N.: Snapchat's augmented reality brand culture: sponsored filters and lenses as digital piecework. Continuum **35**(1), 12–29 (2021). https://doi.org/10.1080/103 04312.2020.1827370

50. Cowan, K., Javornik, A., Jiang, P.: Privacy concerns when using augmented reality face filters? Explaining why and when use avoidance occurs. Psychol. Mark. **38**, 1799–1813 (2021). https://doi.org/10.1002/mar.21576

51. Smink, A.R., et al.: Try online before you buy: how does shopping with augmented reality affect brand responses and personal data disclosure. Electron. Commer. Res. Appl. **35**, 100854 (2019). https://doi.org/10.1016/j.elerap.2019.100854

52. Smink, A.R., et al.: Shopping in augmented reality: the effects of spatial presence, personalization and intrusiveness on app and brand responses. J. Bus. Res. **118**, 474–485 (2020). https://doi.org/10.1016/j.jbusres.2020.07.018

53. Baek, T.H., Yoo, C.Y., Yoon, S.: Augment yourself through virtual mirror: the impact of self-viewing and narcissism on consumer responses. Int. J. Advert. **37**(3), 421–439 (2018). https://doi.org/10.1080/02650487.2016.1244887

54. Carrozzi, A., et al.: What's mine is a hologram? how shared augmented reality augments psychological ownership. J. Interact. Mark. **48**, 71–88 (2019). https://doi.org/10.1016/j.int mar.2019.05.004

55. Huang, T.-L., Mathews, S., Chou, C.Y.: Enhancing online rapport experience via augmented reality. J. Serv. Mark. **33**(7), 851–865 (2019). https://doi.org/10.1108/JSM-12-2018-0366

56. Javornik, A., et al.: Augmented self. The effects of virtual face augmentation on consumers' self-concept. J. Bus. Res. **130**, 170–187 (2021). https://doi.org/10.1016/j.jbusres.2021.03.026

57. Yim, M.Y.-C., Park, S.-Y: "I am not satisfied with my body, so I like augmented reality (AR)". Consumer responses to AR-based product presentations. J. Bus. Res. **100**, 581–589 (2019). https://doi.org/10.1016/j.jbusres.2018.10.041

58. Floch, J.-M.: Semiotics, Marketing and Communication: Beneath the Signs, the Strategies. Palgrave, New York (2001)

59. Féré, J. (dir.): Les dessous des marques. Une lecture des marques comme signes des mythes contemporaines. Ellipses, Paris (2021)

60. Oswald, L.R.: Creating Value: The Theory and Practice of Marketing Semiotics Research. Oxford University Press, Oxford (2015)

61. Asa Berger, A.: The branded self. In: Asa Berger, A. (eds.) Brands and Cultural Analysis, pp. 89–98. Palgrave Macmillan, Cham (2019)

Analysis of the Behavior of E-Sports and Streaming Consumers in Latin America

Cristobal Fernandez-Robin[1]([✉]), Diego Yañez[1], Scott McCoy[2], and Pablo Flores[1]

[1] Departamento de Industrias, Universidad Técnica Federico Santa María, Av. España 1680, Valparaiso, Chile
{cristobal.fernandez,diego.yanez}@usm.cl,
pablo.floresc@alumnos.usm.cl
[2] Mason School of Business, Williamsburg, VA, USA
scott.mccoy@mason.wm.edu

Abstract. The e-sports and streaming industries have experienced explosive growth in recent years, reaching audiences of millions of people around the world. Latin America is a region that has been partly left aside by scientific research in this field, which is mostly because this region is small compared to Asia or North America in terms of e-sports streaming. Therefore, it is necessary to build a model of the final consumers of these industries in order to understand continuance intention in the context of online videogames in this region. This study used the uses and gratifications theory to model the behavior of consumers of e-sports and streaming in the case of Riot Games Latino America Sur, specifically players of League of Legends. A survey was applied to 484 actual players, obtaining a R^2 of continuance intention equal to 0.39, i.e., 39% of the error variance of this factor is explained by its exogenous latent variables. Furthermore, the model concluded that the variables that best predict continuance intention (CI) are social interaction (SI), social presence (SP) and enjoyment (E), while the variables achievement (A), self-presentation (S), fantasy (F) and escapism (RE) are not significant. Finally, a cluster analysis conducted did not identify clear segments among Latin American players.

Keywords: e-Sport · Streaming · Continuance intention

1 Introduction

The e-sport and streaming industries, in addition to be strongly interrelated have experienced exponential growth over the last years. This has generated great interest in their analysis and research. Studies on the topic have comprised the geographical zones with the largest audiences, mainly Asia, North America and Europe. When analyzing the most present countries in the industry based on number of viewers, these are Taiwan (China), Russia, Poland, Germany, Sweden, France, the United Kingdom, Canada, the United States and Brazil [1]. The country where this industry is the most developed is China, which already had 64 e-sports clubs in 2012, with almost 1200 registered athletes [2], showing the predominance of Asia in this field.

G. Meiselwitz (Ed.): HCII 2022, LNCS 13316, pp. 235–247, 2022.
https://doi.org/10.1007/978-3-031-05064-0_18

The most important brands in the world have made large advertising investments in the e-streaming industry. An extrapolation of these numbers suggests that more than US$800 million were invested in marketing in 2019, i.e., almost 1 billion dollars. In addition, the e-streaming audience was composed of more than 50% young people aged 21 to 35 years in 2016 [3].

The concentration of researchers on the regions with more users has limited the analysis of the behavior of these consumers in Latin America. Therefore, this study derives from the need for modeling the final consumers of these industries through the theory of uses and gratifications in a case applied to Riot Games Latinoamérica Sur in order to provide some guidelines for the companies in the industry.

2 Theoretical Background

2.1 E-sports and Sport Streaming

E-sports have been formally defined as an area of sports activities in which people develop and train mental or physical skills for the use of information and communication technologies [4]. In previous years and years close to 2011, both the media and several scholars and videogame developers commented on the relevance of e-sports, not only as new sports events but also as an increasingly important factor in the gaming culture of players [5]. In the World Computer Gaming tournament held in 2010, approximately 450 players from 53 countries participated in 13 official computer game platforms, attracting more than de 9.5 million viewers around the world [6, 7]. E-sports and video gamers facilitate the formation of communities, given the cultural characteristics implied. These communities are different from one another depending on the game and competition style they have, i.e., one-to-one or strategy, among other types, which reflects sociological behaviors in the market [8].

2.2 Uses and Gratifications Theory in Hedonic Information Systems

Originating from research into radio communication, the Uses and Gratifications Theory (U&G) has been widely employed to explain user behavior from a user-level perspective [9]. U&G is theoretically similar to the TAM insofar as it explains continued use of something already chosen. The difference between TAM-based models and U&G is the applied scenario; TAM and the unified model explain on the job technology use in the majority of cases, whereas U&G addresses consumer media use [10].

This theory expanded its scope and has lately been used in different applications related to the Internet and other technologies. Among the multiple existing studies, Mäntymäki and Islam (2015) [11] used the theory of uses and gratifications in users of a freemium music streaming service. Heikkilä et al. (2015) [12] applied the theory in the context of online videogames, while Chunmei Gan, Weijun Wang (2015) [13] performed an analysis on the continued use of social networks. In this way, the theory of uses and gratifications is employed to model the continuance of hedonic information systems (Hedonic IS), which are strongly linked to consumption technologies.

3   Research Model and Hypotheses

The model comprises three types of gratification, namely Hedonic Gratification, Social Gratification and Utilitarian Gratification. Hedonic gratification is represented through the determinants for the degrees of Enjoyment, Fantasy and Escapism. The second type of gratification, social gratification, is expressed through Social Interaction and Social Presence, while the third type is composed of Achievement and Selfpresentation). The final result corresponds to the Continuance Intention of the hedonic SI, in which age and gender act as moderators of each relationship in the model [12] (Fig. 1 and Table 1).

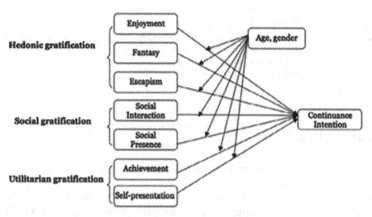

Fig. 1. Model for the Theory of Uses and Gratifications proposed for continuance in hedonic SI (Source: Heikkilä, J., Li, H., Liu, Y., Van der Heijden, H. and Xu, X. 2015)

Table 1. Definition of constructs and hypotheses (created by the authors)

Construct	Definition	Hypothesis
Enjoyment (GD)	The extent to which using an e-sport service is perceived as enjoyable in its own right [14]	Enjoyment will positively affect continuance intention
Fantasy (F)	The degree to which the imagined events or sequences of mental images representing an integration of the demands of all the psyche and reality components are realized in playing an e-sport [15]	Fantasy will positively affect continuance intention
Escapism (ER)	The extent to which playing an e-sport helps players escape unpleasant realities or distract them from problems and pressures [15]	Escapism will positively affect continuance intention
Social Interaction (IS)	The extent to which players use an e-sport as a social environment to interact with others [16]	Social Interaction will positively affect the continuance intention

(continued)

Table 1. (*continued*)

Construct	Definition	Hypothesis
Self-Presentation (A)	The extent to which playing an e-sport will help the player to generate a particular image of self and thereby influence how others perceive and treat the player [17]	Self-presentation will positively affect continuance intention
Achievement (L)	The extent to which an e-sport is played to gain power, progress rapidly, accumulate in-game symbols of wealth or status, interest in analyzing the underlying rules and system in order to optimize character performance and the desire to challenge and compete with others [18]	Achievement will positively affect continuance intention
Social Presence	The extent to which a player's psychological sense of physically interacting and establishing a personal connection with others via playing an e-sport is achieved [19]	Social Presence will positively affect continuance intention
Continuance Intention (IC)	Intention to play e-sports in the future [20]	–

4 Empirical Research

4.1 Measurement Development and Data Collection

To model the behavior of the League of Legends consumer, the Theory of Uses and Gratifications was employed through structural equation modeling (SEM) in the SPSS Amos software. In turn, including the relationships between the independent factors of the model, a cluster analysis was performed using the SPSS Statistics v22 software.

The methodology employed is similar to that found in Heikkilä et al. [12], who applied U&G in video gamers from China in order to assess their continuance intention in social media games. The survey for this paper is an adaptation of the final design of Heikkilä et al. [12] that has been tailored to the context of League of Legends Latinoamérica Sur. The instrument was uploaded to SurveyMonkey and shared among the communities of League of Legends Latinoamérica Sur. 737 surveys were filled out, of which only 566 were complete (77% of the total). However, given that only responses from active players from the Latin American region were desired, the first two questions acted as a filter. Additionally, a section with questions about demographics, frequency of gaming and streaming consumption is incorporated, which included the moderators of the model: age and gender. It may be seen that of the 566 valid responses, only 484 represent actual gamers of Latinoamérica Sur, of which 318 are regular viewers of the stream.

4.2 Analysis and Results

Cluster Analysis. Using the SPSS Statistics v22 software, clustering is conducted in the sample in order to identify segments among the Latin American gamers. This analysis starts with an exploratory phase that uses the hierarchical cluster tool, including variables of the model and of the user profile of respondents and excluding variables associated with the frequency of stream consumption and duration of such sessions, as well as the demographic variables of age and sex, obtaining two and four clusters. In turn, using the bi-step cluster tool, three clusters are obtained, considering the same previous variables; however, the quality obtained is poor.

In this way, three cases are selected for analysis in the conclusive phase, i.e., the segmentation of the sample in two, three and four clusters using the k-media cluster tool (Table 2).

Table 2. Number of cases in each cluster (Source: Created by the authors)

Cases	2 clusters		3 clusters			4 clusters			
	1	2	1	2	3	1	2	3	4
Size	234	250	168	216	100	182	100	121	81

For each case, the variables of seniority and experience had significance above 5%; therefore, this process was conducted again without including these variables. In general, no significant differences exist between the final centers between each cluster for each of the three cases. Among the model variables, a rather linear behavior is observed between clusters, since the higher the agreement in each independent variable of the mode, the higher the continuance intention. This behavior is seen in all of the three cases proposed. In turn, in the cluster of each case, there is a predominance of people who consume streams to an extent. Likewise, a higher continuance intention reflects a higher gaming frequency and a longer duration of each gaming session. Finally, given the above, two clusters are accepted, which will be denominated light gamers (cluster 1) and intensive gamers (cluster 2) (Table 3).

Table 3. Means and standard deviation of each variable per cluster (Source: Created by the authors)

QCL		IC1	IC2	FREC_J	DUR_J	FREC_S	DUR_S	ANT	EXP
Cluster 1 (Light gamer)	Mean	**3.23**	**3.81**	**3.06**	**3.50**	**3.60**	**2.49**	**5.47**	**4.30**
	N	234	234	234	234	142	142	234	234
	SD	1.047	.838	1.253	1.007	1.399	1.219	.840	1.026
Cluster 2 (Intensive gamer)	Media	**3.95**	**4.32**	**2.30**	**4,10**	**3.48**	**2.47**	**5.44**	**4.20**
	N	250	250	250	250	176	176	250	250
	SD	.936	.746	1.193	1.181	1.369	1.304	.859	1.131
Total	Media	3,60	4.07	2.67	3.81	3.53	2.47	5.46	4.25
	N	484	484	484	484	318	318	484	484
	SD	1.053	.831	1.280	1.140	1.382	1.265	.849	1.081

In general, the variables associated with continuance intention, gaming frequency and duration of gaming sessions have means consistent with the classification of each cluster, i.e., light gamers have a lower continuance intention, lower gaming frequency and shorter duration per session than intensive players; however, the values are not significantly distant and there is a high standard deviation (between 20% and 35% of the measuring range). In turn, the variables of frequency of stream consumption, duration of stream viewing session, seniority and experience are even less distant among clusters.

Table 4. Percentage of men and women per cluster (Source: Created by the author)

Classification			SEX		Total
			1 (Men)	2 (Women)	
Cluster	1 (Light gamer)	Values	206	28	234
		% within QCL	**88.0%**	**12.0%**	100.0%
		% within SEX	47.7%	53.8%	48.3%
	2 (Intensive gamer)	Values	226	24	250
		% within QCL	**90.4%**	**9.6%**	100.0%
		% within SEX	52.3%	46.2%	51.7%
Total		Values	432	52	484
		% within QCL	89.3%	10.7%	100.0%
		% within SEX	100.0%	100.0%	100.0%

Analyzing the demographic variables of each group, it is observed that in terms of sex, both clusters are quite similar, with the light gamers cluster having 3% more women than intensive gamers. In the case of the age variable, both clusters have more concentration in the age range between 19 and 24 years, although the intensive gamers segment is 13.5% more concentrated in such a range. Finally, in the percentage of stream consumers, cluster 1 has a lower percentage of viewers than cluster 2 (Tables 4, 5 and 6).

In this way, given the previous results and analysis, the sample is observed to be homogeneous, with the most significant differences between both clusters being the use profile. This is consistent with the quality obtained through the bi-stage cluster tool in the exploratory phase, since the segments are not heterogeneous enough for visualizing different segments within the variables measured in the survey.

U&G Analysis. Based on the analysis of the survey, the R^2 of continuance intention is 0.41, i.e., 41% of the variance in the errors of that endogenous latent variable is explained by its associated exogenous latent variables, as show in Fig. 2. Since this result considers all the exogenous latent variables, this is the maximum possible value in the model. However, the results indicate that achievement (L), self-representation (A), fantasy (F) and escapism (ER) are not significant because they have a p-value above 0.05. In turn, the factors of social interaction (IS), social presence (PS) and degree of enjoyment (GD) were significant, with GD as the most significant. These results are presented in Table 7.

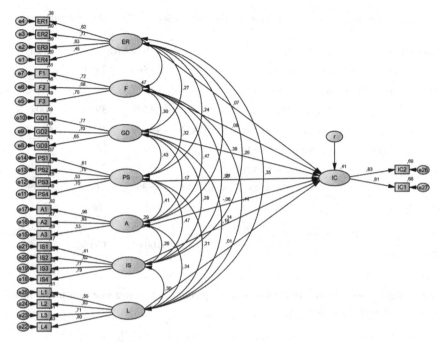

Fig. 2. SEM of the survey applied (Source: Created by the authors)

Table 5. Percentage of age brackets per cluster (Source: Created by the authors)

Classification			Age						Total
			1 (>16)	2 (16–18)	3 (19–24)	4 (25–30)	5 (31–35)	6 (<35)	
Cluster	1 (Light gamer)	Recuento	10	33	158	31	1	1	234
		% within QCL	4.3%	14.1%	67.5%	13.2%	.4%	.4%	100.0%
		% within AGE	28.6%	34.0%	53.9%	55.4%	50.0%	100.0%	48.3%
	2 (Intensive gamer)	Recuento	25	64	135	25	1	0	250
		% within QCL	10.0%	25.6%	54.0%	10.0%	.4%	0.0%	100.0%
		% within AGE	71.4%	66.0%	46.1%	44.6%	50.0%	0.0%	51.7%
Total		Recuento	35	97	293	56	2	1	484
		% within QCL	7.2%	20.0%	60.5%	11.6%	.4%	.2%	100.0%
		% within AGE	100.0%	100.0%	100.0%	100.0%	100.0%	100.0%	100.0%

Table 6. Percentage of stream consumers per cluster (Source: Created by the authors)

Classification			F_STREAM		Total
			1 (Si)	2 (No)	
Cluster	1 (Light player)	Recuento	142	92	234
		% within QCL	**60.7%**	**39.3%**	100.0%
		% within F_STREAM	44.7%	55.4%	48.3%
	2 (Intensive player)	Recuento	176	74	250
		% within QCL	**70.4%**	**29.6%**	100.0%
		% within F_STREAM	55.3%	44.6%	51.7%
Total		Recuento	318	166	484
		% within QCL	65.7%	34.3%	100.0%
		% within F_STREAM	100.0%	100.0%	100.0%

Table 7. Significance of each factor that aims to predict continuance intention in the model (Source: Created by the authors)

			Estimate	S.E.	C.R.	P
IC	<---	L	.007	.036	.190	.850
IC	<---	IS	.103	.044	2.327	.020
IC	<---	A	−.057	.057	−1.008	.313
IC	<---	PS	.179	.060	2.970	.003
IC	<---	GD	.346	.059	5.862	***
IC	<---	F	.060	.056	1.079	.280
IC	<---	ER	.087	.075	1.169	.242

In order to improve the goodness-of-fit index of the model, continuance intention was analyzed considering only the significant exogenous variables. The new R^2 of continuance intention is 0.39, i.e., 39% of the variance in the errors of that endogenous latent this variable is explained by its exogenous variables. With this result, it is possible to notice that factors discarded in the previous step, being non-significant, only contributed 2% to the R^2 of continuance intention (Fig. 3).

The significance of statistics for covariance indicates a dependence among the social interaction, social presence and degree of enjoyment factors, i.e., covariance is different from 0 (Table 8).

In turn, the observable variable of IS1 has a regression value of 0.38 with the factor of social interaction, which is low; therefore, the variable is removed in order to improve the goodness-of-fit statistics.

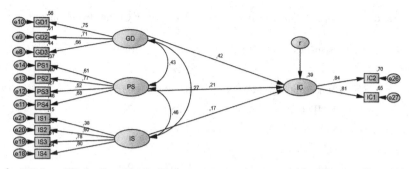

Fig. 3. SEM modified only with significant exogenous latent variables (Source: Created by the authors)

Table 8. Covariance among exogenous latent variables of the modified new model (Source: Created by the authors)

			Estimate	S.E.	C.R.	P
PS	<-->	IS	.359	.053	6.733	***
GD	<-->	PS	.270	.045	6.016	***
GD	<-->	IS	.205	.047	4.338	***

The final R^2 of intention continuance is 0.39, i.e., 39% of the variance in the errors of this factor is explained by its exogenous latent variables as a result of the observable variables present in Fig. 4.

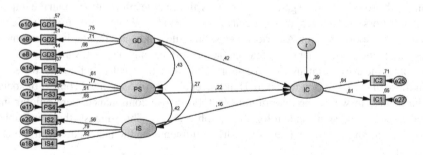

Fig. 4. Final SEM (Source: Created by the authors)

Regarding the goodness-of-fit indexes presented in Table 9, it is observed that CMIN is 130.791 with a significance below 0.05, which indicated that the model is acceptable. The other statistics are within the parameters to accept the model, with RMSEA just in the limit but considered acceptable. Thus, the model is accepted.

Table 9. Goodness-of-fit statistics of the model (Source: Created by the authors)

Statistics	Value	Criterion
CMIN	962.187	
Probability level CMIN	0.000	<0.05
CMIN/DF	3.251	<2–5
GFI	0.869	>0.9
NFI	0.821	>0.9
CFI	0.867	>0.9
RMSEA	0.068	<0.06

5   Discussion

This study allows for a better understanding of the use continuance of a hedonic information system, specifically e-sports in Latin America, through the definition of the factors that influence the continuance intention of the same, as well as the characterization of gamers in a homogeneous group differentiated by some variables of use. Concretely, the study showed that the use continuance of e-sports in Latin America is determined by the latent variables of enjoyment, social presence and social interaction. Additionally, it was confirmed that no other differentiated segments of players exist when using the variables of the U&G model and of use profile.

5.1   Implications

Along with providing online game developers with valuable information about the importance of factors such as enjoyment, social presence and social interaction for the use continuance of e-sports in Latin American users, this study indicates that both geographical location and the game under study may be factors influencing the latent variables that are relevant for the use continuance of an e-sport. Therefore, the results obtained are different from those of the study conducted by Heikkilä et al. [12] in Asia in the context of social media games, in which the determining factors for use continuance were enjoyment, social presence and achievement for all age sub-brackets. This suggests that geographical region and/or analyzed game have a strong influence on the factors determining use continuance.

5.2   Limitations and Future Research

Based on a comparison with the studies above mentioned, future research will need to determine whether both variables, i.e., geographical region and game under study, influence the key factors for the use continuance of e-sports. To this end, two future studies are proposed. The first study should have the same methodology but focusing on another game in Latin America in order to analyze the extent to which the game under study affects use continuance; the second study should be an analysis of League of Legends players in another geographical region in order to verify whether there are changes in the determining factors for use continuance by region. Among the limitations of this study is the fact that not all online games can be generalized; in addition, the results cannot necessarily be transposed to other geographical regions, hence the need for new studies that can provide more robust responses on the incidence of these variables.

Appendix: Survey Translated and Adapted to the Context of League of Legends (Source: Heikkilä, J., Li, H., Liu, Y., Van der Heijden, H. & Xu, X. 2015)

Construct	Item	Measure
Escapism	ER1	I play League of Legends when I feel frustrated
	ER2	I like playing League of Legends when I have a bad day
	ER3	Playing League of Legends releases my anger
	ER4	Playing League of Legends is the best way of disconnecting myself from the world
Fantasy	F1	I play League of Legends to feel things I wouldn't be able to feel in my daily life
	F2	I play League of Legends to pretend I am someone else or that I am in other place
	F3	I play League of Legends to immerse myself in the life of the world of videogames
Degree of Enjoyment	GD1	It generates little….a lot of interest
	GD2	It is not fun…it is fun
	GD3	It seems boring…interesting to me
Social Presence	PS1	I trust that other League of Legends players will help me if I need it
	PS2	I feel very connected to other players in the League of Legends environment
	PS3	In my interactions with other League of Legends players I can be myself and show the type of player/person I really am
	PS4	While I am playing League of Legends I feel I am part of its community
Self-representation	A1	I play League of Legends because I want other players to perceive me as a nice/sympathetic person
	A2	I play League of Legends because I want other players to perceive me as a friendly person
	A3	I play League of Legends because I want other players to perceive me as a skillful
Social Interaction	IS1	I am more open to relate to others through League of Legends than through other means of communication

(continued)

(continued)

Construct	Item	Measure
	IS2	I have a friend network that I have created by playing League of Legends
	IS3	Playing League of Legends allows me to connect with friends in real life
	IS4	Playing League of Legends allows me to keep contact with my friends in real life
Achievement	L1	I play League of Legends to reach a higher level
	L2	I play League of Legends to have more power than others
	L3	I play League of Legends to obtain some equipment/objects that give me more status than other players
	L4	I play League of Legends to prove to other players that I am the best
Continuance Intention	IC1	It will be worth it to keep playing League of Legends in the future
	IC2	I am willing to play League of Legends in the future

References

1. Twitch TV. Twitch retrospective 2015 (2016). Retrieved on 24 April 2017. https://www.twitch.tv/year/2015
2. Xu, H.: The retrospective analysis of China E-sports club. IERI Procedia **2**, 690–695 (2012). https://doi.org/10.1016/j.ieri.2012.06.155
3. Higgins, C.: Newzoo report: brands to spend $325m on eSports marketing in 2016 (2016). Retrieved on 23 April 2017. http://www.mcvuk.com/news/read/newzoo-report-brands-to-spend-325m-on-esports-marketing-in-2016/0164699
4. Wagner, M.: Competing in metagame space – eSports as the first professionalized computer metagame. Space time play – Games, architecture, and urbanism, pp. 182–185 (2007)
5. Borowy, M.: Public Gaming: eSport and Event Marketing in the Experience Economy (Tesis de Master en Artes). University of British Columbia, Canada (2012)
6. World Cyber Games. WCG history (2012). Recuperado de: http://www.wcg.com/renew/history/wcg2010/wcg2010_overview.asp
7. Seo, Y.: Electronic sports: a new marketing landscape of the experience economy. J. Mark. Manag. **29**(13–14), 1542–1560 (2013). https://doi.org/10.1080/0267257X.2013.822906
8. Marcano, B.:. Características sociológicas de videojugadores online y e-sports. El caso de Call of duty. Revista Interuniversitaria 2012, vol. 19, pp. 113–124 (2011). Retrieved on 24 April 2017. http://www.redalyc.org/articulo.oa?id=135025474007
9. Chunmei, G., Chee-Wee, T.: Understanding mobile social media usage: uses and gratification expectancy model. In: PACIS 2017 Proceedings, vol. 212 (2017)
10. Stafford, T.F., Stafford, M.R., Schkade, L.L.: Determining uses and gratifications for the Internet. Decis. Sci. **35**(2), 259–288 (2004)
11. Mäntymäki, M., Islam, A.K.M.N.: Gratifications from using freemium music streaming services: differences between basic and premium users. Presented at the Thirty-Sixth International Conference on Information Systems (n.p.) (2015)

12. Heikkilä, J., Li, H., Liu, Y., Van der Heijden, H., Xu, X.: Modeling hedonic is continuance through the uses and gratifications theory: an empirical study in online games. Comput. Hum. Behav. **48**, 261–272 (2015). https://doi.org/10.1016/j.chb.2015.01.053
13. Gan, C., Li, H.: Understanding the effects of gratifications on the continuance intention to use WeChat in China: a perspective on uses and gratifications. Comput. Hum. Behav. **78**, 306–315 (2018)
14. Davis, F.D., Bagozzi, R.P., Warshaw, P.R.: Extrinsic and INTRINSIC MOTIVATION TO USE COMPUTERS IN WORKPlace. J. Appl. Soc. Psychol. **22**(14), 1111–1132 (1992)
15. Hirschman, E., Holbrook, M.: Hedonic consumption: emerging concepts, methods and propositions. J. Mark. **46**, 92–101 (1982)
16. Ryan, R., Deci, E.: Intrinsic and extrinsic motivations: classic definitions and new directions. Contemp. Educ. Psychol. **25**(1), 54–67 (2000)
17. Goffman, E.: The Presentation of Self in Everyday Life. Doubleday, New York (1959)
18. Yee, N.: Motivations for playing online games. Cyberpsychol. Behav. **9**(6), 772–775 (2006)
19. Biocca, F., Harms, C., Burgoon, J. K., Interface, M., Lansing, E.: Towards a more robust theory and measure of social presence: review and suggested criteria. Presence: Teleoper. Virtual Environ. **12**(5), 456–480 (2003)
20. Bhattacherjee, A.: Understanding information systems continuance: an expectation-confirmation model. MIS Q. **25**(3), 351–370 (2001)

Information Consumer eXperience: A Chilean Case Study

María Paz Godoy[1]([✉]) [iD], Cristian Rusu[2] [iD], and Jonathan Ugalde[1] [iD]

[1] Universidad de Valparaíso, Blanco 951, 2340000 Valparaíso, Chile
mariapaz.godoy@uv.cl, jonathan.ugalde@postgrado.uv.cl
[2] Pontificia Universidad Católica de Valparaíso, Av. Brasil 2241, 2340000 Valparaíso, Chile
cristian.rusu@pucv.cl

Abstract. Costumer eXperience (CX) has been widely studied in the last decade to understand customers behavior. The analysis of CX is important for companies as it allows them to understand customer's perceptions of the interactions (touchpoints) with their products, systems and services. At organizational level, the employees who uses information-related products, systems and/or services for their work into the organization can be seen as information consumers. Therefore, Information Consumer eXperience (ICX) may be considered as a particular case of CX, involving expectations, satisfactions and pains of information consumers inside the organization. ICX analysis the interaction between employees or departments and the organization or information providers departments, through its information products, systems and services offered. This work aims to analyze the ICX in a Chilean university, concerning three aspects: consumer's needs, consumer's behavior, and consumer's experience. We identified a set of customer profiles and associated needs through interviews and surveys. We analyzed the interaction between consumers and the organization information products, systems and services, identifying 11 touchpoints. These touchpoints were used to model the consumer behavior using a Customer Journey Map (CJM) technique. Finally, we evaluate ICX based on an adapted version of SERVQUAL and interviews. The results obtained shows that the consumers of information at the Chilean university have a good experience in general, with some low and high rated evaluation items such as difficulties on information system access and data visualization mechanism respectively.

Keywords: Customer eXperience · Information Consumer eXperience · Information systems · Consumer needs · Customer Journey Map

1 Introduction

Business competition has become very even in recent decades, companies are always developing new strategies to get and keep more customers [1]. This has set the way for Consumer Experience (CX) authors to closely study this topic in recent years. CX is a concept that involves the expectations, satisfactions and pains of customers through interactions with a brand or company, buying their products and services [2]. Improving

G. Meiselwitz (Ed.): HCII 2022, LNCS 13316, pp. 248–267, 2022.
https://doi.org/10.1007/978-3-031-05064-0_19

the CX is a win-win job, companies can improve their profits through better customers engagement meanwhile customers can receive a better experiences and product/service quality, in a virtuous circle. In order to reach that, companies have to work on improve every interaction point (known as touch points) with their costumers, guaranteeing them the max satisfaction on each touch point of their customer journey. Therefore, a good CX management can separate companies from their competition towards an advantageous position [1].

In the same way as a customer with a brand or company, the employees that work with organizational data interacts with several information products, systems or services provided by a company or organization. Generally, organizations have one or more information administration departments that provide access to employees from others departments to the information products, systems and services into the organization. In this way, these employees can be seen as customers or information consumers provided by the organization through its information administration departments. Into an organization the employees from several departments such as sales, people management, financial, operations, executive, among others, uses information products, systems and services in order to do their daily work and decision making, that generally are administrated by informatic or analytics departments. The consumption of information from employees within an organization is composed by several information products, systems and services such as reporting systems, data management systems, data analytics tools, data extraction tools, data visualization services, communications services among others. All these information products, systems and services represent a potential touchpoint to information consumers into the organization. Several studies related with information systems success [3, 4] and user experience [5] have been addressed in the literature. In this work, a CX approach called Information Consumer eXperience (ICX) is used to identify the pains or needs of information consumers to carry out their work in the organization. Therefore, an Information Consumer eXperience (ICX) concept, that involves the expectations, satisfactions and pains of the information consumers inside the organization can be studied as the analysis of the interaction between employees or departments (consumers of information, as a customer role) and the organization or information providers departments (as a company role), through its information products, systems and services offered. Additionally, these touchpoints allow to generate a Consumer Journey Map with the channels, stages and emotions associated to each touchpoint to analyze ICX into a specific organization.

On this work, the ICX concept was analyzed through a study case in a specific Chilean organization, through the identification of the touchpoints between information consumers and the information products, systems and services within the organization. As results, 11 touchpoints were identified and used as central component in a Customer Journey Map (CJM) for the information consumer, identifying consumers emotions and channels associated to each touchpoint. This CJM and the touchpoints founded allowed us to state that the ICX concept is a CX particular case, then an adapted version of SERVQUAL and interviews were performed to evaluate it. The statement than the ICX concept is instance of CX arise a set of research questions to guide this study: What is Information Consumer eXperience (ICX)? What are information consumer needs? What are the existing touchpoints between the information consumers and the organization?

What are the touchpoints most and worst evaluated by information consumers?. The paper is organized as follows. In Sect. 2 background key concepts are described. Related works are discussed in Sect. 3. In Sect. 4 the research methodology is described. Results are presented in Sect. 5. Finally, conclusions and future work are discussed in Sect. 6.

2 Background

2.1 Costumer eXperience (CX)

Although the Customer eXperience (CX) has been widely studied in the literature, it does not have a formal or standard definition. CX is referred to customer's perception produced by his interactions with all products, systems and services offered by a company or organization [6]. As a complex concept, authors have given different definitions of CX in the literature. In [7] six dimensions of CX are described: *Emotional:* associated to consumers feelings and emotions. *Sensorial:* that involves the stimulation of different senses of the customer produced by his interaction with the company. *Cognitive:* related with the conscious mental and thinking processes of the costumers. *Pragmatic:* involved with the practical act of doing a job within a company's product or service. *Lifestyle:* related with consumers values and the beliefs. *Relational:* associated with the social contexts of the costumer and his relationships with other customers or people.

CX involves the customers perception produced by his interaction with one or more touchpoints, which are fundamental components in the elaboration of the Customer Journey Map (CJM). CJM is a strategic management instrument that allows to represent CX in a company on a graphical way, where all touchpoints are identified together with their channels, expectations and emotions associated during the customer interaction [8]. Although there is no unique definition of the CJM structure, in [9] four key elements of CJM are defined: *(i) Persona:* The central element of the CJM which describes the behavior, motivations, habits, interests and needs patterns of the customer. *(ii) Touchpoints:* Represent the interactions points between the costumer and the products and services of the companies. Into the CMJ, touchpoints describe a logical sequence, in some cases grouped by stages, of actions performed by the costumer during the usage of the product or the consumption of the service. *(iii) Channels:* Involves the medium, physical or logic, through the customers interacts with the company's touchpoints. *(iv) Emotions:* The customer perceptions, feelings and moods during his interactions in each touchpoint, reflecting which are the critical points of the customer journey where the customer is satisfied or not, and need to be improved.

2.2 Touchpoints

As it has been mentioned before, CX involves the interactions between a costumer and the products or services offered by a brand or company. These interactions are called touchpoints and in [10] are defined as the moments when costumer's experiences occur as the costumer "touch" a brand or company through the interaction of any piece of their products or services, across a medium or channel in a certain point of time. On this sense, in [6] four categories of touchpoints are proposed: *Brand-owned touchpoints:* interactions which are designed and managed and controlled by the company. *Partner-owned touch-points:* interactions which are designed, managed, and/or controlled by the company together with one or more of its partners. *Customer-owned touchpoints:* those which are not managed or controlled by the company or any of its partners. *Social/external touch-points:* Touchpoints that take place outside the company domain but can be associated to the brand or company products or services.

On other hand, [10] identifies a set of touchpoints components such as atmospheric, technological, communicative, process, employee-customer interaction, customer-customer interaction, and product interaction elements. With all these touchpoints categories and components, is possible identify and understand several touchpoints instances in the analysis of the relationship between the costumer and the products and services of a company.

2.3 Information Consumer eXperience (ICX)

Information Consumer Experience (ICX) involves all the interactions between employees (consumers) and information products, systems and services inside an organization, including tasks such as information usage, information generation, information management, information inter-department sharing, information usage, based team work and decision making. All these interactions represent touchpoints between information consumers employees or departments and the information providers departments inside the organization. Therefore, ICX can be considered as a particular instance of the CX concept and can be aborded using analytical methods from CX domain in order to understand the ICX within an organization, identify different touchpoints, represent ICX through a Customer Journey Map and evaluate it using well known CX evaluation techniques such as SERVQUAL.

3 Related Works

The information consumers within the organization have been addressed in the literature through several studies related with different approaches. The first one is oriented to analyze the dimensions of the information systems success model proposed by [11] with their six factors for the success of information systems: system quality, information quality, system use, user satisfaction, individual impact and organizational impact. [12] studied how user satisfaction is an important factor which affects the use of information systems through the analysis of a set of factors that are involved in as use of the system, system quality, information quality and performance of the user.

Related to information quality, many authors have proposed definitions for this concept, describing the quality as set of characteristics such as useful, current, and accurate [13]. The Information quality has been studied for address Information Systems Success and decision making within organizations. In [4] the impact of information systems on user performance in Tunisian companies was studied, focusing in user satisfaction and their performance and productivity. Later, [14] investigates how this information system dimensions and technological/infrastructural issues, users' IT self-efficacy influence user satisfaction of the university of Ibadan postgraduate school web portal. On other focus, related to desition making and value generation within a organization, [15] addressed the information quality with focus in the improvement of decision making through an auditable information approach, while [16] aborded the value generation through information-intensive services (IISs) use, they identified nine key factors that characterize this data-based value generation: data source, data collection, data, data analysis, information on the data source, information delivery, customer (information user), value in information use, and provider network, to validate the usefulness of these factors for value generation in IISs.

Other approach to address the information consumption into an organization has been assessed since [17] discusses Personal Information Management (PIM) and archiving to design software tools to assist this process and facilitate peoples work with information. A task-based evaluation methodology for PIM evaluation is proposed by [18] to abord its main difficulties: people re-find information from unique personal collections and privacy issues regarding personal information usage and sharing. [19] analyzed the PIM on laptop computer users in an ethnographical study of wireless practice, this study reports on the role of historical interaction resources in a mobile PIM practice as well as the contextual effects on PIM. Their findings revealed a PIM-practice highly connected to use situations not always departing from manipulating files and folders. These studies leave the way for [20] to analyze and proposed a model of the process of digital personal information organization in everyday life situation.

The approach related with User eXperience (UX) and Customer eXperience (CX) has been addressed in different studies since [21] identifies a set of variables that affect the success or failure of end-user computing (EUC), which are related with the work environment within the organization, such as Task technology variables (management activities, task structuredness, task repetitiveness and task interdependence), Organizational time frame, Psychological climate, Systems development backlog, EUC training, Rank of EUC executive and EUC policies. To achieve this, they adopt the [22] categorization of end users. Later, [23] discusses the information consumer needs into the design of software tools about information management and archiving systems, into public health context within the U.S. National Health Service (NHS). They give to consumers' needs a stronger role in determining how information is supplied to them. [24] examined the perceived impacts of information technology use on firm marketing organization performance, proposing a model to associate organizational and end user traits, information quality, system/service quality, among other elements using a system to perceptions of organizational performance impacts through ease of system use, perceived usefulness and attitudes toward system use. This model is elaborated based on the analysis of 403 responses to a survey delivered by a national (United States) mail survey.

Regarding to customer experience of internal information consumption within an organization, [25] studied the Impact, relationship and similarities between service climate (user experience related to a specific service) and customer experience. [26] explores how to construct an information user satisfaction model that involves the information user's behavior and psychological character analysis. Addressing the complex nature of the use perception and its quantification, [26] included cognitive, emotional and behavioral satisfaction measurement, that are related to each other through incentive mechanisms (such as stress, adaption, self-efficacy, risk/reward) and interference factors (such as personal and environment factors, and social background). All this with the objective of bring a stronger theorical basis to the evaluation system of information user satisfaction.

These studies presented empirical and theorical background for the potential application of CX to address the information consumer experience of employees inside a specific organization. In this sense, related to the CX application to several domains, [5] addressed the Programmer eXperience as a UX particular case, where programers interacts with several software development artifacts such as programming environments, design documents, and programming codes in their work. [27] addresses the Student eXperience (SX) concept as a specific case of CX, where students interact with different products, systems and services that their educational institution offers. This approach aims this study in order to assess the information consumers within the organization, because just as SX, the Information Consumer eXperience (ICX) can be seen as a particular case of Costumer eXperience (CX), and previous work indicates that employee's emotions and perception can be assessed in other to analyze the consumption experience of information products, systems or services inside an organization.

4 Methodology

Our study analyzed a Chilean organization, and was structured in three stages: identify information consumer's needs, analysis of touchpoints between information consumers and the organization, and ICX evaluation. These stages, with its data recollection, data analysis and evaluation techniques, are described below.

4.1 Stage 1: Information Consumer's Needs

In the first stage, a survey and interviews were performed in order to recollect data related to the perceptions and feelings of the information consumers into the organization. In this section, these techniques and its structure are described.

Interview. To carry out a preliminary exploration about the perception of the experience of information consumers, an interview was performed. This interview structure is based in four stages (Table 1). The first stage aimed to collect general information and work experience. In a second stage, consumers are asked for their perception of their work environment and its information products, systems or services. The third stage aims on meet consumers experience about the reception and manipulation of the data provided by the organization through its information products, systems and services. Finally, in the fourth stage, consumers are consulted for their perception and evaluation about the information products, systems and services they used in the organization. Interview's structure is presented in Table 1.

Table 1. Structure of the interview performed into a specific Chilean organization.

Stage 1. Questions about position and work experience	
1	In what organization do you work?
2	What is your position? What are your main functions in the organization?
3	What is your career or area of profession?
4	What has been your professional experience inside or outside your organization?
Stage 2. Questions about work experience in the organization	
5	What is your perception or opinion about the efficiency of your organization's work? How would you rate it?
6	Do you think that data to support decision making should be provided by the organization? or should they be compiled by the professionals themselves?
7	What is the basis for making decisions in your work? In experience, intuition, data, or a mixture of the above?
Stage 3. Questions about data manipulation	
8	How important is data in your daily work?
9	In your experience, what types of data do you use the most, quantitative data or qualitative data?
10	Do you use tools or systems not provided by your organization for your daily tasks? (Example: Reports, etc.)
11	Do you think there is a difference between data and information? Can you visualize this difference in your daily tasks?
12	In your organization or in your daily work, is sensitive or confidential data handled? Why are they considered sensitive or confidential?
13	What protocols or practices are considered when working on this type of data?
14	Do you share data or information with the other units or areas of your organization? How is collaborative work in this sense?
Stage 4. Questions about perception of information services	
15	How do you perceive the role of the Official Portal or other information systems in your organization?
16	Do you use the information systems provided by the organization in your daily work or do you use your own records?
17	In your opinion, how would you evaluate the products or services offered by the information systems available to you in your organization?
18	In your opinion, what would be the ideal way for an organization to work with its data and information systems?
19	In your experience, do the information systems provided by your organization need improvement? What are the functionalities or features that you like or dislike the most?

Survey. The structure, questions and general design of the survey is based mainly on the answers obtained in the interviews. Therefore, the survey is made up of four sections (Table 2): a first section focused on demographic information, a second section with questions about individual data usage, a third section with questions about data usage at organization level, and a final section about the organization's Information systems. The responses were measured using a 5-point Likert scale, in order to perform quantitative analysis. Regarding to the experiments, they were performed in an online mode and with a limited number of employees participating.

Table 2. Structure of the survey performed into a specific Chilean organization.

N°	Section	Question	Type
SS1	Personal Data	How old are you?	Optional by Age Range
SS2	Personal Data	What is your academic degree?	Optional Category
SS3	Personal Data	In which unit or direction of the organization do you work?	Optional Category
SS4	Personal Data	How many years of work experience do you have?	Optional Range
SS5	Personal Data	How many years have you been in the organization?	Optional Range
SS6	Personal Data	How would you evaluate your work experience in the organization?	Likert scale 5 levels
SS7	Personal Data	How would you evaluate the labor efficiency in your unit/management?	Likert scale 5 levels
SS8	Individual Usage	How often do you use data in your daily work?	Likert scale 5 levels
SS9	Individual Usage	What kind of data do you use most often?	Optional Category
SS10	Individual Usage	What is the importance of the data in your daily tasks?	Likert scale 5 levels
SS11	Individual Usage	What are you based on to make decisions in your work?	Optional: in experience, in data, or both
SS12	Individual Usage	Do you collect your own data collections?	Likert scale 3 levels
SS13	Organizational Usage	Does the institution provide all the necessary data to fulfill its daily tasks?	Likert scale 3 levels
SS14	Organizational Usage	What data visualization or manipulation tools provided by the organization do you use?	Optional Category

(continued)

Table 2. (*continued*)

N°	Section	Question	Type
SS15	Organizational Usage	What external data manipulation tools do you use?	Optional Category
SS16	Organizational Usage	Do you have access to sensitive or confidential data?	Likert scale 3 levels
SS17	Organizational Usage	Do you use special tools to manipulate sensitive data?	Likert scale 3 levels
SS18	Organizational Usage	What is the scope of dissemination of sensitive data?	Optional Category
SS19	Organizational Usage	Do you share data or information with the other units or areas of your organization?	Likert scale 5 levels
SS20	Organizational Usage	How would you evaluate the collaborative work with other Units/Directorates of your organization?	Likert scale 5 levels
SS21	Products, systems and Services	Do you know the technological tools and information systems offered by the organization for work?	Likert scale 3 levels
SS22	Products, systems and Services	Do you use institutional information systems?	Likert scale 5 levels
SS23	Products, systems and Services	How do you perceive the role of institutional information systems in your organization?	Likert scale 5 levels
SS24	Products, systems and Services	How would you evaluate the services offered by the information systems available to you in your organization?	Likert scale 5 levels
SS25	Products, systems and Services	Do you perceive that institutional information systems work in an integrated way, like a large centralized system?	Likert scale 3 levels
SS26	Products, systems and Services	How would you evaluate the integration of institutional information systems?	Likert scale 5 levels
SS27	Products, systems and Services	What is your opinion about the provision of data and information from the organization to its officials, to help in their work?	Open question

4.2 Stage 2: Touchpoints Analysis

The analysis of the data obtained from the interviews and survey performed in the first stage, allows us to identify the touchpoints where the information consumers interact with the information products, systems and services offered by the organization. These touchpoints represent the items that could influence the perceptions of consumers regarding their experience working with information. In this sense, a Customer Journey Map (CJM) for information consumers is elaborated, in order to involve different channels, stages emotions and perceptions associated to each touchpoint. This CJM has two axis for touchpoint representation. In the horizontal axis each touchpoint is ordered chronologically, while at the vertical axes they are positioned in a consumer evaluation scale, adapted from the responses extracted from interviews and survey performed at the first stage.

4.3 Stage 3: ICX Evaluation

To evaluate the experience of information consumers during their interactions with information products, systems or services provided by the organization, an adaptation of SERVQUAL was used. This evaluation technique is divided into two sections, the first section aims to collect information consumer perceptions while the second aims to collect information consumers expectations. Both sections of the questionnaire consider: 5 questions for Tangible Elements dimension, 4 questions for the Reliability dimension, 4 questions for Responsiveness dimension, 4 questions for the Assurance dimension and 5 questions for the Empathy dimension. The responses to each of the questions were measured using the 5-point Likert scale. Thus, a percentage transformation function is applied to each value of the Likert scale, allowing us to perform quantitative analysis to evaluate CX for information consumers. Table 3 presents the Likert scale used for SERVQUAL.

Table 3. Likert scale used for SERVQUAL responses.

1	2	3	4	5
Strongly disagree	*Disagree*	*Neither agree nor disagree*	*Agree*	*Strongly agree*
0%–20%	20%–40%	40%–60%	60%–80%	80%–100%

4.4 Experimental Set-up

The experiments carried out in this work are based on interviews and survey application. The study population corresponds to the employees of a specific Chilean organization, among directors, academics, researchers and administrative officials of the institution. In total, the organization has 3,564 employees, where 14 of them participated on the surveys and SERVQUAL experiments, and 5 of those 14 participants were interviewed. The chosen employees were selected for the authors as they accomplish 2 criteria: they are known by authors and their responses trustworthy, while they are also representative of the different types of employees into the organization. Therefore, for the 14 participants of the survey, 4 are associated with directive tasks, 4 with academic schools and departments, and 6 administrative work employees were chosen. From the application of the interview, relevant information regarding the sample of the interview was obtained regarding the distribution of gender, age range and academic preparation, which are presented in Fig. 1.

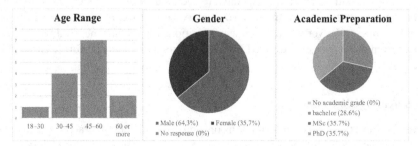

Fig. 1. Sample distribution by age range, gender and academic preparation.

The survey and SERVQUAL adaptation were performed through the online survey platform Google Forms, where the respondents were able to answer all of the responses, reaching a 100% response completion rate for both the survey and SERVQUAL.

5   Results

In this section, the results of this study are presented, describing the stage, touchpoints and CMJ associated to the Information Consumer, into a study case developed in a Chilean specific organization.

5.1   Information Consumer's Needs

From the results of the interviews performed to the information consumers into the Chilean university, 5 needs that impact their work were identified, which are described in Table 4.

Since the needs described above are shared by some groups of consumers, it is possible to identify some information consumer profiles that share similar pains and needs. In Table 5, 3 information consumer profiles were identified.

Every consumer profile arises from different needs association to a certain group of consumers, which are presented in Table 6.

5.2   Touchpoints Analysis

After the analysis of the data collected through the surveys and interviews to the information consumers, 3 main stages of the information customer journey were identified. On

Table 4. Information consumer needs.

ID	Need	Description
N1	Centralized information service	In general, those interviewed consumers point out that there is no centralized information system that integrates all the data that is involved in their work. This implies that information consumers must extract data from different systems or, in some cases, directly from institutional databases, which would decrease the productivity of their work. Therefore, consumers said that a centralized system would improve their productivity, and consequently, the productivity of the organization
N2	Real-time Information Service	Consumers state that it is necessary to have updated data all the time, to use reliable inputs to carry out daily work, especially for an accurate (as possible) decision-making process. In the absence of up-to-date data, decisions and derived actions may not have the expected effects, since the context in which they are applied may changed
N3	Tools for Data manipulation	Information consumers who constantly manipulate data to prepare reports or information products, which are used by other consumers or departments in their decision-making processes, need to have the maximum possible number of tools for data visualization or manipulation. In order to ease their daily work and decision-making processes. If they do not have these types of tools, the consumer would be delayed in their work, delaying the organizational processes, which may affect academic and administrative work
N4	Institutional Information Systems Diffusion	All consumers need to know and use data manipulation tools provided by the organization, to ease their work, while increasing their productivity and organization overall productivity. Therefore, it is necessary to promote the use of information systems and technological tools through their diffusion, otherwise consumers will not be able to access them, as observed in the results of the surveys. This makes it difficult for consumers to work, leading them to frustration and low productivity

(continued)

Table 4. (*continued*)

ID	Need	Description
N5	*Protocols for sensitive data usage*	A need mainly associated with consumers who manipulate data, is the creation of protocols for the use and manipulation of sensitive data, since many do not use special tools to manipulate this type of data, they do not know if these tools exist or need, or are not even aware of working with sensitive data. Safety at the use of data allows consumers to work comfortably when they have to handle sensitive data. When they use sensitive data, consumers are not using the secure tools recommended by the institution, which implies that this data can be filtered and lead legal consequences for consumers and the organization

Table 5. Information consumer needs.

Profile	Description
Executive consumer	Profile for information consumers who generally belong to the executive level of the University, who use data as inputs for high-level strategic decision-making processes, on the policies and management of the institution. Their associated needs are N1, N2 and N4
Academic consumer	Consumers of information about their students from to their academic department, in order to make teaching and administrative decisions about students or his department. This profile is associated to all five needs
Professional consumer	Profile for information consumers who manipulate data to prepare reports or information products, which serve as part of the inputs that executive and academic profiles could use in their decision processes. The needs associated to this profile are N01, N02, N03 y N05

Table 6. Associations between information consumers needs and profiles.

		Priority for profile		
ID	Need	Executive	Professional	Academic
N1	*Centralized information service*	High	High	High
N2	*Real-time Information Service*	High	High	High
N3	*Tools for Data manipulation*	Low	High	High
N4	*Institutional Information Systems Diffusion*	Medium	Medium	Medium
N5	*Protocols for sensitive data usage*	Low	High	Low

the first stage called *Searching*, the information consumer interacts with the touch-points that occurs before the information access and posterior usage, doing a search of the information and/or the product, system or service that can provide this information. Executive Profile consumers does not interact in this stage. The second stage called *Consumption* involves all the touchpoints related to the access and usage of information products, systems and services within the organization. Touchpoints such as information services access request, information service sign in, information visualization and selection. At the third stage of *Application,* after the information consumer has searched, accessed, visualized and selected information through the products, systems or services within the organization, the consumer can download a copy of this information and process it to elaborate reports or other representation form to share it with another consumers, departments or external organizations.

From these stages, a set of 11 touchpoints were identified, through the analysis of the data collected from the personal interviews and performed survey, which are presented in Table 7 and are described below.

With these touchpoints, the CJM of the Information Consumer eXperience into a specific Chilean organization is presented in Fig. 2. This CJM is used to show the perceptions of the information consumers about a specific touchpoint, transforming the map into a two-dimensional axis where the contact points are on the horizontal axis, and a scale of the level of perception of the consumer on the vertical axis. Generally ordered from negative perception to positive perception in an upward direction. In this way, a perception level value can be classified or assigned to each touch point, identifying the best and worst touch points rated by consumers, allowing the organization to take action accordingly.

As can be observed in this CJM the evaluation of the contact points is fair or good, where the best evaluated points of contact correspond to TP05, TP07 and TP11, which are mainly related to the interaction with the data, its visualization and application to work tasks. The worst evaluated touchpoint is TP06, where consumers indicate that access to services is not easy, nor are there clear and socialized instructions to the consumers for correct access to the different information products, systems and services provided by the organization. However, once they enter an information service, their experience improves remarkably.

5.3 ICX Evaluation

Once the SERVQUAL survey was performed, the perceptions and expectations from consumers are compared for each of their 22 statements. These differences are called SERVQUAL scores. Then, the average SERVQUAL scores are calculated for each question and dimension. Finally, the SERVQUAL Service Quality Index (SQI) can be calculated using Eq. 1.

$$\text{Quality Index in Servqual Service (SQI)}$$
$$SQI = Perception - Expectation \tag{1}$$

If the SQI is positive then the quality of the service is good and the perception of consumers exceeds their expectations. When SQI is 0, both expectations and perception

Table 7. Touchpoints of the Information Consumer during his interaction within organization.

ID	Stage	Touchpoint	Category	Compoments
TP01	*Searching*	*Information Search*	*Brand owned*	*Atmospheric*
	Based on an information need, the consumer performs a preliminary search for the information they need on the university's open access websites. These sites are accessible by all employees of the organization, and serve consumers to guide their search to the formal information products, system or services provided by the organization. This point of contact is optional, the consumer may not interact at this point to start their journey and can start on TP2 or TP3			
TP02	*Searching*	*Recomendations from other information costumers*	*Brand owned*	*Costumer-Costumer Interaction*
	In searching for information, the consumer can turn to other consumers for guidance to guide their search. In which another consumer can recommend any of the services that he knows and where the information that the consumer is looking for is found. This point of contact is optional, the consumer may not interact at this point to continue with their journey			
TP03	*Consumption*	*Information Service Access Request*	*Brand owned*	*Thecnological Employee-Customer Interaction*
	In the case of the Managerial Profile and to a lesser extent the Academic Unit profile, when using the reporting service, the consumer makes a request to access an existing report or the creation of a new one, if necessary			
TP04	*Consumption*	*Information Service Credentials Request*	*Brand owned*	*Thecnological Employee-Customer Interaction*
	Once the service that the consumer will use has been defined, the consumer must make a request to obtain their access credentials to the selected service. This interaction takes place the first time the consumer has to access to the selected service, since in the following times he will already have their previously assigned credentials. This contact point only applies to information systems or databases services since they require authentication to be used, the reporting service does not require authentication (the access is restricted to an internal connection to the organization's network or through a VPN connection)			
TP05	*Consumption*	*Response to Information Service Access and Credentials Request*	*Brand owned*	*Thecnological Employee-Customer Interaction*
	Either in response to a report request or a request for access credentials to an information service, the consumer receives in his organizational email a link to a report or his access credentials -as appropriate- with which he will be able to access the service. It is important to note that this point of contact can be optional, since once a request is answered, the consumer can use the response to access again in the future			

(continued)

Table 7. (*continued*)

ID	Stage	Touchpoint	Category	Compoments
TP06	*Consumption*	*Information Service Sign In*	*Brand owned*	*Thecnological Product Interaction*
	Either with a link to a report or with their previously assigned authentication credentials, the consumer can access an information service, through a web browser in the case of Reports or Information Systems, or through a database connection software. Data (Installed on all organizational computers assigned to officials, as standard)			
TP07	*Consumption*	*Information Visualization*	*Brand owned*	*Thecnological Product Interaction*
	At this point of contact, consumers interact with the selected information service, browsing the information it offers, to find the data that can provide a solution to their need for information. The navigation mechanisms may vary according to the selected service, however in all services it is possible to search, explore, filter and view information			
TP08	*Consumption*	*Important Information Selection*	*Brand owned*	*Thecnological Product Interaction*
	After exploring the information offered by the selected service, the consumer can find and select the data that serve to his needs, which they can view or also use in the work activity they are doing, as will be described in points TP09, TP10, TP11			
TP09	*Application*	*Save Information Local Copy*	*Brand owned*	*Thecnological Product Interaction*
	Once the data that the consumer needed has been selected, the information services offer the option of downloading this data, so that the consumer can keep a local copy on their computer, which they can use at will in the framework of its organizational work. It should be noted that this point of contact is optional, since the consumer satisfies their need for information only by viewing data of interest at point TP8			
TP10	Application	Information Proccessing	Social/External	Thecnological
	Once the data that the consumer needed to satisfy their need for information has been selected, the information services offer the option of downloading this data, so that the consumer can keep a local copy on their computer, which they can use at will in the framework of its organizational work. It should be noted that this point of contact is optional, since the consumer satisfies their need for in-formation only by viewing data of interest at point TP8			
TP11	*Application*	*Information Usage into an Organizational Task*	*Social/External*	*Thecnological communicative Costumer-Costumer Interaction*

(*continued*)

Table 7. (*continued*)

ID	Stage	Touchpoint	Category	Compoments
	Whether in the drafting of a report, communication of information to another official or management, or in other administrative tasks, at this last point of contact the consumer finally uses the data (processed or not) obtained from the information service used, to in-corporate them in a work that develops and motivates the consumption of information services			

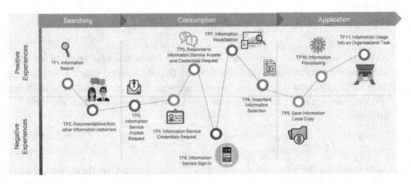

Fig. 2. Customer Journey Map for Information Consumers in a specific Chilean organization.

of consumers are balanced, and the service complies with the quality standards expected by consumers. Whereas, when the SQI is negative, expectations of consumers are higher than their perception. Therefore, the quality of the service does not meet the expectations of consumers. In order to calculate the SQI Service Quality Index, in Table 8 the consumer perception scores and expectation scores are presented. The difference between perception and expectation is then calculated for each evaluation dimension, which can be interpreted as a specific SQI for each dimension. To finally calculate the Overall SQI of the services provided by the organization.

Table 8. Satisfaction SERVQUAL section results by dimension.

Dimension	Perception	Expectation	SQI
Tangible elements	3.25	4.14	−0.89
Reliability	3.23	4.21	−0.98
Responsiveness	2.92	4.32	−1.39
Assurance	3.05	4.41	−1.35
Empathy	2.98	4.41	−1.43
Overall	**3.086**	**4.298**	**−1.212**

The best evaluated dimension is Empathy reaching an average score of 4.41, which indicates that consumers perceive that the organization meets their specific needs in a personalized way. Meanwhile, the worst evaluated dimension corresponds to the Responsiveness dimension with a 2.92 score. The scores of the remaining dimensions vary in a range between 3.05 and 3.25, indicating that the perception of consumers in general is regular or good. Generally, the difference between the perception and expectations of consumers is negative, the dimension that presents a lower quality of service is Responsiveness, with a SQI of -1.39. On the other hand, the dimension that presented the best quality index was the Tangible Elements, with an SQI of -0.89. This can be explained because the expectations in this dimension are not as high as in the rest, and they manage to enhance the perception of consumers. Finally, it can be observed that consumers have similar trends in evaluating both their expectations and their perception of the service received. However, the quality indices are negative, so the organization has a big task on compensate this situation, identifying key needs to increase the perception of the quality of the information service delivered to its employees.

6 Conclusions

This study has been oriented to analyze the Information Consumer eXperience (ICX) as a specific case of Costumer eXperience (CX). To achieve this, feedback from several information consumers from a specific Chilean organization was recollected through interviews and a survey. On this context, 11 touchpoints between the information consumers and the information products, systems or services offered by the organization were identified. Additionally, the channels and emotion of information consumers in different stages of they work were identified in order to elaborate a Customer Journey Map (CJM) of the ICX. This CJM shows that information consumers have pains related with information access into the organization, while they have a good perception about the quality of the data presented within the information products, systems and services provided by the organization.

With these findings, this study has allowed to analyze and affirm that ICX can be seen as a specific case of CX, which can be addressed with some important CX methods such as CJM and the identification of touchpoints between the information consumers and the information products, systems and services offered by the organization. Describing the perceptions, emotions and channels where these touchpoints take place. This gives to ICX some important characteristics from CX, related to the analysis of information consumer perceptions and emotions during his daily work within the organization.

Finally, the results obtained in this study provide an important start point for future work for practitioners and researchers about the analysis of the experience of use of different information products, systems or services within organizations of several industries, size or structure. Regarding to researchers, this study allows to address the ICX concept and find methods and instruments to evaluate it into an organization. Regarding to practitioners and organization, this study represents a call for action to address the experience of their employees when using different information products, systems or services within the organization from a new perspective.

References

1. Keiningham, T., et al.: Customer experience driven business model innovation. J. Bus. Res. **116**, 431–440 (2020)
2. Christopher, M., et al.: Understanding customer experience. Harvard Bus. Rev. **85**(2), 116 (2007)
3. Tatenda, W., Shaun, P.: Identification of User Satisfaction Dimensions for the Evaluation of University Administration Information Systems (2019)
4. Ali, B.M., Younes, B.: The impact of information systems on user performance: an exploratory study. J. Knowl. Manage. Econ. Inf. Technol. ScientificPapers.org **3**(2), 1–10 (2013)
5. Morales, J., Rusu, C., Botella, F., Quinones, D.: Programmer eXperience: a systematic literature review. IEEE Access. **7**(71079–71094), 8727527 (2019)
6. Lemon, K., Verhoef, P.: Understanding customer experience throughout the customer journey. J. Mark. **80**(6), 69–96 (2016)
7. Spiller, N., Noci, G.: How to sustain the customer experience: an overview of experience components that co-create value with the customer. Eur. Manage. J. **25**(5), 395–410 (2007)
8. Temkin, B.D.: Mapping the customer journey. Forrester Res. **3**(1), 20 (2010)
9. Marquez, J., Downey, A., Clement, R.: Walking a mile in the user's shoes: customer journey mapping as a method to understanding the user experience. Internet Ref. Serv. Q. **20**(3–4), 1.135–150 (2015)
10. Stein, A., Ramaseshan, B.: Towards the identification of customer experience touch point elements. J. Retail. Consum. Serv. **30**, 8–19 (2016)
11. Delone, W., McLean, E.: Information systems success: the quest for the dependent variable. Inf. Syst. Res. **3**, 60–95 (1992). https://doi.org/10.1287/isre.3.1.60
12. Igbaria, M., Tan, M.: The consequences of information technology acceptance on subsequent individual performance. Inf. Manage. **32**, 113–121 (1997)
13. Rieh, S.Y.: Judgment of information quality and cognitive authority in the Web. J. Am. Soc. Inf. Sci. **53**, 145–161 (2002)
14. Miss, A.M.B.: Information Systems User Satisfaction: A Survey of the Postgraduate School Portal. University of Ibadan, Nigeria. Library Philosophy and Practice (e-journal), p. 1192 (2014)
15. Azemi, N.A., Zaidi, H., Hussin, N.: Information quality in organization for better decision-making. Int. J. Acad. Res. Bus. Soc. Sci. **7**(12) (2018). Human Resources Management Academic Research Society (HRMARS)
16. Lim, C., Kim, K.-H., Kim, M.-J., Heo, J.-Y., Kim, K.-J., Maglio, P.P.: From data to value: a nine-factor framework for data-based value creation in information-intensive services. Int. J. Inf. Manage. **39**, 121–135 (2018)
17. Peters, R.: Exploring the design space for personal information management tools. In: CHI 2001 Extended Abstracts on Human Factors in Computing Systems (CHI EA 2001), pp. 413–414. Association for Computing Machinery, New York, NY, USA (2001)
18. Elsweiler, D., Ruthven, I.: Towards task-based personal information management evaluations. In: Proceedings of the 30th Annual International ACM SIGIR Conference on Research and Development in Information Retrieval (SIGIR 2007), pp. 23–30. Association for Computing Machinery, New York, NY, USA (2007)
19. Lindroth, T., Bergquist, M.: Breadcrumbs of interaction: situating personal information management. In: Proceedings of the 5th Nordic Conference on Human-Computer Interaction: Building Bridges (NordiCHI 2008), pp. 266–273. Association for Computing Machinery, New York, NY, USA (2008)
20. Oh, K.E.: Personal information organization in everyday life: modeling the process. J. Document. **75**(3), 667–691 (2019)

21. Cheney, P.H., Mann, R.I., Amoroso, D.L.: Organizational factors affecting the success of end-user computing. J. Manag. Inf. Syst. **3**(1), 65–80 (1986)
22. Rockart, J.F., Flannery, L.S.: The management of end user computing. Commun. ACM **26**(10), 776–784 (1983)
23. Hepworth, J.B., Griffin, E., Vidgen, G.A., Woodward, T.: Adopting an information management approach to the design and implementation of information systems. Health Serv. Manage. Res. **5**(2), 115–122 (1992)
24. Stone, R.W., Good, D.J., Baker-Eveleth, L.: The impact of information technology on individual and firm marketing performance. Behav. Inf. Technol. **26**(6), 465–482 (2007)
25. Yang, J., Wang, Y.: A study on the impact of organizational service climate on customer experience. In: 2010 3rd International Conference on Information Management, Innovation Management and Industrial Engineering, vol. 2. IEEE (2010)
26. Zou, J., Yu, Y.: The study of information users satisfaction model based on the user behavior. In: 2012 International Symposium on Information Technologies in Medicine and Education, vol. 2. IEEE (2012)
27. Cano, S., Rusu, C., Matus, N., Quiñones, D., Mercado, I.: Analyzing the student experience concept: a literature review. In: 23rd HCI International Conference, HCII 2021, Proceedings, pp. 174–186 (2021)

The Biodigital Rises: A New Digital Brand Challenge

Marie-Nathalie Jauffret[1] and Frédéric Aubrun[2(✉)]

[1] International University of Monaco, Monaco, Principality of Monaco
mjauffret@omneseducation.com
[2] BBA INSEEC, 25, Rue de l'Université, 69007 Lyon, France
faubrun@inseec.com

Abstract. The research aims to understand the degree of acceptance of biodigital influencers by communication and marketing professionals. The semi-qualitative methodological approach is based on 2 group interviews spaced 3 weeks apart with communication and marketing professionals. The first survey proves that in France in 2021, the majority of respondents do not know these characters. They first express a feeling of fear and lack of ethics at the idea of considering promoting a company or a product and influencing their targets through this virtual technological means. In a second step, a month of reflection later, the second results show that professionals agree to work with biodigitals to stay in step with the market in a digitized and innovative world. The limits of the study consider a context of French culture. The results therefore underline the perception of an innovative digital culture by communication professionals in France. This study proves the existence of an initial reluctance to use biodigitals, but that it is mitigated by a period of reflection. In conclusion, these innovative results allow to understand that a professional in communication or marketing may face a latency period before agreeing to work with biodigitals. This unique research also makes it possible to initiate the literature review concerning biodigitals and to note their potential breakthrough in the field of communication and marketing.

Keywords: Biodigitals · Influencers · Social network

1 Introduction

1.1 Innovate in a Digital Context

Social networks and in particular digital platforms welcome technological and digital innovation in an internationalized context [1]. Almost all areas are affected by this need to communicate digitally to initiate and then enrich relationships with prospects and consumers. Companies are therefore working in this direction to design and implement their marketing and communication plans and activate their brands because "digital innovation has radically changed the nature and structure of new products and services" [1]. Through this digital media, organizations therefore strive to develop competitive and innovative advantages to attract attention and meet the demand of their consumers [2].

G. Meiselwitz (Ed.): HCII 2022, LNCS 13316, pp. 268–277, 2022.
https://doi.org/10.1007/978-3-031-05064-0_20

To support this commercial and advertising communication, many companies employ influencers who broadcast messages to present and promote products and "structure the process of interactive brand communication" [3]. But these characters who work voluntarily or professionally must ensure long-term credibility [4]. Indeed, the constant number of novice and professional influencers tends the market and can also lead to a feeling of weariness [5]. In addition, some influencers run out of steam in the creativity of their posts, in the duration of their missions and find it difficult to measure their return on investment [6]. The risks of click-farm [7] also present themselves to communication managers who cannot always be sure at first glance that influencers are not lying about the real number of their followers. In addition, influencers are human beings who are constantly changing according to the "evolving nature of the brand" [8].

Agencies can therefore have difficulty in managing, in particular, certain whims of stars or the physical traces of their persons (age, weight, etc.) or even the state of health, because any change (even natural) can have a disastrous impact on a communication in progress or to be carried out. Influencers sometimes demonstrate the limits of this function and use [9] in communication and marketing practices.

In summary, companies therefore sometimes engage in influence promotion without being certain that the influencers are loyal to them and respect the image they broadcast and that the posts presented reach the consumer target.

1.2   The Rise of Biodigital Characters

To counter this problem, in this world in digital transformation, social networks give birth to biodigital characters. These new influencers are unalterable over time and have a blurred identity [10] because they mainly define themselves as human, digital human or robot. These virtual representations mainly communicate digitally through videos, visuals and/or texts. By their particularities and their new forms of existence, they bring together communities of followers who follow them assiduously. These biodigitals, beings of a new kind, of all ages and of various origins, therefore, influence several million people today, particularly on the Instagram platform. Strengthened by this new power, these new beings who fascinate by their characteristics which are based on "a notion of ambivalence and divergence of interpretation" [10] play internationally.

They are therefore available to companies to work with they are already doing the same as human influencers who serve to "direct the behavior of targets through blogs, tweets, and the use of other social networks" [11]. By making this new form of communication available and their ability to bring people together in new and innovative ways [12], some companies are using this biodigital influence to try to make consumers aware of their products and/or services on Instagram and to integrate them into their marketing and communication strategies and in particular into their advertising campaigns. Thus, in 2019 Calvin Klein called on the services of a young influential artist, Miquela Sousa, alias @lilmiquela [13], a true symbol of innovation and great technical qualities, to take advantage of its large community of subscribers on Instagram (more than 3 million followers in 2022) notably through a controversial video clip intended to promote this brand [14]. A large Swedish furniture company also uses a biodigital [15]. The latter, called Imma.gram, is a young Japanese woman with 355,000 subscribers (2022), who presents herself as "a virtual girl interested in art, Japanese culture, films and art" [16]. She also works for the brand Maje Paris or Desigual [17]. Shudu.gram [18], who works as a model in London, is also the voice of many brands, including that of Fenty Beauty (2018) and that of Michelob ULTRA Organic Seltzer (2021) for their advertising campaigns. Ella Stoller, born in Israel, also works on advertising campaigns [19]. Using biodigitals therefore allows brands to publicize their discourse in a roundabout way, while helping to anchor these new characters in reality by giving them a commercial role. In this sense, this commercial collaboration allows the brand to move forward hidden, insofar as the consumer's primary objective is to discover the real identity of the biodigital character, to know if it is a robot, a virtual being for example. In this phase of interrogation and "driven by the semiological and semantic questioning of the publications of these new images" [10], the consumer does not therefore directly perceive the post as an advertising context caught up in these new human forms. Advertisers can therefore place their brands without actually being spotted, working on this new axis of hyper-advertising understood as the "search for maximizing the advertising presence", which is perceived in the "semiotic densification of the advertising content of the discourse" [20].

These new influencers are therefore beginning to invest in the place of the international market [12]. Top lists quoting these biodigitals appear on the web to state their new powers and the attention they deserve. Fascinated, their followers "interpret their visual cues in different contexts" [21]. These biodigitals are also beginning to place themselves in cyberspace and initiate marketing and brand communication work in the metaverse, a shared virtual space. It is also possible to find LilMiquela's digital artwork "Rebirth of Venus" for sale "my piece is a meditation on the feeling of letting go of skepticism…" [22]. The advance of biodigitals and the promotion of brands through the hyperpublicity technique therefore promise to be important. However, many companies are not working to promote their brands using this new digital process.

1.3 Questioning the Need to Communicate with Biodigitals

The problem then arises of knowing whether using biodigitals to conquer new targets and/or reach targets already acquired, can retain the interest of companies that have not yet chosen this possibility of digital communication, in particular on the Instagram platform. The research question concerns communication managers to find out why they are not already working on the implementation of this new tool in order to present them to advertisers. Why don't companies already create their own biodigital character in the identity image of their brand, and how to explain the fact that in strategic response to the context of digital innovation that these biodigitals are not already placed in an important way in advertising campaigns? In a context of need for sustainable growth and management, this research proposes to study the degree of acceptance of this innovative phenomenon by communication and marketing professionals. It is a question of questioning the rapid adaptation to change [23, 24] caused by the birth of biodigital and the competitiveness [25, 26] of communication agencies in this digital dynamic. Looking at their understanding and acceptance of this tool to implement desirable changes [27, 28] in this new advertising discourse is rightly interesting in terms of positioning. This new complex context in which the concept of organizational agility can theoretically fit [24, 29, 30] therefore makes it possible to highlight 4 main categories, which make it possible to understand the positioning of agencies and advertisers within the framework of this digital innovation. These are practices oriented towards controlling change, then practices for developing human resources and cooperation practices and finally practices for creating value for customers [31–33]. While taking into account the ever-existing difficulty to well define conceptually the terminology of agility [24, 34] and without omitting general characteristics [35]. Research is being conducted on the new apprehension and possible management of the action of biodigitals, these computer-generated images by communication and marketing professionals to understand their positioning towards this creative subject. In this sense, interviews are therefore carried out in order to discover whether the practice of this tool simply does not hold the interest of professionals and what would be the reasons for this or whether the use of biodigital influencers is a real complex challenge to be faced.

2 Methods and Results

2.1 Qualitative Study with Communication and Marketing Professionals

To answer this problem, we present here a study conducted from a qualitative angle, with 53 adults aged 26 to 63 years. They define themselves as communication or marketing professionals and all work in France in the communication and/or marketing departments of public or private organizations or within communication agencies. Their seniority is on average 12 years. The agency or department in which they work has less than 10 employees. The methodological approach is based on 2 phases of semi-structured interviews spaced 3 weeks apart and lasting at least 30 min. The interviews take place for the first part during half-yearly meetings between professionals and for the second in their agencies. It was decided to position oneself on a face-to-face interview guide, conducted like a conversation without using any presentation of the agility diagnosis [24] so as not to suffer from structural constraints. The terminology of biodigital and virtual character is stated to precisely define these characters upstream according to the definition provided by the literature review [10] and the Instagram posts presenting the 10 most famous biodigitals (in terms of number of subscribers) they are shown. The questions are divided into 4 themes proposed in the literature on organizational agility as stated above [36, 37, 39, 40].

2.2 Results

The results prove that all of the professionals questioned know and practice digital platforms. They are all subscribed to at least more than 10 profiles on the Instagram platform. On the other hand, it results from the thematic analysis that they do not know all the biodigital influencers (78%). The lack of proactivity and responsiveness to this use is explained in particular by a lack of knowledge in the definition of biodigitals and limited access to information [38]. At the visual presentation of these characters, 64% of the people tested think they are human at first glance and then perceive that they are digitized characters. The first results also indicate that professionals refuse or express a feeling of fear at the idea of promoting and influencing their targets through this virtual technological means.

Practices Oriented in the Control of Change. This factor of doubt falls into the first field of the category of practices oriented in the control of change and demonstrates that professionals during their first phase of reflection do not wish to work with this new type of influencer. The lack of knowledge and practice of this non-humanity raising fears of a lack of mastery. During the second interview, the answers are similar because the technological mastery always seems complex to approach. They themselves analyze this fear by the fact of having been easily duped into thinking them human when they thought they were able to apprehend a false digital reality. They consider these biodigitals to be dangerous in their use because of their physical association with humans (87%). They think this approach is unethical and consider the new type of link that can be created between a biodigital character and a potential consumer subscriber complex (92%). They think the potential manipulation relationships (65%) that could develop during conversations between a biodigital character and their followers (consumers approached or acquired) are harmful. Some question the legality of this staging (26%). In addition, the future emotions of target consumers - whether positive or negative - in the face of the mysterious identity of biodigitals make them uncomfortable (68%) because they fear being criticized for a manipulation strategy. In summary, most of them (82%) therefore believe that the effects of the use of a biodigital person on their potential targets (prospected consumers) have not yet been sufficiently examined and that their early use involves an ethical and social risk not yet measured. The innovation of such a process does not seem very ethical to them today because they consider that biodigitals can fascinate by their influence but also manipulate consumers by concealing their real digital identity (80%).

Practices for Developing Human Resources. With regard to the second category, which exposes the practices for developing human resources, the people interviewed in the two parts of the interviews announce that they do not have the autonomy necessary to quickly embark on such a project. A technical reflection on the implementation of graphic design, the identity definition of biodigital to be created within the agency as well as the legal aspect to be dealt with for their clients and the ethical consideration to be studied do not allow rapid decision-making autonomy either. [41]. A team reflection is understood as mandatory by the majority of respondents (82%).

Cooperation Practices. The same is true for the 3rd field, which deals with cooperation practices. Legal and ethical issues are also raised during the two interviews. Professionals indicate that they come up against a potential lack of internal cohesion that may lead them not to carry out this digital innovation project [24, 29] because biodigitals are considered immoral and manipulative (49%). A disagreement that would reign within the agencies themselves would therefore not allow them to offer the use of a biodigital to their clients due to a lack of internal cohesion.

Practices of Creating Value for Customers. In the 4th category addressed, practices of creating value for customers, the creative aspect of these characters is quickly perceived as a tool for the future (98%). Professionals quickly position biodigitals as advertising players on digital platforms (97%) but find it more difficult to understand that the scope of their actions can develop outside the digital field such as on show stages in the form of holograms for example (58%). The second semantic analysis reveals a change in judgment towards these biodigitals. A month of reflection later, the results show that professionals are reformulating their thoughts. By following the dimensions of organizational agility, they consider that using biodigitals to stay in step with the market in a digitized world is interesting for developing a strategic vision because it is innovative. This creativity, synonymous with continuous improvement and strength of proposal for the clientele, could in their view, testify to an enhancement of their skills because the results seem promising. The fact of being able to anticipate the changing demands of customers in an expanding digital market therefore falls within the last theme "practices of creating value for customers" without omitting that an ethical reflection remains latent. More than three-quarters of the interviewees (78%), claim to want to use a biodigital in the exercise of their profession because this channel or communication tool can prove to be very innovative, while others think of the seductive aspect of novelty (58%). They speculate that being able to test new ground with a new form of communication would be very interesting in terms of media coverage (81%). They believe that innovation can help them compete with competitors in France and abroad (64%). On the other hand, the vast majority of interviewees consider that the company they work for and their brands or products could benefit from the creation of a biodigital persona designed exclusively for their own image (91%). A biodigital character can become, in their view, a real and innovative factor of brand identity (87%) thanks to verbal and non-verbal interactions with subscribers. They finally judge that this new kind of virtual being can be inseparable from the regular commitment of consumers (75%) for a brand.

A New Digital Brand Challenge. Reading the results makes it possible to clarify the primary and secondary feelings of communication managers towards the creation and/or use of biodigitals. Indeed, first of all, professionals reject or report their fear of using these new digital beings because of this unprecedented human-machine relationship. Indeed, these sometimes referred to as virtual humans are new to the advertising market and the relationship to reality is troubling [10]. There are therefore obstacles for this machine-human being relationship "between the present which is not in symbiosis and the anticipated future symbiosis" [42]. The use of biodigitals raises questions of ethics and legislation because of the physical resemblances. Secondly, after 3 weeks of reflection, it emerges from this study that the majority of communication professionals show themselves to be attentive to this new form of identity thanks to its innovative aspect after a phase of discovery and reflection (94%). Some of these professionals are determined in exploiting this new form of communication (79%) because they feel capable of mastering them and recommending them to their clients but nevertheless expect to have internal cohesion in the face of this technologically implicative decision. and ethically. In conclusion of these results, with regard to organizational agility within the framework of the consideration of biodigitals, the research demonstrates that communication and marketing professionals consider the practices oriented in the mastery of change, as the biodigitals are considered carriers of the future. In addition, they seize the opportunity of new "customer value creation practices" by understanding the international expansion of these characters adaptable to all messages and all types of contexts. On the other hand, a barrier to their use still remains. In the context of human resource development practices and cooperative practices, it seems difficult to be proactive in creating or using a character. This difficulty is mainly explained by the primary need to agree internally at the level of the teams both on the content and on the form before proposing this project to the client. Added to this essential phase are the ethical, moral and legal obligations incumbent on the agencies to protect themselves from possible pitfalls internally or with regard to the order by advertisers and the reception by consumers. This innovative advance is therefore awaiting verification and experiments carried out by others because of the impact of biodigitals, which they currently consider insufficiently predictable, in particular socially, ethically and legally.

2.3 Limits: Going Beyond French Territory

The limits of the study consider communication and marketing professionals linked only to a territory of French culture. The research nevertheless makes it possible to assess the judgment of actors in the professional field on their perception of an innovative digital culture through biodigitals. This method based on the theory of organizational agility concerning a specific theme, namely the creation and/or use of a biodigital, even if it is carried out in France, is therefore reproducible in other European and international territories. In this possible extension of this unique research in the field of biodigitals, it would also be interesting to study the changes in judgment of professionals over time to find out if they modify their opinions.

3   Conclusion: Between Opportunities and Risks

This unique research makes it possible to initiate the rare literature review dealing with biodigitals which symbolize a new aspect of digital progress. According to the state of this research, communication and marketing professionals consider their jobs to be very innovative. They do not yet use them in advertising campaigns and this "lack of strategy, processes and resources oriented and dedicated to innovation can explain the lack of innovation" [43]. In order to verify the reasons why this commitment in the promotion of brands by these characters is low, this qualitative study is based on the organizational context. The results of the research prove that communication and marketing professionals seem initially reluctant to use them because they perceive above all risk factors with regard to the use of this new form of influencers. After a time of reflection and apprehension of the digital context and after having deciphered the characteristics of this type of tool, they finally announce themselves ready to consider this new form of artificial intelligence. They recognize that biodigitals can cause surprise and curiosity beneficial to brands. They also assess that this factor of astonishment and questioning can multiply the links with consumers and allow the company presenting its biodigital to enter the field of innovation. They nevertheless remain cautious about the creation and/or use of a biodigital. Indeed, professionals hear the internal and external constraints in this digital advance. They establish that an internal consensus must be found within their group because internal relations impact the decision-making process of the teams. This insertion forces in terms of management, to a legal and ethical reflection upstream even if they want just as much "to ensure a sustainable growth of the profits and a better insertion in their environment" [44]. These results therefore show the challenge faced by companies to digitally enhance their brands and the latency time required to initiate a strategy. This innovative research also enriches the scientific literature on the new place of virtual influencers in the management and communication of organizations. It demonstrates the necessary organizational agility of marketing and communication professionals and the new digital challenge for brands posed by the introduction of biodigital influencers.

If "advertising designates the adaptation of the form of the media, of their content, and of the professional practices from which they proceed, to the need to accommodate advertising" [45], biodigital characters can constitute new spaces of expression for brands. They bring commercial communication to literally become one with new organic matter, participating in this sense in an innovative construction of digital identity that is still in its infancy. If the public seems to accept the first collaborations between brands and a new virtual human who represents them, the challenge for communication and marketing professionals remains to tackle this new digital challenge. But to venture conscientiously into this field of communication and marketing with biodigitals in search of media identity, and not risk holding their images and those of brands, professionals consider it necessary upstream to study and measure the possible risks of the creation, presence and influence of a biodigital.

References

1. Nambisan, S., Lyytinen, K., Majchrzak, A., Song, M.: Digital innovation management: reinventing innovation management research in a digital world. MIS Quar. **41**(1), 223–238 (2017)
2. Burnett, J., Moriarty, S.: Introduction to Marketing Communication: An Integrated Approach. Prentice-Hall Inc., Upper Saddle River, NJ (1998)
3. Uzunoğlu, E., Kip, S.M.: Brand communication through digital influencers: leveraging blogger engagement. Int. J. Inf. Manage. **34**(5), 592–602 (2014)
4. Belanche, D., Casaló, L.V., Flavián, M., Ibáñez-Sánchez, S.: Building influencers' credibility on Instagram: effects on followers' attitudes and behavioral responses toward the influencer. J. Retail. Consum. Serv. **61**, 102585 (2021)
5. Bisma, M.A., Pramudita, A.S.: Business model formulation of social-commerce based influencer on instagram platform. J. Organ. Manage. **17**(2), 249–264 (2021)
6. Santiago, J.K., Castelo, I.M.: Digital influencers: an exploratory study of influencer marketing campaign process on instagram. Online J. Appl. Knowl. Manage. **8**(2), 31–52 (2020)
7. Anand, A., Dutta, S., Mukherjee, P.: Influencer marketing with fake followers. IIM Bangalore Research Paper, vol. 580 (2020)
8. Nascimento, T.C.D., Campos, R.D., Suarez, M.: Experimenting, partnering and bonding: a framework for the digital influencer-brand endorsement relationship. J. Mark. Manag. **36**(11–12), 1009–1030 (2020)
9. Riefa, C., Clausen, L.: Towards Fairness in Digital Influencers' Marketing Practices (2019)
10. Jauffret, M.-N., Landaverde Kastberg, V.: Portrait du personnage biodigital. Hermès, La Revue **3**(82), 91–97 (2018)
11. Karen, F., Kristin, G., Karen, M., Freberg, L.A.: Who are the social media influencers? a study of public perceptions of personality. Public Relations Rev. **37**(1), 90–92 (2011)
12. Jauffret, M.-N., Landaverde Kastberg, V.: Biodigital influencers: a new alternative for fighting loneliness. In: Fox, B (Dir.) Emotions and Loneliness in a Networked Society. Palgrave Macmillan (2019)

13. Lilmiquela (2022). https://www.instagram.com/lilmiquela/
14. MyCalvin: I speak my truth in #MyCalvins (2019). .https://www.youtube.com/watch?v= Tphh_h8N-a8
15. Ikea (2020). https://www.youtube.com/watch?v=s586r8PMlSk
16. Imma.gram (2022). https://www.instagram.com/p/CWXu5_6FepL/
17. Maje Paris (2022). (https://www.instagram.com/p/CWQJ82Chb6z/
18. Shudugram (2021). https://www.instagram.com/p/CMksIpTLfYL/?utm_source=ig_embed& utm_campaign=loading
19. Stoller Ella (2020). https://www.youtube.com/watch?v=dCeJ2rS63-M&t=23s
20. Patrin-Leclère, V., Marti de Montety, C., Berthelot-Guiet, K.: La fin de la publicité? Tours et contours de la dépublicitarisation. Le Bord de L'eau, Lormont (2014)
21. Kauppinen-Räisanen, H., Jauffret, M.-N.: Using colour semiotics to explore colour meanings. J. Cetacean Res. Manag. **21**(1), 101–117 (2018)
22. Rebirth of Venus (2022). https://superrare.com/artwork-v2/rebirth-of-venus-16297
23. Dove, R.: Response Ability: The Language, Structure, and Culture of the Agile Enterprise. Wiley, New York (2001)
24. Shafer, R. A.: Creating organizational agility: the human resource dimension. Unpublished Ph.D. dissertation. Cornell University (1997)
25. Lin, C.T., Chiu, H., Chu, P.Y.: Agility index in the supply chain. Int. J. Prod. Econ. **100**(2), 285–299 (2006)
26. Sharifi, H., Zhang, Z: A methodology for achieving agility in manufacturing organisations: an introduction. Int. J. Product. Econ. **62**(1-2), 7–22 (1999)
27. Worley, C.G., Williams, T.D., Lawler III, E.E.: The agility factor: building adaptable organizations for superior performance Jossey-Bass ISBN: 978-1-118-82137-4 (2014)
28. Barrand, J.: Le Manager agile, Vers un nouveau management pour affronter la turbulence. Dunod, Paris (2006)
29. Goldman, S.L., Nagel, R.N., Preiss, K.: Agile competitors and Virtual Organizations: Strategies for Enriching the Customer. Van Nostrand Reinhold, New York (1995)
30. Joroff, M.L., Porter, W.L., Feinberg, B., Kukla, C.: The agile workplace. J. Corpor. Real Estate **5**(4), 293–311 (2003)
31. Goldman, S.L., Nagel, R.N.: Management, technology and agility: the emergence of a new era in manufacturing. Int. J. Technol. Manage. **8**(1–2), 18–38 (1993)
32. Kassim, N.M., Zain, M.: Assessing the measurement of organizational agility. J. Am. Acad. Bus. **4**(1), 174–177 (2004)
33. Mates, G., Gundry, J., Bra-dish, P.: Agile Networking: Competing Through the Internet and Intranets. Prentice Hall PTR, Upper Saddle River, NJ (1998)
34. Sherehiy, B., Karwowski, W., Layer, J.K.: A review of enterprise agility: concepts, frameworks, and attributes. Int. J. Ind. Ergon. **37**(5), 445–460 (2007)
35. Breu, K., Hemingway, C.J., Strathern, M., Bridger, D.: Workforce agility: the new employee strategy for the knowledge economy. J. Inf. Technol. **17**(1), 21–31 (2001)
36. Long, C.: Measuring your strategic agility: a checklist. Consult. Manag. **11**(3), 25–28 (2000)
37. Charbonnier-Voirin, A.: Développement et test partiel des propriétés psychométriques d'une échelle de mesure de l'agilité organisationnelle. M@n@gement **14**(2), 119–156. https://doi.org/10.3917/mana.142.0119 (2011)
38. Rahmouni, M.: Perception des obstacles aux activités d'innovation dans les entreprises tunisiennes. Revue d'économie du développement **22**(3), 69–98 (2014)
39. Amos, J.W.: Agility as an organizational competence. In: Sanchez, R., Heene, A. (eds.) Advances in Applied Business Strategy: Implementing Competence-Based Strategies, pp.1–31. JAI Press, Greenwich, CT (2000)
40. Dyer, L., Shafer, R.A.: Dynamic organizations: achieving marketplace and organizational agility with people (2003)

41. Shafer, R.A., Dyer, L., Kilty, J., Amos, J., Ericksen, J.: Crafting a human resources strategy to foster organizational agility: a case study. Hum. Resour. Manage. **40**(3), 197–211 (2001)
42. Licklider, J.C.R.: IRE man-computer symbiosis. IRE Trans. Hum. Factors Electron. **HFE-1**, 4–11 (1960)
43. Kacioui-Maurin, E., Lazzeri, J., Michon, V.: L'innovation des Prestataires de Services Logistiques (PSL): une analyse par les comportements stratégiques. Logistique Manage. **24**(2), 86–97 (2016)
44. Barzi R.: PME et agilité organisationnelle : étude exploratoire, Innovations 2011/2 (n°35), pages 29 à 45 (2011)
45. Patrin-Leclère, V., Marti de Montety, C. et Berthelot-Guiet, K.: La fin de la publicité ? Tours et contours de la dépublicitarisation. Lormont : Le Bord de L'eau (2014)

Yellow or Blue Dress: How a Product Page Can Impact the Customer Experience

Catalina Montecinos and Camila Bascur[✉]

Pontificia Universidad Católica de Valparaíso, Av. Brasil 2241, 2340000 Valparaíso, Chile
cbascurbarrera@gmail.com

Abstract. As the pandemic has forced a positive digital transformation making online purchases a part of everyday life, eCommerce has seen a booming explosion of usage and sales. Where product information plays a key aspect in the online purchase experience and is one of the many steps to fulfill the jobs to be done by a potential customer.

Although critical problems have also arisen at alarming rates, these include poor or nonexistent Customer Service, lack of purchase support, or product pages lacking information quality, to name a few. For this paper, our study subject will be product detail pages as they are one of the most important steps in a customer's journey. They do not only deliver key information about the product but also make sure that a customer is purchasing in an informed way. Poor or weak product pages not only cause confusion, but also high bouncing rates, and lastly no sales, which in the online world can have a high negative impact.

In this study case, we will present our theoretical background and compare different product pages from Chile's biggest retailers' eCommerce websites to propose a checklist whose main objective is to assure content quality on a product page. Our objective is to gather insights regarding its value for non-designers and stakeholders closer to the decision-making of product design in online retail.

Keywords: Retail · Customer experience · eCommerce · Product pages · Basic product information hierarchy · Information architecture

1 Introduction

As the pandemic has forced a positive digital transformation making online purchases a part of everyday life, eCommerce has seen a booming explosion of usage and sales. Where product information plays a key aspect in the online purchase experience and is one of the many steps to fulfill the jobs to be done by a potential customer.

Katie Sherwin notes "In eCommerce, product pages are critical to the success of a site. Customers need to have enough information to make an informed purchase decision. The product page, or product detail page, is where customers decide whether and what to buy" [1]. In terms of customer experience, poor product pages can have two outcomes: hesitation and abandonment of the website or purchasing the wrong product which leads to poor satisfaction, and therefore a damaged experience with the brand.

G. Meiselwitz (Ed.): HCII 2022, LNCS 13316, pp. 278–291, 2022.
https://doi.org/10.1007/978-3-031-05064-0_21

And what about customer experience? If we take the definition provided by J.J. Garret "the experience the product creates for the people who use it in the real world" [2] then we realize that a product page is indeed a key step in a purchase flow because it helps the customer to make an informed decision. This is crucial in online experiences because the means to ask a salesperson or to try an item before purchasing is almost impossible. Some features can help customers to access missing information about the product or service, such as live chats, chatbots, immersive experiences such as VR, but these technologies demand not only specific technology but also highly motivated customers to invest time when it's easier to just go to the next webpage.

Traditionally Chile has had 3 major players in the retail and eCommerce sectors, being leaders and role models in terms of strategy, business model, and design. These players are Falabella, Paris, and Ripley [3–5]. Just for the past 5 to 4 years, new players such as MercadoLibre [6] and Amazon [7] have been slowly gaining market share. But strong investments, improved services, and greater access of consumers have allowed these players to become aggressive contenders.

This paper will be divided in 4 sections. Where in Sect. 1 is the introduction, with basic data of the problem, in Sect. 2 will handle the theoretical background in which the definitions of Customer Experience, Retail, eCommerce website, and product page can be found. Additionally, it will be included a subsection with relevant cognitive aspects related to the understanding of user interfaces.

Section 3 will expose the analysis of our study case applied to product pages on eCommerce sites within the aforementioned retailers. This is followed by a suggested checklist inspired by good practices for a proper design of a product page, which will include the results of a short survey to experts in the User and Customer Experience field and finally in Sect. 4 conclusions and future work were found.

2 Theoretical Background

2.1 Customer Experience

For this paper, we consider a definition of Customer Experience as the one portrayed by Ch. Gentile, N. Spiller, and G. Noci [8] which is based in regard of the most relevant scientific contributions. They defined it as "the concept of Customer Experience as an evolution of the concept of the relationship between the company and the customer".

They develop this definition further by adding: "*The Customer Experience originates from a set of interactions between a customer and a product, a company, or a part of its organization, which provoke a reaction (LaSalle and Britton, 2003, Shaw and Ivens, 2002). This experience is strictly personal and implies the customer's involvement at different levels (rational, emotional, physical, sensorial, physical, and spiritual) (LaSalle and Britton, 2003, Schmitt, 1999). Its evaluation depends on the comparison between a customer's expectation and the stimuli coming from the interaction with the company and its offering in correspondence of the different moments of contact or touchpoints (LaSalle and Britton, 2003, Shaw and Ivens, 2002).*" [9–11].

In a nutshell, we can consider that the Customer Experience is mainly focused on the relationship between a Business or Brand and its customers. Therefore, an outcome of the perceptions that a customer has after the before, during, and after of their interactions with a Business or brand at a rational, physical, emotional, and psychological level with their different touchpoints, services, or products. This also includes any digital services that a business or brand may have.

We can also add the User Experience as a part of the Customer Experience since this delves into the products of a Business or Brand. These products can be digital or physical, such as kiosks, web pages like eCommerce sites, mobile applications, among others. Usually, the User Experience is more niche centered as it identifies a group of "users" with "common characteristics or behaviors", whereas the Customer Experience has a much broader application since it is centered on the total relationships between a Business/Brand and its segments.

2.2 Retail

The retail industry, as traditionally defined, is the composition of retail outlets that sell merchandise to customers [12]. This also includes products and services offered and sold in stores, through catalogs, and through the internet.

Some types of retail stores as described by L. Godás are [13]:

- Departmental stores: Usually, large stores with a wide range of coexistent categories.
- Specialized stores: These specialize in a specific category like technology, footwear, sports, and outdoor activities, to name a few.
- Supermarkets: These stores come in various sizes from medium to wide stores, have a self-service system, and sell groceries, fresh produce, meat, bakery and dairy products, and occasionally nonfood goods.
- Discount stores: these can be any of the above, but its most particular difference is that products can have bigger discounts as in a regular store.
- Convenience stores: A type of small to medium-size stores in residential areas that have longer opening periods, even during weekends. They have a wide range of products and are often pricier than supermarkets.

In the context of the present, our subject studies are Falabella, Paris, Ripley and MercadoLibre. These are the biggest retail players in the Chilean market and have more than +20 years of trajectory. The only exception to these players is MercadoLibre, a digital marketplace platform that has been gaining market share over the last years. Amazon is also worthy of mention as it inspired our local retailers to create a marketplace logic within their eCommerce sites.

Thanks to these new contenders, users and customers have had new experiences, being able to compare them and demand what in their opinion is a standard of service. One of the main reasons why Mercado Libre has multiplied its market share for the past year. For example, its promise to deliver products within a certain time frame (24–48 h after the purchase) caused a ruckus amongst the biggest players, which lead to changes in the delivery policies of most retailers.

2.3 eCommerce Website

These are defined as: "All transactions that occur digitally between organizations and individuals, through the Internet, which culminate in the payment of the individual's product or service, which consequently is acquired" [14]. In other words, it is a type of specialized website whose main focus is commercial transactions, besides providing information.

There must be noted that multiple criteria for digital commerce exist, and the main three are defined below.

- B2B: Business-to-Business scheme refers to the commerce between two businesses rather than to commerce between a business and an individual consumer. Usually, these transactions are at a wholesale level, and by nature, they are not only higher in quantity, but also in dollar value [15].
- B2C: Business-to-Consumer as the commerce between a business and an individual consumer. It can be applied to any type of direct-to-consumer selling, and is largely associated with online selling, also known as eCommerce or "retailing". There are five types of business models, and these are direct sellers, online intermediaries, advertising-based, community-based, and fee-based [16].
- C2B: Consumer-to-Business commerce as the model where a consumer makes a product or service that a business uses to complete a commercial process or gain a competitive advantage. This model represents a complete change to the traditional business-to-consumer relationship, and the most representative cases evolved from the growth of consumer-generated media and content across different consumer segments. Some of the most iconic examples are content creators that use Youtube, TikTok, Twitch, to list a few [17].

It must be noted that a retailer can indeed have an eCommerce site, which creates a complex relationship that transits between the physical and virtual world, creating not only new opportunities for businesses and customers alike but also new kinds of problems.

Our study subjects can be classified as having a B2C type of relationship, who are physical retailers with a wide presence in the digital world not only to stay relevant but to increase market share and audiences. The only exception to this is MercadoLibre, which is a digital marketplace that does not have physical stores.

2.4 Product Page

Or also known as product-detail pages are critical for the success of an eCommerce site. K. Sherwin from the NNGroup states that *"Customers need to have enough information to make an informed purchase decision. The product page is where users decide whether and what to buy. The page must include complete product information, educating and informing the user about the product in a straightforward way"* [1].

In the digital world customers can't try, touch, or use the item before purchase. Furthermore, asking a sales representative about product specification or any question whatsoever is near to impossible, despite the great advancements of technology such as support platforms embedded on eCommerce sites, chatbots, VR experiences, videos, or 3D images. According to K. Sherwin [1], all these instances have a high interaction cost, that requires highly motivated customers to spend time on a given website or application.

A high interaction cost, which is the sum of efforts -mental and physical- that the customer must deploy in interacting with a site to reach a given goal [18], and weak product pages can harm not only the relationship with the customer but also have negative outcomes. One of the most negative aspects of this phenomenon can lead to high abandonment of the product site, as the customer might go to another site, which can be a competitor's eCommerce page. Additionally, poor or lack of information can lead to legal problems for a business to unsatisfied customers or returned purchases.

A product page needs to answer customers' potential questions and prepare the shopper to be ready to buy. Hence the importance of fully understanding a customer's jobs-to-be-done and building an effective product page that can convey efficiently and effectively the necessary information and keep customers and shoppers satisfied with the purchase flow.

NNGroup points out that the basic information should be [1]: descriptive product name, recognizable images, enlarged view of images, price -including any additional product-specific charges, clear product options -such as color and size and a way to select them, product availability, clear way to add an item to the cart -and clear feedback when it has been added, and concise informative product description.

However, even with this guideline made by one of the most prominent User Experience consultancies we are still witnessing home pages with information overload, dark patterns, and product pages that do not follow the basic information architecture of what is recommended by most experts. Being this sector as competitive as it is, not seeing much improvement regarding these matters is alarming.

Furthermore, besides the changes towards purchase attitudes and behaviors, we also need to consider cognitive aspects of how humans understand information on a given user interface. For this we are going to considerate some of the phenomena listed by S. Durrani and Q. S. Durrani [19] that can affect product pages:

- Placement of text and Images: a customer can identify text quickly when they are displayed in the user's right visual field and images in the left visual field. This aligns directly with the placement of product image and product basic information (text) such as product name, short description, and price.
- Simon effect: users respond faster and more accurately to stimuli that occur in the same relative location as the response. This can be applied to main buttons called "call-to-action", system messages, and other types of notification or interactions that need action by the user.
- Transference: "is the expectations of a user about an interface's behavior based on his/her previous experiences with other interfaces" [20].
- Memory limitation: Based on research short term memory has a limited capacity to hold and process information. This capacity is generally 7 ± 2 items or pieces of information [20].
- Visual search: When a user spends time searching for specific information from a given interface and is not able to find it albeit being present. This phenomenon happens mostly because there is the absence of information hierarchy such as clear categories or visual hints such as bold texts for paragraphs [20].

3   Case Study: Frecuent Problems in eCommerce Retail Stores

As there are plenty of problems that we might encounter, we will mainly focus on problems of understanding and unefficient information architecture on product detail pages. We will analyze the product page of the fashion (garment) of Falabella, Paris, Ripley, and Mercado Libre.

3.1   Chilean Retail

Falabella

Basic information such as images, product name, price, discounts and additional product charges, size and color selection, and product description are present.

Upon further inspection, we can identify the following issues:

- Pictures show a person modeling the garment, but there is no reference upon the size of the modeled garment and the measurements of the male model.
- There is no size chart. Although being the brand is known as Adidas, a size chart is still necessary.
- The description of the product is generic, although acceptable for the type of garment.
- Content on the product specification is also acceptable, being composition and design might lead to misinterpretation. Although images compensate for this issue.
- When reading the comments 11 out of 324 pointed the colors as not matching the actual color of the received product.
- Color miniatures can be misleading and are not representative of the color of the garments. The text is not supporting enough (Fig. 1).

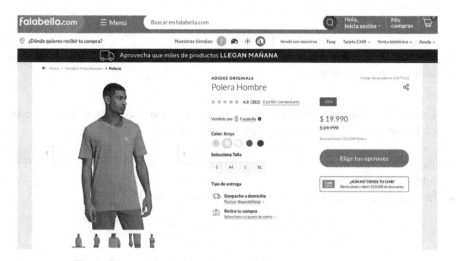

Fig. 1. Product detail page of Falabella showing an Adidas t-shirt.

Paris

As in previous product pages, basic information such as images, product name, price, discounts and additional product charges, size and color selection, and product description are present.

Some identified issues are:

- Pictures show a person modeling the garment, but there is no reference upon the size of the modeled garment and the measurements of the male model.
- There are no comments or reviews, although we could consider this as desirable information.
- The table with the product characteristics has problems of interference. Although it uses bolds for each subcategory, there is more visual importance placed on the rows of the table being the background color grey or white. Which can alter the visual search of information and make it more ineffective (Fig. 2).

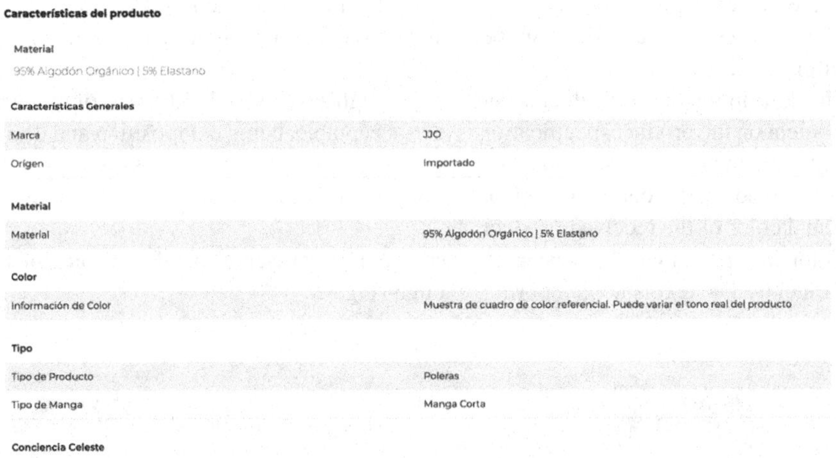

Características del producto

Material

95% Algodón Orgánico | 5% Elastano

Características Generales

Marca   JJO

Origen   Importado

Material

Material   95% Algodón Orgánico | 5% Elastano

Color

Información de Color   Muestra de cuadro de color referencial. Puede variar el tono real del producto

Tipo

Tipo de Producto   Poleras

Tipo de Manga   Manga Corta

Conciencia Celeste

Fig. 2. Table of the product specification where visual importance is placed upon rows rather than subcategories, which are in bolds.

Despite the mentioned issues, there are some positive and relevant aspects to mention, which is how the size chart and color options are portrayed.

- Size chart of the brand, but with vague visual references (they are not enough to understand how to measure).
- Detailed measurements and correspondence to a size (S-XL).

- Color options are displayed in miniatures and accompanied by their color name (Fig. 3).

Fig. 3. Product detail page of Paris showing a JJO t-shirt.

Ripley

Same as previous product pages, basic information such as images, product name, price, discounts and additional product charges, size and color selection, and product description are present.

The following issues were identified:

- Pictures show a person modeling the garment, but there is no reference upon the size of the modeled garment and the measurements of the male model.
- There is no size chart. Although Lacoste is a known brand, it is considered essential information.
- Color miniatures can be misleading and are not representative of the color of the garments. The text is not supporting enough.
- Acceptable product description.

Positive aspects worth mentioning:

- Use of visual hierarchy and supporting icons to convey extra and relevant information. See Fig. 4.
- Proper use of background color on tables. See Fig. 5.

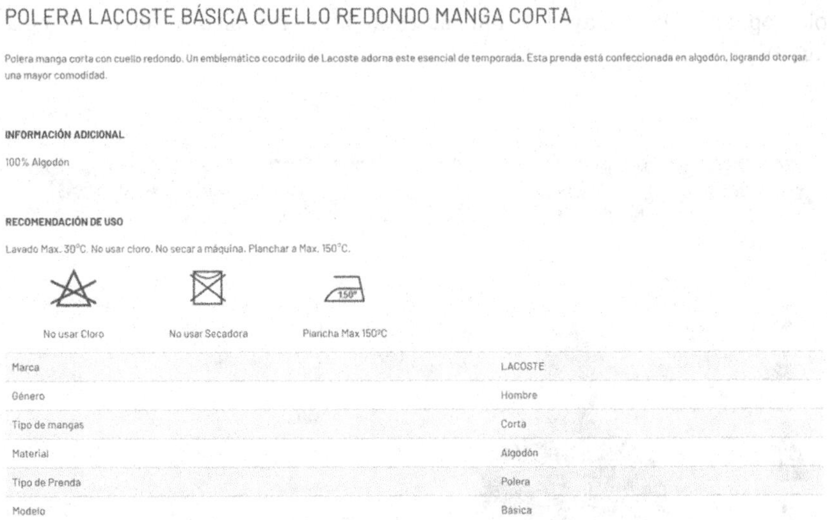

POLERA LACOSTE BÁSICA CUELLO REDONDO MANGA CORTA
Polera manga corta con cuello redondo. Un emblemático cocodrilo de Lacoste adorna este esencial de temporada. Esta prenda está confeccionada en algodón, logrando otorgar una mayor comodidad.
INFORMACIÓN ADICIONAL
100% Algodón
RECOMENDACIÓN DE USO
Lavado Max. 30°C. No usar cloro. No secar a máquina. Planchar a Max. 150°C.
150°
No usar Cloro
No usar Secadora
Plancha Max 150°C
Marca
LACOSTE
Género
Hombre
Tipo de mangas
Corta
Material
Algodón
Tipo de Prenda
Polera
Modelo
Básica

Fig. 4. Product description using visual hierarchy to distinguish titles, subtitles from paragraphs easing lecture. Supportive icons for washing instructions.

R .com
Menú de Categorías
Buscar productos
Bienvenid@
Iniciar Sesión
POLERA LACOSTE BÁSICA CUELLO REDONDO MANGA CORTA
SKU: 2000384906071
(1 Calificaciones)
Polera
Normal
$32.990
Internet
$26.990
Tarjeta Ripley o Chek
$22.990
Descuento
-30%
Con tarjeta Ripley acumulas
184 RipleyPuntos GO
Pide tu Tarjeta Ripley y llévate $10.000 de dcto!
Solicítala aquí
*Aplicable a compras superiores a $20.000
COLOR: Rosado
TALLA: S
S
M
L
XL
XXL
Santiago

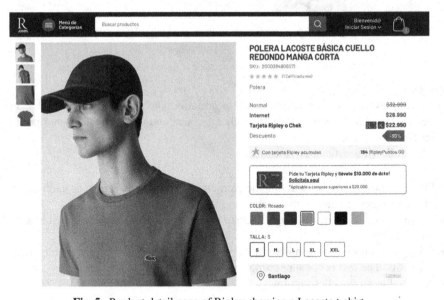

Fig. 5. Product detail page of Ripley showing a Lacoste t-shirt.

Mercado Libre
Basic information such as images, product name, price, discounts and additional product charges, size and color selection, and product description are present.

Nonetheless, upon further analysis, the following potential problems arise.

- Product name with unrecognizable codes that do not provide any informational value to a potential shopper.
- Pictures show a person modeling the garment, but there is no reference upon the size of the modeled garment and the measurements of the male model.
- The size chart does not specify the measurement system, it only relies on numbers with is equivalence for their sizes.
- There are no specifications to take the measurements, just a vague image of what they entail.
- According to the negative comments on the product, the sizes of the garment are poor and not as indicated on the image.
- Others alluded to the poor quality perceived of the fabric.
- While the description has some structure and has relevant information, some of it can be misleading and bias the potential shopper. For example, "Tallas tamaño normal/regular sizes" can be classified as subjective information (Fig. 6).

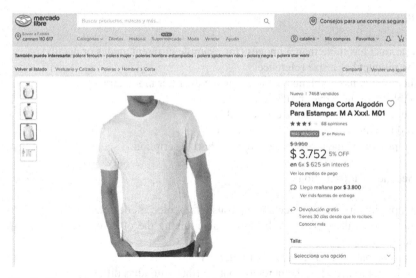

Fig. 6. The product detail page of Mercado Libre shows a plain brandless white t-shirt.

In summary, there is a distinctive visual hierarchy pattern that also supports the basic information that a product detail page needs to support for an informed decision. All basic information was successfully found and easy to identify. Product images were in general acceptable, and product names were short and descriptive in most cases, with being Falabella the poorest in delivering valuable descriptive information, and Mercado Libre delivering cryptic information in its product name (probably seller codification). Size charts were missing on two product pages, which we consider as crucial information, and one size chart albeit being present rendered to be unuseful. This also includes measure references of the male models, which might have provided better context and guidance. Only two product detail pages had miniatures displaying the color accompanied by their name, the other two had misleading color watches accompanied by their name.

All product descriptions were short but somewhat expected for this kind of product. Product characteristics were concise but generic in most cases, are also to be expected by a basic garment.

In terms of the total quantity of contents, the "cleanest" product detail pages were Paris and Falabella. These got straight-to-respond acceptably most jobs-to-be-done without visual distractors. Even if tertiary information was present, it was designed in a minimalistic way so a customer could focus on the product.

Ripley and Mercado Libre product pages had more elements present, which can potentially lead to cognitive overload or the abandonment of a potential purchase.

3.2   Checklist and Good Practices

Considering the above findings a checklist was generated to support other professionals when designing or auditing product pages in an eCommerce context. The main objective of this list is intended to check the quality of the presented information on a product page.

Primary information:

- A product has more than 3 images (for example different angles or details).
- The product has a size reference.
- The product has emblems that might make the offer more attractive.
- Emblems do not cover product images.
- The name of the product is easily readable.
- Product name avoids using cryptic words.
- The product name is accompanied by a short description.

Secondary information:

- The product has easily selectable options (size, color, model, etc.).
- The price of the product is distinguishable among the other prices (normal, offer, conditional).
- Purchase button visible and easy to identify.
- Intuitive interaction of the purchase button (the button has different states to convey extra information).
- Interaction of the purchase button according to user expectancy (phenomena of transference).
- Visual indication of the user interface of the product being added to the bag/shopping cart

Tertiary information:

- Description of product is properly used to describe the product.
- Description of the product indicates the benefits of the product and suggested usage.
- Description of product uses enriched text and visual hierarchy to ease lecture.
- The description of the product is not the same as the characteristics of the product.
- The description of the product is contingent and contextual to the product.

- Product counts with technical characteristics.
- The product page has a review feature.

3.3 Validation

The initial trial of this checklist occurred past 12th of October 2021 and was used by one of the researchers of this paper and other two researchers with different years of experience within the same design team and company.

Each evaluator was assigned a random list of product detail pages to evaluate using this checklist. These were performed anonymously and discussed later in a retrospective session of 30 min.

This first trial showed that prior to the retrospective round some items were unclear and difficult to understand as the phrasing was not as generic. Which also made its application to different products in other categories tricky and hard to apply.

Despite its shortcomings, evaluators pointed out the value of a checklist, especially if oriented to non-specialists and who usually audit content in product pages, also junior designers and content writers might be benefited as well. Yet, the professionals were adamant on technical language adaptation, which might be a potential disincentive for using this checklist.

As for the DELPHI evaluation, due to the sensitivity of the data, and considering the current pandemic we were unable to perform the proposed validation of the checklist. However, we decided to launch a short survey to 5 experts in the Customer Experience and User Experience field in the retail sector. This survey consisted in seeing the same product pages that were used for this paper, then using our proposed checklist to analyze its content quality and components. Afterward, a short survey consisting of 4 open-ended questions was sent to respond anonymously.

There was a common agreement that a checklist might be useful to standardize information hierarchy and quality (5 out of 5). In terms of content audit, our checklist was also acceptable, yet they suggested that some categories or products might have special qualities which our checklist needs to address in a generic way (3 out of 5). One of the surveyed professionals added that the division of primary-secondary-tertiary was not the best approach, as a product page has layers rather than divisions. Something similar was pointed out by another professional who added that according to the tactical strategy, some contents can shift in the hierarchy.

4 Conclusion and Future Work

Product detail pages deliver their core and basic information in an acceptable way. Although, it is worth mentioning that this study only addressed the fashion category and analyzed a basic t-shirt for males. It is necessary to test the same checklist with a wide range of categories and products.

The main problem that most product details pages had was to deliver contextual information such as the measurements of the male model using the garment. This could have helped to put into context the manufacturer's sizes in an efficient way. Some might consider this as non-relevant information, but we are highly contextual beings who need references when visualizing images.

On a cognitive level, we can't do two actions at the same time, and elements such as cross-selling carrousels might appear as distracting. Especially when positioned between the basic product information and the product description and characteristics. A product page should be clear in its interaction funnel and make everything possible to support its customer on the purchase, which also aligns with the business purpose: generate a purchase.

Another relevant point worth mentioning was that product pages are still highly cluttered with information, which makes it difficult for the customer to easily identify relevant information without getting distracted by elements that do not conduce to a purchase: visual advertisement from other services of the brand. Notwithstanding, there are some positive advancements in regards to decluttering product pages by Falabella and Paris.

We can confidently say that in general the potential jobs-to-be-done are answered on most product pages, yet there is still much to improve regardless. For example the quality of product description and how businesses showcase product specifications or characteristics. As the interest of the companies slowly shifts towards a customer-centric logic, there is still a pervasive interest in technological solutions and innovations, rather than putting more effort towards the usability of the contents.

There are plenty of advances in cognitive sciences and studies by agencies such as NNGroup that indicate basic guidelines that might assist in successful sales and experiences, yet online retailers are still behind such advancements.

This can be due to the fact that businesses have other interests or agendas, no control or proper audits upon digital eCommerce sites, or clear and concise guides or recommendations only applicable by experts and not managers or stakeholders who have actual decision power.

The main objective behind our suggested checklist was to provide a useful tool in Spanish with a collection of basic guidelines of necessary elements for a successful product detail page. After carefully analyzing our provided feedback by 5 experts in Customer Experience (or User Experience) and Design it was apparent the utility of a checklist to survey or audit product pages, especially for designers that might come from other niches, or non-designers taking relevant decisions that may impact product detail pages. Some of the points that we need to rework are: creating generic parameters and examples, adding special parameters for border cases, and avoiding technical wording or phrases. Our future work will consist of the refinement of our checklist by applying it to more product categories and asking other product designers and managers to use it on their product page optimization tasks.

References

1. Ecommerce product pages. https://www.nngroup.com/articles/ecommerce-product-pages/. Accessed 11 Feb 2022
2. Garret, J.J.: The Elements of User Experience: User-Centered Design for the Web and Beyond, 2nd edn. New Riders, Indianapolis (2011)
3. Ripley Homepage. https://simple.ripley.cl/. Accessed 08 Feb 2022

4. Falabella Homepage. https://www.falabella.com/falabella-cl. Accessed 08 Feb 2022
5. Paris Homepage. https://www.paris.cl/. Accessed 08 Feb 2022
6. Mercado Libre Homepage. https://www.mercadolibre.cl/. Accessed 08 Feb 2022
7. Amazon Homepage. https://www.amazon.com/. Accessed 05 Feb 2022
8. Gentile, C., Spiller, N., Noci, G.: How to sustain the customer experience: an overview of experience components that co-create value with the customer. Eur. Manage. J. **25**(5), 395–410 (2007)
9. LaSalle, D., Britton, T.: Priceless: Turning Ordinary Products into Extraordinary Experiences, 1st edn. Harvard Business Press, Boston (2003)
10. Shaw, C., Ivens, J.: Building Great Customer Experiences, 1st edn. Palgrave, London (2002)
11. Schmitt, B.: Experiential marketing. J. Mark. Manage. **15**(1–3), 53–67 (1999)
12. Chiles, C.R., Dau, M.T.: An analysis of current supply chain best practices in the retail industry with case studies of Wal-Mart and Amazon.com. Thesis (M. Eng. in Logistics) Massachusetts Institute of Technology, Engineering Systems Division (2005)
13. Godás, L.: La distribución: comercio mayorista y minorista. Offarm **26**(3), 1–140 (2007)
14. Laudon, K.C., Traver, C.G.: e-Commerce, negocios, tecnología y sociedad, Naucalpan de Juaréz, Mexico, Pearson (2009)
15. Business to business. https://www.shopify.com/encyclopedia/business-to-business-b2b. Accessed 08 Feb 2022
16. Business to Consumer. https://www.shopify.com/encyclopedia/business-to-consumer-b2c. Accessed 08 Feb 2022
17. Consumer to Business. https://www.techopedia.com/definition/23258/consumer-to-busine ss-c2b. Accessed 08 Feb 2022
18. Interaction cost definition. https://www.nngroup.com/articles/interaction-cost-definition/. Accessed 08 Feb 2022
19. Durrani, S., Durrani, Q.S.: Applying cognitive psychology to user interfaces. In: Tiwary, U.S., Siddiqui, T.J., Radhakrishna, M., Tiwari, M.D. (eds.) Proceedings of the First International Conference on Intelligent Human Computer Interaction. Springer, New Delhi (2009). https://doi.org/10.1007/978-81-8489-203-1_14
20. Cognitive psychology IA from theory to practice. https://boxesandarrows.com/cognitive-psy chology-ia-from-theory-to-practice/. Accessed 08 Feb 2022

Evaluating Store Features Using Consumer Reviews in Beauty Salons

Ryo Morooka[1](✉), Takashi Namatame[2], and Kohei Otake[3]

[1] Graduate School of Information and Telecommunication Engineering, Tokai University, 2-3-23, Takanawa, Minato-ku, Tokyo 108-8619, Japan
socmyo99@gmail.com

[2] Faculty of Science and Engineering, Chuo University, 1-13-27, Kasuga, Bunkyo-ku, Tokyo 112-8551, Japan
nama@kc.chuo-u.ac.jp

[3] School of Information and Telecommunication Engineering, Tokai University, 2-3-23, Takanawa, Minato-ku, Tokyo 108-8619, Japan
otake@tsc.u-tokai.ac.jp

Abstract. In recent years, the number of beauty salons has been on the rise and competition is intensifying in Japan. It is necessary for stores to understand the characteristics of other stores in the area and the needs of their customers and to come up with strategies to secure customers to keep up with the competition. The purpose of this study is to understand the characteristics of stores using the review data. Specifically, we extract the characteristic words of each store and classify them according to their characteristics to understand the characteristics of beauty salons in the region from the review data using natural language processing. Furthermore, we use the extracted feature words to compare the feature of a target store with those of its competitors. Finally, we attempt to propose a marketing measure to the target store that considers the characteristics of local stores.

Keywords: Beauty salon · Review data · Natural language processing · Cluster analysis

1 Introduction

In recent years, competition among beauty salons have intensified in the beauty salon industry due to an increase in the number of beauty salons, lower prices, and a decrease in the number of customers [1]. In addition, problems such as the declining population and shrinking market due to the declining birthrate and aging population are expected to have a significant impact on the beauty salon industry in the future. Under these circumstances, it can be said that the management strategy of the salon is important.

Figure 1 shows the changes in the number of barber shops and beauty salons based on the Ministry of Health, Labor and Welfare's "The first year of Reiwa Sanitation Report" [2]. From the Fig. 1, the number of barber store has been decreasing year by year, the number of beauty salon has been increasing year by year. In 2019, there were 254,422 beauty salons, which is about 1.36 times more than the 187, 277 beauty salon in the third

© The Author(s), under exclusive license to Springer Nature Switzerland AG 2022
G. Meiselwitz (Ed.): HCII 2022, LNCS 13316, pp. 292–307, 2022.
https://doi.org/10.1007/978-3-031-05064-0_22

year of Heisei. Along with the increase in the number of beauty salon, the number of beauticians has also been increasing year by year. The number of beauticians and beauty salons is expected to continue to increase in the future.

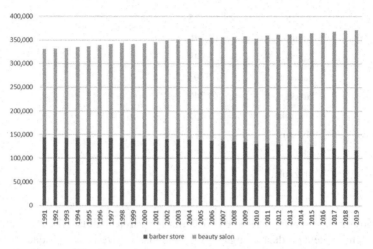

Fig. 1. Trends in barber store and beauty salon

Table 1 and Table 2 show the number of barber stores and beauty salons (top 10) by prefecture from the Ministry of Health, Labor and Welfare's "The first year of Reiwa Sanitation Report" [2]. The number of barber stores and beauty salons is concentrated mainly in the Kanto region and in prefectures with designated cities. Tokyo has many beauty salons (24,088), indicating that competition among salons is fierce. This is followed by Osaka Prefecture with 17,275 beauty salons.

Table 1. Number of barber store by prefecture (Top 10)

Prefecture	Number of barber stores
Tokyo	7,929
Osaka	6,324
Hokkaido	6,258
Aichi	5,419
Saitama	5,160
Kanagawa	4,746
Chiba	4,649
Fukuoka	4,249
Hyogo	3,851
Shizuoka	3,754

Table 2. Number of beauty salons by prefecture (Top 10)

Prefecture	Number of beauty salons
Tokyo	24,088
Osaka	17,275
Aichi	12,636
Kanagawa	11,848
Saitama	11,307
Hokkaido	10,740
Fukuoka	10,155
Hyogo	9,912
Chiba	9,559
Shizuoka	8,487

According to a survey conducted by Yano Research Institute [3], the size of the beauty salon market was decreasing (Fig. 2). The market size is on a gradual downward trend. While the market size is decreasing, the number of barber stores and beauty salons are increasing, suggesting that competition among stores will become fierce.

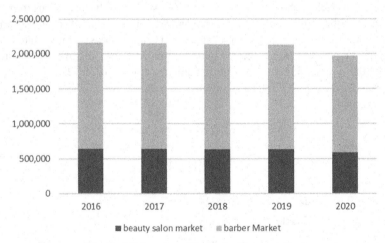

Fig. 2. Market size of barber and beauty salon

Against the backdrop of the above, the number of bankruptcies, closures, and dissolutions of beauty salons are rapidly increasing. According to the "Survey by Tokyo Shoko Research" [4], the number of bankrupt stores in 2000 was 31, but in 2018 it was 95, which is about three times the number of bankrupt stores. 92 stores were bankrupt in 2019 (January-October), and the number of bankruptcies is expected to increase in future. The number of bankruptcies is expected to increase in the future. The number of closed and dissolved businesses has increased significantly from 8 in 2000 to 242 in 2018, a 30-fold increase.

Competition in the beauty salon industry is intensifying due to such factors as the increase in the number of beauticians and beauty salons, the decrease in the size of the market, and the decline in population due to the declining birthrate and aging population. In particular, Tokyo is the prefecture with the largest number of stores in Japan and is considered to be a region where competition is fierce. Therefore, it is important for stores to understand the characteristics of other stores in the area and the needs of their customers, and to develop strategies to secure customers. Word-of-mouth evaluations of stores can be used as a reference when considering strategies to understand the characteristics of local stores and the needs of their customers. However, it is difficult to grasp all the contents of a huge amount of word-of-mouth, summarize them, and consider strategies, and it takes a lot of time and effort.

On the academic side, research targeting beauty salons has been conducted using a variety of approaches. Ohno et al. [5] focused on customers' awareness of beauty and the date of visit. Then, they classified customers' awareness of beauty and predicted the probability of their next visit. From this study, they found that the probability of visiting a store differs depending on the level of sensitivity to beauty. Based on the results, they propose an improvement plan for the DM sending function to increase the repeat rate. Hidaka et al. [6] analyzed the content of users' reviews and the distribution of numerical evaluation scores on a beauty salon information site. In addition, they extracted the users' sweet and spicy level, characteristic words, and preferred treatments. Then, they proposed an interface to support the search of beauty salons by visualizing these information. Sato et al. [7] defined the satisfaction levels of both new and continuing customers in a beauty salon chain. They proposed an optimization for the problem of reallocating stylists to satisfy them. Nonaka et al. [8] identified the factors that cause repeat customers to leave a beauty salon chain. They found that the longer the average interval between visits, the more likely the customer was to become a repeat customer, and the longer the interval, the more likely the customer was to leave the store. In addition, they identified the treatments that are most likely to cause attrition in stores with long and short average intervals between visits. Nishimura et al. [9] analyzed the effect of the cumulative number of customer visits on the revisit interval using a proportional hazards model in order to understand the status of customer revisits. In addition, the estimated retention level was visualized by principal component analysis in order to understand the status transition of revisit. The results of this study show that it is possible to capture the changes in the status of customer revisit in stores and to obtain guidelines for improving the revisit rate.

However, most of these studies have focused on customers, and not enough research has been conducted on the characteristics of the stores themselves. In addition, few studies have compared beauty salons with their competitors in the same region.

2   Purpose of This Study

The purpose of this study is to propose marketing measures that consider the characteristics of the stores using the text data in the review data for beauty salons provided by

Hot Pepper Beauty [10]. Specifically, we extract the characteristic words of each store and classify them according to their characteristics to understand the characteristics of beauty salons in the region from the review data. In addition, we attempt to extract the characteristics of the competing stores. Then, we attempt to propose a marketing measure to the target store that considers the characteristics of local stores.

3 Selection of Regions for Analysis

In this study, we used "Recruit dataset" provided by Recruit Co., Ltd. [11]. The data period is two years from January 11, 2012 to January 9, 2014. In addition, in order to propose specific marketing measures, we use ID-POS data provided by a beauty salon chain that operates mainly in Tokyo.

In this study, the characteristics of stores in a certain region are clarified from the review data, and stores are classified according to their characteristics in the region. We selected regions for analysis to understand the characteristics of stores. We extracted stores with more than 50 reviews posted on Hot Pepper Beauty in the regions where targeted beauty salon chain stores are located, and the region with the largest number of stores was selected for analysis. Based on the idea that it is difficult to understand the characteristics of stores with few reviews and areas with few comparison targets, Ginza was chosen as the target area for analysis in this study. In addition, we obtained the recent review data for the target store in Ginza.

4 Analysis on Understanding the Characteristics of Stores in the Target Area

In this chapter, we attempt to extract the characteristics of stores in Ginza. Specifically, we first extract the feature words in the reviews of each store using the TF-IDF method. Next, we classify the stores with similar features into five clusters using the percentage of occurrences of the feature words.

4.1 Feature Extraction for Each Store Using Review Data

First, we attempt to identify characteristic words by natural language processing using the TF-IDF method to grasp the characteristics of stores in the Ginza area using review data. Specifically, we perform morphological analysis on the review contents of each store using MeCab [12] and separate them by parts of speech. Morphological analysis is a method to divide a document written in natural language into morphemes, which are the smallest units in language. We then performed the TF-IDF method to calculate the importance of words in a document (Eqs. (1)–(3)).

$$\text{TFIDF}_{i,j} = tf_{i,j} \times idf_i \tag{1}$$

$$tf_{i,j} = \frac{n_{i,j}}{\sum_s n_{s,j}} \tag{2}$$

$$idf_i = \log\frac{|D|}{|\{d:d \in t_i\}|} + 1 \tag{3}$$

where

$n_{i,j}$	the frequency of word i in the sentence j,
$\sum_s n_{s,j}$	the frequency of all words in the sentence j,
$|D|$	the total number of all sentences,
$|\{d:d \in t_i\}|$	the number of sentences containing word i.

In addition, stop words were set the words that could be judged as not representing the characteristics of the store were deleted. Among the extracted words, some words were considered to have the same meaning. We judged that using the extracted words as they were in the analysis would affect our understanding of the characteristics of the stores, so we adopted the words with the highest TF-IDF values among the words that could be considered to have the same meaning and deleted the other words.

The top 30 words of TF-IDF values were extracted for each store among the words expressing the features of the store. Categories were set by referring to the questions used in the questionnaire survey on "What makes you choose a beauty salon or beauty salon" conducted by Normalism Co. to determine the evaluation of the extracted words [13]. The categories were "Customer service", "Location", "Treatment", "Date/Time", "Price", "Food/Drink", "Event", "Equipment", and "Other". Moreover, the words categorized as "Other", we classified into "Other (positive)", "Other (negative)", and "Other (unknown)" using the word-emotion polarity correspondence table [14]. In this table, words are assigned a value from -1 to 1. In this table, words are assigned a value from -1 to 1, with words closer to 1 indicating a greater degree of negativity and words closer to 1 indicating a greater degree of positivity. From this, of the words classified as "Other" with reference to the emotion polarity real value assigned to each word, words with a value greater than zero were classified as "Other (positive)", words with a value less than zero were classified as "Other (negative)", and words that could not be classified were classified as "Other (unknown)". This resulted in the following categories: "Customer service," "Location", "Treatment", "Date/Time", "Price", "Food/Drink", "Event", "Equipment", "Other (positive)", "Other (negative)" and "Other (unknown)".

Next, we tagged the top 30 TF-IDF words extracted from the review text for each store into these 11 categories. Figure 3 shows the results of the percentage of TF-IDF values in each category. Here, Store A refers to the target store. In the category of "Customer service", the percentage is high in stores 12 and 26, while it is low in stores 5 and 13. In "Location", the percentage was slightly higher in stores 7 and 13, and lower in the other stores. For "Treatment", the percentage was high in stores 11 and 18, etc., and low in stores 14 and 24, etc. For "Date/Time", the percentage was high in stores 13 and 23, and low in the other stores. As for "Price", the ratio was high in stores 1 and 16, but low in other stores. As for "Food/Drink", the ratio was a little higher in store 3 and store 10, while it was lower in other stores. In "Event", the ratio is high in store 13 and low in other stores. As for "Equipment", the ratio was high in stores 5 and 24, and low in stores 19 and 25. As for "Other (positive)", the percentage was high in stores 12, 14, etc., and low in stores 13, 22, etc. As for "Other (negative)", the percentage was

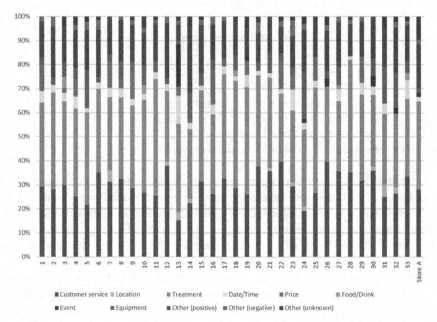

Fig. 3. Percentage of TF-IDF values for each category.

high in stores 20 and 23, while it was low in other stores. In this way, we were able to understand the characteristics of each store.

4.2 Classification of Similar Stores

Next, we conducted cluster analysis based on the percentage of TF-IDF values for each category in each store. Specifically, we conducted hierarchical cluster analysis and we identified the store characteristics of each group.

The dendrogram created by the hierarchical cluster analysis is shown in Fig. 4.

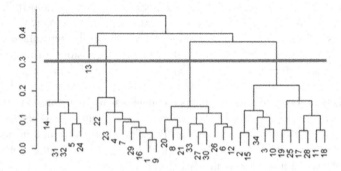

Fig. 4. Cluster analysis results

The values from 1 to 33 in Fig. 4 are the same as the stores in Fig. 3. In Fig. 4, 34 represents the target store. Euclidean distance was used for the distance between the data, and Ward's method was used for the distance between the clusters. As a result of hierarchical cluster analysis, we divided all stores into 5 clusters.

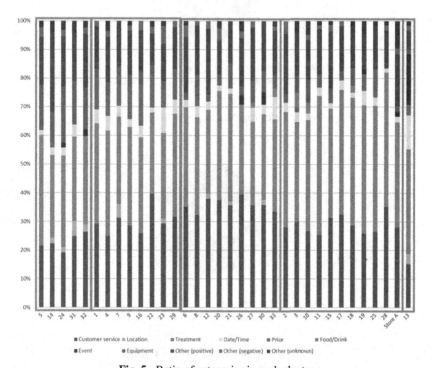

Fig. 5. Ratio of categories in each cluster

Figure 5 shows the ratio of categories in each cluster. The area surrounded by the red box represents each cluster. From left to right, the clusters are Cluster 1, Cluster 2, Cluster 3, Cluster 4 and Cluster 5. Cluster 1 contained 5 stores, Cluster 2 contained 8 stores, Cluster 3 contained 9 stores, Cluster 4 contained 11 stores, and Cluster 5 contained 1 store. Store A was classified in Cluster 4, which has the largest number of stores.

Then, the average value of each cluster category was calculated to understand the characteristics of each cluster. The results are shown in Fig. 6, 7, 8, 9 and 10.

Figure 6 shows the percentage of categories in Cluster 1. In descending order of the percentage, "Treatment" accounted for 32%, "Customer service" accounted for 23%, "Other (positive)" accounted for 20%, and "Equipment" accounted for 15%. One of the characteristics of Cluster 1 is that the TF-IDF values of feature words related to "Equipment" and "Other (positive)" are higher than those of the other clusters. On the other hand, the proportion of TF-IDF values of feature words related to "Customer service" and "Treatment" is lower. Based on these characteristics of the clusters, cluster 1 was named "Comfort-oriented".

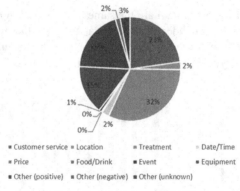

Fig. 6. Percentage of categories in Cluster 1

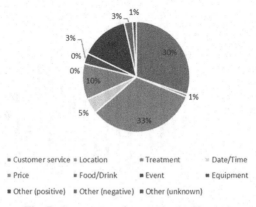

Fig. 7. Percentage of categories in Cluster 2

Figure 7 shows the percentage of categories in Cluster 2. In descending order, "Treatment" accounted for 33%, "Customer service" accounted for 30%, "Other (positive)" accounted for 14%, and "Price" accounted for 10%. One of the characteristics of Cluster 2 is that the TF-IDF values of feature words related to "Date/Time" and "Price" are higher than those of the other clusters. On the other hand, the TF-IDF values of feature words related to "Equipment" and "Other (positive)" are lower. Based on these characteristics of the clusters, we named Cluster 2 as "Price-oriented".

Figure 8 shows the percentage of categories in Cluster 3. In descending order of the percentage, "Customer service" accounted for 36%, "Treatment" accounted for 33%, and "Other (positive)" accounted for 17%. Cluster 3 is characterized by a higher percentage of TF-IDF values for feature words related to "Customer service" than the other clusters. Based on these characteristics of the clusters, Cluster 3 was named "Customer-oriented".

Figure 9 shows the percentage of categories in Cluster 4. In descending order of the percentage, "Treatment" accounted for 42%, "Customer service" accounted for 29%, and "Other (positive)" accounted for 16%. Cluster 4 is characterized by a higher percentage of TF-IDF values for the characteristic word "Treatment" than the other clusters. On the

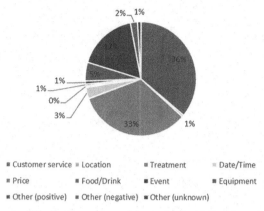

Fig. 8. Percentage of categories in Cluster 3

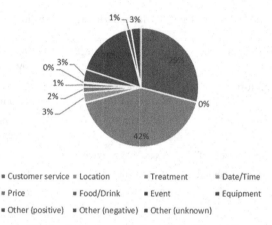

Fig. 9. Percentage of categories in Cluster 4

other hand, the percentage of TF-IDF values of feature words related to "Equipment" is low. Based on these characteristics of the clusters, we named Cluster 4 as "Treatment-oriented".

Figure 10 shows the percentage of categories in Cluster 5. In descending order, "Treatment" accounted for 37%, "Event" for 18%, "Customer service" for 15%, and "Date/Time" for 12%. The characteristic of cluster 5 is that the TF-IDF values of feature words related to "Date/Time" and "Event" are higher than those of the other clusters. On the other hand, the TF-IDF values of feature words related to "Customer service" and "Other (positive)" are lower. Based on these characteristics of the clusters, we named Cluster 5 as "Event-oriented".

A summary of the characteristics and naming of each cluster is shown Table 3.

From Table 3, the TF-IDF values of feature words related to "Customer service" and "Treatment" are high in all clusters. Among them, "Customer service" and "Treatment" have particularly high percentages in Cluster 3 and Cluster 4, respectively.

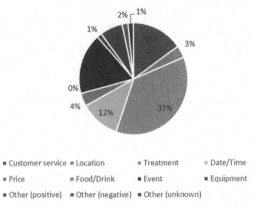

- Customer service   - Location   - Treatment   - Date/Time
- Price   - Food/Drink   - Event   - Equipment
- Other (positive)   - Other (negative) - Other (unknown)

Fig. 10. Percentage of categories in Cluster 5

Table 3. The characteristics and naming of each cluster

Cluster	Cluster's name	Characteristic categories (high percentage)	Characteristic category (low percentage)
Cluster 1	"Comfort-oriented"	"Equipment", "Other (positive)"	"Customer service", "Treatment"
Cluster 2	"Price-oriented"	"Date/Time", "Price"	"Equipment", "Other (positive)"
Cluster 3	"Customer-oriented"	"Customer Service"	
Cluster 4	"Treatment-oriented"	"Treatment"	"Equipment"
Cluster 5	"Event-oriented"	"Date/Time", "Event"	"Customer service", "Other (positive)"

5   Comparison of Store Characteristics in the Ginza Area

Based on the results of the hierarchical cluster analysis, we compared the stores and understand the characteristics of the stores in Ginza. In this study, we focused our analysis on the target store and seven stores located in the vicinity of the target store as competing stores. As for the clusters to which the competing stores belonged, "Treatment-oriented" has three stores, "Customer-oriented" has two stores, "Price-oriented" has one store and "Comfort-oriented" has one store. Including the target store, there are four "Treatment-oriented" stores in this area, indicating that competition among "Treatment-oriented" stores is intense. On the other hand, there is only one "Price-oriented" store, indicating that there is no competition.

Next, we focused on the feature words of each store to understand the characteristics of stores. The extracted words are the top 30 words of TF-IDF value of each store. The extracted words are the top 30 words in the TF-IDF value of each store and are classified into five clusters by cluster analysis. The clusters are as follows.

- **Comfort-oriented:** The TF-IDF values of words related to "Equipment" and "Other (positive)" are high, and the TF-IDF values of "Customer service" and "Treatment" are low. The TF-IDF values of the words "Equipment" and "Other (positive)" are higher in the "Comfort-oriented" category, while the TF-IDF values of "Customer service" and "Treatment" are lower. The stores in the "Comfort-oriented" category are beauty salons that provide a relaxing space and are like a third place like a cafe. This type of store is likely to attract customers who are looking for security and healing. The words categorized as "Equipment" included "キッズスペース(kids space)" and "テラス(terrace)", and each store had its own characteristics. Therefore, it can be assumed that the customer base is different and that there is competition among the "Comfort-oriented" stores in terms of needs. In addition, when the rating of "Equipment" is high, the rating of "Other (positive)" is also high, suggesting that the reviews of "Comfort-oriented" stores tend to have more positive contents, and that the comfort in beauty salons easily gives customers a positive impression. This suggests that comfort in a beauty salon is likely to give a positive impression to customers. This leads to more positive content in the reviews, which in turn gives a good impression to the reviewers.

- **Price-oriented:** The TF-IDF values for "Date/Time" and "Price" are high, while the TF-IDF values for "Equipment" and "Others (positive)" are low. This indicates that stores in this cluster are especially evaluated for the price of their menu items and are less likely to be evaluated for comfort. It is thought that "Price-oriented" stores tend to attract customers who want to get a haircut as cheaply as possible. In the case of the "Price-oriented" stores, the proportion of positive evaluations was lower when the proportion of "Price" was higher. It can be seen that "Price-oriented" restaurants focus on offering low prices for their menu items. In the case of the "Price-oriented" restaurants, they focus on offering the menu at low prices, and when they offer the menu at low prices, they have less time for "Equipment", which is likely to lead to positive evaluations such as comfort, and this is thought to influence the low percentage of "Other (positive)" evaluations.

- **Customer-oriented:** The TF-IDF values for "Customer service" has high ratio. Therefore, the response and attitude of the staff are especially evaluated in the stores in this cluster. In addition, compared to other stores, there are no items with a low evaluation ratio, indicating that the stores in this cluster are well-balanced without any shortcomings. It is thought that the "Customer- oriented" stores attract customers who want to enjoy communication with the staff.

- **Treatment-oriented:** The TF-IDF value ratio for "Treatment" is high and the ratio for "Equipment" is low. This indicates that stores in this cluster are particularly valued for the attractiveness and quality of their menus and products. On the other hand, it is difficult to evaluate the comfort of the beauty salon. It is thought that "Treatment-oriented" stores tend to attract customers who are highly conscious about beauty. The stores in this cluster have the largest number of stores in the Ginza area, and competition is fierce.

- **Event-oriented:** The TF-IDF values for "Date/Time" and "Event" are high, while the TF-IDF values for "Customer service" and "Other (positive)" are low. This indicates that the stores in this cluster are suitable to be used before going to weddings and receptions. It is thought that stores in the "Event-oriented" category are likely to attract customers who will attend weddings and other events held near Ginza. There is only one store classified in this cluster, and it is differentiated from other stores in the Ginza area, so it can be said that it has successfully positioned itself.

From the results of cluster analysis, it can be concluded that there are, "Comfort-oriented", "Price-oriented", "Customer-oriented", "Treatment-oriented" and "Event-oriented" types of stores in Ginza. There are many "Treatment-oriented", followed by "Customer-oriented", "Price-oriented", "Comfort-oriented", and "Event-oriented" types of stores. We found that there are many stores in this order. Near Store A, a total of seven stores were identified three "Treatment-oriented" stores, two "Customer-oriented" stores, one "Price-oriented" store, and one "Comfort-oriented" store. Store A was categorized as a "Treatment-oriented" store and was found to be highly evaluated for its treatment. The fact that there are many "Treatment-oriented" salons in the vicinity of Store A suggests that they are competing for customers who choose salons that focus on treatment. It is necessary to consider strategies to survive during such many competing stores.

Table 4. Feature words extracted from Store A (bottom 10 TF-IDF values)

feature word	category
雰囲気(atmosphere)	"Equipment"
風合い(texture)	"Other (unknown)"
トリートメント(treatment)	"Treatment"
希望(hope)	"Customer service"
マッサージ(massage)	"Treatment"
夏(summer)	"Event"
施術(treatment)	"Treatment"
手入れ(maintenance)	"Treatment"
パーマ(perm)	"Treatment"
スポーティ(sporty)	"Other (unknown)"
厳つい(stern)	"Other (unknown)"

Table 4 shows the words belonging to the bottom 10 TF-IDF values of the feature words extracted from Store A and their respective categories. Many words related to treatment, massage, and perm were extracted at Store A. On the other hand, in competing stores, treatment was extracted near the top 10. This indicates that there are few evaluations of treatments at Store A.

Figure 11 shows the number of orders for each menu category aggregated using the ID-POS data of Store A. From Fig. 11, "cut" being the most common, followed by "Treatment", "Blow-dry, shampoo, hair set", and "color".

From these results, we believe that it is effective to improve the "Treatment" techniques at Store A as a proposed strategy. Specifically, "perm", "massage", and "treatment", which were extracted from the reviews of Store A, are among the lowest ranked

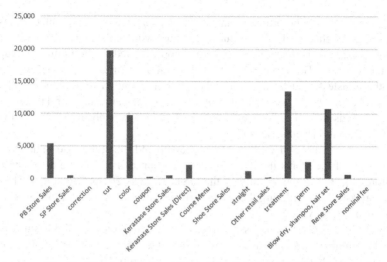

Fig. 11. Number of Menus Ordered by Category (ID-POS Data)

"Treatment" feature words. In particular, "treatment" was ordered second most frequently, but its evaluation was low, suggesting that it would be more effective if the technique of "treatment" could be improved. As a result, it can be confirmed from word-of-mouth that Store A is a store that focuses on various "Treatments". In addition, since there is only one "Customer-oriented" store among the competing stores in the vicinity, it will be effective to improve the "customer service" technology to differentiate Store A from the "Treatment-oriented" stores. By proposing these measures, we believe that Store A will be able to compete more effectively with competing stores in the region and build a relationship of coexistence with stores that are not in a competitive relationship.

6 Conclusion

In this study, using review data of the beauty salon chain store, we conducted clustering to understand the characteristics of stores in Ginza and to propose measures for Store A. Specifically, the TF-IDF method was used to extract the top 30 words of the TF-IDF value that would be the characteristic words using the review data of the stores to be analyzed. Categories were set up and the feature words were classified to understand what kind of feature words existed. Based on the results of the TF-IDF method and hierarchical cluster analysis, we were able to divide the stores in Ginza into five clusters. Compared to the other clusters, Cluster 1 had a higher percentage of TF-IDF values for feature words related to "Equipment" and "Other (positive)", and a lower percentage of TF-IDF values for feature words related to "Customer service" and "Treatment". Cluster 1 was named "Comfort-oriented" because of this. Cluster 2 has a higher percentage of TF-IDF values for feature words related to "Date/Time" and "Price" and a lower percentage of TF-IDF values for feature words related to "Equipment" and "Other (positive)" than the other clusters. Therefore, we named Cluster 2 as "Price-oriented". Cluster 3 has a higher percentage of TF-IDF values for feature words related to "Customer service" than the other clusters. Therefore, we named Cluster 3 as "Customer-oriented". Cluster 4 has a higher percentage of TF-IDF values for feature words related to "Treatment" and a lower percentage of TF-IDF values for feature words related to "Equipment" compared to the other clusters. Therefore, we named cluster 4 as "Comfort-oriented". Compared to the other clusters, Cluster 5 has a higher percentage of TF-IDF values for feature words related to "Date/Time" and "Event" and a lower percentage of TF-IDF values for feature words related to "Customer service" and "Other (positive)". Therefore, we named Cluster 5 as "Event-oriented".

Based on the feature of each cluster, we compared the stores and understand the characteristics of the stores in Ginza. We focused our analysis on the target store and seven stores located in the vicinity of the target store as competing stores. Then, we proposed measures considering the characteristics of Store A and competing stores in the vicinity of Store A.

In our future works, it is necessary to review the categories set in this study and to increase the number of review data of stores in Ginza for analysis. This will enable us to understand the characteristics of stores in the area in more detail.

Acknowledgement. In this paper, we used "Recruit dataset" provided by Recruit Co., Ltd. via IDR Dataset Service of National Institute of Informatics. This work was supported by JSPS KAKENHI Grant Number 19K01945, 21H04600 and 21K13385.

References

1. Ministry of Health, Labour and Welfare. "Overview of the Beauty Industry," https://www.mhlw.go.jp/stf/seisakunitsuite/bunya/kenkou_iryou/kenkou/seikatsu-eisei/seikatsu-eisei03/06.html. Accessed 10 Feb 2022
2. Ministry of Health. Labour and Welfare "The first year of Reiwa Sanitation Report," https://www.mhlw.go.jp/toukei/saikin/hw/eisei_houkoku/19/. Accessed 10 Feb 2022
3. Yano Research Institute, Inc.: "Conducted a survey on the barber and beauty market (2021)". https://www.yano.co.jp/press-release/show/press_id/2690. Accessed 10 Feb 2022
4. Tokyo Shoko Research, Inc., Jan–Oct 2019. Bankruptcies in 'Beauty Salons,' http://www.tsr-net.co.jp/news/analysis/20191111_03.html.10. Accessed 10 Feb 2022
5. Ohno, K., Sone, H.: Study on customer visit prediction at a hairdresser considering the beauty. In: 2019 The Japan Society for Management Information, 1P1-14 (2019)
6. Hidaka, K., Toyoda, T., Ohara, G.: Visualization of beauty salon reputation information and user information considering sweetness and spiciness of reviewers. In: The 79th Information Processing Society of Japan, 2Q-08 (2017)
7. Sato, Y., Saijo, N., Usami, S., Hashimoto, K., Otake, K., Namatame, T.: Store reallocation of beauty salon stylists considering customer's convenience and needs. Oper. Res. **64**(2), 79–86 (2019)
8. Nonaka, M., Otake, K., Namatame, T.: Analysis of the characteristic of customer leave in a hair salon Chain store. In: 2019 The Japan Society for Management Information, 1P1-16 (2019)
9. Nishimura, N., Kobayashi, K., Yoshizumi, S.: Analysis of beauty salon revisit status using constrained proportional hazard model. Oper. Res. **64**(2), 65–72 (2019)
10. Hot Pepper Beauty. https://beauty.hotpepper.jp/. Accessed 10 Feb 2022

11. Recruit Co., Ltd. Hot Pepper Beauty data. Informatics Research Data Repository, National Institute of Informatics (2014). https://doi.org/10.32130/idr.4.1
12. MeCab: Yet Another Part-of-Speech and Morphological Analyzer. http://taku910.github.io/mecab/. Accessed 10 Feb 2022
13. Normalism, Inc.: "What was the trigger or deciding factor in choosing a beauty salon?" https://hairlog.jp/. Accessed 10 Feb 2022 https://hairlog.jp/special/article/9544. Accessed 10 Feb 2022
14. Takamura, H.: Word-Emotion Polarity Correspondence Table. http://www.lr.pi.titech.ac.jp/~takamura/pndic_ja.html. Accessed 10 Feb 2022

The Internet-of-Things and AI and Their Use for Marketers

Marc Oliver Opresnik[✉]

Technische Hochschule Lübeck, Public Corporation, Mönkhofer Weg 239, 23562 Lübeck, Germany
Marc.Oliver.Opresnik@TH-Luebeck.de

Abstract. The current digital transformation, called Industry 4.0 and representing the fourth industrial revolution in manufacturing and industry, influences production of goods and services as well as value chains and business models. Automation, Big Data, AI (artificial intelligence) and IoT (Internet-of-Things) are technologies within Industry 4.0 that create so-called Smart Factories allowing the manufacturer to control the entire production from one platform.

In the future, IoT will play a central role in every-day life and it will open new business and market opportunities as well as it will give market actors room for being active creators.

Keyword: Social media marketing · AI Internet of Things · Artificial intelligence · Marketing planning · Marketing management · Web 2.0 · Marketing 5.0 · Integrated marketing communication · Social computing · Social media

1 Web 2.0 and the Evolution of Digital Marketing

The Internet has changed the way people, organizations and institutions communicate. Accordingly, media planning is undergoing a dramatic change from traditional ATL communication tools such as newspapers and magazines to non-traditional BTL tools such as mobile and Internet marketing. Figure 1 displays that mobile and desktop Internet adspend in Germany is estimated to account for nearly 45% of the adspend market in 2021 [1].

Appropriate software allows the firm to track who is reading and responding along with the types of responses. This enables the firm to segment the audience accordingly, targeting future communications based on recipients' self-reported priorities.

A checklist for launching a successful digital marketing campaign includes the following aspects [2]:

Solid planning. Companies are required to have clear and measurable objectives, and they must carefully plan their campaign.

Excellent content. Firms have to make sure they are offering genuine value to the audience.

Right frequency and timing. Organizations must not overwhelm their audience.

Appropriate use of graphics. Businesses should not get carried away. If graphics add real value and aren't too big, they could be used.

G. Meiselwitz (Ed.): HCII 2022, LNCS 13316, pp. 308–316, 2022.
https://doi.org/10.1007/978-3-031-05064-0_23

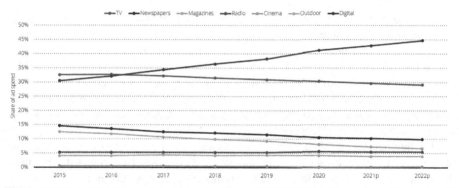

Fig. 1. Development of the media mix in advertisement 2015–2020 in Germany and forecast until 2022 (compared to the previous year) (Source: Statista 2021)

Lead with company's strength. Companies should not bury the best content or offer. They need to ensure it is at the top or at the e-mail equivalent of 'above the fold'.

Link to company's site. This is where the richness of content and interactivity can really reside. Marketers should tease readers so they will link to the site. Advertising can also be incorporated to create a desire in the audience for more information. The Web site catch page is crucial to this tactic and is often where many people falter when integrating traditional advertising with online promotions.

Measure and improve. The ability to measure basics such as open and click-through rates is one of the main advantages of digital marketing, but companies should not stop there. They should also track sales or other conversions and learn from what works and make necessary adjustments.

Web 2.0 websites allows enterprises to do more than just retrieve information, as this was mainly the case with Web 1.0. Web 2.0 transforms broadcast media monologues (one-to-many = Web 1.0) into social media dialogues (many-to-many). The term Web 2.0 was first used in 2004 to describe a new way software developers and end-users started to utilize the internet to create content and applications that were no longer created and published by individuals, but instead continuously modified by all users in a participatory and collaborative fashion. The popularity of the term Web 2.0, along with the increasing use of blogs, wikis, and social networking technologies, has led many in academia and business to work with these 'new' phenomena. For marketers, Web 2.0 offers an opportunity to engage consumers. A growing number of marketers are using Web 2.0 tools to collaborate with consumers on product development, service enhancement and promotion. Companies can use Web 2.0 tools to improve collaboration with both its business partners and consumers. Among other things, company employees have created wikis, which are Web sites that allow users to add, delete and edit content, and to list answers to frequently asked questions about each product, and consumers have added significant contributions. Another Web 2.0 marketing feature is to make sure consumers can use the online community to network among themselves on content that they choose themselves. Besides generating content, the Web 2.0 Internet user tends to proactively bring in a whole new perspective on established processes and approaches, so that the users create innovative ideas for the future development of companies [3].

With the creation of the World Wide Web and Web browsers in 1990s, the Internet was transformed from a mere communication platform into a certifiably revolutionary technology. For consumers, digital technologies have not only provided the means to search for and buy products while saving time and money, but also to socialize and be entertained. The emergence of social networking sites such as Facebook has enabled consumers to spend time socializing, and the development of video streaming and music downloads means that they can be entertained as well. A major challenge for marketers is to tap in to the huge audiences using the net.

The Internet is a global channel of communication, but the advertising messages are often perceived in the local context by the potential customer. Herein lays the dilemma that often causes the results from internet promotion to be less than anticipated.

Traditional media have two capabilities – building brands and direct marketing. In general, most promotional forms are useful for one or the other. The internet however, has the characteristics of both broadcast mass media and direct response advertising.

In the conventional model of communications in the marketplace, there are clear distinctions between the sender, the message and the recipient, and control of the message is with the sender. In 'market space', control of the message is shared between sender and receiver because of the interactivity of the medium, its ability to carry a message back in reply to that sent, and the impact of the information technology on time, space and communication. The above stated impacts on the feedback loop are built into the Internet and on the aspects of interference. In general, interference is more likely to be from internet clutter and less from external sources.

The web represents a change away from a push strategy in international promotion, where a producer focuses on compelling an intermediate to represent the products or services or a distributor to stock its goods, towards a pull strategy in which the producer communicates directly with the customer. In this transition process, promotional costs and other transaction costs are reduced. The differentiating feature of the Internet from other promotional vehicles is that of interactivity. This results in the special feature that Internet combines the attributes of both selling and advertising. Interactivity facilitates a completely innovative approach to reaching potential customers. Unlike television, for example, where the consumer passively observes, with the web there is an active intent to go onto the Internet and more attention to content as a result. In the Inter-net, the potential customer has a high involvement approach to advertising. A continual stream of decisions is demanded from the user. Each click represents a decision and therefore the web is a very high involvement medium. In addition, unlike traditional media, the web is a medium by which the user can click through and obtain more information or purchase the product. Web advertisements can and are often targeted to a user profile that in turn affects the way the message will be received. Increasingly, the ads displayed on the web are specific to user interests and appear as these interests are revealed while the user navigates the web [3].

2   The Internet-of-Things and AI and Their Use for Marketers

The Internet-of-Things (IoT) is a network of interconnected devices, systems and services within the existing Internet infrastructure. The core of the IoT is that it allows for 'all things connected' in the communication between devices and objects, creating a more direct integration between the physical world and computer-based systems.

By capturing and analyzing the data that come from the sensors at the endpoints of the connected objects, the IoT's value lies in its ability to track, measure and create 'smart' devices that bring considerable benefits to individuals and businesses.

Basically, an IoT system consists of three elements [3].

Sensors: Sensors create data about the status of manufacturing equipment and its context, and work as an information interface between physical devices and the Internet. Sensors add connectivity to manufacturing equipment and material components, and are the building blocks of proactive and autonomous repair and maintenance concepts.

Actuators: Actuators are all sorts of components of automated systems that – based on signals from the sensors - drive movement of physical effects, such as moving robots, opening of windows in a house, etc. The IoT builds on Internet-connected actuators, which enable often centralized operators to remote control of a process, and to conduct remote repair and maintenance activities.

IT-Internet ('Cloud') driven services, represented a smart phone app.

For example, a smartphone app, connects the physical objects in a house in order to create a good indoor climate. In this way, IoT may enhance customers' lives and make them 'smarter' (intelligent), while at the same time feed data to develop the firms' competitive advantages, making it possible to more directly, for example, target, monitor and deliver more specific and customized experiences. In order for IoT-oriented organizations to create and capture customer value, they must work together in order to solve customer problems, e.g. in order to create a good in-door climate. The challenge is to get different manufacturers' complementary IoT platforms to work together with the final goal of establishing a smartphone app, that can get the heating system to work together with the air condition system and opening of the windows at the right time.

In online market research there is a trend in moving from active to passive measurements. In other words: from sending out online surveys (with questions to be answered) to observing the online behavior of customers and analyze it by using AI. Social media are a rich source of data on decision-making and buying behavior and can give an accurate picture of the 'sentiment' surrounding a brand.

Online market research has become a combination of research and analysis. Digitalization has provided a significant quantities of customer data (Big Data) readily available. By analyzing this with AI, an accurate picture arises of how customers behave regarding brands and of their attitudes to them.

The digitalization has meant that online market research relies more on analytics nowadays than on research. Companies use search AI and engine analyses, chat sessions, forums and click-through analyses to learn more about the online and offline buying behavior of customers. Companies such as Facebook, Google and Microsoft use their own data to monitor consumer responses to banners, search results, and website formats, usually without the consumer being aware of it (although totally legal). This includes analyzing media habits such as watching TV and listening to online radio. Streaming data can be very accurately analyzed, and they keep track of the time you spend watching or listening, to which stations, when you switch channels, to which channels you switch etc.

The following are the specific techniques that may be used and analyzed with the help of AI [4].

Eyetracking: A technique that uses a special camera that captures the movements of the eyes on the screen.

Mousetracking: Similar to eyetracking, but is more quantitative in nature, as many people can participate online.

Online focus groups: Based on the traditional focus group, a qualitative research form, in which a limited group of people come together online in order to explore awareness, understanding and attitudes related to a brand or a whole category of brands.

Online communities: Allow customers to participate in research over a period of time. For example, a community can be deployed for evaluating a new online advertising campaign.

Social media & Blogs monitoring & analysis: As many companies are becoming active on social media, many new agencies have popped up with a focus on analyzing the massive amount of social media data. Well-known techniques for doing this are the sentiment analyses that allow the companies to see how positively or negatively their company or brand is appearing in social media sentiment.

Smart phone research: The main advantage of mobile research is that you can reach consumers at any time of the day and anywhere. Additionally, people often prefer to fill in surveys on their smart phone, while they are waiting for something else. Another feature is the possibility of GPS registration. The means, for ex-ample, that if you have attended an event, you can receive a survey to evaluate this event immediately afterwards.

Neuroscience: We have seen the emergence of neurotechnology, no longer confirmed to the universities for purely scientific re-search, but now applied in the field of marketing. How our brain reacts to marketing stimuli is now becoming clearer. It is also important to know in which part of the brain this happens, because the location of our brain activity determines whether we store something short term or long term. To do this, an MRI scanner is used.

Facial coding: The webcam is here used to measure people's emotions by looking at their facial expressions. This is especially used to measure the impact of TV or web commercials.

Marketing has historically been about communicating messages and ensuring that it goes to the target persons – framing a product and then deciding what to tell the target market. The next phase takes marketing a step further – not only targeting the target audience but taking the next step for them and integrate a true Service-Dominant logic (SD-logic) by "doing the job for them".

IoT data is real usage data. Compare this to surveys or focus groups marketers have counted on for so long. We used these techniques because they provided us with some helpful insights but there is nothing more powerful than the insights, we can gain from IoT. Teams can see exactly how a customer is using a product, what specific features they are using and which they are not. Just pure facts without any bias or the risk of perception misguiding the feedback. And it is not only how they are using a product. Marketers can also identify design and performance issues, address them immediately and refine over time. Just imagine having a product that is constantly getting better rather than outdated by the next new gadget. When marketers correlate this with other information about their products and customers, they can get a much more sophisticated understanding of the people using their products.

Development and sustainability of IoT marketing is highly dependent on the acquisition of the new skills for the marketer. As the IoT solution becomes a reality, the interactions between consumers and things under-go emergence and contribute something greater than the sum of the parts resulting in new consumer experiences embodying design and complexity. For example, the connected devices in a home can create safe and secure home, with a good indoor climate.

The increasing challenge for marketers is shifting away from the traditional perspectives of marketing, sales and advertising towards design with a focus on architecting the interactions and orchestrating the consumer experiences underpinning IoT.

The role of the marketer greatly changes with IoT and responsibilities include developing IoT driven experiences through consideration of the product flows and integration with key consumer touch points, establishing the overall product interaction with customers and setting up pre-defined actions built on automating customer journeys.

This role is unique from previous marketing roles in the IoT has an ability to actually change customer behaviour for benefit of both the customer and marketer through monitoring the sensors. The data acquisition from sensors has not been available previously to marketers and represents an opportunity to add customer value through servicing and engaging the customer proactively in brand conversations [3].

Basically, the new technologies will enable data-driven, predictive, contextual, augmented and agile marketing. A distinction is made between the three interrelated applications of predictive marketing, contextual marketing and augmented marketing [5, 6].

These three applications build on two organizational disciplines, namely data-driven marketing and agile marketing.

Data-driven Marketing: In Marketing 5.0, sufficient data must be available for all marketing decisions. To facilitate and optimize these decisions, a data ecosystem must be built. This can be achieved by collecting and analyzing big data.

Agile Marketing: Marketing 5.0 requires an agile organization to deal with the ever-changing market. This is achieved through the use of decentralized and cross-functional teams so that products and marketing campaigns can be quickly conceived, designed, developed and validated.

The two disciplines presented enable the deployment of the three applications of so-called Marketing 5.0. It should be emphasized that the three applications are interrelated and not mutually exclusive (Fig. 2).

Companies must first build data-driven capabilities and ultimately the organization's agility in execution will determine the success or failure of the implementation [5, 6].

Predictive Marketing: This application enables companies to envision a market reaction and proactively influence this reaction. This requires the development and use of predictive analytics (e.g., machine learning) to forecast the results of marketing activities.

Contextual Marketing: Depending on the customer context, this application enables the operation of 'one-to-one marketing' in real time and is considered the backbone of marketers. It requires the identification, profiling and servicing of customers with personalized interactions, e.g. through the use of sensors in physical space.

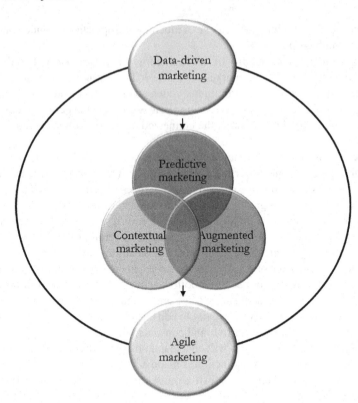

Fig. 2. The five components of Marketing 5.0 [6]

Augmented Marketing: This application enables marketers to merge digital touch-points characterized by speed and convenience with personal touchpoints character-ized by warmth and empathy. This is achieved through the use of digital technologies, e.g. the productivity of marketers in direct customer contact is in-creased by using human-mimicking technologies such as chat-bots.

As described, this marketing approach is based on the so-called next technologies (next tech). Marketers can use next tech to create value along the customer journey and to create a seamless and delightful customer experience.

Next tech is enabled by the maturation of the following six factors [6].

Computing Power: Realizing artificial intelligence with real-time responses requires powerful yet cost-effective hardware. Advances in semiconductor technology, shrinking processor sizes and efficient graphics processors result in more performance and less energy consumption, so that small AI components can be used in self-driving cars, for example.

Open-Source Software: In addition to computing power or hardware, robust software is also required. In order to accelerate development processes that typically take years and to enable rap-id improvements, large companies such as Google and Microsoft make their AI research and algorithms available as open source.

The Internet: Billions of people and machines are now connected through the Internet, with fiber optic cables and the 5G mobile phone standard meeting the growing demand for band-width, making the Internet the foundation for all network-dependent (e.g., blockchain) and interactive (e.g., voice assistants) technologies.

Cloud Computing: This means shared access (based on scalable subscription models) to software and storage systems, e.g. to enable teleworking and to be able to use complex AI executions without having to invest in expensive hardware and software - major providers include Amazon and IBM.

Mobile Devices: The technological advances of mobile devices are such that high-end smartphones are now as powerful as PCs and, for many people, are even the main device for computer services and Internet access. The mobile usability of these devices increases productivity everywhere.

Big Data: The new technologies require the handling of a lot of different data so that, for example, algorithms can learn and be-come better. Data is available in real time and in large quantities. In addition, the cost and complexity of storing and managing da-ta is decreasing.

New technologies will unleash their full potential in the next ten years and fundamentally change marketing. By mimicking human capabilities, market research can be conducted in real time and personalization can be rapid and comprehensive. The contextual nature of the technologies al-lows content, offers and interactions to be tailored to the customer's cur-rent state of mind. The computing power allows for real-time services.

3 Conclusion

The marketer can play a leadership role in making IoT data the means by which marketers can truly understand customers and products. Further-more, marketers can join forces with the heads of engineering, research and development, and sales. The use of IoT data to create more customercentric products, offer new services, and find and sustain new competitive differentiation for the company.

Following steps are involved in the marketer's process of using IoT for gaining more customer insights and using appropriate marketing tools towards target customers:

Analyze customer buying habits across platforms.

Gather previously unobtainable data about how consumers inter-act with devices and products.

Gain deeper insights into where the customer is in the customer journey.

Provide real-time point-of-sale notifications and targeted ads.

Quickly resolve issues of 'getting the job done' and keep customers happy.

References

1. Statista.com: https://de.statista.com/statistik/daten/studie/870786/umfrage/prognose-der-wer bemarktanteile-der-medien-in-deutschland/. Accessed 22 Nov 2021
2. Linkon, N.: Using e-mail marketing to build business, TACTICS, p. 16 (2004)
3. Hollensen, S., Opresnik, M.: Marketing: Principles and Practice, 4th edn. Lübeck (2020)

4. Kotler, P., Hollensen, S., Opresnik, M.: Social Media Marketing – A Practitioner Guide. 5th edn. Lübeck (2022)
5. Gömann, J., Hollensen, S., Opresnik, M.: Customer Experience Management in 100 Minutes. Lübeck (2022)
6. Kotler, P., Kartajaya, H., Setiawan, I.: Marketing 5.0. Technologie für die Menschheit. Frankfurt am Main (2021)

Analyzing Methods, Instruments, and Tools for Evaluating the Customer eXperience

Luis Rojas[(✉)] and Daniela Quiñones

Pontificia Universidad Católica de Valparaíso, Valparaíso, Chile
luis.rojas.c01@mail.pucv.cl, daniela.quinones@pucv.cl

Abstract. There are multiple evaluation approaches (methods, instruments, and tools) that can be used for evaluating the CX0. However, these may not be considered by different companies/organizations because they assume that these are not related to the CX. This research analyze 29 evaluation approaches identified in a previous study (Rojas and Quiñones 2021) used in the areas of usability, user experience (UX), and satisfaction. We differentiate and examine these evaluation approaches indicating: (1) the type of participants required to apply them (experts or users); (2) the overall costs needed to use them (cheap or expensive); (3) some disadvantages or potential risks of them; and (4) the CX dimensions that could be evaluated. We found that: (1) most evaluation approaches (69%) require representative users rather than expert evaluators; (2) most evaluation approach (86,2%) are inexpensive to use since they do not need equipment or training; and (3) the most evaluated CX dimension corresponded to "sensorial", while the least evaluated CX dimension was "emotional".

Keywords: Customer eXperience · Evaluation · Evaluation approaches · Methods · Instruments · Tools

1 Introduction

Understanding the Customer eXperience (CX) is an essential factor for different companies/organizations seeking to increase the number of customers using their products, systems, or services to achieve a competitive advantage in the industry [1]. To accomplish this, it is necessary to use multiple evaluation approaches (methods, instruments, or tools) to effectively evaluate and improve the CX through different interactions the customer's journey.

There are different evaluation approaches that can be used for evaluating the CX. Some of them come from other areas related to the CX, such as usability, user experience (UX), or satisfaction. However, these may not be considered by different companies/organizations because they assume that these are not related to the CX. Nevertheless, some authors propose that CX can be considered an extension of the UX [2, 3], while the usability is a facet of the user experience (UX) [4]. Hence, it would be possible to apply evaluation approaches of these areas to evaluate specific interactions within the CX.

G. Meiselwitz (Ed.): HCII 2022, LNCS 13316, pp. 317–330, 2022.
https://doi.org/10.1007/978-3-031-05064-0_24

This study present an analysis of 29 evaluation approaches identified in a previous study [5]. We analyze and discusses each evaluation approach indicating: (1) the type of participants required to apply them (experts or users); (2) the costs needed to use them (cheap or expensive); (3) some disadvantages or potential risks of them; and (4) the CX dimensions that could be evaluated. The article is organized as follows: Sect. 2 introduces the main concepts related to CX, UX, and mention the work used as a basis. Section 3 presents the research methodology. Section 4 discusses and analyze the evaluation approaches. Finally, Sect. 5 summarizes the conclusions, limitations, and future work.

2 Theoretical Background

The concepts CX and UX, and the baseline work of this study are briefly presented below.

2.1 Customer eXperience (CX) and User eXperience (UX)

There is no widely accepted definition or standard that defines the CX, so there are multiple definitions for this concept. In this study -based on research and the literature- we recognize CX as: "the set of personal and/or subjective responses resulting from customer's direct or indirect interaction with a company through products, systems or services along the customer's journey from the first encounter, remaining even after the last interaction" [6–11].

Unlike the CX, the UX has a standard that defines it. The ISO 9241-210 standard [12] defines User Experience (UX) as "person's perceptions and responses resulting from the use and/or anticipated use of a product, system or service". Despite the existence of the standard, there are other definitions widely used, for instance, Norman and Nielsen [13] states that UX "encompasses all aspects of the end-user's interaction with the company, its services, and its products".

As with the definition of CX, something similar happens with the multiple dimensions that define the CX. There is no consensus among the authors when conceptualizing dimensions for the CX due to the different contexts in which CX is evaluated and studied. For this study, we decided to use the CX dimensions proposed by Gentile et al. [8] because they are defined in a general way, allowing their application to different contexts. The CX dimensions are briefly presented below.

- **Sensorial**: Aim to provide good sensorial experience through any of the five senses (sight, hearing, touch, taste and smell), e.g., aesthetical pleasure, excitement, satisfaction, or sense of beauty.
- **Emotional**: Generation of moods, feelings, emotions to create an affective relation with the company, its brand, or products.
- **Cognitive**: Related to customer's thinking and conscious mental processes, engage customers by using their creativity or problem-solving abilities.
- **Pragmatic**: Associated to practical act of doing something and the concept of usability through all the product life-cycle stages.

- **Lifestyle**: Refers to values and beliefs shared by the company and the customer through the product, its consumption and/or use.
- **Relational**: Involves customer's social context, relationship with other people and their own ideals.

2.2 Previous Work

This study is based on a literature review carried out by Rojas and Quiñones [5]. In the study, the authors analyzed different methodologies used to evaluate the CX by focusing on two research questions relate to: (1) methodologies, processes, stages, or steps used to evaluate the CX (including those that can be used as reference); and (2) methods, instruments or tools included in the identified methodologies. The authors noticed different findings related to the lack of essential factors within evaluation methodologies and the presence of multiple evaluation approaches used in other areas that could be applied to evaluate interactions with products, systems, or services in CX.

That study presented 29 evaluation approaches from different methodologies and frameworks that could be used as reference for evaluating the CX (see Table 1). However, they identified a lack of detail in these because only their name was usually mentioned without delving into them.

Table 1. Evaluation approaches that could be used for evaluating the CX

Methods	Instruments	Tools
• Affinity diagram [14] • Automated usability evaluation software [15] • Blind finger tracking [16] • Card sorting [17] • Co-discovery [18] • Cognitive walkthrough [19] • Eye tracking [20] • Focus group [18] • Heuristic evaluation [21] • Interview [18] • Observations [22] • Survey [23] • Thinking aloud [18] • Valence method [24] • Web usage analysis [15]	• AttrakDiff [25] • Emocards [26] • Hedonic utility scale [27] • Positive and negative affect schedule (PANAS) [28] • Post-study system usability questionnaire (PSSUQ) [29] • Questionnaire [18] • Self-assessment manikin (SAM) [30] • SERVQUAL [31] • System usability scale (SUS) [32] • UX questionnaire (UEQ) [33]	• Cause and effect diagram [34] • Critical to quality (CTQ) tree [34] • Quality function deployment (QFD) [34] • Supply, Input, Process, Output and Customer (SIPOC) [34]

3 Research Methodology

Our study seeks to analyze different evaluation approaches that can be used for evaluating the CX. We defined 2 research questions (see Table 2) using as a basis the results obtained in a previous literature review [5]. To answer these research questions, we considered mainly 3 sources: (1) the original study of each evaluation approach (if possible); (2) different studies that used them; and (3) the experience of the authors using them.

Table 2. Research questions

ID	Research question
RQ1	What features does each evaluation approach have? (participants, costs, and disadvantages)
RQ2	What CX dimension could be evaluated by each evaluation approach?

4   Results and Discussions

The results and discussions related to each research question are presented below.

4.1   What Features Does Each Evaluation Approach Have? (Participants, Costs, and Disadvantages) (RQ2)

It is important to distinguish which types of participant should participate in the different evaluation approaches, i.e., expert evaluators or representative users We identified that most evaluation approaches (69%, 20 of 29) require the presence of representative users to be used (see Fig. 1). For instance, the heuristic evaluation is a method that must be conducted by a small group of usability experts (3–5 evaluators) [21]. On the other hand, co-discovery requires working with groups of 2 users to explore a product or system [18]. The type of participant required to use each evaluation approach are shown in Appendix A.

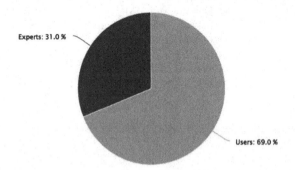

Fig. 1. Type of participants required to apply the evaluation approach

In addition, we analyzed the overall costs to use these evaluation approaches indicating whether they are cheap or expensive for evaluating the CX (see Fig. 2). We noticed that most evaluation approaches (86.2%, 25 of 29) are relatively cheap because they do not need technological devices or expensive resources. For instance, scales such as hedonic utility scale [27], SERVQUAL [31], or UX questionnaire (UEQ) [33] just need users to assign a score to different dimensions so they are inexpensive. In contrast, eye tracking [20] or automated usability evaluation software [15] require equipment and training so unlike other evaluation approaches their costs are higher. The classification of each evaluation approach regarding their cost is presented in Appendix A.

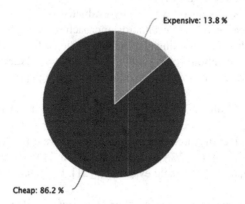

Fig. 2. Overall costs of evaluation approaches to evaluate the CX

Finally, we decided to mention some general disadvantages of each evaluation approach to recognize the potential risks when applying them (see Appendix A). For instance, we detected some evaluation approaches whose results can vary significantly since these depend on emotions, feelings, or moods of users (e.g., emocards [26], positive and negative affect schedule (PANAS) [28], or self-assessment manikin (SAM) [30]). Another disadvantage of certain evaluation approaches is that although they can be considered cheap, their costs can easily increase by including more participants making them expensive (e.g., such as heuristic evaluation [21], interview [18], or survey [23]).

4.2 What CX Dimension Could Be Evaluated by Each Evaluation Approach? (RQ3)

We associated each evaluation approach -used to evaluate the usability, UX, and satisfaction- with the CX dimensions proposed by Gentile et al. [8]. Furthermore, due to their qualitative nature, it is possible that an evaluation approach could be used to evaluate more than one CX dimension. These associations were made after reviewing, analyzing, and discussing each of them. Appendix B shows the association between CX dimensions and the evaluation approaches. Some of the highlights regarding the associations indicate that:

- **Sensorial**: This was the most evaluated CX dimension by the evaluation approaches. We believe it is because most evaluation approaches are focused on evaluating user's perceptions and responses through their senses. We identified 21 associations (72,4%) with this dimension: 11 methods and 10 instruments (e.g., blind finger tracking [16], hedonic utility scale [27], and UX questionnaire [33]).

- **Emotional**: This was the least evaluated CX dimension by the evaluation approaches. We consider that this is related to the difficulty of evaluating emotional aspects due to their subjectivity. We identified 9 associations (31%) with this dimension: 5 instruments and 4 methods (e.g., emocards [26], valence method [24], or positive and negative affect schedule (PANAS) [28]).
- **Cognitive**: This CX dimension was highly evaluated by the evaluation approaches. We think this is because multiple evaluation approaches usually includes elements that evaluate the thoughts and reasoning of users when using different products or services. We identified 20 associations (69%) with this dimension: 12 methods, 4 instruments, and 4 tools (e.g., questionnaire [18], cognitive walkthrough [19], or critical to quality (CTQ) tree [34]).
- **Pragmatic**: This CX dimension was evaluated in half of the evaluation approaches. This is due to the presence of different evaluation approaches related to usability, which are used to identify potential problems in software products or systems. We identified 15 associations (51,7%) with this dimension: 11 methods, and 4 instruments (e.g., thinking aloud [18], heuristic evaluation [21], or system usability scale (SUS) [32]).
- **Lifestyle**: This CX dimension was another of the least evaluated by the evaluation approaches. We assume that it is because the evaluation approaches come from the areas of usability and UX, so their main purpose is not related to evaluate the values shared between customers and companies. We identified 10 associations (34,5%) with this dimension: 6 methods and 4 instruments (e.g., interviews [18], surveys [23], or SERVQUAL [31]).
- **Relational**: This CX dimension was not highly evaluated by the evaluation approaches. As in the previous dimension, we presume this is because these evaluation approaches come from other areas, so they are not designed to evaluate the social context of customers or their relationships with other people. We identified 10 associations (34,5%) with this dimension: 6 methods, and 4 tools (e.g., affinity diagram [14], focus group [18], or observations [22]).

5 Conclusions

This study was conducted to analyze different evaluation approaches identified in a previous literature review [5] through 2 research questions related to: (1) features (participants, cost, and disadvantages); and (2) CX dimension that could be evaluated. To archive this, we reviewed, analyzed, and discussed the 29 evaluation approaches used in distinct methodologies and frameworks where different findings were identified.

Respect to the first research question "What features does each evaluation approach have? (participants, costs, and disadvantages)?", we analyzed in a general way: (1) the type of participant required (representative user or expert evaluator); (2) the costs to apply the evaluation approach (cheap or expensive); and (3) some disadvantages to consider for each of them. Concerning the second research question "What CX dimension could be evaluated by each evaluation approach?", we associated each of them with one or more dimensions proposed by Gentile et al. [8] to identify CX dimensions that could be evaluated.

In summary, we found that most evaluation approaches (69%) require representative users rather than expert evaluators. In general, most evaluation approach (86,2%) are inexpensive to use since they do not need equipment or training. Finally, the most evaluated CX dimension corresponded to "sensorial", while the least evaluated CX dimension was "emotional". We believe that this is because perceptions and responses through the senses are much easier to evaluate than emotions and feelings as the latter are more subjective.

The study performed has some limitations. The first limitation corresponds to the cost of each evaluation approach because it was not indicated in a detailed way why these are considered expensive or cheap. The second limitation relates to the association between CX dimensions and the evaluation approaches because some of these were not linked with certain CX dimensions as these were only partially evaluated. Despite these limitations our work has a great contribution because it is not common to consider evaluation approaches related to usability and UX for evaluating the CX. This is due to lack of knowledge about the relationship between these areas causing not everyone to know how these evaluation approaches work and some of their features.

As a future work, a systematic literature review is planned to provide more detail on each evaluation approach found and to identify others used to evaluate different interactions through the CX. Finally, a methodology or framework for evaluating the CX in a specific domain will be developed with the objective of clearly identifying stages and evaluation approaches needed to evaluate the CX in a holistic way by considering different interactions, channels, and CX dimensions.

Acknowledgments. This work was supported by the School of Informatics Engineering of the Pontificia Universidad Católica de Valparaíso – Chile. Luis Rojas has been granted the "INF-PUCV" Graduate Scholarship. Luis Rojas is supported by Grant ANID BECAS/DOCTORADO NACIONAL, Chile, No 21211272. Daniela Quiñones is supported by Grant ANID (ex CONICYT), Chile, FONDECYT INICIACIÓN, Project N° 11190759.

Appendix A: Participants, Costs and Disadvantages of Each Evaluation Approach

Evaluation approach	Participant	Cost	Disadvantages
Affinity diagram [14]	Experts	Cheap	• It requires having previously collected information • It may require a lot of time depending on the variety of information

(continued)

(*continued*)

Evaluation approach	Participant	Cost	Disadvantages
AttrakDiff [25]	Users	Cheap	• Not much information is available about this instrument • The original publication is in Deutsch
Automated usability evaluation software [15]	Experts	Expensive	• Usually, these software are not free to use • Software with lack of flexibility and customization
Blind finger tracking [16]	Users	Cheap	• A screenshot must be taken each time the user performs a function on the mobile device
Card sorting [17]	Users	Cheap	• This method may not go deep enough • The results can be very variable and inconsistent
Cause and effect diagram [34]	Experts	Cheap	• It is difficult to represent the interrelated nature of problems and causes • It is not very useful to represent complex problems
Co-discovery [18]	Users	Cheap	• The researcher cannot control the direction of the discussion • Not all problems can be identified, only those related to defined tasks
Cognitive walkthrough [19]	Experts	Cheap	• Experts' experience may cause them to overlook problems • Not all problems are identified, only those related to defined tasks
Critical to quality (CTQ) tree [34]	Experts	Cheap	• It depends on other methods to identify needs • It is not very useful to represent complex problems
Emocards [26]	Users	Cheap	• Difficulty in differentiating emotions by users • The method do not measure the actual emotion, it only measure the perceived pleasantness and arousal

(*continued*)

(*continued*)

Evaluation approach	Participant	Cost	Disadvantages
Eye tracking [20]	Users	Expensive	• Eye tracking equipment and training can be expensive • It is difficult for users to control eye position accurately all times
Focus group [18]	Users	Expensive	• Participants usually know they are being observed so the answers might be dishonest • This method is not as efficient in covering maximum depth on a particular issue
Hedonic utility scale [27]	Users	Cheap	• The scale can be interpreted subjectively • Its results may vary depending to the mood of the participant
Heuristic evaluation [21]	Experts	Cheap	• The relevance of the problems identified depends on the experience of the evaluators • Its costs can easily increase if many expert evaluators are required
Interview [18]	Users	Cheap	• Participants usually know they are being observed so the answers might be dishonest • Its costs can easily increase making them expensive
Observations [22]	Experts	Cheap	• The observer had limited control over physical situation • The relevance of the data observed depends on the experience of the evaluator
Positive and negative affect schedule (PANAS) [28]	Users	Cheap	• The scale can be interpreted subjectively • Its results may vary depending to the mood of the participant
Post-study system usability questionnaire (PSSUQ) [29]	Users	Cheap	• There is not as much information available for this instrument as others
Quality function deployment (QFD) [34]	Experts	Cheap	• Categories are based on qualitative aspects and appears to be vague and not very clear

(*continued*)

(*continued*)

Evaluation approach	Participant	Cost	Disadvantages
Questionnaire [18]	Users	Cheap	• Participants may give wrong or unanswered answers • Participants answers might be dishonest
Self-assessment manikin (SAM) [30]	Users	Cheap	• The scale can be interpreted subjectively • Its results may vary depending to the mood of the participant
SERVQUAL [31]	Users	Cheap	• It evaluates customer perception in a general way • It only focuses only on service delivery and not on the outcomes
Supply, Input, Process, Output and Customer (SIPOC) [34]	Experts	Cheap	• The tool is not applicable to all processes • Not very useful to represent complex problems
Survey [23]	Users	Cheap	• Participants may give wrong or unanswered answers • Its costs can easily increase making them expensive
System usability scale (SUS) [32]	Users	Cheap	• The instrument is a subjective measure of perceived usability • The instrument only provide quantitative data so it is difficult to know why participants assigned certain scores
Thinking aloud [18]	Users	Cheap	• Participants limit their responses because they are observed • Not all problems can be identified, only those related to defined tasks
UX questionnaire (UEQ) [33]	Users	Cheap	• Participants may have problems to interpret the items of the scale
Valence method [24]	Users	Cheap	• Participants should use the product or prototype for the first time during the evaluation • Its results may vary depending to the mood of the participant
Web usage analysis [15]	Users	Expensive	• There is not as much information available for this method as others

Appendix B: Association Between CX Dimensions and Evaluation Approaches

Evaluation approach	CX dimensions					
	Sensorial	Emotional	Cognitive	Pragmatic	Lifestyle	Relational
Affinity diagram [14]	X		X		X	X
AttrakDiff [25]	X			X		
Automated usability evaluation software [15]				X		
Blind finger tracking [16]	X		X	X		
Card sorting [17]	X		X	X		
Cause and effect diagram [34]			X			X
Co-discovery [18]	X		X	X		X
Cognitive walkthrough [19]	X		X	X		
Critical to quality (CTQ) tree [34]			X			
Emocards [26]	X	X				
Eye tracking [20]			X	X		
Focus group [18]	X	X			X	X
Hedonic utility scale [27]	X	X			X	
Heuristic evaluation [21]			X	X		
Interview [18]	X	X	X	X	X	X
Observations [22]	X		X		X	X
Positive and negative affect schedule (PANAS) [28]	X	X				
Post-study system usability questionnaire (PSSUQ) [29]	X		X	X		
Quality function deployment (QFD) [34]			X			X
Questionnaire [18]	X	X	X	X	X	X
Self-assessment manikin (SAM) [30]	X	X				
SERVQUAL [31]	X		X		X	

(continued)

(*continued*)

Evaluation approach	CX dimensions					
	Sensorial	Emotional	Cognitive	Pragmatic	Lifestyle	Relational
Supply, Input, Process, Output and Customer (SIPOC) [34]			X			X
Survey [23]	X	X	X	X	X	X
System usability scale (SUS) [32]	X			X		
Thinking aloud [18]	X		X	X		
UX questionnaire (UEQ) [33]	X		X		X	
Valence method [24]	X	X			X	
Web usage analysis [15]			X	X		
Total	21	9	20	15	10	10

References

1. Rawson, A., Duncan, E., Jones, C.: The truth about customer experience. Harv. Bus. Rev. **91**(9), 90–98 (2013)
2. Lewis, J.R.: Usability: lessons learned. and yet to be learned. Int. J. Hum. Comput. Interact. **30**(9), 663–684 (2014). https://doi.org/10.1080/10447318.2014.930311
3. Rusu, V., Rusu, C., Botella, F., Quiñones, D., Bascur, C., Rusu, V.Z.: Customer eXperience: a bridge between service science and human-computer interaction. In: Ahram, T., Karwowski, W., Pickl, S., Taiar, R. (eds.) IHSED 2019. AISC, vol. 1026, pp. 385–390. Springer, Cham (2020). https://doi.org/10.1007/978-3-030-27928-8_59
4. Morville, P.: User Experience Design, Semantic Studios (2005)
5. Rojas, L., Quiñones, D.: Customer eXperience evaluation methodologies: a literature review. ACM Int. Conf. Proc. Ser. (2021). https://doi.org/10.1145/3488392.3488398
6. Schmitt, B.: Experiential marketing. J. Mark. Manag. **15**(1–3), 53–67 (1999)
7. Meyer, C., Schwager, A.: Understanding customer experience. Harv. Bus. Rev. **85**(2), 116–124 (2007). https://doi.org/10.1108/00242539410067746
8. Gentile, C., Spiller, N., Noci, G.: How to sustain the customer experience: an overview of experience components that co-create value with the customer. Eur. Manag. J. **25**(5), 395–410 (2007). https://doi.org/10.1016/j.emj.2007.08.005
9. Verhoef, P.C., Lemon, K.N., Parasuraman, A., Roggeveen, A., Tsiros, M., Schlesinger, L.A.: Customer experience creation: determinants, dynamics and management strategies. J. Retail. **85**(1), 31–41 (2009). https://doi.org/10.1016/j.jretai.2008.11.001
10. Lemke, F., Clark, M., Wilson, H.: Customer experience quality: an exploration in business and consumer contexts using repertory grid technique. J. Acad. Mark. Sci. **39**(6), 846–869 (2011). https://doi.org/10.1007/s11747-010-0219-0
11. Lemon, K.N., Verhoef, P.C.: Understanding customer experience throughout the customer journey. J. Mark. **80**(6), 69–96 (2016). https://doi.org/10.1509/jm.15.0420

12. ISO 9241–210. "ISO 9241–210 : 2010 Ergonomics of human-system interaction—part 210 : Human-centred design for interactive systems. International Standard (2019). https://www. iso.org/standard/77520.html

13. Norman, D., Nielsen, J.: The Definition of User Experience (UX). Nielsen Norman Group. https://www.nngroup.com/articles/definition-user-experience/

14. Dam, R., Siang, T.: Affinity Diagrams – Learn How to Cluster and Bundle Ideas and Fact. Interaction Design Foundation (2020). https://www.interaction-design.org/literature/article/ affinity-diagrams-learn-how-to-cluster-and-bundle-ideas-and-facts

15. Meng, L.: Literature review. In: Gender in Literary Translation. CIS, vol. 3, pp. 9–28. Springer, Singapore (2019). https://doi.org/10.1007/978-981-13-3720-8_2

16. Álvarez, T.: Metodología para la evaluación de la experiencia del usuario de sistemas de software interactivos para usuarios ciegos. Universidad veracruzana (2019)

17. Sherwin, K.: Group Card Sorting: Uncover Users' Mental Models for Better Information Architecture. Nielsen Norman Group (2018). https://www.nngroup.com/articles/card-sorting-definition/

18. Jordan, P.W.: Designing Pleasurable Products: An Introduction to the New Human Factors, vol. 53, no. 9 (2000)

19. Interaction Design Foundation, How to Conduct a Cognitive Walkthrough. Interaction Design Foundation (2020). https://www.interaction-design.org/literature/article/how-to-conduct-a-cognitive-walkthrough

20. Moran, K.: Setup of An Eyetracking Study. Nielsen Norman Group (2019). https://www.nngroup.com/articles/eyetracking-setup.

21. Nielsen, J., Molich, R.: Heuristic evaluation of user interfaces. In: Conference on Human **Factors** in Computing Systems - Proceedings, pp. 249–256 (1990). https://doi.org/10.1145/97243.97281

22. Business Research Methodology, Observation (2011). https://research-methodology.net/research-methods/qualitative-research/observation

23. Hackett, G.: Survey research methods. Pers. Guid. J. **59**(9), 599–604 (1981)

24. Burmester, M., Mast, M., Jäger, K., Homans, H.: Valence method for formative evaluation of user experience. In: Proceedings of the 8th ACM Conference on Designing Interactive Systems, pp. 364–367 (2010)

25. User Interface Design GmbH, Attrakdif (2013). http://www.attrakdiff.de/

26. Desmet, P., Overbeeke, K., Tax, S.: Designing products with added emotional value: development and appllcation of an approach for research through design. Des. J. **4**(1), 32–47 (2001). https://doi.org/10.2752/146069201789378496

27. Voss, K.E., Spangenberg, E.R., Grohmann, B.: Measuring the hedonic and utilitarian dimensions of consumer attitude. J. Mark. Res. **40**(3), 310–320 (2003)

28. Watson, D., Clark, L.A., Tellenge, A.: Development and validation of brief measures of positive and negative affect: the PANAS scales. J. Pers. Soc. Psychol. **1988**(6), 1063–1070 (2017)

29. Lewis, J.R.: Psychometric evaluation of the post-study system usability questionnaire: the PSSUQ. Proc. Hum. Fact. Soc. Ann. Meet. **36**(16), 1259–1260 (1992)

30. Bradley, M.M., Lang, P.J.: Measuring emotion: the self-assessment manikin and the semantic differential. J. Behav. Ther. Exp. Psychiatry **25**(1), 49–59 (1994)

31. Parasuraman, A., Zeithaml, V., Berry, L.: SERVQUAL: a multiple-item scale for measuring consumer perceptions of service quality. J. Retail. **64**(1), 1–30 (1988)

32. Brooke, J.: SUS: A 'Quick and Dirty' Usability Scale. Usability Evaluation in Industry, pp. 207–212 (1996). https://doi.org/10.1201/9781498710411-35

33. Laugwitz, B., Held, T., Schrepp, M.: Construction and evaluation of a user experience questionnaire. In: Symposium of the Austrian HCI and Usability Engineering Group, pp. 63–76 (2008)
34. Tague, N.R.: The Quality Toolbox, vol. 600. ASQ Quality Press Milwaukee (2005)

Evaluating the Post-pandemic Tourist Experience: A Scale for Tourist Experience in Valparaíso, Chile

Virginica Rusu[1](✉) [ID], Leslie Márquez[1], Patricia González[1], and Cristian Rusu[2] [ID]

[1] Universidad de Playa Ancha, Av. Playa Ancha 850, 2340000 Valparaíso, Chile
virginica.rusu@upla.cl
[2] Pontificia Universidad Católica de Valparaíso, Av. Brasil 2241, 2340000 Valparaíso, Chile
cristian.rusu@pucv.cl

Abstract. Tourist eXperience (TX) is a concept discussed by many authors over the last couple of decades. TX can be approached as a particular case of Costumer eXperience (CX). TX evaluation is complex and challenging, due to its multidimensional nature, and because TX is highly personal. General and specific TX scales have been proposed. Tourism was extremely affected by the COVID-19 global pandemic. New concerns and procedures have emerged for safe trips, and they will likely become the norm in the post-pandemic era. Our study aims to develop a scale to evaluate TX in Valparaíso, Chile. We present a preliminary version of the scale, that includes 56 items, grouped in 8 dimensions: emotions, local culture, authenticity of the place, entertainment, services, post-pandemic experience, loyalty, and general perception. It includes 13 original items, and 43 adapted items, from other authors. The scale will be further validated and refined based on experts' judgment, experiments, and statistical validation.

Keywords: Tourist experience · Customer experience · Tourist experience evaluation · Scale · COVID-19

1 Introduction

1.1 A Subsection Sample

"Tourist eXperience" (TX) as a concept has been discussed by many authors. There is still a lack of consensus on its definition, for several reasons: the subjectivity of the issue, how personal the tourist experience can be, and how multidimensional it is. There are, however, some points of coincidence in the study of TX. There is convergence between authors which consider that TX spans through a period that begins when the tourist is planning a trip, and continues even after this trip occurs, through memories about the activities and learning that were acquired. Yang et al. emphasize that tourism is an intangible commodity, and TX is the results of accumulated experiences and memories related to travel [1].

G. Meiselwitz (Ed.): HCII 2022, LNCS 13316, pp. 331–343, 2022.
https://doi.org/10.1007/978-3-031-05064-0_25

TX may be considered as a particular case of Customer eXperience (CX). CX includes all physical and emotional responses that a customer experiences before, during and after coming into contact, directly or indirectly, with a brand/company, during his/her whole "journey", including the post consumption stage [2]. Tourists are specific types of costumers, that are using tourism-related services, products and systems.

CX has a highly interdisciplinary nature; originally proposed in marketing, lately raised interest in several fields. Human-Computer Interaction (HCI) community is showing a growing interest on CX. As other scholars [3], we think that CX is a natural extension of User eXperience (UX), focusing on a person's interaction to all services, systems and products that a company/organization/brand offers [4, 5]. We studied for years the usability and UX of tourism-related websites, as online travel agencies [6–8], virtual museums [9–11], and national parks [12]. We are now using a broader, holistic approach to TX, from a CX point of view [13–15].

The main objective of our study is to develop a scale to evaluate TX in Valparaíso, Chile. In our view, it would allow a proper diagnose that can help making Valparaíso a better tourist destination. The study is carried out knowing that TX is going to be and currently is very different due to the ongoing COVID-19 pandemic; new concerns and procedures have appeared for safe trips, and Valparaíso is no exception.

The current global pandemic context dramatically affects tourism, which is one of the most important economic activities of Valparaíso. The Chilean Undersecretary of Tourism monthly report "Tourism Barometer for January 2021" exposes important data from the sector, and how the national tourism industry has been affected by the COVID-19 pandemic: a decrease of 75.1% in tourism, and 3,395,104 less foreign tourists visited Chile, compared to 2019 [16]. There are hopes that tourism will recover with the massive vaccination. While the pandemic in Chile was at its most critical point, with almost the entire country in quarantine, the tourism sector of Valparaíso was extremely affected; without tourists and with its trademark funiculars closed, much of the trade closed and tourist activity was put in pause. Since the national pandemic situation got better and the government was removing restrictive sanitary measures, tourism in Valparaíso has been slowly reactivated. However, as January 2022, the new wave of pandemic still rises uncertainty, with daily records of new cases.

The paper presents a first version of the scale to evaluate TX in Valparaíso. Section 2 presents relevant concepts that fundament our study: CX and TX. Section 3 documents the development of the scale, based on bibliographical research. Section 4 highlights conclusions and future work.

2   Background

2.1   Costumer eXperience

CX has a complex, multidimensional and highly interdisciplinary nature. There is no unique, general agreed, CX definition. Laming and Mason consider that CX includes "the physical and emotional experiences occurring through the interactions with the product and/or service offering of a brand from point of first direct, conscious contact, through the total journey to the post-consumption stage" [2].

The ISO 9241-210 standard [17] defines the UX as "the perceptions and responses of the person resulting from the use and/or anticipated use of a product, system or service". We consider CX as a natural extension of UX; it focuses on a person's interaction to all services, systems and products that a company/organization/brand offers, instead of a single one [4, 5]. This is one of the reasons why the HCI community is increasingly studying CX.

CX is constructed across a series of "touchpoints" between costumers and a brand/company/organization; touchpoints are the instances when costumers interact with the products, systems or services that the brand is offering. Touchpoints' nature is different, and it highly depends on the products/systems/services involved [18]. Correctly identifying touchpoints is a core part of the CX studies.

Thompson indicates some key issues in CX research: emphasizing quantitative research and underestimating the qualitative aspects of CX; proper interpretation of data; and not stressing the link between CX evaluation and design [19]. In our view, some of the reasons that make CX evaluation complex are: CX is constructed through a sequence of touchpoints; the nature of each touchpoint is (very) different; the experience at one touchpoint may (highly) influence experiences at other touchpoints, across the entire customer's journey; CX has several dimensions; and CX is highly personal [5].

Several sets of CX dimensions/attributes/factors were proposed. Gentile et al. highlight the CX multidimensionality [20]. They synthesize a comprehensive set of CX dimensions: sensorial, emotional, cognitive, pragmatic, lifestyle, and relational.

2.2 Tourist eXperience

Tourism (and associated) services offer is rapidly growing. traditional channels for promotion/sales/feedback are replaced by virtual channels. We examined TX as a special case of CX in previous works, identifying scenarios and touchpoints [4, 5]. TX is strongly related to the quality of the services that are offered [21, 22]. However, general CX definitions are not covering the specificity of TX.

Tung and Ritchie synthesized different TX definitional approaches [23]. They consider TX as "an individual's subjective evaluation and undergoing (i.e., affective, cognitive, and behavioral) of events related to his/her tourist activities which begins before (i.e., planning and preparation), during (i.e., at the destination), and after the trip (i.e., recollection)". They identified four key dimensions of "memorable" TX: affect, expectations, consequentiality, and recollection.

Analyzing several studies, Godovykh and Tasci propose a "comprehensive yet parsimonious" TX definition [24]. In their view, TX is the "totality of cognitive, affective, sensory, and conative responses, on a spectrum of negative to positive, evoked by all stimuli encountered in pre, during, and post phases of consumption affected by situational and brand-related factors filtered through personal differences of consumers, eventually resulting in differential outcomes related to consumers and brands". Their TX models includes four components: emotional, cognitive, sensorial, and conative. They also describe the sequential nature of TX.

Walls et al. propose a framework of factors that influence TX [25]: individual characteristics (e.g., health, culture, previous visits, and demographic features), perceived human interactions in the destination (e.g., the host community's attitude, friendly inter-personal relationships, and service quality), the physical environment (e.g., scenic beauty and landscape, weather, accommodations, and transportation), and situational factors (e.g., the purpose of a trip and one's travel companions).

The current global pandemic dramatically affects tourism. TX currently is and it will remain very different in the post COVID-19 era. Joo et al. studied the perceived risk, emotional solidarity, and support for tourism amidst the COVID-19 pandemic [26]. They indicate that residents express their concerns about the health risks that would accompany tourists. They also highlight the booming of domestic tourism in some countries, due to the international travel restrictions. Hassan and Soliman stress the need to reinforce the good reputation of the destination and to enhance customers' trust in times of crises, like the current global pandemic [27].

3   Developing a Scale for Tourist Experience Evaluation

When examining TX as a concept, and its different dimensions, we did not find a proper scale to evaluate TX in Valparaíso, nor considering the pandemic restrictions. So, the need to develop a new one was even more apparent to us. We did find many definitions and dimensions of TX that helped us designing our own scale, that aims to fulfil Valparaíso's specificity when it comes to tourism. The scale is being developed considering several iterations:

1. A preliminary version of the scale was developed based on literature.
2. The scale is being evaluated by experts, academics, and tourism students. The scale will be refined based on their feedback.
3. The scale will be validated through a pilot test. If necessary, adjustments will be made.
4. The final version of the scale will be applied to tourists, and will be statistically validated.

We constructed the scale based on a significant amount of bibliographical resources. We were mainly looking for TX definitions, TX dimensions (attributes, factors), and scales to evaluate TX.

Gallarza and Gil (2007) proposed a scale for the perceived TX, that includes 11 items, grouped in 9 dimensions: efficiency, service quality, social value, entertainment, esthetics, perceived cost, perceived risk, time and effort, and perceived value [28]. Kim et al. (2010) proposed a 24-item scale to evaluate memorable TX; items were grouped in 7 dimensions: hedonism, novelty, local culture, refreshment, meaningfulness, involvement, and knowledge [29]. Martín-Ruiz et al. (2010) developed a scale to evaluate the experience of a visit to an archeological site; it includes 23 items, classified in 6 components: service experience, service quality, access sacrifice, effort sacrifice, general evaluation, and visitor's intentions [30]. The scale allows calculating an evaluation index. Ali et al. (2014) proposed a 23-item scale to evaluate memorable TX in Malaysian resort hotel; they grouped items in 6 dimensions: education, entertainment, esthetics, escapism, memories, and customer loyalty [31]. Kim (2014) developed a 43-item scale to evaluate the destination attributes associated with memorable experiences; the scale allowed obtaining a 10-attributes construct: infrastructure, accessibility, local culture/history, physiography, activities & events, destination management, quality of service, hospitality, place attachment, and superstructure [32]. Lu et al. (2015) proposed a 14-item scale to evaluate TX at historic districts; items were grouped in 4 dimensions: image, satisfaction, authenticity, and involvement [33]. Sarra et al. (2015) developed a 20-item scale to evaluate TX in Lisbon [34]. Chen and Rahman (2018) proposed a 49-item scale aiming to evaluate the interplay between 5 factors: visitor engagement, cultural contact, memorable tourism experience, intention to recommend, and revisit intention [35]. Coelho and Gosling (2018), developed a 41-item scale to evaluate the memorable TX; items were classified in 10 dimensions: environment, culture, relationship with companions, relationship with tourists, relationship with local agents, dream, emotion, novelty, refreshment, and meaningfulness [36]. Lončarić et al. (2018) proposed a scale to evaluate memorable TX in Croatia; it includes 24 items, grouped in 4 factors: hedonism and novelty, local culture, involvement, and refreshment [37]. Saayman et al. (2018) developed a 7-item scale in order to calculate a tourist well-being index [38]. Torres and Baez (2018) proposed a 21-item scale to evaluate TX in Quito; items were categorized in 5 dimensions: uniqueness, co-creation, entertainment, personal development, and rational quality [39]. All above mentioned scales are evaluating the items using Likert scales of 5 (more frequently) or 7 points.

In order to cover the most important issues that experts have referred, we considered 8 TX dimensions: emotions (8 items), local culture (8 items), authenticity of the place (13 items), entertainment (8 items), services (11 items), post-pandemic experience (4 items), loyalty (2 items), and general perception (2 items). The 56 items were thoroughly reviewed by two UX/CX experts, with computer science and psychology background; items were refined based on their feedback.

Table 1 describes the preliminary scale, indicating its dimensions, the items associated to each dimension, and how items were originated. The scale includes 13 original items and 43 adapted items. 4 new items are COVID-19 pandemic-related, and 8 new items are related to Valparaíso particularity; only 1 new item is general (medical and health services availability).

The preliminary scale was submitted to the judgment of a significant number of tourism experts, academics/scholars, and tourism students. They were asked to evaluate each item using a 5-point Likert scale (1 – not appropriate at all, to 5 – very appropriate). They were also asked to make any comments they considered important, on items individually, as well as any other comments on dimensions, the scale as a whole, and, if necessary, to propose new dimensions and/or items. We are currently evaluating their feedback and will make the necessary adjustments.

The second version of the scale will be validated through a pilot test. If necessary, adjustments will be made. The final version will be then applied to tourists, and will be statistically validated.

The scale was specifically designed to evaluate TX in Valparaíso, Chile. However, if eliminating the 8 items related to Valparaíso, the scale can be used as a general-purpose TX scale. It can also be adapted to other touristic destinations, properly particularizing items specific to Valparaíso. The items can be evaluated using a 5-point or a 7-point Likert scale. A 7-point scale allows a more detailed judgment. Besides, it may be more

Table 1. A preliminary scale for tourist experience in Valparaíso, Chile.

Dimensions	Items	Observations
Emotions (8 items)	It was a liberating experience	Adapted from Kim et al. [29], Chen and Rahman [35], Coelho and Gosling [36], Lončarić et al. [37]
	It was a unique experience	Adapted from Kim et al. [29], Chen and Rahman [35], Coelho and Gosling [36], Lončarić et al. [37]
	It was a revitalizing experience, that took me out of monotony	Adapted from Kim et al. [29], Ali et al. [31], Chen and Rahman [35], Coelho y Gosling [36], Lončarić et al. [37]
	I had fun	Adapted from Gallarza and Gil [28], Kim et al. [29], Lu et al. [33], Coelho and Gosling [36], Lončarić et al. [37], Torres and Baez [39]
	I will remember the emotions and sensations that I felt	Adapted from Ali et al. [31], Coelho and Gosling [36]
	I felt positive emotions in general	Adapted from Martín-Ruiz et al. [30], Ali et al. [31], Coelho y Gosling [36]
	I enjoyed the overall experience	Adapted from Chen y Rahman [35], Lončarić et al. [37]
	I will always remember this experience	Adapted from Kim et al. [29], Ali et al. [31], Chen and Rahman [35], Coelho and Gosling [36], Lončarić et al. [37]
Local culture (8 items)	The relationship with the local community was nice	Adapted from Kim et al. [29], Kim [32], Chen and Rahman [35], Coelho and Gosling [36], Lončarić et al. [37]
	I experienced local traditions and customs	Adapted from Kim et al. [29], Kim [32], Chen and Rahman [35], Coelho and Gosling [36], Lončarić et al. [37]

(*continued*)

Table 1. (*continued*)

Dimensions	Items	Observations
	I participated in activities organized by local communities	Adapted from Lu et al. [33], Chen and Rahman [35]
	The local community organizes activities open to visitors	Adapted from Lu et al. [33]
	I got a good impression of the local community	Adapted from Kim et al. [29], Chen and Rahman [35], Lončarić et al. [37]
	The local community is unique, and different from my own community	Adapted from Coelho and Gosling [36]
	The local community was ready to help and provide information on Valparaíso	Adapted from Kim [32]
	The identity of Valparaíso is remarkable	Adapted from Torres and Baez [39]
Authenticity of the place (13 items)	I learned new things	Adapted from Ali et al. [31]
	I appreciated the historic richness of Valparaíso	Adapted from Lu et al. [33]
	I appreciated the uniqueness of the funiculars ("elevators")	Original
	I appreciated the uniqueness of the trolleys	Original
	I appreciated the uniqueness and importance of the stairs for Valparaíso	Original
	I appreciated the historical case of Valparaiso, as world heritage	Original
	I appreciated the Valparaíso harbor and its commercial relevance	Original
	I appreciated the coast, the sea, and the associated services	Original

(*continued*)

Table 1. (*continued*)

Dimensions	Items	Observations
	I appreciated the gastronomy of Valparaíso	Adapted from Kim [32], Sarra et al. [34], Saayman et al. [38], Torres and Baez [39]
	I appreciated Valparaíso's architecture	Adapted from Kim [32]
	I appreciated the variety of touristic attractions	Adapted from Kim [32]
	Valparaíso offers a significant cultural diversity	Adapted from Lu et al. [33], Coelho and Gosling [36], Torres and Baez [39]
	Valparaíso's climate is pleasant	Adapted from Torres and Baez [39]
Entertainment (8 items)	Guided tours are available	Adapted from Chen and Rahman [35], Coelho and Gosling [36]
	Cultural activities are freely available	Adapted from Lu et al. [33]
	Valparaíso offers cultural attractions (e.g. galleries, cultural centers, museums)	Adapted from Torres and Baez [39]
	Valparaíso offers activities concerning its history	Adapted from Kim [32], Lu et al. [33]
	I enjoyed participating in activities that Valparaíso offers	Adapted from Kim et al. [29], Ali et al. [31], Chen and Rahman [35], Lončarić et al. [37]
	I performed activities that I have never done before	Adapted from Kim et al. [29], Coelho and Gosling [36], Lončarić et al. [37]
	Valparaíso offers night entertainment attractions	Adapted from Sarra et al. [34]
	I enjoyed carnivals and/or festivals specific to Valparaíso	Adapted from Kim [32]
Services (11 items)	Valparaíso offers diverse options of accommodations	Adapted from Sarra et al. [34], Saayman et al. [38]
	Valparaíso offers diverse restaurants/places to eat	Adapted from Sarra et al. [34], Saayman et al. [38]

(*continued*)

Table 1. (*continued*)

Dimensions	Items	Observations
	Valparaíso offers diverse leisure and relaxation services	Adapted from Kim [32]
	Public restrooms are available	Adapted from Martín-Ruiz et al. [30]
	Medical and health services are available	Original
	Valparaíso has public security services	Adapted from Sarra et al. [34]
	Valparaíso offers accessible tourist information services	Adapted from Martín-Ruiz et al. [30], Kim [32], Sarra et al. [34]
	Tourist agents were friendly	Kim [32], Chen y Rahman [35], Coelho y Gosling [36], Lončarić et al. [37]
	Tourism service quality was as promised	Adapted from Gallarza y Gil [28]
	Valparaíso has appropriate signaling for emergency procedures, as for tsunamis and earthquakes	Original
	Secure areas for tsunamis and earthquakes are clearly indicated	Original
Post-pandemic experience (4 items)	I felt safe, without fear of COVID-19 contagion	Original
	I felt that social distance measures where appropriate	Original
	COVID-19 related safety measures where appropriately informed	Original
	COVID-19 related safety measures did not impede that my experience was enjoyable	Original
Loyalty (2 items)	I would recommend Valparaíso as destination to other tourists	Adapted from Ali et al. [31], Chen and Rahman [35]

(*continued*)

Table 1. (continued)

Dimensions	Items	Observations
	I would like to visit Valparaíso again in the future	Martín-Ruiz et al. [30], Ali et al. [31], Chen y Rahman [35]
General perception (2 items)	The experience met my expectations	Adapted from Martín-Ruiz et al. [30], Lu et al. [33]
	I was satisfied with the experience	Adapted from Lu et al. [33], Saayman et al. [38]

familiar to Chilean tourists, as a 7-point scale is generally used in Chile, in many fields, starting with the educational system. Nevertheless, 5-point Likert scales are largely used in TX, and items' evaluation using only 5 levels may be perceived by tourists as easier to perform.

4 Conclusions and Future Work

TX has been discussed for decades, by many authors. there is no consensus on a single, unique definition. TX can be considered as a particular case of CX. In fact, some scholars are specifically referring to costumer/consumer experience in tourism, instead of TX. As there is a growing interest in CX in the HCI community, and the number of tourism-related systems, digital products, and services is continuously growing, the HCI community interest in TX is natural.

Evaluating TX is equally challenging as evaluating CX, for several reasons: TX is multidimensional; TX is constructed through a sequence of touchpoints; the nature of each touchpoint is different; the experience at one touchpoint may (highly) influence experiences at other touchpoints, across the entire tourist journey; and TX is highly personal. Several TX scales were proposed; some of them are general, others are specific; many scales aim to evaluate the "memorable" TX. Tourism was extremely affected by the COVID-19 global pandemic; new concerns and procedures have appeared for safe trips, and they will likely become the norm in the post-pandemic era. That is why TX scales should include specific post-pandemic experience items.

As we did not find a proper scale to evaluate TX in Valparaíso, Chile, nor considering the pandemic restrictions, our study aims to develop a specific TX scale. We propose a preliminary version of the scale, that includes 56 items, grouped in 8 dimensions: emotions, local culture, authenticity of the place, entertainment, services, post-pandemic experience, loyalty, and general perception. We constructed the scale based on a significant amount of bibliographical resources; it includes 13 original items, and 43 adapted from other authors. The scale was reviewed by 2 CX experts, and refined based on their feedback. Even if the scale was specifically designed to evaluate TX in Valparaíso, it can also be adapted to other touristic destinations, properly particularizing the Valparaíso specific items.

The scale is currently being evaluated by a significant number of experts, academics, and tourism students, and it will be refined based on their feedback. It will be further validated through a pilot test and adjustments will be made, if necessary. The final version of the scale will be applied to tourists, and will be statistically validated.

Acknowledgments. This project was financed by Dirección General de Investigación of Universidad de Playa Ancha, Chile (Concurso Regular 2020, code HUM 04-2122).

References

1. Yang, Y., Mao, Z., Zhang, X.: Better sleep, better trip: the effect of sleep quality on tourists' experiences. Ann. Tour. Res. **87**, 103153 (2021)
2. Laming, C., Mason, K.: Customer experience - an analysis of the concept and its performance in airline brands. Res. Transp. Bus. Manag. **10**, 15–25 (2014)
3. Lewis, J.R.: Usability: lessons learned... and yet to be learned. Int. J. Hum.-Comput. Interact. **30**(9), 663–684 (2014)
4. Rusu, V., Rusu, C., Botella, F., Quiñones, D.: Customer experience: is this the ultimate experience? In: Interacción 2018, Proceedings of the XIX International Conference on Human Computer Interaction. ACM (2018)
5. Rusu, V., Rusu, C., Botella, F., Quiñones, D., Bascur, C., Rusu, V.Z.: Customer experience: a bridge between service science and human-computer interaction. In: Ahram, T., Karwowski, W., Pickl, S., Taiar, R. (eds.) IHSED 2019. AISC, vol. 1026, pp. 385–390. Springer, Cham (2020). https://doi.org/10.1007/978-3-030-27928-8_59
6. Rusu, C., Rusu, V., Quiñones, D., Roncagliolo, S., Rusu, V.Z.: Evaluating online travel agencies' usability: what heuristics should we use? In: Meiselwitz, G. (ed.) SCSM 2018. LNCS, vol. 10913, pp. 121–130. Springer, Cham (2018). https://doi.org/10.1007/978-3-319-91521-0_10
7. Rusu, V., Rusu, C., Quiñones, D., Botella, F., Roncagliolo, S., Rusu, V.Z.: On-line travel agencies' usability: evaluator experience. In: Meiselwitz, G. (ed.) SCSM 2019. LNCS, vol. 11579, pp. 452–463. Springer, Cham (2019). https://doi.org/10.1007/978-3-030-21905-5_35
8. Díaz, J., et al.: Website transformation of a Latin American airline: effects of cultural aspects and user experience on business performance. IEEE LA Trans. **17**(5), 766–774 (2019)
9. Rusu, C., Rusu, V.Z., Muñoz, P., Rusu, V., Roncagliolo, S., Quiñones, D.: On user experience in virtual museums. In: Meiselwitz, G. (ed.) SCSM 2017. LNCS, vol. 10282, pp. 127–136. Springer, Cham (2017). https://doi.org/10.1007/978-3-319-58559-8_12
10. Rusu, V.Z., Quiñones, D., Rusu, C., Cáceres, P., Rusu, V., Roncagliolo, S.: Approaches on user experience assessment: user tests, communicability and psychometrics. In: Meiselwitz, G. (ed.) SCSM 2018, LNCS, vol. 10913, pp. 97–111. Springer, Cham (2018). https://doi.org/10.1007/978-3-319-91521-0_8
11. Rusu, V., Rusu, C., Cáceres, P., Rusu, V., Quiñones, D., Muñoz, P.: On user experience evaluation: combining user tests and psychometrics. In: Karwowski, W., Ahram, T. (eds.) IHSI 2018. AISC, vol. 722, pp. 626–632. Springer, Cham (2018). https://doi.org/10.1007/978-3-319-73888-8_97
12. Delgado, D., Zamora, D., Quiñones, D., Rusu, C., Roncagliolo, S., Rusu, V.: User experience heuristics for national park websites. In: Meiselwitz, G. (ed.) SCSM 2020. LNCS, vol. 12195, pp. 194–204. Springer, Cham (2020). https://doi.org/10.1007/978-3-030-49576-3_14
13. Rusu, V., et al.: Assessing the customer eXperience based on quantitative data: virtual travel agencies. In: Marcus, A. (ed.) DUXU 2016. LNCS, vol. 9746, pp. 499–508. Springer, Cham (2016). https://doi.org/10.1007/978-3-319-40409-7_47

14. Rusu, V., Rusu, C., Guzmán, D., Roncagliolo, S., Quiñones, D.: Online travel agencies as social media: analyzing customers' opinions. In: Meiselwitz, G. (ed.) SCSM 2017. LNCS, vol. 10282, pp. 200–209. Springer, Cham (2017). https://doi.org/10.1007/978-3-319-58559-8_17

15. Rusu, V., Rusu, C., Quiñones, D., Roncagliolo, S., Carvajal, V., Muñoz, M.: Customer experience in Valparaiso hostels: analyzing tourists' opinions. In: Meiselwitz, G. (ed.) SCSM 2020. LNCS, vol. 12195, pp. 226–235. Springer, Cham (2020). https://doi.org/10.1007/978-3-030-49576-3_17

16. Subsecretaría de Turismo, Gobierno de Chile. http://www.subturismo.gob.cl/barometros/. Accessed 01 Feb 2022

17. ISO 9241-210: Ergonomics of Human-system Interaction—Part 210: Human-centered Design for Interactive Systems. International Organization for Standardization (2010)

18. Stein, A., Ramaseshan, B.: Towards the identification of customer experience touch point elements. J. Retail. Consum. Serv. **30**, 8–19 (2016)

19. Thompson, M.: The CX tower of Babel: what CX job descriptions tell us about corporate CX initiatives. Interactions **25**(3), 74–77 (2018)

20. Gentile, C., Spiller, N., Noci, G.: How to sustain the customer experience: an overview of experience components that co-create value with the customer. Eur. Manag. J. **25**(5), 395–410 (2007)

21. Tussyadiah, I.: Toward a theoretical foundation for experience design in tourism. J. Trav. Res. **53**(5), 543–564 (2014)

22. Bosangit, C., Hibbert, S., McCabe, S.: If I was going to die I should at least be having fun: travelblogs, meaning and tourist experience. Ann. Tour. Res. **55**, 1–14 (2015)

23. Tung, V., Ritchie, J.R.: Exploring the essence of memorable tourism experiences. Ann. Tour. Res. **38**(4), 1367–1386 (2011)

24. Godovykh, M., Tasci, A.: Customer experience in tourism: a review of definitions, components, and measurements. Tour. Manag. Pers. **35**, 100694 (2020)

25. Walls, A., Okumus, F., Wang, Y., Kwun, D.: An epistemological view of consumer experiences. Int. J. Hosp. Manag. **30**, 10–21 (2011)

26. Joo, D., Xu, W., Lee, J., Lee, C., Woosnam, K.M.: Residents' perceived risk, emotional solidarity, and support for tourism amidst the COVID-19 pandemic. J. Dest. Market. Manag. **19**, 100553 (2021)

27. Hassan, S., Soliman, M.: COVID-19 and repeat visitation: Assessing the role of destination social responsibility, destination reputation, holidaymakers' trust and fear arousal. J. Dest. Market. Manag. **19**, 100495 (2021)

28. Gallarza, M., Gil, I.: La investigación conceptual sobre valor percibido en la experiencia turística. Propuesta de un Modelo Verbal Gráfico. Estudios turísticos **174**, 7–32 (2007)

29. Kim, J., Ritchie, J., McCormick, B.: Development of a scale to measure memorable tourism experiences. J. Trav. Res. **51**(1), 12–25 (2010)

30. Martín-Ruiz, D., Castellanos-Verdugo, M., Oviedo-García, M.: A visitors' evaluation index for a visit to an archaeological site. Tour. Manag. **31**, 590–596 (2010)

31. Ali, F., Hussain, K., Ragavan, N.: Memorable customer experience: examining the effects of customers experience on memories and loyalty in Malaysian resort hotels. Proc. Soc. Behav. Sci. **144**, 273–279 (2014)

32. Kim, J.: The antecedents of memorable tourism experiences: the development of a scale to measure the destination attributes associated with memorable experiences. Tour. Manag. **44**, 34–45 (2014)

33. Lu, L., Chi, C., Liu, Y.: Authenticity, involvement, and image: evaluating tourist experiences at historic districts. Tour. Manag. **50**, 85–96 (2015)

34. Sarra, A., Di Zio, S., Cappucci, M.: A quantitative valuation of tourist experience in Lisbon. Ann. Tour. Res. **53**, 1–16 (2015)

35. Chen, H., Rahman, I.: Cultural tourism: an analysis of engagement, cultural contact, memorable tourism experience and destination loyalty. Tour. Manag. Persp. **26**, 153–163 (2018)
36. Coelho, M., Gosling, M.: Memorable Tourism Experience (MTE): scale proposal and test. Tour. Manag. Stud. **14**(4), 15–24 (2018)
37. Lončarić, D., Dlačić, J., Perišić, M.: What makes summer vacation experience memorable? An empirical study from Croatia. Zbornik Veleučilišta u Rijeci **6**(1), 67–80 (2018)
38. Saayman, M., Li, G., Uysal, M., Song, H.: Tourist satisfaction and subjective well-being: an index approach. Int. J. Tourism Res. **20**, 388–399 (2018)
39. Torres, P., Baez, S.: Tourist experience measurement in Quito city. Rev. Bras. Pesq. Tur. São Paulo **12**(1), 133–156 (2018)

Purchasing Behavior Analysis Model that Considers the Relationship Between Topic Hierarchy and Item Categories

Yuta Sakai[1]([✉]), Yui Matsuoka[2], and Masayuki Goto[1]

[1] Waseda University, Shinjyuku-ku, Tokyo 169-8555, Japan
y-sakai1003@akane.waseda.jp
[2] NTT DATA Corporation, koto-ku, Tokyo 135-6033, Japan

Abstract. With the spread of EC sites, it has become an important work for companies to analyze user preferences contained in accumulated purchase history data and utilize them in marketing measures. A topic model is well known as a method for analyzing user preferences from purchase history data, and a model assuming hierarchy of topics has been proposed as an extension method. The previously proposed PAM (Pachinko Allocation Model) is a highly expressive model in which all upper and lower topics are connected by a network and the relationships between multiple topics can be analyzed. However, PAM is easily affected by the initial values of learning parameters, and it is difficult to obtain stable topics, so the interpretation of the estimated topics becomes unstable. It is dangerous to make business decisions based on the interpretation of such unstable results. Therefore, in this research, instead of using the hierarchy of topics estimated based on the user's purchasing behavior, we use information with a hierarchical structure of "product categories" given by the EC site for managing items. Therefore, we propose a method that is useful for studying measures and that enables hierarchical topic analysis. Finally, the proposed method is applied to the evaluation history data of the actual EC site to analyze the user's preference and show its usefulness.

Keywords: Topic model · Purchase history data · EC site

1 Introduction

With the proliferation of e-commerce sites, it has become an important issue for companies to analyze user preferences contained in the accumulated purchase history data and utilize them in marketing strategies. In general, customers' preferences are diverse, and topic models that can handle data where customer groups with completely different purchasing behaviors are mixed together are recognized as very effective models for marketing policy planning [1,2]. A topic model is known as a method to analyze user preferences based on purchase history data, and a representative method is Latent Dirichlet Allocation (LDA) [3].

G. Meiselwitz (Ed.): HCII 2022, LNCS 13316, pp. 344–358, 2022.
https://doi.org/10.1007/978-3-031-05064-0_26

LDA assumes latent classes (topics) behind the user's purchase behavior, and user preferences can be interpreted from the obtained topic.

On the other hand, user preferences are considered to have hierarchical structures, and as an extension of LDA, hierarchical Latent Dirichlet Allocation (hLDA) [4] and Pachinko Allocation Model (PAM) [5], which assume hierarchical nature in topics, have been proposed. Hierarchical model can take into account the hierarchical and inclusive relationships among topics that generally exist. In hLDA that is general hierarchical topic model, the hierarchy of topics is limited to a branching structure represented by a tree structure, so it is not possible to analyze the relationship between a lower-level topic and multiple higher-level topics. On the other hand, PAM is a model with higher flexibility, in which all higher and lower topics are connected by a network, and the relationships among multiple topics can be analyzed. However, PAM is susceptible to the initial value at the time of training and is difficult to obtain stable topics, which makes the interpretation of topics unstable. Because of instability of parameter estimation on the training phase, it is dangerous to make business decisions based on the interpretation of such unstable results.

Therefore, this research proposes a method that is useful for examining measures and enables hierarchical topic analysis by utilizing hierarchical information of "product category", which is assigned by the e-commerce site to manage items, instead of the hierarchical structure of topics estimated based on users' purchase behavior. Specifically, we apply independent LDAs to the purchase history data of two categories with different granularity and evaluate the relationship between the obtained topics by calculating the topic relevance score. The topic relevance score enables to construct a network structure between upper and lower hierarchies of topics. Because the training of LDA is not easily affected by initial values relatively to PAM, it becomes possible to stably represent the hierarchy of user preferences. Finally, we apply the proposed method to the evaluation history data of an actual e-commerce site to analyze user preferences and show its usefulness. In addition, we evaluate the stability of the topics and show the effectiveness of the proposed method in comparison with PAM.

2   Preliminaries

2.1   Analyzing Customer Purchasing Behavior for EC Sites

First, we describe the e-commerce site that we will be using in this research. There is a huge variety of items on EC sites, and users select the items they want to purchase by browsing EC sites. The purpose of this research is to develop new marketing strategies by analyzing the trends of items that users prefer. Nowadays, the analysis of e-commerce sites is conducted in a variety of situations, and e-commerce sites that handle items of various categories such as Amazon [6] and Rakuten Ichiba [7] are well known. A variety of analysis methods have been used to analyze EC sites, including methods that use latent representations of items and user information embedded in a space for analysis and item recommendation [8], and methods that analyze matrix decomposition of vectors that represent the purchases of users and items [9]. In this research, we focus on topic models that can extract potential user preference patterns based on users' purchase histories. In addition, when analyzing user preference patterns, it is necessary to associate them with "product categories" that are assigned by e-commerce sites to manage items, so that the analysis results can be easily used from the viewpoint of site operators. A product category is information that is assigned in advance by an e-commerce site based on the purpose of use, etc., in order to manage a large number and variety of items, and often has a hierarchical structure such as major categories and subcategories. Table 1 shows some of the categories assigned to the actual items on Rakuten Ichiba items [10] that is a famous EC site of shopping moll type in Jappan.

Table 1. Some of the categories assigned to Rakuten Ichiba items

Major category	Subcategory
Sports, Outdoors	Sportswear, Accessories
	Tennis
	Swimming
Ladies' fashion	Coats, Jackets
	Bottoms
	Dress
Foods	Breads, Jams, Cereals
	Seafood, Fishery products
	Processed meat, Meat products

From Table 1, we can see that for a given major category, there are multiple subcategories. To give a concrete example, an item called "swimsuit" is categorized as "Sports, Outdoors" in the major category and "Swimming" in the minor category. In this research, we will conduct an analysis focusing on the categories of items with this hierarchical structure.

2.2 Topic Model

The topic model is a method that assumes a latent topic behind the process of document generation, and models the word generation according to these topics as a document. Topic models generally represent the co-occurrence relationship between documents and words, and it is possible to represent and analyze the relationship between data with a huge number of dimensions by using "latent topics".

Latent Dirichlet Allocation (LDA) [3] is a topic model proposed by Blei et al. as a kind of language model that assumes that a document is generated from multiple topics. By applying this model to purchase history data, the probability distribution of occurrence of latent topics and the probability distribution of occurrence of items for each topic are assumed for users, and it is possible to analyze user preferences based on topics.

We define the notations used in this research. Let the user set be $\mathcal{U} = \{1,\ldots,U\}$, the itemset be $\mathcal{X} = \{1,\ldots,X\}$, and a set of K latent topics $\mathcal{K} = \{1,\ldots,K\}$. The topic distribution of user $u \in \mathcal{U}$ is denoted by $\boldsymbol{\theta}_u = (\theta_{u,1},\ldots,\theta_{u,K})$, and the topic assignment of the ith item of user u is $z_{u,i}$. The item distribution in topic $k \in \mathcal{K}$ is denoted by $\boldsymbol{\phi}_k = (\phi_{k,1},\ldots,\phi_{k,X})$. Let $x_{u,i} \in \mathcal{X}$ denote the ith item purchased by user u. The simultaneous distribution of each variable $x_{u,i}$, $z_{u,i}$, $\boldsymbol{\phi}_k$, and $\boldsymbol{\theta}_u$ is represented by Eq. (1).

$$p(x_{u,i}, z_{u,i}, \boldsymbol{\phi}_k, \boldsymbol{\theta}_u) = p\left(x_{u,i} \mid z_{u,i}, \boldsymbol{\phi}_k\right) p\left(z_{u,i} \mid \boldsymbol{\theta}_u\right) p\left(\boldsymbol{\phi}_k\right) p\left(\boldsymbol{\theta}_u\right) \qquad (1)$$

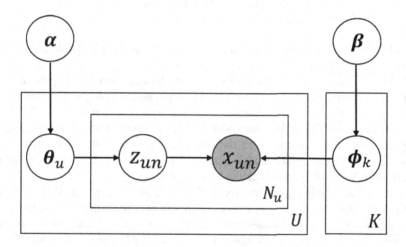

Fig. 1. Graphical model of LDA

The graphical model of LDA is represented by Fig. 1. Here, the topic distribution of user u is $\boldsymbol{\theta}_u$, and the item distribution in topic $k \in \mathcal{K}$ is $\boldsymbol{\phi}_k$, assuming a Dirichlet distribution for the prior distribution. Set the hyperparameter of the Dirichlet distribution assumed for the topic distribution $\boldsymbol{\theta}_u$ of user u to $\boldsymbol{\alpha} = (\alpha_1,\ldots,\alpha_k)$, and Let the hyperparameter of the item distribution $\boldsymbol{\phi}_k$ in topic $k \in \mathcal{K}$ be $\boldsymbol{\beta} = (\beta_1,\ldots,\beta_k)$. By analyzing the topics in detail, we can learn the user's preferences and the nature of the items.

2.3 Hierarchical Topic Model

In this research, we analyze customer preferences in more detail by giving hierarchy to the topics that express latent preferences, since the user's purchase history data has multiple topics. In this paper, we explain the Pachinko Allocation

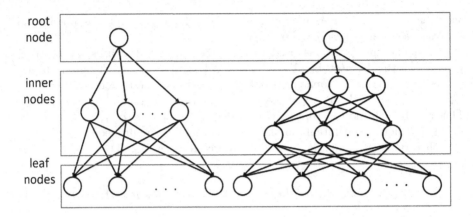

root node

inner nodes

leaf nodes

Fig. 2. LDA and PAM DAG structure

Model (PAM), which is a hierarchical topic model that inspired this research, in comparison with LDA.

PAM is a model that can represent correlations between topics and co-occurrences of multiple topics. This PAM is represented using a directed acyclic graph (DAG) [13], and the differences in the model structure from LDA are shown in Fig. 2. In this DAG, each leaf node represents an item. Internal nodes other than leaf nodes correspond to topics and have a distribution over child nodes. In PAM, the relationships among all topics can be analyzed by co-occurrence relationships with higher-level topics.

Another commonly known hierarchical topic model other than PAM is hLDA [4]. Like PAM, this model represents topics under multiple hierarchies, but because it is based on the Chinese restaurant process [14], it has a tree structure in which a lower level topic belongs to only one of the higher level topics. Therefore, although it is possible to analyze lower-level topics from higher-level topics, it is desirable to have a PAM-like structure in order to analyze higher-level topics based on lower-level topics.

3   Proposed Method

3.1   Overview

In hLDA, the hierarchical structure of topics is limited to a branching structure represented by a tree structure, so it cannot represent relationships such as a network structure between all higher and lower topics. On the other hand, in PAM, all the higher and lower topics are connected by a network, but the parameters of the estimated model are easily affected by the initial values, resulting in topic variation, making it difficult to obtain stable interpretation results. Therefore, expressing the hierarchy of user preferences by analysis using hLDA and PAM is not better for decision making in business.

Therefore, in this research, we consider expressing the hierarchy of user preferences by using LDA, which has high stability against initial values. However, since LDA has only one topic hierarchy, it cannot express the hierarchy as it is. All items on the e-commerce site to be analyzed in this research are assigned product categories that have a hierarchical structure, such as large categories and small categories, in order to manage the huge number of items. Therefore, we consider using the hierarchical information of product categories assigned to the items to express the hierarchy of topics. Specifically, we consider a model that constructs a higher-level LDA and a lower-level LDA with different granularity of hierarchical category information of items, and combines these two LDAs to represent the hierarchy of topics. For this purpose, we first apply LDA to the purchase history data of both major and minor categories to generate topics. Next, we calculate the topic relevance score, which quantifies the strength of the relationship between topics in the large and small categories, and use this value to construct a more stable topic hierarchy than PAM. By using this value, we can construct a more stable topic hierarchy than PAM. This enables us to obtain stable topics by using product categories and to analyze the hierarchy of user preferences.

3.2   Structure of the Proposed Model

A model for topic analysis that takes into account the hierarchical categorical information of items is described below. First, let $x_{u,i}$ denote the ith item purchased by user u in the proposed model as well as in LDA.

In the proposed model, $x_{u,i}$ is defined as $x_{u,i}^B$ and $x_{u,i}^S$, which are one-hot vector representations of products in large (major) and small (sub) categories, respectively. The topics obtained by applying LDA to the purchase history data of the large category of items are defined as B-topics, and the topics obtained from the purchase history data of the small category are defined as S-topics. The number of topics is defined as K and M.

Using these transformed item vectors for each category, we perform LDA for each category. Referring to Eq. (1), the simultaneous distribution of each variable $x_{u,i}^B$, $z_{u,i}$, ϕ_k, and θ_u in the LDA based on the large category is expressed in Eq. (2).

$$p(x_{u,i}^B, z_{u,i}, \phi_k, \theta_u) = p\left(x_{u,i}^B \mid z_{u,i}, \phi_k\right) p\left(z_{u,i} \mid \theta_u\right) p\left(\phi_k\right) p\left(\theta_u\right) \qquad (2)$$

Similarly, the simultaneous distribution of each variable $x_{u,i}^S$, $v_{u,i}$, ϕ_m, and θ_u in the subcategory-based LDA is represented by Eq. (3).

$$p(x_{u,i}^S, v_{u,i}, \phi_m, \theta_u) = p\left(x_{u,i}^S \mid v_{u,i}, \phi_m\right) p\left(v_{u,i} \mid \theta_u\right) p\left(\phi_m\right) p\left(\theta_u\right) \qquad (3)$$

Based on these equations, the proposed method first estimates each topic $\mathcal{Z} = \{z_k \mid 1 \leq k \leq K\}$ and $\mathcal{V} = \{v_m \mid 1 \leq m \leq M\}$, and then estimate the item distributions ϕ_k and ϕ_m in z_k and v_m.

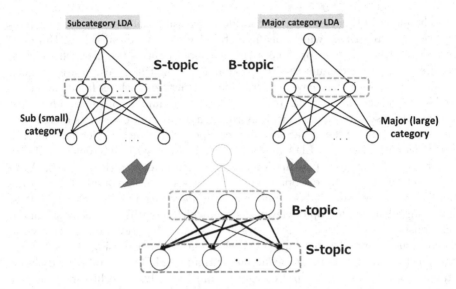

Fig. 3. B-topic and S-topic LDA

After learning each category by LDA, B-topic and S-topic are combined based on the topic relevance score, as shown in Fig. 3. In this way, we can extract topics of different hierarchies based on the same training data and build a model that can be analyzed across multiple topics. In the following, we describe the topic relevance score used here.

3.3 Topic Relevance Score

The topic relevance score is a value that expresses the relationship between the topics of the B-topic and the S-topic. First, in order to calculate the topic relevance score, the generated B-topic and S-topic are connected through the items included in the B-topic. Then, to define the relevance between topics, we utilize the hierarchical structure of the product categories owned by the e-commerce site, such as large and small categories.

Specifically, we assume that a B-topic and an S-topic that contains items belonging to a subcategory of a lower level of the items contained in the B-topic are highly related. For example, the topic of food obtained in the large category and the topic of sweets obtained in the small category have a hierarchical inclu-sion relationship in the product category, and thus can be regarded as highly related. Let the number of large categories be Q, the q-th large category be G_q, the number of small categories belonging to the q-th large category be N_q, and the n-th small category belonging to the q-th large category be G_{qn}. In this case, the topic relevance score can be calculated using Eq. (4) by applying the method [15] of Okawa et al.

$$\gamma_{k,m} = \sum_{q=1}^{Q} p\left(G_q \mid z_k\right) \sum_{n=1}^{N_q} p\left(g_{qn} \mid v_m\right) \tag{4}$$

Here $\gamma_{k,m}$ is defined as the topic relevance score between z_k and v_m, $p\left(G_q \mid z_k\right)$ is the probability that the q-th major category G_q appears under z_k, and $p\left(G_{qn} \mid v_m\right)$ denotes the probability of the appearance of the subcategory G_{qn} belonging to the q-th large category under v_m. For each B-topic and S-topic, we normalize the sum of the topic relevance scores to be 1 using Eqs. (5) and (6), and the affiliation probability of the B-topic's topic with the S-topic's topic is defined by Eq. (6).

$$\widetilde{p}\left(v_m \mid z_k\right) = \frac{\gamma_{k,m}}{\sum_j \gamma_{k,j}} \tag{5}$$

$$\widetilde{p}\left(z_k \mid v_m\right) = \frac{\gamma_{k,m}}{\sum_l \gamma_{l,m}} \tag{6}$$

From the above affiliation probabilities, we can express the hierarchical relationship between each topic based on both large and small categories, and obtain a model with the structure shown in Fig. 3. This makes it possible to analyze the hierarchy of user preferences.

4   Actual Data Analysis

In this section, we analyze the data using actual purchase history data of an e-commerce site. From the analysis results obtained by the proposed method, we discuss the hierarchy of topics using product categories.

4.1   Data Set and Analysis Conditions

In this research, we analyzed the evaluation review data of Rakuten Ichiba in 2019 [10]. We analyzed the evaluation review data of Rakuten Ichiba in 2019 using citedata. Since it is considered that the evaluation review data is basically the evaluation of items purchased by users, we regarded the evaluation review as a purchase history and analyzed it. Of this purchase history data, users with six or fewer evaluations were extracted, and the data of items with two or fewer evaluations were removed in advance for analysis. As a result, the total number of purchase histories was 1,774,493, the number of users was 172,912, and the number of items was 67,498. The average number of purchases by users was 10.26, and the average number of items purchased was 26.29. There are two types of product categories in the experimental data: large category and small category. The numbers of large and small categories are 39 and 437, respectively. The numbers of B-topic (the number of topics in the large category) and S-topic (the number of topics in the small category) were set to $K=6$ and $M=18$, respectively, from the viewpoint of the value of the learning evaluation function and interpretability. All elements of the hyperparameter $\boldsymbol{\alpha}$ used in each model were set to 0.1, $\beta = 0.1$, and the models were trained.

Table 2. Top 5 large categories of each B-topic

	z_0	z_1
Top.1	Sports, Outdoors	Kids, Baby, Maternity
Top.2	Smartphones, Tablets	Daily necessities, Stationery, Handicrafts
Top.3	Car and Motorcycle accessories	Interior, Bedding, Storage
Top.4	Bags, Accessories, Brand-name goods	Pets, Pet goods
Top.5	Men's Fashion	Kitchenware, Tableware and utensils
	z_2	z_3
Top.1	Foods	Beauty, Cosmetics, Perfume
Top.2	Sweets, Confectionery	Diet, Health
Top.3	Water and Soft drinks	Daily necessities, Stationery, Handicrafts
Top.4	Beer and Western liquor	Pharmaceuticals, Contact lenses, Nursing care
Top.5	Daily necessities, Stationery, Handicrafts	Water and Soft drinks
	z_4	z_5
Top.1	Flowers, Garden	Women's Fashion
Top.2	Hobby Goods	Bags, Accessories, Brand-name goods
Top.3	Jewelry, Accessories	Innerwear, Underwear, Nightwear
Top.4	Daily necessities, Stationery, Handicrafts	Shoes
Top.5	Interior, Bedding, Storage	Jewelry, Accessories

4.2 Result

In order to confirm the analysis results of the proposed method, the top five categories of items with high probability of belonging in each topic (B-topic and S-topic) are shown in Table 2 and Table 3.

From Table 2, it can be seen that z_0 is a user who prefers items related to men's hobbies, z_1 is a user whose life has changed after childbirth, z_2 is a user who is highly conscious of beauty, z_3 is a user who tends to purchase food, z_4 is a user who prefers items related to home lifestyle, and z_5 is a user who prefers women's brands and fashion. We can see that z_4 is a topic for users who prefer items related to their home lifestyle, and z_5 is a topic for users who prefer women's brands and fashion. In this large category trend, z_2 and z_3 are topics that belong to the category of items that are used on a daily basis and are likely to be purchased regularly. As an overall topic, we were able to extract the relationship between users' lifestyles and the items they purchase accordingly.

Next, analyzing some specific topics from Table 3, we can see that v_2 is the topic of diet food, v_4 is the topic of food, and v_{11} is the topic of children's products. Comparing with Table 2, we can confirm that more detailed topics are obtained. In particular, v_4 seems to be similar to the topic of z_3, but food tends to appear mainly and beverages do not appear at the top. This indicates that users who prefer foods tend to be interested in other foods and purchase them, and that beverages and foods have different tendencies. In addition, since

Table 3. Top 5 small categories of each S-topic

	v_0	v_1	v_2
Top.1	Women's Jewelry Accessories	Contact lenses and care products	Supplements
Top.2	Bags	CD	Nuts
Top.3	Stationery Office Supplies	Nursing care products	Diet foods
Top.4	Tableware CutleryGlass	Comics	Health foods
Top.5	Wallets and Cases	Body Piercing	Bread, Jam, Cereal
	v_3	v_4	v_5
Top.1	Bedding	Seafood Fishery products	Sundries
Top.2	Storage furniture	Side dish	Tea
Top.3	Sundries	Fruits	Coffee
Top.4	Carpets, Mats, Tatami mats	Processed meat, Meat products	Flavoring
Top.5	Air conditioning appliances	Vegetables	Water
	v_6	v_7	v_8
Top.1	Dog supplies	Tops	Skincare
Top.2	Pet care supplies	Bottoms	Hair care, Styling
Top.3	Chuhai, Highball Cocktail	Women's shoes	Ladies
Top.4	Pet tableware waterers, feeders	Dress	Base make up
Top.5	Air conditioning appliances	Ladies	Body care
	v_9	v_{10}	v_{11}
Top.1	Kids	Tops	Baby
Top.2	Lunchboxes and water bottles	Rice, Millet	Toy
Top.3	Marine sports	Golf	Maternity
Top.4	Stationery Office Supplies	Men's shoes	Party and Event supplies
Top.5	TV game	Men's	Collection
	v_{12}	v_{13}	v_{14}
Top.1	Cat supplies	Gardening agriculture	Handicrafts, Crafts, Fabrics
Top.2	Smoking gear	Flowers and plants	Fortune telling Feng Shui, Power stone
Top.3	Baseball, Softball	Exteriors and Garden furniture	Skateboarding
Top.4	Pet care supplies	Buddhist altar, Buddhist tools and Sacred objects	Stationery Office Supplies
Top.5	Pet tableware waterers, feeders	Interior decorations	Home appliances
	v_{15}	v_{16}	v_{17}
Top.1	Accessories for smartphones and cell phones	PC supplies and consumables	Car accessories
Top.2	Nail polish	Accessories, Parts	Outdoors
Top.3	Cables and conversion adapters for smartphones and tablets	Sportswear accessories	DIY tools
Top.4	Batteries, Chargers	Tablet PC accessories	Cycling
Top.5	Tropical fishes Aquariums	Beer and Western liquor	Motorcycle accessories

beverages are likely to be purchased with other items, they appear in a variety of topics.

In addition, to check the hierarchy of user preferences, the affiliation probability of each S-topic at z_1 is shown in Table 4, and the affiliation probability of each B-topic at v_2 is shown in Table 5.

Table 4. Value of $\widetilde{p}(v_m \mid z_1)$ in z_1

	v_0	v_1	v_2	v_3	v_4	v_5
z_1	0.0551	0.0056	0.0047	0.1320	0.0040	0.0672
	v_6	v_7	v_8	v_9	v_{10}	v_{11}
z_1	0.1247	0.0076	0.0106	0.1327	0.0057	0.1318
	v_{12}	v_{13}	v_{14}	v_{15}	v_{16}	v_{17}
z_1	0.0682	0.0472	0.1505	0.2087	0.0231	0.0084

From Table 4, we can see that the probabilities of belonging to S-topics v_3, v_6, v_9, v_{11}, v_{14}, and v_{15} are high for z_1. These S-topics are the topics of furniture, pet supplies, children's items, maternity items, handicraft items, and smartphone peripherals. It can be seen that "a group that purchases not only children's items but also pet supplies" exists among the z_1 group that tends to purchase children's items and daily necessities due to changes in their lives after giving birth. The high probability of belonging to v_{15} seems to be an unnatural topic, but since nail polish is also included in the topic of smartphone peripherals, we can analyze that it is related to the interest in the design of things that users wear as well as accessories for smartphones and cell phones. When the analysis focuses on topics related to changes in lifestyle, we are able to analyze the detailed trends separately for each topic.

Table 5. Value of $\widetilde{p}(z_k \mid v_2)$ in z_2

	z_0	z_1	z_2	z_3	z_4	z_5
v_2	0.0139	0.0221	**0.6154**	**0.3451**	0.0004	0.0032

Also, from Table 5, the topic of diet food in v_2 has a high probability of belonging to the B-topic z_2 of users who are highly conscious of beauty and to the B-topic z_3 of users who have a high tendency to purchase food. Also, from Table 5, the topic of diet food in v_2 has a high probability of belonging to the B-topic z_2 of users who are highly conscious of beauty and to the B-topic z_3 of users who have a high tendency to purchase food. Therefore, even within the same group that tends to purchase diet foods, there are two aspects: one is the topic of user preference interested in beauty, and the other is the topic of user preference that leads to purchase a variety of foods, not limited to diet foods. If we consider the top-occurring categories of v_2, supplements can be considered only as health foods, while nuts can be considered both as beauty foods and as snacks or sweets for alcoholic beverages, etc. In this way, by analyzing detailed topics separately in terms of larger topics, it is possible to search for the causes of one product category appearing together with other product categories. In conclusion, the proposed method enables us to analyze the hierarchy of user preferences.

5   Experiment to Evaluate the Dependence of Parameters on Initial Values

In this section, we compare the proposed model with PAM, which is one of the methods assuming hierarchy in topics, in order to show that the proposed model is less sensitive to the initial values of parameters in learning.

5.1   Experimental Conditions

The numbers of large and small categories of the experimental data are 39 and 437, respectively, as in purchase data analysis. Experiments were conducted with 100 different initial values of parameters in the proposed model and PAM. Applying the purchase history data of subcategories to PAM, we set the number of super topics as $s_1 = 6$ and that of subtopics as $s_2 = 18$. In evaluating the dependence of parameters on initial values, it is important to focus on the difference of items with high probability of belonging to each topic when interpreting the topics. Therefore, as an evaluation method, the Jaccard coefficients of the top 10 categories with the highest probability of affiliation in each topic obtained by each proposed method and PAM were calculated. The Jaccard coefficient is an index that can measure the degree of agreement between topics.

5.2   Result

The results of topic evaluation by Jaccard coefficient for the top 10 categories of LDA and PAM are shown in Table 6.

Table 6. Jaccard coefficients for the top 10 categories of LDA and PAM

	Jaccard coefficients
Proposed	**0.7112**
PAM	0.5913

From Table 6, the proposed method showed a higher value of Jaccard coefficient than PAM. Therefore, the proposed method is less sensitive to the initial value than PAM, indicating that the proposed method provides stable topic interpretation results.

6   Discussions

6.1   Effectiveness of the Proposed Method

In this research, by applying LDA to each of the large and small categories, which are generally defined by product categories, we were able to obtain interpretation results with different granularity. This made it possible to analyze the user's general preferences for the topic B-topic obtained from the large category and the user's detailed preferences for the topic S-topic obtained from the small category. Furthermore, by using the topic relevance score, which is a value that quantifies the strength of the relationship between B-topic and S-topic, the topics obtained from the large and small categories respectively, it is possible to analyze the user's preferences in more detail. By using the topic relevance score, which is a value that quantifies the strength of the relationship between the B-topic and the S-topic, it is possible to analyze user preferences in more detail. When the S-topic is used as the criterion, it is possible to analyze the different aspects of the preferences of the user groups that purchase the items. In addition, because we analyzed user preferences using categories, we believe that it is possible to send direct mail and issue coupons by category as is in marketing measures in actual business. Similarly, in the design of e-commerce site screens, we can consider measures such as placing categories that are considered to have a high probability of being purchased nearby for groups of users with the same preferences. The proposed method can be applied not only to e-commerce sites but also to retail stores, music and movie viewing sites.

6.2   On Evaluating the Dependence of Parameters on Initial Values

For LDA used in the proposed method and PAM, which is one of the models assuming hierarchy in topics, we conducted real data analysis by changing the initial values of parameters, and confirmed that LDA is not easily affected by the initial values. We can infer from the value of the Jaccard coefficient that user preferences are obtained stably. We confirmed that LDA is less sensitive to the initial values of the parameters. This means that the proposed method using LDA can obtain stable topic interpretation results and provide useful insights for decision making in business.

7   Conclusion and Future Work

In this research, we proposed a hierarchical topic model that can represent the hierarchy of topics by considering the categorical information of items. The novelty of our proposal can be described as follows. The hLDA and PAM, which assume hierarchy, are unable to interpret topics stably, but our proposal resolved these problems by utilizing the pre-defined hierarchical categories of items. Furthermore, by defining the topic relevance score in the proposed analysis, it becomes possible to analyze user preferences based on the topic of each level.

Finally, by applying the proposed method to actual data from an e-commerce site, we show an example of category-based analysis of user preferences, demonstrating the usefulness of the proposed method. The results of this research enabled us to analyze user preferences from a hierarchical perspective using the hierarchical relationship of items that is generally defined in product masters. This enables analysis that reflects the hierarchical structure of items, and is expected to contribute to the planning of more specific measures.

As an extension of the proposed model, we can consider building a model that considers not only the auxiliary information of category information assigned to items, but also the attribute information of users. In this way, we can obtain detailed analysis results by taking into account both the user's attribute information and the item's auxiliary information, and we can expect more user-oriented marketing measures.

Acknowledgements. In this paper, we used "Rakuten Dataset" (https://rit.rakuten.com/data_release/) provided by Rakuten Group, Inc. via IDR Dataset Service of National Institute of Informatics, Japan. We gratefully acknowledge the provision of the precious dataset. This work was supported by JSPS for Scientific Research No. 21H04600.

References

1. Satomura, T.: Integrated analysis of customer data using topic models (Topikku-moderu niyoru kokyakude-ta no tougoutekibunseki). Commun. Oper. Res. Soc. Jpn. **63**(2), 67–74 (2018)
2. Iwata, T., Sawada, H.: Topic model for analyzing purchase data with price information. Data Min. Knowl. Disc. **26**, 559–573 (2013)
3. Blei, D.M., Ng, A.Y., Jordan, M.I.: Latent dirichlet allocation. Mach. Learn. **45**(1), 5–32 (2001)
4. Blei, D.M., Griffiths, T.L., Jordan, M.I., Tenenbaum, J.B.: Hierarchical topic models and the nested Chinese restaurant process. In: Advances in Neural Information Processing Systems, pp. 17–24 (2004)
5. Li, W., McCallum, A.: Pachinko allocation: DAG-structured mixture models of topic correlations. In: Proceedings of the 23rd International Conference on Machine Learning, pp. 577–584 (2006)
6. Amazon. https://www.amazon.co.jp/
7. Rakuten Ichiba. https://www.rakuten.co.jp/
8. He, R., Wang-Cheng, K., McAuley, J.: Translationbased recommendation. In: 11th ACM Conference on Recommender Systems, pp. 161–169 (2017)
9. Kohjima, M., Matsubayashi, T., Sawada, H.: Non-negative multiple matrix factorization for consumer behavior pattern extraction by considering attribution information. J. Jpn. Soc. Artif. Intell. **30**(6), SP1-G, 745–754 (2015)
10. Rakuten Group Inc.: Rakuten Ichiba Data. National Institute of Informatics National Institute of Informatics (NII) Data Repository for Informatics Research (Dataset) (2014). https://doi.org/10.32130/idr.2.1
11. Iwata, T., Watanabe, S., Yamada, T., Ueda, N.: Topic tracking model for purchase behavior analysis. IEICE Trans. Inf. Syst. **J93-D**(6), 978–987 (2010)

12. Iwata, T., Sawada, H.: Topic model for analyzing purchase data with price information. Data Min. Knowl. Disc. **26**(3), 559–573 (2012)
13. Thulasiraman, K., Swamy, M.N.S.: Graphs: Theory and Algorithms. Wiley, Hoboken (2011)
14. Blei, D.M., Griffiths, T.L., Jordan, M.I.: The nested Chinese restaurant process and Bayesian nonparametric inference of topic hierarchies. J. ACM (JACM) **57**(2), 1–30 (2010)
15. Okawa, J., Kumoi, G., Goto, M.: Relationship analysis of query and answer documents based on latent dirichlet allocation and its application. J. Manag. Inf. Soc. **29**(1), 39–54 (2020)
16. Iwata, T.: Topic Model. Kodansha, in Japanese (2015)
17. George, E.I., McCulloch, R.E.: Variable selection via Gibbs sampling. J. Am. Stat. Assoc. **88**(423), 881–889 (1993)
18. Ovsjanikov, M., Chen, Y.: Topic modeling for personalized recommendation of volatile items. In: Proceedings of ECML/PKDD 2010, pp. 483–498 (2010)
19. Wang, J., Huang, P., Zhao, H., Zhang, Z., Zhao, B., Lee, D.L.: Billion-scale commodity embedding for e-commerce recommendation in Alibaba. In: KDD 2018, pp. 839–848 (2018)

Resale Price Prediction Model for Used Electrical Products Using Deep Neural Network

Shinnosuke Terasawa[1], Kohei Otake[2], and Takashi Namatame[3(✉)]

[1] Graduate School of Science and Engineering, Chuo University, 1-13-27, Kasuga, Bunkyo-ku, Tokyo 112-8551, Japan

[2] School of Information and Telecommunication Engineering, Tokai University, 2-3-23, Takanawa, Minato-ku, Tokyo 108-8619, Japan
otake@tsc.u-tokai.ac.jp

[3] Faculty of Science and Engineering, Chuo University, 1-13-27, Kasuga, Bunkyo-ku, Tokyo 112-8551, Japan
nama@kc.chuo-u.ac.jp

Abstract. This study suggested the Deep Neural Network (DNN) model to estimate the ratio of reuse price to list price in the electrical industry, so that it can help to decide resale price. In reuse industry, the pricing is particularly important. First, we constructed one multiple regression model and two DNN models. The DNN models are divided according to the handling methods of categorical variables, One-hot vector and entity embedding. We introduced some explanatory variables in consideration the complicated consumer's emotion for products price. Next, we utilized and evaluated these models. As the result, DNN with entity embedding is the best model based on correlation coefficient and RSME. However, we found that this model did not fit for the data of bulk buying. Lastly, we mentioned the problem of this model to improve accuracy.

Keywords: Deep Neural Network · Neural network · Reuse item pricing

1 Introduction

Reuse market in Japan has been growing since 2009, this market's size estimated to reach 2.4 trillion yen by 2020 [1]. Even in the pandemic of COVID-19, the entire market has expanding, but the expansion of the reuse market in EC (e-commerce) is remarkable. There is not only the trend of flea market application but environmental consideration by attention for SDGs in this background. Pricing of used goods is one of the issues that should be mentioned in the reuse market, which is expected to grow in the future. In the C to C reuse market, the exhibiters have to decide the price of reused goods, and it is important to set the appropriate price that will induce purchase. In the general reuse industry, profits are made by reselling the reuse goods purchased from consumers, that is, the price at the time of purchasing the reuse goods from consumers linked to the price at the time which it is resold. Hence the pricing is important as well.

G. Meiselwitz (Ed.): HCII 2022, LNCS 13316, pp. 359–374, 2022.
https://doi.org/10.1007/978-3-031-05064-0_27

2 Purpose of This Study

There has already been a lot of study for pricing, and it is found that many factors affect pricing [2]. Although who can decide the price is seller, it is also true that the consumer's feelings of price influence the pricing. In this study, we use the sales data of companies that sell not only new electric products but used ones at both real-stores and ECs. We will consider how much it should be discounted from the list price of a new product when it is resold, instead of estimating the resale price directly. By estimating the resale price in this way, we believe that it can also be used for setting price when purchasing reuse goods from consumers. For the estimation model of the ratio of reuse price to list price, in other words $(1 - Discount)$, we use multiple regression analysis and neural network technique with some explanatory variables that can be considered as factors of price fluctuations. In addition, we evaluate these models respectively and select the optimum one.

3 Datasets

In this study, we use the sales data provided by the company that sells new and used electrical products at both real-stores and EC. In particular, we focus on 580 types of reuse goods sales data that has 500 and more transactions. Table 1 shows the summary of datasets of this study.

Table 1. The summary of datasets

Period	2017/1/1–2021/8/31
Number of products	580
Number of sales transaction	1,010,399

We collect the release date of products and the number of searched on Google apart from above datasets. We explain the detail of variables used in this study below.

3.1 Objective Variable

The "Ratio of reuse price to list price" (hereinafter, this is called "RRP") as an objective variable used in the estimate models calculated by Eq. 1. The numerator "The actual resale price of reuse goods" is the amount actually paid by the consumer at the time of purchase after using points and coupons. This is because consumers themselves thought that they would refer to the price on the premise of using points and coupons when making a purchase. The denominator "The list price of the new goods" is the price set by the target company for new products.

$$RRP = \frac{The\ actual\ resale\ price\ of\ reuse\ goods}{The\ list\ price\ of\ the\ new\ goods} \tag{1}$$

3.2 Explanatory Variables

In this section, we explain the continuous and categorical variables separately as explanatory variables.

Continuous Variables. There are 4 continuous variables: "Elapsed days", "Purchased points", "New goods cost" and "Google search count".

Elapsed Days. It's an elapsed-days from the release date of the new good to the point of sales date of purchased the reuse one. We introduce to consider the oldness.

No. of Purchased. It's the number of purchased for each product by the date when each used goods was purchased. We introduced to consider the trend.

New Goods Cost. It's a price when purchasing the new goods. We introduce to consider the price range.

Google Search Count. It's the number of times the product name was searched on the search engine Google in the week in which it was purchased. We introduced to consider the topicality. This data was collected using Google Trend.

Categorical Variables. There are 2 categorical variables: "Store" and "Goods category". Details shown below.

Store. The target company in this study has 33 real stores and 5 EC. We classified these sales channel into 6 and labeled 1 to 6. Table 2 shows the label number and classification.

Table 2. The label number of stores

Label	Classification	Number of sales transactions
1	"Flagship shop"	334,450
2	"Central of Tokyo", "Osaka", "Yokohama"	330,032
3	"Suburbs of Tokyo", "Saitama"	90,121
4	"Provincial city"	129,471
5	"Downtown"	39,259
6	"e-commerce"	88,066

Goods Category. We use the category number attached to each product by the target company, but we combined the categories that have low number of sales transactions into one category. Table 3 shows the label number of goods categories.

Table 3. The label number of goods categories

Label	Category	Number of sales transactions
1	"Game"	640,540
2	"PC-soft"	296,645
3	"Others"	73,214

4 Estimation Models

In this study, we use the multiple regression analysis and neural network to estimate the RRP. We construct two types neural networks separately depending on how categorical variables are handled, One-Hot Vector and Entity Embedding. Hence we construct 3 types models. In the training of all models, we divide the all data randomly into 80% for training data and the remaining 20% for test data, and the same training and test data are used so that there is no difference between the models. We describe the details of constructed models below.

4.1 Multiple Regression

Multiple regression is one of the liner regression models, and it is a model that estimate the objective variable by liner function with explanatory variables. The linear regression model models the relationship between cause and effect for a phenomenon. In particularly in multiple regression, explanatory variables $(x_1, \ldots, x_M)$ can be formulate an objective variable (y) as Eq. 2. This function is straight line that fits best for the data in the M dimensional space.

$$y = \sum_{m=1}^{M} w_m x_m + b \tag{2}$$

w: The weights of explanatory variables, : The intercept.

Since the objective variable is a ratio in this study, we believe that it is difficult to express it as a liner function. Therefore, we utilize logit transformation for the objective variable. The logit transformation is to convert using Eq. 3.

$$R = \frac{1}{1 + e^{-f(x)}}$$
$$e^{-f(x)}R = 1 - R$$
$$f(x) = \log R - \log(1 - R) \tag{3}$$
$$\log \frac{R}{1 - R} = f(x)$$

$f(x)$: The linear function, : The objective variable.

Table 4 shows the correlation coefficients between the explanatory variables (continuous variables), and we confirmed that there is no multicollinearity. We standardize each explanatory variable distribution so that the mean is 0 and the variance is 1.

Table 4. The correlation coefficients

	Elapsed days	Purchased points	New goods cost	Google search count
Elapsed days	1.000	0.164	0.205	−0.096
Purchased points	0.164	1.000	−0.103	0.096
New goods cost	0.205	−0.103	1.000	−0.213
Google search count	−0.096	0.096	−0.213	1.000

Table 5 shows the result of the multiple regression. We select variables using Akaike's Information Criterion (AIC) and treat the categorical variables as factor types, Therefore, the result based on the partial regression coefficient of label = 1 as 0.

Table 5. Result of multiple regression

	Coefficient	P value
Intercept	0.739	0.000
Elapsed days	−0.316	0.000
Purchased points	0.115	0.000
New goods cost	0.045	0.000
Google search count	0.262	0.000
Store 2	0.036	0.000
Store 3	0.083	0.000
Store 4	0.092	0.000
Store 5	−0.016	0.026
Store 6	−0.237	0.000
Category 2	−0.231	0.000
Category 3	0.066	0.000

As shown in Table 5, all coefficients are 5% significant. At this time, the adjusted R-squared is 0.126.

4.2 Neural Network

Neural network (NN) is one of the algorithms in the field of artificial intelligence, and is a technology that simulates the learning function of the human brain with a computer. The learning function is reproduced by combining artificial neurons that imitate nerve cells in the brain. This artificial neuron is called the perceptron, Fig. 1 shows the perceptron takes two inputs and outputs one value.

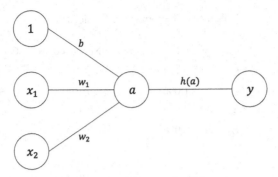

Fig. 1. The structure of perceptron

In this time, the sum of inputs a can be expressed as Eq. 4 using weight w and bias b. $h(x)$ is called activation function, and it decides the shape of an output – namely, the output $y = h(a)$.

$$a = b + w_1x_1 + w_2x_2 \tag{4}$$

Figure 2 shows NN is a combination of perceptrons, and has one input layer and on output layer, and multiple hidden layers.

Input layer takes initial information as a value and hand over to the hidden layer. The hidden layer execute various analyzes on the information taking from input layer. Each unit adds the information from the units of the previous layer, converts it with the activation function, and transmits it to the next layer. Therefore, the more hidden layers there are, the more complex the analysis becomes possible. Among them, NN which has 3 or more hidden layers is called "Deep Neural Network" (DNN).

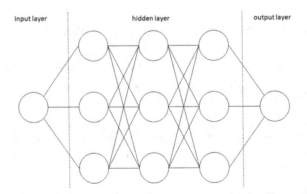

Fig. 2. The structure of neural network

The weights in constructed model learn to minimize the margin outputs and true values. At this time, we have to define the loss function to calculate this margin. In this study, we use mean square error (MSE) as a loss function. MSE is calculated as Eq. 5 for n numbers data.

$$MSE = \frac{1}{n}\sum_{i=1}^{n}(\hat{y}_i - y_i)^2 \tag{5}$$

Even if we change parameters randomly to minimize the loss function, it could not be learned well. The optimization function is used to obtain this optimum parameter efficiently. In this study, we use RMSprop as optimization function. The RMSprop is a way to obtain the optimum parameter quickly by adjusting the learning rate in the Stochastic Gradient Descent (SGD). SGD calculate gradient from the data only for mini-batch-size and update the parameters. At this time, if the leaning ratio is too high, there is a possibility cause vibration. Then the RMSprop changes the learning rate according to the gradient as Eq. 6.

$$E\left[g^2\right]_t = \beta E\left[g^2\right]_{t-1} + (1-\beta)\left(\frac{\delta C}{\delta w}\right)^2$$

$$w_t = w_{t-1} - \frac{\eta}{\sqrt{E\left[g^2\right]_t}} \frac{\delta C}{\delta w} \tag{6}$$

$E\left[g^2\right]$: The moving average of squared gradient, : The learning rate,
$\frac{\delta C}{\delta w}$: The gradient of loss function for weight, : The moving average parameter.

In this study, we utilize a DNN model to estimate the RRP with reference to Namatame's paper [3]. And we construct 2 types DNN models according to how handle categorical variables "One-Hot Vector" and "Entity Embedding". We explain details of these models.

One-Hot Vector. One-hot vector is a vector that consists of 0s in all cells with the exception of a single 1 in a cell. Using goods category labels as an example (Table 3), if the category of a certain goods is a "Game", the label is 2, so that the category is expressed as category = (0, 1, 0) using one-hot vector. By expressing the categorical variables using one-hot vector, it becomes possible to use the categorical variables for training as the explanatory variables even if there is no continuous relationship between the categories. However, looking at the data in 1 row, it has a disadvantage that as the number of labels in categorical variables increase, the cell with 0 so does. Therefore, the data becomes sparse, and the calculate cost tend to be high.

In this study, we construct DNN model using data expressing "Store" and "Category" using one-hot vector and 4 kinds of continuous variables as one input. Figure 3 shows the constructed DNN model, and Table 6 shows the parameters set in the model construction. Since the training doesn't go well when the number of hidden layers is 3, finally it is changed to 4. As an activation function, we tried the ReLU-function, but because of its low accuracy, we use the sigmoid-function.

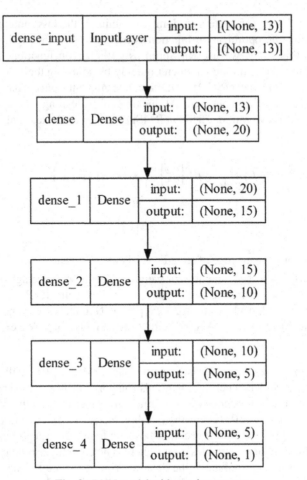

Fig. 3. DNN model with one-hot vector

Table 6. Parameters of the DNN model with one-hot vector

	Number of units	Activation function
1st hidden layer	20	Sigmoid
2nd hidden layer	15	Sigmoid
3rd hidden layer	10	Sigmoid
4th hidden layer	5	Sigmoid

We train the constructed model. In the training process, the batch size is set to 32, and the cross-validation ratio is set to 20%. To avoid overfit, the maximum epoch number is set to 1000, and if there is no improvement within 15 epochs, the training is stopped.

Figure 4 shows the transition of the loss function. The training is stopped 307 epochs, at this time "loss" is 0.018514 and "val_loss" is 0.018543.

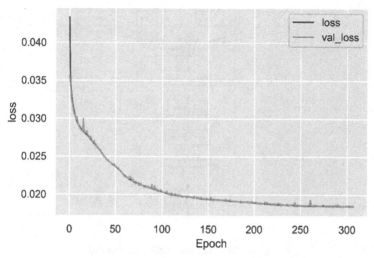

Fig. 4. Transition of loss function of DNN model with one-hot vector

Entity Embedding. The entity embedding is one of the encoding methods to handle the categorical variables. It becomes possible to train each weight of categorical variables by using the embedding layer for the categorical variables [4]. The one-hot vector only extracts the index whose value is 1 from the weight matrix. Therefore, in order to extract a specific index, create a matrix with a voluntary number of dimensions. This is called "Embedding Matrix" and defined as Eq. 7. Then the number of dimension m need to set as $m \leq n - 1$, where n is the number of labels of categorical variables. And it is recommended generally as $m = \sqrt[4]{n}$ [5].

$$EmbeddingMatrix = \begin{pmatrix} w_{11} & w_{12} & \cdots & w_{1m} \\ w_{21} & w_{22} & \cdots & w_{2m} \\ \vdots & \vdots & \ddots & \vdots \\ w_{n1} & w_{n2} & \cdots & w_{nm} \end{pmatrix} \tag{7}$$

In this study, we construct DNN model that inputs 6 explanatory variables, 4 continuous variables and 2 categorical variables, separately. We combine the embedded categorical variables and the continuous variables at fully connected layer, and the hidden layer is set to 5 layers. Figure 5 shows the constructed DNN model with embedding layer, and Table 7 shows the parameters set in the model construction. Then the number of dimension of Embedding layer is set to 2.

We train the constructed model. In the training process, the batch size is set to 32, and the cross-validation rate is set to 20%. To avoid overfit, the maximum epoch number is set to 1000, and if there is no improvement within 15 epochs, the training is stopped.

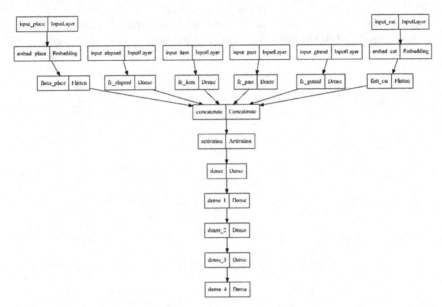

Fig. 5. DNN model with entity embedding

Table 7. Parameters of the DNN model with entity embedding

	Number of units	Activation function
1st hidden layer	204	Sigmoid
2nd hidden layer	96	Sigmoid
3rd hidden layer	48	Sigmoid
4th hidden layer	24	Sigmoid
5th hidden layer	12	Sigmoid

Figure 6 shows the transition of the loss function. The training is stopped 142 epochs, at this time "loss" is 0.009211 and "val_loss" is 0.009134. And the loss value is halved than the DNN with One-Hot vector.

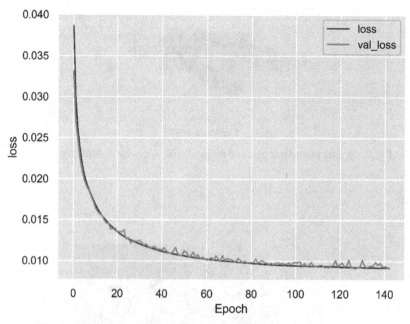

Fig. 6. Transition of loss function of DNN model with entity embedding

5   Model Evaluation

In this chapter, we evaluate three models structured in Sect. 4. And we select one model as the optimal RRP estimation model. In Sect. 5.2, we check the accuracy of selected model.

5.1   Model Selection

In this section, we evaluate three models constructed in Sect. 4. As the evaluation points of view, we use correlation coefficients and Root Mean Squared Error (RMSE) between the predicted values and test data.

Figure 7, 8 and 9 shows that the scatter plot of test data and the predicted values by three constructed models respectively. Table 8 shows the correlation coefficients and RMSE of these models.

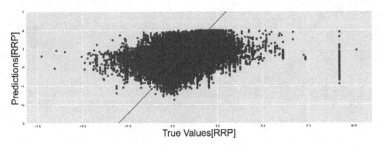

Fig. 7. Scatter plot of test data and the predicted values by multiple regression

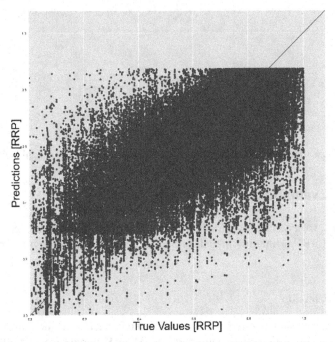

Fig. 8. Scatter plot of test data and the predicted values by DNN model with one-hot vector

As shown in Fig. 7, the multiple regression can hardly analyze, especially the data where near 0 and 1 does not predict well. As shown in Fig. 8, the prediction accuracy around 0 is not well, and the predicted values are not beyond 0.85. As shown in Fig. 9, almost all data learned well, but there is a small amount of data in the lower right and upper left. Upon checking the details of these data, it is found that one consumer is purchasing sixty same goods at the same time. In this case, since only the explanatory variable "No. of Purchased" fluctuates, we consider that the accuracy has dropped due to the influence of one variable.

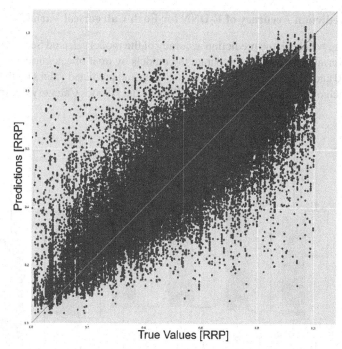

Fig. 9. Scatter plot of test data and the predicted values by DNN model with entity embedding

Table 8. Correlation coefficients and RSS

	Multiple regression	DNN with one-hot vector	DNN with entity embedding
Correlation coefficient	0.355	0.796	0.907
RMSE	1.167	0.136	0.095

As shown in Table 8, the DNN model with embedding layer, which has a high correlation coefficient and a low RSS and RSME, is selected as the estimation model of the RRP at the time of resale of electrical goods, which was the purpose of this study.

5.2 The Prediction Accuracy of E-DNN for Each Categorical Variable

In this section, we check the prediction accuracy of the model selected Sect. 5.1 for each categorical variable, because we separate the models by treat of categorical variables.

Figure 10 and 11 are the boxplots of the test data and predicted values by the selected model for each of the categorical variables "Store" and "Goods Category", respectively.

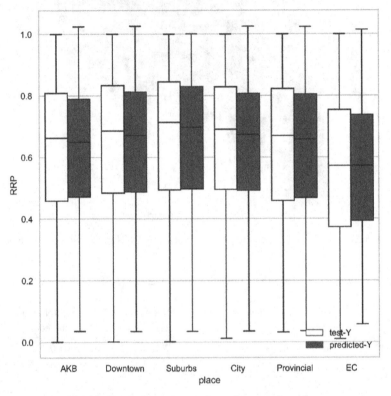

Fig. 10. Prediction accuracy for each store of purchase

From Fig. 10 and 11, it can be seen that the estimation is successful. However, in all labels, the median of predicted values is lower than median the of test data, on the other hands, in (Store) = {1, 2, 4, 6} and (Category) = 2, the distribution of predicted values exceed the distribution of test data.

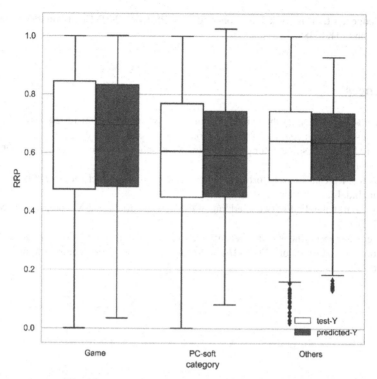

Fig. 11. Prediction accuracy for each goods category

6   Conclusion

In this study, we estimate the ratio of reuse price to list price for predict the optimal discount rate of the reuse electrical goods from sales data. For estimation, we construct and evaluate three types models (multiple regression, DNN with one-hot vector, DNN with entity embedding) by correlation coefficient and RSME. As a result, we select the DNN model with entity embedding from Table 8.

We consider that this model is so practical for estimate the discount rate at the time of resale because it has high accuracy and the used explanatory variables are easy to obtain. In particularly, by enabling discount rate estimation, we can refer for purchase price when purchasing the reuse goods from consumers. Accordingly, this lead to an increase in profitability in the reuse industry.

However, some problems remain in this study. Since the dataset for training is excerpted some goods with larger numbers of transactions from all data, this model is unlikely to apply to data with a small number of transactions.

Another problem is that the explanatory variables do not include product condition data. The condition of reuse goods is very important factor for the selling price in the reuse market and it is expected that the resale price will be greatly affected. Therefore, for our future work, it will be necessary to introduce the condition of the product as data.

Acknowledgement. This work was supported by JSPS KAKENHI Grant Number 19K01945, 21H04600 and 21K13385.

References

1. Recycle Mail: Estimating the market size of the reuse industry 2021 (2020 version). https://www.recycle-tsushin.com/news/detail_6396.php. Accessed 20 Jan 2022
2. Ueda, T.: Marketing strategy for price decision. Gakushuin Univ. Econ. Theory Collect. **31**(4), 185–208 (1995). (in Japanese)
3. Namatame, T., Asai, Y., Motoyoshi, N., Saito, Y.: Analysis of contract price in a B2B automobile auction. Ind. Eng. Manage. Syst. **8**(4), 201–212 (2009)
4. Guo, C., Barkhahn, F.: Entity embedding of categorical variables, arXiv preprint arXiv:1604.06737 (2016)
5. Google Developers: Introducing TensorFlow Feature Columns, 20 November 2017. https://developers.googleblog.com/2017/11/introducing-tensorflow-feature-columns.html. Accessed 20 Jan 2022

An Indicator to Measure the Relationship Between Firms and Consumers Based on the Subjective Well-Being of Consumers: Promoting Corporate Social Contribution Activities to Maintain Socially Sustainable Development

Masao Ueda[✉] [iD]

Yokohama City University, 22-2 Seto, Kanazawa, Yokohama, Japan
m_ueda@yokohama-cu.ac.jp

Abstract. Since corporate social contribution activities affect consumers as a whole and not just the firm's customers, it is important to develop a quantitative understanding of the relationship between companies and consumers. In this study, we propose a new indicator to measure the relationship between firms and consumers, focusing on the consumer's subjective well-being (SWB). We confirm through empirical analysis a positive relationship between SWB and the firm's marketing activities. The data were obtained from 2,025 online monitors and were analyzed using a zero-inflated gamma model and a binary logit model with an assumed mixed effect for the SWB term. Results showed that the fixed effect parameter for SWB is positive for the four firms selected from the retail and manufacturing sectors, indicating that SWB can be used to effectively measure the relationship between firms and consumers. This study establishes SWB as such an indicator—one that can be effectively used to promote the sustainable development of society as a whole.

Keywords: Customer relationship management · Subjective well-being · Mixed effect model

1 Introduction

In the past, firms have focused on building a strong relationship with their customers in order to earn a profit and sustain their business. Today, firms are regarded as members of society and are expected to not only earn a profit but also to contribute positively to the society in which they operate. This trend was highlighted in a statement by the Business Roundtable in August 2019, which noted that corporations should pursue the benefit of all stakeholders and not just that of its shareholders (Business Roundtable 2019). By engaging in social contribution activities, a firm affects not only its customers but also those consumers who do not purchase its goods or services. The more social activities that a firm pursues, the more consumers it affects and the more it builds a relationship with those consumers. Furthermore, the role of consumers is changing—from simply purchasing goods and services to sharing the firm's advertisements, investing in its stocks, and raising awareness of the firm's positive activities via social media or through direct verbal communication. These new consumer roles can provide substantial benefit to the firm. Accordingly, firms need to recognize not only the importance of their customers, but also the importance of consumers in general.

In the past, firms have focused on building a strong relationship with their customers in order to earn a profit and sustain their business. Today, firms are regarded as members of society and are expected to not only earn a profit but also to contribute positively to the society in which they operate. This trend was highlighted in a statement by the Business Roundtable in August 2019, which noted that corporations should pursue the benefit of all stakeholders and not just that of its shareholders (Business Roundtable 2019). By engaging in social contribution activities, a firm affects not only its customers but also those consumers who do not purchase its goods or services. The more social activities that a firm pursues, the more consumers it affects and the more it builds a relationship with those consumers. Furthermore, the role of consumers is changing—from simply purchasing goods and services to sharing the firm's advertisements, investing in its stocks, and raising awareness of the firm's positive activities via social media or through direct verbal communication. These new consumer roles can provide substantial benefit to the firm. Accordingly, firms need to recognize not only the importance of their customers, but also the importance of consumers in general.

In this context, the ability to assess the firm-consumer relationship using measurable indicators in order to evaluate the firm's activities becomes significant. Without such indicators, one-sided, firm-based social activities may have unintended consequences, as the social influence of the firm's activities cannot be accurately evaluated. Several indicators exist to help firms manage their customer relationships using direct customer metrics such as satisfaction, loyalty, recency, frequency, and monetary value. However, such indicators for managing and assessing the relationship between firms and the broader group of consumers in general have not been widely promulgated.

One of the candidate indicators for measuring the relationship between the firm and consumers is consumer subjective well-being (SWB). Subjective well-being is a cognitive evaluation of life that can include satisfaction with life in general or satisfaction with various domains in one's life (Diener et al. 2000). Conducting or supporting social activities, environment conservation activities, and arts and cultural support activities can enable firms to improve the subjective well-being of consumers. However, the actual effect on the firm of such efforts has not been extensively addressed in prior research, nor has the usefulness of employing consumer SWB as a management indicator been convincingly confirmed. In order to legitimize SWB and the firm's socially conscious activities as a useful marketing tool, it is necessary to determine whether consumer SWB significantly affects business performance. Evidence should cite links between consumer SWB and marketing or consumer behavior variable (e.g., purchase volume, recommendations to others, etc.). It can be argued that firms are established to provide products and services that satisfy the needs of consumers generally, including those who are not direct customers, and that the subjective well-being of consumers will improve if their needs are met by the firm's products and services. Given this premise, the consumers' level of subjective well-being is likely to link to a firm's sales and profits. What is needed in this era of Sustainable Development Goals (SDGs) is an indicator capable of connecting the sales and profits of the firm to its social contribution activities.

2 Previous Research

The application of SWB has gained significant "real world" traction in recent years. Stiglitz et al. (2009) suggest that the value of SWB should be used along with gross domestic product (GDP) to better understand the state of a country's economy. In fact, the office for national statistics in the United Kingdom[1] and the EU[2,3] give SWB values as well as GDP figures on their web sites. Research related to SWB has mainly been in the fields of social psychology, politics, and economics. The main focus of such research has been to clarify those factors that influence SWB. Dolan et al. (2008) review previous studies showing that income, age, gender, race, health status, etc., all have some influence on SWB. In addition, various studies have been conducted on the relationship between happiness and life. For example, Lyubomirsky et al. (2005) reviewed the relationship between happiness and success in life.

In the fields of marketing and consumer behavior, consumer SWB has received scant attention. Indeed, Suranyi-Unger (1981) indicated that well-being was not of primary interest in consumer behavior. However, there have been several related studies in the areas of marketing and consumer behavior. These studies have mainly examined the relationship between consumption and SWB. For example, Dunn et al. (2008) concluded that spending money affects one's SWB, and Oropesa (1995) found that the enjoyment of the shopping experience has a positive effect on SWB. Zhong and Mitchell (2010) further investigated the relationship between hedonic consumption and the SWB of the consumer. In another study, Ganglmair-Wooliscroft and Lawson (2011) found that SWB variables were not uniform among consumers, showing differences in consumer SWB values among various consumer segments.

None of the studies cited above directly address the issue of using consumer SWB as a management tool. As members of society, firms today are expected to engage in activities that make a positive social contribution; however, they also need to turn a profit to remain a going concern. If the social contribution activities of the firm both increase consumer SWB and, at the same time, work to the firm's economic benefit, the case for using SWB to help direct the firm's managerial choices and marketing strategies becomes compelling.

As noted earlier, customer satisfaction is commonly used as an indicator of a company's marketing performance since it has a well-established relationship with variables that influence marketing success. Cooil et al. (2007) found a positive relation between customer satisfaction and share of wallet. Gustafsson et al. (2005) clarified the relationship between customer satisfaction and customer retention, while Lim et al. (2020) explored the relationship between customer satisfaction and future sales costs. To utilize

---

[1] https://www.ons.gov.uk/peoplepopulationandcommunity/wellbeing.

[2] https://ec.europa.eu/eurostat/web/quality-of-life.

[3] The EU site presents the data as overall life satisfaction or happiness.

the SWB of consumers as an indicator of the firm's performance and as an important factor in its marketing management, it is necessary to show a similar positive relationship between consumer SWB and variables that influence the company's marketing effectiveness. Based on this premise, the following empirical analysis was conducted.

3 Data and Analysis Model

3.1 Data

Two types of data were used in our study: purchase history data and consumer survey data. The purchase history data were used to establish purchase behavior; the survey data were used to calculate SWB metrics. More specifically, the purchase history data provide information on the daily consumer shopping behavior of 25-year-old residents of Tokyo and Kanagawa prefectures over the period from July 1, 2018 to June 30, 2019. The consumer survey data come from an online survey conducted between July 26 to August 6, 2019. Both sets of data were acquired from the same monitors, all of whom belonged to the online research firm, Internet Research, Inc.

In this study, we sought SWB information for 14 firms in seven industries. To avoid bias toward any specific industry, two firms in each of the seven industries were selected. The seven industries included food manufacturers, liquor manufacturers, daily necessities manufacturers, railways, mobile phone carriers, convenience stores, and online shopping sites[4]. The purchase history data for firms in four of the seven industries— liquor manufacturers, daily necessities manufacturers, convenience stores, and online shopping—were ultimately selected for a full analysis. To eliminate the effect of order when asking the study participants about their SWB as it related to the fourteen firms, each item was randomly presented to the monitors along with a check item noted later. The degree of subjective well-being associated with each firm was measured by the responses of the survey participants and their reaction times when answering the following research question: "In addition to providing products and services, current firms are engaged in various activities such as environmental protection activities, cultural support, and community support. Do these activities contribute to the happiness of your life?" This question was based on consideration of previous research. The responding monitor was then asked to select one of two dichotomous alternatives as an answer, i.e., "Yes" or "No."

To survey degrees of SWB, a number of prior studies have used multiple survey items; others have used just a single item (Diener et al. 2000; Graham et al. 2004; Lucas et al. 2004). Considering the large volume of information being gathered from the monitors in our study, we chose to use a single item. Our concern was that the use of multiple items to confirm the SWB that a monitor associated with each of the fourteen firms would cause the monitors to exercise less care in their responses in general, thus negatively affecting the quality of the data used for analysis. We chose dichotomous alternatives rather Likert scales based on the observation that many survey participants

---

[4] There were two reasons for including railway companies and mobile phone carriers in the survey items. One reason is to prevent the monitors from becoming aware of what the firm to be analyzed is. The other reason is to stabilize the average reaction time for each item.

would be using smartphones rather than personal computers to register their responses. Since the screen of a smartphone is quite narrow, it is much easier to respond to survey items that involve dichotomous alternatives rather than Likert scales.

Given that Likert scales were not used in the survey, the strength of the consumer's SWB attitude was measured according to the monitor's reaction time, following Fazio (1990), who showed that reaction time was suitable for measuring the associative strength of memory. If the monitor felt strongly that the firm contributed to his/her well-being (i.e., it was strongly connected to memory), it could be expected that reaction time would be faster. Thus, reaction time was used for weighting in this study. Specifically, if the reaction time of a monitor when responding to the item for a certain firm was faster than the overall average reaction time for that particular item, a weight of 1 was given to his/her response; otherwise, a weight of 0.5 was applied. The consumer's SWB score was then calculated by multiplying the result (yes = 1, or no = −1) by the appropriate weight. Thus, the consumers' SWB score could take one of the following four values: −1.0, −0.5, 0.5, or 1.0[5].

It is well known that reaction times often show outliers. Many methods have been used to check these outliers (Ratcliff 1993). To maintain data quality in this study, the maximum reaction time and the checked item were used. The checked item, "Push right button, please," was used to determine whether the monitor was careful and attentive in their response. If a monitor pushed the "Yes" button shown at the left rather than the right, it was judged that he or she was a careless monitor. This check item was presented at random. This approach enabled us to exclude monitors having a maximum reaction time ≥ 60 s[6] and those who reacted incorrectly to the check item. The final number of monitors for the analysis was 2,025.

The purpose of the current study was to determine whether a consumer's SWB affects his/her marketing-related behaviors. Marketing-related behaviors include not only purchasing goods and services, but also word-of-mouth communications, recommendations for certain goods and services, and online searching of related web pages. If there is such a link, understanding its nature is an important matter for the firm. In this study, data on purchase volume serve as purchase history data; data related to word-of mouth communications, recommendations, and web-searches were obtained via an extensive web survey. In the web survey, respondents were asked to answer the following items with a simple "Yes" or "No":

- Word-of Mouth: Have you ever talked about the following firms in the last three months?
- Recommendations: Have you recommended the products and services of the following firms to your family, friends and acquaintances in the last three months?
- Web searches: Have you searched for products, services, etc., on the homepage of the following firms in the last three months?

---

[5] The converted data had better model convergence than the unconverted data.

[6] This criterion was determined based on consideration of the distribution of the obtained reaction time data.

3.2 Analysis Model

A separate analysis was conducted for each of two industries: retail and manufacturing. The retail group consisted of two convenience stores and two online retailers. In the manufacturing group, two liquor manufacturers and two daily-goods manufacturers were analyzed. Purchase volume, word-of-mouth communications, recommendations, and web page searches served as the pertinent marketing indicators. Purchase volume is an indicator that relates directly to sales and profits, while word-of-mouth, recommendations, and web searches are important to the firm as indicators of its ability to stimulate communication among consumers. Importantly, word-of-mouth communication, product recommendations, and web search behaviors are not limited to a firm's customers but rather can involve a much broader group of consumers who do not purchase or have not purchased the firm's goods or service. In order to examine the relation between these indicators and the SWB of consumers, we developed the two analytical models.

A zero-inflated gamma distribution was used to model purchase volume. As shown in Fig. 1, the purchase volume distribution for the four manufacturing firms is strongly skewed in the positive direction. The purchase volume distribution for retail also tended to be similar to that for manufacturers. As a consequence, applying the gamma distribution was considered. However, as can be seen in the figure, the purchase volume of 0 appeared extremely frequently in the data, which meant that applying a simple gamma distribution would be inappropriate. Hence, purchase volume was assumed to be a zero-inflated gamma distribution, as modeled in Eqs. (1) through (9).

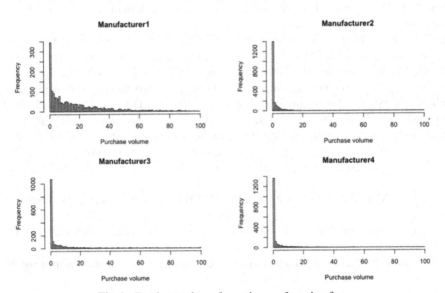

Fig. 1. Purchase volume for each manufacturing firm

The zero-inflated gamma distribution has three parameters: θ, α, and β. θ is the Bernoulli distribution parameter, and α and β are parameters of the gamma distribution. In our model, purchase rate is expressed by θ in Eq. (2), while the mean value of purchase volume, μ, is expressed as α and β in Eq. (6). Given that our aim was to determine whether the value of consumer SWB is positive, that is, whether it is common among firms that consumer SWB positively influences the firm's purchase rate and volume, fixed and random effects are assumed for the consumer SWB term in Eqs. (3) and (7). Gender term is used as covariates, and fixed effect is assumed. It is well known that a consumer's gender affects his/her purchase behavior; for example, female consumers have a tendency to purchase more daily goods than males. The reason for using loyalty as a covariate in Eq. (7) is to eliminate its effect on sales volume, i.e., as the loyalty value increases, purchase volume can be expected to increase. Since there are differences in the loyalty indicator between companies, we assumed the random effect in addition to the fixed effect[7].

$$p\left(y_{ij}^c | \theta_j^c, \alpha_j^c, \beta_j^c\right)$$

$$= \begin{cases} bernoulli(0|\theta_j^c) & \text{if } y_{ij}^c = 0 \\ bernoulli(1|\theta_j^c) \times Gamma(y_{if}^c | \alpha_j^c \beta_j^c) & \text{if } y_{ij}^c > 0 \end{cases} \quad (1)$$

$$\theta_j^c = 1/1 + \exp\left(-Z_j^c\right) \quad (2)$$

$$Z_j^c = a_0^c + \left(a_1^c + a_{1j}^c\right) * cSWB_{ij}^c + a_2^c * Gender_i \quad (3)$$

$$a_{1j}^c \sim normal(0, sa_1) \quad (4)$$

$$sa_1 \sim half\ cauchy(0, 1) \quad (5)$$

$$\mu_j^c = \alpha_j^c / \beta_j^c \quad (6)$$

$$\mu_j^c = b_0^c + \left(b_1^c + b_{1j}^c\right) * cSWB_{ij}^c + b_2^c * Gender_i + \left(b_3^c + b_{3j}^c\right) * loyalty_{ij} \quad (7)$$

$$b_{1j}^c \sim normal(0, sb_1), b_{3j}^c \sim normal(0, sb_3) \quad (8)$$

$$sb_1 \sim halfcauchy(0, 1), sb_3 \sim halfcauchy(0, 1) \quad (9)$$

Here, y_{ij}^c represents the number of purchases ($y_{ij}^c = 0$ is a non-purchase) by monitor i ($i = 1$ to $2{,}025$) from firm j ($j = 1$ to 4) in industry category c (1 = manufacturer, 2 = retailer). θ_j^c is assumed to be a random effect for firm j and is the Bernoulli distribution parameter; α_j^c and β_j^c are random effects for firm j and are parameters of the gamma distribution; a_{1j}^c, b_{1j}^c, and b_{3j}^c are random effects parameters for firm j (otherwise a fixed effect parameter); sa_1, sb_1, sb_3, are standard deviations and are assumed to follow the half-Cauchy distribution in Eqs. (5) and (9). The $loyalty_{ij}$ term represents the number

---

[7] The parameters sa_1, sb_1, and sd_1 follow a weakly informative prior distribution, as shown in Eqs. (5) and (9). Gelman (2006) recommended a half-Cauchy prior distribution when the number of groups for analysis is small for a variance parameter

of days on which monitor i purchased items sold by firm j or used the shop of firm j, divided by the number of days on which monitor i purchased items in the category or at a shop in the category ($0 <= loyalty_{ij} <= 1$).

Because the three marketing-related behaviors included in this study—word-of-mouth, recommendations, and web searches—are treated as dichotomous variables, they follow a Bernoulli distribution. The analytical model is described in Eqs. (10) through (13). The reason for using purchase days as a covariate is similar to the reason noted above—if one has many opportunities to make a purchase, it is natural to conclude that there are increased opportunities to engage in these three behaviours.

$$p\left(B_{ijk}^c = 1|\delta_j^c\right) = 1/\left(1 + exp\left(Z_j^c\right)\right) \tag{10}$$

$$Z_j^c = d_0^c + \left(d_1^c + d_{1j}^c\right) * cSWB_{ij}^c + d_2^c * Gender_i + \left(d_3^c + d_{3j}^c\right) * loyalty_{ij} \tag{11}$$

$$d_{1j}^c \sim normal(0, sd_1), d_{3j}^c \sim normal(0, sd_3) \tag{12}$$

$$sd_1 \sim halfcauchy(0, 1), sd_3 \sim halfcauchy(0, 1) \tag{13}$$

Here, $B_{ijk}^c = 1$ indicates the exercise of behavior k ($k = 1$ to 3, where 1 = engaging in word-of-mouth, 2 = making a recommendation to others, 3 = conducting a web search) by monitor i ($i = 1$ to 2,025) involving firm j ($j = 1$ to 4) in industry category c (1 = manufacturer, 2 = retailer); δ_j^c is assumed to be a random effect and is the Bernoulli distribution parameter d_{1j}^c and d_{3j}^c are random effect parameters for firm j (otherwise, a fixed effect parameter); See the above for the same terms and parameters as in Eqs. (1) through (9).

The parameters in these models were estimated using the Markov chain Monte Carlo method (MCMC) in RStan v.2.21.2 and R v.4.0.3. The No-U-Turn Sampler was used for the sampling algorithm. The MCMC steps were repeated 800 times. The first 400 iterations were treated as the burn-in period. The final 400 iterations were used to estimate the posterior distribution of the parameters. Convergence was monitored visually and confirmed using the Rhat value, which was found to be below 1.1 (Gelman et al. 2014).

4 Results

According to Fig. 2[8], the purchase volume by those who answered "yes" to the SWB item is substantial, indicating a positive relationship between SWB and purchase volume. However, Fig. 2 shows the results of a rather simple calculation. To make the case for a positive relationship, it is necessary to confirm whether the same tendency is shown in a statistical model that includes covariates. Similarly, it is necessary to confirm not only the purchase result but also the behavior such as word-of-mouth using the statistical model given in Eqs. (10) to (13).

---

[8] The horizontal axis represents the firms being analyzed: M1 and M2 are liquor manufacturers, M3 and M4 are daily necessities manufacturers, R1 and R2 are convenience stores, and R3 and R4 are online shopping sites.

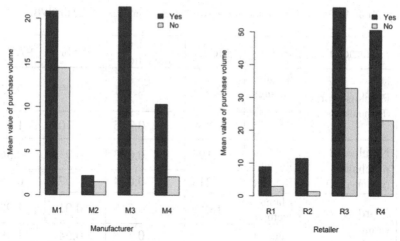

Fig. 2. SWB response and purchase volume (Left: manufacturers, Right: retailers)

The estimation results of the fixed effect consumer SWB parameters, a_1^c, b_1^c, and d_1^c, are shown in Table 1. Although one parameter on web searches for retailer is not significant (i.e., the credible interval contain 0), the parameters regarding consumer SWB were statistically significant and positive. The parameter a_1^c, which related consumer SWB to purchase rate, was 0.411 for manufacturers and 0.869 for retailers. The purchase volume parameter b_1^c was 0.195 for manufacturers and 0.213 for retailers. The results in Table 1 indicate that, if the consumer's SWB is high, the number of users, purchase volume, and the rate of each behavior—word-of-mouth, and recommendations—have the same tendency for all four firms in each of the two industries. This result shows that the level of consumer SWB reflects the tendency of positive effects on number of users, purchase volume, and each of the behaviors. On the other hand, not all random effect parameters for consumer SWB are statistically significant.

In this study, usage (purchase) day loyalty and gender were included as covariates. Table 2 showed that fixed-effect parameters related to loyalty are not statistically significant except for in parameters on the number of purchase, word of mouth, and recommendation for retailers. On the other hand, the gender parameter indicates significant value except for word-of-mouth for manufacturers. Among significant parameters, only recommendation for retailers show a negative value, otherwise is positive. From the fact that most of the parameters on gender were significant, it can be understood that the gender term is necessary as a covariate in this model.

Table 1. Estimation results for the fixed-effect parameters related to SWB.

Parameter		Industry	Mean	Standard deviation	2.5%	97.5%
a_1^c	Purchase rate (Bernoulli dist.)	Manu-facturer	0.411	0.161	0.090	0.758
		Retailer	0.869	0.355	0.105	1.550
b_1^c	Number of purchases (gamma dist.)	Manu-facturer	0.195	0.083	0.035	0.362
		Retailer	0.213	0.064	0.074	0.354
d_1^c	Word of mouth	Manu-facturer	1.056	0.510	0.012	1.986
		Retailer	0.950	0.208	0.541	1.397
	Recommenda-tion	Manu-facturer	1.463	0.324	0.701	2.087
		Retailer	1.279	0.204	0.900	1.722
	Web searches	Manu-facturer	1.209	0.332	0.469	1.957
		Retailer	0.904	0.637	-0.576	2.007

Note: The item on gray cells indicates that it is not statistically significant since the item included 0 between credible intervals.

Table 2. Estimation results for the fixed-effect parameters related to Loyalty.

Parameter		Industry	Mean	Standard deviation	2.5%	97.5%
b_3^c	Number of purchases (gamma dist.)	Manu-facturer	4.019	0.402	3.214	4.865
		Retailer	2.008	0.298	1.391	2.603
d_3^c	Word of mouth	Manu-facturer	-0.363	1.782	-4.707	2.658
		Retailer	1.055	0.430	0.309	1.755
	Recommen-dation	Manu-facturer	1.202	0.886	-0.769	2.924
		Retailer	0.999	0.217	0.567	1.450
	Web searches	Manu-facturer	0.491	1.003	-1.818	2.150
		Retailer	1.061	0.752	-0.171	2.342

Note: The item on gray cells indicates that it is not statistically since the item included 0 between credible intervals.

5 Discussion and Conclusions

This study aimed to clarify the relationship between consumer SWB and consumer behavior as it relates to the firm and its marketing performance (as shown by such factors as purchase volume, purchase rate, word-of-mouth communications, recommendations, and web searches). Analysis results indicated a positive relationship. The analytical model was applied to four firms in the manufacturing industry and four firms in the retail industry and confirmed that the effect of consumer SWB was common among all four firms in each of the two industries. Furthermore, the model included gender and loyalty covariates that were used to isolate the effect of consumer SWB on the dependent variable. The estimated parameters on number of purchases, "b_3^c", had positive signs, showing loyalty had a positive effect on the dependent variables. However, some parameters regarding consumer communication were significant statistically and some were not. This estimation result is reasonable because behaviors such as word-of-mouth are not so strongly related to loyalty compared to the number of purchases. As can be seen here, a number of the estimated parameters on the gender term were significant except for web searches for retailers; however, the signs of the parameters differed between firms in the two categories.

A zero-inflated gamma distribution model was used to show the magnitude of the effect of consumer SWB on purchase rate and purchase volume. The fixed parameter of consumer SWB had a positive sign for firms in both the manufacturing and retail industries. The purchase rate and volume are directly related to sales and profits; therefore, the consumer SWB can be a meaningful indicator for business management. As for the word-of-mouth and recommendations, the fixed parameter for consumer SWB was also positive. This suggests that consumers who have a high degree of SWB with respect to the firm are more likely to take favorable actions based on the firm's advertising and communications.

This study makes both an academic and business contribution. Academically, it expands the area of research on customer relationship management (CRM). Until now, CRM research has focused on how customers can bring financial profits to the firm through customer acquisition, development, and retention (Kamakura et al. 2005). Although Ascarza et al. (2017) mentioned that a CRM program can affect non-target customers and pursued research that considers non-target customers, our study more clearly extends the scope of research that is principally customer-centered to research that is more broadly consumer-centered.

Our proposal of a new indicator that is relevant to both consumer and customer relations management represents another academic contribution. Given the diversity of customer behavior, using indicators that can effectively capture and characterize various behaviors is important. Database marketing firms often use RFM (Recency, Frequency, and Monetary value) as an indicator in customer management (Blattberg et al. 2008). Various other studies have been conducted on indicators related to CRM. For example, Yang (2004) proposed an index, M/R (monetary value divided by recency), based on RFM. Zhang et al. (2013, 2015) proposed an index that they call "clumpiness." However, few of these previous studies have attempted to measure the relationship with the broader category of consumers—as is done in our study. Perhaps equally important is the fact that SWB has heretofore rarely been a topic of study in marketing and consumer behavior.

Our expectation is that our results will spur increased interest among researchers in this area.

As for the business contribution of our study, we have proposed an indicator to help manage consumer relations in today's era of SDGs. According to our results, a company's performance can be effectively measured in terms of consumer SWB. We offer evidence that higher levels of SWB link to favorable performance factors such as purchase rate, product recommendations and web page searches. Based on our findings, it seems clear that a high level of consumer SWB is desirable for firms and that SWB can be used as an effective indicator of its relationship with customers and, by extension, its relationship with consumers.

In the past, the role of consumers were mainly the role of customers to purchase products and services provided by firms, however nowadays, the role of consumers are diverged, they have the role of mediators who mediate advertisements or the role of a communicator who conveys the goodness of product or service. Given that the role of consumers has changed significantly in recent years, traditional indicators seem less equipped to fully measure the relationship between the firm and consumers. By showing the significance of SWB, our study gives firms a way to assess their relationship with consumers and provides direction for managing the firm's activities. There seems little question that firms will continue to contribute to society, both for their own sustainability and for the further development of society. However, to carry out such activities indefinitely, an indicator to measure the effectiveness of the firm's social contribution activities is needed. Our study establishes SWB as such an indicator—one that can be effectively used to promote the sustainable development of society as a whole.

This study is not without limitations. Most prominent among them is the fact that the number of companies analyzed is quite small and the analysis covers only a single year. As for future research, if SWB can be effectively used to evaluate a firm's marketing performance, extending the approach to analyze the relationship between consumer SWB and other performance indicators such as the firm's stock price or profit margin would seem a logical next step. Luo and Bhattacharya (2006) demonstrated that customer satisfaction positively affects a firm's market value. Extending this idea to the relationship between consumer SWB and firm value offers fertile ground for future research.

References

Ascarza, E., Ebbes, P., Netzer, O., Danielson, M.: Beyond the target customer: social effects of customer relationship management campaigns. J. Mark. Res. **54**(3), 347–363 (2017)

Blattberg, R.C., Kim, B.D., Neslin, S.A.: Database Marketing: Analyzing and Managing Customers. Springer, New York (2008)

Business Roundtable: Business Roundtable Redefines the Purpose of a Corporation to Promote 'An Economy That Serves All Americans' (2019). https://www.businessroundtable.org/bus iness-roundtable-redefines-the-purpose-of-a-corporation-to-promote-an-economy-that-ser ves-all-americans

Cooil, B., Keiningham, T.L., Aksoy, L., Hsu, M.: A longitudinal analysis of customer satisfaction and share of wallet: investigating the moderating effect of customer characteristics. J. Mark. **71**(1), 67–83 (2007)

Diener, E., Gohm, C.L., Suh, E., Oishi, S.: Similarity of the relations between marital status and subjective well-being across cultures. J. Cross Cult. Psychol. **31**, 419–436 (2000)

Dunn, E.W., Aknin, L.B., Norton, M.I.: Spending money on others promotes happiness. Science **319**(21), 1687–1688 (2008)

Dolan, P., Peasgood, T., White, M.: Do we really know what makes us happy? A review of the economic literature on the factors associated with subjective well-being. J. Econ. Psychol. **29**(1), 94–122 (2008)

Fazio, R.H.: Practical guide to the use of response latency. In: Hendrick, C.A., Clark, M.S. (eds.) Research Methods in Personality and Social Psychology, pp. 74–97. Saga, California (1990)

Ganglmair-Wooliscroft, A., Lawson, R.: Subjective well-being of different consumer lifestyle segments. J. Macromark. **31**(2), 172–183 (2011)

Gelman, A., Carlin, J.B., Stern, H.S., Dunson, D.B., Vehtari, A., Rubin, D.B.: Bayesian Data Analysis, 3rd edn. CRC Press, Florida (2014)

Gelman, A.: Prior distributions for variance parameters in hierarchical models. Bayesian Anal. **1**, 515–533 (2006)

Graham, C., Eggers, A., Sukhtankar, S.: Does happiness pay? An exploration based on panel data from Russia. J. Econ. Behav. Organ. **55**(3), 319–342 (2004)

Gustafsson, A., Johnson, M.D., Roos, I.: The effects of customer satisfaction, relationship commitment dimensions, and triggers on customer retention. J. Mark. **69**(4), 210–218 (2005)

Kamakura, W., et al.: Choice models and customer relationship management. Market. Lett. **16**(3, 4), 279–291 (2005)

Lim, L.G., Tuli, K.R., Grewal, R.: Customer satisfaction and its impact on the future costs of selling. J. Mark. **84**(4), 23–44 (2020)

Luo, X., Bhattacharya, C.B.: Corporate social responsibility, customer satisfaction, and market value. J. Mark. **70**(4), 1–18 (2006)

Lucas, R.E., Clark, A., Georgellis, Y., Diener, E.: Unemployment alters the set point for life satisfaction. Psychol. Sci. **15**(1), 8–13 (2004)

Lyubomirsky, S., King, L., Diener, E.: The benefits of frequent positive affect: does happiness lead to success? Psychol. Bull. **131**(6), 803–855 (2005)

Oropesa, R.S.: Consumer possessions, consumer passions, and subjective well-being. Sociol. Forum **10**(2), 215–244 (1995)

Ratcliff, R.: Methods for dealing with reaction time outliers. Psychol. Bull. **114**(3), 510–532 (1993)

Stiglitz, J.E., Sen, A., Fitoussi, J.P.: Report by the Commission on the Measurement of Economic Performance and Social Progress (2009). https://ec.europa.eu/eurostat/documents/813 1721/8131772/Stiglitz-Sen-Fitoussi-Commission-report.pdf

Suranyi-Unger, T.Jr.: Consumer behavior and consumer well-being: an economist's digest. J. Consum. Res. **8**(2), 132–143 (1981)

Yang, A.X.: How to develop new approaches to RFM segmentation. J. Target. Meas. Anal. Mark. **13**(1), 50–60 (2004)

Zhong, J.Y., Mitchell, V.W.: A mechanism model of the effect of hedonic product consumption on well-being. J. Consum. Psychol. **20**(2), 152–162 (2010)

Zhang, Y., Bradlow, E.T., Small, D.S.: New measures of clumpiness for incidence data. J. Appl. Stat. **40**(11), 2533–2548 (2013)

Zhang, Y., Bradlow, E.T., Small, D.S.: Predicting customer value using clumpiness: from RFM to RFMC. Mark. Sci. **34**(2), 179–307 (2015)

Evaluation of Analysis Model for Products with Coefficients of Binary Classifiers and Consideration of Way to Improve

Ayako Yamagiwa[1]([✉]) and Masayuki Goto[2]

[1] School of Creative Science and Engineering of Waseda University,
Okubo Shinjuku 3-4-1, Tokyo, Japan
saxophone_0105@ruri.waseda.jp
[2] Waseda University, Okubo Shinjuku 3-4-1, Tokyo, Japan

Abstract. Purchasing actions on e-commerce sites have become very common for general consumers in recent years. Products that were used to be bought at offline shops are purchased are also handled. Such products, like gifts or durable consumer goods, are often purchased infrequently and whose prefer items change each time they are purchased. A lot of methods are proposed for analysis purchase history data in order to improve customer satisfaction. However, most of them focus on the co-occurrence relationship between customers and products and treat products purchased by the same customer as similar. Then, it is difficult to use the conventional product analysis methods that have been proposed for purchase history data is difficult for some kinds of data mentioned before.

Therefore, the authors have proposed an analysis method with extracting features of products by using the coefficients of binary classifiers that discriminates product purchases or not. In this study, we conduct experiments with artificial data in order to evaluate our method. Specifically, we verify how accurately the coefficients can be estimated and under what circumstances they can be estimated more accurately.

Keywords: Product analysis · Feature embedding · Binary classifiers

1 Introduction

In recent years, many purchasing activities have been carried out through EC sites with the development of internet technology and the widespread use of information terminals such as PCs and smartphones. In addition, not only customers can buy products without visiting physical stores but also shops do not have to hold a real shop and easily deploy service. Thus, the scale of the EC market and the rate of EC adoption in Japan has been increasing [5] as shown

This work was supported by JSPS KAKENHI Grant Number 21H04600.

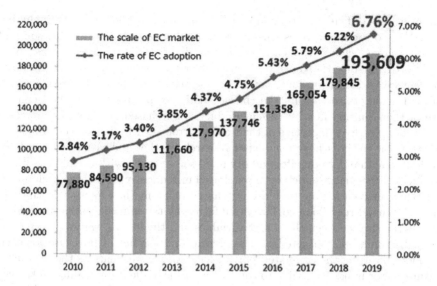

Fig. 1. English translated FY2019 international economic research project for the establishment of an integrated domestic and international economic growth strategy (market research on electronic identification systems) [5].

in Fig. 1 published by the Ministry of Economy, Trade and Industry. The purchasing behavior on EC sites is accumulated as log data by each company, and the importance of utilizing this large amount of data for business is increasing [4]. Especially for B2C (Business to Customer companies), constantly reviewing the product lineup and matching it to market need is one of the essential elements to improve customer satisfaction and ensure continuous sales. In order to achieve that, it is necessary to analyze the characteristics of each product, such as whether the products currently being marketed meet consumers' needs. Companies can promote customer willingness to purchase if creating a product line up is possible that matches customer preferences and satisfies their needs.

The most traditionally basic method of product analysis is to use product attribute information. However, although this method allows grouping of products, it does not reflect customer preferences. Therefore, it is inadequate as an analysis for capturing customer needs. With purchase history data have been utilized in various ways, many methods have been proposed to analyze the characteristics of products such as the evaluation of similarity between products with their features vector based on customer preferences. Item2Vec [3], one of the representative methods, has recently been applied to the customer behavior data of various products and service such as music, movies, games, and daily necessities on EC sites. In much literature, its effectiveness has been demonstrated [2,9,14,26]. This method is based on the co-occurrence relationship between customers and products and constructs a feature space in which products purchased by the same customer are regarded as similar and can be embedded nearby.

However, it is difficult to apply most of the methods studied recently, including Item2Vec, to product groups with a small number of purchases per person and their preference changed by each purchasing due to above characteristics.

In order to solve the above problem, authors proposed a method to estimate the feature vector of products using the coefficients of the classifiers [25]. This method attempts to capture the characteristics of products from the perspective of the situation in which each product is purchased and does not analyze products from the perspective of their co-occurrence with the same customer. In practice, the authors have conducted research on the application of the above method to actual data on gifts and obtained some results with them. The object products of the that research were purchased infrequently and whose preferences tend to change each time they are purchased. This method focuses on the fact that the partial regression coefficients inferred by the binary classifier represent the relationship between the target variables and the feature values [21]. Learning a discriminator that predicts the presence or absence of purchase for each product and using the estimated partial regression coefficients as the product's feature vector make it possible to conduct analysis without depending on the co-occurrence relationship between customers and products. Here, we should note about that the numbers of positive and negative examples in the training data set and the data used for training affect the estimation results of the binary classifiers. If we train a binary classifier with a certain product as positive examples, that mean the product was purchased and other negative examples, there will be a large imbalance between the number of positive and negative examples. Then, appropriately sampling the negative examples is necessary to reduce the size of negative data. In addition, the discriminative boundaries can be changed by which negative examples are chosen. This is because the binary classifier tries to learn the boundary that discriminates between positive and negative examples. Thus, we need care about how to chose the negative examples.

In this paper, we investigate the performance of our proposed method by using artificial purchase history data and conduct experiments for the following two purposes. The first is to evaluate the pros and cons of feature analysis using coefficients. In general, the coefficients learned by a binary classifier in a linear regression model indicate the relationship between the target variable and the explanatory variables. And when the coefficient of an explanatory variable has a positive value, it can be said to have a positive effect on the target variable as well. If the size and sign of the estimated coefficients are consistent with the true values, it is possible to analyze under what circumstances a product is likely to be bought and use this information for corporate product development and marketing. Secondly, we investigate the conditions for ensuring more accurate estimation. As mentioned above, proper sampling of negative examples is necessary when generating data for training a binary classifier. By assessing what kind of negative example sampling is appropriate, we try to identify conditions that should be taken into account to improve the estimation accuracy. Thus, the purpose of this paper is to clarify the validity of the proposed method and the factors for its further use.

2 Related Work

In recent years, machine learning has been increasingly used in the field of marketing [8]. According to Gerrikagoitia et al. [8], there are various trends that companies want to achieve through machine learning, such as Interactive & media-rich, Real-time automation, Customer-journey focus and Personalization. This research aims to model customer preferences using purchase histories, and approaches personalization among the above trends.

It is common for customers with the same attributes to have different preferences. And there is no correct data for analyzing individual customer preferences based on purchase history data. Here, the word "correct" means that the true pairs of customers and their preferences. Thus, most machine learning methods for analyzing customer preferences are unsupervised learning methods. Traditional methods for unsupervised learning include clustering using k-means, principal component analysis, and dimensionality reduction using factor analysis. In these methods, the product itself or the attributes of the customer who purchased the product are used to analyze the product. In addition, unsupervised learning methods that have been developed in recent years include topic models, methods using matrix factorization [13], and methods for learning distributed representations [3]. For example, regarding topic models, research has been done to analyze customer purchasing behavior and products by modeling the co-occurrence relationship between each customer and the purchased product using latent classes [11,12,16]. As for methods that use matrix decomposition, research has been done on using the output of multiple low-dimensional matrices that approximate the matrices representing the customer's product purchase presence and evaluation value information to analyze products and customers [15,24]. There has also been a lot of research using distributed representations, including Item2Vec using product purchase information by the same customer [3] and its application research [1,2,9,14,17,18,23], and a method for estimating the distributed representation of products considering the purchase order [10,20,22], and so on, have been applied to various problems.

One of the problems with the conventionally studied methods is that they cannot learn parameters when the number of purchases by the same customer is insufficient. Then, there are cases where conventional methods cannot be applied. And it is also one of the problems that they cannot interpret the meaning of the parameters estimated by the model. As a result, because of the difficulty in interpreting the parameters, it is difficult to conduct analysis by combining the obtained variance representation with human knowledge, or to utilize the obtained parameters for new product development. Here, the regression model is one of the models that can interpret the parameters. If we can learn the feature vectors of the products using the coefficients estimated by the regression model, it will be possible to interpret the obtained feature vectors. In practice, in Fujii et al.'s study [7], the regression model is used to predict the evaluation values of products and the estimated partial regression coefficients are used to interpret the reasons for recommending the products to customers. According to Fujii et al., it is possible to interpret the regression coefficients obtained by using actual observable features, and it has been shown that it is possible to show. For example, the reason for recommending an item to one user can be shown as because of another similar user has purchased it. Furthermore, since the regression model does not require that the products be purchased by the same customer, it can be applied to product groups that could not be analyzed in the past.

3 The Authors' Method [25]

3.1 Conception

Conventional product analysis methods based on purchase history data attempt to evaluate product characteristics and the degree of similarity between products based on the co-occurrence of products by the same customer. However, there are some product groups with a small number of purchases per person and its purpose is changed by each time, such as gifts which are the subject of this study, and the conventional methods cannot be directly applied to them. Therefore, authors focus on the fact that the partial regression coefficients of each feature learned in the regression model represent the relationship with the target variable. And they consider obtaining a vector representation from the estimated values to represent the characteristics of the products. Specifically, we use the partial regression coefficients obtained when learning a binary classifier that discriminates whether or not each product is purchased by using information such as customer attributes obtained from purchase history data as the feature values. Here, the obtained partial regression coefficients are considered to represent relationships between target variables and explanatory examples such as the customer attributes and situations. Thus, products with similar vector representations can be regarded as similar in terms of the conditions under which they are likely to be purchased. The authors' proposed method enables product analysis based on purchase history data, even for product groups that have been difficult to analyze with conventional methods. And it allows us to utilize the knowledge gained in product design that is currently based only on the experience of the person in charge.

3.2 Learning Steps of the Method

The learning steps of the proposed method are shown below.

1. Creating the training data-set
2. Training the binary classifiers
3. Representing vectors of products using coefficients and analyzing similarities between products

Creating the Training Data-Set. In order to train a binary classifier to discriminate the purchase of a certain product A, authors create a data-set with the purchase data of product A as positive examples and the purchase data of other products as negative examples. Here, if all the data stored on the site is used, the negative example data will be "all the data that did not purchase product A", and the number of data will be extremely biased. When a binary classifier is applied to training data with such an unbalanced number of positive and negative examples, the coefficients cannot be estimated properly. The coefficients obtained from such unbalanced training data do not truly stand for the characteristics of the data [6]. Therefore, it is necessary to under-sample the negative example data appropriately to match the number of positive and negative examples. It should also be noted that the estimated coefficients will differ depending on how the negative examples are sampled.

Training the Binary Classifiers. In the artificial data generated in this paper, it is assumed that the probability of a certain product being purchased is influenced by each variable and their interaction. Therefore, in training a binary classifier, we will use FM [19], which represents the interaction by the product of the interaction matrices and allows us to evaluate the interaction with few parameters.

For a binary classifier that estimates whether or not a certain product A has been purchased, the objective variable $y^A(\boldsymbol{x})$ is a variable that takes 1 when a certain product A has been purchased and -1 when another product has been purchased, and let $\boldsymbol{x}^A$ denote the feature value. For the sake of clarity, the feature value is also described as $\boldsymbol{x}^A$ with the name of product, A. However, the order of the feature value vector does not change for each product because the order does not depend on which product is the target. Then $\boldsymbol{x}$ always has a constant domain of definition regardless of which product purchase is treated as the target variable.

From the following Eq. (1), the coefficients representing the direct effect of each variable $\boldsymbol{w}^A = (w_0^A, w_1^A, ..., w_d^A)$ and the matrix representing the interaction $\boldsymbol{V}^A \in \mathcal{R}^{d \times k}$ are learned. Here, note that $\boldsymbol{V}^A = (\boldsymbol{v}_1^{A^\top}, \boldsymbol{v}_2^{A^\top}, ..., \boldsymbol{v}_d^{A^\top})^\top$, $\boldsymbol{v}_i^A = (v_{i1}^A, v_{i2}^A, ..., v_{ik}^A)^\top$.

$$\hat{y}^A(\boldsymbol{x}) = w_0^A + \sum_{i=1}^{d} w_i^A x_i^A + \sum_{i=1}^{d} \sum_{j=i+1}^{d} \langle \boldsymbol{v}_i^A, \boldsymbol{v}_j^A \rangle x_i^A x_j^A \qquad (1)$$

$$\langle \boldsymbol{v}_i^A, \boldsymbol{v}_j^A \rangle = \sum_{l=1}^{k} v_{il}^A v_{jl}^A \qquad (2)$$

The loss function to be minimized when learning $\boldsymbol{w}^A$ and $\boldsymbol{V}^A$ is expressed by the following Eq. (3). where $\hat{y}^A$ is the predicted value.

$$\ln\left(\exp(-y^A \hat{y}^A) + 1\right) + \lambda_w \|\boldsymbol{w}^A\| + \lambda_v \|\boldsymbol{V}^A\| \qquad (3)$$

Here, $\|\boldsymbol{\alpha}\|$ represents Euclidean norms of vector $\boldsymbol{\alpha}$ or matrix $\boldsymbol{\alpha}$. And λ_w and λ_v are regularization parameters to prevent over-learning of parameters. In this study, the alternating least squares method is used to estimate the parameters.

Representing Vectors of Products Using Coefficients and Analyzing Similarities Between Products. This section describes a method for evaluating the similarity of products using partial regression coefficients obtained from a trained binary classifier. When creating the training data in this study, it should be noted that for each piece of information in the purchase data, qualitative variables are transformed using dummy variables in order to apply FM. Figure 2 shows the interaction matrix to be learned in FM and the $d \times d$-dimensional matrix $\boldsymbol{V}^A \boldsymbol{V}^{A\top}$ that shows the interaction between the features obtained from it. Authors focus on the right diagonal component because the $d \times d$-dimensional matrix $\boldsymbol{V}^A \boldsymbol{V}^{A\top}$ shown in Fig. 2 is a diagonal matrix. Here, the feature $\boldsymbol{x}$ is a 1-hot vector with a dummy variable for each qualitative variable so that its values are 0 and 1. Then, in the $d \times d$-dimensional matrix, there are apparent interactions between the same qualitative variables caused by the introduction of dummy variables, and it is not appropriate to use its value for similarity evaluation. Therefore, the areas to be used for similarity analysis in this study are the direct effect $\boldsymbol{w}$ and the upper right part of Fig. 2. However, note that the main purpose of this paper is not to evaluate the similarity between products, but to evaluate the estimation accuracy of the obtained coefficients themselves.

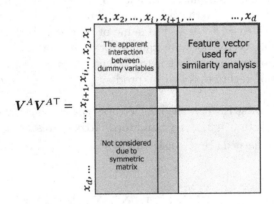

Fig. 2. A part for similarity analysis.

4   Experiment

4.1   A Detail of Artificial Data

In this section, we explain the details of the generated artificial data, including the preconditions for the data structure and the method of generating the purchase history data.

Data Structure Assumptions. The artificial data generated in this paper mimics purchase history data. We assume that each product has a set of features that indicate how likely or unlikely it is to be purchased when each observed variable is given. The features consist of the direct effect of the observed variable and the interaction effect of each combination of them. Furthermore, assume that each product belongs to one of the C clusters, and that the feature value is generated from a standard normal distribution with different means for each cluster. The average of each features is assumed to be 0, and the variance of the direct effect is assumed to be 0.2, the variance of the interaction is assumed to be 0.1. And the value of the center vector of each cluster is assumed to be in the range of -0.5 to 0.5.

The direct effect of the actual data generated as the number of cluster $c = 3$ is shown in the Fig. 3 below. The number of categorical observed variables was set to 5, the number of types of values that each categorical variable can take was set to 4. As a result, for each categorical variable, the final number of feature dimensions was 20, since it is converted into a 1-hot vector representing the presence or absence of each element. And the number of products belonging to each category was set to 10. Note that The sum of the values of the center vectors of each cluster is set to zero, so that there is no difference in the ease of being purchased by the clusters.

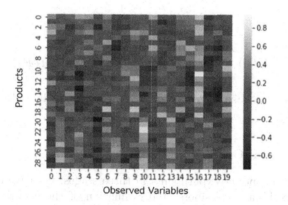

Fig. 3. Generated direct effect features (number of clusters 3).

The feature values of a product are shown below in Fig. 4 for the interaction of the certain data generated as the number of cluster $c = 3$. For convenience, the feature for the apparent interaction between dummy variables is set to zero.

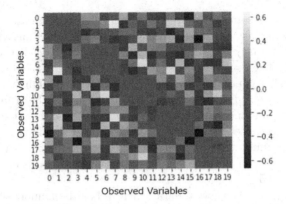

Fig. 4. Generated interaction effect features (number of clusters 3).

Generate of Purchase History Data. We respectively defined the value of the n-th products as α_n and β_n for the generated feature vectors of direct effect and interaction shown in the Sect. 4.1. For each purchase, the purchase probability $P_i(x)$ for each product is obtained using the following Eq. 4 with the observed variables $x = \{x_0, x_1, ..., x_D\}$. Here, x_0 is a bias term and $x_0 = 1$ for all data.

$$P_n(x) = \frac{1}{1 + e^{-f_n(x)}} \tag{4}$$

$$f_n(x) = \sum_{d=0}^{D} \alpha_{n,d} x_d + \sum_{d=1}^{D} \sum_{d'=d+1}^{D} \beta_{n,d,d'} x_d x_{d'} \tag{5}$$

We created the purchase history data by probabilistically selecting products according to $P_n(x)$.

4.2 Experimental Condition

In this paper, we conduct experiments in three stages: negative example selection, training of binary classifiers, and evaluation of the accuracy of the estimated features. For the negative example selection method, we use the following methods to compare their accuracy.

1. Randomly selected from all of data
2. Randomly select from products in the same cluster
3. Randomly select products from the same cluster with noise
4. Randomly select products from different clusters
5. Randomly select from products in different clusters with noise

An annotation "with noise" means that randomly select a certain percentage as noise. As to a phase of training of binary classifiers, the Factorization Machine is used as the binary classifier in the experiment.

Finally, in the accuracy evaluation, we evaluate whether the coefficients obtained by the binary classifier are able to estimate the true values. Here, considering the usage of the estimated features obtained by this method, it is not necessary to estimate the actual values themselves. This is because the important point in product design and policy planning is "which observed variables have a positive impact" and "what is the relationship between the size of these variables." For this purpose, it is sufficient to understand the relative relationships among the feature values. Thus, we consider using the standardized value of each element of the matrix. Here, the standardizing was done in a way that is proportional to the original value. From the above perspective, the following Eq. 6 and Eq. 7 are used to evaluate the estimation accuracy. These mean a mean square error (MSE) between standardized estimated features and standardized true features.

$$\text{MSE}_\alpha = \frac{1}{N}\sum_{n=1}^{N}\frac{1}{D}\sum_{d=1}^{D}(\hat{\alpha}_{n,d}^{\text{standard}} - \alpha_{n,d}^{\text{standard}})^2 \tag{6}$$

$$\text{MSE}_\beta = \frac{1}{N}\sum_{n=1}^{N}\frac{1}{D \times (D-1)}\sum_{d=1}^{D}\sum_{d'=d+1}^{D}(\hat{\beta}_{n,d,d'}^{\text{standard}} - \beta_{n,d,d'}^{\text{standard}})^2 \tag{7}$$

Here, N is the number of kinds of products, D is the dimension of visible variance x and $\hat{}$ means $\cdot$ is estimated one. And features with the description of "standard" on the right shoulder indicate that they have been standardized using the above method.

4.3   Experimental Result

Evaluation of Estimation Accuracy. We will examine the degree of accuracy of the estimation. The following figure shows the average trend of the accuracy when the number of interaction dimensions k is changed in the data with 3 clusters and 10 trials were conducted. The selection of negative examples is random, the regularization terms are all set to 0.01, and the number of purchase histories generated is 5,000.

Figure 5 that the accuracy changes with the change in k for both MAE_α and MAE_β. When $k = 0$, it means that interaction is not considered, which is equivalent to estimation by multiple regression analysis. For example, the MAE for $k = 4$, which is the lowest value for the estimation accuracy of $\hat{\alpha}$, is 0.11, which means that it can be estimated with a certain accuracy. On the other hand, the minimum value of MAE_β is 0.20 at $k = 2$, indicating that the estimation accuracy is lower than that of alpha. This can be attributed to the fact that beta is a feature given to the combination of multiple observed variables, then the number of data available for estimating the feature is less than the direct effect.

In addition, we perform a qualitative evaluation. The heat map of the α estimates and the true values after standardization is shown in Fig. 6.

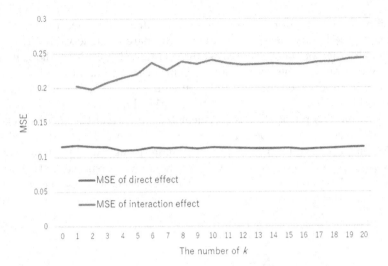

Fig. 5. Change in accuracy of feature estimation by interaction dimensionality k (number of clusters 3).

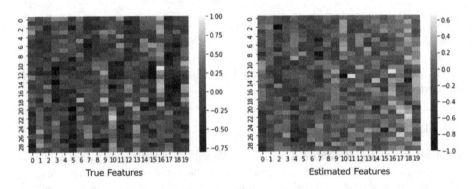

Fig. 6. Heat-map of α true and estimates values (after standardized).

According to the Fig. 6, it can be said that the approximate trend can be estimated. And it is reasonable to evaluate the relationship between each variable and the target variable by using the authors' method.

Next, we evaluate the estimation accuracy for data with the number of cluster $c = 4$ in the same way. The following figure shows the change in accuracy when the dimension k of the interaction matrix is changed. The Fig. 7 shows that the accuracy is generally worse than that for $c = 3$, with a minimum of 0.12. The same trend was observed for MAE_β, where the accuracy was still lower. Even at $c = 4$, the MAE was below a certain level, suggesting that using the features obtained from the coefficients to conduct product analysis has a certain effect.

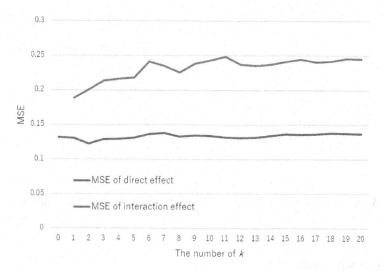

Fig. 7. Change in accuracy of feature estimation by interaction dimensionality k (number of clusters 4).

Accuracy Change by Negative Example Selection Method. The change in accuracy as the number of interaction matrix dimensions k changes is shown in Fig. 8 for the accuracy of feature estimation by negative example selection. The left figure shows the estimation accuracy of the direct effect feature α, and the right figure shows the estimation accuracy of the interaction feature β. Note that for the with noise method, it is assumed that there is a 20% probability that a cluster will become a negative example even if it does not belong to the negative example selection target.

From Fig. 8, the direct effect was the lowest when negative examples were selected from the same category, and the next lowest when noise was included in the selection from the same category. This may be due to the fact that products in the same category have similar features, so when they are selected as negative examples, proper estimation is not possible. On the other hand, random, different categories, and different categories-with-noise methods all showed better MAE, with the best value of 0.12 under the condition of selecting from different categories and setting $k = 3$. As to interaction features, there was no significant difference in the accuracy between the negative example selection methods. The best value was obtained when the negative examples were selected with different categories with noise and trained with $k = 1$. These results confirm that the negative example selection method has an impact on the obtained features. Furthermore, it was shown that it is effective to select products belonging to different clusters from the target product as negative examples in order to improve accuracy.

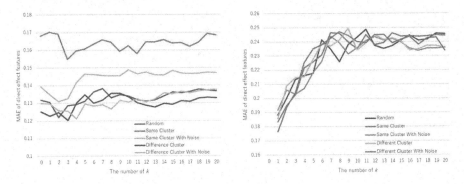

Fig. 8. Accuracy of feature estimation by negative example selection (number of clusters 4).

5   Consideration

Conducted experiments make it clear that the authors' method can also estimate the features of each product that have a small number of purchases per customer and are difficult to be regarded as similar even if they are purchased by the same customers. This method does not use any information on whether or not a product has been purchased by the same customer. Therefore, we can apply this method onto the products group that conventional methods can not be applied.

In addition, from the experiments in which the negative example selection method was varied, it became clear that it was necessary to select products belonging to a different cluster from the positive example target products as negative examples. Here, we discuss whether such a negative example selection is possible or not. When we conducted clustering based on the direct effect features obtained using the authors' method, we were able to estimate the clusters correctly both when the number of clusters was 3 and when the number of clusters was 4. Therefore, we can conclude that even if we don't have cluster data of each products, we can estimated and use the information for select of negative sampling under this condition. Furthermore, even for real data, it is possible to obtain cluster information to a certain extent by using only the direct effects at first, and then re-selecting negative examples appropriately based on the direct effects, to achieve more accurate feature estimation.

6   Conclusion and Future Work

In this paper, we examined the effectiveness and applicability of the feature analysis method proposed by the authors using artificial data. Specifically, it is a method that learns a binary classifier that predicts whether or not a certain product has been purchased based on purchase history data. And it considers the coefficients of the estimated variables as feature values. As a result of verification using artificial data, the method showed a certain level of accuracy, and the validity of the method was clarified. In addition, it made clear that the estimation accuracy depends on how negative examples are selected in the data selection process when learning the binary classifier. Future tasks include proposing a negative example selection method to improve the estimation accuracy and improving the expressiveness of the model.

References

1. Barkan, O., Caciularu, A., Katz, O., Koenigstein, N.: Attentive item2vec: neural attentive user representations. In: IEEE International Conference on Acoustics, Speech and Signal Processing, pp. 3377–3381. IEEE (2020)
2. Barkan, O., Caciularu, A., Rejwan, I., Katz, O., Weill, J., Malkiel, I., Koenigstein, N.: Cold item recommendations via hierarchical item2vec. In: 2020 IEEE International Conference on Data Mining, pp. 912–917. IEEE (2020)
3. Barkan, O., Koenigstein, N.: Item2vec: neural item embedding for collaborative filtering. In: IEEE 26th International Workshop on Machine Learning for Signal Processing, pp. 1–6. IEEE (2016)
4. Burt, S., Sparks, L.: E-commerce and the retail process: a review. J. Retail. Consum. Serv. **10**(5), 275–286 (2003)
5. Ministry of Economy and IT Industry: Fiscal year 2019 international economic research project for the establishment of an integrated domestic and international economic growth strategy (market research on electronic identification systems) (2020)
6. Fernández, A., García, S., Galar, M., Prati, R.C., Krawczyk, B., Herrera, F.: Learning From Imbalanced Data Sets, vol. 11. Springer, Cham (2018). https://doi.org/10.1007/978-3-319-98074-4
7. Fujii, R., Okamoto, K.: Model-based collaborative filtering with transparency using linear regression. JSAI **35**(1), D-J61_1 (2020)
8. Gerrikagoitia, J.K., Castander, I., Rebón, F., Alzua-Sorzabal, A.: New trends of intelligent e-marketing based on web mining for e-shops. Proc. Soc. Behav. Sci. **175**(1), 75–83 (2015)
9. Gui, Y., Xu, Z.: Training recurrent neural network on distributed representation space for session-based recommendation. In: 2018 International Joint Conference on Neural Networks, pp. 1–6. IEEE (2018)
10. He, R., Kang, W.C., McAuley, J.: Translation-based recommendation. In: Proceedings of the Eleventh ACM Conference on Recommender Systems, pp. 161–169 (2017)
11. Hotoda, M., Kumoi, G., Goto, M.: A study on customer purchase behavior analysis based on hidden topic Markov models. Indust. Eng. Manage. Syst. **20**(1), 48–60 (2021)
12. Jin, J., Geng, Q., Mou, H., Chen, C.: Author-subject-topic model for reviewer recommendation. J. Inf. Sci. **45**(4), 554–570 (2019)
13. Koren, Y., Bell, R., Volinsky, C.: Matrix factorization techniques for recommender systems. Computer **42**(8), 30–37 (2009)
14. Li, Z., Zhao, H., Liu, Q., Huang, Z., Mei, T., Chen, E.: Learning from history and present: next-item recommendation via discriminatively exploiting user behaviors. In: Proceedings of the 24th ACM SIGKDD International Conference on Knowledge Discovery and Data Mining, pp. 1734–1743 (2018)

15. Lu, Y., Dong, R., Smyth, B.: Coevolutionary recommendation model: mutual learning between ratings and reviews. In: Proceedings of the 2018 World Wide Web Conference, pp. 773–782 (2018)
16. Park, E.O., Chae, B.K., Kwon, J., Kim, W.H.: The effects of green restaurant attributes on customer satisfaction using the structural topic model on online customer reviews. Sustainability **12**(7), 2843 (2020)
17. Pei, W., Yang, J., Sun, Z., Zhang, J., Bozzon, A., Tax, D.M.: Interacting attention-gated recurrent networks for recommendation. In: Proceedings of the 2017 ACM on Conference on Information and Knowledge Management, pp. 1459–1468 (2017)
18. Rahutomo, R., Perbangsa, A.S., Soeparno, H., Pardamean, B.: Embedding model design for producing book recommendation. In: 2019 International Conference on Information Management and Technology, vol. 1, pp. 537–541. IEEE (2019)
19. Rendle, S.: Factorization machines. In: 2010 IEEE International Conference on Data Mining, pp. 995–1000. IEEE (2010)
20. Sun, Z., Yang, J., Zhang, J., Bozzon, A., Huang, L.K., Xu, C.: Recurrent knowledge graph embedding for effective recommendation. In: Proceedings of the 12th ACM Conference on Recommender Systems, pp. 297–305 (2018)
21. Takamitsu, S.: Regression Analysis. Asakura Publishing, Tokyo (1979)
22. Tang, J., Wang, K.: Personalized top-n sequential recommendation via convolutional sequence embedding. In: Proceedings of the Eleventh ACM International Conference on Web Search and Data Mining, pp. 565–573 (2018)
23. Tran, T., Lee, K., Liao, Y., Lee, D.: Regularizing matrix factorization with user and item embeddings for recommendation. In: Proceedings of the 27th ACM International Conference on Information and Knowledge Management, pp. 687–696 (2018)
24. Xu, C.: A novel recommendation method based on social network using matrix factorization technique. Inf. Process. Manage. **54**(3), 463–474 (2018)
25. Yamagiwa, A., Kumoi, G., Goto, M.: An analytical model based on purchase history for products with low multiple purchases from each customer. IEICE J105–D(5) (2022). (in press)
26. Yoon, Y.C., Lee, J.W.: Movie recommendation using metadata based word2vec algorithm. In: 2018 International Conference on Platform Technology and Service (PlatCon), pp. 1–6. IEEE (2018)

Clustering and Feature Analysis of Shoes Brands Using Questionnaire Data and Word-of-Mouth Review Data

Haruki Yamaguchi[1]($\boxtimes$), Kohei Otake[2], and Takashi Namatame[3]

[1] Graduate School of Science and Engineering, Chuo University, 1-13-27, Kasuga, Bunkyo-ku, Tokyo 112-8551, Japan
a18.jyet@g.chuo-u.ac.jp
[2] School of Information and Telecommunication Engineering, Tokai University, 2-3-23, Takanawa, Minato-ku, Tokyo 108-8619, Japan
otake@tsc.u-tokai.ac.jp
[3] Faculty of Science and Engineering, Chuo University, 1-13-27, Kasuga, Bunkyo-ku, Tokyo 112-8551, Japan
nama@kc.chuo-u.ac.jp

Abstract. Currently, competition for customers in the shoes industry is intensifying due to the entry from other industries such as the apparel industry. Therefore, we believe that it is an important issue for each brand to understand the values of its customers and to differentiate itself from other brands in order to build a strong relationship among them. In this study, we use a questionnaire data to understand the values of customers who own each shoes brand, and believe brands that have customers with similar values as brands that are likely to compete with each other. In addition, using a word-of-mouth review data of EC site, we identify differences in the directionality of each shoes brand based on the composition of word-of-mouth reviews for each brand. Based on these results and the demographic data of each brand owners obtained from the questionnaire data, we discuss the points that should be differentiated among some brands that are likely to compete with each other in terms of customer values.

Keywords: Consumer's value · Shoes brand · Hierarchical cluster analysis · Factor analysis

1 Introduction

Nowadays, shoes industry is becoming increasingly competitive, with many companies from other industries entering the market [1, 2]. In order to survive in such a competitive environment, it is important to build and maintain strong relationships between brands and customers [3]. In order to create such a relationship, it is necessary to build a relationship of trust with customers by understanding their values and selling products that match those values.

G. Meiselwitz (Ed.): HCII 2022, LNCS 13316, pp. 403–421, 2022.
https://doi.org/10.1007/978-3-031-05064-0_30

In addition, in recent years, the purchase process has changed due to the advancement of information transmission technologies such as SNS, and consumers are now transmitting their evaluations of products and brands on SNS and reviews on mail order sites after purchasing products. In addition, the word of mouth can help consumers decide whether or not to make a purchase [4]. Word-of-mouth review data is useful not only for customers, but also for the brands that sell the products. We believe that reviews of own products can help us understand what we can do to improve own products, while reviews of competitors' products are useful for comparison with own. Therefore, word-of-mouth review data of a product is useful in differentiating it from competitors.

Furthermore, it is now easier than in the past to obtain various types of information, including written data such as reviews and numerical data such as sales. Therefore, it is important to analyze data from multiple sources in a complex manner rather than analyzing only a single data set.

2 Purpose

In this study, we focus on the customer's values and evaluation of the product at the time of purchase in a shoes brand. For each brand, securing a fixed number of customers who continue to buy from the brand will stabilize business performance. Therefore, the values of customers who own the products of their own brand are important information that leads to continuous purchasing. In addition, product evaluations at the time of purchase enable us to understand customers' impressions of own brand and other brands, which is important information for retaining existing customers and acquiring new customers. Therefore, this study analyzes the values of customers who support each shoes brand, and treats brands with customers with similar values as brands that are likely to become competitors. Moreover, based on the aspect of product evaluation, the points that should be differentiated from those of the competition will be examined.

3 Data

In this section, we describe the summary of "large-scale questionnaire data on consumer lifestyles targeting approximately 30,000 people" and the "Rakuten product review data" which are used in this study.

3.1 Questionnaire Data

In this study, we use large-scale questionnaire data on consumer lifestyles of about 30,000 people (hereinafter referred to as "questionnaire data") conducted in 2015, which was provided by a Japanese research company. We used data from responses to the following seven questions.

- Values of purchasing and ownership: 5-point scale questions on purchasing and ownership
- Values of information and lifestyle: 5-point scale question on information and lifestyle

- Owned brands of footwear (female): Question indicating whether women own 123 footwear brands
- Owned brands of footwear (men): Question indicating whether men own 118 footwear brands
- Points to consider important when purchasing footwear: Questions about important factors when purchasing shoes (16 choices)
- Demographic data (age and occupation).

The questions on values (purchasing and ownership) and values (information and lifestyle) are as follows (Tables 1 and 2).

Table 1. Values (purchasing and ownership) question contents

Question no.	Question contents
Q124_1	I'm not one to care about brands or reputation as long as I like it
Q124_2	I tend to buy things on impulse when I intuitively like them
Q124_3	I often find myself unintentionally coveting things that other people around me have
Q124_4	I'm the kind of person who actually buys new products and tries them out
Q124_5	I often shop based on sales rankings
Q124_6	I think the higher price tag is worth it
Q124_7	Once we like a product or brand, we tend to keep buying it
Q124_8	I want to use good things as carefully as possible for as long as possible
Q124_9	I like to own branded stuff
Q124_10	I think I only want to put things around me that I like
Q124_11	You want to have something as different from the people around you as possible
Q124_12	Shopping is often a matter of not compromising until you find what you really want
Q124_13	I think it shows your personality in what kind of shopping you do
Q124_14	I think shopping is fun

The number of respondents to this questionnaire data is as follows.

- The number of male respondents: 13,113
- The number of female respondents: 14,978
- The number of male respondents who did not answer "None" for the brand they own: 5656
- The number of female respondents who did not answer "None" for the brand they own: 9747

Table 2. Values (information and lifestyle) question contents

Question no.	Question contents
Q125_1	I'm always checking for new products
Q125_2	It's hard to keep track of one thing after another that I want
Q125_3	I'm sick and tired of being misinformed
Q125_4	People around me often ask me for advice
Q125_5	When I do something with my friends, I'm more likely to be invited than to invite them
Q125_6	I don't think I'm very good at giving advice to people
Q125_7	I think I'm the type that gets hot and cold easily
Q125_8	I like to go out to places that are popular and visited by many people
Q125_9	I would rather have a stable life with less risk than an exciting but risky life
Q125_10	I would rather avoid trouble with others by not asserting myself than by asserting myself even if it means fighting with others
Q125_11	I cherish my leisure time and strongly desire to enrich it
Q125_12	Work is my purpose in life, and I want to live my life around work
Q125_13	I'm concerned about how I'm perceived by others
Q125_14	I want to be recognized by the people around me

3.2 Word-of-Mouth Review Data

In this study, we use product review data from the Rakuten dataset (2015) (hereafter referred to as "word-of-mouth review data") provided by Rakuten Group, Inc. via IDR Dataset Service of National Institute of Informatics [5]. From word-of-mouth review data, the following two items were used.

- Product name
- Description of review

Word-of-mouth review data consists of product reviews of various categories. Therefore, it is necessary to extract and analyze only the data of shoe products. In addition, the questionnaire data and word-of-mouth review data were taken separately. Therefore, it is necessary to extract only the review data of brands that are commonly included in both of them so that these can be consistent. The following shows the procedure for extracting analytical data from word-of-mouth review data.

1. From word-of-mouth review data, we extracted data containing any of the following seven words in the product name column: " 靴(shoes), シューズ(shoes), ブーツ(boots), サンダル(sandals), パンプス(pumps), スニーカー(sneakers), 厚底(thick soles),ローファー(loafers)". With these processes, we extracted product data related to shoes from word-of-mouth review data.

2. From the data extracted from the product data related to shoes, we extracted data that included the names of male and female brands in the questionnaire data as product names, and created word-of-mouth review data for male brands and word-of-mouth review data for female brands. This was done to ensure consistency between the questionnaire data and the word-of-mouth review data.

3. From the word-of-mouth review data, which was consistent with the questionnaire data, the sample size of each brand was aggregated, and we selected only brands with a sample size of 100 or more as dataset for analysis.

As a result of extraction, 68 brands for men and 56 brands for women were included in the analysis.

4 Analysis Methods

In this section, we explain the analysis methods used in this study.

4.1 Factor Analysis

Factor analysis is a multivariate analysis method for estimating the latent factors that exist behind the observed variables obtained through experiments. In this study, we conducted an exploratory factor analysis, which is a factor analysis without hypotheses about the factor structure. Exploratory factor analysis is a method of estimating factor loadings from a factor to an observed variable by assuming that there are factor loadings from all factors to all observed variables. Each factor does not have a pre-defined name, but is interpreted from the relationship of the factor loadings to the observed variables to determine what the factor indicates. Therefore, in order to make it easier to interpret the factors, varimax rotation was used in this study.

In this study, from the viewpoint of cluster interpretation in the clustering to be conducted later, factor analysis was conducted on the response data of values (purchase and ownership) and values (information and lifestyle) in the questionnaire data to interpret the values of customers. From the obtained factor scores of the respondents' values (purchasing and ownership) and values (information and lifestyle), and from the response data of the brands owned by each respondent, the factor scores of the values of the respondents who own each brand were averaged, and the average factor score was defined as the "factor score of customers who support the brand" (hereinafter referred to as the value factor score of the brand). After analyzing the data, we treated the data separately for males and females, as described above.

The number of factors was determined using the result of parallel analysis. Parallel analysis is an analysis method in which the eigenvalues calculated by factor analysis from the data for analysis are compared with the eigenvalues calculated from the correlation matrix of random numbers generated with the same sample size as the data for analysis, for each number of factors, and the number of factors when the eigenvalues of the data for analysis are higher than those of the random number data is considered to be the appropriate number of factors.

4.2 Hierarchical Cluster Analysis

Hierarchical clustering is a method of clustering all data into a hierarchical structure by comparing the data one by one, grouping the similar data into clusters, and repeating the process of grouping the data or clusters that are most similar to the clusters. There are multiple ways to calculate the similarity between the data, and the clustering results will vary depending on the method selected. There are multiple ways to calculate the similarity between the data, and the clustering results will vary depending on the method selected. In this study, we chose the Ward's method, which creates clusters from the smallest sum of squares of each data.

In this study, in order to subdivide the clusters from the viewpoint of determining the brands that are likely to become competitors because the values of the customers who own each brand are similar, we divided the value factor score of the brand into "purchase and ownership" and "information and lifestyle" and performed hierarchical clustering for each. Finally, by combining these results into one, the result of clustering is the number of clusters multiplied by the number of clusters for " purchase and ownership" and "information and lifestyle" respectively.

Furthermore, in this study, we used the NbClust package in R to determine the optimal number of clusters for each data. The NbClust package is a package that provides 30 indices for determining the number of clusters and proposes to user the best clustering scheme from the different results obtained by varying all combinations of number of clusters, distance measures, and clustering methods [5].

4.3 Word Frequency Analysis

Word frequency analysis is an analysis method that calculates the document frequency in which a particular word appears.

In this study, as a means of analyzing the differences in product evaluation among brands, we took the method of analyzing the differences in the review composition of each brand. In order to analyze the differences in review composition, word frequency analysis was performed on word-of-mouth review data. The frequency of occurrence was measured using the following 12 words, which are related to the evaluation of shoes and appear in most brand reviews: size, right size, cute, color, different colors, hue, design, cheap, comfortable, light, child, and work. Based on these frequencies of occurrence, we calculated the composition ratio of the 12 words for each brand from Eq. (1), and used these values to evaluate the brands from the aspect of product evaluation using review contents.

Word composition ratio of word i in a certain brand

$$= \frac{\text{Frequency of occurrence of word } i \text{ in a certain brand}}{\sum_{j \in A} \text{Frequency of occurrence of word } j \text{ in a certain brand}}$$

$A = \{$ size, right size, cute, color, different colors, hue, design, cheap, comfortable, light, child, work $\}$

$$(1)$$

4.4 Hierarchical Clustering Using Cosine Similarity

Cosine similarity is a similarity calculation method used to compare documents in a vector space model. It outputs the similarity between vectors as a cosine value of the angle between the vectors, so if the angle is close to 1, the direction of the vectors are close, and if it is close to -1, the direction of the vectors are opposite.

In this study, we calculated the cosine similarity for each brand using the word composition ratio calculated from the word frequency analysis, as in Eq. (2), and performed hierarchical clustering based on it. This allowed us to analyze the differences in the evaluation of brand proximity from the aspect of values and the aspect of product evaluation.

$$\text{Cosine similarity between brands A and B} = \cos(\boldsymbol{a}, \boldsymbol{b}) = \frac{\boldsymbol{a} \cdot \boldsymbol{b}}{\|\boldsymbol{a}\| \|\boldsymbol{b}\|}$$

$$\text{Vector of 12-word composition ratios for brand A:} \boldsymbol{a} = (a_1, a_2, \ldots, a_{12})^T \quad (2)$$

$$\text{Vector of 12-word composition ratios for brand B:} \boldsymbol{b} = (b_1, b_2, \ldots, b_{12})^T$$

5   Result

In this section, we present the results of the analysis conducted for the male and female brands.

5.1 Hierarchical Clustering Using Large Scale Questionnaire Data

Both male and female brands could be divided into six clusters.

Male Brands. We extract 6 factors about "purchasing and ownership" and "information and lifestyle" respectively, and each factor could be interpreted as follows.

- Values (purchasing and ownership)

  ML1: Brand-conscious
  ML2: Choosy
  ML3: Impulsive
  ML4: Following crowds
  ML5: Originality
  ML6: Price-conscious and likes to shop

- Values (information and lifestyle)

  ML1.1: Likes new things
  ML2.1: Advisor
  ML3.1: Hardworking

ML4.1: Approval desire
ML5.1: Avoid conflicts and troubles
ML6.1: Low self-esteem

The value of factor scores of the brands were calculated from the factor scores of each respondent in these six factors and the brands owned by the respondents. Based on the value factor scores of the brands, hierarchical clustering was conducted, and the shoes brands were classified into six clusters. The factor scores for each cluster are shown in Fig. 1, and based on the interpretation of each factor described above, the six clusters were defined as follows.

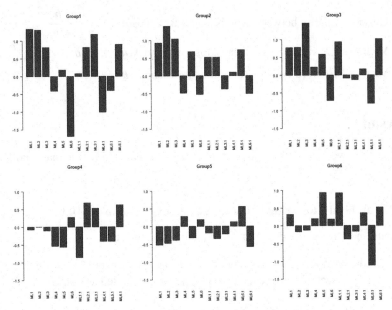

Fig. 1. Factor scores for each value cluster for male brands

• Interpreting clusters

group 1: Hardworking and having an obsession with brands.
group 2: Choosy and have uniqueness
group 3: Impulsive and likes new things
group 4: Price-conscious and likes to shop
group 5: Less particular about and avoid conflicts and troubles (plain)
group 6: Pioneer, influencer

The brands that were included in each of the six clusters are shown in Table 3. Table 3 shows the results of clustering for all male brands included in the questionnaire data.

Table 3. Male value cluster classification brand

Group	Classified brands	Number of brands
1	A.Testoni, Jhonston&Murphy, Jhon Lobb, Tony Lama, Bally, Marelli	6
2	Ugg, Alden, Keen, J.M.Weston, Takeo Kikuchi, Church's, Tod's, Trippen, Paraboot, Buttero, Moreschi	11
3	Gucci, Crockett&Jones, Salvatore Ferragam, Danner, Diesel, Red Wing	6
4	Valentino, Hermes, Scotch Grain, Dunhill, Chippewa, Trussardi, Bass, Hush Puppies, Haruta, Footjoy, Brooks, Pro-Keds, Pedala, Bobson, Bon Step, Madras, Mephisto, Lacoste, Lancel, Lanvin, Regal, Le Coq Sportif, Renoma	23
5	Asics, Adidas, Admiral, Umbro, Yves Saint Laurent, Airwalk, Ecco, Edwin, Onitsuka Tiger, Kansai Yamamoto, Camper, Katharine Hamnett, Washington Ginza Tokyo, Clarks, Crocs, K·Swiss, Converse, The North Face, Spingle Move, Spalding, Cedar Crest, Dunlop, Champion, 通勤快足(Business Express), Diadora, Timberland, Dragon Beard, Tricker's, Nike, New Balance, Burberry, Hydro-tech, Patrick, Vans, Pierre Cardin, Hiraki, Fila, Whoop-de-doo, Puma, Bridgestone, Hawkins, Madras Modello, Mizuno, Merrell, Muji, Mobus, Mont-bell, United Arrows, Yonex, Lee, Reebok, Rockport, World March	53
6	Alfredo Bannister, L.L.Bean, Gravis, Cole Haan, Columbia, Zara, Santoni, Skechers, Dc Shoes, Dr. Martens, Dolce&Gabbana, Visaruno, Birkenstock, Prada, Paul smith, Polo Ralph Lauren, Yanko, Ralph lauren, Louis Vuitton	19

Female Brands. We extract 6 factors about "purchasing and ownership" and "information and lifestyle" respectively, and each factor could be interpreted as follows.

- Values (purchasing and ownership)

  ML1: Believe that what we buy shows our personality
  ML2: Following crowds
  ML3: High price stability orientation
  ML4: Impulsive
  ML5: Brand-conscious
  ML6: Unique and selective orientation

- Values (information and lifestyle)

  ML1.1: Approval desire
  ML2.1: Advisor
  ML3.1: Avoid conflicts and troubles

ML4.1: Following crowds
ML5.1: Hardworking
ML6.1: Impulsive

The value factor scores of the brands were calculated from the factor scores of each respondent in these six factors and the brands owned by the respondents. Based on the value factor scores of the brands, hierarchical clustering was conducted, and the shoes brands were classified into six clusters. The factor scores for each cluster are shown in Fig. 2, and based on the interpretation of each factor described above, the six clusters were defined as follows.

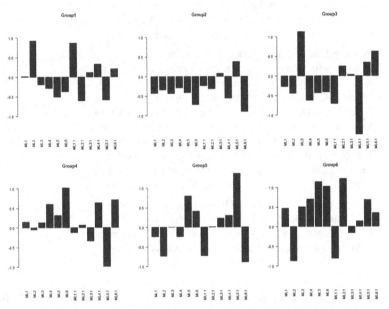

Fig. 2. Factor scores for each value cluster for female brands

- Interpreting clusters

group 1: Following crowds
group 2: Plain
group 3: High price stability orientation
group 4: Impulsive and Unique and selective orientation
group 5: Work-centric
group 6: Brand-conscious and go-getter

The brands that were included in each of the six clusters are shown in Table 4. Table 4 shows the results of clustering for all female brands included in the questionnaire data.

Table 4. Female value cluster classification brand

Group	Classified brands	Number of brands
1	Earth Music&Ecology, R&E, Akakura, Ugg, あしながおじさん(Ashinagaojisan), Adidas, Anna Sui, Untitled, Ingni, Esperanza, Odette e Odile, Oriental Traffic, Camui Water Massage, Crocs, Koos, Cocue, Converse, Gu, Jelly Beans, Shimamura, Strawberry-Fields, VII XII XXX, Tsumori Chisato, Tory Burch, Nike, 23区(Nijusanku), Natural, Beauty, Basic, New Balance, Nuovo, Barclay, Haruta, Vans, Birkenstock, Puma, Pool Side, Bobson, Mare Mare, Michel Klein. Minnetonka, Miu Miu, Muji, Le Coq Sportif, Repetto, Lowrys Farm	44
2	Asics, Ecco, Elle, Elegance Himiko, Ginza Kanematsu, Ginza Yoshinoya, Washington Ginza Tokyo, Coca, Skechers, Diana, Timberland, Hush Puppies, Patrick, Pansy, Pitti, Himiko, Hiraki, Fila, Pedala, Benetton, Benebis, Hawkins, Marie Claire, Mizuno, Mihama, Mode Kaori, Yonex, Regal, Reebok Riz Raffinee, Wacoal	31
3	Clark, Saya, Trippen, No Name, Madras, Merrell	6
4	Alfredo Bannister, Emu, Onitsuka Tiger, Cavacava, Jimmy Choo, Jill Stuart, Diesel, Dr. Martens, Bridget Birkin, Mode et Jacomo, Wano Nano	11
5	Yves Saint Laurent, Bally, Margaret Howell	3
6	Hermes, Camper, Gucci, Christian Dior, Christian Louboutin, Courrèges, Chloé, Coach, Cole Haan, Salvatore Ferragam, Chanel, Charles Jourdan, Sergio Rossi, Sonia Rykiel, Tod's, Trussardi, Nine West, Nina Ricci, Pinky&Dianne, Fin, Fendi, Prada, Bruno Magli, Marc Jacobs, Manolo Blahnik, Ralph Lauren, Louis Vuitton, Rebecca Taylor	28

5.2 Hierarchical Clustering by Using Cosine Similarity of Word Composition Ratios

Cosine similarity was calculated from the word composition ratio of the word-of-mouth review data, and hierarchical clustering was performed. The results of the clustering were plotted in the form of a dendrogram.

Male Brand. Figure 3 shows a dendrogram of male brands.

Female Brand. Figure 4 shows a dendrogram of female brands.

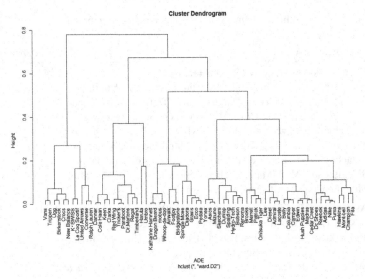

Fig. 3. A dendrogram created from the word composition ratio of male brands

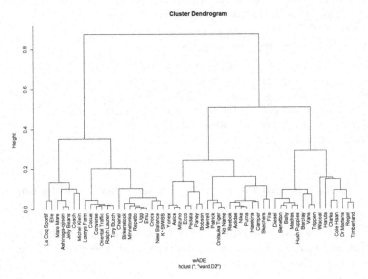

Fig. 4. A dendrogram created from the word composition ratio of female brands

6 Discussion

6.1 Comparison of Value and Product Evaluation Clustering

In this section, we compare and discuss the results of clustering of values and product evaluations.

From the clustering results of product evaluation (Figs. 3 and 4), the mass-market sneaker brands such as Asics, Yonex, Mizuno, Adidas, Puma, and Nike, which were classified in the same cluster in the male value cluster, were separated to form small groups in "Asics, Yonex, Mizuno" and "Adidas, Puma, Nike" respectively. This separation is similar to the results obtained when clustering female brands by value. However, the word-of-mouth review data with clustering of product evaluation does not have gender data of the reviewers. Therefore, we considered that if the proportion of female reviewers was large in the word-of-mouth review data, the reviews might have been tailored to women's values. Reebok, a brand aligned with these sports sneaker brands, was classified in the same group 2 as "Asics, Yonex, and Mizuno" in the women's value cluster (Table 4), but was next to "Adidas, Puma, and Nike" in the product evaluation cluster (Fig. 4). Therefore, we believed that Reebok's product direction was similar to that of Adidas, Puma, and Nike, but that the values of the customers who actually purchased and owned the products were similar to those of Asics, Yonex, and Mizuno.

In the women's value cluster, UGG and Emu, which sell shoes made of the same mouton material, were classified in different clusters. However, in the clustering of product evaluations (Fig. 4), UGG and Emu were found next to each other. Although there were no words directly related to mouton material in the 12 words subjected to word frequency analysis in this study, similar shoes brands were lined up in this way. Nevertheless, not all brands have similar designs and categories next to each other in the dendrogram of product evaluation. For example, among women's brands, No Name and Dr. Martens, which sell the same thick-soled shoes and boots, and among men's brands, Converse and Diesel, which are the same foreign sneaker brands, are not next to each other in the dendrogram of product evaluation. Therefore, the clustering of product evaluations was more difficult to interpret than the value clusters, although the clustering of product evaluations showed different brand similarity tendencies than the clustering of values. In addition, it is highly possible that there are brands for which differences in product evaluations could not be discriminated using only the 12 words extracted in the word frequency analysis, and we believe that there are areas for improvement in the clustering of product evaluations.

6.2 Evaluation of Sneaker Brands for the Masses

In this section, we discuss the factors that divide the aforementioned six mass-market sneaker brands into two sub-groups: "Asics, Yonex, and Mizuno", and "Adidas, Puma, and Nike".

Initially, the ratio of respondents who answered "points to consider important when purchasing footwear" for these brands is shown in Tables 5 and 6.

When we look at the "functions and performance" and "design" in Tables 5 and 6, we can see that although there is not a large difference in the values, "Asics, Yonex, and Mizuno" and "Adidas, Puma, and Nike" show a coherent trend of values, respectively. For both males and females, the ratio of "functions and performance" was from 1.5 to 2.0% higher for "Asics, Yonex, and Mizuno" than for "Adidas, Puma, and Nike". On the other hand, "design" was from 1.0 to 2.0% higher in "Adidas, Puma, and Nike" than in "Asics, Yonex, and Mizuno".Therefore, we believed that there might be a difference between "Asics, Yonex, and Mizuno", which emphasize functionality, and "Adidas, Puma, and

Table 5. Male Ratio of responses to "Points to consider important when purchasing footwear"

brandname	Comfortable	Quality	Functions and performance	Durability	Price	Manufacturer	Brand	Design	Color	Materiality	Size	Many dealers	There's a store I frequent	Word of mouth and reputation
Asics	0.1630	0.0808	0.1009	0.0786	0.1412	0.0769	0.0475	0.0712	0.0818	0.0494	0.0940	0.0033	0.0088	0.0027
Yonex	0.1553	0.0875	0.1065	0.0822	0.1347	0.0693	0.0434	0.0632	0.0822	0.0563	0.1035	0.0053	0.0068	0.0038
Mizuno	0.1567	0.0837	0.1011	0.0801	0.1384	0.0763	0.0459	0.0677	0.0847	0.0508	0.0986	0.0036	0.0099	0.0025
Adidas	0.1568	0.0801	0.0855	0.0685	0.1425	0.0813	0.0584	0.0846	0.0882	0.0497	0.0903	0.0032	0.0077	0.0033
Puma	0.1503	0.0782	0.0827	0.0710	0.1412	0.0814	0.0577	0.0843	0.0941	0.0527	0.0915	0.0029	0.0085	0.0035
Nike	0.1603	0.0801	0.0871	0.0692	0.1429	0.0798	0.0589	0.0822	0.0884	0.0484	0.0897	0.0030	0.0071	0.0029

Table 6. Female Ratio of responses to "Points to consider important when purchasing footwear"

brandname	Comfortable	Quality	Functions and performance	Durability	Price	Manufacturer	Brand	Design	Color	Materiality	Size	Many dealers	There's a store I frequent	Word of mouth and reputation
Asics	0.1527	0.0829	0.0935	0.0654	0.1153	0.0538	0.0403	0.0844	0.1008	0.0825	0.1097	0.0033	0.0108	0.0046
Yonex	0.1509	0.0862	0.1063	0.0654	0.1078	0.0520	0.0379	0.0736	0.1063	0.0870	0.1071	0.0037	0.0112	0.0045
Mizuno	0.1524	0.0829	0.0997	0.0610	0.1184	0.0559	0.0308	0.0820	0.1048	0.0783	0.1146	0.0042	0.0103	0.0047
Adidas	0.1466	0.0762	0.0790	0.0583	0.1241	0.0555	0.0446	0.0952	0.1099	0.0789	0.1112	0.0041	0.0112	0.0051
Puma	0.1531	0.0672	0.0761	0.0507	0.1211	0.0549	0.0504	0.1040	0.1129	0.0767	0.1145	0.0038	0.0101	0.0044
Nike	0.1500	0.0746	0.0825	0.0586	0.1192	0.0576	0.0473	0.0950	0.1095	0.0789	0.1099	0.0040	0.0089	0.0040

Nike", which emphasize design. However, since these values are small differences, we will also consider the value of the word composition ratio.

Table 7. Word composition ratio of the six brands

Brandname	Size	Right size	Cute	Color	Different colors	Hue	Design	Cheap	Comfortable	Light	Child	Work
Asics	0.145	0.006	0.046	0.079	0.021	0.010	0.127	0.129	0.128	0.192	0.097	0.021
Yonex	0.171	0.004	0.025	0.104	0.017	0.011	0.146	0.147	0.146	0.142	0.081	0.006
Mizuno	0.165	0.004	0.044	0.081	0.011	0.008	0.154	0.137	0.121	0.172	0.099	0.003
Adidas	0.231	0.004	0.096	0.083	0.016	0.014	0.153	0.114	0.092	0.128	0.057	0.006
Puma	0.192	0.011	0.122	0.103	0.023	0.013	0.140	0.123	0.075	0.123	0.058	0.015
Nike	0.214	0.012	0.112	0.124	0.018	0.017	0.126	0.106	0.087	0.107	0.071	0.006

The values of the word composition ratio of the six brands are shown in Table 7. In the case of Asics, Yonex, and Mizuno, the ratio of words indicating functionality, such as "comfortable" and "light," and in the case of Adidas, Puma, and Nike, the ratio of words indicating design, such as "cute," were markedly higher than those of "Points to consider important when purchasing footwear".

From these results, we believed that there were differences between "Asics, Yonex, Mizuno" and "Adidas, Puma, Nike" in terms of "functionality for competition and other uses" and "design that is easy to choose for the light users".

6.3 Proposals for Differentiation for Brands

In this section, we discuss the points that should be differentiated for each brand as described in the purpose of this study. The brands under consideration were those with similar product categories sold in clusters with a relatively large number of classified brands. The points that should be differentiated will be discussed by focusing on the aspects of values and product evaluation, and using demographic data as a supplement.

6.3.1 Male Brands

In the men's value cluster, Skechers and Dc Shoes, which were classified in the same cluster 6 (Pioneer, Influencer), are not universally known brands in Japan, but they are major sneaker brands overseas. Looking at the word composition ratios for Skechers and Dc Shoes (Table 8), Skechers has a relatively large proportion of words related to shoe functionality, such as "comfortable, light," while Dc Shoes has a relatively large proportion of words related to design and price, such as "design, cheap". In other words, Skechers is evaluated by customers for its functionality, while Dc Shoes is evaluated for its design and price. In terms of age group (Fig. 5), Skechers showed no owners in their 20s and a large percentage in their 40s to 60s, while Dc shoes showed a large percentage in their 20s to 30s. From these considerations, we thought that Skechers should differentiate itself in terms of functionality, such as comfort, which older generations demand, while Dc shoes should differentiate themselves in terms of design and affordability, which younger generations demand.

Table 8. Word composition ratio of Skechers, Dc Shoes

Brandname	Size	Right size	Cute	Color	Different colors	Hue	Design	Cheap	Comfortable	Light	Child	Work
Skechers	0.176	0.012	0.129	0.064	0.038	0.006	0.104	0.067	0.130	0.229	0.025	0.020
Dc Shoes	0.238	0.000	0.188	0.063	0.025	0.025	0.138	0.113	0.063	0.100	0.050	0.000

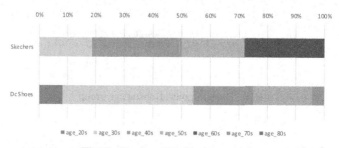

Fig. 5. Skechers, Dc Shoes age group

Similarly, we consider the points of differentiation for Hush Puppies and Bobson, which sell leather casual shoes and are classified as cluster 2 in the men's value cluster. The results of the word composition ratios (Table 9) showed that "cute, design, cheap" was relatively high for Hush Puppies, while "comfortable, light" was relatively high for Bobson. This difference in word composition ratio is similar to that for Skechers and Dc Shoes, but the difference is not as pronounced as for Skechers and Dc Shoes. The difference in the word composition ratio of "comfortable, light", which represents functionality, is relatively large, but the difference in the word composition ratio of "cute, design, cheap" is slightly smaller than in Table 8. Looking at the differences in age groups (Fig. 6), Hush Puppies showed a large proportion of people in their 20s to 40s, while the Bobson showed a small proportion of people in their 20s to 40s. This suggests that Hush Puppies are favored by a relatively younger generation, and therefore price and design are more important, while Bobson are favored by a relatively older generation, and therefore functionality such as comfort and lightness are more important than price and design. This suggests that Hush Puppies are favored by a relatively younger generation, and therefore price and design are more important, while Bobson are favored by a relatively older generation, and therefore functionality such as comfort and lightness are more important than price and design. Therefore, we believed that Hush Puppies should be differentiated by emphasizing price and design, which are demanded by younger generations, while Bobson should be differentiated by emphasizing functionality such as comfort and lightness, which are demanded by older generations.

Table 9. Word composition ratio of Hush Puppies, Bobson

Brandname	Size	Right size	Cute	Color	Different colors	Hue	Design	Cheap	Comfortable	Light	Child	Work
Hush Puppies	0.248	0.000	0.081	0.090	0.038	0.005	0.195	0.110	0.119	0.090	0.005	0.019
Bobson	0.169	0.000	0.042	0.078	0.030	0.018	0.163	0.078	0.175	0.223	0.012	0.012

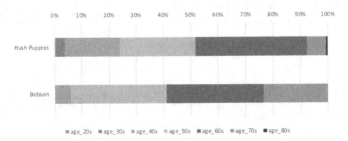

Fig. 6. Hush Puppies, Bobson age group

Female Brands. In the women's value cluster, we discuss the differentiation of the leather shoe brands Barclay, Haruta, and Lowrys Farm, which are classified in the same cluster 1 (following crowds). Looking at the word composition ratios of Barclay, Haruta, and Lowrys Farm (Table 10), Barclay has a large composition ratio of words expressing design, such as "color, different colors, design," Haruta has a large composition ratio of words expressing "size, cheap, child", and Lowrys Farm has a large composition ratio of words expressing "cute". These results show that there is a difference in that Barclay is valued for its design, which is different from "cute," while Lowry's Farm is valued for its design in the "cute" direction. In the case of Haruta, the high percentage of the word "child" suggests that parents are buying the products for their children to go to school, and size and price are also important. Lowrys Farm was also shown to be favored by the younger age group (Fig. 7). Therefore, we thought that Barclay should differentiate itself by emphasizing design that is supported by the middle class, Haruta by emphasizing affordable prices and sizes that fit children's feet as school shoes for children, and Lowrys Farm by emphasizing design that is supported by young people in their 20s and 30s.

Table 10. Word composition ratio of Barclay, Haruta and Lowrys Farm

Brandname	Size	Right size	Cute	Color	Different colors	Hue	Design	Cheap	Comfortable	Light	Child	Work
Barclay	0.248	0.006	0.065	0.155	0.097	0.019	0.187	0.058	0.097	0.019	0.000	0.013
Haruta	0.323	0.009	0.057	0.083	0.009	0.004	0.043	0.252	0.064	0.021	0.130	0.004
Lowrys Farm	0.182	0.020	0.253	0.111	0.040	0.020	0.101	0.121	0.101	0.020	0.010	0.020

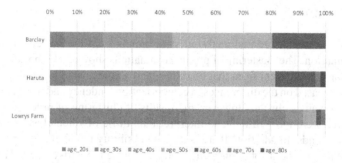

Fig. 7. Barclay, Haruta and Lowrys Farm age group

Similarly, we discuss the points of differentiation for Ecco and Elle, which sell a wide range of products from sneakers to leather shoes and are classified as cluster 2 in the women's value cluster. The results of the word composition ratios (Table 11) show that Ecco has a relatively high level of "comfortable" and a slightly higher level of "size, right size, color"; Elle has a relatively high level of "cute" and a slightly higher level of "design". In terms of age groups (Fig. 8), Ecco showed a large proportion of people in their 60s to 80s and Elle showed a large proportion of people in their 20s to 40s. Therefore, we believed that Ecco should be differentiated in terms of comfort and color-related design for the older generation, and Elle should be differentiated in terms of cute design for the younger generation.

Table 11. Word composition ratio of Ecco, Elle

Brandname	Size	Right size	Cute	Color	Different colors	Hue	Design	Cheap	Comfortable	Light	Child	Work
Ecco	0.204	0.022	0.032	0.081	0.043	0.011	0.199	0.097	0.199	0.091	0.005	0.016
Elle	0.142	0.005	0.260	0.059	0.039	0.010	0.211	0.083	0.088	0.098	0.000	0.005

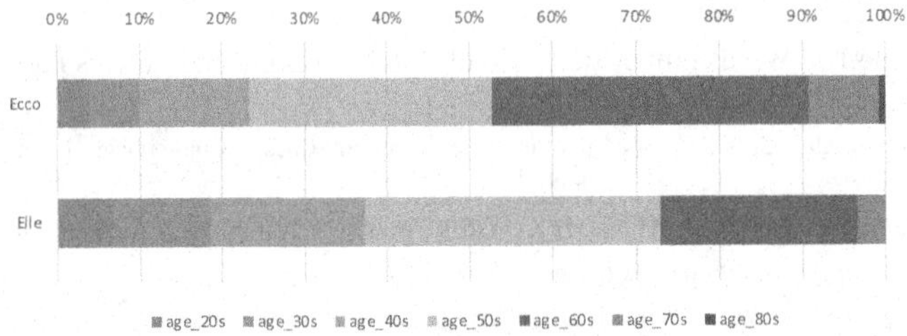

Fig. 8. Ecco, Elle age group

7 Conclusion

In this study, we compared and analyzed shoe brands from the aspects of values and product evaluation. The clustering of product evaluations showed a brand categorization tendency that was different from that of values, and we were able to consider points of differentiation based on the differences in categorization tendency and word composition ratio from the values cluster. However, the results of clustering of product evaluations by themselves were more difficult to interpret than those of value clusters in terms of classification trends. In addition, there is a high possibility that there are brands whose product evaluations could not be discriminated only by the 12 words extracted in the word frequency analysis, and we thought that the clustering of product evaluations should be improved.

Through these analyses, we were able to obtain results that support the fact that the mass-market sneaker brands "Asics, Yonex, and Mizuno" and "Adidas, Puma, and Nike" differ in terms of "functionality for competition" and "design that is easy to choose for the light users", respectively.

We were not able to examine the points that should be differentiated from competing brands for all brands, but we did examine them for some brands. Overall, brands with a large number of older owners tended to demand functionality, while brands with a large number of younger supporters tended to demand design. However, when examining more specific differentiation among them, the 12-word composition ratio used in this study left insufficient information to point out points of differentiation.

One of the future works of this study is that the number of brands classified in each cluster has become biased. Therefore, from the viewpoint of interpretability, we believed that we should have further subdivided the data into only those clusters with a large number of brands.

In addition, the 12 words used in the word frequency analysis were not enough to fully consider the points that should be differentiated in detail. Therefore, as an future work, we believed that it was necessary to strengthen the analysis method by organizing various words, including those other than the 12 words in this study, into directions such as "functionality" and "design" and evaluating the strength of each direction.

Acknowledgement. This work was supported by JSPS KAKENHI Grant Number 19K01945, 21H04600 and 21K13385.

References

1. ITmedia Business ONLINE: Not accepted at the time, but ...... UNIQLO re-enters the shoes business, 22 April 2015. https://www.itmedia.co.jp/makoto/articles/1504/22/news120.html. Accessed 1 Dec 2021
2. Gyokaidoukou search.com: What are the issues and problems in the shoes industry? 18 June 2021. https://gyokai-search.com/7-kutu-issue.html. Accessed 17 Dec 2021
3. Hato, M.: A review of brand image research and future challenges. J. Univ. Market. Distrib. Sci. Distrib. Sci. Bus. Admin. **33**(2), 1–19 (2021)
4. Taniguchi, Y.: Research on Strategic Product Planning Based on Word-of-Mouth Data Analysis
5. Rakuten Group, Inc.: Rakuten Dataset. Informatics Research Data Repository, National Institute of Informatics (2020). https://doi.org/10.32130/idr.2.1
6. R Documentation NbClust (versions 3.0). https://www.rdocumentation.org/packages/NbClust/versions/3.0/topics/NbClust. Accessed 18 Dec 2021
7. Kitajima, Y., Namatame, T., Otake, K.: A study on key brands that promote consumer brand transition - through analysis using a consumer value questionnaire. In: The Japan Society for Management Information 2019 Fall National Conference (2019)

Corner-Shopping: Studying Attitudes and Consumer Behavior on the Cornershop App

Diego Yáñez[✉], Cristóbal Fernández-Robin, and Florencia Bohle

Universidad Técnica Federico Santa María, Valparaíso, Chile
{diego.yanez,cristobal.fernandez}@usm.cl,
florencia.bohle@sansano.usm.cl

Abstract. Online shopping is one of the most popular online activities world-wide, in 2020, retail e-commerce sales worldwide amounted to 4.28 trillion US dollars and e-retail revenues are projected to grow to 5.4 trillion US dollars in 2022. Cornershop was born in 2015 with an initial capital of US $ 300 thousand. They managed to raise US $ 30 million and in just six years later, and after Uber announced that it would take 100% of the company, it was valued at no less than US $ 3,000 million. The present study aimed to model the continuity of use of the Cornershop app. The proposed model was made up of six latent variables, based on UTAUT2 which 8 hypotheses were proposed to explain the Behavioral Intention (BI) to use Cornershop. To obtain data, a survey was applied through SurveyMonkey, which consisted of 32 questions, intended to measure observable variables associated with the latent constructs of the model, and study the demographic profile of respondent that are users of Cornershop. Based on these results, it is possible to conclude that Performance Expectancy, Habit, Price Value, Hedonic Motivation and Utilitarian Motivation, are statistically significant when predicting Behavioral Intention to use Cornershop. Other results, conclusions, and theoretical and practical recommendations are further discussed along the paper.

Keywords: E-commerce · Consumer behavior · Delivery · Online shopping

1 Introduction

This study arose from the significant growth experienced by e-commerce and the importance that this tool has gained in multiple companies around the world, which has been potentiated by the development of mobile commerce and over the last years by the COVID-19 pandemic.

In this way, the power achieved by this sales channel has potentiated the development of different industries, such as the delivery industry, in which, in Chile, one of the main stakeholders is the Chilean company Cornershop. This company was founded in 2015 and directly targeted the retail sector, specifically the delivery of products from the supermarket.

Based on data from the Chilean Fiscalía Nacional Económica [13], the rapid growth of the company allowed it to reach about $160 billion dollars in sales during 2019. By

G. Meiselwitz (Ed.): HCII 2022, LNCS 13316, pp. 422–435, 2022.
https://doi.org/10.1007/978-3-031-05064-0_31

2021, the Chilean start-up was purchased by the North American company Uber for an amount of $1.4 billion dollars, becoming one of the first Chilean companies to achieve the status of "unicorn" in the market, after which, it appreciated by $3 billion dollars. Currently, Cornershop is present in seven countries in the Americas, such as the United States, Mexico, and Chile, and it is progressively entering the European market [12].

Given the significant growth experienced by the existing digital sales channels and the success of Cornershop, this study has the objective of examining the e-commerce service offered by this Chilean delivery company through the implementation of the Information and Communication Technology Acceptance Model to identify the factors that significantly influence Chilean users' behavioral intention to use the app.

Once the research objectives were defined, the methodological phase of the study was implemented, which was divided into three important stages: model design and specification, design and implementation of the data collection instrument and construction of a structural equation model (SEM).

2 Literature Review

The first stage consisted of a conceptual phase, which started with an extensive review of background information about the e-commerce industry and a literature review on the models and theories related to the use and acceptance of Information and Communication Technologies (ICTs).

E-commerce, as it is currently known, dates to 1981, when the German company Holidays conducted its first commercial transaction through the Internet. In 1992, the first online shop project emerged, which had a system that allowed users to buy and sell books online using the internet. This platform evolved over the years and became Books, the first online store. Based on the above, by 1998, there were several companies, such as Amazon, eBay, Zappos and Ritmoteca, among others, with a business strategy based on e-commerce, which strongly revolutionized the digital purchase system [5]. According to the current estimates, everything indicates that this market will record increasing numbers year after year. Therefore, from 2021 to 2025, e-ecommerce revenues from final consumption will increase from 3.3 trillion dollars in 2021 to more than 4.2 trillion dollars in 2025. The sector with the highest turnover in this period will be fashion, with a $900 billion turnover this year [16]. The Latin American and Caribbean e-commerce market will reach a retail sales value around $80.5 billion dollars this year. By 2025, this number is expected to surpass 105.5 billion dollars. Both numbers would be the highest ever recorded for this sector, which continues growing year by year and increasing its participation in national economies. In 2020, the application of restrictions during the COVID-19 pandemic led to an unprecedented online sales boom, marking a turning point in the e-commerce market of the region [19]. However, some countries will do better than others. Although the reign of Brazil and Mexico in regional e-commerce will remain untouched in the coming years, other economies such as Argentina, Chile and Peru are expected to experience much faster growth. According to the analysis of Americas Market Intelligence (AMI), e-commerce in Chile will continue growing at a constant pace during the coming years, reaching 28% in the 2020–2024 period and generating an estimate of $35.4 billion dollars in returns.

The technology acceptance model or TAM [9] is one of the most widespread models in research in the field. TAM was specially designed for the prediction of information system acceptance by a user in an organization [25]. According to Davis [9], there are two critical factors that determine the use of ICTs by a significant group of individuals. The first one corresponds to perceived usefulness (PU), which is defined as the extent to which people believe that by using a specific system, their work performance will improve. The second factor is the perceived ease of use (PEOU), which indicates the extent to which people believe that by using a specific system, it will take less effort to perform tasks. TAM2 [21] incorporates new variables linked to social influence and cognitive processes, which directly affect perceived usefulness and ease of use [7]. In turn, the extension of TAM2, the technology acceptance model 3 (TAM3), proposes that ease of use is influenced or determined by the variables of anxiety, enjoyment and self-sufficiency in regard to technology, in addition to perception of enjoyment, objective usefulness and perception of external control. These last three variables are directly related to PEOU [23].

The unified technology acceptance and use model or UTAUT corresponds to a technology acceptance model whose objective is to predict the intention of users to use an information system as well as their subsequent behavior towards it [22]. Finally, the unified technology acceptance and use model 2 [24] arises as an extension of UTAUT aimed at analyzing the intention to use consumer technologies.

In this way, considering research by diverse authors, a model is designed based on the UTAUT2 [24], and characterized by a high predictive level compared to other technology acceptance models previously developed [18].

The model built and presented in Fig. 1 contained a total of seven latent variables, from which eight hypotheses were proposed for explaining the behavior of the endogenous latent variables of behavioral intention (BI). These variables, together with their associated hypotheses are presented below.

The latent endogenous variable of behavioral intention (BI) refers to the determination of individuals or users to perform a specific behavior [1, 9]. In this way, this study seeks to identify which are the variables or factors that significantly influence acceptance and use of the delivery app Cornershop by Chilean users.

The endogenous variable of performance expectancy (PE) is associated with the extent in which the use of a specific technology or system helps or benefits consumers in the performance of their activities. This variable significantly affects the behavioral intention (BI) for a specific technology by individuals [24].

H1. *The usefulness expectation of users influences the behavioral intention of the Cornershop app.*

Expected effort (EE) corresponds to one of the exogenous latent variables of the model, which seeks to indicate the degree of ease of use perceived by individuals in terms of the use of a specific technology, directly influencing behavioral intention (BI) [24].In addition to the above, this study considers that this variable has a direct effect on the endogenous variable of performance expectancy (PE), which is associated with the fact that if consumers perceive a technology as easy to use, they also believe that the technology is more useful and therefor there is a stronger behavioral intention (BI).

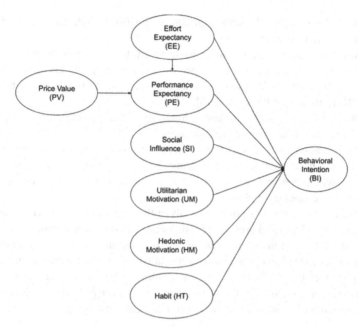

Fig. 1. Proposed model to measure the continuity of use of the Cronershop app.

H2. *Effort expectancy by the consumer positively influences the behavioral intention of the Cornershop app.*

H3. *Effort expectancy by consumers positively influences performance expectancy of the Cornershop app.*

The exogenous latent variable price value (PV) refers to the cognitive compensation between the perceived benefit from the use of a specific technology and the monetary cost of using it [24].In connection, this variable can be applied to the context of use of digital tools for commercialization, associating the concept of "perceived benefit" with the performance expected by the consumer when using a specific platform, and the "cost", the monetary expense linked to the payment for the service received. Therefore, this research model proposes the existence of a direct influence of the exogenous variable on performance expectancy (PE).

H4. *Price value positively influences the performance expectancy of the Cornershop app.*

Another exogenous latent variable of the model is social influence (SI), which is associated with the extent to which individuals perceive that people they are close to and value believe that the use of certain technology is important [10], influencing the intention to use it.

H5. *Social influence influences behavioral intention of consumers of the Cornershop app.*

In the context of this study, the exogenous latent variable of habit (HT) refers to the ease or the habit of individuals to use a specific technology or system. This construct becomes a predictor of behavioral intention (BI) and significantly influences it [24].

H6. *The habit of using delivery applications positively influences the behavioral intention to use the Cornershop app.*

The exogenous latent variable of hedonic motivation (HM) is defined as the fun or pleasure derived from the use of a specific technology [24]. Therefore, from the perspective of consumers, the variable at stake plays a relevant role in the behavioral intention (BI) to use a specific system [6].

H7. *The hedonic motivation to use delivery applications positively influences the behavioral intention to use the Cornershop app.*

COVID-19 has brought about the implementation of a series of sanitary measures in Chile, due to which e-commerce, including the delivery industry, has experienced a significant growth in demand since consumers need to search for alternatives to acquire goods when they cannot do it physically.

In connection with the last point, to analyze the effect of the pandemic on behavioral intention (BI), the model proposed for this study included a new exogenous variable denominated utilitarian motivation (UM), which is associated with the utilitarian dimension of consumer behavior as it focuses on the satisfaction of a functional or economic need [2, 4], even if the satisfaction of the same does not provide any enjoyment [3].

H8. *In the current sanitary context, utilitarian motivation for the use of delivery apps positively influences the behavioral intention of the Cornershop app.*

3 Methodology

The methodology of the study comprised three stages: model design and specification, design and implementation of the data collection instrument and construction of a structural equation model (SEM). The first stage of literature reviewed served to establish the model in Fig. 1, which corresponds to an extended UTAUT2.

To test the proposed extension for UTAUT2, a survey was conducted through the digital platform SurveyMonkey during May 2021 (first pandemic peak). The design of the survey was based on the validated UTAUT2 questionnaire, which was adapted to the objectives of the present study and complemented with related research.

The questionnaire for the proposed model had as target audience young people and adults from different communities in Chile who used or had used the delivery platform Cornershop through the app available in the App Store and Google Play.

The sampling technique used in the implementation of the data collection tool was non-probabilistic sampling, whose application had the advantages of being fast, simple, and economical, as the samples are selected based on their availability [17]. It should be noted that the survey was disseminated mainly through digital channels, such as Instagram, Facebook, and WhatsApp.

The survey contained 32 questions, among which 24 corresponded to items associated with measurable observable variables that aimed to represent the underlying factors of the model presented in Fig. 1. The attitudes and degrees of conformity with the proposed statements were measured though a 5-point Likert scale that ranged from 1, corresponding to "totally disagree", to 5, "Totally agree". In addition to the factors for measuring the proposed construct, some questions were asked that aimed to measure the purchasing habits of users and the profile or demographic characteristics of the sample obtained.

For the analysis and study of these data, the software Microsoft Excel, IBM SPSS Statistics v27 and IBM SPSS Amos v27 were employed. Finally, the conclusions and practical implications of this work are discussed.

4 Results

After applying the survey, a total of 465 responses were obtained, of which 248 were valid for the study, as these belonged to individuals who use or have used the e-commerce service of the company Cornershop. In this way, the responses considered for this study analysis corresponded to 71.10% of respondents who reported regularly using delivery applications. It is noteworthy that around 25.00% of responses were from people who do not often use delivery apps, while of the 75.00% of respondents that do use them, 29.00% had never employed the Cornershop app for that service (Fig. 2).

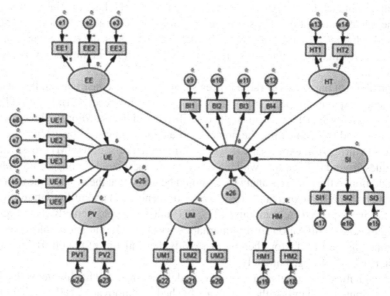

Fig. 2. Diagram of measurement and structural model, which explain the relationships between the variables involved. Source: created for this study.

Regarding gender the sample was composed of mostly women, who accounted for 54.31% of the total. In addition, with respect to the age range of the sample, most respondents are between 18 and 34 years of age, making up 81.22% of the total sample. Based on these results, the mean age of the sample is 30 years. As for the civil status, most participants reported being single, 76.65% of the sample, which is directly correlated with the dominant age range. Finally, the educational level of the sample was analyzed which indicate that more than 50.00% of respondents completed technical or university studies.

428   D. Yáñez et al.

After analyzing the demographic profile of the sample, a study of the shopping habits of the users interviewed was conducted. Among the questions, respondents were asked to indicate the frequency with which they use the app. Based on this, 30.86% of consumers report using the application more than once a month, while the second largest group, corresponding to 30.04% of the sample, reports using the service once in three months.

Finally, the goods or products with the highest demand in the app studied are groceries, with 90.53% of responses, which reflects the leading position attained by Cornershop within the sales segment associated with supermarket products. These products are followed by chocolate and sweet shop products, with 26.75% of responses, products from restaurants/coffee shops with 23.46% and health products such as medicine and personal care items with 22.22%.

To verify the reliability of the instrument used in this study, the Cronbach's alpha index was used, which corresponds to an internal consistency model based on the mean of the correlations of the observable variables of the model, which is applied to analyze the reliability of the items expected to measure the same construct or latent variable [8].

As for the values defined as "acceptable" for the index, several authors propose different acceptance ranges. However, for the analysis of the latent variables that compose the model under study, the scale recommended by George and Mallery [15] was employed, which is presented in Table 1. From the above, using the IBM SPSS Statistics Base V27 software, the Cronbach's alpha values for each latent variable of the model were obtained.

An analysis of the results in Table 1 reveals that most of the constructs studied, namely performance expectancy (PE), price value (PV), social influence (SI), habit (HT) and behavioral intention (BI), present high reliability coefficients, whose values oscillate between 0.8 and 0.9, indicating the presence of a "good" internal consistency for such variables. In turn, effort expectancy (EE) and utilitarian motivation (UM) present alphas with values around 0.7 and 0.8, which are within the "acceptable" consistency values.

In addition to the previous analysis, it should be noted that the alpha values obtained for the variables effort expectancy (EE), social influence (SI) and utilitarian motivation (UM) can be improved by removing EE3, SI1 and UM3, respectively. However, the only significant modification to the internal consistency coefficient would take place by eliminating the EE3 factor, thereby increasing the statistics of the effort expectancy variable (EE) to 0.9, approximately.

Although most constructs that form the model demonstrated having items that positively contribute to reliability, the latent variable hedonic motivation (HM) did not reach favorable reliability values, obtaining a Cronbach's alpha significantly lower than the expected optimal values.

Subsequently, the parameters of structural model were analyzed through the maximum likelihood estimation. First, the statistical significance level of the predicting latent variables over the endogenous latent variables was studied through the analysis of the p-values associated with each of them. In this way, as observed in Table 2, both effort expectancy (EE) and social influence (SI) demonstrated being the only variables with p-values above 0.05; therefore, hypothesis 2 and 5, associated with the direct influence of these variables on behavioral intention (BI), are rejected.

Table 1. Cronbach's alpha associated with the model constructs.

Construct	Cronbach's Alpha	Item	Cronbach's Alpha if item deleted
Effort expectancy	.785	EE1	.616
		EE2	.543
		EE3	.904
Usefulness expectation	.843	UE1	.796
		UE2	.803
		UE3	.783
		UE4	.842
		UE5	.830
Price value	.875	PV1	–
		PV2	–
Social influence	.817	SI1	.837
		SI2	.690
		SI3	.714
Habit	.882	HT1	–
		HT2	–
Hedonic motivation	.421	HM1	–
		HM2	–
Utilitarian motivation	.726	UM1	.539
		UM2	.614
		UM3	.781
Intention to use	.835	BI1	.773
		BI2	.821
		BI3	.756
		BI4	.812

Given the results obtained for statistical significance of the predicting variables, the standardized regression coefficients of the model were studied, which allowed for categorizing the relative importance of each latent variable in the equations that model the behavior of the dependent variables of the model [20].

In addition to the coefficients obtained for the latent variables of the model, the standardized regression estimators of the observed variables were studied in order to measure to what extent the design indicators represent their constructs. Therefore, items with a standardized factor load above 0.40 were considered effective indicators of their corresponding latent variables [14] (Table 3).

In this way, it can be concluded that the total of items that form the model that was built presented factor loads with acceptable magnitudes, significantly influencing their

Table 2. SEM results.

Item	Estimate	S.E.	C.R.	P-value
UE ← EE	.272	.04	6.757	***
UE ← PV	.228	.038	5.93	***
BI ← EE	.001	.05	.018	.986
BI ← UE	.493	.113	4.372	***
BI ← SI	-.015	.037	-.415	.678
BI ← UM	.247	.072	3.431	***
BI ← HM	.548	.168	3.268	.001
BI ← HT	.326	.04	8.121	***

Table 3. Standardized regression coefficients for latent variables. Regression coefficients estimated for the significant latent variables in the model. Source: created for this study.

Item	Standardized Estimate
UE ← EE	.523
UE ← PV	.487
BI ← UE	.375
BI ← UM	.247
BI ← HM	.456
BI ← HT	.634

corresponding latent variables. However, it should be noted that although the factors EE3 and HM2 have a relevant impact on the variables of effort expectancy (EE) and hedonic motivation (HM), respectively, these present low standardized loads that are close to the established limit.

Finally, in order to study the structural fit of the model, the determination coefficient (R^2) was calculated for the endogenous latent variables of performance expectancy (PE) and behavioral intention (BI). Based on the above, the predicting latent variables of performance expectancy (PE), which are effort expectancy (EE) and price value (PV), explain 51% of its variance. In turn, regarding the results obtained for the behavioral intention construct (BI), 81% of its variability is explained by the predicting variables performance expectancy (PE), habit (HT), hedonic motivation (HM) and utilitarian motivation (UM).

Finally, to verify the degree of coupling existing among sample data and data obtained from the model built, the absolute, incremental and parsimony fit levels of the model were analyzed.

For the absolute fit analysis, whose indicators seek to determine the extent to which the model predicts the variance matrix and observed covariance [11], the Chi-square (Cmin) and the root mean square error of approximation (RMSEA) indexes were calculated. Cmin had a value of 623.772, with a significance below 0.05, indicating an acceptable absolute fit. In addition, a value of 2.556 was obtained for ratio chi-square, which represents the division between Cmin and the degrees of freedom of the model (df). Even when this last value is within the allowed range, it is very close to the acceptable limit.

In turn, the RMSEA index had a value of 0.058, satisfactorily meeting the acceptability criterion proposed for this index, indicating an adequate absolute fit index.

For incremental fit, which allows for measuring the fit of the model proposed by comparing it with a null model that is taken as a reference [11], the goodness indexes of comparative adjustment (CFI) and normed fit (NFI) were calculated, obtaining 0.851 and 0.781, respectively. Although these values are relatively close to 1, they do not meet the acceptability criteria proposed for them, which implies that the proposed model does not reach the incremental fit levels desired.

Finally, regarding the parsimonious fit, whose measure allows for relating quality of model fit to the number of estimated coefficients required to reach such a fit level [11], the parsimonious normed fit index was calculated, which had a value 0.635, within the acceptable range. Based on this result, it may be concluded that the studied model has a parsimonious fit that was adequate but improvable.

5 Conclusions

Thanks to the results obtained in this study, a series of conclusions were drawn, which are associated with the different hypotheses proposed for each variable that forms the proposed model.

First, regarding the variable of performance expectancy (PE), a causal relationship with behavioral intention (BI) is revealed, which is defined by the third highest standardized regression coefficient among the predicting variables of the model, with a value of 0.38. Although this last value is positive—which allows for the assertion that the higher the performance expectancy of the app, the stronger the intensity of the customers' intention to use it when making a purchase—it indicates a small causality, from which it can be inferred that consumers do not consider the reliability, efficacy, efficiency, or complexity of the app to be critical factors in the decision to use it.

When analyzing the relationship between effort expectancy (EE) and behavioral intention (BI), whose standardized regression coefficient was 0.0, it may be concluded that there is no direct causality between these variables. It is noteworthy that this exogenous variable proved to be non-significant in the prediction of behavioral intention (BI) of the application, which indicates that the app is considered easy to use or understand by consumers, and the variable does not significantly influence the decision or desire to use. The latter may be related to the age range of the sample studied, which is mostly made up of young people aged 18 to 34, who have a high degree of familiarity with this technology and therefore assume that they could use any type of digital platform, diminishing the importance of the complexity of its use.

In turn, when analyzing the influence of effort expectancy (EE) on performance expectancy (PE), for which a coefficient of 0.51 was obtained, it may be concluded that as Cornershop users consider this app easier to use, they also believe this technology is more useful or efficient and therefore have an incentive to use it.

It should be noted that at the time of studying the consistency of effort expectancy (EE), the observable variable EE3 showed a low correlation with the other items of the underlying latent variable, which indicates that the fact that the app is enabled for its use and easy to access for consumers does not imply that is simple to use.

The variable of price value (PV) had a standardized regression coefficient of 0.41, which indicates that although such a factor has a positive impact on performance expectancy (PE) (as the service price/quality ratio improves, consumers are more convinced that the app is useful for the purchase of certain products), it is not decisive in the perception of users about its performance or productivity. This result may be attributed to the mean age of the analyzed sample (30 years), which is directly related to its educational level and the possibility that these consumers currently have a paid job, somehow reducing sensitivity to the price variable. Regarding the latter, it is recommended that future research analyzes the socioeconomic status of the users of this app to identify the income level of its consumers.

Based on the influence level of social influence (SI) over the behavioral intention (BI) to use the Cornershop app, it may be concluded that there is practically no degree of causality between the variables, since the value of the estimated regression coefficient was very small (−0.03). This indicates a negative effect of social influence (SI) on behavioral intention (BI), which implies that the more importance that users give to the opinion of people close to them, the less the desire to use the app to satisfy their shopping needs. However, the variable under study was demonstrated to be non-significant in the prediction of behavioral intention (BI) and therefore this factor does not directly influence the decision of users to use the app.

The variable of habit (HT) turned out to be the factor with the highest impact on behavioral intention (BI), with a standardized regression coefficient of 0.63, which indicates positive causality from this variable. This would suggest that the higher the degree of ease users perceive in using the app to make a purchase, the more their intention to use it at the moment of wanting to satisfy such a need. The importance consumers give to the variable of habit (HT) can be attributed to the familiarity of the current society with the constant use of mobile apps to satisfy diverse objectives or needs, which is reflected in the percentage of respondents that often use delivery apps.

Regarding the variable of hedonic motivation (HM), this had a standardized regression coefficient of 0.46, becoming the second construct in impact on behavioral intention (BI). However, since the value of the estimator is not high enough, it may be concluded that although there is an increase in the intention to use the app as the enjoyment derived from using it increases, this is not a critical factor in the user's decision.

It should be noted that, thanks to the reliability analysis performed on the constructs that form the model, it was revealed that the analyzed variable (HM) had an insufficient internal consistency associated with the low correlation and number of items composing it. This generates a considerable loss of validity in the factor.

In turn, after the analysis of the regression coefficient obtained for the utilitarian motivation variable (UM), whose value was 0.25, it is concluded that, although the sanitary conditions and norms imposed in Chile due to the COVID-19 pandemic generated an increase in the behavioral intention (BI) of the app, the causality of this variable is low, implying little importance given by consumers to this construct. The result is attributable to the efficient citizen vaccination process, which has allowed for more freedom of movement in the different regions and communities of Chile, reducing the need for using mobile apps to purchase goods or products.

Considering the variables with the strongest effect on the prediction of behavioral intention (BI), a series of recommendations for enhancing them are presented below.

First, in order to increase the performance expectancy (PE) of the app by consumers, some decisive aspects related to the perception of users about the performance and efficiency of the app need to be addressed. Therefore, one of the points that would improve the productivity of the Cornershop app is related to the increase of shops that have the products in highest demand for users.

In addition to the above, it is recommended to improve information regarding the shops and products sold in them, as well as the information associated with the product return process and the communication channels for dealing with misplaced orders. Finally, in order to increase the efficiency and efficacy of the service, working on new strategies and tools for training human capital (shoppers) is fundamental.

In turn, to improve effort expectancy (EE), i.e., the effort expected by the user, it is recommended to work on perfecting the order and clarity of the information presented, which would allow for more understanding about how to use the app. This is crucial when trying to attract older age segments, as users above 55 years of age are less familiar with the use of mobile apps, which is why the order and clarity of data exhibited is key.

To improve the price/quality perception or value price (PV) of the service offered by Cornershop, it is recommended to work on a marketing strategy that shows the quality of the service, as well as its advantages and benefits.

Regarding the potentiation of the variable of habit (HT), which has a direct effect on behavioral intention, it is important to create an experience that transforms the desire to shop on the app into something natural and frequent. Therefore, it is recommended to increase the number of ads or reminders that encourage the use of the app, as well as messages communicating deals and discounts for costumers.

Finally, based on the results of the hedonic motivation variable (HM), it is recommended to offer a fun and pleasant experience that attracts new customers and boosts the desire to using the app for future purchases. Thus, one way to increase pleasure during use is the intensification and improvement of deals, such as a reduction of shipping costs for products in high demand or the accumulation of points per purchase (which can become discounts for users), among others.

References

1. Ajzen, I., Fishbein, M.: Belief, attitude, intention and behaviour: an introduction to theory and research (1975)
2. Babin, B., Darden, W., Griffin, M.: Measuring hedonic and utilitarian shopping value. J. Consum. Res. **20**(4), 644–654 (1994)

3. Babin, B., Chebat, J., Michon, R.: Perceived appropriateness and its effect on quality, affect and behavior. J. Retail. Consum. Serv. **11**(5), 287–298 (2004)
4. Batra, R., Ahotla, O.: Measuring the hedonic and utilitarian sources of consumer attitudes. Mark. Lett. **2**(1), 159–170 (1991). https://doi.org/10.1007/BF00436035
5. Bahillo, L.: Historia de Internet: cómo nació y cuál fue su evolución. Marketing4ecommerce, 17 May 2021. https://marketing4ecommerce.cl/historia-de-internet/#:~:text=%C2%BFCu% C3%A1ndo%20naci%C3%B3%20Internet%3F%20(al,as%C3%AD%20la%20red%20A rpa%20Internet
6. Brown, S., Venkatesh, V.: Model of adoption of technology in households: a baseline model test and extension incorporating household life cycle. MIS Q. **29**(3), 399–436 (2005)
7. Cabero, J., Barroso, J., Llorente, M.: Technology acceptance model and realidad aumentada: estudio en desarrollo. Revista Lasallista de investigación. **13**(2), 18–26 (2016)
8. Campo-Arias, A., Oviedo, H.: Aproximación al uso del coeficiente alfa de Cronbach. Revista Colombiana de Psiquiatría **34**(4), 573–580 (2005)
9. Davis, F.: Perceived usefulness, perceived ease of use and user acceptance of information technology. MIS Q. **13**(3), 319–340 (1989)
10. Díaz, M., Loraas, T.: Aprender nuevos usos de la tecnología durante un trabajo de auditoría: contextualizar modelos generales para avanzar en la comprensión pragmática. Revista Internacional de Sistemas de Información Contable **11**(1), 61–77 (2010)
11. Escobedo, M., Hernández, J., Estebané, V., Martínez, G.: Modelos de ecuaciones estructurales: Características, fases, construcción, aplicación y resultados. SciELO. **18**(55), 16–22 (2016)
12. Fajardo, D.: Uber adquirirá el 100% de Cornershop y pagará US$ 1.400 millones por el 47% que aún no tenía. La Tercera, 21 June 2021. https://www.latercera.com/pulso/noticia/sigue-la-oleada-de-startups-chilenas-uber-adquiere-el-100-de-cornershop/CWGBOTL4SFBIBIF LNXJSIWOBDY/
13. Fiscalía Nacional Económica. Fiscalía Nacional Económica, Gobierno de Chile. Informe de Aprobación de Adquisición de control sobre Delivery Technologies SpA por parte de Walmart Chile S.A., 21 January 2019. https://www.fne.gob.cl/informe-de-aprobacion-de-adquisicion-de-control-sobre-delivery-technologies-spa-por-parte-de-walmart-chile-s-a/
14. Gaeta, M., Cavazos, J., Sánchez, A., Rosário, P., Hogemann, J.: Propiedades psicométricas de la versión mexicana del Cuestionario para la Evaluación de Metas Académicas (CEMA). Revista Latinoamericana de Psicología. **47**(1), 16–24 (2015)
15. George, D., Mallery, P.: IBM SPSS Statistics 26 Step by Step: A Simple Guide and Reference. Routledge, Routledge (2019)
16. Mena, M.: Cuánto factura el comercio electrónico en el mundo. Statista, 22, November 2021. https://es.statista.com/grafico/26228/ingresos-por-ventas-minoristas-de-comercio-electronico-a-nivel-mundial/
17. Otzen, T, Manterola, C.: Técnicas de Muestreo sobre una Población a Estudio. SciELO. **35**(1), 227–232 (2017)
18. Palos, P., Reyes, A., Ramon, J.: Modelos de Adopción de Tecnologías de Información y Cloud Computing en las Organizaciones. Información Tecnológica **30**(30), 3–12 (2019)
19. Pasquali, M.: El comercio electrónico no para de crecer en América Latina. Statista, 25 November 2021. https://es.statista.com/grafico/22835/boom-del-e-commerce-en-latinoame rica/
20. Stock, J., Watson, M.: Introducción a la Econometría. Pearson Educación, Pearson (2012)
21. Venkatesh, V., Davis, F.: A theoretical extension of the technology acceptance model: four longitudinal field studies. Manage. Sci. **46**(2), 186–204 (2000)
22. Venkatesh, V., Morris, M., Davis, G., Davis, F.: User acceptance of information technology: toward a unified view. MIS Q. **27**(3), 425–478 (2003)
23. Venkatesh, V., Bala, H.: Modelo de aceptación de tecnología 3 y una agenda de investigación sobre intervenciones. Decis. Sci. **39**(2), 273–315 (2008)

24. Venkatesh, V., Thong, J.: Consumer acceptance and use of information technology: extending the unified theory of acceptance and use of technology. MIS Q. **36**(1), 157–178 (2012)
25. Young, L., Rivas, L., Chaparro, J.: Modelo de aceptación tecnológica (TAM): un estudio de la influencia de la cultura nacional y del perfil del usuario en el uso de las TIC. INNOVAR. Revista de Ciencias Administrativas y Sociales **20**(36), 187–203 (2010)

Author Index

Printed in the United States
by Baker & Taylor Publisher Services